Instant Access to Powerful eResources for:

Creating the Enterprise

First Edition

by Gartner/Bellamy

ERESOURCES INCLUDED:

- **Enterprise Online**
  Offers a robust set of online multimedia learning tools, including Small Business School videos, quizzing, glossary, and more.

- **Student Companion Site**
  Additional study aids

Tear out card missing?

If you did not buy a new textbook, the tear-out portion of this card may be missing or the Access Code on this card may have already been used. Access Codes can be used only once and are not transferable.

© 2008 South-Western, a part of Cengage Learning.

ISBN-13: 978-0-324-58680-0
ISBN-10: 0-324-58680-9

SOUTH-WESTERN
CENGAGE Learning™

TO GET STARTED:

1. Launch a web browser and go to **academic.cengage.com**

2. Click on "Create an Account" under Student eResource Registration.

3. Enter the Access Code below exactly as it appears.

ACCESS CODE

PPQBL89P3WXGWW

4. Follow the prompts to create your account.

5. Record your email address and password for future visits.

Email:

Password:

NOT...
the eR...
is com...

D1402777

For technical support, go to

academic.cengage.com/support

creating the
ENTERPRISE

William B. Gartner
Clemson University

— *with* —

Marlene G. Bellamy

THOMSON

SOUTH-WESTERN

Australia · Brazil · Canada · Mexico · Singapore · Spain · United Kingdom · United States

THOMSON
™
SOUTH-WESTERN

Creating the Enterprise
William B. Gartner with Marlene G. Bellamy

VP/Editorial Director:
Jack W. Calhoun

Editor-in-Chief:
Melissa Acuna

Senior Acquisitions Editor:
Michele Rhoades

Developmental Editor:
Ohlinger Publishing Services

Editorial Assistant:
Ruth Belanger

Marketing Manager:
Clinton Kernen

Senior Marketing Coordinator:
Sarah Rose

Senior Marketing Communications Manager:
Jim Overly

Senior Content Project Manager:
Kim Kusnerak

Technology Project Manager:
Kristen Meere

Manufacturing Buyer:
Doug Wilke

Production House:
Integra Software Services Pvt. Ltd

Printer:
Transcontinental
Louiseville, PQ

Senior Art Director:
Tippy McIntosh

Cover/Internal Designer:
c miller design

Cover Image:
© PhotoDisc Imaging and Ryan McVay

Library of Congress Control Number:
2007905889

For more information about our products, contact us at:

Thomson Learning Academic
Resource Center

1-800-423-0563

Thomson Higher Education
5191 Natorp Boulevard
Mason, OH 45040
USA

WBG—Maryse and Ellison:

The lights begin to twinkle from the rocks:
The long day wanes: the slow moon climbs: deep
Sighs filled with many voices. Come, they call,
'Tis not too late to seek a newer world.' [—with apologies to Tennyson]

MGB—

To my husband Don and my daughter Rebecca, who supported my need to write
when the muse was with me, even if it meant well into the evening and on weekends,
and to my Siamese cat Sabrina, who provided a special brand of editorial
oversight with her forays across the keyboard.

Enterprise—(1) a willingness to take initiative;
(2) an organized, systematic, and purposeful activity;
(3) a project that is complicated and risky.

Enterpriser—one who undertakes an enterprise.

This is a book about how to make things happen. We purposely use the words *enterprise* and *enterpriser* throughout the book, rather than words like *entrepreneur* and *manager*. Our goal is to give you a new mindset, where you see yourself as an enterpriser: someone who takes initiative to organize a project, in situations with some complications and risk. When someone makes things happen, they are enterprising.

We are all willing to take initiative in situations where we know we will immediately benefit from our actions. If you invested $100 in U.S. series EE savings bond on May 1, 2007, you would receive $103.40 on May 1, 2008. That return is certain. The particular action of investing money has a specific future consequence. But what about other types of activities you could undertake, where the outcomes are much more uncertain? If you invested $100 in the creation of a new business, how much would you likely receive a year from now? For most new efforts, it is probably difficult to know the specific outcomes from particular actions. So the question then becomes, Under what conditions are you willing to take initiative?

You may be familiar with the phrase "Fools rush in where angels fear to tread." In situations where we can take initiative, the challenge is determining, to the best of our knowledge and abilities, whether our future actions will be successful or foolish. Jobs and careers are unstable and short term, frequently putting us in situations where we have to make judgments about our future: "Is this course of action a good one to take?"

Creating the Enterprise focuses on developing the skills you will need to evaluate and actualize opportunities that will be best for *your* life. We are less likely to take foolish actions when we know who we are and what we want—if we can better determine whether certain opportunities are worthy of our time and effort and are feasible. We can risk being foolish when we know what the consequences of foolishness are. (As we know from Shakespeare, sometimes playing the part of the fool is the smart way to go.)

The process of getting things done is not, typically, something that can be done alone. It would be difficult to achieve anything without the involvement and assistance of other people and organizations. Try to name some activities that you can do that don't involve resources, products, materials, or the interaction and involvement of other people. (We can think of only a few actions: singing and talking—to yourself). If you write something, you are probably using a pencil or pen and paper made by someone else that has been shipped and delivered to a store, where you purchased them. To write, then, depends on other people for the materials to write with. Few of us make our own clothes, build our own houses, grow our own food, or create our own entertainment. We live primarily in an organizational world, where our ability to make things happen requires that we understand how to create and develop enterprises to achieve our goals.

The abilities and skills to achieve our goals require that we learn about how to organize the activities and efforts of others in a systematic and purposeful way. When we create an enterprise, we are concerned with how all of the various interactions among "others"—customers, employees, suppliers, government regulators, competitors—play out in a way that provides benefits for ourselves and others. An important paradox of the enterprising process is that successful enterprisers are also those individuals who provide the most value and benefits to others. Enterprisers are involved in creating "win-win" situations.

Finally, the process of enterprising is complicated and risky. Even with thorough preparation and analysis, there are no certainties that a particular enterprise will be successful. Successful enterprisers have the insight and willingness to judge and navigate the risks and uncertainties that are inherent in all future activities. When events don't turn out as planned, enterprisers have the resilience, fortitude, and adaptability to change. Failing is a part of the process of learning. There are no guarantees in the world of enterprise. That makes it all the more fun, interesting, and rewarding when events play out in your favor.

In the world of enterprise, your choice is to get into the game, rather than watch from the sidelines.

Development of the Text

How many times have you heard these phrases:

- The world is different now.

- Times have changed.

- I remember when. . .

- The way things used to be. . .

Well, our lives *are* different. We just need to watch the news or read the paper to see that our lives are no longer what they used to be. The world is more complicated. There is more competition. We live in a time when people vie for jobs and resources not only locally or nationally, but also internationally. What people do in India or China or Botswana or Chile affects us in Detroit or San Antonio or Yakima or Red Rock. There is no denying that the ways that people were successful in the past may not provide the same game plan for success in the future.

Few individuals are going to work in the same job for an entire career. At various points in our lives we might work for a large company, be self-employed, expand self-employment into a business with employees, engage in independent consulting, start a business for another organization, or work in a smaller company. Indeed, we often have multiple "jobs" at the same time: working full time for a large company while we have a "part-time" business on the side, or undertaking some consulting while we are working at starting our own business. In a world where everyone is likely to bounce from working in a small or a large business, from being an employee or an employer, from serving as a consultant or a client, we will need a new mindset, along with new skills and knowledge, to take advantage of these new and ever-changing opportunities.

We decided to write *Creating the Enterprise* because "enterpriser" is not a unique kind of personality, a special kind of job or role, or a unique lifestyle. It seemed to us that the word *entrepreneur* carries too much baggage about individuals who have a special set of personality characteristics, skills, abilities, or achievements—Bill Gates, Richard Branson, and Mark Cuban, for example—that then put them in a category of individuals that few others believe they can achieve. Entrepreneurship seems to be about business success, rather than about how people go about accomplishing things. The words *manager* or *business owner* seemed too passive. "To manage" seems more reactive, like tending sheep, rather than an activity that is proactive and oriented toward risk taking and achievement.

So we chose the word *enterprise* to constantly remind you that the mindset, skills, and abilities we offer in this textbook require a different way of thinking. Becoming an "enterpriser"—someone who undertakes an enterprise—is a goal that anyone can achieve. "To enterprise," then, is not a choice that only a few people will be making. In the future, we will all need to be enterprisers.

Organization of the Text

This textbook is organized into 12 chapters and 4 appendixes. The approach of *Creating the Enterprise* concerns itself with analysis on three levels: by person, business, and environment. It also proposes three stages of change: recognizing and developing opportunities, progress and growth, and transition. *Creating the Enterprise* focuses on the first stage of change: recognizing and developing opportunities. A subsequent textbook, *Enterprise*, will provide a comprehensive exploration of all three stages of the life of an enterprise.

Understanding how "to enterprise" involves navigating among the three levels of analysis and the three stages of change. The three levels of analysis help students realize that their success in enterprise (business level) is dependent on their context (environment level), and their interests, goals, skills, and abilities (person level). In addition, enterprise success is evolutionary, rather than static.

The Environment

A central theme of *Creating the Enterprise* is that enterprisers have to be attentive to what's going on, internally and externally. Enterprises exist in a world and national economy, a political and regulatory system, a financial and banking system, an industry, and in a space where social networks and relationships among customers, suppliers, investors, and other community stakeholders matter. By addressing these environmental topics, students will be better prepared to make successful business decisions.

The Person

The textbook challenges students to explore their personal goals to see how their own lives mesh with their professional objectives. *Creating the Enterprise* focuses on developing enterprising ways of thinking and enterprising skills, rather than worrying whether a person has the right kind of motivations or the right personality to be an entrepreneur or small business owner. All individuals are enterprisers! Everyone, at some point in their lives, has to initiate, plan, and execute new ideas and projects.

Creating the Enterprise looks at four ways that entrepreneurs think about their situations and their approaches to solving problems that relate to enterprising success. Through self-assessments and other exercises, students are trained to adopt an enterprising mindset. These ways of thinking include:

- Attribution—how you explain the past

- Expectancies—how you explain the future

- Optimism—expecting good things will happen

- Problem solving—attitudes and skills to accomplish planned goals and handle unforeseen issues

Enterprisers need the knowledge and capabilities to get what they want and to get the resources they need. *Creating the Enterprise* addresses skills involving personal planning and goal setting, networking, negotiation, and persuasion. Enterprise is a form of action. By developing these important skills, students improve the likelihood of succeeding in their enterprising interests.

The Business

At the level of the business, *Creating the Enterprise* focuses on the characteristics of enterprise success. The core feature of this discussion involves developing a business concept and exploring each enterprise's business model. The business concept is the enterprise's story and answers the 4Cs:

- Customer: Who is the customer?

- Consideration: What does the customer want?

- Connection: How is this consideration going to be provided?

- Commitment: Are you committed to this opportunity?

In developing the business model, the formula for how an enterprise makes money, we add a fifth C:

- Capital: Can you make money doing this?

Stages of Change

Creating the Enterprise sets the stage for considering the life cycle of the person, business, and environment. Personal and business success is evolutionary. It's a given that an individual and a business will change over time. As economic and industry conditions change, enterprisers need skills to recognize how these environmental factors will impact their personal and business success. Enterprise ownership, like any other job, represents something temporary in everyone's work career. Being able to navigate through the transitions between start-up, ownership, and management, and divestment of an enterprise takes critical skills. Individuals need capabilities to separate themselves from their enterprises. We all need skills to reap the benefits of our present activities and free ourselves to undertake new challenges with new rewards.

Creating the Enterprise explores the first stage in the life of an enterprise: its emergence. Recognizing and developing opportunities will be useful skills, not only for starting and developing a business but also in a multitude of personal situations. *Creating the Enterprise* suggests that recognizing and developing opportunities also occurs in other business settings (corporations, governments, nonprofits), as well as in personal projects, team projects, and other venues where goals are identified and realized.

This book presents the skills necessary to set, manage, and monitor personal goals and aspirations and offers practical examples of these skills. An important perspective of *Creating the Enterprise* is its affirmation of all types of enterprises as outcomes of an individual's choices and interests. Enterprisers must select enterprises that are appropriate for their own goals, abilities, and skills, and that fit the context of the business's industry and environment. These choices and factors will determine, in part, a business's growth. We celebrate what are typically called lifestyle businesses—businesses that do not have rapid rates in sales or employee growth. High-growth enterprises are often inappropriate for many enterprisers and for many industries. Students should not be ashamed to choose a very small or low-growth business that supports their goals and interests. Many small enterprises provide substantial financial rewards without the hassles of managing employees. Small is beautiful!

Part 1—An Enterprising Framework

The first five chapters of the book provide a basis for thinking about the nature of an enterprise in terms of context (person, business, and environment) and process (emergence, newness, and transformation). Context and process matter because the businesses enterprisers develop significantly impact their personal goals and aspirations. Each enterprise has its own needs and demands that are different from the needs and demands of the enterpriser. Enterprisers must recognize the contextual factors that influence the situations they encounter to reach their own goals.

At the level of the person, we will also look at the variety of people who are likely to become enterprisers. We begin to describe how enterprisers can think about their situations and take action. We will also explore the essential skills that enterprisers need: goal setting, persuasion, negotiation, and networking.

Turning to the level of the business, students learn about the ways that businesses are legally formed. These legal forms (sole proprietorship, partnership, corporation, and not-for-profit) offer different ways for an enterpriser to develop a business. They both enable and limit how an enterprise can function and act in certain situations. Finally, we look at the legal and regulatory environment that increasingly plays a significant role in how businesses operate.

Part 2—The Enterprising Process

This section of the book explores how opportunities are recognized, developed, and exploited through the process of creating opportunities, determining feasibility, and business planning. Enterprisers work to leverage their own skills and pay attention to the ways that the environment changes. The creation of an opportunity occurs when the skills, knowledge, and interests of the enterpriser intersect with an ever-changing environment. Enterprisers also develop habits that can increase their luck. While there are many opportunities that might be worth pursuing, the process of feasibility analysis explores whether an opportunity is actually possible and whether it will make money. For those opportunities that are feasible, an enterpriser will enhance the likelihood of starting an enterprise by developing a business plan. From our perspective, a business plan lays out the specific resources, tasks, and activities necessary to transform an opportunity into an ongoing business.

Part 3—Enterprising Strategies

A unique feature of this textbook is its focus on the many different ways that enterprisers go about starting new enterprises. There is no one right way to develop a successful enterprise. We offer insights into eight major pathways that combine an enterpriser's personal capabilities and experiences, start-up actions, enterprise strategies, and environmental characteristics into an archetype (a model or format) for enterprise success. Two of the major ways that enterprisers develop businesses (purchasing an existing business and franchising) are explored in detail.

Part 4—The Enterprising Mind

Creating the Enterprise is fundamentally a book that focuses on creating successful individuals. The final section of the book reemphasizes the importance of one's own values and goals, and it explores how these values are heavily influenced by the kinds of commitments we make and the kinds of stories we tell about ourselves to others. There are significant ways that individuals can readjust their thinking to become more aware of the many possibilities and options in their future. Enterprisers need to be grounded in how they will satisfy the four different goals of a well-lived life: achievement, significance, legacy, and happiness.

Chapter Structure

Each chapter is organized in a similar manner.

1. Key Concepts—The chapter opens with an outline of its fundamental objectives.

2. Introduction—It offers some insights into key issues and problems the chapter will address.

3. Topics—They provide examples, descriptions, and analysis of ideas and subjects critical for enterprising.

4. Case—Each chapter has a case that requires students to make decisions by applying the topic material.

5. Enterprising Ethics and An Enterprising World boxes—Each chapter provides brief box material that emphasizes the ethical and global implications of the chapter's topics.

6. Summary—Important highlights of the topics in each chapter are provided.

7. Review Questions—Questions specific to the chapter material reemphasize critical ideas and issues.

8. Applying What You've Learned—Exercises offer students the chance to apply the topic material and relate it to their own experiences and to enterprise opportunities.

9. Enterprisers on the Web—This section points to materials, exercises, examples, ideas, and issues that students can easily access through the Web, expanding their options for learning about enterprising. (*Note:* all of the URLs used in these exercises were active at the time of publication. If you find an inactive URL, try going to the homepage of the site and search for the article or resource referenced in the exercise.)

Key Features of the Text

This textbook should appeal to students across a wide range of institutions. The following are key features of the text:

- Emphasis on an enterprising mindset that sees opportunities in a wide variety of situations

- A focus on personal and professional skills through such topics as goal setting, persuasion, negotiation, and networking

- A multilevel framework for evaluating situations based on characteristics of the person, business, and environment

- A consistent accent on the ethical issues enterprisers face in day-to-day situations

- A recognition of the global issues confronting enterprisers and enterprises

- Opportunities to apply concepts and knowledge through cases and exercises.

Supplements

Instructor's Resource CD-ROM (ISBN 0-324-36560-8)

This CD provides instructors with "one-stop shopping" for various teaching resources, including the chapter PowerPoint slides, the Instructor's Manual, and the Computerized Test Bank.

PowerPoint Presentation Slides

Developed by Charlie T. Cook, University of West Alabama, in close coordination with the text authors, the slides provide a comprehensive review of each chapter in the book. Also available online at http://www.thomsonedu.com/management/gartner.

Instructor's Manual

The instructor's manual for *Creating the Enterprise* was prepared by Mary E. Gorman, Ph.D., University of Cincinnati, and includes the following content:

- Key Concepts as described in the text.

- Chapter Outline of main headings with developed lecture notes and references to all exhibits.

- Developed Answers for the discussion questions that accompany the two box features, An Enterprising World and Enterprising Ethics.

- Developed Answers for the Enterprisers Video Case Studies discussion questions.

- Answers to Review Questions.

- Suggested Answers and Suggested Instructor Strategies for the activities presented in Applying What You've Learned.

- Suggested Instructor Strategies for the activities in Enterprisers on the Web.

Also available online at http://www.thomsonedu.com/management/gartner.

Test Bank

The ExamView computerized testing system is an easy-to-use test-creation program that is compatible with Microsoft Windows and Macintosh and enables instructors to create printed tests, Internet tests, and LAN-based tests quickly. The QuickTest Wizard lets test generators assemble a test in minutes, using a step-by-step selection process.

Instructors can choose from over 800 questions in true/false, multiple choice, and short essay formats. The printed test bank can be downloaded at http://www.thomsonedu.com/management/gartner.

Gartner Creating Product Support Website (http://www.thomsonedu.com/management/gartner)

Instructors can go to this site to download the text supplements and glossary.

Enterprise Online (www.thomsonedu.com/management/enterpriseonline)

This site, access to which is available with every new book via a bind-in card, offers broad instructional and student support, including:

- Interactive Quizzes—These quizzes (available for every chapter) offer students a quick check of their understanding of the chapter material.

- Complete Sample Business Plan—The Beau-Ties business plan is discussed in Chapter 8, Business Plans and Planning, and the entire plan can be viewed here.

- Small Business School Videos to accompany Enterprisers Case Studies—Small Business School, the series on PBS stations, is hosting the video materials for this book. At the special link provided, students are taken inside the largest video library in the world about small companies. On PBS since 1994, every episode delves inside the mind of an owner to discover why the business was started and what steps that owner had to take to turn an idea into profits. Owners from San Diego to Boston and from Miami to Seattle talk to the camera and tell their own story about what it takes to start, run, and grow a business. Watch, listen, and learn.

- Flashcards—Students can test their understanding of key terms using them.

Final Remarks

This book is a collaborative effort to develop a text that provides the latest knowledge and insights about enterprise in a style that is accessible, easy to read, and interesting. Thank you for considering this text.

William B. Gartner
Arthur M. Spiro Professor of Entrepreneurial Leadership
Clemson University

Marlene G. Bellamy
Writeline Associates

Acknowledgements

The creation and development of this book has been an enterprise, itself. There are so many people who have played a significant role in turning this book from an idea into a reality. We have had opportunities to work with many innovative and enthusiastic colleagues at various universities who have been so important to our development as teachers and writers. We are particularly indebted to Tom O'Malia and Bill Crookston at the University of Southern California for their insights and collaborative efforts to imbue inspiration and passion into the practice of entrepreneurship. Caron St. John at Clemson University has shown how to develop students into collaborative innovators and community entrepreneurs. At Thomson Learning, John Szilagyi played a significant role in convincing us of the value of developing a new approach toward a textbook that looks at entrepreneurship, management, and small business. Michele Rhodes has continued to provide a stable and constant route for the completion of this work through the ups-and-downs of the corporate landscape. And Monica Ohlinger (Ohlinger Publishing Services) was the glue that kept this project from falling apart; without her constant encouragement, humorous cajoling, and determination toward deadlines, this book would not have been completed.

For their helpful suggestions during the preparation of this book, we are especially grateful to the following individuals:

Robin Anderson, University of Portland

Marilyn Besich, MSU, Great Falls College of Technology

Dr. Dorothy S. Gleckner, Bergen Community College

Jack P. Doo, Jr., California State University, Stanislaus

Dr. Todd A. Finkle, Fitzgerald Institute for Entrepreneurial Studies, University of Akron

Barbara Frazier, Western Michigan University

Dr. Dorothy S. Gleckner, Bergen Community College

Mary E. Gorman, University of Cincinnati

Daniel R. Hogan, Jr., Loyola University in New Orleans

Norma Juma, University of Texas at Arlington

Karen G. Killinger, Salt Lake Community College

Richard Kimbrough, University of Nebraska, Lincoln

Antoinette (Toni) Knechtges, Eastern Michigan University

Donald L. Lester, Ph.D., Arkansas State University

Gideon D. Markman, Ph.D., University of Georgia

John V. Mullane, Middle Tennessee State University

Margo Reign, University of Delaware

William J. Rossi, University of Florida

Dr. Milton Silver Ph.D., Le Bow College of Business, Drexel University

Marcene Sonneborn, Syracuse University

Kenneth R. Taurman, Jr., JD, Indiana University Southeast

Amy M. Tomas, Ph.D., University of Vermont

Dr. Robert Wyatt, Drury University

brief contents

contents

about the authors

William B. Gartner is the Arthur M. Spiro Professor of Entrepreneurial Leadership at Clemson University. He received all of his degrees (B.A., MBA, and Ph.D.) from the University of Washington. Prior to joining Clemson University he was on the faculty at the University of Virginia, Georgetown University, San Francisco State University, and the University of Southern California. In 2005 he received the FSF–NUTEK Award, which is an international award for outstanding accomplishments in entrepreneurship and small business research that was instituted by the Swedish Foundation for Small Business Research (FSF) and the Swedish Business Development Agency (NUTEK). Professor Gartner is one of the co-founders of the Entrepreneurship Research Consortium, which initiated, developed, and managed the Panel Study of Entrepreneurial Dynamics (PSED). The PSED is a longitudinal dataset on enterprisers in the process of starting businesses (http://www.psed.info). His research has been published in the *Journal of Business Venturing, Entrepreneurship Theory and Practice,* the *Academy of Management Review, Journal of Management,* and the *Journal of Small Business Management,* and he has received funding from the Kauffman Foundation, Coleman Foundation, U.S. Department of Education, U.S. Small Business Administration, the Small Business Foundation of America, the *Los Angeles Times,* the Pacific Gas and Electric Company, the Corporate Design Foundation, and the National Endowment for the Arts. His research explores how enterprisers find and identify opportunities, recognize and solve start-up problems, and undertake actions to successfully launch new businesses.

Marlene G. Bellamy formed Writeline Associates in 1990, after 13 years as an investment and corporate banker. She has applied her finance experience to the academic and corporate arenas, collaborating with authors and publishers on 15 major college- and graduate-level business textbooks and related educational materials. Her contributions include chapters; special features such as chapter-opening vignettes, practitioner and investor interviews, boxes, and case studies; and instructor's manuals for corporate finance, investing, marketing, management, introduction to business, and personal finance textbooks. She has also provided corporate communication services in finance, marketing, and technology to units of Deloitte & Touche LLP, for whom she co-authored annual reports on the software industry, wrote and edited several technology-oriented newsletters, and prepared marketing communications materials. She lives in La Jolla, California, and received her B.A. from Smith College and MBA from Boston College.

part **1**

An Enterprising Framework

chapter 1

Enterprise: Creating a Framework for Success

1. An enterprise is a business that is conceived and managed by independent, energetic individuals who systematically seek results that serve their personal and professional objectives. To enterprise is to take initiative in an organized way.

2. People take initiative in a variety of different contexts. While some individuals may work independently to accomplish specific goals, others may organize and coordinate their efforts with others who strive for a common goal. Organizations have proven to be important social entities that benefit all individuals involved.

3. The sum total of all human activity, individual and organizational, occurs in the context of the environment.

4. Change is the only constant in all human activity. Evolutionary theory can be used to explain how this change occurs.

Suppose your biggest love in life is surfing the waves in Southern California and hanging out with surfer friends on the beach. You enjoy good stories, simple food, and the beauty of nature. The last thing you want to do is cut your hair, put on a suit, and sit behind a desk from 9 to 5. Then suppose your parents, who have worked hard all of their lives in the restaurant business, keep nagging you to "Grow up and get a 'real job.'"

This chapter features a case that describes how three brothers in this situation, Wing Lam, Ed Lee, and Mingo Lee, created Wahoo's Tacos, a restaurant chain that enables them to keep their love of surfing and to combine it with special abilities and insights they developed from early childhood. Enterprisers with an independent, energetic spirit, they followed their passion, created a unique small business, and grew it into a successful, fun enterprise.

Let's now look at the organizational world, where small businesses like Wahoo's play an important role, and learn how businesses interact with their environment.

1.0 An Organizational World

Organizations are so pervasive in our economy that it is nearly impossible to consider what the world would be like without them. An **organization** is simply an entity that involves people doing work for a purpose. Take a moment and think about all of the organizations that you come in contact with during each day. How many organizations do you think you could identify? An organization was likely involved in building your house or apartment; making the sheets on the bed; manufacturing the carpet; providing the toothpaste; and growing, delivering, and selling the food you eat. Organizations provide the electricity for the lights. Organizations set up the traffic lights and stop signs to regulate traffic and enforce traffic laws. Organizations provide the entertainment you watch and the opportunity to watch or participate in a sport. From the moment you get up in the morning until you go to bed at night, you are in constant contact with products and services that are provided by organizations. Most of our day-to-day activities involve or are impacted by organizations.

To succeed in an organizational world, it is important to understand how to create, manage, own, and operate these organizations. This is the focus of *Creating the Enterprise*. Throughout this book, you will study the role of **enterprisers**, individuals who engage in activities that initiate and then direct an organization to serve their purposes. Enterprisers are involved in all aspects of the

organization
An entity that involves people doing work for a purpose.

enterpriser
An individual who engages in activities to initiate and then direct an organization to serve his or her purposes.

life of organizations, from starting businesses, managing and owning businesses, purchasing or inheriting businesses, and selling businesses. The ability to enterprise encompasses activities beyond the scope of what is typically considered as entrepreneurship.

Entrepreneurship is one form of enterprise. **Entrepreneurs** are individuals who are involved in the start-up of a business. This textbook looks beyond the process of business start-up to consider all of the ways that individuals can take initiative and be proactive in businesses. In fact, this book should be helpful in teaching you how to be successful in any business situation. A **business** is an organization that is started and operated for the purposes of its owners. Typically, a business is started and managed so that it provides a profit for its owners. A **profit** is the money left over after all expenses are paid. This book explores the environment in which businesses operate and the stages of inception, growth, and transition most businesses pass through. In addition, this book provides you with the skills and knowledge you need to seize entrepreneurial opportunities and use businesses to your advantage.

When most people think about businesses in the United States, they often assume that most businesses are big corporations such as General Electric, Exxon, or Procter and Gamble. Yet, the reality is quite the opposite: *Nearly all businesses in the United States are small businesses!* According to the Small Business Administration, there are about 25 million businesses in the United States, of which about 19 million have no employees. Based on tax returns, the majority of these businesses—about 19 million, or 82 percent—had sales of less than $100,000. About 85 percent of these businesses employ fewer than 20 people, and most of these businesses are sole-proprietorships (owned by a single person). In fact, 99 percent of all businesses in the United States have fewer than 500 employees, which qualify them as small businesses.[1] Similarly, most European businesses are considered small. About 93 percent of all firms in Europe have fewer than nine employees.[2] Since most businesses are small businesses, it makes sense to understand how these organizations are successfully started and operated.

Large businesses have a dominant role in our economy, providing employment for over 50 percent of the U.S. workforce. In addition, of about 5 million corporations that operate in the United States, the largest 9 percent control about 97 percent of all corporate assets. In comparison, it might appear that the economic and employment impact of small businesses is relatively minor. In fact, small businesses represent a powerful economic force in the United States:

- Small businesses created a significant proportion—60 to 80 percent—of new jobs in the United States within the last decade. In fact, during recessions, small businesses create nearly all new jobs in the economy while large firms reduce their employment.

- Small businesses are a major source of innovation in technology and new product development in nearly all industries in the United States.

- Small businesses account for approximately one half of all private sector goods and services produced in the United States. In terms of scale, American small businesses would rank as the third largest economy in the world, next to the United States' economy as a whole, and Japan.

---

entrepreneur
An individual involved in the start-up of a business.

business
An organization that is started and operated for the purposes of its owners.

profit
The money left over after all expenses are paid.

- Small businesses provide an important pathway for social and economic advancement, especially for women, minorities, and immigrants.

- Small businesses play a leadership role in local neighborhood and community development. Studies have found that compared to large businesses, small businesses contribute at nearly twice the level of funding per employee to local community organizations.[3]

In addition, small firms form the seedbed for all growing firms in the United States. Every large firm was once a small business. While firms such as Microsoft, Yahoo!, Home Depot, and Cisco rank as large corporations today, each of these organizations began with a smart business idea pursued by a zealous entrepreneur. Exhibit 1.1 lists some of the largest high-growth U.S. corporations, when they were founded, and their 2005 revenues.

This chapter outlines the basic concepts of enterprise. We offer a process for leveraging your efforts toward business success. In addition, we offer a framework for thinking about businesses in the larger context of the nation and the world.

exhibit 1.1   Selected High-Growth Firms

Firm	Year Started	Fiscal Year 2005 Revenue ($ billions)
Amazon	1995	8.5
Amgen	1980	12.4
Apple Computer	1977	17.3
Cisco	1984	22.0
Dell Inc.	1984	55.9
eBay	1995	4.6
Genentech	1976	6.6
Google	1998	6.1
Home Depot	1978	81.5
Hewlett Packard	1939	86.7
Intel	1969	38.8
Microsoft	1976	39.8
Oracle	1977	11.8
Qualcomm	1985	5.7
Starbucks	1985	6.4
Texas Instruments	1930	13.4
Walmart	1962	288.0
Yahoo!	1994	5.3

1.1 The Context of Enterprise: Levels of Business Activity

Take a minute to consider all of the businesses that are profiled in this book. These businesses engage in very different kinds of activities to achieve their goals. They operate in a variety of contexts—farms, factories, services, retail, and restaurants—in a variety of business formats. Think, for example, about all of the different kinds of restaurants that exist: fast-food, sit-down, fine-dining, ethnic. Businesses employ many different types of people with various skills and abilities in each business format. As a way to understand all of this variation in enterprise, this book looks at three major levels of activity: *persons, businesses,* and *environment,* as illustrated in Exhibit 1.2.

Persons

At the simplest level, a *person* can create and exchange goods and services with others. In this scenario, a single person undertakes all of the activities necessary

exhibit 1.2   **Three Major Levels of Business Activity**

to make a product or provide a service and then engages in exchanges with others. For example, if you were interested in selling music CDs, you could be involved in composing the music, playing all of the instruments and singing all of the lyrics, recording the CD, making copies of the CD, and selling each CD. Yet engaging in all of these different activities is time consuming and complicated. Few individuals are gifted at doing a variety of tasks well, or find doing all of these tasks interesting and fun. But what if you are a highly talented guitarist and enjoy performing more than all of the other activities? Wouldn't it be more efficient and rewarding for you to focus on performing and delegate all other activities to other specialists?

This is not a new idea by any means. Adam Smith, in his 1776 book *The Wealth of Nations,* offered an example of individuals undertaking all of the tasks in manufacturing a specific product: pins. He described how one individual could manufacture 20 pins each day. Each person performed every aspect of pin manufacture: cutting the wire, pounding the tip of the wire to make a point, and flattening the rear of the wire to make the head of the pin. Once the pins were manufactured, each individual went out and sold these pins, using this money to purchase more wire to make more pins. Smith pointed out that when individuals combined their efforts at pin making, they could dramatically increase the number of pins produced. By forming groups, each pin maker specialized in one activity, thereby increasing the efficiency of each person's actions. One person cut the wire, one person made pinpoints, and one person made pinheads. By combining their efforts and specializing in one activity, a group of ten pin makers increased their production of pins to 48,000 pins a day, or 4,800 pins for each person in the group. That is a significant increase in productivity!

The Business

Clearly, individuals who collectively organize and coordinate their efforts are significantly more efficient than individuals performing every task alone. Let's return to our original example of making and selling CDs. Assume that a group of individuals agrees to work together in the CD venture. The members divide the individual tasks of composing, performing, recording, manufacturing, and marketing the CDs among themselves based on their talents and interests. This group performs all of the functions of a business—an organization that is started and operated for the purposes of its owners. Dividing all the functions of the business among the group results in a significant increase in productivity. Therefore, businesses exist because they can more effectively create goods and services than individuals working independently.

The Environment

The level of the **environment** is the entire context of activities that surrounds the operation of a business. There are so many different issues to consider when recognizing the environment that, at this point, this section will only highlight some of the environment's important features. All of the businesses that are involved in making and selling CDs are identified as an **industry**, a group of businesses

environment
The entire context of activities that surrounds the operation of a business.

industry
A group of businesses producing similar products and services.

producing similar products and services—in this case, the music-recording industry. An industry can be defined in many different ways. We could define the music industry as all of the people who are paid to produce, perform, record, distribute, and sell CDs. Or we can narrow the definition of the industry to only those individuals and businesses that are paid to produce rock or classical music CDs. The collection of all industries is considered a **community**. For example, we think of all of the different industries involved in music as the music industry. This includes industries involved in making musical instruments and recording equipment, and companies involved in transporting and setting up the stage and equipment for musical performances, as well as service industries such as advertisers and concert promoters.

community
A collection of related industries.

The environment also consists of the *state* or *national* level, where all communities of organizations in a particular geographic area are regulated. At the state or national level, governments regulate and coordinate all of the business, economic, and social activities in a specified area. Finally, the environment consists of all the physical, social, economic, and political features of the world we inhabit. In creating, making, and selling CDs, we would need to consider the legal issues involved with the ownership of the music performed. With changes in technology, it is now possible to record and exchange songs performed by others over the Internet. Should each individual have the right to record music that was created by others for free? The intellectual property rights of music creators and performers are regulated by their respective nations. Compensation for the creators of intellectual property is a political decision that will have a significant impact on the growth and viability of particular industries, including the music industry.

These three levels of activity—individual, business, and environment—are the primary ways we will explore how enterprise occurs. While the focus of this book is on the business level as the primary form of enterprise, we always need to recognize our role at the individual level and the effect of the environment on business activity. In fact, we believe that one of the unique features of this book is its emphasis on individual-level issues for determining business success. Your success is as important as the success of the business you are involved in.

1.2 The Process of Enterprise: An Evolutionary Perspective

One word summarizes the evolutionary perspective of business: *change.* All businesses will change over time. This change takes place in various forms—size, legal form, location, financial stability, ownership, management, and goods and services offered, to name just a few.

emergence
The first stage of a business's life cycle: New venture formation.

As shown in Exhibit 1.3, three processes foster change in businesses: emergence, newness, and transformation. The first process, **emergence**, involves great change as new businesses form and initiate new projects. These new businesses are the result of blind variations or intentional variations. A *blind variation* is a change that occurs by accident, chance, or luck. An *intentional variation* is the

exhibit 1.3   **Three Processes for Change**

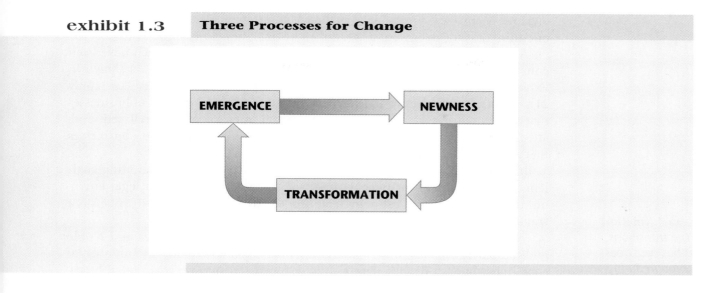

result of the conscious efforts of individuals or other businesses to create a new way to solve a perceived problem through business creation.

Most new businesses are likely to be a combination of blind and intentional variations. For example, the idea behind The Republic of Tea, a business that imports, manufactures, and distributes high quality teas and tea accessories, arose out of a chance meeting between two entrepreneurs who were flying home from a conference. As these two entrepreneurs talked about their likes and dislikes about the food service on airlines, they discovered that they both enjoyed drinking high quality teas and had problems finding sources for purchasing such teas. From that fortunate occurrence, they agreed on a plan to start a tea importing and sales business.

Once a business is successfully created, it then faces the problems of *newness,* the second phase of the evolutionary process. The process of **newness** involves developing and managing a fledgling business so that it survives and flourishes. This is a challenging stage, and statistics indicate the grim fact that few new businesses grow—most eventually fail. Academics have coined the term "the liability of newness" to describe findings that new businesses fail at higher rates than older and larger businesses. Not only do most new businesses fail, they also do not grow very large. Only 5 percent of all new businesses ever grow to larger than 20 employees. Much of the focus of this book is on the challenges of managing and growing a new and small firm.

According to the Small Business Administration, about 581,000 new businesses with employees were launched in 2004. Of those new firms, about 95 percent had less than 20 employees. In that same year, almost as many terminated operations—and again, 95 percent of those had less than 20 employees. Also, in 2004, another 336,000 people started firms that had no employees.[4]

Starting and stopping businesses is a normal part of the dynamics of a healthy economy. Businesses that close are not necessarily failures. About 60 percent become inactive, while others formally close. Many are sold or transferred to new

newness
The stage in a business's life cycle that involves developing and managing a fledgling business so that it survives and flourishes.

owners.[5] Many were profitable over their lifetime; based on a recent study, about one-third of businesses were successful at the time they closed.[6]

According to studies of the survival rates of new business, which have been consistent over the past 50 years, most new and small firms fail. As shown in Exhibit 1.4, businesses are more likely to fail if they are small. After ten years, only 21 percent of businesses of all sizes have survived, while 62 percent of businesses that have hired five or more employees are still in existence.[7] Overall, ten years after start-up, nearly 80 percent of businesses had failed.[8] In sum, most businesses that are started do not last very long.

If a small business survives its early years, it may face more daunting challenges from changes in its economic, social, technological, and legal environments. To survive these inevitable upheavals, businesses must undergo a **transformation** to adapt to these changing circumstances.

With the growth of book "super-store" chains such as Barnes and Noble and the emergence of online booksellers such as Amazon.com, the number of small retail bookstores has significantly declined. To survive, small retail bookstores must transform themselves by offering other types of services and benefits besides carrying general books. For example, Hennesey and Ingalls, a bookstore in Santa Monica, California, has survived and prospered by catering to customers who want to browse among a comprehensive collection of books on the arts and architecture. This bookstore prides itself on having salespeople with a thorough knowledge of arts and architecture books who can assist customers in finding books that meet their interests and needs.

transformation
The transitions a business goes through during its life cycle to adapt to changing circumstances.

The Life Cycle of Enterprise

The three change processes we've just described correspond to the three broad stages of the **life cycle of enterprise**:

1. New venture formation (emergence)

2. Progress and growth (newness)

3. Transition and change (transformation)

life cycle of enterprise
The three stages of an enterprise's life: emergence, newness, and transition.

exhibit 1.4

Businesses Survival Rates

Years	Companies of All Sizes (%)	Companies That Hired 1–4 People (%)	Companies That Hired 5 or More People (%)
After 2 years	76	92	94
After 4 years	47	80	87
After 6 years	38	76	79
After 8 years	29	53	70
After 10 years	21	41	62

Source: The State of Small Business: A Report of the President, 1997 (Washington, DC: U.S. Small Business Administration, 1997), p. 129.

New Venture Formation

New venture formation, the stage where the enterprise emerges, focuses on learning how to successfully start and initiate new ventures and then on combining the resources and competencies necessary to be successful. During this entrepreneurial stage, the enterpriser must recognize and discover opportunities, analyze feasibility, develop a business plan, and determine the best start-up path. This might be forming a completely new company, purchasing a franchise unit, or buying an existing business. We'll explore these topics in Part 2 of this book.

The skills required during this stage will prove valuable in many different contexts, not just in creating businesses. They are applicable in other settings such as corporations, government organizations, and nonprofits, as well as in personal projects, team projects, and other venues where goals need to be identified and realized.

Progress and Growth

Once an enterprise is launched, how do you ensure its ongoing success and overcome the liability of newness? During the progress and growth stage, the primary objective is to manage, monitor, and grow personal and professional achievements. In this book, you will explore the skills for managing and monitoring personal goals and aspirations, as well as the techniques and skills to operate an ongoing business. One important perspective of *Creating the Enterprise* involves the affirmation of all kinds of businesses as outcomes of an individual's choices and interests and the environment in which the business competes. "Lifestyle" businesses, that is, businesses that do not have rapid rates of growth, are celebrated in this book. All businesses could be considered "lifestyle" businesses, because the growth of a business is partly determined by choices made by the business's entrepreneurs, the skills and abilities of these entrepreneurs, and environmental and industry factors. Entrepreneurs must be aware of the businesses that match their goals, abilities, and skills. It is important to learn when a business should stay small and when a business should grow. In any case, enabling a business to successfully operate, whether it is small or large, growing or stable, involves important enterprise skills.

It is possible for some businesses to enter a steady stage of maturity, where in essence the business could be put on autopilot, without a significant need to change. But this is not realistic for most businesses in today's fast-moving climate; they must keep adapting to survive.

Transition and Change

Just as individuals age and their interests and goals change over time, a business also ages and changes. Its transformation may be caused by changes in the environment or by the aging of an industry. For example, only a handful of businesses in the United States manufacture covered wagons, or horse-drawn carriages, or any other kinds of vehicles that require animals for locomotion. Yet a few such businesses do exist and are very successful.

Thus, the final transition and change stage of the enterprise life cycle is characterized by the following actions:

- Enterprisers evaluate their personal and professional achievements. They celebrate their accomplishments with the expectation of moving on to new opportunities, or they take time to enjoy the benefits of their success.

- Enterprisers study the changes in the current environment and reevaluate their goals and priorities in light of environmental changes.

- Enterprisers make decisions about the future, such as selling a business, taking the business to the public through a stock offering, or transferring the management of the business to someone else. This is often a very difficult and emotional time. If the business has not been successful, the entrepreneur faces the trauma of bankruptcy or dissolution.

Taking a Global Perspective

Change is occurring not only in how businesses compete against each other, but in many other ways as well. Now more than ever, companies are required to plan for business activities that extend beyond the United States' borders. In fact, part of the transformation process for a new business may include adapting its business model to accommodate the needs or utilize the resources of a new nation. Since 1990, 30 new nations have been recognized and offered membership in the United Nations. Not only do new nations emerge, but the demographic characteristics of existing nations change as well. Industrialized countries such as Japan and Italy are experiencing declining rates of population growth. The expected population change in Italy is from 58 million people in 2001 to 42 million people in 2050. Japan is expected to decline from 127 million people in 2001 to 101 million people in 2050. Other countries such as Brazil and India have populations that are very young and growing. In Brazil, 30 percent of the population is under the age of 15, and the country is expected to grow from 184 million people in 2005 to 260 million people in 2050. In India, 36 percent of the population is under the age of 15, and the country is expected to grow from 1.1 billion people in 2005 to 1.6 billion people in 2050.[9] Such changes in population will affect not only these nations but others who locate plants there and export goods to them.

Changes in population and economic conditions contribute to entrepreneurial activity in other countries as well as in the United States. In the An Enterprising World box, you'll discover which countries have the highest rates of early-stage entrepreneurial activity and why.

Evolving Industries

Industries are also changing. The invention of new technologies, such as the emergence of the Internet, drives the formation of new industries and companies. In the mid- to late 1990s, venture capitalists funded thousands of Internet businesses. Some, like Amazon.com, Yahoo!, and Google, were incredible success stories. The majority of the new Internet-related companies in the business-to-consumer sector, however, failed. Those that survived learned how to adapt the

Entrepreneurship Goes Global

Most people think that the United States is the most enterprising country in the world. Well, it's not! By any number of measures of entrepreneurship, other countries have a higher percentage of people who are more enterprising.

Over the past seven years, a number of countries have participated in the Global Entrepreneurship Monitor, an ongoing study that measures entrepreneurial activities in a way that allows comparisons between countries. The 2005 report is based on data from 35 nations grouped into middle-income, high-growth and high-income, and low-growth categories according to per capita GDP and GDP growth rate.

One key measure of entrepreneurial activity is "early-stage entrepreneurial activity," the percentage of people who are involved in starting businesses and those who have started businesses within the past four years. In the most recent study, Venezuela scores 25 percent on this measure, which means that one out of every four people in that country are either starting a business or own a new business. Of the countries participating in this study, the United States ranks sixth, with an early-stage entrepreneurial activity rate of 12.4 percent—about half of Venezuela's rate. Exhibit 1.5 shows the early-stage entrepreneurial activity for each of the 35 countries.

As you look at this chart, you may wonder why some countries rank lower in terms of their enterprising activity than others. Countries like Hungary, Japan, Belgium, and Sweden ranked at the bottom, while Venezuela, Thailand, New Zealand, and Jamaica ranked near the top. For one thing, individuals have different motivations

An Enterprising World

exhibit 1.5

Early-Stage Entrepreneurial Activity by Country

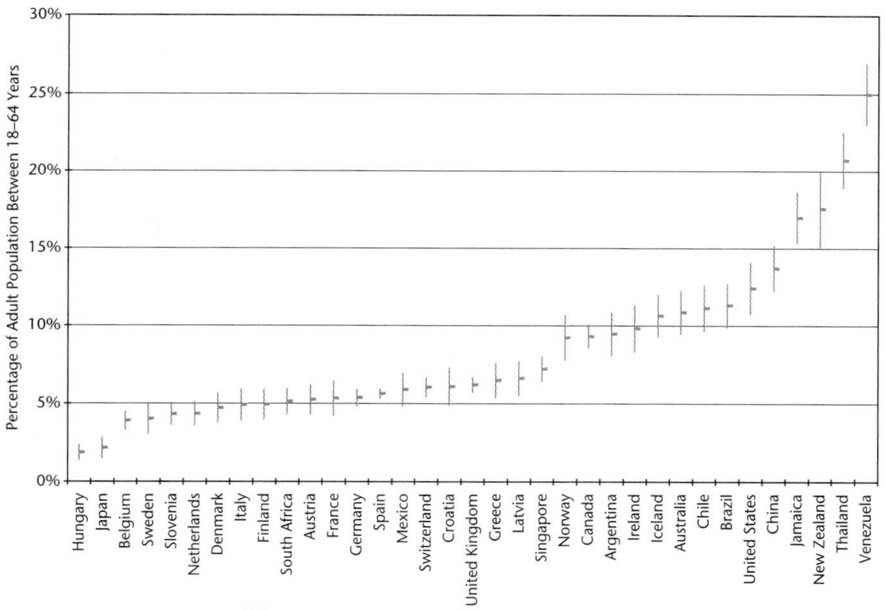

Source: Maria Minniti, Bill Bygrave, and Erkko Autio, *Global Entrepreneurship Monitor 2005 Executive Report,* January 12, 2006, p. 16, http://www.gemconsortium.org/.

(continued)

for starting businesses. The authors of the GEM report have identified two main reasons why enterprisers start new ventures:

- Opportunity: They see an opportunity to exploit by starting a business.

- Necessity: They start a business because they have no other choice. There are no jobs for them to take.

The ratio of opportunity- to necessity-based entrepreneurship also varies greatly around the world, as you can see in Exhibit 1.6. Countries such as New Zealand, Denmark, and the United States have very high ratios of opportunity enterprisers, which means that most entrepreneurs who are starting businesses see opportunities to exploit. In other countries—for example, France, Brazil, and South Africa—necessity enterprisers account for nearly 50 percent of all start-ups. In general, high-income countries exhibit a higher ratio of opportunity-driven to necessity-driven business owners than do middle-income countries.

Again, we might ask why countries differ significantly in the ratio of necessity to opportunity enterprisers. Why would France have such a high percentage of necessity entrepreneurs, while Belgium, its neighbor, has such a low percentage of necessity entrepreneurs? Both are in the high-income cluster. One reason for this difference involves the strict labor laws in France, which make it difficult for companies to fire employees. Since companies cannot fire employees, they are often shy about hiring new employees, so many people in France cannot get jobs. Individuals in France, therefore, are more likely to turn to necessity enterprising.

exhibit 1.6   **Opportunity- to Necessity-Based Early-Stage Entrepreneurship**

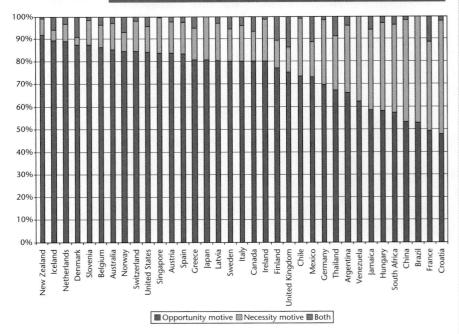

Source: Maria Minniti, Bill Bygrave, and Erkko Autio, *Global Entrepreneurship Monitor 2005 Executive Report*, January 12, 2006, p. 16, http://www.gemconsortium.org/.

Discussion Questions

1. What types of economic situations create a business environment that supports entrepreneurship?

2. What are some reasons that the ratio of necessity versus opportunity enterprisers differs so greatly from country to country?

3. In looking at Exhibits 1.5 and 1.6, do you think that necessity entrepreneurs seem to be important for promoting economic growth in certain kinds of countries?

Source: Maria Minniti, *Global Entrepreneurship Monitor 2005 Executive Report,* January 2, 2006, http://www.gemconsortium.org/.

early business models to their advantage and to develop new ones as the new technology evolved. The Internet also forced companies and even whole industries to change their business models and to implement new ways of operating that take advantage of the Internet and electronic commerce (e-commerce).

The success and failure rates of businesses in a particular industry are an indication of an industry's health. An industry is considered healthy when it rewards businesses that satisfy customer needs through innovation and lower prices. These businesses will experience growth through higher sales. Businesses that don't satisfy customer needs, on the other hand, will experience decreases in growth and sales. Keen enterprisers should be alert to industry changes to help them avoid some of the big mistakes made by dot-com businesses.

Individual tastes and preferences change, often in contradictory ways. Such changes may drive industry trends. For example, obesity has become a worldwide epidemic as the rate of obesity increases at an alarming rate. In the United States, as many as 65 percent of adults are either overweight or obese, 16 percent of children and adolescents ages 6 to 19 are overweight, and another 15 percent are at risk of becoming overweight.[10] At the same time, Americans consume huge amounts of snack foods, pushing snack food industry sales to almost $10 billion! Although there has been an increasing interest in healthier snack foods, sales of high-calorie nuts, corn chips, and potato chips have remained high. And consumers appear to prefer flavored varieties that are higher in carbohydrates and salt.[11] Yet the weight loss industry is booming as Americans spend billions on diet programs, foods, and supplements each year. Companies such as NutriSystem and Weight Watchers International report high revenue growth as consumers look for help in the fight against fat.[12]

If change is likely to occur in all aspects of our lives—individual, business, and environment—it makes sense to prepare ourselves for this inevitability.

1.3 Pursuing Personal Success

A fundamental premise of this book is that the pursuit of success in business should be a way to promote your success in life. We believe that you should give this personal success a higher priority than the success of the businesses and organizations in which you are involved. The focus of *Creating the Enterprise* is primarily on *you* and therefore it emphasizes the tradeoffs each person makes between personal and business priorities.

Being unaware of these tradeoffs may lead to decisions that do not benefit either the business or the individual. For example, an owner of a growing clothing retail business may decide to expand her business by renting and renovating space adjacent to her current store. She will require funds to pay for fixtures (such as clothes racks, wall racks, shelves, and display cases), additional space, and additional inventory (such as clothes and accessories). If the business does not have sufficient surplus funds to pay for this expansion, it will need to borrow money from lenders, such as banks, or take on additional investors. Many lenders require that the owner of the business cosign for a business loan. Cosigning obligates the owner to pay for the loan if the business cannot make the payments to the bank. If the expansion of the business does not generate enough profits from additional sales to pay back the loan, the owner of the business would have to pay this debt. Thus, the owner's decisions about expanding her business could place personal assets and savings at risk.

The idea of placing more value on your personal and professional aspirations may seem to be a selfish and self-centered perspective that appears to contradict other important values. Why should generous, kind, or altruistic people develop a self-serving attitude? How can persons who put themselves first work together in organizations? Wouldn't selfishness lead to everyone working alone? On the contrary, the pursuit of individual goals can actually benefit everyone else as well.

Know Thyself

This book is grounded in a philosophy of "self-actualization ethics," which emphasizes the unique value and importance of each person.[13] You are unique. No other person in the world is like you. Indeed, there has never been, nor will there ever be another person like you. You have certain qualities and abilities that no one else has. In the philosophy of "self-actualization ethics," it is each person's priority to realize his or her unique capabilities and gifts. In this philosophy, everyone benefits when each person pursues his or her unique capabilities. Much like Adam Smith's example of the pin makers, when each person strives for excellence on a particular set of tasks, and also coordinates those efforts with others, everyone achieves more. Each person's obligation, therefore, is to excel at his or her own unique capabilities.

To pursue this uniqueness, you must first discover your special abilities. Aspire to "Know thyself," taking the time and effort to discover your unique skills and abilities. For most of us, this is not an easy task. We may have some sense of our strengths and weaknesses in certain types of jobs. We may have accumulated enough experience to know the kinds of situations we enjoy and the kinds of people we like. Yet we may be unclear about what we should be doing with our lives and how we might go about achieving our capabilities. We devote many parts of this book to exercises that will help you discover your values, goals, and capabilities. Self-knowledge makes it easier to make decisions and expend the time and energy to accomplish tasks.

Even when we have gained knowledge about our unique abilities and gifts, we still must undertake the responsibility to achieve these capabilities. Personal excellence takes time and energy. Fully utilizing your unique capabilities takes a lot of work. For example, a gifted athlete may be endowed with superb hand–eye coordination, nimbleness, and speed. But this talented athlete still needs training and practice to fully maximize his or her potential.

Changes in Disposition, Cognitions, and Actions

Just as a talented athlete needs training and practice, each of us should identify our unique abilities and gifts and develop them so we can reach our personal and professional goals. Each person is a composite set of dispositions, cognitions, and actions. Together, these characteristics may create a powerful foundation for building a rewarding and successful life.

A **disposition** is a set of personality characteristics that is likely to remain stable in nearly all situations, such as a person's temperament, character, or personality. If a person has a disposition toward eating sweets, we would assume that this person would enjoy sweets in most situations. Knowing about this "sweet tooth" allows us to make predictions about the kinds of foods that person might choose in most situations.

People vary on a number of personal dimensions, such as aggression, shyness, optimism, intelligence, sociability, self-control, and flexibility. These personal dimensions are characteristics that influence a person's behavior in all situations. For instance, a person with a shy disposition will find it more difficult than other people to be outgoing and is therefore less likely to meet and greet new people in social functions. That doesn't mean that shy people can't meet and greet new people; it simply means that it will be more difficult for them. Individual dispositions may constrain certain thoughts and actions, but they do not prevent them.

The psychologist and educator Howard Gardner suggests that people vary on different dimensions of their personality. These dimensions support various kinds of activities and occupations. Exhibit 1.7 briefly describes Gardner's **seven intelligences**. Gardner believes that each individual has strengths and weaknesses across all seven intelligences and should recognize how to best use those unique capabilities. It is unlikely that any one individual will have exceptional talents in all seven intelligences. What Gardner suggests is that we should seek to discover our own unique profile of intelligences, and work toward enhancing and building them.

Your **cognitions**, thought processes that reveal what and how you think, significantly influence what you are likely to do. For example, psychologists have found that people who were diagnosed with depression were likely to experience "learned helplessness."[14] Learned helplessness is a condition where individuals evaluate negative events in their lives and think that the causes of these problems are enduring and pervasive personal defects. People with these attributes are likely to do nothing. They become helpless because they think that the characteristics of the situation cannot change. By not taking action to dispel

disposition
A set of personality characteristics that generally remains stable in nearly all situations, such as a person's temperament, character, or personality.

seven intelligences
The seven different types of intelligences that people may possess, as categorized by Howard Gardner: musical, bodily-kinesthetic, logical-mathematical, linguistic, spatial, interpersonal, and intrapersonal.

cognition
Thought process that reveals what and how you think, significantly influencing what you are likely to do.

exhibit 1.7   **Howard Gardner's Seven Intelligences**

Musical Intelligence. The ability to perform and compose music. Some individuals have a natural ability to pick up a musical instrument and play it almost immediately, while others with a very low musical intelligence cannot carry a tune.

Bodily-Kinesthetic Intelligence. The ability to control one's body, which would be seen in an individual's movement, balance, agility, and grace. Individuals who excel in sports, such as Tiger Woods and LeBron James, display a natural sense of how their bodies should act in demanding physical situations.

Logical-Mathematical Intelligence. The ability to mentally process logical problems and equations.

Linguistic Intelligence. The ability to utilize language. A person's ability to construct and comprehend language will vary, but this trait is universal. Some people have exceptional abilities to learn many different languages and use language in creative ways—for example, gifted writers and public speakers like Barack Obama.

Spatial Intelligence. The ability to perceive and interpret objects in the physical world, as well as to abstractly comprehend and manipulate these objects mentally. Spatial intelligence is used to comprehend shapes and images in three dimensions.

Interpersonal Intelligence. The ability to interact with others, understand them, and interpret their behavior. Interpersonal intelligence is manifest in how people are able to discern the moods, temperaments, intentions, and motivations of others.

Intrapersonal Intelligence. The ability to understand and sense our "self," that is, who we are, what feelings we have, and why we are the way we are. A strong intrapersonal intelligence can lead to self-esteem and self-enhancement, and a strong character can help us solve internal problems. Others often do not recognize intrapersonal intelligence unless we show it as an emotion, such as anger or joy, or as something tangible, such as a painting or a poem.

Source: Adapted from Howard Gardner, *Frames of Mind: The Theory of Multiple Intelligences* (New York: Basic Books, 1983).

their beliefs about a particular situation, they are unable to prove whether these attributions are correct. They learn to be hopeless and then act helpless. Fortunately, we can modify our thinking process and learn to overcome this and other cognitions.

Finally, we want to behave and act in ways that support our personal values and goals. This book helps you develop behaviors that enhance the satisfaction you get from both your personal and professional endeavors. For example, you will learn about goal setting in Chapter 3. The activities involved in goal setting enable you to identify, set, and achieve goals for your own life. Goal setting is also key to business success and significantly improves the performance of employees in most business settings.

Creating the Enterprise provides a multitude of ways to increase your chances at personal and business success. These involve

- *Exploring your dispositions* to gain a realistic understanding of your inherent capabilities and the values and beliefs that motivate you.

- *Probing your thinking* to discover how your perceptions of your circumstances significantly influence the kinds of choices you consider.

- *Identifying new skills and behaviors* to increase ways to take control of your situations and influence your destiny.

Enterprisers 1.4

Wahoo's Surfs Its Way to Success

Dressed in shorts and sandals and sporting a laid-back, surfer-bum attitude, Wing Lam, Ed Lee, and Mingo Lee may not look like successful entrepreneurs. But behind the casual demeanor lies plenty of business savvy. From Santa Ana, in Southern California surf country, the three Lam brothers run Wahoo's Fish Taco. Since opening their first restaurant in 1988, they have grown their company to over 30 locations in Southern California and Colorado, each generating more than $1 million in annual revenue. The company's plans call for selective growth in other areas as well.

How did the brothers turn a love of surfing and surfer food into such a success story? For one thing, they come from a family of restaurateurs. Their parents, refugees from communist China, opened one of Brazil's first Chinese restaurants. In 1975, the Lees and their three Brazilian-born sons immigrated to Southern California and opened Chinese restaurants on Balboa Island in upscale Newport Beach and in Costa Mesa. When the senior Lees were ready to retire, they offered to turn the restaurants over to the boys.

"We had no desire to put on the white shirt, black pants, and the bow tie," recalls Wing Lam, who wanted to strike out in a different direction. With their parents pushing them to get "real jobs," the brothers looked for a way to earn a living and still have time to surf. Operating a restaurant was the logical choice. "All of us grew up in this type of business," explains Mingo Lee. "In Brazil, we lived on the third floor over our restaurant. From the day you were able to walk, you knew what was going on in the operation. We stood on Coke crates, peeling shrimp and washing dishes."

The Wahoo's concept grew out of the brothers' surfing trips to Baja California. They based their menu on the beach food they and their friends liked to eat. "Literally, the day before we opened, I actually sat in the kitchen and wrote things down, and tried a couple of things, and said, 'We're opening tomorrow,'" says Wing.

Although this would be risky for many other aspiring enterprisers, the brothers' boyhood experiences gave them an instinctual feel for the business. "When you cook all your life, you just know what goes with what," Mingo continues. After cooking up the first batches of beans, rice, and fish, they looked at each other and said, "Hey, that was okay!" The brothers also wanted to create a special feeling. "Sure the food's going to be good," says Mingo. "We felt confident in our menu, but we wanted people to walk in and actually experience something—sort of a getaway to our favorite spots down in Baja." They designed a place that would appeal to their own "Boarding Tribe"—surfers, snowboarders, and skateboarders—and have expanded to include all extreme sports enthusiasts.

The approach worked. Wahoo's reflects the brothers' personalities and Southern California lifestyle. Stroll into a Wahoo's restaurant, and you'll see happy customers digging into plates

(continued)

of fresh food, piled high and priced low. It's noisy, friendly, and even chaotic. The walls are plastered with real surf gear and posters from surfing, skateboard, and snowboard companies—a custom that began when employees from local surfing apparel manufacturers who ate at Wahoo's put up banners to mark their favorite booths. Wahoo's became the cool place to eat. "Instead of importing what's fashionable in New York, we're exporting our own culture," Wing says. Although just about all ages will find something good to eat at Wahoo's, its target customers are young men 18 to 24 years old, who eat out almost six times a week and are the biggest consumers of commercially prepared food in the United States, according to the National Restaurant Association.

"It looks easy on the outside," says Mingo, who is in charge of the finance area. But behind the casual and upbeat atmosphere of a Wahoo's eatery are a theme concept, carefully developed food preparation systems, and employee training programs. "Our parents gave us the tools by sending us to school, giving us the extra edge that they didn't have growing up," he says. Each brother has a business degree and speaks several languages.

They started small, originally planning on each brother running one store. As sole proprietors, they could keep operations simple and use their dad's "old school" methods. "You just keep everything between the ears," explains Mingo. "When you show up each morning, you put your inventory together. You just never have any paperwork in place."

This plan worked for those first three stores. As the Wahoo's concept gained acceptance and the fourth and fifth stores were coming on line, the brothers realized they needed better systems for growth. They set up administrative procedures, such as standard inventory sheets and computerized payroll. From there the brothers divided managerial responsibilities among

themselves and added a fourth partner, Steve Karfaridis, who joined them in 1990 as director of operations.

Mingo is chief financial officer, handling all the finances and other corporate departments like human resources. "I am cheap to the core," he says. "I cut every corner that is not needed. I am concerned about the bottom line." Wing is in charge of marketing, including promotions and fundraisers, while Ed focuses on planning. "I handle the development of the restaurants," Ed explains. "I find real estate and make sure that it's within Mingo's budget, then build it out." Steve, an experienced restaurateur, serves as director of operations and implemented standardized methods and employee training programs that were critical to the chain's ability to grow. Keeping it simple was key. "We had created a training program that's based on single page modules," Steve says. Another company-wide practice is the ten-second rule. Ten seconds is the maximum amount of time a plate of food will wait in the pass-through or a customer will stand at the register before someone greets them. The company also prides itself on developing employees and promoting managers from within.

Part of the chain's unique quality comes from its marketing philosophy: "If you discount yourself, you cheapen the image that you have built all these years," explains Wing. "It's either full-price or it is free; there is nothing in-between. If we are going to give something, we give it with no strings attached."

From the beginning, Wahoo's gave away a lot of food at sporting events patronized by its core market groups. As Wahoo's helped other groups and stores promote themselves, they introduced potential customers to the great-tasting food the restaurants featured. Wing Lam believes that offering free food at community gatherings is cheaper and much more effective than relying on more traditional marketing methods. "Once they taste it, see it, smell it, and touch it, they connect it to you," he says. "Everyone wants to support a local business as opposed to a large corporate entity to which they are not attached. They see you being a part of the community and want to interact with you, support you because you are supporting the community. The giving comes back tenfold."

Discussion Questions

As you read the other sections of Chapter 1, keep in mind some of the insights and ideas of this story. The following questions will help you think about issues this chapter introduces:

1. What special abilities (or behaviors or instincts) did the founders of Wahoo's possess that were instrumental in their success as entrepreneurs?

2. How important is individual choice in determining an individual's success?

3. What environmental factors played a significant role in the early success of Wahoo's?

4. What kinds of actions did the founders of the business take to initiate the development of Wahoo's?

5. What obstacles should the founders of Wahoo's anticipate as they expand this business?

6. If you were thinking about starting a restaurant, how would you start this process?

Source: Adapted with permission from Small Business School, the series on PBS, at http://SmallBusinessSchool.com.

1.5 Business: The Organizational Imperative

Businesses are their own entities and need to be treated as if they are uniquely their own persons. The **organizational imperative** states that a business has its own needs and objectives that are separate from the needs and objectives of any of the business's other stakeholders.[15] For example, many high-technology firms need substantial amounts of funds from outside investors to grow and prosper. This financing supports research and product development, as well as the expansion of production facilities. When the founders of many high-technology firms raise capital from other investors, they often find themselves "fired" from their roles as managers of these new, larger firms. They may not have the substantial managerial expertise and background required to run the resulting high-growth business. Most successful high-growth technology firms need managers and leaders with experience at running and operating high-growth businesses. Therefore, it may not be in the best interest of the firm to have inexperienced managers in charge. Who, then, has the authority to make decisions about the needs and objectives of the business?

   Determining who will make the decisions about a business's needs and objectives is based on the legal format of the business. In Chapter 4 we will explore all of the details that characterize various legal forms of businesses, such as sole proprietorships, partnerships, and corporations. The characteristics of these legal

organizational imperative
Concept that a business has its own needs and objectives separate from the needs and objectives of any of the business's other stakeholders.

forms of business have many different implications for how the business will be managed and operated.

At this point, let's consider two major dimensions by which the interests of the business are determined. The *control dimension* involves determining who will manage the business. The person who manages the business makes decisions about the business's day-to-day operations. The *ownership dimension* involves determining who will share in the benefits of the business.

In most businesses, the individual who owns the business also controls the business. The goals and purposes of the business are determined by the *owner/manager* of the business. Sole proprietors are an example of a business where the manager is typically also the owner. When businesses need more capital to expand and grow, as in the high-technology example mentioned earlier, they require more people to invest in the business. Investors often ask for some ownership in the business as a way to insure that they gain benefits from the business's success. If a substantial number of people are owners of a business, their ability to control the day-to-day operations of the business become more limited. Think about the difficulty of operating a business if it had 10,000 owners who all wanted to run the business. Larger businesses usually separate the functions of ownership from the functions of control. Managers will make the day-to-day decisions about the needs and objectives of the business, while the shareholders will receive the benefits of ownership in the business through rising stock prices or dividends.

Imagine, then, that a business can become of a size where it no longer needs its original founders or owners to survive and flourish. Few businesses that last longer than ten years keep their founding owners and managers. McDonald's no longer has the involvement of its original founders, the McDonald Brothers, or Ray Kroc, the person who took the McDonald Brothers' original concept and expanded it into an international company.

As these examples demonstrate, you are not your business—and the business is not you. While most entrepreneurs start businesses to support their own personal goals, it is very likely that as a business grows and matures, the goals of the business and the goals of its founder will change and diverge. It is important to be able to see when your personal goals and values no longer correspond to the needs and objectives of the business, and then, make appropriate choices to benefit both yourself and the business, if possible.

1.6 The Environment: No One Is an Island

No one is an island. We are all connected to each other. Our decisions affect a multitude of other people, and their concerns and issues will also affect our ability to make decisions. This requires an understanding of the *environment* in which enterprise occurs. As noted earlier, the environment includes the entire physical universe and all of its human and social activity. Simply put, the environment is everything that is not you. We have seen that human and social activity can be organized in many different ways. We all have different priorities, interests, and goals. All of the individuals, groups, communities, businesses, and governments in the environment have different and competing interests and concerns.

Balancing Stakeholder Interests

Suppose we want to use more electricity to power home appliances, TVs, and computers, and we decide to build more hydroelectric dams as a way to generate this electricity. A new dam will flood many square miles of land, displacing people living in towns and farms along the river. The flooded land will be lost for farming or any other activity. A new dam may disrupt the migratory patterns of fish in the river, so that fewer fish are able to survive. While some people will benefit from the electricity the dam generates, other people will be harmed, and the physical and natural environment will also be changed. How can we acknowledge all of the different people and factors that comprise such a decision? A way to understand this constellation of cooperative and competing interests among other people and the physical and natural environment is through *stakeholder theory*.

Stakeholders are entities that have a legitimate interest in the processes and activities of a business. Exhibit 1.8 illustrates nine broad categories of stakeholders. To make effective decisions about you and your business, you must consider stakeholder theory, which recognizes the interests of every possible individual, group, or other entity that may have some connection to you and your business. Stakeholder theory has proven very valuable in helping us understand all of the forces that affect a business.

stakeholder
An entity that has a legitimate interest in the processes and activities of a business.

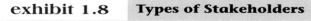

exhibit 1.8   **Types of Stakeholders**

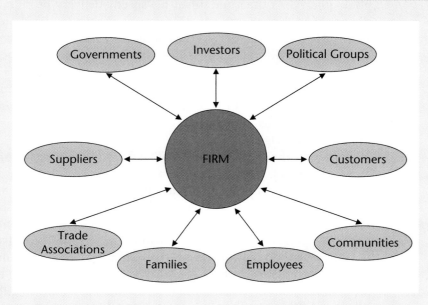

Stakeholder Theory in Action

To demonstrate the effects of these various stakeholders on the operations of a business, let's consider the ramifications of starting a pizza delivery business.

First, it is important to recognize the influence of your *family* on business decisions. Most entrepreneurs depend on their families to help them start and build their businesses so that families are often significantly involved in the decisions you'll make. Families typically provide both emotional and financial support for most budding entrepreneurs. Let's assume that your parents invested $25,000 in the business and also promised to help out on weekends. Tradeoffs between family needs and business needs will surface. For example, decisions to expand the pizza delivery business may mean that you have to use personal income to buy a larger pizza oven instead of spending for other personal needs. As a result, you may have to decide if cash generated by the business should pay for a larger pizza oven, purchase a new family car, or pay tuition for the children's schooling. How many hours should you devote to your business versus the number of hours spent with your family? Should the pizza delivery business be open until 2 AM to serve late-night customers? How many hours will you have available for your family if you work at the pizza delivery business until it closes? Should your family members work for the business? And what salaries and benefits should your family members receive if they do work for the business? Balancing decisions involved with family and business are often the most difficult for entrepreneurs to make.

All firms will have *customers* who are concerned about the success and operation of the business. The decisions you make about the quality of your products and the level of the service you provide will influence them. For example, you may advertise that you will deliver pizzas to your customers within 30 minutes of receiving their telephone order, a great benefit to customers who want a hot pizza quickly. At the same time, this speedy delivery promise will involve other stakeholders. Your pizza truck drivers may have to speed along neighborhood streets. How will members of the community respond to seeing your pizza delivery trucks speeding along their streets? Will the *community* be angry about a 30-minute delivery guarantee that may make their streets less safe for their children? How should you balance the interests of your customers who want pizza delivered in 30 minutes with that of the members of the neighborhood who are not buying your pizzas but who want your delivery trucks to drive slowly and safely through their neighborhoods?

The community might form *political groups* who might protest and demonstrate at your pizza store to prevent you from delivering pizzas in 30 minutes. These political groups could initiate and promote legislation to make food delivery businesses illegal in their communities. Other stakeholders may also influence your ability to deliver pizzas within 30 minutes. The city *government* can pass a law preventing any business within the city limits to advertise and promise to guarantee food deliveries within 30 minutes. The government could monitor the safe-driving behaviors of your drivers by issuing speeding tickets if they drive too fast. In addition, the city will have an interest in knowing that your pizzas are safe to eat. The city will have regulations and inspectors to monitor the operation of your business by specifying health standards, licenses, and building and food safety codes. Without the proper licenses to operate your business, the city can prevent you from operating. You will need to ensure that your pizza business is located in an area that is zoned for businesses that can serve and deliver food.

Your pizza business will likely have *employees* who take phone orders, make the pizzas, and deliver pizzas. These employees have their own interests and concerns. For example, the pizza delivery drivers will be concerned about their safety when making deliveries and may not want to drive to certain locations to deliver pizzas—say, a city park—that are not houses or apartment buildings. Such delivery spots may be more likely to be places where drivers are often robbed and killed, particularly late at night. Should a driver be allowed to say, "I won't deliver a pizza to that location"? You will have to balance the concerns of your pizza drivers with the needs of some customers who want a pizza delivered to a park or street corner.

Your pizza business will also purchase food, boxes, and equipment from *suppliers*. These businesses hope that your company will be successful so that you will buy more supplies from them over time. As your business expands, they will benefit through increased sales. Your business also depends on the ability of your suppliers to provide quality materials on time and at reasonable prices. What if your pizza business uses real Italian mozzarella cheese as an important ingredient and your cheese supplier cannot acquire the cheese you want because of shipping problems from Italy to the United States? What would you say to your customers if you did not have the real Italian mozzarella cheese you advertise? Should you close your business until you have real Italian cheese? Should you try to find another source of supply? Should you substitute Italian cheese with American cheese? What should you tell your customers, and should you price your pizzas differently because of this change?

As this pizza delivery business example illustrates, every business is connected in very complicated ways to multiple stakeholders who affect the business's success. Decisions that affect one group of stakeholders may have a profound effect on other stakeholders. Each group must be considered. More than likely, each group will make its views known. As an enterpriser, you have to be proactive in ascertaining the views and interests of all of the stakeholders that impact your business.

Ethical Behavior

Enterprisers make many types of business decisions in the course of a day. In addition to considering stakeholder needs, they must also take into account what they believe to be right and wrong. The owner of our pizza delivery business has choices in how to run the company and the standards he or she sets. These actions shape the ethics of the organization. **Ethics** refers to the standards of moral behavior used to determine whether something is right or wrong. Examples of unethical behavior include lying, unauthorized use of someone else's property, giving false impressions, bribing someone to get business, and failing to disclose information. Suppose our pizza delivery business owner doesn't tell customers

ethics
A set of moral standards and values that helps individuals choose between right and wrong.

that deliveries to addresses outside a five-mile zone carry an extra charge. This is unethical because it misleads customers about the total cost of their orders.

Managing businesses ethically has many benefits, including keeping customers loyal, attracting new customers, and retaining employees. Throughout this book, we will address ethical concerns that enterprisers face when starting and operating their businesses.

As we make transactions with other people, we can choose to act ethically so that everyone wins or act in ways that cause the enterpriser to win and the other party to lose. The Enterprising Ethics box presents a framework for evaluating such interactions.

enterprising ethics

Who Benefits?

Our lives are a series of transactions between other people. These transactions occur whenever a person is involved with another person and represent experiences where there can be gains or losses between the two parties. When person A initiates an activity with person B, it has an effect on both A and B. We can diagram these transactions as a two-by-two matrix that shows gain or loss between party A and party B.

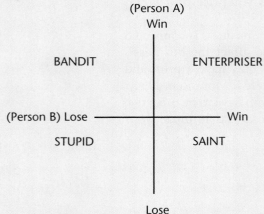

In our view, people who initiate an activity where both A and B win are *enterprisers*. They create situations where everyone gains. When you sell a product or provide a service, ideally the buyer of your product is better off because the transaction fills a need. You are also better off because you make money through the transaction.

A person who initiates an activity where he or she loses and the other person wins is a *saint*: Person

A's actions result in a situation where A is worse off, but B is better off. For example, some people start businesses and sell products at prices below their costs to gain customers. While their customers benefit, the enterpriser eventually goes out of business. In this situation, others benefit while the enterpriser doesn't.

On the other side of the spectrum is the *bandit*. In this case, party A initiates an action where he or she gains but party B loses. Certainly, there are individuals who start businesses that eventually defraud others, where the business doesn't provide benefits to anyone other than the owners. Only the owners win, while everyone else is worse off. We would hope that most of these people go to jail for such actions, but you can probably think of people who personally gained through their actions while others have not. The recent Enron, Tyco, WorldCom, and other corporate scandals are examples of such situations. Bandits can exist at small companies, too. Unscrupulous contractors with no credentials offer to fix a roof or driveway, take a sizable deposit, and don't return or do slipshod work. Get-rich-quick schemes also promise big profits. Unsuspecting customers pay for the materials, only to discover that the only one who gets rich quick is the promoter—who is clearly a bandit.

Finally, we have situations where A initiates an activity that ends up with losses for both A and B. In this case, A is *stupid*. People who cause accidents fall into this category. There are also individuals who initiate activities that they hope will be successful but which eventually fail. So not only does the initiator fail, but so do any others who are involved. Employees, customers, investors, and suppliers all are worse off, too.

While this framework may seem to be an oversimplification of interactions between people, it helps us think about the types of situations that might occur when people initiate new activities.

Discussion Questions

1. Give examples of enterprises that fit into these four quadrants.

2. Are people in other countries rewarded differently for being in each of these four quadrants? Are there some countries that expect people to act as saints rather than as enterprisers? Can you think of countries where people are more likely to act as bandits?

3. How would you characterize former Enron executives Kenneth Lay and Jeffrey Skilling: bandits or stupid?

4. What kinds of laws and regulations would you enact to promote more enterprisers versus bandits, saints, or stupid people?

Source: Carlo M. Cipolla, "The Basic Laws of Human Stupidity," *Whole Earth Review,* Spring 1987, pp. 2–7, http://www.mentalsoup.com/mentalsoup/index.html.

1.7　Summary

1. We live in a world where organizations have a profound effect on our day-to-day activities. To succeed in an organizational world, we need to understand how to create and control these organizations.

2. An organization is an activity-based system (work gets done) that is socially constructed (involves other people), goal directed (has a purpose), and is bounded (there is a distinction between members and non-members). There are many ways to compare and contrast the different types of organizations. For-profit versus not-for-profit organizations (differentiated by a purpose to make money) and private versus public organizations (differentiated by how membership is determined) are two ways that we can compare different types of organizations. A business is defined as an organization that is created for the purpose of generating value for its owners.

3. An enterpriser is one who undertakes an enterprise. To be *enterprising* is to be marked by an independent, energetic spirit and by a readiness to undertake or experiment.

4. A primary reason for focusing on small businesses is that most organizations are small. About 98 percent of all businesses in the United States have fewer than 100 employees. Small businesses create most of the new jobs in the economy. Small businesses are a significant source of innovations in technology and of new products, and are significant in the creation of new markets. Small businesses are a major pathway for the economic and social advancement of women, minorities, and immigrants.

5.   Business activity occurs across three levels: person, business, and environment. At each level, there are forces that push for change. In an evolutionary perspective, change occurs through a cycle of emergence, newness, and transformation. In emergence, change occurs as persons, businesses, and forces in the environment seek variation. A variation is a difference in how things currently are. As enterprisers strive to develop new ways of doing things, they face the problem of newness. Most new things fail. If a business survives its early years, then it is likely to face ongoing changes in the environment. Environmental change is inevitable as individual tastes and preferences change, new technologies are introduced, and social, demographic, environmental, and economic changes occur.

6.   The three forces of change also apply to the life cycle of an enterprise. In the new venture formation stage, the focus is on starting and initiating new projects. During the progress and growth stage, the focus is on managing, monitoring, operating, and growing personal and business achievements. In the final stage, transition and change, the focus turns to reevaluating prior successes and achievements, recognizing changes in the environment and in personal goals and priorities, and making decisions about the future.

7.   In an organizational world, it is important for all individuals to take an active role in their personal success. In "self-actualization ethics," every individual seeks to pursue his or her unique qualities and abilities. It is important to "know thyself" and seek an understanding of how one's disposition affects and is affected by one's way of thinking (cognitions) and actions.

8.   The actions of individuals and businesses take place within the context of an environment. An environment involves everyone and everything that is not about you. Anyone affected by a specific business is a stakeholder of that business. Most businesses are likely to have investors, customers, communities, employees, trade associations, suppliers, governments, political groups, and family members of the owners of the business as stakeholders.

9.   The organizational imperative states that a business has its own purpose and objectives, as well as its own needs and resource requirements that are separate from the goals, objectives, and needs of the owners and managers of the business. Two major dimensions by which the interests of a business are determined are control and ownership.

Review Questions

1. What is required in order to succeed in a world of organizations?

2. What is the difference between an "enterpriser" and an "entrepreneur"?

3. In what ways do small businesses contribute to the economy?

4. How might changes in one of the three levels of business activity (person, business, environment) affect the other levels of business activity?

5. Study Exhibit 1.4. What reasons might explain why businesses with more employees are likely to survive at higher rates than businesses without employees?

6. Why would a philosophy of "placing yourself first," that is, self-actualization ethics, be of benefit to others?

7. Differentiate between disposition, cognition, and action and give examples of each.

8. What negative characteristics in attributing problems seem to lead to "learned helplessness"?

9. Identify and define Howard Gardner's seven intelligences.

10. Study Exhibit 1.8. Identify specific stakeholders for each category that would be affected by a business that manufactured bicycles.

11. Explain the concept of "organization imperative."

12. What are the two major dimensions by which the interests of a business are determined?

13. Where might opportunity recognition and development skills be utilized?

14. What characterizes the transition and change stage of an enterprise life cycle?

Applying What You've Learned

1. The first step in developing your future career plans is to examine your own life and goals. Here are some questions to get you started.

   (a) Do I have personal goals for my personal life?
   (b) Do I function efficiently and effectively?
   (c) Do I plan my daily schedule for maximum efficiency?
   (d) Have I set aside specific time each week to upgrade my knowledge and professional proficiency?
   (e) Do I work well with others?
   (f) Am I working to develop stronger leadership qualities?
   (g) Do I participate in community, civic, or church activities?
   (h) Do I have a positive attitude?
   (i) How well do I organize my work and home life?

   (j) Am I an asset to my community?

2. The primary activity for developing your own abilities and knowledge as an enterpriser is through networking. (This topic will be covered in more detail in Chapter 4.) Each week you should contact ten "strangers" (individuals with whom you have not had any previous personal contact) about aspects of enterprising that will be of benefit to you. These strangers can be entrepreneurs, experts, customers, or suppliers in an industry you are interested in; or venture enablers such as accountants, lawyers, and investors. Keep a log of these strangers. Provide a name and contact information (address, phone number, e-mail address) for each stranger. How did you get the name of this stranger? Why did you contact this stranger? What benefits were you hoping

to offer this stranger? What benefits were you hoping this stranger would offer you? What other contacts was this stranger able to offer you to help you achieve your goals?

3. Review the descriptions of Howard Gardner's Seven Intelligences in Exhibit 1.7. Which of these are among your strengths? Weaknesses?

4. Choose a business in your area, such as a restaurant, grocery store, or gas station. Identify all of the different stakeholders that are affected by this business (e.g., customers, employees, government). How does this business *succeed* with each stakeholder group? How similar, or different, are the measures of success for each stakeholder group?

5. Look around your house and choose an object that you use frequently (e.g., pen, pencil, cup). How might this product be improved? Think about how you would go about the process of taking your ideas and developing them into a product that other people would buy. What would you need to make your idea become real?

Enterprisers on the Web

1. Go to the home page of Wahoo's Fish Tacos, http://www.wahoos.com, and use the information you find to answer the following questions:

   (a) What does the home page say about the style and priorities of this business?
   (b) Explore the Events, Photos, and Contests pages. How do these pages demonstrate the underlying marketing philosophy Wing Lam describes?
   (c) Read the latest news about Wahoo's on its News and Media page. What more can you learn about the reasons for Wahoo's success?

2. Using an online article database like Find Articles (http://www.findarticles.com) or InfoTrak, read what others are saying about this company. How do others perceive Wahoo's, and how does this compare to how Wahoo's sees itself?

3. Go to http://geography.miningco.com/science/geography/cs/worldpopulation/ and explore demographic changes in the population of the world and the United States. This site provides many different pathways to find demographic, social, and economic data on all regions and countries of the world. What kinds of changes are likely to occur in the world over the next 25 years? What kinds of changes are likely to occur in the United States over the next 25 years?

4. Go to *Inc.* magazine's website: http://www.inc.com/. Explore the various sections of this site. What kinds of resources are available for enterprisers?

5. Go to the GEM Consortium website, http://www.gemconsortium.org/, and explore the most recent version of the Global Entrepreneurship Monitor (GEM), which tracks entrepreneurial activity in dozens of countries throughout the world. Which countries appear to be engaged in more entrepreneurial activity, and what reasons does the report offer to explain these higher levels? Give several reasons why the United States is not the most entrepreneurial country.

6. Use one of the Internet directories (e.g., Yahoo!) to find a directory of businesses in your area. How many different kinds of businesses are identified in this directory? Why are there so many of the same kinds of businesses (restaurants, dry cleaners, retailers)? Are there any kinds of businesses that seem to be missing that might be successful in your area?

End Notes

1. "Frequently Asked Questions: Small Business Statistics and Research," *Small Business Administration, Office of Advocacy,* http://www.sba.gov (April 30, 2006).

2. Zoetermeer, *The European Observatory for SMEs: First Annual Report* (The Netherlands: European Network for SME Research and EIM Small Business Research and Consultancy, 1993).

3. "Frequently Asked Questions," *Small Business Administration, Office of Advocacy,* October 15, 2005, http://www.sba.gov.

4. *The Small Business Economy 2005: A Report to the President,* U.S. Small Business Administration (Washington, DC: Government Printing Office, 2005), p. 8.

5. William J. Dennis, *Business Starts and Stops* (Washington, DC: National Federation of Independent Business, 1999).

6. Brian Headd, "Redefining Business Success: Distinguishing between Closure and Failure," *Small Business Economics,* August 2003, pp. 51–61.

7. *The State of Small Business: A Report to the President,* U.S. Small Business Administration (Washington, DC: Government Printing Office, 1997).

8. William J. Dennis, *Business Starts and Stops* (Washington, DC: National Federation of Independent Business, 1999).

9. *2005 World Population Data Sheet*, Population Reference Bureau (Washington, DC: Population Reference Bureau, 2005), http://www.prb.org.

10. Eileen Marie Simoneau, "Get a Move on at Grandma's," *Orlando Sentinel*, March 12, 2006, p. J1; and Dixie E. Snider, "Obesity Statistics Still Grim," *Atlanta Journal-Constitution*, February 25, 2005, p. A15.

11. Greg Masters, "Peanuts or Pork Rinds?" *Retail Merchandiser*, July 2005, pp. 26–29.

12. Christopher Palmeri, "How NutriSystem Got Fat and Happy," *Business Week*, September 19, 2005, pp. 82–84; and Tatiana Serafin, "The Fat of the Land," *Forbes*, April 10, 2006, p. 104.

13. David L. Norton, *Personal Destinies: A Philosophy of Ethical Individualism* (Princeton, NJ: Princeton University Press, 1977).

14. Martin Seligman, *Learned Optimism* (New York: Pocket Books, 1998).

15. William G. Scott and David K. Hart, *Organizational America* (Boston: Houghton Mifflin Company, 1979).

chapter 2

Enterprisers

Key Concepts

1. Entrepreneurship is a universal social and economic activity in the United States. Because being an enterpriser is more about *doing* than about *being*, nearly everyone has the same potential to become an enterpriser.

2. Enterprisers come from all backgrounds, ages, and experiences. Some characteristics (demographic and personal) can increase the likelihood of becoming an enterpriser. Although individuals can't change demographics—ethnicity, gender, and age—they do have some control over personal characteristics. Education, for example, is a primary driver of entrepreneurship.

3. Successful enterprisers are more likely to think differently from other individuals. They are more likely to view their situations optimistically, focus on ways to leverage their means (current resources and capabilities at hand) to come up with a variety of solutions (ends), and engage in accomplishing "small wins."

Suppose you are an African American male, the youngest of seven children, who grew up in a Texas ghetto. The biggest support in your life is your grandmother, who insists that you put God first, your family second, and everything else after that. Your father is a doorman who wants you to grow up to be a businessman. You start your first business venture as a child, mowing lawns for 50 cents. Its success encourages you to follow your entrepreneurial instincts and acquire those characteristics and dispositions that help you prosper.

This chapter introduces a case about how a determined young man from government housing, Albert Black, went to college on a football scholarship and built a successful business in spite of many setbacks while he still maintained the values his grandmother instilled in him. As you read this chapter, you will learn how you, too, can enhance your chances of becoming a successful enterpriser.

2.0 Enterprisers

"Am I an entrepreneur?" It's a common question that many people ask before they embark upon their journey as enterprisers. When we see successful people, we often wonder whether they have "something special" that makes them different from other people. Do enterprisers have personality characteristics that make them unique? We don't think so. In terms of their personalities, enterprisers are just like everyone else. Although you might suspect that most enterprisers are outgoing, sales-oriented people, in fact, all personality types are represented. Introverts who avoid risks at all costs are just as likely to be successful enterprisers, under the right circumstances, as extroverts and risk takers. Successful enterprisers find business situations that match their personal characteristics and skills.

This chapter explores a variety of dispositional and cognitive characteristics that determine whether enterprisers are different from other people. **Dispositional characteristics** are natural or acquired habits or characteristic tendencies in a person or thing. **Cognitive characteristics** are intellectual rather than physical—the ability to think, learn, and remember—and include mental processes such as comprehension, reasoning, perception, decision-making, planning, and learning. As you will discover, enterprisers are of all ages and come from all kinds of backgrounds and experiences. No personality characteristic prevents a person from becoming an entrepreneur. Certain characteristics, however, seem to increase the chance of becoming an enterpriser and achieving success.

dispositional characteristics
A person's natural or acquired habits or characteristic tendencies.

cognitive characteristics
Intellectual rather than physical traits— the ability to think, learn, and remember. Examples include comprehension, reasoning, perception, decision making, planning, and learning.

For example, people who already earn a lot of money are more likely to start businesses than those who earn less. Knowing this fact doesn't prevent individuals who earn less money from becoming enterprisers. The statistics provide a sense of the *relative probabilities* of success for someone in a particular category. So when we talk about the following dispositional and cognitive characteristics, think of them as providing some individuals with a slight advantage at the starting line. Being rich is an advantage, but it doesn't guarantee future success—just as being poor doesn't prevent a person from becoming successful. You are likely to share some of the characteristics of successful enterprisers.

Our basic philosophy is that being an enterpriser is more about *doing* than about *being*. In Chapter 3 we cover some fundamental behaviors that you can practice to become a better enterpriser. Enterprising is not about *who you are*; it is about *what you do* with your life. Enterprising is a mindset and a way of acting.[1] Yet we all worry about whether we have the "right stuff" to become an enterpriser.

As we discussed in Chapter 1, we think about individuals in terms of dispositions, cognitions, and actions. *Dispositions* are a person's characteristics, what a person has at hand at a particular moment in time. *Cognitions* are the way a person thinks, and *actions* are what a person does—behaviors.

We hope that by the end of this chapter you will agree that nearly everyone can become an enterpriser *if that is what they truly desire* and if they undertake the actions necessary to achieve this goal. As we mentioned earlier, learning about the dispositions and cognitive characteristics—for example, age, gender, marital status, and optimism—should offer encouragement by demonstrating that nearly everyone has the chance to become an enterpriser.

The Panel Study of Entrepreneurial Dynamics

Until recently we have had surprisingly little systematic evidence about the fundamental nature of the individuals involved in business start-up or the entrepreneurial process. The fall 2002 publication of an introduction and overview to the Panel Study of Entrepreneurial Dynamics (PSED) provides important research to substantially enhance our understanding of entrepreneurship.[2]

New business formation is one of the most important indicators of economic growth around the world. The self-sufficiency and independence that lead individuals to create new businesses significantly affect economic growth, innovation, and job creation. Entrepreneurs have played a major role in shaping the business environment in the United States. Of today's Fortune 200 corporations, about 97 percent had entrepreneurial beginnings. Think about the personal computer, Internet, and biotechnology industries. Many leading companies in these sectors didn't even exist 25 years ago! And it's not just technology firms. With Starbucks Coffee, Howard Schultz changed the way the world thinks about a cup of coffee, while Fred Smith's Federal Express revolutionized the small-package delivery system and gave us an alternative to the U.S. Postal Service. Schultz and Smith are two examples of how **nascent entrepreneurs**, individuals who undertake the efforts necessary to initiate and start new businesses, create new industries (overnight delivery) or change and restructure how businesses in established industries compete.

nascent entrepreneurs
Individuals who undertake the efforts necessary to initiate and start new businesses.

The PSED focused on four fundamental questions:

1. Who is involved in starting businesses in the United States?

2. How do they go about the process of starting firms?

3. Which of these business start-up efforts result in new firms?

4. Why are some of these business start-up efforts successful in creating new firms?

Through questionnaires and detailed interviews with 830 nascent entrepreneurs, the PSED gathered information about the type and sequence of start-up activities, the sources and kinds of resources nascent entrepreneurs used, work and career experience, social networks, perceptions of entrepreneurial climate, risk assessment, social skills assessment, competitive strategy, and future expectations.

The PSED is unique in several ways. By collecting information while entrepreneurs were starting their firms, the study gathered knowledge of their *current* expectations and thought processes rather than the reminiscences of entrepreneurs *after the fact*. Second, the PSED sample reflects a variety of attempts to get into business, not just of those individuals who successfully started firms. By following these start-up efforts over time, the PSED sample helps to differentiate characteristics of successful and failed efforts to create new businesses. Finally, the PSED included not only nascent entrepreneurs but also a comparison group. The PSED can be used to compare nascent entrepreneurs to the population of working-age adults across a wide variety of demographic, economic, social, and psychological factors.

Key Findings of the PSED Study

The results of the PSED indicate that all groups and types of individual are involved in the new business formation process. The highlights of the study include these findings:

- Entrepreneurial activity in the United States is widespread. Approximately 10.1 million adults in the United States are trying to start new businesses at any time, either as individuals or in teams.

- Men are twice as likely to start new businesses as women.

- Enterprisers span all adult age groups. Among the most active are young men aged 25–34; those over 65 are less likely to start businesses.

- African Americans are about 50 percent more likely to start a new business than whites.

- Education significantly predicts emergent entrepreneurship, particularly for African Americans and Hispanics.

- Those with higher incomes are more likely to be involved in starting a business.

- Where people live affects entrepreneurial activity. The presence of certain economic, demographic, and educational factors contribute to higher entrepreneurial activity in more urban areas.

Clearly, entrepreneurship is a universal social and economic activity in the United States.

2.1 The Demographics of Enterprisers

Americans devote a lot of energy to entrepreneurial activity.[3] Today, over 10 million adults in the United States are involved in new business creation. In fact, 6 percent of all U.S. adults over the age of 18 are trying to start new firms. Even though men and women are roughly equal in numbers in the population, men are almost twice as likely to start businesses as women. For men 18 years and older, the rate is 8 percent, almost twice the 4.5 percent rate for women 18 and older.

People like to work together when they try to start businesses. While over 40 percent of new businesses are formed as sole proprietorships, the average start-up team is about 1.8 people,[4] suggesting that nascent entrepreneurs are attempting to form well over 5 million new firms. Compare this to figures for marriages and births in the United States: According to the *Statistical Abstract of the United States: 2006*, there are about 2.2 million marriages and 4.1 million live births in the United States each year.[5] In short, the creation of a new firm is more widespread than the creation of a new household or the birth of a baby!

Age and Gender

Age and gender are correlated to whether individuals initiate efforts to start a new business. While men and women of all ages engage in the entrepreneurial process, this activity is more likely to occur in certain age groups. As Exhibit 2.1 shows, the highest prevalence rate for both men and women is among those 25–54 years old—the prime years for work success.

exhibit 2.1 | **Nascent Entrepreneurs by Age and Gender**

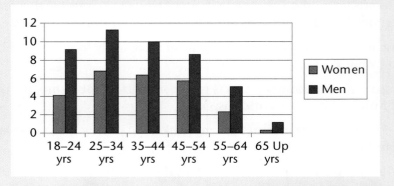

Ethnicity

Ethnic background influences the likelihood that individuals will start new businesses. Based strictly on numbers, there are more white entrepreneurs. As we see in Exhibit 2.2, however, the PSED estimates that the rate of business formation by African American men and women is about 50 percent higher than for whites, and for Hispanic men it is about 20 percent higher than for white men. Many people may find these findings surprising because earlier studies of minority enterprise indicated that blacks and Hispanics were less likely to be self-employed than whites.[6] However, both groups have always had strong traditions of business ownership.[7]

2.2 Personal Characteristics of Enterprisers

Demographic characteristics are those characteristics that one is basically "born with." You cannot change your ethnicity, gender, and age. Individuals do have some control over the following personal characteristics, however.

Education

Given the many educational programs available to prospective enterprisers, it comes as no surprise that schooling plays an influential role in the entrepreneurial process. As Exhibit 2.3 confirms, individuals who finish high school and complete some additional education or training are more likely to try to start a new business venture. However, the impact varies substantially by ethnic group. Post–college graduation training significantly increases the likelihood of black men and women and Hispanic men becoming entrepreneurs.

You, the reader of this textbook, are likely to be a person who is getting a college degree. This places you in a category of people who are more likely to start businesses. Education is the one major factor that people can leverage to improve their chances of becoming a successful enterpriser.

exhibit 2.2   **Nascent Entrepreneurs by Gender and Ethnic Identity**

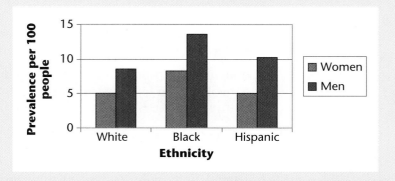

exhibit 2.3

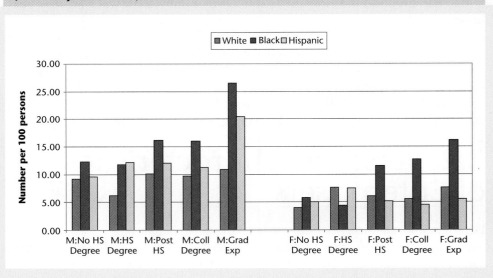

Nascent Entrepreneurs by Ethnic Identity and Education (18–54 years old)

Household Income

Like education, household income influences the likelihood that an individual will start a new business. The higher the household income, the greater a person's tendency to participate in start-up activities. Most people can't easily change the amount of money they earn—at least in the short term. Yet there is considerable evidence that household income is highly correlated with education. We can all position ourselves to achieve higher incomes by acquiring more education. *Education is, therefore, the primary driver of entrepreneurship.*

Marital Status and Household Characteristics

The PSED study also considered whether characteristics such as marital status, size of household, and age of children in the household have an impact on entrepreneurial activities:

* Marital status and the number of people living in a household have a small effect on whether individuals start new business.

* Respondents with children in the household are more likely to report being involved in a business start-up.

Labor Force Participation

Do people start new businesses out of desperation, because they have lost employment or cannot find a job? You might think so, but the PSED results do not support this popular belief. The rate of business start-ups for those 18 and older with-full time jobs is 8 percent, versus 7 percent for those working part time. In contrast, the rate is about 5 percent for those not currently working (such as the unemployed, students, and homemakers), and about 1 percent among those who are retired (5 percent among those retired but under 65 years old). Active participation in the workforce seems to have a positive impact on entrepreneurial activity, with little variation by gender or ethnic group.

Having a job provides a number of advantages for people considering starting a business. People with jobs are likely to be closer to potential customers, and therefore see new opportunities for products and services. People with jobs are more likely to have connections to suppliers, as well as have a deeper knowledge of how a particular industry works so that opportunities can be more easily identified and exploited.

2.3 Cognitive Characteristics: Career Reasons

Do enterprisers start businesses for different reasons from those individuals who have other kinds of careers? Do they think differently from others? As we mentioned earlier, many people believe that enterprisers are "different" from others, and that enterprisers have a greater desire for higher levels of financial success, autonomy, and independence. A recent study using the PSED compared nascent entrepreneurs to nonentrepreneurs on six career motives:[8]

1. *Innovation* involves reasons that describe an individual's intention to accomplish something new, such as developing an idea for a product and being innovative and on technology's cutting edge.

2. *Independence* describes an individual's desire for freedom, control, and flexibility in the use of one's time.

3. *Recognition* refers to an individual's intention to have status, approval, respect, and recognition from family, friends, and those in the community.

4. *Roles* describe an individual's desire to follow family traditions or follow the example of others one admires.

5. *Financial* success involves an individual's intention to earn more money and achieve financial security for himself or herself, spouse, and children.

6. *Self-realization* refers to the pursuit of self-directed goals—for example, challenging oneself, fulfilling a personal vision, leading and motivating others, and greatly influencing an organization.

More Alike than Different

The results of this study were surprising. As we see in Exhibit 2.4, there were no significant differences between nascent entrepreneurs and the comparison group on four of the scales—*innovation, independence, financial success,* and *self-realization*—but significant differences on two of the scales—*recognition* and

exhibit 2.4

Reasons for Choosing a Career, Nascent Entrepreneurs vs. Nonentrepreneurs

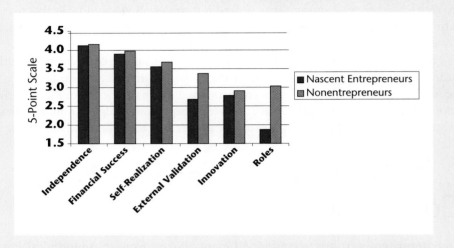

roles. The analysis also showed that for all six reasons, the nascent entrepreneurs were likely to have *lower* scores than the non-entrepreneurs, overall.

In addition, all respondents (the nascent entrepreneurs and the non-entrepreneurs) were likely to rank the importance of the six reasons in the same order. *Independence* was the most important career reason, followed by *financial success, self-realization, recognition, innovation,* and *roles.* Interestingly, the more significant differences between nascent entrepreneurs and nonentrepreneurs occurred on scales that were rated as *less* important by both groups (such as *roles*).

Finally, the analysis showed a small but significant difference between men and women. Men had higher scores on *financial success* and *innovation* than women, regardless of their category. It is important to note that although the score women assigned to financial success was lower than that given by men, women still saw financial success as an important reason in career choice and equal in their ranking to self-realization.

Universal Values

The insights from this study suggest that for individuals in the United States, the desire for financial success, independence, self-realization, and innovation is universal. In fact, in studies of individuals from countries around the world, the reasons people give for why they work are surprisingly similar. An international research consortium, the Work Importance Study (WIS), analyzed data on the importance of work and or work values from 11 countries.[9] The study identified five factors and compared them cross-nationally:

- *Individualistic orientation* (autonomy, lifestyle, creativity, personal development)

- *Orientation toward self-actualization* (ability utilization, altruism, aesthetics)

- *Social orientation* (social relations, social interaction, variety, working conditions)

- *Utilitarian orientation* (economics, advancement, prestige, achievement)

- *Adventurous orientation* (risk, variety, physical activity)

The findings indicated that the career value structures of individuals were surprisingly similar. In all the countries studied, the self-realization values (personal development, ability utilization, and achievement) are ranked highly, whereas people place little importance on risk taking and the desire for authority and prestige.[10]

Given these similarities, then, what differentiates enterprisers from others? Basically, enterprisers are less likely to care about how other people view their pursuit of success and do things themselves. They pursue financial success, independence, self-realization, and innovation on their own terms.

enterprising ethics

What Does a Kazaa Do, Anyway?

Imagine starting a company based on a product that you believed had a great future—even though you were not sure how people would use it! Niklas Zennström and Jan Friis did just that. Zennström, who earned business and computer science degrees at Uppsala University in Sweden, met Friis at Swedish telecom provider Tele2 in the 1990s. Tele2, the first Internet service provider in Sweden, now serves more than 30 million customers in 22 countries with fixed and mobile telephony, broadband, and cable television—successfully challenging the government monopolies.

These European technology entrepreneurs parlayed their prior telecommunications expertise into Kazaa, a company they developed around the commercialization of their proprietary peer-to-peer file-sharing software and launched in 2001. To date, the software has been downloaded onto more than 389 million computers worldwide. The original company was incorporated in the Netherlands.

Although Zennström thought the technology was promising, he admits he was not sure how people would use it. Some possibilities included sharing software and videos. "So we made it as open

as possible and then we thought we'd see what people used it for," he says. "It was more a technical proof of concept that it was possible to transfer files between two end users rather than going through servers."

The software is free; all revenues come from advertisers who place ads on the Kazaa website. As users tried Kazaa software and liked it, it became the world's top download. Still, the partners did not expect the company to become so successful as a tool for music downloads. They attribute its popularity to the very user-friendly technology and interface, which was easier to use than rivals such as Napster.

An important difference between Kazaa and the now-defunct Napster was technology. Kazaa's peer-to-peer technology does not rely on central servers that are controlled by the company, as with Napster. Instead, users download the software to their own PCs, and the software automatically connects individual users to each other directly over the Internet—with no central management point. Kazaa provides the software but neither has control over how it is used nor knowledge of what users are doing when they are

(continued)

online. Kazaa and other file-sharing networks continue to maintain that their software has many legal uses and they should not be held accountable when users deploy the applications illegally.

This difference became important as the popularity of music- and movie-sharing services soared. Music publishers in many countries, including Australia and the United States, sued Kazaa and other file-sharing companies for copyright violations. After a Netherlands court ruled against Kazaa, Zennström quickly restructured the company, giving the software code to a company with operations on a British island known to be a tax haven and in Estonia, which has lax intellectual property regulations. They sold the Kazaa interface and the license for the file-sharing technology to Sharman Networks, a newly formed Australian company incorporated in Vanuatu, an island nation in the South Pacific. Because Vanuatu levies no taxes and does not release financial information about its companies, the companies are able to avoid regulation and legal challenges. However, major recording and movie studios soon sued Sharman Networks for copyright infringements.

Discussion Questions

1. How responsible are Nicholas Zennström and Jan Friis for the ways their creation is used? Should entrepreneurs care if others use their products or services in illegal ways? What steps could they take to prevent this from happening?

2. Why did Kazaa's acquirer, Sharman Networks, incorporate in Vanuatu? Discuss the ethical implications of incorporating in a country solely to avoid legal liability for the use of Kazaa's peer-to-peer file-sharing programs.

3. Visit the website for Kazaa, http://www.kazaa.com. What types of advisories are posted on the site? Do you think they protect Kazaa from legal action, and why?

4. Do a Web search to learn the outcome of the lawsuits against Sharman Networks/Kazaa. Summarize your findings and discuss whether you agree with the decisions.

Sources: Jane Black, "Napster's Sons: Singing a Different Tune?" *Business Week*, February 21, 2002, http://www.businessweek.com; Ted Bridis, " 'Kazaa' Makers Settle Piracy Lawsuits," Associated Press, July; 28, 2006, http://www.businessweek.com; "How Skype and Kazaa Changed the Net," BBC Click Online, June 17, 2005, http://news.bbc.co.uk; Kazaa website, http://www.kazaa.com (July 30, 2006); "Kazaa," http://en.wikipedia.org (July 30, 2006); Andy Reinhardt, "2005 Stars of Europe—Innovators: Niklas Zennström," *Business Week*, May 30, 2005, http://www.businessweek.com; and Todd Woody, "The Race to Kill Kazaa," *Wired*, February 2003, http://www.wired.com.

2.4 Cognitive Characteristics: Optimism

How we think about what happens to us, and how we think about what *will* happen to us, is vital for enabling us to take actions that can make a difference in our lives. Thinking optimistically involves viewing our past and future situations in a way that we don't get stuck and not take action when necessary. Living life successfully involves a certain level of risk taking. You will often be in situations where you need to take action, but you will not be sure whether your actions will result in the outcomes you intend. There is always a chance that your actions may turn out differently from what you intended.

Research on success has found that individuals who take action are more successful than those who don't, *even if those actions are not necessarily the best or the right actions*. Much of this book is about learning the skills and abilities to determine the right actions to take. However, simply knowing what to do does not necessarily lead to action. You must still take action—and you should put yourself in the right frame of mind to take action.

Positive Thinking

People who are more likely to take action are probably also optimists. An **optimist** is a person who believes that good things will happen. It sounds simple: Just believe that your actions will result in good outcomes. But it is not always easy to adopt this mindset. We encounter situations where we feel discouraged and hopeless or *pessimistic*, that bad things will happen, no matter what we do. This section discusses how to think about our situations so that we become optimists and take actions that lead to good outcomes!

optimist
A person who believes that good things will happen.

What characterizes an optimistic viewpoint? Individuals make three attributions about their experiences:[11]

- First, we make a judgment about whether the situation is *internal*. Is it about us or our efforts, or is the situation *external* to us? For example, if a person was involved in an automobile accident, an internal attribution would be, "I caused the accident," while an external attribution would be, "A dog jumped in front of the car, and I swerved to avoid hitting the dog."

- Second, we determine whether the situation is *stable*, likely to exist for a while, or *variable*. "I caused the accident because I have poor vision," is a stable attribution. Poor vision isn't something that is quickly corrected. "I was answering the cell phone when the accident occurred," is temporary; it occurred only in that moment.

- The third type of attribution involves a judgment about whether the cause is *global* and will extend into other situations or is *specific* to the incident. "I always fail to pay attention," is a global attribution compared to, "I just didn't see the car come out of the driveway until it was too late," which is a specific attribution.

Consider a good situation you have recently experienced. For example, imagine that you just took an exam and received the highest grade in the class. An optimist offers internal/stable/global attributions for this situation, such as, "I always do well on multiple choice exams." This comment indicates that you consider your success to be because of you (an internal attribution) and that you believe you'll be successful in taking other exams in the future (a stable and global attribution). A pessimist will offer attributions that are the opposite of the optimist's—an external/temporary/specific attribution of the situation, such as, "The professor gave an easy test today." The pessimist doesn't attribute any of the success to himself or herself (an external attribution) and doesn't believe that this good event will last or have any significance for other situations (a temporary and specific event).

Optimists attribute external/temporary/specific causes to bad situations. For example, if an optimist gets a poor grade on an exam, the optimistic attribution would be, "The professor put questions on the exam on material that we didn't cover in class." The poor grade is due to an external situation that is also temporary and specific to this one exam. The pessimist will offer an internal/stable/global attribution for a poor exam score, "I'm not very smart," which attributes the poor exam score to himself or herself and suggests that such poor performance on this one exam is likely to occur on other exams as well.

Believe in Yourself

The previous examples were for attributions that people make about their past, explanations for the causes of what happened to them. Individuals also offer their expectations for what they believe will occur in future situations. The same patterns hold true. An optimist will offer explanations about future situations indicating that he/she expects good things will occur. These good things will result from his/her own efforts (internal), will continue (stable), and will extend to other situations in his/her life (global). The pessimist, on the other hand, doesn't expect that his/her own efforts will help good things occur (external). Any good things that do happen will be short-lived (temporary) and apply only to that situation (specific).

Because optimists expect good things to happen, they are likely to put effort into achieving their expectations. Pessimists, who expect that bad things will happen, tend to give up too soon, thinking that their efforts will be for naught. Certainly, there are many situations where one should give up, but giving up is appropriate only when there are other goals that might be more attainable, achievable, or appropriate. *Giving up, and doing nothing, is not an option for an enterpriser.*

An optimistic way of thinking about our lives provides tremendous benefits, even in difficult situations. For example, in studies of students who are making the adjustment to college life, researchers found that students with higher levels of optimism were less stressed, less depressed, less lonely, and had more social support.[12] In studies of cancer patients, optimists were more likely to have less distress and were more likely to be able to cope with the difficulty of having cancer and undergoing treatment.[13] In work situations, optimists are likely to be more problem-focused than pessimists. Pessimists often avoid dealing with problems by escapism, overeating, and overdrinking.[14]

As Exhibit 2.5 clearly illustrates, researchers have found that optimists are more able to engage in the kinds of behaviors that enable them to cope with difficult situations. Optimists exhibit less stress in difficult times and accept the situations they are in. They are proactive in looking for solutions. Their pessimistic counterparts are likely to be in denial and not do anything to improve their lot.[15]

There are relatively few, if any, situations where it is better to be a pessimist. Indeed, researchers suggest that pessimistic thinking often cripples individuals from undertaking any action on important goals in their lives. When individuals are hobbled by thoughts that their actions will result in bad outcomes, they fall into a state of lethargy, where it seems impossible to do anything that might

exhibit 2.5   **Coping Tendencies of Optimists and Pessimists**

Optimists	Pessimists
Information seeking	Suppression of thoughts
Active coping and planning	Giving up
Positive framing	Self-distraction
Seeking benefit	Cognitive avoidance
Use of humor	Focus on distress
Acceptance	Overt denial

Source: M. F. Scheier, C. S. Carver, and A. W. Bridges, "Optimism, Pessimism, and Psychological Well Being," in E. C. Chang (Ed.), *Optimism, Pessimism: Implications for Theory Research and Practice* (Washington, DC: American Psychological Association, 2001), Exhibit 9.1, p. 204. Reprinted with permission of C. S. Carver.

improve the situation. Believe that your efforts will lead to success, and your chances of success will increase!

2.5 Cognitive Characteristics: Ends and Means

We can approach problems in two ways: focusing on the ends or on the means. When we have a particular problem to solve, the *ends* of the problem are the characteristics of the problem itself. The *means* refer to the capabilities necessary to solve a particular problem. In most situations, we tend to focus on developing the means to satisfy particular ends.[16] The differences between ends and means may, at this point, seem rather trivial. However, these two approaches yield very different—but equally important—ways to accomplish our goals. Here is a simple example of the difference between ends and means.

Imagine a chef is assigned the task of cooking dinner. The task can be organized in two ways. In the first, the host or client picks out a menu in advance. All the chef needs to do is list the ingredients needed, shop for them, and then actually cook the meal. This is a process of focusing on ends. *It begins with a given menu and concentrates on selecting effective ways to prepare that particular meal.*

In the second case, the host asks the chef to look through the cupboards in the kitchen for possible ingredients and utensils and then cook a meal. Here, the chef has to imagine possible menus based on the given ingredients and utensils, select the menu, and then prepare the meal. This is a process of focusing on means. *It begins with given ingredients and utensils and focuses on preparing one of many possible meals with them.*[17]

Ends

When we focus on *ends*, we *start* with the solution. Most problem solving uses this approach. Assume that you love dogs and are also artistic. Frustrated in your current job at a public relations firm, you decide you want to start a canine-themed business. From your experience with your own large dogs, you know that currently available dog collars and leashes don't do a good job of letting the handler control large dogs, and you choose to focus on designing attractive and effective products that solve this problem. As you develop your plans, you would perform certain steps to create your dog collar and leash business, including the following:

- Determine the resources necessary to make collars and leashes, such as the supplies, equipment, and employees to make and assemble them.

- Gather market information about the people who purchase collars and leashes and where they are likely to purchase them (such as pet stores).

- Make contacts with retail stores who might display your company's collars and leashes for customers to purchase.

We begin with a specific goal, or end: a collar and leash business. We then work out the means to achieve that goal.

When we start with ends, we use our creativity to generate the necessary means to achieve given ends. Indeed, we often hear of individuals who identify new means to solve particular ends. Our entrepreneur will need supplies (means)—for example, nylon webbing, buckles, and fasteners—for the collar and leash business, yet may have very little money to purchase these supplies. The creative enterpriser might convince a supplier to provide the necessary materials on credit or offer the supplier a partnership in the new business as a way to obtain the necessary materials to make the collars and leashes.

Means

Focusing on *means* takes a different approach to the situation. We begin with what we have at hand. Let's assume that the general problem is the same as before: controlling large dogs. What might we already have available to us that could control large dogs?

We might first consider our ability to train a large dog to obey our commands. Rather than starting a collar and leash company, we might consider using our dog-handling skills to open a training school for large dogs. We could take our dog to a park where dogs can run and play without leashes and demonstrate our abilities to control our dog without a leash. Other dog owners may notice our well-behaved dog and ask for tips on dog training. We could turn these queries into sales by suggesting that we will train their dogs for a fee.

We could also put up fliers announcing our dog-training classes. The training classes could grow into a substantial business. We might end up training other people to teach the classes and generate revenues from their activities. We might then decide to write a book on dog training as another possible way to help people control their dogs. We might consider conducting seminars on dog training or developing a television show or video about this topic.

By focusing on our *means*—what we have currently available to use—we can expand the many ways that our skills and abilities in controlling large dogs might develop into a business. These become the starting point for achievement.

Differences Between Ends and Means

Let's consider the ways these two approaches differ and how companies might apply them in developing a business strategy. Exhibit 2.6 summarizes the major differences between ends and means.

It is important to understand that efforts toward accomplishing a goal are likely to combine both ends and means. Few situations are likely to be pure forms of one or the other. These approaches are points of view about how individuals accomplish activities. Enterprisers should explore both and can be effective using either approach.

exhibit 2.6	Ends vs. Means	
Ends versus Means Categories	**Focus on Ends**	**Focus on Means**
Givens	End is a given	Means and capabilities are a given
Decision-making criteria	Choose between means to achieve a given effect	Choose between possible ends that can be created with given means
	Selection of means based on expected return	Selection of ends based on affordable loss or acceptable risk
	Outcome dependent: Choosing means is driven by the characteristics of the outcome that the decision makers wants to create and their knowledge of possible means	Actor dependent: Given specific means, choice of outcome is driven by characteristics of the actors and their ability to discover and use contingencies
Competencies employed	Exploiting knowledge	Exploiting contingencies
Nature of unknowns	Focus on the predictable aspects of an uncertain future	Focus on the controllable aspects of an unpredictable future
Underlying logic	To the extent we can predict the future, we can control it	To the extent we can control the future, we do not need to predict it
Outcomes	Market share in existing markets through competitive strategies	New markets created through alliances and other cooperative strategies

Source: Adapted from S. D. Sarasvathy, "Causation and Effectuation: Toward a Theoretical Shift from Economic Inevitability to Entrepreneurial Contingency," *Academy of Management Review* 26 no. 2 (2001), p. 251.

2.6 Exploring Ends and Means: Powell's Books versus Amazon.com

To more clearly illustrate the distinctions between means and ends, let's look at two Internet companies that represent these contrasting styles: Internet businesses Powells.com and Amazon.com. We'll start with the givens of each firm's situation and then compare each in terms of the categories in Exhibit 2.6.

Givens

In the Ends approach, the enterpriser starts with the desired effect (outcome). Amazon.com started operations in July 1995. The company's objective was to use the Internet to change the way people purchased books. Founder Jeff Bezos set about acquiring the resources necessary to start an online bookstore, including selling stock in his company. Bezos also formed an alliance with a major distributor of books to gain access to a nearly unlimited inventory of books that could be shipped to customers.

In the Means approach, the enterprise starts with current capabilities. Powell's Books is a used and new bookstore that began operations in Portland, Oregon, in 1971. The company's sales grew to the point where the store occupied an entire city block, and the company transformed itself into "Powell's City of Books." Powell's increased book sales by branching out into specialized types of books: technical books, travel books, and books for gardeners and cooks. The company's growth was evolutionary. As customers requested certain kinds of books, Powell's Books offered them. With a reputation for having a comprehensive stock of both used and new books, Powell's Books had customers from all over the world who used mail and phone orders to buy books without entering the Portland bookstore.

When companies like Amazon.com began to show that many book buyers were using the Internet to purchase books, Powell's Books decided to pursue this approach as well—but with a difference. Powell's Books' primary effort built on current capabilities and involved the development of a computerized database to identify the books they already owned. In the past, its salespeople had to physically go into the book stacks and find out whether it had a new or used copy of a book in inventory. The decision to offer books on the Internet was, for Powell's Books, a decision about expending the effort to identify the resources they already owned.

Decision-making

In the Ends approach, the enterpriser chooses means based on the desired goals. Jeff Bezos' goal of creating the leading Internet bookseller required him to seek substantial resources to achieve his objective. In addition to selling equity to the public, he also raised two billion dollars by selling bonds that could, at a later date, be converted into stock if the price of Amazon stock continued to rise. With over four billion dollars to spend, Bezos could invest substantial resources to create an innovative and easy-to-use Internet site, build warehouses and distribution centers to distribute books, and buy a substantial amount of inventory to be able to ship books upon order.

In the Means approach, the enterpriser chooses possible effects given the capabilities and resources on hand. Powell's Books decided to sell books on the Internet as one of many possible ways they could sell books to customers. While Powell's Books was tentatively establishing an Internet presence, they were also opening other stores in the Portland area. Its investment in the website also involved upgrading the firm's inventory management system. Powell's Books made choices to expand based on enhancing current capabilities. The investment in building a website was a minor cost when compared to the cost of their overall operations. The risk of failing to sell books on the Internet would be an affordable risk for Powell's Books.

Competencies

In the Ends approach, the enterpriser exploits knowledge. Amazon.com was a pioneer in online retailing. One of its major innovations was "one-click" purchasing. The company spent millions of dollars to develop and patent a simple, convenient way to buy books at its Internet site. Customers could make a purchase without having to enter relevant customer information each time they visited the site. With "one-click," a database kept the customer's address, credit card information, and any other information that Amazon.com would need to complete the book sale. Initially, the "one-click" system was new knowledge that only Amazon.com could exploit and use.

In the Means approach, the enterpriser exploits contingencies. Powell's Books was an established bookseller, so it could pursue opportunities based on its existing capabilities. It already had a massive inventory of used and new books to sell. Adding Internet sales was a natural extension of its current mail and phone order sales process. Powell's exploited its strength in various ways, such as expanding its downtown store, opening other stores in the area, and increasing nonlocal orders with the addition of capabilities for ordering books online. The means—books—were the same. How Powell's sold the books—the ends—changed as Powell's customers asked for different ways to purchase books.

Unknowns and Logic

In the Ends approach, the enterpriser seeks to predict the characteristics of an uncertain future, because if one can predict the future, one can control it. Amazon.com's focus has been to capture a growing share of all book sales by encouraging book buyers to purchase via the Internet. To predict its ability to achieve its desired market share, Amazon.com must estimate the number of people who will purchase books using the Internet and compare this to the number who purchase through other channels like bookstores and mail and phone sales. If Amazon.com improves the incentives—say, by offering free shipping, larger price discounts, or faster shipping—will more people purchase from Amazon.com instead of Powell's? Once the company has greater insight into the mindset of book buyers and knows how different incentives increase sales, it can adapt these incentives to cater to these buyers.

In the Means approach, the enterpriser seeks to control aspects of the unpredictable future, because if one can control the future, one does not have to predict it. Powell's Books attempts to control the various ways that a person might want to purchase a book. Certainly, in Portland, Oregon, a book purchaser can buy a book by driving to the downtown location, visiting one of the many branch stores, placing a phone order, buying through catalog mail order, or using the Internet. If Powell's Books provides a variety of options for purchasing books, Powell's is there no matter which option a customer chooses!

Outcomes

In the Ends approach, the enterpriser seeks to increase market share in existing markets. For this category, the roles of Powell's Books and Amazon.com are reversed. Powell's Books wants to increase its market share of new and used book sales, particularly in the Portland, Oregon, area.

In the Means approach, the enterpriser seeks new markets through alliances and other cooperative strategies. Amazon.com sought a variety of strategic alliances to pursue new opportunities. Any book owner can list used books for sale on the Amazon.com site. Amazon.com, which at no cost to itself essentially gains a vast number of potential partners, earns a percentage on each used book sale. Amazon.com has also greatly expanded its online offerings through strategic alliances. Site visitors can buy much more than books at Amazon.com. It has teamed up with a wide variety of companies, many of whom have their own e-commerce sites, to offer a wide variety of other products and services—from apparel to electronics, home furnishings, jewelry, sporting goods, magazine subscriptions, photo finishing, and more. Nordstrom, Macy's, Foot Locker, Sephora, Target, Office Depot, Cooking.com, eToys, TigerDirect, J&R Music, and Computer World are just a few of the retailers whose products customers can buy through Amazon.com. The partners earn a percentage of the revenues from these jointly shared transactions. It's a win-win situation: Amazon attracts more visitors to its site because it offers so many products and can boast of having "the earth's largest selection," and the other merchants benefit from Amazon's online retailing expertise and huge customer base.

What is important to take away from these comparisons between ends and means is an appreciation that *enterprisers must explore both.* Enterprisers can be effective using either approach. Knowing which approach will be more appropriate for you will depend on your circumstances and on thoroughly knowing your own capabilities.

A Swede, a Dane, and Technology Equal a Global Success Story

Swedish entrepreneur Niklas Zennström and his Danish partner Jan Friis, whom we met earlier, exemplify global entrepreneurship at its best. The founders of Kazaa, which was formed in the Netherlands, sold the company to Sharman Networks, an Australian company, in 2002, and quickly moved on to their second venture. Skype Technologies, an even more lucrative business, was incorporated in Luxembourg in 2003 and based in London and Tallinn, Estonia.

The technological foundation for both Kazaa and Skype is peer-to-peer networking of user computers. Kazaa users were able to share music and video files between computers. With Skype, the technology was adapted for telephone calls. By downloading Skype's free software, users can make free, high-quality calls to another Skype user who is also online—anywhere in the world—using an Internet connection and headsets or microphones plugged into their computers. Now available in 27 languages, Skype's customer base grew to more than 54 million users in its first two years and is currently expanding at a rate of about 150,000 users a day.

"Skype has blazed a new trail," says Ian Cox of Juniper Research Ltd. Not only does it advance Voice over Internet Protocol (VoIP) technology, but it also presents a very different business model. While the software and basic computer-to-computer phone service, video calls, chats, and some conference calls are free, Skype earns revenues from fee-based premium features. SykpeOut lets Skype users call from PCs to landline and mobile phones worldwide, for rates averaging about $0.02 per minute. Voicemail costs $20 per year, and SkypeIn offers a phone number and voicemail for $30 per year. Personalized services such as ring tones cost $1.20 to $1.95. By partnering with hardware and software companies, Skype is able to offer new services and products, such as headphones and WiFi phones.

Even more interesting is its ability to grow without spending much money. Unlike traditional telecommunications providers, Skype has no investment in capital equipment or marketing. Its customers use their own computers and Internet connections to make calls and invite others to join. As more people join to use the free services, Skype has more opportunities to sell its premium services. As Zennström explains, "We want to make as little money as possible per user, [because] we don't have any cost per user, but we want a lot of them."

Skype's success in the VoIP sector attracted the attention of major new media companies such as Google, News Corp., Yahoo!, MSN, and AOL. In September 2005, Skype surprised everyone by accepting a $2.6 billion acquisition offer from eBay, which will also pay a $1.5 billion bonus if Skype meets financial performance goals. Why eBay? The two companies can help each other grow. eBay is the largest in the United States, while Skype has more presence internationally. Other synergies include a stronger link with eBay's PayPal online payment unit and the ability of eBay users to speak to each other via Skype. A major plus for Zennström and Friis, however, was eBay's promise to let them continue to develop Skype to become the dominant Internet communications provider, for all media, internationally. "When Yahoo! and Microsoft buy companies, they typically disintegrate them," says Zennström.

The eBay–Skype partnership is working. By mid-2006, Skype had more than 100 million registered users and keeps offering improved usability and more features. While they continued to work at Skype, Zennström and Friis began

(continued)

An Enterprising World

developing their third project, code-named the "Venice Project," a communications venture that builds on file-sharing software technologies—this time for distributing TV shows and other forms of video over the Web.

Discussion Questions

1. What dispositional and cognitive characteristics do Zennström and Friis display, and how do these traits contribute to their success?

2. Is the story of Skype an example of ends or means? Explain your answer with specific examples. What does your answer tell you about Zennström and Friis?

3. Discuss the implications of Skype's business model and how it relates to means and ends.

4. How did Zennström and Friis use small wins to grow Skype?

Sources: "About Tele2," http://www.tele2.com, July 27, 2006; "How Skype and Kazaa Changed the Net," BBC Click Online, June 17, 2005, http://news.bbc.co.uk; Olga Kharif, "Skype Piles It On," *Business Week*, May 3, 2006, http://www.businessweek.com; "Q&A: Skype's Niklas Zennström," Red Herring, November 21, 2005, http://www.redherring.com; Andy Reinhardt, "2005 Stars of Europe–Innovators: Niklas Zennström," *Business Week*, May 30, 2005, http://www.businessweek.com; Steve Rosenbush, "Kazaa, Skype, and now 'The Venice Project,' " *Business Week*, July 24, 2006, http://www.businessweek.com; "Skype's 'Aha!' Experience," *Business Week*, September 19, 2005, http://www.businessweek.com.

2.7 Small Wins: The Building Blocks of Enterprise

Moving on from disposition and cognitions, then, we need to think about how to position ourselves for success. Based on where you are at this moment, it might seem that you can't do much to change anything in your life. That would indeed feel depressing! Yet there is a strategy for moving forward: small wins.

Given your situation, if you wanted to become an enterpriser, what would you do? Where would you start the process? The tasks and activities involved in enterprising may seem daunting at the outset. Just look at all the chapters in this book—so much to learn and to do! Taking the first steps toward achieving a major goal may seem overwhelming, difficult, and complicated. Enterprising, with all it involves, is not easy.

Anything of significance, whether it's a new craft project such as building a bookcase or starting a new business venture, takes time to achieve. After all, Rome wasn't built in a day! Yet we often fail to take this basic concept into account when we begin something new, forgetting that significant accomplishments rarely result from big actions. Rather, they emerge from a series of small activities.

Even gigantic organizations like Ford Motor Company started small. Henry Ford began his first effort in the automobile industry in 1896 while working full time for the Edison Illuminating Company. He devoted his evenings and nights to building his first car, the "quadracycle," which he completed in 1898. When this automobile was completed, he sold it for $200 and used the proceeds to invest in his first automobile company, the Detroit Automobile Company. This company was started in 1899 and failed in 1901. Undaunted, he started another automobile company, the Henry Ford Company, in 1901, and this company failed too! It was on his third try, when he started the Ford Motor Company in 1903, that he finally succeeded. We often forget that big companies start out small, and that enterprisers often fail before they learn how to succeed.

A Journey of a Thousand Miles Begins with a Single Step

Most accomplishments begin with the idea of **small wins**, which are achievable, tangible accomplishments that are within a person's capabilities and produce visible results.[18] A series of small wins creates a pattern of visible success that attracts supporters to your cause and deters possible competitors. Put into practice, the concept of small wins helps companies make steady progress toward improved performance. Actions that may initially appear to be rather simple and trivial often solve seemingly difficult and impossible problems.

For example, Greyhound of Canada was losing customers. When it asked customers why they were not riding its buses, they offered a variety of responses. Some preferred other means of transportation, and others complained of inconvenient bus routes, schedules, and bus terminals.

Although unable to identify an obvious solution that would bring back its customers, one senior vice president, John Munro, decided to take action—an action that seemed trivial but ultimately proved to be a small win that was successful. Munro decided that the restrooms in the bus terminals needed to be kept immaculately clean. To demonstrate Greyhound's commitment to cleanliness, Munro held black-tie dinners in the restrooms. Over 70 percent of the station managers began keeping their restrooms clean, and Greyhound hired janitorial services to bring the others into compliance. The result was an overall increase in customers, with a 10 percent increase in women customers.[19]

How could something as simple as clean restrooms increase the number of customers riding the bus? To customers, clean restrooms translated into safety and comfort. Customers felt that the company was being attentive to their needs. Greyhound of Canada did much more to attract new customers, but cleaning the restrooms was a start. And although it wasn't initially apparent that customers thought that clean restrooms were an important part of the bus riding experience, it was a small win that Greyhound of Canada could immediately achieve. Small wins, such as having clean restrooms, are how individuals and businesses begin the process of accomplishment.

small wins
Achievable, tangible accomplishments that are within a person's capabilities and produce visible results.

Characteristics of Small Wins

From a psychological perspective, small wins reduce the stress and anxiety that individuals feel when faced with situations they perceive as overwhelmingly complicated and difficult. Under pressure, they are less able to apply the right skills to solve a problem and tend to respond less effectively.

The small win approach helps them to see problems as being within the scope of their abilities and effort instead of impossible to solve. The result is a feeling of "I can do this," rather than tension and helplessness. Small wins, therefore, are very much about how we describe problems in the first place. With the small wins perspective, we define problems so that our efforts and capabilities matter—and thereby increase our ability to successfully resolve them.

The small wins concept is not the same as breaking down a large task into small steps. Small wins typically don't follow a linear progression from one step to the next. They do, however, move in the same general direction toward a goal.

Given the importance of small wins to achieving larger goals, we need to build them into our daily lives. We need to discover opportunities and then find ways to improve the situation through some action that is within our control. Although they are hard to design, small wins are easy to recognize from their five identifying characteristics.

Ability to Control Actions

When Mary T. Meagher won three gold medals in swimming at the 1984 Los Angeles Olympics, she ascribed her success not to practicing more than other swimmers but to two fundamental changes in her practice routine. First, she arrived at swimming practice on time, which gave her a sense that every minute of her training counted. Second, she made sure to do all her practice turns correctly, according to the competitive rules. This meant always touching the side of the pool with two hands, not sometimes touching with one hand. Within a year of implementing these two small changes, Meagher was the world record holder in the butterfly. As she points out, "People don't know how ordinary success is."[20]

Meagher could control her ability to arrive to practice on time. She could control whether she did her turns correctly during practice. Both activities were within her capabilities. Her small wins didn't involve doing more of the same thing but doing something differently. By simply controlling her own actions, she made a major change in the outcome.

Willingness to Take Action

Small wins include some action and the belief that our actions will make a difference. This optimistic view of our activities is what motivates us to proceed, even though we know that we have no guarantee of success. The alternative is doing nothing, which leads to neither success nor failure. Think of a small win as an experiment, where we can test our assumptions about the situations we face and discover whether our beliefs are valid or not. Often allies (as well as detractors) come to the forefront only when we take action.

To save the redwood trees, 23-year-old Julia Butterfly Hill, a preacher's daughter, climbed a redwood tree and lived in it for more than two years. Her action helped identify supporters such as various environmental groups, government bureaucrats, and wealthy donors, as well as opponents, including logging companies and loggers. By bringing together and mobilizing the supporters, she saved many hundreds of redwood trees.[21]

Hill had no guarantee that her actions would save any redwood trees, let alone the tree she was living in. And she never expected her crusade to last two years. Each day brought its own problems and opportunities, which she faced with the same positive attitude that took her up the tree in the first place. She experienced a series of small wins by acting on her intentions.

Activities that Stand Alone

A small win is a completed outcome. Take the process of making "cold calls," calling strangers on the telephone to sell a product or service or arrange a meeting with a potential investor. Every cold call is a small win that stands alone. Each phone call results in a completed outcome: The person responding to the phone call hangs up, asks for more information, agrees to a meeting, or makes some other choice. It is a completed accomplishment—whether the call's outcome is a success or a failure. Individuals who make cold calls can learn from each attempt, using each phone call to explore what kinds of pitches are likely to result in a higher chance of a sale.

Communicating an Intent

Any action, no matter how small, signals likely future intentions. For example, at CNN, Ted Turner instituted a $100 fine for any CNN employee who used the word *foreign*. Turner felt that the word *foreign* did not make sense in a global economy, and that news knew no borders. Simply fining those individuals who used the word *foreign* sent a strong message that he wanted CNN staffers to think globally.[22]

Emphasis on Details

Small wins occur because people don't overlook the specifics of their own situations. All the examples mentioned above involve noticing things that others appeared to miss. When we pay close attention to the specifics of the situation at hand, we gain the intimate knowledge to discern the small ways we can make changes. Munro's knowledge of buses and bus terminals provided insight into what small things could be changed, such as bathrooms. Meagher's knowledge of swimming helped her to identify changes she might make in her swim practice. Hill's knowledge of redwood trees enabled her to live in one. Developing detailed knowledge of the situations we face provides a significant advantage, particularly if we are looking for those small ways to leverage a task into meaningful action.

Inherent in the small win perspective is a view of situations where the future is ambiguous, subject to interpretation and change, malleable, and within our grasp. Because the future is not predetermined, our actions can make a difference. Small wins provide options. They may appear to amount to little, but because they are in fact wins, they encourage us to keep taking positive action.[23]

When you consider all the activities necessary to successfully enterprise, remember to create small wins. Choose activities that are within your knowledge and capabilities. Understand the details and intricacies of the situation. Seek accomplishments that can stand alone. Treat each action as an experiment, and then learn from it.

2.8 Enterprisers

On Target Hits the Bull's-Eye

Albert Black is a self-proclaimed capitalist. The baby of seven children, Albert grew up in Dallas, Texas, in government-subsidized housing (Frasier Courts) and started his first business when he was just eight years old. Today, he is CEO of On Target Supplies and Logistics, which provides business services and logistics management for companies. In 2002 the company employed 117 people and had revenues of over $28 million. His customer list includes the who's who of Dallas: EDS, Texas Instruments, Southwestern Bell, Texas Utilities, NationsBank, and Lone Star Gas. On Target services large corporations throughout Texas, Oklahoma, Louisiana, Arkansas, and Missouri from its offices and warehouses in Dallas and other Texas locations. In 1998, the kid from the projects was named Ernst & Young's Entrepreneur of the Year. On Target is also on the Inner City 100 list and Black is recognized as a leading minority entrepreneur.

"For me, the roots of capitalism took place right here in Frasier Courts," Black recalls. "I remember going up to the office and renting a push mower, knocking on doors and cutting yards for 50 cents." His lawn service prospered to the extent that he incorporated it when he was 19. Black continued to own Best Friends Lawn Service until he sold it in 1985.

He credits his grandmother with instilling the character traits that have helped him reach success: treat people with compassion, always look out for the other fellow, do what you say you're going do, take care of others before you take care of yourself, tell the truth, love and expect to be loved, and put God first, your family second, and everything else somewhere after that. His mother also influenced him: "She didn't think that she should expect anything but the best from her children, and that drives the way we run On Target Supplies and Logistics now." "You may live in the ghetto, but you're not ghetto material," she would

tell her children. "And I don't—I won't—stand for you acting that way."

Soon after his 1982 college graduation, he started On Target to provide businesses with custodial supplies and janitorial services. Black had to get a second job while he built the company's business, and for ten years worked from 5 PM to 1 AM. "I had a goal," he says. "Not only would I earn income, I would pick up a skill set, a management ability, a competency that I could bring into my company and make it work."

Black and his wife Gwyneith worked hard to start On Target, often spending 14–16 hours a day and using their own car to make deliveries. They tried many different ways to spread the word about On Target's services. When trade fairs, direct mail, and cold-calling didn't work, they came up with a novel approach that did.

On Target became involved in communities, providing leadership for nonprofit organizations in and around town. Volunteering for those nonprofits gave Black and his company the opportunity to network, gaining exposure and business connections, while also "doing good" for the city of Dallas by sharing skills.

This approach worked, and On Target's business began to grow. Within five years, however, Black realized that the market had changed, with large companies turning to outsourced janitorial services. He redefined On Target's services to focus on supply distribution and logistics services and acquired his first big corporate account, Lone Star Gas Company. "I think our ability to listen, to plan, to present, to perform, to review, and to adjust is what corporate clients need today more than any other time in their history," says Black. On Target demonstrated its flexibility and ability to add value for the customer. Normally products went from On Target's loading dock to Lone Star's. "We came in with a strategy to take it to desktop distribution, and for the same price," says Black. "That saved them time. It saved them money. It saved them inventory expense."

Black credits his education—a bachelor's degree from the University of Texas at Dallas and an MBA from Southern Methodist University—with giving him a better foundation for management and leadership. As a result, he has made continuing education a priority at On Target, which pays for employees to pursue the next highest educational degree in a business-focused area. "As a company, we're willing to pay for it. As a CEO or a leader, I'm willing to insist on it," Black asserts. "There's no written policy that employees must go to college and achieve a bachelor's degree or you will be fired, but I think everybody around here knows that when Albert's sitting down with you and gives you that old south Dallas smile and insists or suggests that you go to college, I think they get the message."

In addition to what Black calls traditional financial income, On Target promises employees two other important incomes: educational and psychological. The company does more than pay for college. "If you come to work with us, you will know how to run a business," Black says. "We have absolute open-book accounting. You would know every expense in this business. You will know every revenue stream. You will know all the cost of sales. You will know how to run a business in a couple of years. That's the educational income." Black then supports employees who want to start their own businesses in areas serving complementary parts of On Target's market. More than ten former employees have taken advantage of this program to take the entrepreneurial plunge themselves.

Psychological income means feeling good about what you're doing for the company. "An esprit de corps, the attitude that says, 'Together we can climb mountains and win battles'—that's what we offer people, that psychological income of making a contribution every day."

To Black, financial income is the least important of the three, although he recognizes that for some it is the most important. Even here, however, his employees have reason to be happy, because the company pays above-market wages. "We like to bring people in, and over the course of their career here give them above-the-industry average, and then so much above the industry average that their desire to leave is based on the first two—psychological and educational income—and not financial considerations."

Never content with the status quo, Black encourages his employees to keep learning. The company gives each employee 60 hours of training annually to develop a well-trained, highly motivated, and customer-service–oriented staff. "We have a great sense of security that our employees are trained on a greater level than that of our competitors," Black says.

"We have to continuously resharpen the saw, find new information, new strategies, new principles, new foundations to employ in our business," he explains. "If we don't do that, well, we can look to be fired as the leaders of our organizations. How do people fire us? They quit. I think leadership and the mandate on leadership is to get the job done. If it means an ultimate sacrifice of giving all of your time and energy, all of your hopes, dreams, aspirations, and prayers toward that endeavor, I think that's what we must do."

Black's efforts in Dallas and throughout Texas have corrected many misconceptions. "Myths about small business—that we cannot capitalize ourselves in order to finance growth; myths about minority businesses—that we can't put together the type of management team necessary to take advantage of market opportunity; myths about black people, African Americans, that we do not have the right stuff in order to take full advantage of the American free-enterprise system." "I've dispelled a lot of myths," he says. "I get a chance to hire people, improve infrastructure, pay taxes, provide leadership, and get rich along the way."

(continued)

Discussion Questions

1. Does Albert Black fit the characteristics (demographic and cognitive) of an entrepreneur described in this chapter? If so, why? And, if not, why not?

2. Why is Albert Black successful?

3. Are there characteristics that all entrepreneurs must have in order to be successful?

What evidence would you offer to support your viewpoint?

4. What advantages or disadvantages does a person's family background provide? Can these be gained in other ways?

5. Are there any "small wins" in how Albert Black has developed and managed his business?

Source: Adapted with permission from Small Business School, the series on PBS, at http://SmallBusinessSchool.com.

2.9 Summary

1. Enterprisers come from all backgrounds, ages, and experiences. No one specific personality characteristic will prevent a person from becoming an entrepreneur, although some dispositional and cognitive characteristics may provide a slight advantage to those considering entrepreneurship. In fact, enterprisers represent all personality types. Successful enterprisers find business situations that match their personal characteristics and skills.

2. Entrepreneurship is a universal social and economic activity in the United States and is an important indicator of economic growth around the world. Research from the Panel Study of Entrepreneurial Dynamics (PSED) enhances our understanding of entrepreneurship. It focuses on nascent entrepreneurs—individuals who initiate and start new businesses, create new industries, or change how businesses in established industries compete. According to the PSED, entrepreneurial activity in the United States is widespread. All groups and types of individual participate in the new business formation process, with about 10.1 million adults in the United States trying to start new businesses at any time, either as individuals or in teams.

3. If we look at the demographics of nascent entrepreneurs, we find that they span all adult age groups, with the highest activity among young men aged 25–34. Men are twice as likely to start new businesses as women. Black men and women are about 50 percent more likely to start a business than white men and women, with business formation by Hispanic men about 20 percent higher than for white men. Hispanic and white women have comparable rates of business formation, with both groups lagging considerably behind black women. Those with higher incomes are more likely to be involved in starting a business. Where people live affects entrepreneurial activity. The presence of certain economic, demographic, and educational

factors contributes to higher entrepreneurial activity in more urban areas.

4. Education is an important predictor of entrepreneurial activity for all individuals, and one that individuals can use to their advantage. Those who finish high school and complete some additional education or training are more likely to try to start a new business venture. For white men and women, there is a slight increase of participation with higher levels of education. Education has a greater impact for blacks and Hispanics. Black men and women and Hispanic men reporting any post–college graduation training are two to three times more likely to be involved in a firm start-up.

5. In terms of other personal characteristics, marital status, size of household, and age of children in the household have a minimal impact on entrepreneurial activities. Contrary to popular belief, jobholders in all ethnic groups report a higher incidence of entrepreneurial activity than those who are unemployed. People with jobs have more opportunities to identify ideas for products and services, make connections to suppliers, and acquire industry knowledge.

6. Many career motives of nascent entrepreneurs and a comparison group of nonentrepreneurs are similar, particularly in four areas: innovation, independence, financial success, and self-realization. There were significant differences in only two areas: recognition and roles.

    In addition, all respondents tended to rank the six career reasons in the same order of importance. Independence was first, followed by financial success, self-realization, recognition, innovation, and roles. These findings hold true in other countries as well. Self-realization values (personal development, ability utilization, and achievement) are ranked highly, whereas people place little importance on risk taking and the desire for authority and prestige. Regardless of where they live, enterprisers are less likely to care about how other people view their pursuit of success and to pursue financial success, independence, self-realization, and innovation on their own terms.

7. Individuals who take action are more successful than those who don't. People who are more likely to take action are probably also optimists. You can put yourself in an optimistic mindset so that you will be more likely to take action. We make three judgments about a situation: is it internal or external to us, stable or variable, and global or specific? Optimists attribute external/temporary/specific causes to bad situations. The pessimist, on the other hand, will offer an internal/stable/global attribution. Optimists also expect good things will occur in the future from their own efforts (internal), will continue (stable), and will extend to other situations in their lives (global). As a result, they are likely to put effort into achieving their expectations. Pessimists, who expect that bad things will happen, tend to give up too soon, thinking that their efforts will be wasted.

8. We can approach problems and accomplish activities in two ways. We can focus on the *ends*, starting with a specific goal and then

generating the necessary solution. Most problem solving uses this approach. When we emphasize the *means* approach, we look at what we have currently available to use and make these the starting point for achievement. Then we use our skills and abilities to solve the problem. Few situations call for pure forms of means or ends approaches. Typically people combine both methods to accomplish a goal. Exhibit 2.6 summarizes the major differences in these approaches. It's important to know which approach is more appropriate in a particular situation.

9. Small wins—achievable, tangible accomplishments that are within a person's capabilities and produce visible results—occur because people pay close attention to the specifics of the situation at hand. We then notice the specifics of situations that others appeared to miss, discovering small ways we can make changes and leverage a task into meaningful action. Small wins reduce stress and anxiety by helping us to see problems as within our capabilities instead of as overwhelming. They provide options, and by creating the feeling that we can do this, encourage us to keep taking positive action. The five identifying characteristics of small wins are ability to control actions, willingness to take action, activities that stand alone, communicating an intent, and emphasis on details.

Review Questions

1. Approximately 6 percent of all U.S. adults are involved in starting businesses. Why aren't more (or less) people involved in starting a business?

2. At what age groups are people more likely to be involved in starting businesses? Why are they more likely to start businesses at that age?

3. Why are men more likely to start businesses than women? What factors might account for this difference?

4. Why would African Americans and Hispanics be more likely to start a business than whites?

5. How important is education for starting a business? Why?

6. Who is more likely to start a business: someone who is unemployed, working full time, or working part time?

7. Are the reasons that nascent entrepreneurs offer for starting businesses different than the reasons that other people give for their career choices?

8. Who is an optimist? What are the characteristics of optimistic thinking? Why is it important to think optimistically?

9. What are the differences between focusing on ends versus focusing on means? Provide some examples of how an enterpriser might start a business using an ends focus and some examples of how an enterpriser might instead take a means focus.

10. What is a small win? What are the characteristics of small wins? Why is it important to focus on small wins rather than on "big wins?"

Applying What You've Learned

1. What personal characteristics might help or hinder your ability to become an enterpriser?

2. Interview an entrepreneur to discover what personal characteristics and reasons are offered for starting a business. Use the following questions to guide your discussion

   - What is the opportunity the entrepreneur decided to pursue?
   - What influenced the entrepreneur to identify and pursue this opportunity?
   - How did the entrepreneur's background (family history, prior education, and work experience) affect the opportunity discovered?
   - How did the entrepreneur evaluate the opportunity?
   - What criteria did the entrepreneur use to determine whether to pursue the opportunity?
   - What were the perceived risks of this opportunity and how did the entrepreneur expect to manage them?

3. Identify three experiences you recently had (e.g., got an exam back, had lunch, went on a date). How did you think about those experiences in the attributional framework (internal/external, stable/variable, global/specific)? Were your thoughts optimistic? If not, why not? Would it have been more helpful for you to think of these experiences in an optimistic perspective?

4. Think of a business that you would like to start. How would you start this business if you focused on means? How would you start this business if you focused on ends?

5. Kazaa, the subject of this chapter's Enterprising Ethics box, is a good example of the unforeseen consequences of entrepreneurial action when the focus is on means rather than ends. Identify the different ways that Kazaa focuses on means in the process of developing the company. What other outcomes (ends) might result from the Kazaa file-sharing software? Can you identify other types of businesses that could be created? Discuss whether these businesses would be legal or ethical.

6. Revisit the story of Skype in the Enterprising World box. If you were a consultant to Zennström and Friis, on what basis would you recommend that they evaluate the various acquisition offers? Which factors would influence you most? Or would you suggest that they keep the company independent, and why?

7. What small wins did you accomplish today? What small wins might you accomplish tomorrow? How might these small wins help you become an enterpriser?

Enterprisers on the Web

1. Are you optimistic? Take the "Optimism Exam" on our website. Did the results surprise you?

2. The Panel Study of Entrepreneurial Dynamics (PSED) is an ongoing research effort. Check out its website at http://www.psed.info for its recent research activities. In the Publications section, look through the annotated bibliography of research publications using the PSED data. Choose an article that is of interest to you and find it on the Web. What do the findings of this article tell you about people who are entrepreneurs? How are these people similar or different from other people?

3. Who is using the "small wins" strategy, and how? Type "small wins" into any Web search engine and select two examples, one of which involves enterprisers. Describe the situation and explain how others have modified the "small wins" strategy to fit their objectives and interests. When might a "big wins" strategy work better than "small wins" ?

4. The Martin Seligman website http://www.psych.upenn.edu/seligman/ has numerous resources for exploring the value of an optimistic mindset and other ways of thinking that are helpful for enterprising. After taking the optimism exam on this website, are you an optimist? Why do you think your score on the optimism exam turned out the way it did? What do you find are your core strengths and values? How might these strengths direct you?

5. The web business eBay (http://www.ebay.com), the leader in online auctions, is an example of a means-focused business. Visit the eBay website and determine how eBay uses the means of the online auction to sell products on the Web. Next, discuss the ways eBay has branched out from the original auction format. Has it been effective, and why? Finally, identify other websites that utilize the means of an online auction and discuss how well this works. (Hint: Think of any goods or services that you might want to purchase on the Web. Use a search engine to locate other sites where on-line auctions take place.)

End Notes

1. William B. Gartner, "Who Is an Entrepreneur? Is the Wrong Question," *American Journal of Small Business* 12 no. 4 (1988), pp. 11–32.

2. Paul D. Reynolds, Nancy M. Carter, William B. Gartner, Patricia G. Greene, and Larry W. Cox, "The Entrepreneur Next Door: Characteristics of Individuals Starting Companies in America" (Kansas City, MO: E. M. Kauffman Foundation, 2002).

3. Paul D. Reynolds, S. M. Camp, W. D. Bygrave, E. Autio, and M. Hay, *Global Entrepreneurship Monitor: 2001 Executive Report* (Kansas City, MO: Kauffman Center for Entrepreneurial Leadership, 2001).

4. M. Ruef, H. E. Aldrich, and Nancy M. Carter, "Don't Go to Strangers: Homophily, Strong Ties and Isolation in the Formation of Organizational Founding Teams" (Chicago: American Sociological Association National Meetings, 2002).

5. "Table 72: Live Births, Deaths, Marriages, and Divorces: 1950 to 2003," *Statistical Abstract of the United States: 2006*, 125th ed. (Washington, DC, 2005: U.S. Census Bureau, 2006), p. 64.

6. U.S. Department of Commerce, *The State of Small Business: A Report of the President* (Washington, DC: U.S. Government Printing Office, 1996).

7. J. S. Butler, *Entrepreneurship and Self Help Among Black Americans: A Reconsideration of Race and Economics* (Albany, NY: State University of New York Press, 1991); and P. G. Greene and J. S. Butler, "The Minority Community as a Natural Business Incubator," *Journal of Business Research* 36 no. 1 (1996), pp. 51–59.

8. Nancy M. Carter, William B. Gartner, K. G. Shaver, and E. J. Gatewood, "The Career Reasons of Nascent Entrepreneurs," *Journal of Business Venturing* 18 no. 1 (2003), pp. 13–40.

9. Donald E. Super, Branimir Sverko, and Charles M. Super (Eds), *Life Roles, Values and Careers: International Findings of the Work Importance Study* (San Francisco: Jossey-Bass, 1995).

10. Branimir Sverko and Donald E. Super, "The Findings of the Work Importance Study," in D. E. Super, B. Sverko, and C. M. Super (Eds), *Life Roles, Values and Careers: International Findings of the Work Importance Study* (San Francisco: Jossey-Bass, 1995), pp. 349–358.

11. Martin E. P. Seligman, *Learned Optimism* (New York: Pocket Books, 1998).

12. M. F. Scheier and C. S. Carver, "Effects of Optimism on Psychological and Physical Well-Being. Theoretical Overview and Empirical Update," *Cognitive Therapy and Research* 16 no. 2 (1992), pp. 201–228.

13. N. J. Christman, "Uncertainty and Adjustment During Radiotherapy," *Nursing Research* 39 no. 1 (1990), pp. 17–20, 47.

14. D. Strutton and J. Lumpkin, "Relationship between Optimism and Coping Strategies in the Work Environment," *Psychological Reports* 71 (1992), pp. 1179–1186.

15. M. F. Scheier, C. S. Carver, and A. W. Bridges, "Optimism, Pessimism, and Psychological Well Being," in E. C. Chang (Ed.), *Optimism & Pessimism: Implications for Theory, Research and Practice* (Washington, DC: American Psychological Association, 2001), pp. 189–216.

16. S. D. Sarasvathy, "Causation and Effectuation: Toward a Theoretical Shift from Economic Inevitability to Entrepreneurial Contingency," *Academy of Management Review* 26 no. 2 (2001), pp. 243–263.

17. Ibid., p. 245.

18. Karl E. Weick, "Small Wins: Redefining the Scale of Social Problems," *American Psychologist* 39 no. 1 (1984), pp. 40–49.

19. Thomas J. Peters, *Patterns of Winning and Losing: Effects on Approach and Avoidance by Friends and Enemies*, Unpublished doctoral dissertation, Stanford University, 1977.

20. Karl E. Weick, "Small Wins in Organizational Life," *Dividend* (Ann Arbor, MI: University of Michigan School of Business), 24 no. 1 (1993), pp. 2–6.

21. J. B. Hill, *The Legacy of Luna: The Story of a Tree, A Woman, and the Struggle to Save the Redwoods* (San Francisco: HarperSanFrancisco, 2000).

22. Weick, "Small Wins in Organizational Life."

23. Weick, "Small Wins: Redefining the Scale of Social Problems," p. 48.

chapter 3

Enterprising Fundamentals

1. Achievement depends upon actions. These actions have two primary purposes: managing yourself and managing your situation.

2. Skills such as goal setting, time management, persuasion, negotiation, and networking are fundamental to future success, whether you are starting, operating, or selling a business.

3. Managing yourself starts with setting goals to determine direction, and then managing your time so that you can initiate the actions necessary to reach those goals. Enterprisers must also manage situations by interacting with others using persuasion and negotiation techniques. By building networks, enterprisers expand the range of interactions and gain competitive advantage.

Suppose, when you were in college, you were responsible for booking campus entertainment and dances. You quickly discovered the difference that proper lighting made in the overall staging of a performance. It didn't take long for you to realize that you had a knack for the complexities—and opportunities— involved in developing quality lighting packages that would become the industry standard.

This chapter presents the case of David and Janet Milly, who focused on their mission, "making money doing lights," set goals related to their mission, managed their time effectively, and used their networks to build a client base. They grew their company into a successful theatrical lighting company for top musical performers but remained committed to servicing the lighting needs of various small organizations in their own community.

In this chapter you will learn these and other practical personal skills you will need to manage yourself and your situation as you build an enterprise.

3.0 Essentials for Enterprisers

Enterprising involves action. Many people have the right attitudes, motivations, abilities, and skills, yet they don't undertake the necessary activities to achieve success. After watching an important sporting event, we have all played Monday morning quarterback—second-guessing the coach and players as to why and how they won or lost the game. Analysis helps us understand the factors that lead to success or failure. However, it is impossible to win a game by just watching! Only those who play get a chance to win (or lose). Many people can describe what should have happened or speculate on what should have been done. But knowing what to do without actually doing it results in nothing.

Enterprisers are doers. They act. They accomplish.

Achievement depends on your actions. Your actions can change your present circumstances, much like using a ship's rudder to change direction. Moving the rudder might not lead to a quick change in course, but soon the ship is sailing in a new direction. Even though it may appear that actions don't result in immediate changes, actions do pull you in certain directions, and you may soon find yourself on a different path.

This chapter provides you with a set of practical "action tools" and skills that will help you achieve success. It highlights the kinds of activities that everyone needs to undertake to be successful: goal setting, time management, persuasion, negotiation, and networking. These skills lay the groundwork for all enterprisers, whether they are starting, operating, or selling a business.

These enterprising fundamentals have a sound basis in the theories of organizational behavior. **Organizational behavior** is the study of people and how they act in organizations. Organizational behavior researchers tend to study people who work in large organizations, but their findings are relevant for enterprisers as well. We will introduce you to some of the academic theory that demonstrates why these skills are important to acquire and use, and then show how you, as an enterpriser, can apply them.

Enterprising fundamentals involve two kinds of skills: *Skills to manage yourself,* such as goal setting and time management, and *skills to manage your situation,* like persuasion, negotiation, and networking.

organizational behavior
The study of people and how they act in organizations.

Managing Yourself

In organizational behavior terms, achievement is defined as a function of ability and effort. You need both ability (your skills and knowledge) *and* effort (the time devoted to the task at hand) to accomplish work.

$$Work = Ability \times Effort$$

In the absence of the other, neither ability nor effort is enough. Smart people who don't put in the effort won't succeed, and people who work hard but don't have the right skills and knowledge won't succeed.

One of the major reasons you are going to school is to acquire the skills and knowledge necessary to succeed in life. What we often underestimate in determining whether people will be successful is their dedication to putting in the necessary time and energy. We believe *the most critical factor for achieving your goals is the amount of time you have available.*

A number of years ago, John Sloboda, a researcher in England, interviewed over 250 music students attending prestigious academies in England to discover whether success as a musician was a function of ability or effort. He looked at how each student did on a national examination of musical ability. The results showed that a student's ranking on musical ability was highly related to the number of hours a student practiced. Students who scored the highest on the music examination were likely to practice eight times more than the lowest performing students. "People have this idea that there are those who learn better than others, can get further on less effort," Sloboda says. "On average, our data refuted that. Whether you're a dropout or at the best school, where you end up can be predicted by how much you practice."[1] Managing your time, therefore, is the best way for you to manage your life. If you don't have time to accomplish critical tasks in life, you won't achieve your goals.

Another way to look at the importance of time in managing your life is to consider your life as the "100,000 hour problem."[2] Think about what you want to accomplish in your life as a "job" and calculate the number of hours you have for this job over your lifetime. Assume that you begin working at age 20 and plan to retire when you are 70. If you work a 40-hour week, then you have 2,080 hours a year of work. With two weeks (80 hours) off per year for vacation, your work year is about 2,000 hours. If you work 50 years at 2,000 hours a year, you have 100,000 hours to accomplish what you want. That is your life!

When you think about it, 100,000 hours is not a lot of time. So to be an effective enterpriser, you must allocate the time to enterprise.

Managing Your Situation

Enterprisers, as we have defined them, involve other people. It is impossible to start or run a business without the involvement of others, whether they are employees, customers, or investors. In a new enterprise, it is a challenge to convince someone to purchase what may be an untested product or take a chance on your new service. You must be able to negotiate with suppliers for better prices, as well as payment terms that will enable your enterprise to grow. And, it is impossible to know everything about running a successful enterprise, so, you will need advice and mentoring from a variety of people that you can depend on. So, managing the involvement of others is critical to whether the enterprise will flourish or not. Your ability to build your enterprise will depend on leveraging the strengths of others.

In Exhibit 3.1, you might think of the five activities of goal setting, time management, persuasion, negotiation, and networking as a series of concentric circles. While each activity might be considered separate from the others, each activity is

exhibit 3.1　　**An Enterpriser's Skill Set**

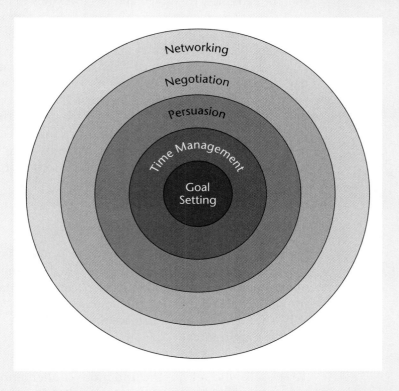

dependent on the other. At the center of your actions is goal setting. Without a clear sense of your goals, using your time wisely, and utilizing your network and your ability to persuade and negotiate with others are useless. And, time management skills will influence your ability to engage others in your enterprise. Negotiation depends on your skills and persuasion. And, networking depends on how skilled you are at using the other skills.

3.1 Goal Setting: The Key to Time Management

The phone is ringing as you walk into your office. Your sales manager tells you that he finally got an appointment with the CEO of the company you've been courting for weeks. Your assistant reminds you to call a new customer. Your calendar shows that you have a meeting with your accounts officer—at the same time you are supposed to meet with the CEO. It's only 8 AM, and it's clear that your day won't be going as planned. By 4:30 PM, you've also helped your purchasing manager with supplier problems, dashed off to do some errands, and interviewed a job applicant—but most of the items on your original to-do list remain undone.

Sound familiar? We all have days like this, where carefully made plans get tossed aside to solve crises. Have too many of these days, however, and you will soon be extremely frustrated and feel like you will never achieve your goals.

Look at the matrix in Exhibit 3.2, which was developed by Stephen Covey in his book *First Things First*. He looks at two key issues: the importance of the problems one faces, and their urgency.

Most tasks we mentioned—and as Covey sees it, most of what we do in our day-to-day lives—fall into Quadrants 3 and 4, with a few in Quadrant 1. Quadrant 3 tasks are urgent and unimportant; activities that *other people* want but won't necessarily help us achieve our own goals. Quadrant 4 tasks, not urgent and unimportant, can end up taking most of our time. Many of these tasks involve short-term activities that steal valuable time from what should be our primary focus: achieving our long-term goals. Goal-setting activities are part of Quadrant 2, which Covey calls the Quadrant of Quality.[3]

Why Set Goals?

Formulating goals isn't easy, but the process is an essential component of personal and professional success. Goal setting involves specifying future objectives or accomplishments. Basically, it entails determining a direction for actions and indicating the amount or quality of work to be accomplished. When we develop our goals, we must also define our priorities and determine what is important.

Two broad findings emerge from laboratory and field research on goal setting:

1. People who set specific and more challenging goals achieve more than people who set no goals, or are asked to "do their best."

exhibit 3.2   **Types of Problems**

	URGENT	NOT URGENT
IMPORTANT	**QUADRANT 1** Crises Pressing problems Deadline-driven projects	**QUADRANT 2** Preparation Prevention Values clarification Planning
UNIMPORTANT	**QUADRANT 3** Interruptions Some mail Some meetings Many popular activities	**QUADRANT 4** Trivia, busywork Some phone calls Time wasters Irrelevant mail Excessive TV

Source: Stephen R. Covey, A. Roger Merrill, and Rebecca R. Merrill, *First Things First* (New York: Simon & Schuster, 1995), p. 37.

2. People who set specific and more challenging goals achieve more than people who set easy goals.[4]

    In other words:

- Specific goals direct action better than vague or general goals.

- A difficult goal leads to better performance than easy or no goals, because people will try harder to achieve a more difficult goal.

- Effort is important for achievement.

- We all need to be challenged in order to achieve.

    While these points may seem obvious, very often we neglect them in planning our lives.

    To be useful, goals must have certain characteristics. They must be specific, results-focused, measurable, realistically attainable, relevant, and have a time frame for accomplishment. Suppose one of your goals is to earn more money. While this is an admirable goal, it is too vague to be useful. How much more money? Over what time period? Earning $300 more over the next three years meets this goal—but is that what you really meant? A better goal would be, increase earnings by $2,000 in 12 months by getting a promotion. This goal statement is specific, measurable, and has a time period for completion—increase by $2,000 by getting a promotion within a year. It is results-focused and relevant—a promotion improves your career and your financial situation; and it is realistic—it is possible to accomplish this in a year.

Perhaps you are very ambitious and decide you want to start a new company within three months. This goal is specific and has a time frame. But is it realistically attainable? Not really. A goal that is beyond your reach—or too easily met—has little meaning. Well-designed goals challenge you, but are attainable with hard work. The basics of sound goal setting are summarized in Exhibit 3.3.

Rhonda Abrams, a small-business planning consultant, has two rules that capture the essence of goal setting:

1. You can't reach a goal you haven't set.

2. If you want something, you also have to "do" something.[5]

Never underestimate the importance of these two rules. A study by Harvard psychologists in the early 1980s looked at people who considered themselves happy. The shared characteristics of this group were not wealth, success, love, or health—however, they knew what they wanted, and they were taking steps to get it.[6]

From Wishes to Goals

We all have plans for the future, many things we want to achieve. Some are vague, like "I want to make lots of money." These are dreams or wishes, not goals. They are not specific enough to qualify. We do, of course, have personal goals—buying a new car, starting a family, or learning a new hobby or skill—and business goals—meeting a sales quota or developing a new advertising campaign.

How can we move from wishes to goals, and then on to results? The first step is to sort out our true motivations and goals, those that are meaningful and relevant for *us,* not for others. Once we identify them, we can take the appropriate actions to accomplish our objectives. Rink Dickinson's goal was to create a company that would be an agent for social change by improving the lives of coffee growers. The Enterprising Ethics box tells how Equal Exchange fulfilled Dickinson's goal.

---

exhibit 3.3   **How to Set Effective Goals**

1. Specify the general objective or tasks to be done.
2. Specify how the performance in question will be measured.
3. Specify the standard or target to be reached.
4. Specify the time span involved.
5. Prioritize goals.
6. Rate goals by difficulty and importance.

Source: Adapted from E. A. Locke and G. P. Latham, *Goal Setting* (Englewood Cliffs, NJ: Prentice-Hall, 1984), pp. 27–41.

enterprising ethics

Equal Exchange Plays Fair

When you buy coffee, tea, sugar, cocoa, or chocolate, you probably don't think about where the product was grown and by whom. Rink Dickinson, however, was concerned about the human rights of the poor coffee growers in Central America. He and two other managers at a New England food cooperative wanted to forge a closer connection between consumers and the farmers. The result was Equal Exchange, the oldest fair trade company in the United States.

Dickinson struggled to raise financing for his new venture. The company's unique business model combined a private, for-profit enterprise with a nonprofit mission. Most investors thought he was crazy. Why pay coffee growers a hefty premium rather than buy for the lowest price possible? Dickinson wanted his company not only to sell high-quality food products, but also to be an agent for social change, improving the lives of farmers and giving them more control over their economic futures.

Fairness to farmers was at the core of his strategy. By importing coffee directly from farmer cooperatives, he could streamline the conventional coffee supply chain. Cutting out middlemen freed up additional money to pay the farmers higher prices per pound while maintaining fair prices to consumers. This would support small farming communities and improve the lives of the farmers and their families. His vision went further and included promoting ecologically sustainable farming practices, educating consumers about fair trade issues, and structuring the company on democratic principles.

In 1986, he obtained $100,000 from like-minded investors to start Equal Exchange. In 1990, the company formalized its worker-owner cooperative structure, and in 1991 became part of the European Fair Trade network. Today the West Bridgewater, Massachusetts, company has 70 worker-owners—none of whom earn more than three times the lowest staff member's salary—and sells coffee, tea, cocoa mix, and other chocolate products from 30 farmer cooperatives in 15 countries. Equal Exchange's customers include about 2,000 restaurants, major supermarkets, natural food stores, consumer coops, cafes, universities, fair trade retailers, and places of worship. In 2005, it generated more than $20 million in revenues and earned a profit while remaining true to its founders' vision and values. It describes itself as a "self-sustaining but not wealth-accumulating enterprise," keeping its margins well below industry averages.

The mission of Equal Exchange is "to build long-term trade partnerships that are economically just and environmentally sound, to foster mutually beneficial relationships between farmers and consumers, and to demonstrate, through our success, the contribution of worker co-operatives and Fair Trade to a more equitable, democratic, and sustainable world." It was a pioneer in adopting fair trade—a voluntary program to create an alternative market for traditionally disadvantaged producers in developing countries, usually small-scale farmers—and has crusaded aggressively for its acceptance. Today more than 400 companies offer some fair trade coffee. The company's efforts have significantly benefited the growers and their communities by providing additional income for education, health care facilities, and other projects.

Dickinson's job is not yet done, however. He continues to raise the consciousness of consumers as well as other businesses and is looking for other areas to apply fair trade standards, such as family farmers within the United States.

Discussion Questions

1. What goals led to the formation of Equal Exchange?

2. What kinds of companies and individuals might want to be involved in Equal Exchange? Why would they want to be involved?

3. Are there other ways that an enterprise could be founded that would meet the same goals as Equal Exchange? Who would most likely benefit if the company was designed solely as a for-profit enterprise?

4. What are the benefits to each party involved in organizing this company as a cooperative?

Sources: Sandy Coleman, "Grounds for Success," *Boston Globe,* February 26, 2006, http://www.boston.com; Equal Exchange website, http://www. equalexchange.com (September 20, 2006); and G. Jeffrey Macdonald, "How to Brew Justice," Time.com, December 11, 2005, http://www.time.com.

Setting Priorities

Because some goals are more important than others, *setting priorities* is the next step in the goal-setting process. This will help you find a balance between personal and professional goals and also manage your time more effectively.

How do you set priorities among your goals? Start with what you love, not what you do well. This passion keeps you motivated to make the effort to reach your goals. To figure out what you want, you have to be willing to fantasize, to shut down the self-doubts that hold you back. For example, you may have an idea for a business, but that inner voice tells you that no one will like the product, you're not smart enough to run a company, you can't raise the money, and so on.[7] You give up before you investigate to see if your ideas are feasible. Take another look at Exhibit 3.2, focusing on Quadrant 2. How can you organize your life so that you have time for the goals that are priorities, so that you put first things first? According to Covey, you should start with the following steps:[8]

Step 1. Create a personal mission statement and connect with it. Ask yourself three questions: What is most important to me? What gives my life meaning? What do I want to be and do in my life? Then write a personal mission statement that sums up your answers and summarizes your long-term goals. It should define your values, principles, most important roles, relationships, and what matters most to you in life. Your mission statement should form the basis of your future goals and decisions, guiding you toward meeting your objectives. If you need help in formulating your mission statement, work through the Mission Formulator at the Franklin Covey website: http://www.franklincovey.com.

Step 2: State your short- and mid-term objectives. Start by identifying the many roles you have: entrepreneur, manager, employee, spouse, parent, son/daughter, student, hospital volunteer, community member, and so on. Include personal goals that enrich you physically, socially, emotionally, mentally, and spiritually. This step increases your overall effectiveness and provides a foundation for success. Then choose one or two major (Quadrant 2) goals that you'd like to accomplish for each role. These should relate to your mission statement. Set a reasonable time frame to meet these goals.

Take a look at the Goal-Setting Worksheet in Exhibit 3.4, which lists the roles, goals, and action steps for Marianna Ravden, a 28-year-old marketing research analyst who wants to start a gift basket business. As you can see, Marianna's goals are more specific and make it easier for her to develop an action plan to reach her goals. Ranking the goals according to degree of priority is another important component of this worksheet. Filling it out offers one way to identify and set priorities for goals and then take the actions to achieve them. Take a moment to fill out your own goal-setting worksheet, which will become an important time management tool.

Managing Your Goals

Now that you've identified your goals, you need to prioritize them. Because you won't be able to accomplish all of your goals at once, you must choose one,

exhibit 3.4   **Goal-Setting Worksheet**

NAME: MARIANNA RAVDEN   DATE: AUGUST 15, 2008

Role	Related Goals	Priority	Action Steps
Enterpriser	1. Find customers	High	• Get directory of companies in local area • Create a brochure of gift baskets • Make up sample gift baskets • Make appointments with corporate event planners and marketing representatives
	2. Locate suppliers of unique foods and gift items	High	
	3. Arrange for delivery helpers	Low	
Mother	Take care of kids	Very high	Morning wakeup
	Keep up the household		Meals
	Pay bills		Transportation to school
			Homework
			Fun
Spouse	Spend time with husband	Very high	

most critical goal to accomplish. If you feel anxious that you have a number of equally important goals, consider these four different strategies to accomplish your goals:

- *Simultaneous goals:* If you have a number of goals, you may want to work on several at a time.

- *Sequential goals:* Change goals after working on one for a set time period.

- *Alternating goals:* Devote alternating blocks of time to different goals.

- *Multiple goals:* Design activities to combine two or three goals into the same situation.

Recognize that accomplishing your goals takes time, and that you won't satisfy all these goals immediately. Goal setting is an ongoing process. As you move through different life stages, your goals will change, as will your priorities. You will also face conflicts when determining priorities. But the more you clarify your goals, the easier it will be to manage them.

Getting Time on Your Side

Like many of us, Renée Madison, owner of a small computer consulting company, has a hectic life. On any day she might find herself developing or presenting proposals for new clients, meeting with employees to discuss scheduling and management of projects for current clients, and making troubleshooting visits. While she is juggling these tasks, she must field numerous phone calls and emails that interrupt her day. She also worries about finding the time to market her services to more clients so that she can grow her business and whether she'll be able to attend her son's soccer game after school.

While your specific activities and problem areas may be different, you can probably identify with Renée's concerns about using time efficiently, both at work and at home. Like her, you may find yourself moving from one crisis to another, sitting in unnecessary meetings, or getting bogged down in paperwork. At the end of each day, you are frustrated with what you *haven't* accomplished.

Learning and using time management techniques is one of the best gifts you can give yourself. It will pay off over and over again. As you gain control of your time, you will be more productive, reduce the stress in your life, enjoy work more, and balance work and personal time. Enterprisers in particular need to be excellent time managers, because there is no manager to monitor what they do. If you spend the day on low-priority activities, you will never be able to start or grow your business. See Appendix A for a discussion of some of the best practices in time management and how to incorporate them into your lifestyle.

3.2 Persuasion

persuasion
Deliberately seeking attitude change through communication—using your personal influence to get someone to do or believe something.

Persuasion involves deliberately seeking attitude change through communication: using your personal influence to get someone to do or believe something. It is similar to negotiation and has the same objective: Helping other people meet *their* needs through involvement with *your* goals. Like negotiation, persuasion is based on creating "win-win" situations. However, persuasion is more subtle, because the other person probably doesn't realize that a negotiation is underway! It is proactive and requires you to have a clear idea of what you want, discover what the other person desires, and then figure out how to meet the other person's needs—and at the same time get what *you* want.

The Six Principles of Effective Persuasion

Some people are born persuaders. Not only do they naturally use charisma and eloquence to get others to do what they ask, they do it in a way that makes others eager to cooperate. But ask them what they do that is special, and they may not be able to tell you. Behavioral science studies, however, have identified six basic principles that appeal in predictable ways to fundamental human needs and desires.[9] Armed with this knowledge, you can apply these principles to become a skilled persuader.

The six principles of effective persuasion—liking, reciprocity, social proof, consistency, authority, and scarcity—are not mysterious or profound. Rather, they are common sense, obvious, and intuitive, explaining how people evaluate information and make decisions. Persuasion is all about attitudes and how you deal with others. Successful persuaders really pay attention to other persons. Exhibit 3.5 defines the six principles and illustrates how they can be applied in business settings.

Why are these six principles so powerful? Think about it. Isn't it easier to get a coworker's cooperation for a project when you've already become friends? Establishing areas of common interest creates goodwill that carries over to other areas. Praise also creates goodwill between people. Such positive comments make the other person like you and more willing to do what you ask at a future date. Praise can help you nurture good relationships and mend poor ones. When someone you like favors a product or idea, you are more likely to view it positively, too.

exhibit 3.5   **The Six Principles of Persuasion**

Principle	Definition	Application	Examples
Liking	People like those who like them.	Find *similarities* with others and offer *real praise.*	Create bonds, like a shared interest in a sport or hobby, with a recent hire during informal conversations. Use genuine praise to generate liking, even in a manager with whom you've had disagreements.
Reciprocity	People repay in kind.	Give what you want to receive; modeling a desired behavior makes others more likely to adopt it.	Lend a staff member to another manager who needs help to meet a deadline, and you're more likely to get help when you need it. Giving seasonal gifts increases the recipient's willingness to want to work with you.
Social Proof	People follow the lead of similar others.	Use peer power to persuade others.	Use testimonials from satisfied customers, especially those companies similar to your prospect. Convince an employee to support a new corporate initiative to get others to buy in.
Consistency	People align with their clear commitments.	Get others to make commitments that are active, public, and voluntary.	Ask an employee to confirm in a *written* memo a commitment to complete a project by a certain date.
Authority	People defer to experts.	Establish your expertise; it may not be as obvious as you think.	Find ways to work into conversation how you solved a problem similar to one the client faces or a particular skill you have mastered.
Scarcity	People want more of items that have limited availability.	Emphasize unique benefits and exclusive information.	Use limited-time, one-of-a-kind offers; share exclusive or advance information with key managers.

The six principles work best when you apply several at once. The combined effect is much more powerful. For example, during a seemingly casual conversation before a meeting, you can convey information about your areas of expertise and also ask questions that show your interest in the other person and gain valuable information to help establish similarities.

Persuasion is not the same as coercion. In fact, intimidating a person into agreement or being dishonest is counterproductive and manipulative. Unless the commitment feels voluntary, the other person will follow through begrudgingly, if at all. Persuasion is a mutually beneficial activity.[10]

In Exhibit 3.6 you'll find tips to increase your persuasiveness based on Dale Carnegie's famous book *How to Win Friends and Influence People*. These ideas are very basic, but you'd be surprised at how often people ignore them and act in ways that harm relationships.

Ready, Set, Persuade!

Have you ever made a presentation that you thought went perfectly, only to learn that your proposal wasn't approved? You covered all the bases with well-organized data supporting your argument and delivered the report in a forceful yet pleasant manner. What went wrong?

Preparation Pays Off

In mastering effective persuasion techniques, you should not only incorporate the six principles of persuasion in your presentations and discussions but also

exhibit 3.6	**How to Become More Persuasive**

1. Become genuinely interested in other people.
2. Be friendly.
3. Make a good first impression: smile.
4. Remember that a person's name is to that person the sweetest and most important sound in any language.
5. Be a good listener. Encourage others to talk about themselves and let them do most of the talking.
6. Talk in terms of the other person's interests.
7. Make the other person feel important—and do it sincerely.
8. Be sympathetic with the other person's ideas and desires and try to see things from the other person's point of view.
9. Avoid criticism and complaints.
10. Show respect for the other person's opinions. Never say, "You're wrong."
11. Make the person happy about doing the thing you suggest.

Source: Adapted from Dale Carnegie, *How to Win Friends and Influence People,* Revised ed. (New York: Pocket Books, 1982).

give careful thought to the *receiver* of the message, as well as to content, context, and delivery. Who is the primary decision maker, and how can you tailor your presentation to his or her style? Will you be in a casual setting or a formal meeting? Clearly, you wouldn't want to introduce a complex proposal during the social hour before a luncheon meeting. However, you could use this time to build rapport with someone you'll be meeting with next week to discuss a proposal.

The more you know about a person's values and needs, the better you can tailor your presentation to be consistent with what you've learned and persuade him or her to accept your point of view. If you are meeting with your boss or other company managers, you may have some clues to the decision maker's personality and "hot buttons." When you are dealing with a sales presentation to a potential client, you many not have the information you need. But listening carefully to the questions the person asks, asking good questions, and watching for other hints can help you respond appropriately.

Building Rapport

Developing *rapport* is essential to successful persuasion and relates to the first principle of persuasion, liking. When people have a high degree of rapport between them, they communicate more effectively. The other person understands clearly what you are thinking; both parties feel like they are on the same wavelength.[11]

You build rapport when you model the other person's gestures, movement, words, and mood, as well as show sincere concern and interest in the other person's needs. If you are talking to a calm, quiet person who speaks slowly, you should adapt to his or her tone. Nonverbal communication conveys your message as well, so use positive body language.

Questions are a good way to demonstrate your interest. Start with questions that discover values, and then follow up with related ones to define values and identify needs, and use that to incorporate mutual benefits into your presentation. Suppose you are the founder of a company that develops sales management software and will be making a presentation to a potential client. In your preliminary discussions with the client, you may have a conversation such as the one below:

Q: What is most important to you in buying software?

A: It should be easy to use.

Q: Why is this most important to you?

A: Our sales and marketing staff complain about our present systems and don't want to use them.

Q: What do you need most from your new software system?

A: Integration of marketing, sales, and inventory management systems.

Q: What do you require from the company that provides your software?

A: Good customer service.

Q: How do you define good customer service?

A: When we call for tech support, we get prompt answers to our problems.

You'll also ask about technical requirements, the hardware platform, price considerations, and similar needs.

With this key information—users of the product, environment in which it will be used, desired results, and problems with existing products—you can customize your presentation and demonstrate how your software's features address those issues. You will also be able to describe your company in a way that highlights its attention to customer service, offering examples of how it responds to customer calls.

Here are a few more points to help you make persuasive, win-win presentations:[12]

1. *Plan for a brief presentation, but also be ready to expand into a longer one.* The ability to explain your ideas briefly but clearly in less than a minute is a valuable skill. Some decision makers want the bottom line right away, while others want the supporting facts as well. Prepare several versions to cover all bases.

2. *State the objective concisely, early in the presentation.* Tell the other person why you wanted the meeting and how you can help meet his or her exact needs. For example: "I want to show you how your company can save about $20,000 with our inventory management software."

3. *Make your verbal and nonverbal communications agree.* Your tone of voice, body language, and overall style should be consistent and fit the situation. Don't forget to smile when discussing positive events. Know what your gestures say. Using a natural tone creates a warm environment.

4. *Listen attentively.* A good listener inspires confidence. Ask open-ended questions to get a better understanding of the other person, and allow plenty of time for the answer.

5. *Use client-centered thinking.* It's not enough to state the benefits of your proposal. You must answer the question, "What's in it for me?" for the other person. Do your employees care that you are adding a bond fund as a new investment option to the company's 401(k) plan? Probably not, until you explain that the bond fund offers an alternative to the stock offerings so that they can build more diversified portfolios.

3.3 Enterprisers

Theatrical Lighting Systems

Based in Huntsville, Alabama, with crews all over the country, Theatrical Lighting Systems (TLS) has a slogan: "We light the stars." Since 1981, David and Janet Milly's company has been creating lighting magic for performers like Tony Bennett, Lee Greenwood, Johnny Cash, and many others. Revenues come from lighting sales and rentals, and there's a division dedicated to the design and installation of permanent lighting systems that integrate both house and theatrical lighting.

"About 25 years ago, when I got into the business, entertainers would perform in a building and just flip the houselights on," says David Lilly. "Then people moved up to two or three lights for the performers, and they'd turn the house-lights off. So the lighting business evolved from nothing to sophisticated half-million dollar lighting systems with computer controls and all that."

As performers discovered the benefits of good lighting, TLS began to grow. "If it's dark, people are looking around; they don't know what to look at," David explains. "You bring the light up—Boom!—that's what they focus their attention on, and it is the energy of a show. If the entertainer's moving around, the lights are moving around. If the entertainer is doing a slow ballad, the lights are a slow ballad. So lighting sets the mood and the tempo for the show and for the entertainer."

Because David understood lighting better than sound, he chose to specialize in lighting and not expand into other areas. "In the long run, it's paid off," he says. "Our mission statement, 'Making money doing lights,' keeps us focused."

Today the company has 30 employees and close to $5 million in revenues from three revenue streams: selling equipment to churches, schools, arenas, and nightclubs; consulting with architects to design light packages for permanent installation; and providing lighting packages for road shows with and without personnel. In 2002, TLS moved into a 57,000 sq ft. headquarters facility that is renovated to include administrative offices, a showroom, a demonstration room, a studio, and a repair lab. The new facility allows TLS to set up, test, and program multiple entertainment lighting systems simultaneously. In addition to this centralized hub for daily activities, the company has several branch sales offices.

Despite its growth and success, TLS remains committed to the small customers who were essential to establishing the business. If a local deejay, private party, small church, or little theater needs lighting, TLS is ready to help. "We've got what they need. We do the larger gigs—but we never forget the little guy," says David.

David's wife Janet has been his partner since the early days. At first she thought of TLS as just

a small operation. After David took her to see several businesses which she considered large players in the industry, she discovered that they were not much larger than TLS. This helped the couple develop their vision for the company's future.

In the beginning, David and Janet did everything themselves, from operating the lights to managing the business. Once it started to grow, David recognized that he needed to concentrate on managing and hire others for the actual lighting projects. "Even though I felt that nobody could do it as well as I could, I had to force myself to send other people out," he says. "What I did best was run the business, and what the people I hired could do best was the lighting." Learning to delegate was one of the hardest lessons for him to learn, and he still finds that giving employees responsibility and authority is difficult, and that the people side of running his own company is the most challenging. "Selling the product, or stocking the product, or coming up with what to sell—that's the easy part," he explains. "Hiring the right people, keeping them pumped up all the time—that's the hardest part of being in business. That's a theme you're going to hear from me forever: Hire the right people, and you will be successful. You hire the wrong people, and you won't be."

Treating those people well is another part of the TLS formula for success. The Millys consider their employees part of their family. "When they get in trouble, they come to you," says Janet. "If they have a wreck, it affects your insurance. It's a constant thing. And, of course, we feel an obligation, also, to make sure that they can make a living and they can support their families. That's important to us."

David also acknowledges his own limitations and is willing to look outside the company for insight. When he was feeling frustrated with the company's growth, he hired a consultant to analyze the business practices that had evolved without much critical thinking. The consultant identified some inefficiencies—for example,

(continued)

too many people reported to David—and made several restructuring suggestions that David implemented.

He and Janet also recognize the value of networking. On the local scene, TLS belongs to the Huntsville/Madison County Chamber of Commerce, which David considers the best promoter of Huntsville and its community. "If a city is good to you, you've got to give something back," he says. He has also been active in the Entertainment Services and Technology Association, which has been instrumental in establishing standards for safety and self-regulation across the country. At trade shows, he and his colleagues share ideas about a variety of industry topics like leasing versus buying equipment and the latest information technology systems. "People who want to start businesses should study the competition," encourages David. "I learn so much from them. It's simpler to see what's been successful than to go out and make your own mistakes."

David has some important advice for would-be entrepreneurs. "Be sure you have a competitive spirit—or find something else to do. Business is definitely a competitive sport."

Discussion Questions

As you read the remainder of Chapter 3, you might want to keep in mind some of the insights and ideas in this case study. Answer the following questions that relate to the case study:

1. Evaluate the TLS mission statement, "Making money doing lights." What kinds of goals did David and Janet set for themselves and their business? Do they relate to the mission statement? Did these goals affect their ability to grow to a $5 million business?

2. What kinds of activities do David and Janet spend their time on? Which kinds of activities do you think might be the best use of their time?

3. How might TLS find new customers? Whom do the Millys know that might help them grow and manage their business?

4. How might TLS learn what other competitors are doing in the lighting industry?

5. How can the Millys expand their business without incurring additional risks? What risks does TLS face?

Sources: Adapted with permission from Small Business School, the series on PBS, at http://SmallBusinessSchool.com; and from material in the video "Invent an Industry from Theatrical Lighting", Small Business 2000, and on the TLS Inc. website, http://www.tlsinc.com.

3.4 Negotiation

When you hear the term *negotiation,* you may think first of executives working out a joint venture, labor unions negotiating with management, attorneys negotiating a pretrial settlement, or diplomats trying to bring about peace in the Middle East. However, negotiation is not just reserved for high-level situations or formal settings. We negotiate all the time, for minor as well as critical reasons. Asking for a raise, purchasing products from a supplier, deciding where to go on vacation, trying to get the best price on a new car—these, too, are negotiations. And regardless of the situation, the process is basically the same.

negotiation
Back-and-forth communication process by which two parties try to reach a mutually acceptable solution to a problem or to accomplish something that neither party could do on its own.

Negotiation involves two parties trying to reach a mutually acceptable solution to a problem or to accomplish something that neither party could do on its own. The goal is to satisfy both parties' interests and achieve a "win-win" situation where each party gains something it wants in exchange for making concessions and feels treated fairly. To be successful, therefore, negotiators must pay attention to their own goals and objectives and the other participants' goals and objectives.[13]

Negotiating Styles

How do people negotiate? Some approach negotiation as an adversarial process: what one side gives up, the other side gets, and vice versa. This negotiating style focuses on victory and fighting hard for one's position. While you may win, the cost may be high in terms of the future relationship with the other party. At the other end of the spectrum is the negotiator who makes concessions to avoid personal conflict; the goal here is reaching an agreement. Even though the outcome seems positive and fosters future relationships, this softer style often results in a less satisfactory agreement and makes it hard to separate the people from the negotiating process. The negotiator may feel exploited.

A better method, described in Roger Fisher's and William Ury's book *Getting to Yes*, is *principled negotiation* or *negotiation on the merits*.[14] This technique applies to most negotiation situations and produces mutually satisfactory results using a friendly rather than an adversarial approach. The key elements of this clear-cut negotiating style are the following:

- **People:** *Keep the people and the problem separate.* Deal with emotions separately from the substantive issues. Be soft on the people and hard on the problem.

- **Interests:** *Focus on interests, not positions.* Interests define the problem; by identifying shared desires and concerns, the way to reconcile conflict becomes more apparent. When you think primarily in terms of gaining acceptance for your position, you lose sight of what you really want, instead of looking for mutual interests.

- **Options:** *Develop multiple possibilities before making any decisions.* It's tough to develop creative solutions when you are under pressure. Instead of quickly looking for one solution, look for many mutually acceptable alternatives and discuss which is best for all concerned.

- **Criteria:** *Base the result on an objective standard.* Discuss and choose fair standards acceptable to all parties—for example, precedent, moral standards, professional standards, market value, replacement cost, competitive prices. Then you can negotiate the issues in terms of the search for an outside principle, instead of pressure from the other party.

To sum up, think of negotiation as problem solving rather than as driving a hard bargain or making trade-offs to get what you want. As Ronald Shapiro, James Dale, and Mark Jankowski explain in their book, *The Power of Nice*, the best way to get what *you* want is to help the *other* side get what it wants. If you first identify the needs of each party and clarify the interests of each side, the discussions proceed within a framework of mutual problem solving. The spirit of cooperation replaces a confrontational, winner-takes-all attitude.

Structuring the Negotiation

Each negotiation has three broad stages: analysis, planning, and proposing. The first two preparatory steps build a solid foundation for all successful negotiations and may, in fact, take longer than the actual discussion of the proposal. Within these stages you'll have other steps. For example, the face-to-face proposing includes stating your proposal, asking questions to clarify objectives and interests, generating options, and reaching an agreement.

Lack of adequate preparation is often the reason that people feel dissatisfied after negotiating. Exhibit 3.7 lists the seven elements of a successful negotiation that arise from the four key points of principled negotiation. These provide a useful framework to use throughout the negotiation preparation process by creating options, building relationships, and facilitating communication. Note that these points are similar to good persuasive techniques: to build relationships, establish areas of common interests, which promotes liking. Reciprocity is at the heart of the negotiating process: your goal is a mutually beneficial outcome. Good preparation, clear communication, understanding of the other party's interests, and rapport between parties improve the odds of success, whether you are persuading or negotiating.

The amount of time you spend on each element will depend on the complexity and importance of the situation you are negotiating.

exhibit 3.7

Seven Steps to Negotiating Success

1. **Know each party's interests and priorities.** Probe deeply and go beyond position to understand each party's needs, wants, and concerns. You are more likely to reach a successful outcome when you build on interests. Remember that money is not usually the priority.

2. **Create many options for solutions.** The first idea may not be the best. By exploring possible agreements or parts of an agreement and not getting stuck on one outcome, you increase the potential to maximize joint gains.

3. **Know the BATNA (best alternative to a negotiated agreement).** What happens if you can't reach an agreement? What is the other party's fallback position? Your objective is to find an agreement that is better than the BATNA.

4. **Legitimize your requests.** Using external standards or precedents when setting quantitative values provides the basis for a fair agreement and builds trust.

5. **Communicate efficiently; listen carefully and deliver a clear message.** Good two-way communication helps reach agreement more quickly and clarifies the underlying assumptions. Know what you are listening for.

6. **Build a relationship with the other party.** Separating the people issues from the substantive issues will help to preserve and enhance the relationship.

7. **Don't commit until you've compared your options to your BATNA.** Know what issues to include in the agreement and the steps to take to reach an agreement.

Source: Adapted from Roger Fisher and Kris Frieswick, "Doctor YES," *CFO,* September 2001, http://www.findarticles.com; and Roger Fisher and Danny Ertel, *Getting Ready to Negotiate* (New York: Penguin Books, 1995), pp. 6–7, 14–16.

Generating Options

Options are at the heart of principled negotiation.[15] Typically people get bogged down in particular positions and viewpoints. They think they have the one right answer—their own—and it is reasonable. Until they consider other ways to approach their situation, they remain stuck with opposing positions.

Here's an example of negotiating based on position, and how the situation can be turned around when options and interests enter the picture. You just had your annual performance review and have requested a $3,000 salary increase. Your boss tells you that isn't possible this year; he can only offer you $1,500. Naturally, you are upset by this low offer. This is a classic win-lose scenario: you win only if your boss loses, and vice versa. You each have stated your position, and now the bargaining begins. If you were to bargain from these fixed positions only, you might try to compromise at the midway point. Would either of you be really satisfied? Probably not.

Let's add some important interests. What do you really care about? Is it the money alone, or are you interested in professional growth, finishing your college degree, or perhaps moving to a different department within the company? Your manager's interests are to run a profitable department, work with talented employees who do high-level work, boost employee morale, and get promoted.

Look at these interests and assign priorities. If professional growth is really important, you can propose a number of options that address these interests, such as additional on-the-job training and company-paid educational benefits that give you additional skills, opportunity to work on a broader range of projects, and assistance in working toward a promotion to a position with even greater salary potential. These options keep the interests of your boss in mind: you become a more productive and competent employee and demonstrate to higher management how well your boss develops employees' abilities. The potential now exists for mutual gain.

As you develop options, resist the temptation to judge them. Brainstorm without trying to decide, so that you generate lots of ideas that can lead to other possible solutions. Then broaden your options. Don't look for the best answer, but rather to gather as many options from which you can eventually choose. Apply different types of thinking to the situation—both real world and theoretical—to analyze the problem and what can be done to solve it, as shown in Exhibit 3.8. Going down and up the steps and revisiting the theory behind a good option will help you come up with others.

Consider the Alternative

Suppose your negotiation doesn't work and you decide to walk away without reaching agreement. What is your best alternative to a negotiated agreement, or **BATNA**?[16] Knowing your BATNA ahead of time, and making educated guesses about the other party's BATNA, sets a baseline for the negotiation. The BATNA becomes the standard against which you should evaluate any proposal. To succeed, *an acceptable agreement must be better than the BATNA.*

Many people plan to walk away if they don't get what they want. But the critical thing to consider is, "Walk away to *what?*" Exploring the BATNAs on each side helps the parties think through their options and often results in negotiators

BATNA (best alternative to a negotiated agreement) *What each party will do if the negotiation process fails to reach an acceptable agreement.*

| exhibit 3.8 | **Four Steps to Create Broad Options** |

Step 4: Develop action ideas. These are specific steps that could address the problem at hand.

Step 3: List possible strategies/solutions. Think about what might be done, in theory, and develop broad ideas.

Step 2: Analyze the problem. Identify its symptoms and suggest causes. What's missing, and what may hinder resolution?

Step 1: What is the problem? Define the problem and its symptoms factually. Make sure you are solving the right problem!

Source: "Circle Chart: The Four Basic Steps in Inventing Options" from *Getting to Yes,* 2nd ed. by Roger Fisher, William Ury, and Bruce Patton. Copyright © 1981, 1991 by Roger Fisher and William Ury. Adapted and reprinted by permission of Houghton Mifflin Co. All rights reserved.

going back to the table to generate other solutions. If each side's BATNAs are worse than options in the negotiated agreement, then the parties are likely to continue negotiating. Your BATNA gives you more flexibility to investigate solutions, rather than reject them out of hand.

In addition, a strong BATNA can give you leverage to reach a deal. If your BATNA seems viable to the other party, your threat to stop negotiating is real. Going into a negotiation without a BATNA makes you vulnerable and unsure of when to stop negotiating. BATNAs will help you focus on your objectives and look into ways to meet them outside of the negotiation. The better your BATNA, the better your negotiated agreement has to be to top it. Your BATNA will also give you more confidence to negotiate.

To develop your BATNA, ask yourself questions like,

- What are the alternatives that satisfy my interests if we cannot agree?

- What are the pluses and minuses of these alternatives?

- Which is my BATNA—the one I will really choose—and how can I improve it?

- What alternatives does the other side have, and what are the merits of each?

- Which looks best, and how can I lessen its attractiveness (make it harder to achieve, convince that it is unwise or costly, etc.)?

Clearly, we have only skimmed the surface of the negotiation process. There is much more to learn about effective communication, style, timing, structuring the discussion process, dealing with challenging situations and difficult people, and similar topics. But understanding how to set the stage for a negotiation by identifying interests, options, and alternatives will get you started on the path to negotiating success.

3.5 Networking

You've probably been networking all your life. When you ask friends to recommend a good restaurant, an auto mechanic, gym, or movie, you are networking. You also network in the workplace as you find out about job opportunities, learn what your competitor is doing, and gather resources you will need to start, run, and manage a business. As you go about your daily life, you interact with many different types of networks.

What Is a Network?

A person's **network** is the sum total of his or her relationships and involves all of the connections that a person has with other people. Exhibit 3.9

network
The total of a person's relationships and connections with other people.

exhibit 3.9   **A Local Bicycle Store's Network**

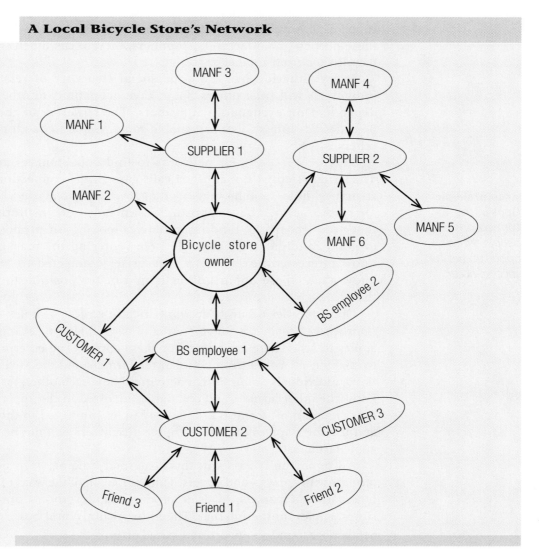

diagrams these relationships and connections among people who are involved with a local bicycle store. The bicycle store's owner is connected to suppliers and manufacturers who provide bicycles and bicycle accessories to the store. Some of these suppliers are connected to other bicycle manufacturers. Think about the different manufacturers and suppliers and how they both compete and work with each other, and how all of these relationships affect the bicycle store owner.

Consider also the people who visit the store to purchase bicycles and accessories. These customers interact with the store's owner and employees. As previous customers share their experiences with others, these word-of-mouth connections generate new customers. At the center of all of these relationships (manufacturers, suppliers, employees, customers) is the bicycle store's owner.

From its particular network of relationships, the bicycle store derives a competitive advantage over other bicycle shops that do not have such a network. Not every bicycle shop will have the same relationships to various manufacturers and suppliers of bicycles, or to particular customers. The unique connections between these parties (manufacturers, suppliers, bicycle customers) differentiate one bicycle shop from another.

Every situation has a unique social structure of relationships: Some individuals will trust others, some have obligations to others, and some are dependent on exchanges with others. The *structure* of these relationships provides advantages that can enable some people to be more successful than others.

structural holes
Gaps in the connections among people, where opportunities for success occur.

Enterprisers use their networks to find opportunities and exploit them. The social scientist Ronald Burt calls gaps in the connections among people **structural holes**, and he suggests that *structural holes are where opportunities for success occur.* These opportunities include new institutions and projects that need leadership, funding initiatives looking for proposals, jobs in need of good candidates, or valuable items entering the market for which you know interested buyers.[17] An enterpriser connected to other people who know about these opportunities is in a better position to find and pursue them.

Opportunities occur in networks rich in structural holes—that is, *in situations where people are not connected to each other.* For example, farmers have apples to sell. There are buyers for these apples. The enterpriser fills the hole by making the connection between the farmers and the buyers. In most situations, individuals doing similar activities know each other; farmers are likely to know the other farmers and companies involved in the apple business. On the other hand, most farmers are unlikely to be connected to those who purchase and use their apples—and most apple purchasers will not be connected to the apple farmers.

An opportunity exists in this structural hole between potential sellers—farmers with apples—and buyers. Think about all of the ways to fill this structural hole: farmer's markets, roadside produce stands, grocery stores, specialty food stores, apples on the Internet. The Enterprising World box explains how Brian Scudamore found an opportunity based on junk.

Junk Money

Have you ever noticed a business or service and asked yourself, "Why don't I do that, too?" Brian Scudamore, a college student in Vancouver, Canada, acted on his impulse after he noticed a junk-hauling truck. With an old truck and a clever name and slogan—"The Rubbish Boys: We'll Stash Your Trash in a Flash!"—he was in business. After several successful summers operating one truck, the young entrepreneur realized that many more people needed his services—and not just during the summer. By 1993 business was so good that he made The Rubbish Boys a full-time business and added two more trucks.

By 1996, the firm was generating $1 million in revenues, and Scudamore saw the potential to move into other markets in Canada and the United States. Under the new name 1-800-GOT-JUNK?, he decided to expand by selling franchises that would use the same name and operate with the business processes Scudamore developed. The idea caught on, and today 1-800-GOT-JUNK? is the world's largest junk removal service, with more than 270 franchises in the United States, Canada, Australia, and the United Kingdom. It ranked 292 on *Entrepreneur*'s 2006 Top Franchises list and 78 on its fastest-growing franchises list.

The business concept behind 1-800-GOT-JUNK? is very basic: Customers contact the company by phone or online at http://www.1800gotjunk.com to schedule pickups of nonhazardous items they no longer want and that may not qualify for municipal or other types of trash collection. The company offers 2-hour appointment windows and calls with an exact time shortly before arrival. Fully licensed, uniformed drivers evaluate the job on-site and present customers with a no-obligation price quote before beginning the job. Then they load the indicated items from the customer's site and even clean up after themselves. From furniture and appliances to truckloads of ceramic knick-knacks, mattresses, construction debris, and yard refuse—as long as two people can lift it, the company's trucks haul it to dumps, local charities, or recycling facilities. Prices are based on the volume items take in the truck and also include any dump or recycling fees.

Customers love and value the service: Through fall 2006, the company's trucks hauled away almost 800,000 tons of junk for more than 756,000 customers worldwide. Customers praise the company for saving them time and money and for the excellent customer service.

Despite the idea's simplicity, Scudamore was the first to develop the fragmented junk removal business into a recognized brand offering professional service. His idea appealed to franchisees because it wasn't a complex business, had low start-up costs, and demand was high. He also embraced technology to improve efficiency through JunkNet, a scheduling and operations management program.

Another key selling point was the commitment to a strategic vision and growth plan, which is clearly communicated to both headquarters employees and franchisees, who praise Scudamore's leadership and the quality of his management team. Employees at the headquarters are enthusiastic about the corporate culture Scudamore has created. They cite the company's passion for its vision and feel a strong sense of dedication to achieving that vision. They feel valued for their contributions, praising the supportive team environment, upbeat culture, responsive management, availability of flextime, generous profit sharing, and the excitement of being part of a rapidly growing company.

(continued)

The future is bright for 1-800-GOT-JUNK? and Scudamore. Starbucks printed a quote from him on more than 10 million cups as part of its "The Way I See It" campaign. The company hauls away junk on the popular *Extreme Makeover: Home Edition* television series, and the company was named the best to work for in British Columbia in 2004 and 2005. Not bad for a guy who made it big with junk!

Discussion Questions

1. Why did Brian Scudamore choose the United States, the United Kingdom, and Australia to start his international expansion? Discuss the feasibility of starting and developing this business in other countries, citing specific examples.

2. What kinds of legal and environmental regulations might prevent this business from succeeding in certain areas?

3. What goals did Scudamore set when starting and developing the 1-800-GOT-JUNK? concept? What additional goals did he use to guide the company's growth?

4. If you were Brian Scudamore, how would you manage your time during the early stages of the start-up process? What should be his priorities? List the kinds of activities he is likely to encounter and consider the amount of time he has to accomplish them. How will these activities and priorities change as the business grows?

5. How might you use the six principles of persuasion to recruit people to become franchisees for 1-800-GOT-JUNK?

6. What kind of network of people does Brian Scudamore need to develop and grow 1-800-GOT-JUNK? List the kinds of people that would be most helpful for developing this business. How might he go about finding and meeting these people?

Sources: "1-800-GOT-JUNK? Announces Massive Australian Franchise Expansion Plan," 1-800-GOT-JUNK? press release, March 31, 2006, http://www.1800gotjunk.com; 1-800-GOT-JUNK website, http://www.1800gotjunk.com (September 17, 2006); Justin Martin, "From Cash to Trash," *Fortune Small Business*, November 2003, http://money.cnn.com/magazines/fsb/; Christina Occhipinti, "Life in the Dumps," *Westchester County Business Journal*, February 20, 2006, p. 19; and "Starbucks To Feature 1-800-GOT-JUNK? CEO on Coffee Cups across North America," 1-800-GOT-JUNK? press release, January 20, 2006, http://www.1800gotjunk.com.

Advantages of Networking

Enterprisers who network gain a number of benefits. The first benefit involves *access*, or receiving a valuable piece of information and knowing who can use it.[18] For example, most job leads come from word of mouth. In fact, the Society for Human Resource Management found that 95 percent of all job applicants and personnel departments used networking and personal contacts to fill positions, and that both groups rated networking to be the most effective way to get a job.[19] Unless you are part of the network where a job opportunity is discussed, you won't be able to take advantage of the information and apply for the job.

The second benefit involves *timing*, that is, when a person might receive information that may have significant value. For example, suppose an enterpriser knew that a shopping center was going to be built in a particular area before others did. He or she could purchase land in the area at advantageous prices, well before most people knew about plans for the new facility.

Finally, enterprisers benefit from *referrals* they receive through a network. Being connected to other people who know about you provides legitimacy. Learning from a customer that the bicycle store's owner provides excellent service carries more weight than a newspaper ad for the store. Who would you more likely trust? The word of a friend, or an advertisement?

Clearly, when enterprisers have connections to people that others don't have, called "social asymmetry," they build relationships within and beyond the firm. These relationships form their *social capital*, which is just as important as the production-oriented, asset-based financial capital and human capital necessary to deliver goods or services. You build your social capital as you develop your networks because you

- Know people with "useful" information.
- Know people who are trustworthy (reliable information).
- Establish a large and diverse (nonredundant contacts) network.

The result of building up your social capital is new friends and associates and greater self-confidence. The more people you know, the more able you are to be in the center of a web of people with no connections to each other. Then you can fill the structural holes that exist, to everyone's benefit.

The Networking Process

Now that we know what a network is and the advantages networks bring, let's look at how to build your network and use it effectively. First, you must identify people to contact and figure out where to find those you don't already know. Then you need to approach them to share or acquire information.

Networking is the process of asking people you know (or could get to know through others) for information, advice, ideas, or help, as you plan and pursue your goals. It's a two-way street. First, you build up a wealth of contacts that help you find what *you* need. You share advice, ideas, leads, and resources with others—and, in turn, you receive information and assistance when you need it. Networking is a life skill you will use extensively for both personal and business reasons. The more you network, the higher your chances of success.

According to Susan RoAne, author of *How to Work a Room: The Secrets of Savvy Networking*, and *What Do I Say Next?*, networking is not a work style but a lifestyle that enhances our personal and professional lives. The best networkers are savvy and have common sense. They may not even realize they are networking. They're sharing themselves and their ideas. They may not have the biggest titles. What they do have is a huge contact base that they are willing to use to help someone else.[20]

networking
The process of asking people you know (or could get to know through others) for information, advice, ideas, or help, as you plan and pursue your goals.

Building Your Network

Think that you don't have a lot of networking contacts? Once you start making a list of potential resources, you may be surprised at how many people you do know! Include *everyone* who might be helpful, even if you are not sure. Use the categories listed in

exhibit 3.10   **Categories of Networking Contacts**

Use this list to develop your own networking lists. Refine the categories to suit your personal needs.

- People in a position to influence
- People who know others
- Coworkers/former coworkers
- Clients/former clients
- Professionals: bankers, lawyers, accountants
- Colleagues and competitors
- Family/ex-family/extended family/friends
- Neighbors/former neighbors
- Former classmates
- Service providers, local merchants
- Associates from organizations: charities, religious organizations, clubs, civic groups
- Special interest groups: sports, community
- Trade associations and professional associations

Exhibit 3.10 as a starting point, and sort your lists by group. Personal information management software can simplify the task of maintaining and organizing your lists.

To expand your circle of contacts, consider joining a networking club that covers your area of interest. For example, some specialize in job seekers, while others focus on small business owners. Alumni group gatherings often provide excellent networking opportunities. To find a professional organization in your field of interest, check out the Gateway to Associations at the American Society of Association Executives' website, http://www.asaenet.org (click on "Find Associations, People, and Businesses").

Work-related conferences and meetings are obvious places to network. However, remember that you have a networking opportunity any time you are in a room with a group of people. Certain events are better than others, but never miss a chance to add new people to your network. Regularly check local business periodicals for calendars of business and organizational events. Social and cultural events that may attract potential customers or people who you want to get to know also present networking possibilities.

Using Your Network

Now that you've begun developing your network and discovered the best places for networking, you are ready to use your network to your advantage. You must be proactive and

- *Feed the list*. Continually update, correct, and add as you make other contacts.

- *Nurture your list.* Keep in touch; send articles of interest, birthday greetings, and such. Try to call those on your lists at least once a year to see how they're doing or what they might need. Communicate trust and mutual support.

- *Use the list.* Take advantage of all opportunities, formal and informal. Whenever you start something—a new marketing program, a career move, buying a house or car—think of your network. Tapping into those resources may save you money.[21]

Think of your list as a valuable reference tool. You can use it for many reasons, from recommending a garden service to a neighbor to finding an internship for a college student.

Never forget that *networking is a reciprocal process.* It involves using your resources and being a resource for others. We may have better contacts in some areas than others, and we are likely to know others who can fill in our gaps. Don't underestimate yourself; we all have a lot to offer. List your job responsibilities, job and general skills, and hobbies. Once you think about what you do well, you'll be more confident and better prepared to share your information.

Networking Basics

Networking is a win-win proposition. By developing relationships with people whom you don't know, you can provide an invaluable service by filling in structural holes. Like the bicycle store's owner and farmers in the prior section, you can be the link between groups of other people.

Look for ways to "exploit differences" among relationships. For example, if you have a friend who wants to rent a room in her house, and another friend is looking for a room to rent, you are "exploiting" the differences between these two friends by linking them together.

The fundamentals of networking are simple: Prepare, show up, and interact. Conversation is the key to making connections. The secret of conversation is to ask questions. The better your questions, the higher the quality of the information you receive. A brief conversation may lead to a relationship, which may then lead to new business.

Let's assume you are attending a meeting of high-technology business owners that will be on campus next week. To get the most out of your networking opportunity, *plan ahead.* Think about who will be at the meeting. If possible, get a list of registrants from the event sponsor. Decide who you'd like to meet and set up a few meetings ahead of time. Set goals so that you know what you want to accomplish. Make notes on the subjects you want to discuss and what you want to find out. This helps you to structure your discussions. Create interest with a clear, interesting self-introduction that you deliver with energy and confidence. Preparing it in advance helps to put you at ease and serves as an ice-breaker. Remember to make eye contact and use positive body language. Adapt the introduction to suit the event.

Focus on meeting new people. It's easy and more comfortable to head for familiar faces, but that approach won't yield the highest networking returns. Spend most of your time with people you don't know. As you talk to people, gain their interest with powerful questions. Look for ways to help. Instead of telling people what you do, share insights that help solve problems.

exhibit 3.11 | **Strategies for Networking Success**

1. **Plan ahead.**
2. **Set goals.**
3. **Develop a brief self-introduction.**
4. **Know how you can help.**
5. **Don't be afraid to ask.**
6. **Know *how* to ask.**
7. **Practice by doing.**
8. **Be aware of time.**
9. **Meet new people.**
10. **Follow up.**
11. **Establish trust.**

Don't be afraid to ask for information. It's a myth to think that people will know what you need and offer to help. Most people are happy to help when you ask. If you don't ask, the answer is always no! *How* you ask is just as important as asking. Remember the fundamentals of persuasion and incorporate those techniques when you request assistance. If you have established rapport, you are more likely to succeed. The best networkers ask in a way that lets people say yes—and gives them room to say no.

Networking may feel awkward at first, but the more you practice, the easier it gets. You'll learn to make the most of every networking opportunity. You should try to meet as many people as possible. By limiting the time you spend with each person, you can "work the room." Spending three minutes per person means you can make about 20 contacts in an hour. Chatting for ten minutes lowers that to six per hour. For large events, try to minimize the time per person, so you can talk to more people.

Good networkers establish trust with their contacts. They treat people with respect, courtesy, and integrity, using their resources appropriately. Reinforce the contacts you made by getting in touch afterwards. Always acknowledge the leads, ideas, information, and support you receive. If you promise to provide information, do so promptly. Follow up in a timely and appropriately persistent manner and you will build a solid network.[22] Exhibit 3.11 summarizes these key tips for networking success.

3.6 Summary

1. Achievement requires action. Enterprisers leverage their abilities and their effort to get their goals accomplished: Work = Ability × Effort. Both ability and effort are required; one without the other is insufficient. To achieve their goals, enterprisers must manage themselves and others.

Managing yourself begins with determining your goals and then allocating the time necessary to accomplish them. Enterprisers must also depend on the efforts, skills, and abilities of others in developing an enterprise. The fundamental tasks involved in managing others are persuasion, negotiation, and networking.

2. Many unimportant activities consume the majority of our time. To achieve our goals, we need to put our effort into tasks that are important, but not urgent. These tasks fall into Quadrant 2, which Steven Covey calls the Quadrant of Quality. We all need to be challenged in order to achieve. Those who set goals accomplish significantly more than people who don't. Those who set harder or more specific goals achieve more than people who set easy or vague goals.

3. Goals must be specific, results-focused, measurable, realistically attainable, relevant, and have a time frame. To create goals, you must identify your true values and the priorities for your life. Developing a personal mission statement helps you determine what is most important to you and what you want to do with your life.

4. Much of the hard work of goal setting is in making choices to prioritize one's goals. Ways to manage multiple goals include pursuing simultaneous goals by moonlighting between different goals; alternating between goals by devoting alternating blocks of time to different goals; choosing sequential goals, where goals are changed over a period of time; or engaging in actualizing multiple goals, where one combines two or three goals within the same set of activities.

5. Time management techniques increase productivity. Achieving one's goals requires a yearly, monthly, weekly, and daily plan of action. A weekly plan directs our efforts by linking the day-to-day activities to goals.

6. Persuasion involves efforts to change the attitudes and behaviors of others through communication. People are persuaded when they believe their own interests will be achieved. An enterpriser can use six principles to persuade others: *Liking:* people are persuaded by those who they feel are like them. *Reciprocity:* Those who give—get. People repay in kind. *Social proof:* Peer pressure will persuade others. *Consistency:* People often change their behaviors if they are asked to make commitments that are active, public, and voluntary. *Authority:* We often defer to the judgment and knowledge of experts. *Scarcity:* People want things that are unique and exclusive. A persuasive individual understands the other person's values and needs and addresses these issues, creating win-win situations, where both parties see benefits in working together.

7. Negotiation involves two parties who are trying to reach a mutually acceptable solution to a problem or to accomplish something that neither party could do on its own. The best approach to negotiating is looking for win-win situations between the two parties. Successful

negotiating involves four key elements: (1) Keeping the people and the problem separate; (2) focusing on interests rather than positions; (3) developing multiple options; and (4) basing the result on an objective standard.

8. Most negotiations involve seven steps: (1) Know each party's interests and priorities. (2) Create many options for solutions. (3) Know each party's BATNA. (4) Legitimize your requests. (5) Communicate efficiently. (6) Build a relationship with the other party. (7) Don't commit until you've compared your options to your BATNA.

9. The most critical aspect of the negotiating process is creating options. To develop options, (1) identify the problem to be solved; (2) analyze the problem for its specific symptoms and causes; (3) look for possible strategies/solutions; and (4) develop action ideas that might match the strategies/solutions. The alternative to a successful agreement is your BATNA. Reaching clarity about your BATNA can help you evaluate your options when negotiating.

10. A person's network is the sum total of his or her relationships, all the connections that a person has with other people. Enterprisers use their networks to find opportunities and exploit them. Opportunities occur in a network where there are no connections between some people (e.g., buyers) and others (e.g., suppliers). Enterprisers fill these "structural holes," those areas where there are no connections. Having a diverse network of relationships to other people provides a number of advantages. A network provides *access* to information that others might not have, *timing* benefits to those who gain information before others, and *referrals* that offer legitimacy (others can vouch for you). Enterprisers seek to build networks that involve people who have a lot of knowledge, are trustworthy, and diverse.

11. The networking process begins with the relationships your already have. Most people know more people than they realize. You can expand this base of contacts systematically by asking everyone for help in pursuing your goals. When asking for help you need to remember to return the favors given to you. Contacts with others need to be nurtured.

Review Questions

1. Why do you need both ability and effort to accomplish work? Do you agree with Sloboda's findings?

2. How do the five activities of managing yourself and others interrelate?

3. Differentiate between the four types of problems and give examples of each that you have experienced lately.

4. Why should you set goals? Define the characteristics of effective goals. Fill in Exhibit 3.4 with three goals you wish to accomplish in the next year and one you wish to achieve in five years.

5. What are the four techniques for managing goals? Apply them to develop a strategy to achieve the goals you listed in question 4.

6. Describe the six principles of persuasion. Give an example of how you would use each in a business and a personal setting.

7. Differentiate between persuasion and negotiation. How can you use elements of persuasion when you negotiate?

8. What are the four elements of principled negotiation? Why is this style so effective? Summarize the steps you'd take to prepare for a negotiation to buy a new car, using Exhibits 3.7 and 3.8 as guides.

9. What is the BATNA, and how can it help you become a more effective negotiator?

10. What is a personal network? Why is networking so essential to an enterpriser's success?

11. Describe the steps you'd take to expand your current network.

Applying What You've Learned[23]

1. Much of the work of goal setting involves figuring out what you want to do with your life. Begin by answering the following questions:

   (a) What is "meaningful work" ?
   (b) What is the job from heaven and the job from hell?
   (c) Change the characteristics of the job from hell into that of the job from heaven.
   (d) Write scenarios about what the future job might look like.
   (e) Make a temporary permanent commitment to pursue the job from heaven.

2. What do you really want to accomplish in your life, and how can you overcome the blocks that get in your way? Use the questions below to learn the answers:

   (a) What are your escape dreams?
   (b) If you had all the freedom in the world, what would you do?
   (c) What would you do if you were bold? What would you do if you knew for sure you would succeed in making your dreams come true?

3. Write your own autobiography. Look back on your life 50 years from now. Write about what you accomplished, the places you went, and the people you met. What were your joys? What gave you the most pleasure doing? What will people remember you for?

4. Develop a plan to use each of the six principles of persuasion to convince someone to

   (a) Purchase a specific type of car
   (b) Take a course in a new area
   (c) Go out on a date with a friend
   (d) Invest in a new restaurant

5. Divide the class into small groups. Have each person choose one of these situations and take turns role-playing these situations. The remaining group members should provide feedback on how persuasive the person was and how to improve the presentation.

6. Using the seven steps to negotiating success in Exhibit 3.7, demonstrate to your group how to use each step to negotiate in one of the following situations:

   (a) Pricing a new car
   (b) Investing in a new restaurant
   (c) Going out on a first date.
   (d) How does your negotiation strategy change if you are in a different role—the seller of a car versus the buyer of the car?

7. Who's in your network? Using the categories in Exhibit 3.10, list all your contacts, and consider how each of these contacts might be helpful for pursuing your goals.

8. Each day contact a person that you don't know, but who might be helpful in pursuing your goals. Call a stranger each day, Monday through Friday. Ask each person you know for the names and phone numbers of other helpful people. What did you learn from this activity?

9. Part of the networking process is getting used to meeting and talking with people that you don't know. Have everyone in the class meet and greet each other. Consider the class as a "networking event" and have the class mingle together, with each person introducing him/herself to others, individually. Have the class members talk to each other about their goals and what kinds of help they might need. By the end of the process, this group of students will make enough contacts to benefit many classmates.

Enterprisers on the Web

1. Develop your personal mission statement with the assistance of the Mission Formulator at the Franklin Covey website: http://www.franklincovey.com/missionbuilder/index.html. Did the results surprise you?

2. How well do you network? Take the quiz "What's Your Schmooze Quotient?" at http://www.susanroane.com/quiz.html. How well did you score? Develop a list of steps you can take to improve your networking ability.

3. Go to Mind Tools, http://www.mindtools.com/pages/main/newMN_HTE.htm, and look at their section on time management. Download the time management section, or read all of the articles online. Which time management activity did you find most helpful to pursue? In what areas of your life do you need to manage your time more effectively?

4. Virginia Tech has a website, http://www.ucc.vt.edu/lynch/TimeManagement.htm, that can help you better manage your role as a student. Go through the exercises in this website as a way to leverage your time and energy. Have you created a semester schedule? Assessed and planned your weekly schedule? Do you adjust your daily schedule? Have you evaluated where you invest your time each day? What kinds of tradeoffs do you need to make between the various activities that are important for you to be successful as an enterprising student?

5. The Persuasion Map at Read-Write-Think, http://www.readwritethink.org/materials/persuasion_map/, takes you through a set of questions and exercises to increase your ability to persuade. Choose a topic and person you want to persuade (e.g., going to a movie that you want to see, buying a car or a house) and see how this site can help you develop ways to convince others.

6. Your emotions and the emotions of those you are negotiating with are critical factors affecting your ability to negotiate. Go to Beyond Reason, http://www.beyond-reason.net/, and download their Emotions Preparation Tool workbook (found under Practical Negotiation Tools). Use the exercises in this workbook to consider how you would negotiate a house purchase, the sale of a restaurant, a divorce.

End Notes

1. Malcolm Gladwell, "Examined Life," *New Yorker*, December 17, 2001, p. 91.

2. Michael Warshaw, "Get a Life," *Fast Company*, June 1998, pp. 138–142.

3. Stephen R. Covey, A. Roger Merrill, and Rebecca R. Merrill, *First Things First* (New York: Simon & Schuster, 1995), p. 37.

4. G. P. Latham and T. W. Lee, "Goal Setting," in E. A. Locke (Ed.), *Generalizing from Laboratory to Field Settings* (Lexington, MA: Lexington Books, 1986), pp. 101–118; and E. A. Locke and G. P. Latham, *Goal Setting* (Englewood Cliffs, NJ: Prentice-Hall, 1984), pp. 27–41.

5. Rhonda Abrams, "Path to Success Begins with Action Plan," Gannett News Service, June 6, 2002, http://www.RhondaOnline.com.

6. Barbara Sher, *I Could Do Anything . . . If I Only Knew What It Was* (New York: Dell Publishing, 1994), pp. 2–6.

7. Ibid.

8. Covey, Merrill, and Merrill. *First Things First*, pp. 77–102; and Lori Ioannou, "Stephen Covey On Time Management," *FSB* (*Fortune Small Business*), June 1, 2002, p. 73.

9. Ibid., pp. 72–74.

10. Ibid., p. 79.

11. Section based on Kevin Hogan, *The Psychology of Persuasion* (Gretna, LA: Pelican Publishing Company, 1996), pp. 167–197.

12. Adapted from Robert Heller and Tim Hindle, "Communicating Clearly," *Essential Manager's Manual* (New York: DK Publishing, Inc., 1998), pp. 18–31; and Hogan, *The Psychology of Persuasion*, pp. 189–197.

13. Resources used to prepare this module include Heller and Hindle, "Negotiating Successfully," pp. 558–625; Roger Fisher and Danny Ertel, *Getting Ready to Negotiate* (New York: Penguin Books, 1995); Roger Fisher, William Ury, and Bruce Patton, *Getting to Yes*, 2nd ed. (New York: Penguin Books, 1991); Roy J. Lewicki, David M. Saunders, and John W. Minton, *Essentials of Negotiation* (New York: McGraw-Hill Irwin, 2000).

14. Fisher and Ury, *Getting to Yes*, pp. 3–14.

15. Section based on Fisher and Ertel, *Getting Ready to Negotiate*, pp. 21–44; and Fisher and Ury, *Getting to Yes*, pp. 56–80.

16. Section based on Fisher and Ertel, *Getting Ready to Negotiate*, pp. 45–60; Fisher and Ury, *Getting to Yes*, pp. 97–102; and James K. Sebenius, "Six Habits of Merely Effective Negotiators," *Harvard Business Review*, April 2001, pp. 93–94.

17. Ronald S. Burt, *Structural Holes: The Social Structure of Competition* (Cambridge, MA: Harvard University Press, 1992), p. 13.

18. Ibid.

19. "Study Reports Job Seekers, HR Depts. Rely on Personal Contacts," *Nation's Restaurant News*, April 23, 2001, http://www.findarticles.com.

20. Susan RoAne, "Create a Network of Colleagues, Cronies, Clients and Friends," Susan RoAne website, http://www.susanroane.com/articles/connect.html (June 13, 2002).

21. Haidee E. Allerton, "Personal Networking," *Training & Development*, October, 2000, http://www.findarticles.com.

22. Section based on Jeffrey Gitomer, "Networking Fundamentals That Work," *Business Journal*, January 21, 2000, http://www.findarticles.com; and Susan RoAne, "Nuances of Networking: A Savvy Approach for the Next Century," http://www.susanroane.com/articles/nuance.html (June 13, 2002).

23. Questions 1–4 from *I Could Do Anything if Only I Knew What It Was*, by Barbara Sher, Copyright © 1994 by Barbara Sher. Used by permission of Dell Publishing, a division of Random House.

chapter 4

What Is an Enterprise?

Key Concepts

1. The choice of a business's legal entity affects how the business will be run, managed, and perceived in the world.

2. The three major legal forms for an enterprise are sole-proprietorship, partnership, and corporation. Other legal forms include limited liability companies, franchises, joint ventures, cooperatives, and not-for-profit organizations.

3. Each form has benefits and liabilities that can significantly affect how the enterprise is controlled and owned.

Suppose a high school guidance counselor suggests that you consider architecture as a profession because you get such good grades in both math and art. You go off to Europe to tour all of its major architectural sites and, as a result, you become convinced that studying architecture is right for you. But after graduation and several years as an associate at a large, prestigious firm in Los Angeles, you become disillusioned with the lack of creative flexibility you have at your firm. In your frustration, you begin to question the wisdom of your career choice.

This chapter describes the case of Ronald Altoon and Jim Porter, two innovative architects, who, with a third colleague, created a partnership that allowed all of them to use their individual talents to serve clients well and, consequently, grow a successful international firm. As you read this chapter, you will learn about the different organizational structures you can choose for your enterprise and the advantages and disadvantages of each form.

4.0 What Is an Enterprise?

As we mentioned in Chapter 1, an enterprise is created for the purposes of its owners. Individuals create enterprises for all kinds of reasons—to develop a new product, such as the Dyson "Cyclone" vacuum cleaner; to meet a customer need, such as a Web-design studio; or to serve the needs of the enterprise's owner, such as a fly fishing guide service. Two dimensions reveal the purposes of an enterprise's owners: *control*, designating who will manage the enterprise, and *ownership*, identifying who will share in the benefits of the enterprise.

The legal form of the enterprise determines how both control and ownership will be handled. Why focus on the legal form of the enterprise before looking at how an enterprise is actually started or how an enterprise would effectively be operated? While the legal form of an enterprise won't, intrinsically, determine whether the enterprise will be successful, choosing a particular legal form affects a variety of issues such as how the enterprise will be taxed and who will be responsible for its legal liabilities. Therefore, the legal form of the enterprise might be considered the "face" of the business—how it is seen by others, particularly others who are involved with regulating and taxing businesses.

The legal forms of an enterprise available to enterprisers who want to share in the benefits of their business are typically sole-proprietorship, partnership, and corporation. A number of other "hybrid" legal forms such as cooperatives and franchises have characteristics found in the three basic types. In addition, enterprises could be formed as "nonprofit" organizations, where individuals don't directly benefit from any surpluses the enterprise might generate but can still operate the business, as well as benefit through salaries and other forms of remuneration.

Although sole-proprietorships are the most popular legal form of business, they tend to remain small. Corporations, which account for only 20 percent of all businesses, generate about 83 percent of total sales and 53 percent of profits. Exhibit 4.1 compares the three basic legal forms in terms of numbers, sales, and profits.

The following are the major questions that we need to address when thinking about the legal form of enterprises are:

- Who will be in control of the enterprise?

- How will the benefits of the enterprise be shared and distributed?

- Who is liable for the actions of the enterprise?

- Who is responsible for any taxes the enterprise must pay?

- What are the differences in legal and administrative costs?

- What is the desired lifespan of the business?

- Will you need to raise capital from outside investors?

- How can owners of the business transfer their investment to others?

In Chapter 1 we discussed the contribution of the various types of businesses to the overall economy in the United States. One point to remember, though, is that all large businesses started, at some point, small. The choice to stay small or grow is one aspect of choosing the appropriate legal form. It is much easier, for example, to grow an enterprise that is formed as a corporation than it is to grow a sole-proprietorship or a partnership. This is not always the case, however. Kinko's started as a sole-proprietorship, and grew as founder Paul Orfelea formed separate partnerships with individuals at different locations around the United States. Before Kinko's was sold to a private investment banking company, Kinko's

| **exhibit 4.1** | **Comparison of Forms of Business Organization** |

Firm	Number (%)	Sales (%)	Profits (%)
Sole Proprietorships	72	5	21
Partnerships	8	12	26
Corporations	20	83	53

Source: Internal Revenue Service, as reported in Table 725, U.S. Bureau of the Census, *Statistical Abstract of the United States, 2006*, 125th ed. (Washington, DC: Government Printing Office, 2005), p. 503.

consisted of 450 separate partnerships. In 2004, FedEx acquired Kinko's, which currently operates as FedEx Kinko's Office and Print Centers and is part of the renamed FedEx Kinko's corporation.[1]

Choosing the best form for a business is no easy task. Enterprisers should consult a lawyer before choosing the legal form of their organization. While an enterpriser may be well versed in many of the legal issues involved with each form of organization, qualified legal help can often spot potential problems in a partnership agreement or in articles of incorporation that can easily be over-looked by enterprisers using many of the forms that are available for partnership agreements or self-incorporation legal kits. Good lawyers are masters at spotting legal problems and issues that often have serious consequences to the business. Please seek legal advice.

4.1 The Sole-Proprietorship: A Solo Act

A sole-proprietorship can be best thought of as a one-person show: You are the enterprise! If you, as an individual, engage in business activities, you are acting as a sole-proprietorship. A **sole-proprietorship** is completely owned and operated by one individual.

Many sole-proprietors undertake business activities using a different name. For example, if the sole-proprietor's name is William Gartner, William could do business without using his own name by filing a *dba* (doing business as), typically with the city or county in which William resides. If William were running a flower store, he could file a *dba* for "Fast Delivery Flowers" and operate under that name (if no other business has registered that name as its business name).

sole-proprietorship
A business that is established, owned, operated, and often financed by one person.

Why Go the Solo Route?

Going it alone has many plusses:

- *It's easy to start.* By engaging in business activity, an individual is acting as a sole-proprietorship. Doing business would require a "business permit" granted by the city or county in which one resides. This permit is typically easy to obtain. There are also a few other licensing require-ments and regulations applying to sole-proprietorships. For example, most cities and counties have zoning ordinances that require certain types of businesses to locate only in certain areas. There might also be health permits if the business is involved with food.

- *All benefits of the enterprise go to the owner.* Since the sole-proprietor is the enterprise, any income generated by the enterprise is the individual's income.

- *Complete control of the business.* Since the enterprise is the individual, the sole-proprietor is responsible for all of the enterprise's operations and does not have to answer to anyone else when making decisions. For example, the owner of a bakery can decide to open at 8:30 AM and close at 3 PM—even though bakeries typically open much earlier in the morning.

- *Fewer governmental regulations.* Other ways of organizing the business, such as partnerships and corporations, have more legal requirements and regulations to consider. Regardless of the legal form of business chosen, the firm will still be responsible for such legal and regulatory requirements as business permits, zoning permits, health and safety permits, and employee safeguards.

- *Taxed at the individual rate.* Since the sole-proprietor is the enterprise, all earnings of the business are taxed as income to the individual. For some individuals, this may mean a lower tax rate, compared to the tax rates if using other legal forms of business.

- *Easy to stop.* The sole-proprietor can end the business at any time without interference from others.

Drawbacks to Going It Alone

On the flip side, there are also disadvantages to the sole-proprietorship form of enterprise.

- *Unlimited liability.* Since the enterprise is the individual, the activities of the enterprise can put all assets of the sole-proprietorship at risk. If the business fails, the liabilities of the business are the exclusive responsibility of the sole-proprietor, whose assets can be used to make up any claims against the business. Note that many business risks, such as a restaurant customer getting food poisoning or a defective enterprise product harming a customer, can be managed by purchasing insurance for these risks.

- *Business losses are considered the individual's losses.* Since the enterprise is the individual, any losses generated by the enterprise become the losses of the individual.

In summary, for some kinds of businesses, such as consulting practices and other kinds of service businesses (which depend on the expertise and skills of just one individual), sole-proprietorships are often the best way to operate. For businesses that depend on the skills and abilities of more than one person, it is usually better to organize as a partnership or corporation. Luckily, it is very easy for an individual to change from a sole-proprietorship into another legal business form.

partnership
An association of two or more persons who agree to operate a business together for profit.

4.2 Partnerships: Teaming Up

A **partnership** involves two or more individuals who agree to operate a business together for a profit. Suppose Fast Delivery Flowers is very successful and William Gartner wants to expand to another location or add related gift products. Rather than bear all the risk himself, he could bring in a partner to share the workload and also make an investment in the business.

In all cases, a partnership should involve a signed written agreement between the partners. It is possible to have a partnership based on an oral commitment between individuals, but when there is conflict between partners, such a commitment can be interpreted in different ways.

A partnership agreement will typically specify the partnership's name, the purpose of the business, the financial contributions of each partner, the management responsibilities of each partner, the salaries and profit percentages that each partner will receive, as well as agreements about how to resolve partnership disputes, the process for dissolving the partnership, and distributing any partnership assets.

There are two types of partnerships: general and limited. All individuals involved in a **general partnership** share in the profits and the management responsibilities of the business, as well as any liabilities that the business might generate. In a **limited partnership**, there are two types of partners: general partners, who share in profits, management responsibilities, and all liabilities; and limited partners, who do not share in the management of the business. The liability of limited partners in the business is limited to their investment, but they will share some portion of the profits and losses of the business. Limited partners typically are investors: individuals who are willing to invest in a business and share in the profits, but who are not interested in managing the day-to-day operations of the business.

general partnership
All individuals share in the profits and the management responsibilities of the business, as well as any liabilities that the business might generate.

limited partnership
There are two types of partners: general partners, who share in profits, management responsibilities, and all liabilities; and limited partners, who do not share in the management of the business.

Advantages of Sharing the Load

Partnerships offer several advantages:

- *Ease of formation.* Much like a sole-proprietorship, a partnership between individuals is easy to form. The legal regulations involving partnerships are not complicated; however, most partnerships involve contracts between the partners that can be expensive and difficult to create and to have all of the partners agree.

- *Fewer government regulations.* Again, much like sole-proprietorships, partnerships involve little government regulatory requirements. The state government registers and regulates most partnerships.

- *Taxation of profits at the individual rate.* Like sole-proprietorships, the profits of the business are directly passed through to the partners of the business, so there is no specific income tax on partnerships. The partners, themselves, are personally responsible for paying income taxes on their portion of the profits or losses generated by the partnership.

Problems with Partnerships

Even though having one or more partners can serve a business well, there is also a downside:

- *Unlimited liability.* All general partners are responsible for the actions of any of the partners in the partnership. For example, Thomas Jefferson was involved in a business partnership where his partner took on debts in the name of the partnership and promptly squandered all of the money. Jefferson was obligated to pay these debts, and, the only way he could generate enough funds was to sell all his books to the U.S. government. (This collection of books became the basis for the Library of Congress.) In many states, the laws for partnerships have been modified so that individuals can form limited liability partnerships (LLPs) that limit the liability of each partner to their own actions in the business.

- *Partnership conflicts.* All enterprises change over time, and the interests of the partners in an enterprise change as well. While business partners may begin their partnership with similar goals, these goals can diverge. Consider two individuals who form a partnership out of college. Both are single and put an equal amount of time and money into the partnership with the expectation that both will work equally hard, to insure that the business grows and is profitable. After five years, one of the partners gets married and decides to have a family. This partner wants to work fewer hours and use more of the profits of the partnership for his own personal use (e.g., buy a house, take more vacations), instead of investing his portion of the profits back into the business. The other partner sees new opportunities for the growth of the business and wants both partners to invest most of their profits to develop these new opportunities. How can such a dilemma be resolved when the goals of these two partners diverge? Partnerships have high rates of failure over time because of difficulties in resolving differences among partners.

Finding a Partner

Most people form partnerships with people whom they already know—trusted friends and family members, rather than "strangers." Yet partnerships formed between close friends and family are often the most difficult partnerships to manage and keep alive over a period of time. In this chapter's Enterprising Ethics box you'll meet two friends who ran into problems when they became business partners and founded an Internet company.

In a business, partners need to talk candidly about problems and point out ways that the other partner may need to change. Individuals who have been in supportive relationships with friends and family members often find it very difficult to be in situations where there is conflict—and all partnerships will experience conflicts. How partners recognize and resolve these conflicts is a key aspect of whether their partnership will survive. Exhibit 4.2 provides a list of possible questions to ask a prospective partner. We will explore many of these questions in later chapters of this book when we look at various ways that enterprises can transform their businesses.

exhibit 4.2   **Picking the Perfect Partner**

Here are some questions for potential partners to ask themselves and each other:

1. What are you looking for in a partner?

2. What do you bring to a partnership?

3. Why are you willing to begin an enterprise with partners? What advantages do you see to such an arrangement? What disadvantages do you see to such an arrangement?

4. How will important decisions in the business be made? If one partner wants to invest the profits of the enterprise while the other partner wants to pay these profits to the partners as salaries, how will this conflict be resolved?

5. How will conflicts among the partners be resolved? Remember, in any enterprise, there must be someone who is ultimately in charge, and who can make the final decision for the business. Unresolved decisions in an enterprise will cause a business to flounder.

6. How can partners leave the enterprise, whether for personal reasons or due to conflicts that cannot be resolved? How will each partner's share of the business be valued? If the partnership's assets are tied up in inventory, plant and equipment, how will a partner who wants to leave be paid?

7. Finally, since many partnerships are begun between spouses or "significant others," both partners should ask themselves whether they really want to be with this partner 24 hours a day, sharing not only the partnership of the enterprise, but the family partnership as well.

enterprising ethics

Why govWorks *Didn't* Work

The concept for govWorks was simple: provide a way for individuals to pay parking tickets, register cars, and transact other routine local government business online. The company would make its money from fees. Childhood buddies Kaleil Tuzman and Tom Herman estimated that the potential market for their services was $450 billion. So with dollar signs in their eyes but little actual experience running a company, they convinced two other friends to join them. Pooling their resources, they came up with $200,000 in start-up funds. In 1999 they began working on the technology for the website. As investor interest grew, they successfully raised $60 million from leading venture capital funds.

With lots of money available to bring their vision to life, the founders quickly staffed up to develop the software for the site. As the site began to take shape, govWorks looked further afield and, like many other dot-coms, took a bigger-is-better mentality. The potential to make millions from tapping the power of the Internet got in the way of sound business practices. Before it had fully developed its primary concept, it formed a joint venture with Cotesa Holding, Ltd., to take the idea into Latin America and also acquired several companies, including Jobs-in-Government, a business that posted government positions. Soon it had 250 employees to pay—and little revenue, because municipal governments weren't signing on for govWorks' electronic payment services.

(continued)

govWorks then decided to offer its software to local governments on a fee basis, cooperating with the municipalities' existing online strategies instead of competing with them. It was too late, however, because rival EzGov got the jump on govWorks and had already launched a site based on this business model. govWorks laid off 60 employees in April 2000. As more competitors entered the market, even offering free bill payment, govWorks had to cut its prices. Costs continued to far outpace revenues, expected financing was withdrawn, and additional layoffs reduced the staff to 60 by November 2000. The company struggled for a few more months, but by early 2001, govWorks had joined the ranks of dot-com has-beens. It "starred" in *Startup.com*, a documentary film that tells the story of the company's founders, their friendship, and govWork's brief but turbulent history. govWorks also earned the tenth slot on CNet's Top 10 list of failed dot-coms.

At first glance, Tuzman and Herman seemed like ideal partners with complementary capabilities. Tuzman, a former investment banker, was the consummate salesman, while Herman brought the technical expertise. Over the course of the following 18 months, the pair's friendship was tested to its limits by the challenges of running a fast-growing Internet company. They differed on critical management issues, such as the right direction in which to take the company. Eventually Tuzman, who was CEO, forced COO Herman to leave the company. Herman felt that Tuzman made him the scapegoat and was protecting himself. Despite his anger at being dismissed over these disagreements and asking for financial compensation for his original investment, Herman later said, "I did (and do) agree with his belief that you need *one* CEO who makes these decisions. When the CEO makes the decision, the rest of the company needs to get on board and make it happen."

What went wrong? According to Tom Herman, the basic business concept was sound—and has been executed successfully by other companies. The major mistake was trying to market directly to consumers rather than partnering with government agencies.

govWorks also grew too quickly, without an organizational structure or consistent operational plan. It added staff without organizing them effectively or having clear job descriptions. It tried to go in too many directions at once. The founders were blinded by their early successes in raising funding and lost sight of their original business concept, chasing instead after Internet riches. Their egos got in the way of good sense. To make matters worse, the venture capital investors had their own ideas of how the company should be run.

Despite their troubles, Herman and Tuzman remained friends and continue to work together on several other business ventures. "There was no benefit to me, to Kaleil, or to any third party for us to be negative or not get along," says Herman.

Discussion Questions

1. If possible, view the movie *Startup.com* for more background. What lessons in entrepreneurship did you learn?

2. What were the expectations of the two partners in terms of how the company would evolve and what role each founder would take? What went wrong between them, and how could they have prevented their problems?

3. Is it ethical to make promises to investors and potential employees about the growth expectations of govWorks.com? Do you think, for example, that new employees were aware of the risk of this new venture? What responsibilities do the founders of the business have to their new employees when the business takes a downturn and they must lay off most of the staff?

4. How do venture capital companies "manage" the possible failure of their investments? Do they have a right to ask the founders to leave the venture?

5. How did Tuzman and Herman preserve their friendship despite the failure of govWorks? Suggest reasons that the pair has continued to work together on subsequent ventures.

Sources: Kent German, "Top 10 Dot-Com Flops," *CNet*, July 28, 2005, http://cnet.com; Anni Layne, "Close Encounters of the Dotcom," *Fast Company*, May 2001, http://www.FastCompany.com; Ryan Naraine, "Anatomy of a Distressed Dot-com: govWorks," January 12, 2001, http://www.atnewyork.com; Online Q&A with Thomas J. Herman, Co-founder, govWorks.com, WashingtonPost.com, July 18, 2001, http://www.publicdatasystems.com/wash_post_071801.htm.

4.3 Corporations: Structured for Growth

Assume that after operating Fast Delivery Flowers for three years, William Gartner and his partner want to expand even further and open additional locations in neighboring states. Bringing in more partners could be a cumbersome process, so instead they choose to form a corporation and raise money for the company's growth by selling equity to investors.

A **corporation** is a legal entity that is separate from its owners. A corporation is considered to be, legally, much like a person. A corporation can own property, borrow money, and can sue and be sued by other individuals and corporations. The corporation, rather than its owners, is liable for its debts and actions and is a taxable entity. The laws of the state where the corporation is chartered govern how the corporation can act and how it is structured.

Many people are under the mistaken impression that because a corporation is solely liable for any debts, the owners of a corporation can have the corporation borrow money or lease cars and equipment and then be personally immune from any liabilities if the corporation can't make loan or lease payments. Most lenders are unlikely to lend money to a corporation unless there are guarantees that any loans will be paid back. To insure this, many banks and lenders require that the owners of the corporation personally guarantee any of the corporation's loans or leases.

Corporations have three organizational components: stockholders, directors, and officers.

- **Stockholders** or **shareholders** own the corporation through shares of stock. This ownership provides them with certain rights. While stockholders don't participate in management of the firm (unless they are also officers), they may share in the corporation's profits by receiving dividends, and they can sell or transfer their shares. Stockholders can attend annual meetings, elect the board of directors, and vote on matters that affect the corporation, in accordance with its charter and bylaws. Each share of stock generally carries one vote.

- A **board of directors**, elected by the stockholders, is responsible for the overall management of the corporation. The directors set major corporate goals and policies, hire corporate officers, and oversee the firm's operations and finances. Small firms may have as few as three directors, whereas large corporations usually have 15 to 25. Corporate boards usually have both corporate executives and outside directors (not employed by the organization), chosen for their professional and personal expertise. Outside directors often bring a fresh view to the corporation's activities because they are independent of the firm.

corporation
A legal entity with an existence and life separate from its owners who are not personally liable for the entity's debts. A corporation is chartered by the state in which it is formed and can own property, enter into contracts, sue and be sued, and engage in business operations under the terms of its charter.

stockholders
The owners of a corporation who hold shares of stock that provide certain rights; also known as shareholders.

board of directors
A group of people elected by the stockholders to handle the overall management of a corporation, such as setting corporate goals and policies, hiring corporate officers, and overseeing the firm's operations and finances.

officers

In a corporation, these individuals are hired by the board and responsible for achieving corporate goals and policies. They include top management such as the president and chief executive officer (CEO), vice-presidents, treasurer, and secretary.

- The **officers** of a corporation, hired by the board, are responsible for achieving corporate goals and policies. These include top management such as the president and chief executive officer (CEO), vice-presidents, treasurer, and secretary. Officers may also serve on the board and own stock.

Enterprisers involved in small corporations are likely to have overlapping roles among the three groups. For example, the firm's owners (stockholders) may also be the corporation's officers and board members. Since the role of the board is to create policy and procedures to guide the corporation's officers who implement the goals of the corporation, many enterprisers will seek to find independent outside directors to provide a different perspective on the operations of the business. When enterprisers play all three roles in the company (owner, director, and officer), it is very hard to see the big picture when the day-to-day operating of a company often consumes all of the enterpriser's time and energy. Since the management of an enterprise will be covered in subsequent chapters in this book, we will look at the critical role of the board of directors in the growth and development of an enterprise.

Board of Directors

As a *fiduciary agent* of the corporation, a member of the Board of Directors has a legal responsibility to the stockholders of the corporation for the operations of the corporation. A growing body of laws and regulations makes directors personally responsible for the actions of the corporation. For example, stockholders can sue a director if the chief financial officer was found to misstate earnings, or an employee was found to have embezzled substantial amounts of money from the corporation and the board had not set into place a control system to closely monitor these employees' behaviors. Since a board member might be personally sued and liable for a corporation's actions, most outside board members require the enterprise to pay for liability insurance that covers any legal fees, possible fines, or monetary judgments. Members of a board of directors may even face criminal charges for the actions of a corporation.

Given the increasing personal liability that an individual can have as a board member, fewer individuals are likely to accept opportunities to serve on boards without considerable benefits. While some individuals will serve on a board of directors for nonfinancial reasons, most people have so many competing demands for their time that some form of compensation is necessary if you want them to pay attention to the affairs of your business. Such compensation varies. Some corporations pay their board members to attend each meeting, while others pay with stock or provide stock options.

There are a number of advantages to having board members who are not family, friends, or employees of the corporation. These outside board members often bring different, more objective views of the corporation's operations and strategies, as well as insights into how other companies are managed and operated. They also can provide helpful business contacts, such as lawyers, accountants, consultants, and prospective employees and investors, as well as contacts with suppliers and customers.

It should be noted that some enterprisers have a *board of advisors* to supplement the corporation's legally mandated board of directors. This group provides advice to the owner of a corporation. These individuals are not legally involved in the direction and operations of the corporation; rather, they offer insights and recommendations only to the owner. A board of advisors can avoid the personal legal liability, since its members are not fiduciary agents of the corporation.

The Incorporation Process

Creating a corporation involves more steps than the other forms of business we've discussed thus far. Each state sets its own registration procedures, fees, taxes, and laws regulating corporations. A firm doesn't have to incorporate in its home state; in fact, it may be advantageous to incorporate elsewhere. For example, Delaware's pro-corporate policies make it a popular state of incorporation for many companies, including about half the Fortune 500. Nevada is another corporation-friendly state.

Incorporating a company involves these main steps:

- Choosing the company's name

- Writing the articles of incorporation (also called a charter or certificate of incorporation in some states)

- Filing the articles of incorporation at the appropriate state office, usually the secretary of state's office

- Paying required fees and taxes

- Holding an organizational meeting

- Adopting bylaws, electing directors, and passing the first operating resolutions.

Exhibit 4.3 describes the components of the articles of incorporation.

Most states now have websites from which you can download the necessary forms to incorporate. For example, following this link will take you to the form for the state of Oregon: http://www.filinginoregon.com/forms/business.htm.

Types of Corporations

The two most common corporate forms are the C and S corporations. C corporations are the "basic" or conventional type of corporation. Small businesses have another option to achieve liability protection, the S corporation.

The S corporation also has stockholders, directors, and officers but receives special tax treatment from the Internal Revenue Service (IRS). By electing S corporation status, an enterprise's taxation is similar to a sole-proprietorship or partnership rather than the corporation paying corporate income taxes. Profits or losses pass directly to the stockholders and are taxed as personal income of the shareholders, thereby avoiding double taxation of corporate profits (once to the corporation and again to the shareholders). As with C corporations, the owners of an S corporation are not personally liable for the corporation's debts. The tax advantages and the liability protection are the major benefits of S corporations.

C corporation
A conventional or basic corporate form of organization.

S corporation
A hybrid entity that is organized like a corporation, with stockholders, directors, and officers, but taxed like a partnership, with income and losses flowing through to the stockholders and taxed as their personal income.

exhibit 4.3 | Articles of Incorporation

A company's articles of incorporation are prepared on a form authorized or supplied by the state of incorporation. Articles of incorporation usually include the following key items:

- Name of the corporation
- The company's purpose/type of business
- Types of stock and number of shares of each type to issue
- Life of the corporation (usually "perpetual," meaning with no time limit)
- Initial capital investment by stockholder
- Methods for transferring share of stock
- Address of the corporate office
- Names and addresses of the first board of directors
- Name and addresses of the incorporators
- Other public information the incorporators wish to include

To qualify as an S corporation, the company must

- Be an eligible entity (a domestic corporation, a partnership, or a single-member or multiple-member limited liability company).
- Have fewer than 100 shareholders.
- Limit shareholders to individuals who are U.S. citizens or residents; no corporate shareholders are allowed.
- Have only one class of stock.
- Allocate profits and losses to shareholders proportionate to each one's interest in the business.
- Use the calendar year as its fiscal year.

Most states recognize S corporations and give them the same tax treatment as the federal government. S corporation stockholders would include their shares of the profit or loss when they file state income taxes. However, there are some exceptions, so it's important to check with the state income tax agency in any states where the S corporation will do business to ask about the tax treatment before choosing this type of corporation.

The Corporate Advantage

Why go through all the formalities to form a corporation rather than choose a sole-proprietorship or partnership? There are several major reasons:

- *Stockholders are not liable for corporate debts.* This is perhaps the most important advantage corporations offer. The corporation is a legal entity that exists separately from its owners. If a corporation runs out of money, its creditors can go after the company's assets to repay the debt. The maximum the shareholders of a corporation can lose is their investment in company stock.

- *Credibility and stability.* Customers and vendors may perceive a corporation as more credible and long-lived than a sole-proprietorship or partnership. The corporate form implies a strong commitment to the business venture.

- *Tax advantages.* Corporations can reduce taxable income by deducting operating expenses and employee benefits such as insurance, travel, and qualified retirement plans. Tax rates may be lower than for other business forms.

- *Perpetual life.* A corporation has an unlimited life. Its existence is not tied to any particular person, so that the illness or death of an officer or stockholder does not end the corporation.

- *Greater access to capital.* A corporation can raise funding in several ways including selling stock and creating new types of stock with different voting or profit characteristics. The separation between personal and business liability makes it easier to attract investors. Bank loans are more available to corporations as well. Access to capital is necessary for growth.

- *Ease of ownership transfer.* The ownership of the corporation is easily transferred through the sale of stock and doesn't disrupt business operations.

- *Ability to be anonymous.* Unlike a sole-proprietorship or partnership, the owners of a corporation can have anonymity if they wish.

- *Management advantages.* Corporations have a broad base of management where all decisions are made by the board of directors, not shareholders. It's also easier for corporations, because of the advantages listed above, to attract and retain talented employees.

Drawbacks to Incorporating

Not everything about the corporate form is an advantage:

- *More difficult and costly to form.* As we've seen, setting up and operating a corporation is more complex than a sole-proprietorship or partnership. Not only are there more forms to file, but initial formation fees, filing fees, and annual state fees can run to thousands of dollars. These costs are partially offset by lower insurance costs.

- *More formalities and regulations.* Corporations must hold regular meetings of the board of directors and shareholders and keep written corporate minutes. They are also subject to numerous state and federal laws.

- *Double taxation.* Not only do corporations pay federal and state taxes on profits, but currently any profits distributed to stockholders are also taxed as personal income. (Congress is evaluating proposals to eliminate taxation at the personal level.)

Exhibit 4.4 summarizes the key characteristics of the three major legal forms of business organization.

exhibit 4.4 — Comparison of Major Forms of Business Organization

	Sole Proprietorship	Partnership	Corporation
Profits and Losses	Owner receives all profits *and* bears all losses.	Partners share profits and losses.	Limited liability protects owners from losing more than they invest.
Ease and Cost of Formation	Easy; low organizational costs.	Easy; relatively low organizational costs.	Complex to form; more expensive to incorporate.
Liability	Unlimited liability; proprietor's total wealth can be taken to pay business debts.	Owners have unlimited liability; may have to cover debts of other, less financially sound partners.	Limited liability.
Taxation	Company's income taxed as personal income of proprietor.	Partnership income taxed as personal income of partners.	Receives certain tax advantages. But double taxation: both corporate profits and dividends paid to owners are taxed.
Access to Financial Resources	Ability to raise funds limited to owner's resources.	Fund-raising ability is enhanced by multiple owners.	Greater access to financial resources allows growth.
Management Responsibilities and Skills	Proprietor has all responsibilities; may have limited skills and management expertise.	More expertise and managerial skill available.	Can attract employees with specialized skills.
Life Span/ Continuity	Easy to terminate; also, business terminates if owner dies.	Dissolves or must reorganize when partner dies.	Perpetual life; difficult to terminate.
Transfer of Ownership		Difficult to transfer ownership, liquidate or terminate.	Easy to transfer ownership through sale of stock.
Growth Potential	Limited to owner's abilities and resources.	Limitations on growth.	Can achieve large size due to marketability of stock (ownership).
Employees and Benefits	Limited long range opportunities and benefits for employees.	Opportunity to become partner; more limited benefits than corporations.	Greater opportunities for advancement; offers more benefits.
Other Factors	Owner has sole control over company. Can maintain secrecy.	Potential for conflicts between partners.	Subject to more government regulation; financial reporting requirements make operations public.

4.4 Specialized Organizational Forms

While most new businesses choose one of the three dominant forms of business organization, several other options are worth considering: the limited liability company (LLC), professional corporations and professional LLCs, franchising, joint ventures, and cooperatives.

The Limited Liability Company (LLC)

A relatively new form of business is becoming more popular with enterprisers. The **limited liability company (LLC)** is a structure created for tax purposes. It combines the advantages of a corporation with the tax advantages of a partnership or S corporation. An LLC can also be a sole-proprietorship, a partnership, a C corporation, or an S corporation depending on the particular circumstances.

limited liability company (LLC) *A hybrid organization that offers the same liability protection as a corporation but may be taxed as either a partnership or a corporation.*

Like corporations, LLCs are separate legal entities that protect personal assets from business liabilities. Members are not personally liable for the debts of the LLC. However, LLCs don't issue stock but are owned by individuals such as company managers. LLCs are easier to form and have fewer restrictions than corporations. They are owned by members, who hold membership interests. Like partnerships and S corporations, any profits or losses pass to the owners and are taxed as personal income, thus avoiding double taxation.

The LLC's flexibility and simplicity make it attractive to many business owners. An LLC has no required structure (board of directors and corporate officers) or corporate formalities such as minutes or resolutions. It can distribute income as it chooses, rather than to all shareholders. Unlike the S corporation, the number or type of members is not restricted in the LLC. Transfer of ownership, however, is harder for LLCs than for corporations. The LLC must be terminated if a member dies or becomes bankrupt.

All states recognize the LLC, although actual regulations may vary. Establishing a LLC requires filing Articles of Organization with the appropriate state agency and paying any fees.

Professional Corporations or LLCs

Professional service providers such as physicians, attorneys, accountants, architects, or consultants may set up professional corporations (PCs) or professional limited liability companies (PLLCs). States often require that certain types of professionals form professional or regular corporations to operate. The definition of professional services varies from state to state. In most cases, professions that require a license must set up their practices as PCs or PLLCs. They require the approval of the appropriate state licensing agency in addition to the filing of standard documents. In some states, professionals can choose whether to incorporate as a PC or a C or an S corporation.

Franchising

franchising
A form of business ownership involving a contractual arrangement where a parent business (the franchisor) provides an investor (the franchisee) with the rights to sell products or services in exchange for fees and/or royalty payments.

franchisor
Parent company that owns and controls the rights to offer the franchise's product concept to the franchisee.

franchisee
The individual or company that owns one or more franchises and sells goods or services in accordance with the terms set by the franchisor.

franchise license agreement
The principal legal document that defines the terms of the relationship between the franchisor and franchisee, including the license to use the franchisor's brand for a specified time period, payment terms, and operating restrictions.

If you want to go into business for yourself but don't want to start a totally new company, franchising may be for you. Franchising has become an important way for enterprisers to start and grow businesses. In this chapter we offer just a brief introduction. Chapter 11, "New Venture Creation Pathways: Franchising," provides a more detailed discussion of the franchise process as a route to business ownership.

Franchising is a form of business organization that involves a specific relationship between a **franchisor** who supplies the business concept and/or product and a **franchisee** who operates a franchise business unit. It includes a licensed trademark, a specific marketing plan, and a fee from the franchisee to the franchisor for the right to sell the franchisor's product or services in a specific territory.

Starting a franchise requires the same amount of work as starting an independent venture. However, the franchisor provides guidance on the operations, marketing, and management of the business—important contacts and knowledge to help you build your business. Most franchisees form corporations to own the assets of the franchise and are licensed to operate the franchisor's business system. They chose this "packaged" route to business ownership because they believe that using the franchisor's brand and systems will minimize the risks that start-ups face and enable them to be more successful than when going out on their own. A recent Gallup Poll of franchisees found that more than 94 percent considered themselves successful and that over 75 percent would buy their franchise again if they had to do it over.

The operations of a franchise are governed by a **franchise license agreement**, which specifies the rights and obligations of the franchisor and franchisee. It grants the franchisee the right to use the franchisor's business name, trademark, and logo. This contract includes provisions outlining how the franchisee will operate the franchise, the services provided by the franchisor, and the financial terms of the arrangement. For example, it may require the franchisee to maintain designated inventory levels, buy a standard equipment package, sustain sales and service levels, and participate in franchisor advertising and promotional programs. The franchisor generally provides a proven company name, symbols, operating procedures, managerial and accounting procedures, and price discounts for supplies, as well as assistance with financing, site selection, construction, management development, and manager and employee training.

Why Buy a Franchise?

The franchise alternative can provide a quicker route to business ownership with the following advantages:

- *Proven product with nationally recognized name.* Rather than start a small business with one local unit, a franchisee becomes part of a chain of locations with a recognized name and brand identity. You don't have to reinvent the wheel, because the business comes with a proven track record, standard goods and services, and national advertising. Because customers are already familiar with the company and its products, the franchisee has a lower risk and improved likelihood for success. Franchisees also benefit from the combined strength of the franchisee group, achieving economies of scale in purchasing materials, supplies, and services such as advertising.

- *Marketing support.* The franchisor provides national and local advertising programs to promote the business. Such pooled advertising has broader reach than possible for most independent business owners. In addition, the brand is already established and carries greater clout.

- *Standardized operating concept and procedures.* The franchisor provides an established operating format and procedures for running the franchise, including operations, management, and accounting. This also contributes to reduced risk.

- *Management training and assistance.* In essence, the franchisor serves as a management consultant for the franchisee. The franchisor has already developed a successful format for its business and transfers it to the franchisee. Initial training programs and manuals cover how to start and operate the business, and ongoing programs to train managers and employees. The franchisees themselves are another valuable resource for support and ideas.

- *Financial assistance.* A proven concept with brand identity is easier to finance than a new small business. Most franchisors offer financing advice to their franchisees, such as financial management, lender referrals, and assistance with loan applications. Many franchisors offer payment plans, loans for real estate and equipment, and short-term credit to buy supplies.

- *Expansion opportunities.* Franchisees who succeed with one unit and enjoy being part of the larger franchise network often acquire additional units.

Disadvantages of a Franchisee

As attractive as franchising sounds, it is not for everyone. Its disadvantages include

- *Loss of control and operating flexibility.* The franchisee gives up operating freedom in exchange for the franchisor's proven system. You must be willing to take direction from the franchisor in all areas, including design for facilities, operating guidelines, and other standardized procedures. You may have to buy supplies from the franchisor or its approved suppliers—even if you can find a less expensive source elsewhere. The franchise agreement is a binding contract that may be difficult to end if you have problems.

- *High start-up and ongoing costs.* Franchising comes with a price that may be higher than starting an independent business. Costs will vary depending on the industry; a fast food franchise, for example, will have a much higher start-up cost for equipment than a business services franchise. Franchisees pay a front-end franchise fee and ongoing fees and/or royalties, typically tied to a percentage of sales. These cut into franchisee profits, as do contributions to national and local advertising programs.

- *Success tied to the larger franchise organization.* Your reputation is tied to that of the overall franchise network. Even though you are doing en exemplary job running your own unit, problems with other franchisees or with the franchisor could adversely affect your business.

Joint Ventures

joint venture
An alliance between two or more companies to pursue a specific project for a specified time period.

A **joint venture** brings together two or more entities in a relationship for a mutually beneficial business purpose, usually for a specified time period. Typically, each participant contributes assets and shares risks. The parties to a joint venture can be individuals, groups of individuals, companies, or corporations.

Participants form joint ventures for various reasons, including access to new markets, products, or technology. Two companies may join forces to take on a project that is too large for one of them to handle alone. Both large and small companies can benefit from joint ventures. Often a small company will join a larger company in the same industry to gain broader product distribution and marketing. Joint ventures are subject to state laws and are treated like partnerships for income tax purposes. They may also be structured as corporations and governed accordingly.

Joint ventures are also popular with companies that want to enter overseas markets. Some countries require a joint venture with a local, well-established company to do business within their borders. In other cases, it makes good business sense. For example, a joint venture with a company based in another country provides local relationships, customers, and knowledge of business regulations. The company that wants to enter the foreign market brings products or new technologies not currently available in that country. The Enterprising World box describes a business that has partnered with Nepalese rug factories.

Cooperatives

cooperatives
Legal entities typically formed by people with similar interests, such as customers or suppliers, to reduce costs and gain economic power. A cooperative has limited liability, an unlimited life span, an elected board of directors, and an administrative staff; all profits are distributed to the member-owners in proportion to their contributions.

Yet another business form, the **cooperative**, belongs to and operates for its members—the people who have organized it—to provide themselves with goods and services they need. Cooperatives share some features with corporations, such as operating as a legal entity, limited liability, an unlimited life span, an elected board of directors, and an administrative staff. The member-owners share in the management and control of the organization and meet regularly. The elected directors hire managers to run the cooperative to serve the members' interests. Members buy shares in the cooperative to provide capital for a strong and efficient operation. They also pay annual fees and share in any profits, which are distributed to members in proportion to their contributions. Cooperatives do not retain any profits and are therefore not taxed.

Cooperatives operate in almost all sectors of the economy and offer just about any good or service—for example, business services, child care, credit services, equipment, food and food services, health care, housing, insurance,

Cutting the Rug in Nepal

The idea for Stephanie Odegard's carpet company began with a Peace Corps assignment in Fiji. The former department store buyer worked with native artisans, showing them how to adapt their crafts for Western tastes. She continued this work at the United Nations and the World Bank, serving as a consultant to craftspeople in developing nations. A business trip to Nepal introduced her to the beautiful rugs produced by Tibetan refugees, who left their homeland after China annexed Tibet in 1959 and during Mao's oppressive Cultural Revolution in the late 1960s and 1970s.

In 1987 she started Odegard Rare and Custom Carpets. She had a dual mission for this business: developing a profitable business to showcase high-quality, hand-woven Nepalese carpets and at the same time improving the lives of the native craftspeople. A quote from Mahatma Gandhi, which she had seen many years before in an Indian railroad station, provided the inspiration to create a socially conscious business. It encourages a person who has doubts to "ask yourself if the step you contemplate [will] lead to comfort for the hungry and spiritually starving millions."

Odegard first developed contemporary interpretations of ancient and traditional Asian textile designs that would suit American clients more than traditional tribal patterns. Odegard also increased the knots per square inch to produce more luxurious carpets and developed dyes for more modern colors. She created her designs in New York and contracted the production to four locally owned factories in Nepal.

The rugs were a difficult sell at first, and the company almost went bankrupt in 1993. Then Odegard discovered that interior designers and architects were the best market for her expensive and unique products. Business took off, and today Odegard, Inc., is one of the major Tibetan rug importers in the United States, generating about $10 million in sales each year. Its rugs grace the floors of museums, luxury hotels, and celebrity homes. Recently she added home accessories, jewelry, and shawls through the Stephanie Odegard Collections.

Doing business with Nepali factories was challenging. Handmade rugs are very labor-intensive, and these factories employ more than 10,000 workers. Of particular concern to Odegard were the working conditions in these and other rug factories. By raising awareness of Tibetan and Nepalese carpets in the design community, she was able to command high prices. In return, she paid her weavers fair wages, rather than exploiting them. She also opposed using children to make the rugs. Factory owners claimed that the children worked faster and did better work—for lower wages. Odegard became a major supporter of the Rugmark Foundation, which works to end child labor in India, Pakistan, and Nepal and provide children with educational opportunities. All her rugs carry the Rugmark label to indicate that no child labor was used to make the rug, and she serves on Rugmark's board. Odegard and her company have won numerous awards for both her exceptional products and her philanthropic activities, among them a 2001 award from the Peace Corps for promoting international economic development, respecting cultural diversity, and creating a model workplace for employees.

All her decisions continue to be guided by the Gandhi quote. As she explains, "I think, 'Is it going to benefit my business, which benefits many people?' The idea that each of us can raise the standards in this world and conduct business on a meaningful level has made a big difference in my life."

An Enterprising World

Discussion Questions

1. What special challenges did Stephanie Odegard face when forming a company that imports all its products from a developing country? What form of business organization should Odegard use, and why?

2. Should Odegard consider forming a partnership with her factory owners? If so, what different types of laws might apply to an international venture such as this one? How might the risks and rewards of the carpet factory be allocated between the partners?

3. Suggest other organizational structures that might work for this enterprise.

4. How has Odegard been able to combine social responsibility and business success?

Sources: "Giants of Design: Stephanie Odegard," *House Beautiful*, June 2004, http://www.odegardinc.com; Nancy Hass, "Good Weaves Meet Good Deeds," *New York Times*, September 25, 2002, http://www. nytimes.com; Odegard website, http://www.odegardinc.com (September 29, 2006).

seller (producer-owned) cooperatives
Individual producers who join together to compete more effectively with large producers. Members jointly support market development, national advertising, and other business activities.

legal and professional services, and product marketing. Over 120 million people are members of 48,000 U.S. cooperatives. Cooperatives can take one of several forms:

- **Seller,** or **producer-owned, cooperatives:** Popular in agriculture and small businesses, members jointly support market development, national advertising, and other business activities. Agricultural and artisan cooperatives focus on processing and marketing goods and providing credit, equipment, and production supplies. Retailers and small businesses organize cooperatives to provide supplies or common services. Some familiar agricultural cooperatives are Sunkist (citrus products), Land O'Lakes (dairy products), Ocean Spray (cranberries and juices), Blue Diamond (nuts), and Farmland Industries (feed, fertilizer, petroleum, and grain).

buyer cooperatives
Consumer-owned or business cooperatives that combine members' purchasing power to buy goods or services in volume, at lower prices.

- **Buyer cooperatives:** These may be consumer-owned or business cooperatives. They combine members' purchasing power to buy goods or services in volume, at lower prices. For small businesses, cooperatives also improve efficiency and strengthen their competitive position. Food cooperatives, credit unions, health maintenance organizations, mutual insurance companies, hardware and other consumer goods retailers, and rural electric cooperatives are examples of buyer cooperatives. Ace Hardware is one of the largest cooperatives in the United States.

worker-owned cooperatives
Employee–owned and controlled businesses.

- **Worker-owned cooperatives:** These are employee–owned and controlled businesses. Found in many industries, worker cooperatives include employee-owned food stores, processing companies, restaurants, taxicab companies, sewing companies, timber processors, and light and heavy industries.[2]

4.5 Not-for-Profit Organizations

not-for-profit organization
An organization that is exempt from most state and federal income taxes and has a purpose that that will benefit others.

In some circumstances, an enterpriser might consider choosing a legal form of business that involves a not-for-profit tax status, which is described in the U.S. Internal Revenue Code (IRC) as a 501 (c) organization. A **not-for-profit organization** is defined as an organization that is exempt from most state and federal income taxes, and has a purpose that that will be of benefit to others. In addition, the individuals responsible for operating the not-for-profit organization cannot substantially benefit from the organization, though they can take salaries and be reimbursed for their expenses. Under the IRC there are many different kinds of 501 (c) organizations such as: 501 (c) (3) charitable organizations, 501 (c) (4) civic leagues and social welfare organizations, 501 (c) (7) social clubs, and 501 (c) 19 veterans' organizations. It should also be noted that there are other kinds of not-for-profit organizations under the IRC, such as 501 (d) religious associations, 501 (e) cooperative hospital service associations, and 501 (f) cooperative educational associations.

In this section we will focus on 501 (c) (3) organizations, which are charitable organizations that focus on such activities as: "the relief of the poor, the distressed, or the underprivileged; advancement of religion; advancement of education or science; erection or maintenance of public buildings, monuments, or works; lessening the burdens of government; lessening of neighborhood tensions; elimination of prejudice and discrimination; defense of human and civil rights secured by law; and combating community deterioration and juvenile delinquency."[3] A 501 (c) (3) organization could be an amateur baseball league, a literary magazine, a school or day-care center, a soup kitchen, a church, or any variety of organizations whose primary purpose is to benefit others.

Not-for-Profit Advantages

Why would you decide to start an enterprise as a not-for-profit organization? There are several advantages:

- Ability to receive contributions and gifts from others, the value of which can be deducted as a charitable contribution on personal income tax statements. For example, if you are interested in starting an organization that would help young single mothers graduate from high school, it is unlikely that these women could afford to pay the full costs of your services. A not-for-profit organization could solicit donations from others (which are tax deductible to them) that could be used to pay the expenses of these educational programs. The government, in essence, is willing to provide a tax subsidy to enterprisers who are willing to start and operate organizations that help others.

  To receive money from other foundations, or from many government agencies in the form of grants or donations, most organizations have to be not-for-profit organizations. For example, some foundations give grants for educational activities, but these grants must be given to other nonprofit organizations, rather than to individuals or for-profit businesses.

- *Exemption from federal and state income taxes.* Any revenues raised and profits earned by the non-for-profit organization can be devoted to charitable purposes, rather than to paying a percentage for taxes—as long as the organization's activities are related to the purpose of the organization.

- *Limited liability.* By organizing as a not-for-profit corporation, members of the organization obtain the same kinds of personal liability protections granted to for-profit corporations.

- *Other financial benefits.* Not-for-profit organizations also gain special postage rates as well as exemptions from certain property taxes on real estate and other property that is owned.

The difference between "related" and "unrelated" activities can be confusing. To clarify these, the IRS has designated some activities non-taxable, even if they aren't related to the nonprofit's purpose. Here's a quick rundown of the activities that aren't taxed:

- Activities in which nearly all the work is done by volunteers

- Activities carried on primarily for the benefit of members, students, patients, officers, or employees (such as a hospital gift shop for patients or employees)

- Sales of merchandise that has been mostly donated to the nonprofit (such as a thrift store)

- Rental or exchange of mailing lists of donors or members

- Distribution of items worth less than $5 as incentives for donating money (such as stamps or preprinted mailing labels)[4]

Not-for-Profit Disadvantages

As with all forms of business organization, not-for-profit organizations have some disadvantages. These include rules that limit their activities:

- *No contributions to political campaigns.* Nonprofit corporations with a 501(c) (3) tax exemption (the most common) may not participate in political campaigns or contribute money to them. Doing so may result in revocation of their nonprofit status and assessment of a special excise tax against the organization and its managers.

- *Limitations on lobbying activities.* Tax-exempt 501(c) (3) nonprofits that influence legislation to any "substantial degree" may lose their nonprofit status. The IRS does permit tax-exempt nonprofits to spend a limited amount on political activities.

- *No distributions of profits to members, officers, or directors.* By definition, a nonprofit corporation cannot be organized to financially benefit its members, officers, or directors. However, it may pay reasonable salaries and expense reimbursements.

- *Payment of taxes on income from "unrelated activities."* A nonprofit organization sometimes earns income from activities that aren't directly related to its nonprofit purpose—for example, the administrator of a nonprofit medical clinic may collect a consulting fee for advising other nonprofits. Any such income over $1,000, even if the group uses it to fund its tax-exempt activities, is subject to corporate income taxes on such unrelated income.

- *Prohibition on earning substantial profits from unrelated activities.* Spending too much time on unrelated activities or generating "substantial" income from them may jeopardize the group's nonprofit status. It's advisable to consult a lawyer or tax expert with experience in nonprofit law before engaging in such activities.

- *Dissolution of a nonprofit corporation requires distribution of its assets to another tax-exempt group.* Since tax-exempt organizations and their assets have no owners, they can never be sold. To disband the organization, its directors must donate its assets to another nonprofit group. This also means that once property goes into a nonprofit corporation, it cannot later be distributed to a member or director.

A good resource for more information on not-for-profit organizations is Nolo.com, http://www.nolo.com.

Enterprisers 4.6

A Well-Designed Partnership

In 1984, Ronald Altoon and Jim Porter left a large architectural firm to start their own business. Since Altoon + Porter opened its doors, it has designed and put into construction projects worth over $3.5 billion in 24 countries. The firm now has seven partners and employs more than 50 people. In addition to the Los Angeles headquarters, offices in Amsterdam and Hong Kong provide the firm's planning, urban design, architecture, interior architecture, and graphic design to a global clientele.

The pair traveled different routes before deciding to form their own firm. A high school guidance counselor suggested the career to Altoon because he was good in math and art. Even though architecture history and art history were his favorite classes in architecture school, he tried to transfer out three times. To find out if this was the right career for him, he bought a cheap ticket to Europe and, with a friend, visited every important architectural landmark in Europe. "I came back so charged up that I knew this is what I wanted to be a part of," he says.

After three years at a very large, prominent architectural firm in downtown Los Angeles, Altoon discovered that a large firm, as good as it was, did not satisfy his needs as an individual. He then switched to a much smaller firm, staying a year until he outgrew it. Next he went to work for Frank Gehry, a famous and innovative architect. "In three and a half years there, I probably got the equivalent of six years' worth of experience," Altoon recalls. "It was an extraordinary time, with very bright and capable people." He met his future partner, Jim Porter, in Gehry's office.

(continued)

Porter's interest in drawing, creating spaces, and the building process started when he was a child. However, he came from a musical family and worked full time in that field for a while until his dad, also a musician, urged him to learn an "honest profession." That led him back to his original creative pursuits and architecture. He, too, joined Gehry's firm, where he met Altoon. Eighteen months later, Porter left Gehry to join a large commercial firm. He invited Altoon to head up the design department of their six-office, 115-person firm.

Over time the friends became leaders of that firm, serving on the management committee and board and becoming stockholders. Although they managed the firm for a year, they were unable to gain financial and business control. "We thought, 'Hey, there's actually more risk to staying here and taking on all of this baggage, as opposed to going into business for ourselves,'" says Porter. "We've never looked back."

With another colleague from the larger firm, they formed a partnership—a structure common to many architectural firms. "We set up a three-legged stool, in effect, that had strengths in all key areas of the practice: the business, the design, and the technical aspects," says Jim. They were determined to avoid a major difficulty they observed in other small architecture firms. "They are so focused on the design issue, they can't focus at the same time on the management or the technical issues of projects," Altoon explains.

Instead of structuring the firm on a departmental basis or as studios under one partner, Altoon and Porter combined the best of both into a matrix management system. Every partner has an area of expertise. One partner is responsible for the legal, accounting, insurance, and contracts for all projects. Altoon is the partner in charge of design, while others handle project management or technical services. This system has served the firm well. "Instead of each project getting the eyes of one partner, they get the eyes of all partners, who all have a vested interest in every project," Altoon says. The partners assign the employees best suited to a particular project, client, or venue.

Unlike many architects, Ronald Altoon and Jim Porter left their egos at the door and focused on the customer. They built their architectural firm using product power, not star power. Their attention to project management and technical details, as well as design, paid off. Personal relationships and high-quality work also contributed to the firm's rapid growth. Revenues tripled in each of its first three years. "I would say most of our business comes to us by referral," Altoon says. "The best way to get business is to serve your clients well, have them come back, and have them refer you to other people. We are also very active across the board in the partnership, in industry organizations. We've been involved in the Urban Land Institute, the International Council of Shopping Centers, and the American Institute of Architects."

In the firm's seventh year, Altoon began feeling dissatisfied with the firm's emphasis on retail projects. He missed the institutional and public projects he had done at other firms but didn't see that there was room for this type of work at Altoon + Porter. He tendered his resignation—but with a seven-year timeframe. "Because it took us seven years together to build the firm, I figured I owed them seven years out the door," Altoon says. "So I said, 'If we're not there in seven years, I want you to know right now that I'm going to go do something else.'" The firm was able to accommodate his wishes, and 20 years later it is still going strong.

The partners recognize the advantages of working as a team. "I'm the one that tends to be willing to take whatever risks we need to take," says Altoon. "I can't do that unless I have partners that keep everything in balance." He also focuses on leadership creation: "We have to breed leaders in our firm. It's not just leaders of projects, or how we conduct our practice, but it's creating leaders in the greater community."

As the partnership moves ahead, it faces new challenges. "I'd like to see us have a bigger impact," says Porter. "I think there's enough talent here in this pool of partners and senior people that we should be able to produce more work at this same quality level."

Discussion Questions

1. Why is the partnership form of business organization popular with professional services firms like Altoon+Porter?

2. How might this partnership be structured in a different way? Are there other legal forms of business that architects can choose?

3. How would this partnership go about attracting new partners to the firm? What should the partnership look for in attracting someone to become a partner? At the other end, how should partners who wish to leave be compensated for their prior contributions?

4. As the needs of the partners in the partnership change, how should differences among the partners be resolved?

Source: Adapted with permission from Small Business School, the series on PBS, at http://SmallBusinessSchool.com.

4.7 Summary

1. Choosing the appropriate legal form of business for an enterprise determines how both control and ownership will be handled, how the enterprise will be taxed, who will be responsible for its legal liabilities, and how it will be managed and perceived by those who interact with it, from employees, customers, and suppliers to regulators and taxing entities.

2. Sole-proprietorships are easy and inexpensive to form. The owner has the rights to all profits and exerts control over the business. These businesses have low levels of government regulation, no special taxes, and are easy to dissolve. On the other hand, the owner has unlimited liability for debts, personally absorbs all business losses, and must make a large time commitment to the business to be economically successful. It may be hard to raise capital and attract employees.

3. Partnerships can take one of two forms: a general partnership, where the partners co-own the assets, share the profits, and are each individually liable for all debts and contracts of the partnership; or a limited partnership controlled by one or more general partners with unlimited liability and limited partners. Financial partners, whose liability is limited to their investment, are not involved in the firm's operations. Partnerships enjoy ease of formation, availability of capital, diversity of managerial expertise, greater flexibility to respond to changing business conditions, and relative freedom from government control. Unlimited liability for general partners, potential for conflict between partners, limited life, sharing of profits, and difficulty leaving the partnership are among the disadvantages.

4. The organizational structure of a corporation, a legal entity chartered by a state, includes stockholders who own the corporation, a board of directors elected by the stockholders to govern the firm, and officers responsible for implementing the board's goals and policies. Stockholders can sell or transfer their shares, and are entitled to receive profits in the form of dividends. The major advantage of corporations is limited liability. Others include ease of transferring ownership, stable business life, and ability to attract financing. Corporations, however, are subject to double taxation of profits, more costly and complex to form, and subject to many government restrictions.

5. The S corporation offers special tax status. It is organized like a corporation but taxed like a partnership, with income and losses flowing through to the stockholders and taxed as their personal income. Another organizational alternative is the limited liability company (LLC). It provides limited liability for its owners but also is taxed like a partnership or a corporation, making it attractive to many small firms.

6. Franchising involves an agreement between a franchisor, who supplies a business concept and goods or services, and a franchisee, an individual or company that buys the right to sell the franchisor's products in a specific area. A franchise provides an established business concept, use of a recognized brand name, a proven product, operating methods, management training and assistance, and financial assistance. Franchises can be costly to start and restrict operating freedom because the franchisee must conform to the franchisor's standard procedures.

7. Two or more companies can form a joint venture to undertake a special project. They can structure joint ventures through partnerships or special purpose corporations. Companies can reduce the risk of new enterprises by using joint ventures to pool management expertise, technology, products, and financial and operational resources.

8. Cooperatives are collectively owned by individuals or businesses with similar interests that combine to achieve more economic power. Cooperatives distribute all profits to their members. Three types of cooperatives are buyer, seller, and worker-owned.

9. A not-for-profit organization is one whose primary purpose is to benefit others rather than make a profit. It is exempt from most state and federal income taxes. In addition, the individuals responsible for operating the not-for-profit organization cannot substantially benefit from the organization. Gifts and contributions to these organizations are deductible from the donors' personal income taxes. Not-for-profit corporations enjoy the same personal liability protections that are granted to for-profit corporations. They also gain special postage rates as well as exemptions from certain property taxes. To qualify for these advantages, not-for-profit organizations must follow certain restrictions. For example, they should not contribute to political campaigns and are limited in their lobbying activities.

Review Questions

1. Summarize the advantages of forming and operating a sole-proprietorship. What types of business are well suited for this legal form?

2. How do partnerships compare with sole-proprietorships in the following areas: ease of formation and termination, ownership transfer, taxation, growth potential, and owner's liability?

3. Differentiate between general and limited partnerships.

4. What are the benefits and drawbacks of incorporating? Describe the corporate structure.

5. Why are S corporations and limited liability companies (LLCs) attractive to enterprisers?

6. Explain why franchising is an increasingly popular route to business ownership. Who are the key parties in a franchise relationship?

7. Describe why enterprisers should be familiar with joint ventures and cooperatives.

8. Under what circumstances might an enterpriser choose to form a not-for-profit corporation, and why?

Applying What You've Learned

1. A good friend plans to start a computer training and consulting business. While she has considerable technical experience, she lacks business knowledge and has asked you for advice on how to choose a legal form for the business. What information would you need to help her decide? Tell her the pros and cons of at least two possible alternatives.

2. Your friend's computer consultancy has been very successful, and she wants to take in a partner to expand the business. She has several possible candidates. What are the key characteristics she should look for in a potential partner? Develop a list of questions for her to use in her interviews.

3. Your uncle has decided to form a partnership with his daughter in a retail and wholesale bakery business. His daughter will be running the business full time, and he sees his role as an investor (he will be contributing 90 percent of the funds to start and operate the bakery) and will offer her advice from time to time. She has five years' experience as a bread and pastry

chef at an upscale restaurant; he has 25 years' experience running a deli and sandwich shop. He has asked you for your advice about what the benefits and liabilities of a partnership would be. What legal form of business would you suggest he consider? Why?

4. A neighbor has owned and operated a very successful hamburger stand for the past ten years. Her business has recently gained significant notoriety after a food reviewer from the city newspaper rated her hamburgers as the "best in the state." Since this review, the hamburger stand has had customers waiting in long lines. She has been approached by a number of wealthy individuals who would like to see her expand her business to other locations around the city and state. Some other people have approached her to consider franchising her business. She is worried that other locations will not have the same quality since she won't be able to manage these locations' day-to-day operations. Which of the legal forms of business might best help her expand her

business and insure that she can maintain the quality of her hamburgers, and why would you recommend this form?

5. The elementary school in your neighborhood is so bad that many of the parents are thinking of starting an alternative school for their children. They have identified a number of the top-ranked teachers in the school district who have all agreed to teach at this new alternative school if a location can be found and money can be raised to insure that they are paid for the first year of teaching. Each parent is willing to put up $5,000 to fund the new school. What would be the advantages and disadvantages to each parent if the school were organized as a for-profit corporation, versus organizing the school as a nonprofit corporation?

Enterprisers on the Web

1. There are many different businesses on the Web that promise to do much of the legal activities necessary for incorporating a business. Use a search engines such as Yahoo! or Google and type "incorporation" to find many of these companies. What specific services do these companies offer and for what price? What are the pros and cons of using one of these services to incorporate rather than using a lawyer?

2. Nearly all city and county governments have information on their websites about the process and the legal forms necessary to file for a business license. Search the Web to find out what your city or county requires you to do in order to start a business and summarize the requirements to get a business license.

3. Every state has information on the process and the forms required to incorporate a business. Search the Web to find out what your state requires you to do to incorporate your business. Choose another state, such as Nevada or Delaware, which is known as a good place to incorporate. Compare the two states and explain which one you would choose to incorporate your business.

4. The following sites provide a wealth of information on the benefits and problems with franchising. The IFA (International Franchise Association) is the trade association that works to promote and regulate franchising in ways that benefit all franchisors and franchisees (http://www.franchise.org). The IFA site has seven readings that provide a good overview of franchising issues. Please be sure to cover the last two readings: "Most Frequently Asked Questions About Franchising" and "Self-Evaluation: Is Franchising for You?" The Federal Trade Commission is the government agency responsible for monitoring and regulating franchises (http://www.ftc.gov). The FTC site provides links to many resources on franchising, as well as details on the legal responsibilities of franchisors and franchisees. What kinds of problems should a prospective franchisee look for when considering a franchise? What kinds of *scams* are typical in the franchise industry?

5. Besides the IFA, *Entrepreneur* magazine is a good source for information on franchising. *Entrepreneur* magazine conducts a number of surveys of the franchise industry and they seek to ascertain new franchising trends and issues. Browse its Franchise Zone site (http://www.entrepreneur.com/franchises/index.html), which includes lots of advice on choosing and starting a franchise and databases such as the Franchise 500, Top New Franchises, and Fast-Growing Franchises, and more. What features do you find most useful and why? Compare this site

to the IFA site. Which would you prefer to use, and why?

6. Using *Entrepreneur* (http://www.entrepreneur.com/franchises/index.html) and/or the IFA site (http://www.franchise.org), go to the "Franchise Mall" and search franchises by category. Find five franchise opportunities that are of interest to you and explain why. Both sites will provide links to the franchise businesses you will be exploring. Using the resources at these two sites and the franchisor sites, answer the following questions about these five franchise opportunities

(a) What kinds of resources are necessary to participate in these five franchise opportunities?

(b) What are the up-front costs involved with pursuing each franchise? What are the ongoing costs for each franchise?

(c) What are the capabilities of the entrepreneurs these franchises seek?

(d) What are the advantages that each franchise promotes?

(e) What are the advantages of a franchisor that is small and new, versus a franchisor that is large and established?

(f) What kinds of help and support does each franchisor offer?

(g) Of the five franchises analyzed, which franchise seems to be better than the others? Why? Summarize your findings in report form and submit it to your instructor.

End Notes

1. "FedEx Kinko's," *Wikipedia*, http://en.wikipedia.org (September 21, 2006); FedEx Kinko's Website, http://www.fedex.com (September 22, 2006).

2. Cooperative section based on material from the National Cooperative Business Association Website, http://www.ncba.coop.

3. "Exemption Requirements," *Internal Revenue Service*, http://www.irs.gov/charities/index.html (September 28, 2006).

4. "Tax Concerns When Your Nonprofit Corporation Earns Money," *Nolo.com*, http://nolo.com (September 29, 2006).

chapter 5

The Legal and Regulatory Environment of Business

Key Concepts

1. Businesses cannot operate without recognizing the importance of the regulatory and legal environment. Enterprisers who do not obey the law could face serious civil and criminal penalties. Ignorance of the law is not a legal defense.

2. A complex body of laws and regulations governs most business behavior. These laws and regulations occur at the federal, state, and local levels. An enterpriser should consult a lawyer for help navigating through all of the laws and regulations that might face the new endeavor.

3. Obeying the law is not the same thing as good ethical conduct—although one is not likely to have good ethical conduct unless one obeys the laws.

Suppose you worked in a hospital long enough to know all about caring for geriatric patients. You know that this market is growing quickly, so it should be profitable. Even more important, you are confident that you can start a small business that will provide medical care that could make a difference in the lives of older Americans. But then suppose that no bank will loan you enough money to get started.

This chapter showcases JoAnn Corn, a former hospital administrator, who had both the vision and the determination to enter the fast-developing health care industry with a variety of services ranging from in-home nursing care to trips abroad tailored for an aging population. As you read this chapter, you will learn about the many different types of regulation and legal issues that she had to consider when starting and operating this type of business.

5.0 Laws and Regulations: A Framework for Order

One of the ways that stakeholders connect to your enterprise is through our system of laws and regulations. We focus on the legal and regulatory environment of business early in the book because enterprisers need to understand the legal system to avoid problems in developing and operating their businesses. Enterprisers may violate some law or regulation unintentionally. However, ignorance of the law is not a reasonable defense. We are responsible for obeying laws—even if we didn't know that these laws existed.

Even something as simple as using your own name as the name of your business could create legal problems. For example, if your last name is "McDonald," you cannot use your name for your business because the McDonald's Corporation owns that name for a variety of businesses.

The issue of zoning and permits is another legal issue confronting an enterpriser. Most cities have regulations that allow certain kinds of activities in an area, while barring others. For example, an enterpriser could not convert a home into a manufacturing center. Cities often enact zoning laws to protect an enterpriser's neighbors from the noise and traffic that might occur with a home-based business.

Conflicts arise from misunderstandings, unmet expectations, unfair competitive practices, and many other sources. Even though you should hire a lawyer to help you navigate through the laws that affect your business venture, you also should familiarize yourself with the regulations that affect your business so that you understand your rights as a consumer and as an enterpriser, and avoid disputes with customers and suppliers.

What are the most common types of legal problems that an enterpriser might encounter? A recent survey of Inc. 500 companies revealed that about 50 percent have disputes with customers, while supplier problems affected 24 percent. Other categories included patent litigation (15 percent), fraud (8 percent), product liability (4 percent), and employee injury (2 percent).[1]

This chapter provides a brief introduction to the basic structure of the legal environment and the types of legal issues that every enterprise is likely to encounter. After an overview of the regulatory environment in which businesses operate, we describe the fundamental concepts of business law, including torts, agency, property, and sales law. Then we examine in greater detail such key areas as naming, licensing/permits, and contracts, emphasizing issues that impact the start-up and growth phases. Finally, we briefly describe the court system and alternative dispute resolution methods.

The Purpose of Laws and Regulations

law
A statute enacted and enforced to establish rules of conduct for a society.

Laws are statutes enacted and enforced to establish rules of conduct for a society. We may take some of these laws for granted. We trust that health professionals are properly licensed, that only registered voters can vote, and that food and drug products meet Food and Drug Administration (FDA) standards. Without laws to impose a sense of order, we'd live in chaos and disorder rather than in a smoothly functioning society. Over time, the system and the laws change in response to the economic, political, and social environment. Enterprisers must stay informed about legislation that affects their businesses.

The legal system also regulates how we conduct business. For instance, a person may purchase a cell phone and agree to a one-year plan that provides a certain number of minutes as talk time for a monthly fee. If the person uses more minutes in a month, the cell phone contract should include how much the additional minutes will cost. If the cell phone malfunctions, the contract should include provisions for returning the phone and getting credit for days the cell phone was not in service. The contract should also provide ways to resolve conflicts that arise.

business law
Regulations that provide a standardized environment to conduct commercial dealings.

This simple example illustrates how a contract between the customer and the service provider facilitates business transactions. The legal system includes laws for contracts that define how each party to a transaction will act and specify what will occur if one of the parties does not live up to the agreement. Contract law is one area of **business law**, the regulations that provide a standardized environment in which to conduct commercial dealings. We'll look at the key areas of business law later in this chapter.

5.1 The Regulatory Environment

Suppose you decide to form a company to develop a weight-loss pill you will make from plants growing in your backyard. Of course, you want to advertise that people who took these pills achieved significant weight loss. Before you move ahead with production and distribution, however, you discover that your business could be subject to numerous regulatory agencies:

- The FDA would be concerned about the medical value of your pills.

- The Federal Trade Commission would carefully scrutinize your weight-loss claims to determine whether they were false or deceptive.

- If the pills were considered a type of food, state and local health boards would inspect your place of operation to see if it meets certain standards of cleanliness.

- Local zoning regulations could limit your ability to make the product in your home.

- If you hire employees, you must comply with employment and tax regulations.

- If you decide to sell stock, you must follow the Securities and Exchange Commission's regulations.

As an enterpriser, you will be subject to a host of government regulations in the normal course of business. Government regulation has another side for enterprisers: More regulation means higher compliance costs. The burden on small companies can be quite heavy in terms of costs and time. For example, the Small Business Administration estimates that compared to larger firms, firms with fewer than 20 employees spend 60 percent more per employee to comply with federal regulations and about twice as much on tax compliance.

Government Regulation and Administrative Agencies

The federal government has the authority to regulate businesses and business practices, and strives to find the best balance between regulation and allowing free enterprise to determine business practices. State and local governments may also enact laws that regulate businesses. The primary purpose of government regulation is to prevent improper conduct by one business against another. Among the many areas to which government regulations apply are production, distribution, financing, pricing, competitive practices, trade, and interstate transportation.

Administrative agencies, organizations created by governments to develop, implement, and enforce regulations pertinent to a specialized area, exist at all levels. Some well-known federal agencies are the Federal Trade Commission, the FDA, the Internal Revenue Service, and the Securities and Exchange Commission. State agencies include public utility commissions and professional licensing boards, while local governments have zoning boards and planning commissions.

Today's agencies deal with everything from securities regulations to employment practices, exports and imports, and environmental protection. They have legislative, executive, and judicial responsibilities. They make rules, implement policies, investigate possible violations, conduct hearings pertaining to alleged

administrative agencies
Organizations created by all levels of government to develop, implement, and enforce regulations pertinent to a specialized area.

violations, and impose penalties when infractions occur. Exhibit 5.1 lists many of the agencies that regulate business activities and protect consumers.

exhibit 5.1

Major Federal Agencies That Regulate Businesses

Agency	Major Responsibilities
Consumer Product Safety Commission (CPSC)	Establishes and enforces consumer product safety standards under the Consumer Products Safety Act; protects consumers from unreasonable risk of injury from products through product recalls.
Environmental Protection Agency (EPA)	Establishes and enforces standards for environmental protection, including air quality and water purity; conducts research on harmful effects of pollution; works to prevent pollution of environment by various offenders.
Equal Employment Opportunity Commission (EEOC)	Prevents discrimination in employment practices; investigates and resolves claims of discrimination in employment.
Federal Aviation Agency (FAA)	Regulates the airline industry.
Federal Communications Commission (FCC)	Regulates the communication industry's interstate commerce, including television and radio.
Federal Energy Regulatory Commission (FERC)	Regulates natural gas sales and pricing, pipelines, wholesale gas and electric rates, and importing/exporting of gas and electricity.
Federal Trade Commission (FTC)	Regulates broad range of business practices including those involving fair competition, false advertising, mail fraud, misleading pricing, and packaging and labeling issues.
Food and Drug Administration (FDA)	Regulates sale and distribution of food and drug products; protects against unsafe, misbranded, or adulterated products.
Surface Transportation Board (STB)	Regulates interstate rail, truck, bus, and shipping companies with regard to rates and finances.
National Labor Relations Board (NLRB)	Administers the National Labor Relations Act by conducting elections to determine whether or not employees want union representation, and by investigating and remedying unfair labor practices by employers and unions.
Occupational Safety and Health Administration (OSHA)	Develops and oversees policies that promote safety and health at work.
Securities and Exchange Commission (SEC)	Regulates the securities industry, including trading and preventing fraud.

Laws Regulating Competition and Pricing

One of the first major regulatory concerns facing the federal government was preventing unfair practices that restricted competition between businesses. In the late 1800s, large firms (trusts) were able to monopolize certain industries, including oil, railroads, steel, sugar, and tobacco. The trusts' size and power allowed them to control trade, push smaller firms out of business, and then set high prices. Congress took steps to regulate the competitive environment by passing the Sherman Anti-Trust Act in 1890. This act prohibits monopolies and any contracts, mergers, or conspiracies in restraint of trade through practices that control prices and exclude competitors. These include price fixing, agreements between competitors to divide markets, and boycotts in restraint of trade.

To strengthen its trust-busting efforts and correct vaguely worded clauses in the Sherman Act, Congress passed the Clayton Act in 1914. The Clayton Act more specifically defined and made illegal a number of business activities that reduced competition:

- *Price discrimination:* offering different prices to customers who are buying on the same terms.

- *Exclusive dealing:* preventing a customer from buying goods from a competitor.

- *Tying contracts:* requiring a customer to purchase unwanted products to get the one they need.

- *Interlocking directorates:* placing board members on boards of competing firms.

- *Community of interests:* buying large blocks of stock of a competing firm with the intent to reduce competition.

That same year Congress passed the Federal Trade Commission Act, creating the Federal Trade Commission (FTC) and giving it the authority to define and monitor unfair trade practices that curtail competition and take action against offenders. In 1938 an amendment to the FTC Act placed regulation of advertising under the FTC's control. The five-member FTC is one of the most powerful government agencies, with broad powers to enforce laws relating to fair business practices.

Subsequent congressional acts amended the Clayton Act to further promote fair prices and encourage competition:

- The Robinson-Patman Act of 1936 prevents a supplier from charging lower prices to customers who buy in large volume, unless they offer the same terms to all customers or can prove that such quantity discounts result in lower production and sales costs. It was passed so that large chain stores could not use their purchasing power to gain discounted prices based on quantity.

- The Celler-Kefauver Act of 1950, also called the Antimerger Act, prohibits companies from acquiring a company by purchasing its assets if the resulting merger or acquisition restricts trade. It also extended antitrust regulation to any merger that lessens competition, not just those in the same industry that create a monopoly, and gave the FTC and the Department of Justice the power to approve all mergers.

Consumer Protection Regulations

In addition to laws regulating the competitive environment, Congress has passed numerous regulations that protect consumers from adverse actions by businesses. Before starting any business, an enterpriser should become familiar with the laws that apply to that industry, as well as employment regulations.

consumerism
A social movement that emphasizes strengthening buyer rights and powers with regard to sellers.

Consumerism, a social movement that emphasizes strengthening buyer rights and powers with regard to sellers, has become an important driver of consumer protection legislation. Buyers should be able to

- Refuse to buy a product.

- Assume that products on the market are safe.

- Expect that the seller will fairly represent its products.

- Obtain sufficient information about products.

    Sellers also have rights and powers. They may

- Introduce any type of product as long as it is not harmful or, if it is considered hazardous, provide appropriate warnings.

- Set prices at any level as long as similar classes of buyers receive the same price, in accordance with price discrimination laws.

- Promote the product in ways that do not interfere with fair competition.

- Develop any advertising messages, as long as they are not misleading or deceptive.

- Offer buying incentives.

Consumer protection legislation covers a broad range of issues, including product labeling, product safety, consumer credit practices, and persons with disabilities. Exhibit 5.2 summarizes key consumer protections laws.

Employment Laws

Employment practices are also subject to federal regulation. These laws protect job applicants and employees from discrimination in hiring, training, job placement, promotions, and compensation. Other laws cover payment of wages, pensions, and employee safety. Exhibit 5.3 lists the most important employment and labor laws.

exhibit 5.2

Consumer Protection Legislation

Law	Date Passed	Description
Fair Credit Reporting Act	1971	Gives consumers access to their credit reports if those reports are a reason for the denial of credit.
Magnuson-Moss Warranty Act	1975	Requires that warranties be written in easy-to-understand language, instead of legalese, and disclose all terms.
Nutrition Labeling and Education Act	1990	Mandates that food products regulated by the FDA must have labels providing accurate nutritional information.

exhibit 5.3

Employment-Related Legislation

Law	Date Passed	Description
Social Security Act	1935	Establishes Social Security Administration and provides retirement income and health care for seniors.
Fair Labor Standards Act	1938	Sets minimum wage levels and overtime pay.
Equal Pay Act	1963	Prohibits pay differentials based on gender.
Civil Rights Act	1964	Prohibits employment discrimination based on race, color, religion, gender, or national origin.
Age Discrimination Act	1967	Protects workers who are over 40 years old.
Occupational Safety and Health Act (OSHA)	1970	Protects worker safety.
Pension Reform Act	1974	Sets minimum requirements for private pensions.
Americans with Disabilities Act	1990	Prohibits discrimination based on mental or physical disabilities.

These are just a few of the many different regulations that may apply to your business. Educating yourself about them in the early stages of your business development plan can prevent problems with suppliers, customers, employers, stockholders, and competitors. The websites listed in Exhibit 5.4 can help you research the many laws and regulations that apply to your business.

exhibit 5.4

Web Resources for Laws and Regulations

FindLaw (**http://www.findlaw.com**): One of the best overall sites to begin a search for information on laws and regulations.

Legal Information Institute (**http://www.law.cornell.edu/topics/index.htm**): Offers a series of "Law About" pages with brief summaries of law topics with links to key primary source material and other Internet and offline resources.

U.S. Code (**http://www.law.cornell.edu/uscode**): A searchable version of the U.S. Code.

LawGuru (**http://www.lawguru.com**): A good site for researching legal issues.

Nolo.com (**http://www.nolo.com**): A legal information site whose goal is to make the law more understandable for lay people; includes a law dictionary, legal encyclopedia, and articles on a variety of personal and business legal topics.

5.2 Basics of Business Law

In addition to government regulation, businesses must comply with many business laws in the course of their daily operations. Laws that apply to business activities fall into several major categories, including contracts, torts, property, agency, bankruptcy, and intellectual property. Contracts, which are an important part of any business's activities, are covered in greater detail later in the chapter.

Torts

tort
Civil (noncriminal) act that injures a person or property and does not arise from a breach of contract.

compensatory damages
Monetary award to repay the victim for actual loss and suffering.

punitive damages
Monetary payments that greatly exceed actual losses; intended to punish the wrongdoer.

A **tort** is a civil (noncriminal) act that injures a person or property and does not arise from a breach of contract. The injured party has the right to sue the wrongdoer for monetary damages as compensation. Types of torts include physical injury, emotional distress, fraud, defamation of character, sexual harassment, and medical malpractice. For example, if a florist's delivery van is involved in an accident and the driver is at fault, an injured person could sue the driver and the company for damages. A company that violates zoning regulations would also be subject to tort law.

If the wrongdoer is convicted in court, he or she will be required to pay **compensatory damages** to the victim for actual loss and for suffering. Severe wrongdoing may result in the award of **punitive damages**, monetary payments that punish the wrongdoer and deter others by imposing fines that greatly exceed the actual losses. A well-known tort case is *Stella Liebeck* v. *McDonald's Corporation*. Liebeck, an elderly woman, suffered third-degree burns after spilling very hot coffee from McDonald's on her lap. She asked McDonald's to pay $20,000 to cover her two years of medical treatments. When the company offered $800, Liebeck sued and received $2.9 million dollars, of which $2.7 million represented punitive damages. As in many such cases, upon appeal the total award was reduced to just $640,000.[2]

Although most torts do not involve crimes, in some cases an act may be both a tort and a crime. If someone assaulted and injured you, that person could be tried in criminal court for violating a public law that prohibits assault as well as having to pay compensatory damages.

Types of Torts

Torts can be intentional or unintentional. Negligence and product liability are two categories of unintentional torts.

Intentional torts occur when the wrongdoer deliberately undertakes an action that could injure another party. Examples of intentional torts include making false statements to harm someone's reputation. When the offense is written or aired publicly on radio or television, it is called *libel. Slander* refers to oral statements. If you owned a café and spread false stories about getting food poisoning after eating at a competitor's restaurant, the competitor could sue you for slander. Other examples of intentional torts are trespassing, assault, and invasion of privacy.

Most tort cases fall into the negligence category. **Negligence** occurs when the defendant does not use a reasonable amount of care to protect others from injury. The earlier example of the auto accident involving the florist's driver would be considered negligence if the injured party claimed the driver was driving recklessly. The vague definition of negligence has resulted in different interpretations of the term and made this area of tort law controversial.

Product Liability

A related area of tort law is **product liability**, which holds manufacturers and sellers responsible for injuries caused by defects in their products. Product liability claims can include negligence or strict liability, which are torts, or misrepresentation or breach of warranty, which come under contract law. Product liability suits can be based on one of three types of defect:

- *Design defects:* Flaws intrinsic to the product and are there before the item is manufactured.

- *Manufacturing defects:* Defects that arise during manufacturing or construction; may affect a limited number of items but not all.

- *Marketing defects:* Defects arising from improper instructions and warnings about possible dangers related to the product.

Strict liability extends the concept of product liability. A manufacturer or seller can be held liable for *any* defects in a product, even if these parties have exercised reasonable care in designing, making, and selling the product.

Product liability lawsuits are costly and can drag on for many years with appeals. Automobile manufacturers are frequently the defendants in product liability suits. Ford Motor Co. was held liable for injuries resulting in a child's paralysis and ordered to pay $33 million in compensatory damages. A defective latch on a rear fold-down seat was blamed for the injury.[3] Another case dragged on for 11 years. Lee Raskin sued Ford Motor Co. claiming that defects in her 1988

intentional tort
Deliberate action that could injure another party.

negligence
Failure to use a reasonable amount of care to protect others from injury.

product liability
Concept which holds manufacturers and sellers responsible for injuries caused by defects in their products.

strict liability
Type of liability that holds a manufacturer or seller liable for any defects in a product, even if these parties have exercised reasonable care in designing, making, and selling the product.

Ford Escort driver's seat and restraint systems made injuries sustained during a 1992 accident worse. In the first trial, the court dismissed her claim as without merit. Upon appeal, this decision was overturned in her favor. In 2003, 11 years later, the Pennsylvania Supreme Court upheld the original verdict in Ford's favor, and Raskin's lawyer was considering yet another appeal.[4]

Other recent examples of product defects include the following:

- In April 2004 General Motors recalled over 100,000 Chevrolet Malibu cars because of problems with the antilock brake system and seat-belt anchors.

- Homeowners sued Goodyear Tire & Rubber Co. for manufacturing Entran II hoses, claiming that these hoses used in radiant heating systems leaked under normal conditions.[5]

- Toymaker Mattel had to recall its Batmobile toy because of sharp points on rear tail wings that have cut children. The company redesigned the car and is sending replacement wings upon request.[6]

Because product liability cases fall under state jurisdiction, laws can vary by state. In an effort to standardize regulation, the Department of Commerce developed a Model Uniform Products Liability Act (MUPLA) for voluntary use by the states.

The UCC, Sales Law, and Warranties

Most sales transactions fall under state jurisdiction. Prior to 1952, each state had its own laws regulating business practices, making it difficult for companies to do business across state lines. To facilitate interstate commerce, all states except Louisiana adopted as statutory law the **Uniform Commercial Code (UCC)**, which establishes a standard set of laws that apply to business transactions. (Louisiana has enacted portions of the UCC.) The UCC includes 13 articles that govern many areas of commercial law. One of the most important to enterprisers is Article 2, which controls all aspects of the sale, whether between merchants and consumers or business-to-business transactions.

Article 2 establishes laws for the sale of most goods and services, with the exception of leases (covered in Article 2a), secured transactions (regulated by Article 9), investment securities, personal services, and real estate. Among the provisions are rules for transfer of ownership from seller to buyer, buyer and seller rights, making offers, inspecting goods, delivery, transfer of ownership, and warranties. All transactions in excess of $500 must have a written sales agreement. Article 2 also includes guidelines to resolve problems arising from sales.[7]

Warranties, the sellers' promise to stand behind their products after the sale, are also covered by Article 2. These can take several forms. **Express warranties** are statements by the seller that the buyer can interpret as fact, such as indications of quality and performance. The following are examples of express warranties that give the buyer specific information about product performance or features:

statutory law
Law written by legislative bodies (the U.S. Congress, state legislatures, local governments); incorporation and bankruptcy laws are examples of statutory laws.

Uniform Commercial Code (UCC)
Set of business laws that provide a standard way for businesses to operate.

express warranties
Indications by the seller that the buyer can interpret as fact, such as descriptions of an item, promises of quality and performance, or samples of products; written warranties must indicate whether they are full or limited.

- A written 90-day warranty that comes with a factory-refurbished copy machine

- An ad for a digital camera that describes the camera as "3.2 megapixels, 3x optical zoom"

- A sample photo from a demonstration model of a color printer

- A salesperson's claim that a copy machine can handle your office work-load of 4,000 copies a month

Express warranties can be either full or limited. *Full warranties* require that during the warranty period the seller must replace or repair a defective product, within a reasonable time, at no charge to the buyer—regardless of whether the buyer registers the product. A *limited warranty* offers less protection. For example, restrictions imposed by limited warranties include coverage only for parts or repairs, charging handling fees for the repair, refunding only a portion of the item's cost, requiring the buyer to return a registration card to be valid, and eliminating certain types of repairs from the warranty.

Under the Magnuson-Moss Warranty Act, express warranties for consumer goods valued at more than $10 must clearly state whether they are full or limited. The Act also states that a warranty must clearly describe what it covers, the remedies offered in the case of a defective product, the length of the warranty period, and contact information for customer service.

Implied warranties are unwritten but specified by law. They grant certain protections to the buyer: the title to the goods is valid, the merchandise will perform as advertised, and the item will serve its intended purpose.

Clearly, enterprisers who produce goods or provide services should be aware of the laws regarding warranties. Even if they do not offer an express warranty, they are bound by the implied warranties mentioned above. Under implied warranties, sellers can be held liable for as long as four years after the sale.

Agency Law

Agency law deals with certain contractual relationships. **Agency** refers to a situation where one party, the *agent,* agrees to represent and act on behalf of another party, the *principal.* Enterprisers may use agents to rent or buy office space, obtain property or health insurance, hire accountants and consultants, or make investments. A firm that outsources some of its operations will also enter into agency relationships.

Each party has certain responsibilities in an agency relationship. For example, the principal must compensate the agent according to the contract between the parties, reimburse the agent for related business expenses, and be cooperative. The principal is held liable for an agent's actions on his or her behalf. Usually the principal transfers authority to the agent using formal document called a *power of attorney.* The agent's obligations include loyalty to the principal, performance of the agreed-upon tasks, accountability, and notification.

implied warranties
Unwritten warranties specified by law that grant certain protections to the buyer, including warranties of title, merchantability (merchandise will perform as advertised), and fitness for a particular purpose (the item will serve its intended purpose).

agency
Situation where one party, the agent, *agrees to represent and act on behalf of another party, the* principal.

Property Law

As an enterpriser you are likely to own property, whether it's office equipment or real estate, and should understand your rights regarding that property. The law defines property as anything of value that one can own and the rights that go with that ownership. Property is a very broad category and is typically divided into three major categories:

real property
Land and anything permanently attached to it.

personal property
All property other than real property.

intellectual property
Property arising from a person's creative activities.

- **Real property:** Land and anything permanently attached to it.

- **Personal property:** All property other than real property.

- **Intellectual property:** Property arising from a person's creative activities.

Personal property can also be *tangible*, anything having physical existence, or *intangible*, existing through written documentation that grants legal rights. Merchandise for sale, cars, books, and appliances are examples of tangible property, while bank accounts, stock certificates, insurance policies, and trademarks are types of intangible property. We will discuss rights with regard to tangible property in this section and consider intellectual property, which includes copyrights, patents, and trademarks, in the following section.

deed
Written document that transfers ownership of real property from one party to another.

lease
Written agreement that temporarily transfers interest in real estate or other tangible assets to the user for a specified time period.

Many business transactions involve the transfer of property ownership. The law requires written documents for all transfers of real estate. If Wahoo's Tacos buys a site to build a new restaurant, the current owner will give Wahoo's a **deed** that transfers title, or the right of ownership, to the property. Wahoo's may also be able to arrange for temporary use of a site or an existing restaurant through a **lease**, a written agreement that transfers real estate or other tangible assets to the user for a specified time period in exchange for payment of rent.

Property law dictates when ownership of personal property transfers to the buyer. Such determination is based on the form of payment. Title passes immediately upon payment in full—for example, writing a check for the entire amount to buy a new computer for your office. For goods purchased using installment payments, title transfers when the buyer takes possession of the items because the buyer has agreed, usually in writing, to make the payments. If you arrange to buy a new copier by paying $59 per month for three years, you receive title to the machine when it is installed in your office.

Intellectual Property

Enterprisers are creative people likely to come up with inventions, distinctive corporate logos and product packaging, and computer programs as they build their companies. These examples of intellectual property are assets that need special legal protection to prevent unauthorized copying. Rights to intellectual property are secured in one of three ways: patents, copyrights, and trademarks. If you don't protect your creative endeavors, anyone can steal your ideas.

Copyrights

copyright
Gives the creator of an original work the exclusive rights to publish, perform, copy, or sell the work.

Copyrights protect authors of written material by giving them exclusive rights to publish, perform, copy, or sell an original work. The copyright period extends for the life of the author plus 70 years. Copyrights apply to any written work, as well as to computer software, artworks, photographs, architectural designs, musical compositions, plays, and video and audio productions. It is important to understand that the copyright doesn't protect the idea but rather the form in which the idea is expressed.

Claiming a copyright is easy: You automatically have one for any original work you create. Just place the copyright symbol "©" or the word *copyright* on your work, along with the year and your name. To formalize a copyright, however, you should register your copyright with the Copyright Office, along with a copy of the work.

Patents

A **patent** is a legal right granted to an inventor that gives the owner exclusive rights to make, use, or sell a product or process for 20 years from the date the patent application was filed. To qualify for a patent, an invention must be new, useful, and not obvious to an ordinary person. Inventions can be machines, products, or methods. Improvements to inventions also qualify for patent protection.

patent
Exclusive right to make, use, or sell the product or process for 20 years from the date the patent application was filed.

Patenting an invention is a time-consuming and expensive process. It requires the inventor to file a lengthy application with the United States Patent and Trademark Office. It may take two years for the office to review an application and approve a patent. Because patent law is a specialized area, consult a patent attorney before beginning the process.

Trademarks

Another important area of intellectual property law that enterprisers may overlook is **trademarks**, or commercial identifiers. These are the words, names, slogans, packaging, colors, or symbols that identify a company and its goods. *Service marks* are similar to trademarks but apply to a company's services rather than products. For example, most legal company names are protected, as are brand names. General Motors' company name and its many brands—Chevrolet, Buick, Cadillac, GMC—are protected by trademark law. So are symbols, such as the Apple Computer apple and McDonald's Golden Arches. Slogans, such as "Northwestern Mutual, the Quiet Company" and UPS's "What can Brown do for you?" are also considered registered service marks.

trademark
Words, names, slogans, packaging, colors, or symbols that identify a company and its goods and services.

A recognizable brand or company symbol is a valuable asset and marketing tool. Trademarks serve as advertisements and also indicate standards of quality to consumers. The Patent and Trademark Office reviews applications for trademarks and grants exclusive rights to a brand name or symbol for an initial period of 20 years. The trademark can be renewed indefinitely as long as the owner continues to protect the exclusive use of the trademark. If you look closely at advertisements, you will see the symbols "®" and "™". These symbols show that a company has registered its rights to use the slogan. Financial institutions and telecommunications companies will place "SM" after their slogans.

Within a local service area, a small business may establish rights to a trademark simply by using it. However, before going into new market areas, businesses should perform a trademark search to be sure the trademark is not in use and register the trademark to prevent others from using it. Enterprisers should also consider the message that the brand name or trademark they use sends to consumers. The Enterprising Ethics box describes a situation where a consumer sued a company because he believed its trademark was misleading.

enterprising ethics

What's in a Name?

Can you rely on a brand name or trademark to describe a product? Paul Bass, a Miami, Florida, lawyer, believes that consumers should be able to make that assumption. He purchased vitamin E bearing the "Nature Made" trademark thinking it was derived from natural sources but then discovered that—product name notwithstanding—it was a *synthetic* form of the vitamin. Bass promptly sued Pharmavite, the California-based manufacturer, for deceptive advertising under the Florida Deceptive Trade Practices Act. Because the Lanham Act, a federal law, regulates the rights to use a trademark, the case was subsequently sent to federal court.

Nature Made is one of the leading brands of vitamins and supplements in the United States. Its products include a wide range of vitamins, minerals, supplements, and herbal products. On the Frequently Asked Questions (FAQ) page of its website, Pharmavite claims that

Nature Made® and Nature's Resource® product lines are made to strict quality standards of purity, potency, and release. Most all products are produced without artificial colors or preservatives. The few products that do contain artificial colors will state this in the ingredient listing on the label.

The company also says that:

All Nature Made® products meet or exceed strict quality standards of the U.S. Food and Drug Administration and the United States Pharmacopoeia (USP). We guarantee the potency of all labeled ingredients as long as the product has been properly stored and is within its shelf life.

Nowhere does it state that its products are totally natural. Why does this matter to Paul Bass? In many cases the natural and synthetic versions of vitamins are identical. This does not hold true for vitamin E, however. Natural vitamin E is derived from vegetable oils and called d-alpha-tocopherol; the synthetic form is chemically derived and called dl-alpha-tocopherol. Why does this matter? According to some research studies, the body absorbs and retains natural vitamin E better than the synthetic one. The Nature Made FAQ claims that some studies show "both natural and synthetic forms of vitamin E to be absorbed equally well, while other studies show that the natural form is slightly better absorbed in the body."

Discussion Questions

1. Who should regulate the claims made by companies about the characteristics of their products, particularly when a product might have medical or nutritional value?

2. Is it reasonable for a buyer of a product named Nature Made to assume that the product is 100 percent natural?

3. Does the fine print on the package describing the source of the vitamin as "synthetic" resolve any complaints buyers of the product might have?

4. Should individuals have the right to sue for damages for the purchase of a product that is less than $25.00 in value? What harm has Mr. Bass really suffered?

Sources: Nature Made website, http://www.naturemade.com (October 31, 2006); Pharmavite website, http://www.pharmavite.com (October 31, 2006); "When Is a Trademark Deceptive Advertising?" *The Nutritional and Dietary Supplement Law Blog,* June 18, 2006, http://nutrisuplaw.com/.

Bankruptcy Law

Despite an enterpriser's best intentions, he or she may get into financial difficulties and be unable to meet the firm's financial obligations to its creditors. When a company's assets are inadequate to pay its debt, it is insolvent and may decide to file for bankruptcy. **Bankruptcy** is a legal procedure that helps debtors restructure their financial obligations and equitably distribute assets to creditors, thereby resolving their debts. Bankruptcy proceedings are governed by the Bankruptcy Reform Act and heard in United States Bankruptcy Courts, which are a specialized type of District Court.

bankruptcy
Situation where an individual or business cannot meet financial obligations and seeks legal protection to repay or restructure debts.

Bankruptcy can be *voluntary,* where the debtor files the petition of bankruptcy, or *involuntary,* when initiated by the creditors. Certain actions may trigger an involuntary bankruptcy, such as not paying principal or interest when due, hiding or transferring property to defraud creditors, or providing a written statement of not being able to pay debts.

Debtors have three ways to resolve a bankruptcy filing. Chapters 7 and 11 of the Bankruptcy Reform Act apply to businesses or individuals and generally have a court-appointed trustee who supervises the proceedings and protects creditor interests, while Chapter 13 is for individuals only:

- *Chapter 7, Liquidation:* Can be voluntary or involuntary. All nonexempt business assets are sold, and the proceeds are distributed to the creditors in accordance with the Act, and the business goes out of existence. Exhibit 5.5 shows the basic steps in a Chapter 7 filing. This is the most common form of bankruptcy.

- *Chapter 11, Reorganization:* Can be voluntary or involuntary. Allows a company to reorganize (reduce costs and restructure operations), continue operating, and propose a plan to repay a portion of debts. Companies have time to reduce costs. If the court approves the

exhibit 5.5   **Bankruptcy Proceedings under Chapter 7**

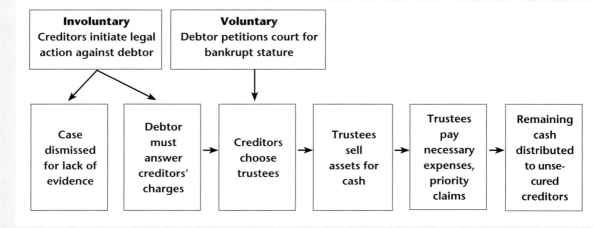

reorganization plan, the remainder is written off and the company makes a fresh start.

- *Chapter 13, Adjustment:* Voluntary only. Similar to Chapter 11, individuals (including small business owners) with regular income can file in court a plan to repay all or a portion of the debts over a three- to five-year period. If the repayment plan is approved, the debt is considered fully discharged. The debtor does not lose any assets.

5.3 Legal Issues at Start-up

While the primary emphasis during the start-up of a business is preparing to provide goods or services that benefit other people, there are a number of legal issues that an enterpriser should consider at this time. This section will cover two critical issues: naming the business and obtaining the proper licenses and permits.

What's in a Name?

Selecting a name for your business is not as easy as it may seem. For example, someone could already legally own your name for business purposes. Anyone with the last name "Dell" would be unable to name an electronics business "Dell's." Common words such as "apple" have been trademarked to identify electronic products made by the Apple Computer Corporation, while Apple Records has trademarked the name for music products.

Coming up with a name that other enterprises have not claimed can take a significant amount of time and money. In fact, there are businesses that specialize in identifying unique business names. Some companies pay firms hundreds of thousands of dollars to come up with company and product names that are novel, memorable, and can be legally protected.

Protecting Your Name

With the rise of electronic commerce, local businesses can more easily have a global presence by selling through a website. Even if you don't intend to sell online, you might have an informational website. The addition of an online presence brings businesses into direct or indirect competition with firms that may be half a world away. Without a unique name, potential customers in the next state may have problems finding your site.

In general, the wider the reach of your business—the more customers and the broader the geographic coverage your business is likely to have—the more important it is to have a business name that can be protected. As a general guideline, if you intend to use your own name for a small business or one-person service business and will operate only in a local market, you can probably use the name without running into trademark problems. Otherwise, you should research your proposed name carefully.

Why should you put so much effort into selecting and protecting your business name? If you invested resources in advertising a business name that already belongs legally to another company, you could be sued and have to pay damages for infringing on its name. Devote time and money to choosing a business name that you will be able to legally protect as your business grows in the future.

The Selection Process

The first step in the business and product name selection process is considering where you expect your new venture to go in the future. Any enterpriser who anticipates that the business may become larger than a sole-proprietorship should plan to get a trademark or service mark for the business. As you learned earlier, you can protect your exclusive rights to use your trade or service mark by registering it (your unique name or symbol).

Enforcement of your trade or service mark is your responsibility. If others use your trademark, you must inform them that they are infringing on your mark and that they should stop. If they continue, you will need to go to court and seek an injunction. Legal action is expensive, as it will surely require a lawyer.

An easy way to begin creating a trade or service mark is to check the federal government's trademark database, TESS (Trademark Electronic Search Service), to determine whether other businesses are using your proposed name, and the kinds of goods or services to which their marks apply. (You'll find TESS at the U.S. Patent and Trademark Office website, http://www.uspto.gov.) Conflicts could occur if your proposed name is a synonym, a phonetic equivalent, an alternative spelling, or an already registered name or mark.

In addition, you should also search the yellow pages (locally and nationally), the Internet, newspapers, industry trade journals, and magazines to discover whether any business might be using a name that you are considering. In most cases, the first user of a name will have rights to that name, even if it isn't registered.

As we discussed in Chapter 4, state law may specify some aspects of the name you might select for your business. Obviously, you cannot use "Inc." or "LLC" in the name of your business unless your business was actually incorporated or formed as a limited liability corporation and registered with your state. Each state has laws about the use of names for corporations, so be sure to check with the state office to see if other corporations have rights to use your proposed name in your state. State laws also specify words that you can't use in your corporate name at all or unless you are a certain type of business.

Many businesses often conduct business under an assumed or fictitious name. For example, a partnership may not want to name the business for all of the partners (e.g., Van Gogh, Monet, Manet, and Matisse) and use a name such as "The French Painters" for the business. In many states, sole-proprietors and partnerships are required to register their assumed or fictitious names with a local city or county office. In addition, these names are often published in the local newspaper's public notice section, listing which individuals and partnerships are "doing business as" (DBA) under a particular name. Some states require a DBA filing to open a business bank account or to conduct any contractual or legal matters using the business name. If a corporation or LLC is doing business using a different name than the one on file with the state, it must complete an assumed or fictitious name registration.

Licenses and Permits

Nearly every start-up enterprise needs licenses and permits from various federal, state, and local governments. Permits and licenses are required for two primary reasons: (1) to generate revenues for various government agencies and (2) to protect the public for various health, safety, and aesthetic reasons. Without the proper permits and licenses, you could be prevented from operating your business and may have to pay fines and penalties. Suppose, for example, that an enterpriser puts a large neon sign above the entrance to a retail store. If that business location is in a zone that does not permit neon signs, the local government could require the enterpriser to take down the neon sign, pay damages, or even close the business.

Obtaining the necessary licenses and permits can be a significant hurdle for enterprisers. For example, if you were thinking about starting a restaurant, you would have to obtain a multitude of different licenses and permits to establish your business, including

- A zoning permit from the city or county approving that your location is zoned for restaurants, with sufficient parking for the restaurant's capacity.

- Health department permits to serve food and licenses indicating that your kitchen and food storage areas are sanitary and will keep food safe and at the right temperatures.

- Licenses from the city, county, and state to serve alcohol.

Because you will have employees, you will also need to register with the federal, state, county, and city governments and make payments for employee taxes, social security benefits, and state unemployment benefits.

It may be tricky to find out which licenses and permits your enterprise requires and file the applications. Contact a local government business development agency in your area to get help determining which licenses and permits your business will need. Ignorance of the law is not a reasonable defense. Don't assume that you can start your enterprise or take actions on building, hiring employees, or making any sales without notifying the proper government authorities. You may want to have a lawyer or a business development agency help you fill out the necessary documents.

Federal Licenses and Permits

Many of the employee- and tax-related permissions and regulations occur at the federal level. For example, if your business

- Hires an employee or uses an independent contractor, you should consider applying for an employer identification number (Form SS-4).

- Has employees, you will need to withhold income tax and Social Security taxes from paychecks, and pay this money (along with your employer contribution for Social Security tax) to the federal government.

- Hires independent contractors, you will need to file IRS Form 1099 for each.

- Will be an S corporation, you must file Form 2553 (Election by a Small Business Corporation).

- Exports goods or services, it may need to obtain export licenses from a government agency.

Various federal government agencies regulate specialized business activities: the Security and Exchange Commission regulates investment advisors; the Federal Motor Carrier Safety Administration, moving and trucking companies; and the Food and Drug Administration, drug manufacturing. If your business reaches a certain number of employees, you may need to comply with the federal Occupational Safety and Health Act (OSHA), which requires certain safety provisions and may decide to inspect your premises.

Exporting is another area that involves a host of complex regulations and government agencies, both at home and abroad.[8] Lists of approved products for export, tariffs, export licenses, and antiboycott regulations are just some of the regulatory issues you will encounter in the United States. Exhibit 5.6 lists some of the government agencies that regulate exporting. In addition, each country where you sell has its own import laws to consider. Trade barriers such as restrictions on the ports of entry and issues regarding compliance with the more than 250 trade agreements between the United States and other nations further complicate the exporting process. The Enterprising World box provides additional information on export regulations and the penalties for violating them.

exhibit 5.6	**Agencies That Regulate or License Exports**
	U.S. Department of State regulates exports of defense articles and defense services.
	U.S. Department of Commerce, Bureau of Industry and Security (BIS) implements and enforces the Export Administration Regulations (EAR) that regulate exports of most dual-use commercial items—items that have both a commercial application and a potential for weapons of mass destruction, conventional arms, or terrorist end-use. Dual-use items range from the surprisingly mundane—chemicals used in ballpoint pens that could also be used in weapons—to sophisticated technologies and equipment. (More specialized exports fall under the jurisdiction of other U.S. government agencies.)
	Nuclear Regulatory Commission licenses nuclear material and equipment.
	U.S. Department of Agriculture monitors the export of animal and plant products.
	Department of the Interior controls the export of endangered fish and wildlife species.
	Food and Drug Administration licenses medical devices and drugs.
	Bureau of Customs and Border Protection and Bureau of Immigration and Customs Enforcement ensure that all goods entering and exiting the United States are in accordance with all U.S. laws and regulations.

The Dangers of Exports

You might think that selling your goods or services in foreign countries is a simple matter of finding a buyer who wants your products. You must decide which items are good candidates to export, where to sell these goods, how to price them for foreign markets, what payment methods to use for exporting, and how to get them to consumers. You must also comply with many more government regulations: export laws in the United States and import laws in the countries where you plan to sell. Without a thorough understanding of U.S. export laws, enterprisers might unknowingly violate one of the regulations. In addition to losing export privileges, possible administrative or criminal penalties include fines ranging from $11,000 to $1 million per violation and prison sentences.

First, an enterpriser should determine whether the item to be exported requires a license. Although most export transactions do not require specific approval or licenses from the U.S. government, certain product categories call for special licensing. These include sophisticated and high-technology products, such as software and hardware, and technical information, and products with defense, strategic, weapons development, proliferation or law enforcement applications. The need for a license is based on such factors as the item's technical characteristics, destination, end-user, and end-use. Once a company receives a license, it must comply with the specific terms of that license. (The Bureau of Industry and Security website, http://www.bis.doc.gov, provides detailed information to help companies comply with export control regulations.)

In 2000, Roper Scientific, Inc., exported night vision cameras to South Korea, Japan, Italy, and other countries without obtaining the proper licenses or retaining required export control documents. Roper also made false statements on a Shipper's Export Declaration. The company, which voluntarily self-disclosed the violations and cooperated fully with the BIS investigation, paid a $422,000 administrative penalty. In 2003, Worldwide Sports & Recreation, which does business as Bushnell Corporation, was convicted for illegally exporting Night Ranger™ night vision devices to Japan and 14 other countries, from 1995 to 1997, without BIS export licenses. Bushnell's sentence in the criminal case was $650,000 in fines and five years' probation. The company also had to pay $223,000 in administrative penalties and was given a one-year suspended denial of export privileges.

Even exporting ordinary items that are not usually subject to export controls can cause problems, as it did for 3-G Mermet Corporation. The company ran afoul of special export controls and authorizations for exports to countries declared to be "state sponsors of terrorism" when it tried to send window shade fabric through its French parent company to Iran without authorization from the Department of the Treasury's Office of Foreign Assets Control (OFAC). 3-G Mermet paid a $17,500 administrative penalty and agreed to set up an export management system.

Transshipment, or using an intermediary country to bypass U.S. export regulations, was the downfall of Ebara International Corporation and its founder and former CEO Everett Hylton. Ebara sold special pumps to Iran by first selling them to a French company. Hylton also falsified documents. The company received a harsh criminal penalty—a $6.3 million fine—and Hylton was fined $10,000 and sentenced to three years' probation. He also had to pay a $99,000 administrative penalty.

Discussion Questions

1. How could the export of sunglasses become a violation of U.S. exporting laws?

2. How would you make sure that the products or services you were exporting did not violate U.S. export laws?

3. How might other countries go about avoiding compliance with these U.S. export laws?

4. Should the U.S. government have the right to prevent subsidiaries of U.S. companies that are operating in other countries from having the opportunity to export products or services made in those countries?

Sources: Bureau of Industry and Security website, http://www.bis.doc.gov (November 1, 2006); *Don't Let This Happen to You!: An Introduction to U.S. Export Control Law*, Bureau of Industry and Security, April 2005, http://www.bis.doc.gov; and International Trade Association website, http://trade.gov (November 1, 2006).

State Licenses and Permits

Nearly all states require licenses for certain occupations such as accountants, architects, auto mechanics, barbers, building contractors, cosmetologists, dentists, doctors, insurance agents, lawyers, pharmacists, and real estate agents. The list of regulated occupations varies from state to state, so an enterpriser should check to find out which occupations may require a license. The requirements for a license may also vary. For example, some states require that an individual must have a law degree and have passed the state bar exam in order to get a license to practice law. Some states—California is one—only require that an individual pass the state bar exam. Some occupations, such as architecture and real estate, often require individuals to work with a licensed practitioner for a number of years before becoming eligible for a license. Many licenses are of a limited duration, so that individuals might need to show continued improvement in their skills (through courses or seminars).

Nearly all states require businesses to register with a state agency. Your enterprise is likely to need a state tax identification number. Most retail businesses are likely to need a state tax license and submit sale taxes that are collected in a timely manner (quarterly or monthly). If your business has employees, there will be a state agency that requires your enterprise to pay state unemployment taxes and worker's compensation insurance. If one of your employees is injured while working for you, your business will need worker's compensation insurance to pay for his or her medical bills and lost wages. Some businesses will also need specific state licenses to sell items such as alcohol, food, and gasoline. Finally, your business may need state environmental permits if your business emits anything into the air or water or the business uses potentially dangerous chemicals and materials. Dry-cleaning businesses, which use chemicals for cleaning, are likely to need such permits.

Local Permits and Licenses

Local authorities also have numerous rules an enterpriser must follow. In many areas, your business will need a city or county business license, even if your business is a sole-proprietorship. Many states, cities, and counties share taxpayer information with the federal government, so that income reported on a taxpayer's federal tax return on Schedule C (business income) can be matched with state, county, and city business tax records to see whether local taxes have been paid. There are often significant financial penalties for individuals who fail to pay local taxes on income reported on their federal income tax statements. Some cities and counties require businesses to pay taxes on property, such as furniture and equipment, and on inventory, as well as taxes on gross sales or on net income from the business.

If you will be selling food, it is likely that you will need licenses and permits from the health department. They will certify your food preparation areas, such as counters, food storage refrigerators, and cooking equipment. Your business may need sinks and dishwashing areas of a certain size and need to be completely free of any pests. Many localities require a "Certificate of Occupancy" that indicates your business location is safe and has properly working doors and windows, exit signs, and emergency lighting. This certificate is often granted through the local fire department.

Most local governments will require permits for any construction. Permits are typically required for electrical, plumbing, heating and ventilating work, and may require an inspector to certify that the work is done correctly. Check to see which building codes may be enforced *before* signing a lease or buying property. For example, if you purchase an older two-story building, you may find that you must install an elevator to meet the requirements of the Americans with Disabilities Act to accommodate employees or customers who cannot use the stairs. Doorways and hallways in older buildings may also be too small to meet current building code requirements. An experienced building contractor can help determine whether significant changes may be necessary to bring a work area up to code.

Finally, the location for your business must be zoned for the appropriate kind of business usage, such as retail, light manufacturing, or commercial. If customers will come to your establishment, your business may need to provide off-street parking. Some commercial areas may have limits on the number of certain kinds of businesses allowed, such as restaurants, gas stations, and liquor stores. An area zoned as a historical district may require that the outside signs, paint color, and changes to the building's façade be approved by a city department. In some cities it may be illegal to operate certain kinds of home-based businesses.

While the number of permits and licenses that may be required for you to start your business may seem overwhelming, there are a number of ways you can get help and assistance. Most local chambers of commerce have ample experience with helping newer and smaller businesses identify the necessary permits and licenses for your area. In addition, contact the trade association for your type of business for insights into laws and regulations governing your type of business. Finally, ask owners of businesses similar to yours for referrals for lawyers with whom they have worked on licensing and permits.

5.4 Contracts

John sees an advertisement that says "Earn $10,000 a week as a court reporter." John calls and talks to a person who says that his court reporting business is so busy that he needs to hire outside contractors to process all of the transcripts. These contractors can earn up to $10,000 a week processing transcripts using special software that costs $2,500. John asks the business owner to send him a contract before he sends any money. The contract states that the $2,500 is for the purchase of the software only. John calls the owner and asks, "If I send you the money, what guarantee do I have that I will get $10,000 a week in business?" The owner says "Well, as I said, I've got more than enough work here. Once you buy the software, you'll be getting business from me." So John buys the software—but he never receives any work from the owner of the court reporting business. John decides to go to court and sue to get his money back. Does John have a chance of winning this dispute?

Enterprisers use contracts for many types of business transactions, from buying and selling goods and services to hiring employees. Because contract law is complex, we will summarize the basic requirements for a binding contract and the remedies if the promises made in the contract are not upheld. Before entering into any contracts, however, enterprisers should consult an attorney to make sure that the contract meets all conditions for enforceability.

A **contract** is a legally enforceable agreement between two or more parties with regard to the performance of a specific action. Contracts can be express or implied. *Express contracts* spell out the terms in words, in writing or orally—for example, a boutique owner giving a jewelry designer a written purchase order for 100 necklaces that states the price of each style and the date of delivery. *Implied contracts* are derived from the actions of the parties and inferred by law. When you use the phone or electricity in your home or business, you have an implied contract with the utility company: the company will provide you with the service and you promise to pay the bill.

contract
A legally enforceable agreement between two or more parties with regard to the performance of a specific action.

Requirements of a Valid Contract

To be valid, a contract must contain the following six essential elements:

- *Agreement:* One party must make a clear oral or written offer to enter into an agreement with another party, and the receiving party must indicate clearly that he or she has accepted that offer. The offer must be specific, firm, and communicated clearly so that the parties understand what is to take place under the terms of the contract. A discussion of a job and the possible price does not constitute a contract because the offer is still tentative and subject to further negotiation.

- *Consent:* Both parties must agree voluntarily to the terms of the contract and must communicate their agreement. If pressure, fraud, unintentional misrepresentation, or honest mistakes are involved, the contract is not valid.

consideration
The exchange of something of value; must be present to have a valid contract.

- *Consideration:* To be valid, a contract must involve **consideration,** the exchange of something of value.

- *Contractual capacity:* The parties to the contract must be legally able to enter into contracts. The law prohibits minors (in most states, those under 18), drug and alcohol addicts, convicts, and the mentally incompetent from entering into contracts.

- *Legality:* The contract's purpose must be legal for it to be enforceable. A contract to remodel a facility without bringing it up to required building codes would not be valid because to do so intentionally is illegal.

- *Proper form:* Contracts do not have to be written to be valid. A phone order is considered a valid contract. Some states require written contracts for the sale of goods costing more than $500, the sale of real estate, terms that cannot be fulfilled in one year, and promises to pay the debts of another party. To prevent later misunderstandings of contract terms, it is a good idea to get most contracts in writing.

In the example of the court reporting transcript business, John signed a written contract indicating that he was purchasing "computer software only" for $2,500. The written contract would take precedence over any verbal agreements that might have been offered by the court reporting transcript business owner. So based on contract law, John would not have a good case.

Consideration is one of the most important elements of a valid contract and differentiates it from a gift. For example, suppose you hire Painter Brothers to repaint your office and agree to pay $650 plus the cost of materials. Because they did such a great job and finished three days earlier than expected, you tell the workmen that you are so pleased and will include a $125 bonus for them. Are you legally bound to pay the bonus? Under the terms of the contract, Painter Brothers is entitled to receive consideration—$650 plus reimbursement for materials—in exchange for their painting services (your consideration). You did not receive any additional consideration for the bonus payment, so you are not obligated by law to make that payment. Similarly, if you offer to help a friend install a new computer, at no cost, and your friend accepts your generous offer, you do not have a binding contract. Your friend did not give you any consideration in exchange for your time and efforts.

A few other points with regard to contracts are worth remembering:

- Written contracts are a good idea even if not required by state law. These do not have to be formal or lengthy as long as they clearly spell out the terms of performance.

- Unless the contract includes a specific expiration date, the offer remains valid for a reasonable time. What's reasonable depends on the type of business and the facts of the situation. For example, perishable items obviously require prompt acceptance. To avoid possible misunderstanding, your offer should state a deadline for acceptance. You should also accept or reject an offer promptly.

- The person making the offer has the right to rescind it at any time prior to acceptance. If you are still considering an offer to paint your office for

$650 and Painter Brothers decides that it really needs $700, it can revoke the offer because no contract exists until acceptance.

- No contract exists until the parties reach an agreement. For example, when you called Painter Brothers, they stated a price of $750 to paint your office. You responded that you can only pay $575. So far, no contract exists because you are still in negotiations. When you accept a counteroffer of $650 and communicate this to Painter Brothers, you have a valid contract, even though you haven't signed a formal document.

- You can't break a contract if you later decide you made a mistake, such as agreeing to pay too much for a used car. If you enter into a valid contract, you are probably bound to pay the agreed-upon amount, unless the courts decide that under the doctrines of fraud or misrepresentation the price is grossly unfair.

- If you sign a contract based on a false statement by the offering party, you have grounds to break the contract. This holds true even if the other person does not intentionally misrepresent the item or service. Suppose you buy a copier because the salesperson tells you that he thinks it is capable of making 5,000 copies a month. Once you have it on site, it continually breaks down—although your monthly copying volume is only 4,000 copies. You have legal grounds to cancel the contract and return the copier.

- You can rescind a contract if you discover you have misunderstood it. For example, you call a seller who advertised a computer and printer for sale. She names a price, which you assume is for both items. However, she assumed it was for the computer only. Although you had an honest understanding of what the price included and both acted in good faith, you could cancel the contract. (As noted earlier, however, if you agree to a price for an item, you can't get out of the contract if you later discover that you overpaid.)

Exhibit 5.7 provides a checklist of the clauses a typical contract would include. You may want to develop a basic contract and use attachments to describe the performance requirements. This allows you to tailor the contract to each transaction without having to write a totally new document.

Be sure to check the laws in your state, which may require specific clauses for certain types of contracts. You can often find sample contract forms applicable to your line of work that include such clauses. The legal sources on the Web (Exhibit 5.2) provide sample contract forms. If possible, choose wording that is easy to understand. For more complex transactions, consult a lawyer who can review your contract to make sure that it accomplishes your objectives and protects you.

Breach of Contract

In most cases, the parties fulfill their obligations under the terms of the contract (this is called *performance*) and the contract expires. Sometimes the parties come to a mutual agreement to end the contract. If one party does not perform as required, however, a **breach of contract** occurs. For example, suppose you hired Painter

breach of contract *When one party does not perform as required under the contract terms.*

exhibit 5.7

Summary of Contract Clauses

The following list summarizes the key clauses you may want to include when writing a contract. You don't need all of them to have a valid contract, and the actual clauses will vary depending on the type of transaction.

- Names and addresses of the parties.
- Dates when each party signs the contract to provide evidence that the parties entered into an agreement.
- Preamble ("recitals"), a brief background description of the parties.
- Description of the agreement between parties. This may be supplemented by attachments or exhibits that provide a more thorough description and clarify the project. Referring to the attachment in the contract makes it part of the contract.
- Delivery date.
- Length of contract period.
- Price.
- Payment terms: in full, installments, interim payments tied to performance.
- Warranties.
- Conditions for termination.
- Penalties for nonperformance.
- Dispute resolution procedures.

Brothers to paint a newly leased clothing store before you move in, and the contract specifies a completion date that allows you several days to move your inventory to the new location and set it up before the lease expires. Unfortunately, moving day arrives and the painters have not yet started. Under contract law, you have several remedies:

- Cancel the contract, thereby ending your obligation to make any payments to Painter Brothers.

- Sue for damages. If you and Painter Brothers cannot work out terms, even with the assistance of your lawyers, you may have to go to court. Damages can take several forms. You can have Painter Brothers honor their contract to paint and compensate you for lost sales (which you must be able to prove with some degree of certainty). You could hire another painter who could do the job more quickly but at a higher cost and sue Painter Brothers for the extra cost.

Some contracts include clauses covering *liquidated damages*, which spell out the monetary damages owed in the case of a breach of contract. In this example, you might indicate that Painter Brothers would owe you a set amount for each day beyond the contract's stated completion date. Because timing is critical to your opening the store in its new location, including a liquidated damages clause in your contract is a good business decision.

5.5 Resolving Disputes

When disagreements arise, individuals, enterprises, and governments have several options for dispute resolution. They can use the court system or other alternative processes such as mediation or arbitration.

The Court System

Disputes that call for a trial are initiated and resolved through the court system. The court system, or judiciary branch of our government, is responsible for interpreting the law and resolving disputes. The United States has a multilevel (federal, state, and local) court system to accomplish these objectives. The appropriate court for a particular case depends on the type of case and where it arises. For example, a zoning dispute between a city and a business would come under the jurisdiction of a state or local court. A newspaper that believes its constitutional right to freedom of the press has been violated would bring the case to a federal court.

The federal court system deals with issues that involve violations of federal law (criminal cases), civil cases that involve disputes with the U.S. federal government, conflicts between individuals or enterprises residing in different states involving damages of $75,000 or more, and cases that involve issues with the U.S. Constitution or federal laws and treaties. These include disputes regarding patents, bankruptcy, taxes, immigration, postal matters, international trade, U.S. claims, Indian tribes, and military appeals.

Civil courts handle cases between individuals or businesses, such as fraud, personal injury, product liability, unfair competition, and slander or libel. Criminal cases involve violations of a public law and might deal with burglary, theft, forgery, and income tax fraud.

judiciary
Branch of government that interprets and applies the law to resolve disputes for individuals, enterprises, and government. It uses a multilevel court system to accomplish these objectives.

Alternative Dispute Resolution

In many situations, a trial is not the best way to settle a dispute. Trials take a long time, and they are also expensive. The parties involved may instead choose a nonjudicial procedure such as arbitration or mediation. Another reason that businesses and individuals like settling disputes out of court is privacy. In most cases, the testimony and settlements can be kept confidential rather than become a matter of public record. **Alternative dispute resolution (ADR)** refers to a method of resolution that takes place outside a courtroom. The two most common out-of-court methods are arbitration and mediation.

Arbitration is a method of ADR in which an impartial third party (the arbitrator or arbitration panel) hears the evidence and makes a ruling. Often the chosen arbitrator has expertise specific to the industry. Because the procedures for arbitration, such as rules for presenting evidence, are less formal than those used for trials, cases are often settled more quickly and at lower cost.

alternative dispute resolution (ADR)
Nonjudicial method of resolving disputes.

arbitration
Out-of-court method of dispute resolution whereby an impartial third party (the arbitrator or arbitration panel) hears the evidence and makes a ruling.

Arbitration may be binding—the parties must abide by the arbitrator's decision—or nonbinding, where the arbitrator recommends a decision but the parties are not obligated to follow it. Settlements reached through binding arbitration are not subject to appeal unless one party can prove fraud or corruption. Contracts, such as those between financial institutions or health care providers and customers, often include clauses requiring mandatory arbitration in the event of a dispute. Arbitration is often used to settle workplace disputes between employees and employers, such as allegations of discrimination.

mediation
Less formal dispute resolution process that uses a neutral third party (the mediator) *to help the parties negotiate a mutually agreeable solution.*

In **mediation**, the parties work together, with the assistance of a trained mediator, to arrive at a mutually agreeable solution. The mediator facilitates the process by helping the parties establish procedures to follow and negotiate a settlement. While the mediator may make recommendations, the parties are under no obligation to accept them. Mediation is more flexible than arbitration and focuses on getting the parties to compromise where necessary to resolve the dispute.

Other options for out-of-court settlements include:

- *Med–Arb:* This hybrid method allows an arbitrator to act as a mediator. In this role, the third party will also attempt to bring about compromise to settle a dispute.

- *Reference to a Third Person:* The parties to a dispute may agree to have disputes decided by a designated third party. Often such a provision is included in a contract. For example, insurance companies that cannot agree on the amount of a loss often turn to independent appraisers to arrive at the settlement amount.

5.6 Business Ethics and the Law

You've recently opened a restaurant serving Cajun food on a street adjacent to a residential community. In keeping with the restaurant's theme, you feature live New Orleans–style jazz music Thursday through Saturday evenings. You have all the required permits but you have heard that your neighbors object to the music. What would you do?

Or perhaps you have just started a consulting business and are bidding on a project. It calls for more in-house resources than you have on your staff, but you know you can hire independent contractors to fill the gaps. Is it okay to present your proposal as if you already have the necessary expertise and personnel?

business ethics
Application of moral standards and values to business situations.

No laws prevent you from offering entertainment at your restaurant, but should you? Are you lying if you imply in your project bid that your firm is larger than it actually is? These are examples of ethical dilemmas that enterprisers frequently face as they interact with customers, suppliers, employees, creditors, investors or competitors. *Ethics* refers to moral standards and values that help individuals choose between right and wrong. Similarly, **business ethics** applies moral standards to business situations.

Both personal and business ethics derive from various sources, including the law and customary practices. Suppose you sell a used laptop computer and include the phrase "As Is" on the sales contract. If the hard drive fails two days later, you have no legal obligation to repair the laptop. However, your personal code of ethical conduct and fairness may prompt you to fix it anyway.

Ethical guidelines help us decide what to do when we know that an action is legal but question whether we should go ahead and do it. You have the legal right to have live music in your restaurant—but do you want to annoy the neighbors who could then keep patrons away? On ethical grounds you'd want to consider the best interests of the community. You might hold a community meeting and discuss your plans with residents to find out if they do object. You could also agree to control the music's level after a certain hour and provide a way for community residents to register complaints if problems arise.

Many questions of ethical practices involve more weighty issues than restaurant music, of course. Lying about a company's profits, manipulating accounting rules, sexual harassment, employment discrimination, withholding important product information, running misleading advertisements, conflicts of interest, and similar behaviors are examples of unethical business conduct.

Benefits of Ethical Conduct

Enterprisers who follow and encourage ethical personal and business practices build trust with stakeholders and set the values for others to follow. Developing a good reputation can provide a competitive advantage and, in the long run, lead to higher profits. In fact, numerous studies demonstrate that companies with strong value systems are more likely to succeed and survive. Those whose ethical lapses come to light—Enron and Tyco are two notable examples—must struggle to overcome their bad reputations and rebuild trust with stakeholders.

When companies do not act ethically, the government may step in to prevent further breaches. The result is more regulation and higher compliance costs. As noted earlier in the chapter, many laws and regulations arose in response to business abuses—for example, consumer safety regulations and product labeling laws.

However, the "right" course of action is not always easy to determine. The interests of one stakeholder group can conflict with another's. Reducing prices on your product could win you more customers but could lower earnings, which would harm your investors. Balancing these competing interests requires looking at a potential action from a variety of viewpoints. Other questions that can help you analyze a situation include,

- Have you correctly identified the problem and those affected by it?

- Would the proposed action injure anyone?

- Can you discuss your decision with those affected by it?

- Would you be comfortable telling other people close to you, both at work or at home, about the planned action?

- Could you justify your decision in a public forum?[9]

Many businesses adopt formal, written codes of ethical conduct to guide managers and employees. The code describes the firm's expectations and policies in terms of conduct toward other employees, customers, and vendors. Typically, a code of ethics will address such issues as honesty and integrity, respect in interpersonal dealings, product quality, trust, responsibility, fair disclosure, and confidentiality. It may specifically prohibit certain actions, such as engaging in transactions for personal gain, conflicts of interest, taking or giving bribes, and abuse or misuse of company property. While it is impossible to cover every situation, the guidelines in a company's code convey an overall attitude toward ethical conduct and create an environment that supports it.

Resolving Ethical Dilemmas

Let's return to the ethical dilemma posed at the beginning of the section: whether to play jazz at your restaurant. The questions posed earlier are one starting point. Several other models offer different frameworks for analysis:

- *The Three-Question Test:* Asking yourself the following three questions is a quick way to get a handle on your problem: Is it legal? Is it balanced? How does it make me feel? Many major corporations recommend this test to their employees. Clearly, if the proposed action violates a law, you need go no further, as compliance with the law takes precedence. Balance refers to fairness and asks you to consider your decision from other viewpoints. The final question personalizes the issue by asking you to examine your conscience.

- *Front-Page-of-the-Newspaper Test:* How would you feel if a reporter published an objective story about your decision on the front page of your local newspaper?

- The Wall Street Journal *Model:* This is another three-question test. Does the conduct comply with the law? What does the decision contribute to the company's stakeholders? What are the consequences of the decision?[10]

Applying the various tests to the music issue, we see that it is legal to play music at your restaurant as long as you comply with any local laws that require it to stop at a certain hour. In terms of balance, you should consider the views of your neighbors and discuss your plans with them. If you were indeed considerate of the community's interests, you would have no problem reading about the entertainment in the paper. On the other hand, if you did not consult with the residents and simply decided to play loud music anyway because it was legal to do so, you would not pass the balance or consequences tests. Nor would you be happy to read about the angry citizens in the newspaper story!

Enterprisers 5.7

A Healthy Regard for the Law

Denver-based Health Care Resources Group (HRG) is riding the wave of the health care future. Specializing in providing home health care—with "home" meaning the house you owned for years, a long-term care facility, or a retirement center— the company is well positioned to serve an aging population that wants to remain as independent as possible. HRG's 250 part-time and 100 full-time employees can help the firm's clients stay in their own homes or receive additional care in a long-term care facility. Its health care providers deliver oxygen and other physician-directed procedures to the patients, wherever they live.

JoAnn Corn, the company's founder, is a former hospital administrator who understood that the demand for temporary and home health nursing care was growing and could be profitable. "I knew there was a marketplace and I knew the people," JoAnn recalls. The first company she started was too small. "If you had a bad month or if the money didn't come in, the clients didn't pay in time, you were in a bad predicament."

She then formed a company with only Medicare clients, and the two businesses balanced each other. "Maybe the private company didn't do so well one month, but the Medicare company would pick up," she explains. The third business provided oxygen for clients and was started in response to client needs. Instead of referring them to Lincare, a large national provider, Corn could go to one of her own businesses. This led her to wonder, "Why can't we eventually get one-stop shopping, where any home care need that they have can come from us?"

Her next venture was in long-term care such as nursing homes. "Let's staff the retirement centers and the assisted living sections of the retirement centers," she thought. After that came a school to provide more advanced training for her employees. "We're dealing with sick people.

You need quality. You need knowledge. You need a certain type of individual working for you. So we started the school and we became certified." HRG's school now teaches aides for other long-term care facilities and is a separate business process center.

Recognizing that people with health problems have a difficult time traveling, Corn acquired a travel agency. "We'll take 15 or 20 clients that have either respiratory problems or are diabetic and are afraid to leave the country because of the health care in other countries," she says. A physician who is familiar with the travelers' medical history accompanies them. "A lot of people with health conditions love to travel, but they don't want to take the chance of going overseas. They just need us to put the trips together."

Like most start-up businesses, Corn's young companies were stretched for cash and she had to come up with some creative strategies to manage cash flow. She didn't yet have enough of a history to obtain bank financing. Being in the health care industry made it even more difficult, however, because the payment cycle often involved reimbursement from insurance companies and Medicare. "I always offered a discount for payment in advance," says Corn. "But some customers would make us wait, 60, 70, 80 days." This strained the company's finances, especially when the Internal Revenue Service's payroll taxes were due every two weeks. Sometimes Corn delayed paying these taxes to have the cash for other expenses, knowing that she'd have to pay additional penalties.

To get the quality personnel she needed to grow the company, she recruited employees from big, national health care companies. "They train their people well," she says. However, the bureaucratic mindset at a larger firm often makes people

(continued)

unhappy, so Corn offers more flexible hours that attracts workers.

Discussion Questions

1. What federal, state, and local regulations did JoAnn Corn have to consider when starting HRG's various business units? List the many different types of agencies and laws that would have jurisdiction over her companies.

2. What form of business organization would you suggest that Corn use for her company? What advantages does it offer? Should she avoid any particular form, and why?

3. A home health care business involves hiring people to work in people's homes. Who is liable when a home health care worker is injured at another person's home? If a home health care worker steals from a patient? What might a home health care company do to prevent the possibility that some of their home health care workers would steal from clients?

4. Who would be responsible if a home health care company failed to deliver oxygen and a patient died?

5. What are the legal and ethical implications of not paying payroll taxes on time? Should a business ever put itself in the position of violating the law in order to continue to operate?

Source: Adapted with permission from Small Business School, the series on PBS, and at http://SmallBusinessSchool.com.

5.8 Summary

1. Businesses cannot operate without recognizing the importance of the regulatory and legal environment. Laws establish rules of conduct for a society, including the way it transacts business. Enterprisers should become familiar with the many federal, state, and local laws that apply to their actions before starting a business. Ignorance of the law does not provide a valid excuse for breaking that law. Enterprisers should consult a lawyer for advice on the laws that pertain to their business. Doing so will avoid conflicts arising from improperly drafted contracts, misunderstandings, unmet expectations, unfair competitive practices, and many other sources.

2. Government regulation of businesses, whether at the federal, state, or local level, is designed to set standards of fair conduct for all businesses to follow. It covers all aspects of business. Government regulations take the form of laws passed by Congress or state legislatures and rulings from administrative agencies, organizations created by governments, to develop, implement, and enforce regulations in a specialized area. These agencies deal with both economic and social matters. The Federal Trade Commission, the Food and Drug Administration, the Internal Revenue Service, and the Securities and Exchange Commission are among the many federal agencies, while public utilities commissions and licensing boards are examples of state agencies. Agencies have broad powers to make rules, apply congressional policies, investigate and conduct hearings pertaining to alleged violations, and set penalties when companies break rules.

3. Early federal regulatory legislation focused on competitive practices. The Sherman Anti-Trust Act, passed in 1890, promotes competition by preventing monopolies, mergers, or other actions that restrain trades. The Clayton Antitrust Act clarified regulation regarding price discrimination, exclusive dealing, tying contracts, and other areas, and the Federal Trade Commission Act created the Federal Trade Commission to oversee business practices. The Robinson Patman Act of 1936 also regulates prices. More recently, the emphasis has shifted to consumer protection regulation that deals with rights of buyers and sellers, including such issues as product safety, warranties, product labeling, and consumer credit. Many employment practices also fall under federal regulations, which prohibit discrimination in hiring, promoting, and compensation; set minimum wages and private pension requirements; and regulate workplace safety.

4. Business law is a specialized field that creates the standards for commercial transactions. It includes contracts, torts, sales, property, agency, bankruptcy, and intellectual property. Torts deal with civil acts that injure a person or property. Torts may be intentional or unintentional or result from negligence. If found at fault, the wrongdoer may be required to pay damages to the victim. Product liability is another area of tort law.

5. The Uniform Commercial Code (UCC) establishes a standard set of laws that apply to business transactions. Article 2 of the UCC governs business to business transactions or those between merchants and consumers, including warranties, which describe what the seller will do if the product is defective or performs improperly. Express warranties are specific statements that the buyer can interpret as fact and can be full or limited. Implied warranties, while unwritten and unspecific, convey certain protections under the law.

6. Agency law deals with situations where a principal hires another party to act as agent on the principal's behalf. It defines the responsibilities of both parties.

7. The law governs property transactions involving real property, personal property, and intellectual property. Intellectual property law protects your recorded work through copyright, invention by means of a patent, and business name or unique identifier with a trademark.

8. A business that cannot pay its debts may have to file for bankruptcy protection. The firm's creditors can also initiate bankruptcy proceedings in certain situations. Under Chapter 7 of the Bankruptcy Reform Act, liquidations, the unencumbered assets of the business are sold and the proceeds used to repay creditors. The business no longer exists. With Chapter 11, a company reorganizes and continues to operate while repaying a portion of its debts according to a plan filed with the court. Chapter 13 is similar to Chapter 11 but applies to individuals, not businesses.

9. An enterpriser should be aware of legal issues that affect business start-ups. You could be sued if you choose a name that another company has already legally claimed. The more customers and the broader the geographic coverage your business is likely to have, the more important it is to have a business name that can be protected by trademark. In addition, an enterpriser should find out what licenses and permits are required for the type of business he or she plans to operate.

10. Contracts, legally enforceable agreements between parties with regard to performance of a specific action, are an essential part of doing business. Valid contracts must include agreement, consent, consideration, contractual capacity, legality, and proper form. Contracts can be written or oral. If one party to the contract fails to perform, the other party can sue for breach of contract and either cancel the contract or sue for damages.

11. Disputes that require a trial are initiated and resolved through the court system. Both the federal and state court systems include trial courts, appellate courts, and a supreme court. Civil lawsuits usually start with the filing of a complaint by the party who initiates the dispute process (the plaintiff). In criminal cases, the prosecutor initiates the process. The defendant is the party who must respond to the lawsuit. Formal procedures govern the investigation process and the trial itself. Arbitration and mediation offer nonjudicial means to resolve disputes that can save time and money.

12. Enterprisers who follow and encourage ethical personal and business practices build trust with stakeholders and set the values for others to follow. Developing a good reputation can provide a competitive advantage and lead to higher profits. A written code of ethics describes a firm's expectations of employees in dealing with other employees, customers, and suppliers. The three-question test, the front-page-of-the-newspaper test, and *The Wall Street Journal* model are among the models enterprisers can use to resolve ethical dilemmas.

Review Questions

1. What is a law, and why should enterprisers understand the legal and regulatory environment within which they operate? List several business-related circumstances that require knowledge of legal issues.

2. Explain the role of administrative agencies in regulating businesses. Give examples of three federal and two state agencies and their areas of responsibility.

3. Why were competitive practices a major concern for the federal government in the late 1800s? How do the provisions of the Sherman, Clayton, and Robinson Patman Acts prevent abuses?

4. Define consumerism and describe three key laws that protect consumers.

5. Which employment practices fall under federal jurisdiction, and how are they regulated?

6. What is business law, and what types of transactions does it cover?

7. Differentiate between intentional and unintentional torts. List several specific examples of each. What are the two categories of penalties that may be imposed on a business found guilty of wrongdoing in a tort case?

8. How does the Uniform Commercial Code (UCC) facilitate interstate commerce? What are the principal areas covered by Article 2 of the UCC?

9. How do express warranties differ from implied warranties?

10. Define the three categories of property and discuss the types of laws that apply to each. How do copyrights, patents, and trademarks protect intellectual property rights?

11. Explain the differences between Chapter 7, Chapter 11, and Chapter 13 bankruptcy filings.

12. Describe the types of legal issues an enterpriser should consider when starting a new company.

13. What is a contract, and what six elements must a valid contract contain? What remedies do you have in the case of a breach of contract?

14. How are conflicts resolved through the court system? Describe the two most popular alternative dispute resolution processes an enterpriser can use.

15. What are the benefits of operating a business ethically? If you were a business owner, would you develop a written code of ethics, and why?

Applying What You've Learned

1. Imagine that you were thinking of starting the following three kinds of businesses: a pizza delivery business, a biotechnology firm that would eventually manufacture and sell drugs to cure cancer, and a web page–design business.

    (a) What kinds of federal, state and local agencies are likely to regulate each of these businesses?
    (b) What kinds of laws would each business be subject to?
    (c) What should be the first legal steps that each business should take?
    (d) What kinds of legal liabilities might each business face?

2. Look through the last week of a major newspaper (for example, *The Wall Street Journal, USA Today,* or *The New York Times*) and identify companies that are facing legal issues. What are some of these issues? What kinds of actions were these businesses alleged to have undertaken that have gotten them into trouble? What could they have done to avoid these legal issues?

3. Look through the last week of a major newspaper (e.g., *The Wall Street Journal, USA Today,* or *The New York Times*) and identify companies that are in bankruptcy. Which kinds of bankruptcy are these firms in? What steps are these firms taking to get out of bankruptcy? What steps are their creditors taking to get their money back?

4. Pick a business that you would like to start.

    (a) What legal issues will this business face at the federal, state, and local level?
    (b) Interview the owners of two businesses similar to the one that you would like to start about the legal and regulatory issues that they face. How do they respond to these issues? How do they use lawyers to help them with their legal needs, and how much do these lawyers charge for their services?

5. Using the format guidelines for contracts outlined in Exhibit 5.6, write a contract

about the course you are using this book for, including

- Names and addresses of the parties.
- Dates that each party signs the contract. Evidence that the parties entered into an agreement.
- Preamble ("recitals"). Brief description providing background on the parties.
- Description of the agreement between parties. This may be supplemented by attachments or exhibits that provide a more thorough description and clarify the project. Referring to the attachment in the contract makes it part of the contract.
- Delivery date.
- Length of contract period.
- Price.
- Payment terms: in full, installments, interim payments tied to performance.
- Warranties.
- Conditions for termination.
- Penalties for nonperformance.
- Dispute resolution procedures.

Use your course syllabus, college catalogue, and other materials provided by your school as resources for writing your contract. How much of the contract for your course is currently "implied," "verbally agreed to," or written out?

6. Find a small claims court in your area. When it is in session, observe the kinds of legal disputes that are adjudicated. What kinds of disputes seem to take up the majority of the court's time? How are disputes resolved in favor of one party versus another?

7. Look in the newspaper for current disputes between businesses or between a business and its employees or customers. Select one and use it to answer the following questions:

   (a) What are the major issues involved in this dispute, and why do the two parties disagree?
   (b) Why are these parties willing to go to court to resolve their differences?
   (c) Would you recommend an alternative dispute resolution process, and why?
   (d) If you were mediating this dispute, what additional information would you need in order to resolve this dispute fairly?
   (e) How would you resolve this dispute?

8. Describe the types of ethical issues an enterpriser might face in the following areas: human resources, marketing, financing, and production. Are these issues different than those facing larger companies, and why?

Enterprisers on the Web

1. Think of a name for the kind of business you would like to start. Search the Web to find out what other businesses are using this name. What kinds of legal steps have these businesses undertaken to protect this name? Have these businesses trademarked their name?

2. Using any one of the major search engines, find federal, state, and local governments that would likely regulate the kind of business you are considering starting. What kinds of forms are you required to fill out? How much are the fees?

3. Find the major trade association for the business you are interested in starting. Identify the kinds of legal issues that the trade association is concerned with. Are these legal issues at the federal, state or local levels? What is the trade association doing about these legal issues?

4. Search the Web for corporate codes of ethics and find several examples. How do they differ, and how are they similar? Does the company's industry make a difference in the content of the code?

5. One of the best sites for online business ethics resources is the University of Illinois Web-Miner Business Ethics site, http://www.web-miner.com/busethics#top.

Divide the class into small groups. Have each group go to the Case Studies section and select one case that interests them. After identifying the key ethical issues in the case, the group should analyze the dilemma using the questions and models presented in the text and prepare a brief report for the class that includes a recommended course of action.

End Notes

1. "Brief Profiles of 2003 Inc. 500 Companies," *Inc.,* October 15, 2003, http://www.inc.com.

2. "McDonald's Coffee Case," *Wikipedia,* April 29, 2004, http://en.wikipedia.org/wiki/McDonald%27s_coffee_case.

3. Beth Warren, "Ford Must Pay for Girl's Injury," *The Atlanta Journal-Constitution,* March 3, 2004, p. B1.

4. Eric Freedman, "Court Upholds Verdict for Ford in Defect Suit," *Automotive News,* December 22, 2003, p. 18.

5. "Homeowners with Leaking Radiant Heating Systems Involving Entran II Hose Could Benefit from Proposed International Settlement," *U.S. Newswire,* April 23, 2004, http://proquest.umi.com.

6. "Mattel's Batmobiles Are Recalled as Wings Pose Hazard to Kids," *The Wall Street Journal,* April 15, 2004, p. 1.

7. "Sales Law: An Overview," *Legal Information Institute,* May 4, 2004, http://www.law.cornell.edu/topics/sales.html.

8. Bureau of Industry and Security website, http://www.bis.doc.gov (October 31, 2006); "Export Basics," *Export.gov,* http://www.export.gov (November 2, 2006); International Trade Administration website, http://www.ita.doc.gov (November 1, 2006); and International Trade Association website, http://trade.gov (November 1, 2006).

9. Ivan Fox, David P. Twomey, and Marianne Moody, *Anderson's Business Law & the Regulatory Environment: Principles & Cases,* 14th ed. (Cincinnati, OH: West Legal Studies in Business, Thomson Learning, 2001), pp. 28–30, 44.

10. Ibid., pp. 43–45.

chapter 6

Discovering Opportunities

Key Concepts

1. Business opportunities are favorable events involving customers, consideration, connection, and commitment that have the potential to become a successful business. Recognizing opportunities requires understanding the context in which the "4 Cs" of an opportunity might prove viable. Successful businesses are based on business opportunities that are different from existing businesses.

2. Opportunities occur because the environment is constantly changing. Enterprisers leverage their background and skills to discover opportunities from sources that others might overlook, such as unexpected occurrences, incongruities, process needs, changes in industry and market, demographics, perception, and new knowledge. They pay attention to environmental trends and know-how to enhance their luck.

3. The challenge of identifying a viable opportunity to pursue involves factors such as leveraging your experience, increasing mindfulness, and making your own luck. In addition, enterprisers must evaluate the fit between an opportunity and their personal goals.

Suppose you love fabrics and colors—sewing them and wearing them—but your nursing job forces you to wear the same drab uniform every day. Out of frustration, you start to sew more appealing scrubs for your own wear. Much to your surprise, your coworkers want your designs, too, and two years later word has spread about your great products. Then suppose your husband introduces you to a businessperson with apparel manufacturing experience.

This chapter presents the case of Sue Callaway, a San Diego nurse, and her husband and partners who turned a sideline home business into a major company that changed the look of uniform clothing for millions of health care workers. She recognized a great idea and took the necessary steps to convert it from an opportunity to a business concept and then to a successful enterprise.

6.0 What Is an Opportunity?

Where do enterprisers find opportunities for successful businesses? Are entrepreneurs just lucky individuals who stumble upon an idea for a successful business? Successful enterprisers are more aware of their surroundings. They understand the context in which an opportunity might prove viable and systematically seek opportunities. Enterprisers then use a variety of techniques to evaluate the related environmental and industry factors to identify opportunities that are worth further study. In other words, by their actions they create what others may call luck.

Because environments and industries change, savvy entrepreneurs need to think ahead and consider how environmental changes might affect present opportunities. The purpose of this chapter is to help you recognize the many different paths for finding opportunities. We will explore ways to increase your awareness of environmental characteristics that will affect these opportunities, as well as help you understand how environments might change over time and give rise to new opportunities. Then we'll explain how to turn an opportunity into a successful business by developing a business model that includes a sound business concept and a viable financial plan. As a result, you'll have the tools to make your own luck.

More than Ideas

We define opportunities in a unique way. Opportunities are not just ideas, but also take into account four features of a situation: customers, consideration, connection, and commitment:

customers
Those who buy an enterpriser's goods or services.

connection
How enterprisers will identify and reach specific customers.

commitment
The enterpriser's dedication to the idea and willingness to implement it.

- **Customers:** Who will buy an enterpriser's good or services?

- **Consideration (see Chapter 5):** Do the enterpriser's specific goods or services provide significant value to the customer?

- **Connection:** How will an enterpriser identify and reach specific customers? This is often called the channel of distribution.

- **Commitment:** Is the enterpriser committed to the idea and willing to execute it to create an actual business? People bring their own unique interests to a situation. Few people seem to be able to create successful businesses solely on whether the business will make a lot of money. Nearly all enterprisers start and build businesses because their businesses reflect their own passions and values.

For example, a chain of adult day care centers might be a great idea for a business. As the population ages, demand may increase for a place for elderly people to go for daytime supervision. While this might seem to be a great idea, does it meet the test of these 4 Cs? Exhibit 6.1 presents the 4 Cs for this opportunity.

Opportunity recognition, then, is about paying attention to your own situation and seeing your own life as a set of favorable events that you can turn into a

exhibit 6.1

The 4 Cs of an Opportunity: Adult Day Care Centers

- **Customers:** In this case, the most likely customers are the relatives who serve as the caretaker for the elderly person. These are the people who would pay to have someone else look after their loved one during the day.

- **Consideration:** The price of using the adult day care center must offer an advantage or benefit to the person who pays the fee. Having someone else supervise and monitor an older person at an adult day care center might be an important benefit to a spouse or sibling who is exhausted from giving 24-hour care.

- **Connection:** An adult day care center would have to find customers who would find this service of value and also have the money to pay for this service. Finding customers can often be expensive and time consuming. This opportunity could be implemented at a specific location, where older individuals are picked up from their homes and taken to the care center, or by individual caretakers who go to the older person's home and provide one-to-one services.

- **Commitment:** Not everyone is likely to be interested in adult day care, even though the adult day care business might prove to be very profitable. An enterpriser who had problems finding good care for an aging parent might be more motivated to implement this idea and have the passion and commitment to make it work.

successful business. An enterpriser's primary activity is recognizing a situation as a "favorable event" and evaluating its business potential using the 4 Cs.

It's Not Just Luck

Enterprisers are often seen as lucky people. In fact, studies suggest that entrepreneurs make their own luck because they devote substantially more effort to scanning the environment than individuals in other occupations. Scanning the environment typically represents the amount of time entrepreneurs spend reading newspapers and popular and trade magazines and also talking with other people, including strangers. Entrepreneurs are prolific gatherers of information; they pay attention to their surroundings and they ask questions.

Opportunities come from a variety of sources. As you might expect, most opportunities arise from previous work experiences. The business environment offers chances to make connections among the various individuals necessary to transform ideas into viable businesses: customers, suppliers, employees, and investors. As they work, enterprisers navigate among these networks of individuals. They find opportunities because markets are inefficient: people do not have the same information nor do they have the same relationships. Entrepreneurs can exploit these gaps in knowledge and connections among people.

Enterprisers also understand that changing environments create both challenges and opportunities. For example, health care businesses are likely to be affected by changes in government regulations and reimbursement policies as well as by changes in technology. Failure to recognize and plan for possible changes in health care regulation could prove to be extremely harmful to a new medical care company.

The development of an opportunity requires a lot of hard work and effort—dedicated commitment. Such commitment is the result of choosing an opportunity that is aligned with the entrepreneur's goals and interests. Opportunities that don't match the entrepreneur's interests and goals will not be sufficiently exploited. Later in the chapter we'll provide a series of exercises that help you explore your personal goals and interests, so that you can screen out those opportunities that can't meet your personal criteria.

One last point: The initial process of enterprising involves *variation*. Starting an enterprise that will be successful involves doing something different from other businesses that exist. Because each enterpriser brings unique skills and experiences to the situation, the enterprise he or she creates will be distinct from one another enterpriser might develop. The resulting business can provide a unique set of benefits to customers.

6.1 The Business Concept

Ideas are not opportunities. Opportunities don't exist unless they include the four constructs defined earlier—customers, connections, consideration, and commitment. What most people call opportunities are really just ideas. So each of the following does not qualify yet as an opportunity: the Internet (a connection), doughnuts (a product with a set of considerations or benefits), elderly people (a general description of a customer), or "I love pets" (a commitment to one's passion). An idea becomes an opportunity, or business concept, when it covers all four elements.

Understanding this key concept is fundamental to opportunity recognition. We may start with one aspect of the opportunity (business concept), such as "I love pets," and then we begin to think of customers, ways to connect to those customers, what benefits those customers are likely to want, and how committed we are to following through and obtaining funding. Once we have all four, the opportunity can become a reality.

The ability to come up with business concepts is more of a projective and creative process rather than an analytical process. The process involves looking for new ways that differences in the 4 Cs can be combined. Overall, this means asking, "What if?" What if people didn't buy their books at a bookstore? Consider all the different ways that books can be sold. You might first think of selling books on the Internet, like Amazon.com or bn.com. Yet one of the fastest growing distribution channels for books has been discount merchandisers such as Wal-Mart and Costco. We will explore this process further when we look at how to develop a concept grid.

Telling the Story

The business concept forms half of the business model, while the other part is about numbers, or profitability. (We will address feasibility analysis and profitability in the following chapter.)

A **business concept** is the story that an enterpriser tells about the kind of opportunity he or she wants to develop. The story has to talk about the four characteristics of **opportunities**: customers, connections, consideration, and commitment. The way to evaluate a business concept is to ask:

- Does this story hold up?

- Does it make sense?

- Do the four characteristics of the story fit together?

For example, suppose you are thinking about starting a hamburger delivery service. Many food items, such as pizza and Chinese food, are home delivered so perhaps people would like hamburgers delivered as well. The business concept is home delivery of hamburgers. The customers are people who want home delivery; their benefit (consideration) is that they don't have to leave home to get a hamburger; the connection is through your delivery service; and you are interested in pursuing this business because you are interested in food.

What you would do next is explore whether the hamburger delivery service holds up as a story. Is a delivered hamburger something that people really want (does it offer the customer significant consideration or value?). Do enough people want such a service? Is home delivery of hamburgers a reasonable way for people to enjoy hamburgers? This issue involves exploring the different ways that

opportunity or business concept
Favorable events involving customers, consideration, connection, and commitment (the 4 Cs) that have the potential to become a successful business.

people are connected to getting hamburgers, such as drive-through windows, sit-down restaurants, hamburger chains such as McDonald's and Wendy's, home-made hamburgers, and hamburgers in the frozen food section in the grocery store. Each connection has advantages and disadvantages, and each connection delivers certain considerations to the customer.

Once you have convinced yourself that the story seems reasonable, you need to consider the final part of the business model: Does it make money? The numbers are based on assumptions about how the four business concept characteristics work together.

An interesting business concept may not work because of the numbers. Take the online home grocery business. The business concept for companies like Home Grocer, Webvan, and Peapod involved people placing online grocery orders that would be selected and packed at an automated warehouse and delivered to customers' doorsteps. The enterprisers believed that this type of service wouldn't be significantly more expensive than going to the grocery store because the business would make it up in volume. What they didn't include in the financial equation was the time element, a key factor that increased the cost of operating a home grocery delivery business.

Think about how we shop for groceries: we drive to the store and spend half an hour or longer going up and down the aisles selecting products. We discount this time at the store (we don't pay ourselves to do this activity)—but we aren't necessarily willing to pay someone else to take the time to do this for us.

The Internet grocery store was a great business concept: customers valued home delivery of items if the cost was the same as going to the grocery store themselves. However, once the additional labor cost of selecting, packing, and delivering the groceries was included, the business simply didn't work at the prices the service charged. So a great story does not always translate into a viable business financially.

Peapod, one of the surviving online grocers, has succeeded by paying attention to its customers and the environment and adapting its business concept accordingly. Peapod's first business concept was to use personal shoppers to fill orders at local supermarkets that would give Peapod a 6 percent discount. However, Peapod discovered that the cost to fill a $100 order was $40! So Peapod changed its business concept to use centralized distribution centers to fulfill orders.[1] Peapod's concept changed again when it became a subsidiary of Royal Ahold, a major international grocer, in 2000. It now uses a "clicks and bricks" concept and partners with Ahold's U.S. supermarket chains, including Stop & Shop and Giant Food. Certain parts of its business concept remained constant, such as its commitment to quality, customer service, the proprietary Stay Fresh delivery system, state-of-the-art order-fulfillment technology, and proprietary transportation routing system.[2]

Enterprisers should focus on both customers and consideration. They need to identify a group of people with needs that the enterprise can fulfill. At some fundamental level, the concept development process starts when someone asks, "What causes you pain?" If finding a cure for your pain is important and another person can provide it, you have the beginning of a business concept that might be worth pursuing.

The Business Concept Grid

A good way to visualize the business concept is a grid that demonstrates the relationship between the 4 Cs. These variables are interdependently manipulated to develop a coherent story about the nature of an opportunity. As Exhibit 6.2 illustrates, the grid is a table with the 4 Cs across the top.

Let's use "chocolate" as the basic idea from which we want to generate concepts (opportunities). First, we would think about the many different categories of customers who would be interested in buying chocolate and place them in column one. Next we would think about all of the ways that chocolate products could be connected to each customer—for example, all the different places an enterpriser might provide opportunities for kids to buy chocolate—and list them in the customer column as in Exhibit 6.1.

For each customer and connection, we then identify all of the ways that we can provide consideration for that option. For example, let's take kids as the customer, and movie theaters as the connection for providing chocolate.

Given this particular connection, it probably makes sense that chocolate products sold in movie theaters tend to be larger than the sizes sold in other places, and, the kinds of chocolate products are often less "messy" (e.g., M&Ms), rather than something like a hot fudge sundae that would be difficult to eat while watching a movie.

Finally, enterprisers have to think about whether the particular configuration of customer, connection, and consideration is appealing for them to pursue. In this example, are you excited about selling candy to children? How do you feel about working to increase candy purchases in movie theaters? If you aren't really passionate about this concept, then you probably shouldn't pursue it—even though it might prove to be very profitable.

One of the major ways for enterprisers to succeed is to think about new ways to connect to customers. For example, Dell sells computers directly to customers through the Internet and through mail order, rather than through retail stores. Customers can order exactly what they want, and the computer is "made to order" for them. This is different from a customer going to a retail store (different connection) and buying what the retailer has on the shelves of the store.

exhibit 6.2

The Business Concept Grid

Customer	Connection	Consideration	Commitment
Kids	Grocery stores		
	Candy stores		
	Movie theaters	(1) Can't go out to other places and buy while movie is showing.	Loves movie theaters.
		(2) Extra treat besides the movie as special occasion.	Enjoys selling.
		(3) Must be able to eat it in the dark.	Likes candy.
	Ice cream stores		
	Vending machines		
	Halloween		

We can start the concept grid in any area. For example, we might start with the connection "movie theater," and consider the types of customers who might be attracted to a movie theater: kids, adults, couples on dates, movie buffs, and so on. Then, we could think about the various considerations that each group of customers would want from their movie experience. For example, what kids might want from their movie experience could be very different from what a movie buff might want. Not only would the movies be different, but also the kinds of seats and snacks a movie buff might prefer could be different from what we'd offer for kids. An enterpriser might be passionate about serving some kinds of customers and not others. An enterpriser who is a film buff may show classic movies, art films, and foreign films more often than mainstream titles. Another enterpriser may target the family market. Each customer, then, has different ways to connect to certain kinds of considerations.

The concept grid provides a visual way of realizing that each category of the concept (customer, connection, consideration, commitment) can be a starting point for developing a viable concept. For many enterprisers, their concept will begin with their passion. Starting with a love of fishing, for example, an enterpriser could think of numerous opportunities that might involve fishing (a commercial fishing boat, offering fishing tours, creating fishing supplies (like lures), a fishing school, etc.).

Enterprisers can work at leveraging their ideas into concepts through effectuation. Begin with what you have (the customers you already know, the connections you already have, the considerations that you can already provide, and the commitments you want to pursue), and look to discover a business concept that might work from combinations of what you already have.

6.2 Sources of Opportunity (the Environment)

Now that we know what opportunities are, how do we find them? We should start with the big picture view—the environment—and then take a closer look at how an opportunity fits with an individual's personality, needs, and talents. The environment includes not only the business environment—a company or an industry—but also the broader social, intellectual, economic, political, regulatory, and global environments.

This section introduces you to several approaches to environmental analysis. First, we'll examine Peter Drucker's strategies for what he calls "systematic innovation." Then we'll consider trend analysis and describe several resources for this important phase of opportunity recognition.

Disciplined Innovation

Because the world is changing every day, a constant stream of new opportunities emerges through changes in the environment. Management expert Peter Drucker believes that innovation is more than inspiration or luck. It takes a different type of hard work—knowing instead of doing. "Above all, innovation is work rather than genius…hard, focused, purposeful work," he writes. "If diligence, persistence, and commitment are lacking, talent, ingenuity, and knowledge are of no avail."[3] His classic 1985 book *Innovation and Entrepreneurship* describes seven sources of opportunities that he considers essential to successful **systematic innovation:**[4]

systematic innovation
As defined by Peter Drucker, a purposeful and organized search for and analysis of changes and the opportunities these changes create.

1. *Unexpected Occurrences:* Individuals capitalize on unexpected successes or see things that don't work and realize that this "failure" indicates some other kind of opportunity. For example, IBM originally thought the science sector would be the primary users of computers. The company quickly switched its focus when initial demand for computers came from businesses that needed to automate payroll calculations for payroll. This unexpected success led to IBM's leadership role in the computer industry. The Ford Motor Company learned through the failure of the Edsel that buyers bought cars because of their identification with a lifestyle, and because of this insight, the company designed the Mustang.

2. *Incongruities:* Incongruities occur when expectations and results don't match. Logically we would expect that companies and industries that grow and become more efficient would in turn earn higher profits. In some cases, the reverse might be true because of incongruities between reality and the basic assumptions about how success in the industry occurs.

   For example, during the first part of the 20th century, the shipping industry was in decline despite the introduction of faster and more fuel-efficient ships to transport cargo. Yet fewer goods were being shipped. The problem lay not in the time a ship was at sea, but rather on the number of days a ship was in port. The opportunity recognition centered on finding ways to speed up loading and unloading cargo to reduce the number of days that ships were in port. Once the industry converted to container ships and roll-on and roll-off ships, the shipping sector grew and returned to profitability. A more recent incongruity involves the Internet grocery business. Knowing that many consumers hate to grocery shop—in one study they ranked it next to last on a list of favorite household tasks—companies like Webvan, Peapod, and Home Grocer were sure that their online supermarket services would attract lots of customers. To their dismay, they discovered that their early assumptions based on such studies were wrong. Shoppers weren't willing to pay more for the convenience and the time they saved.

3. *Process Needs:* Another source of opportunity is identifying changes in how things work. One reason for growth in the pharmaceutical industry is the use of drugs, rather than surgery or other treatment methods, to combat disease. For example, rather than have patients with depression see a psychiatrist weekly, doctors can treat many cases of depression with drugs, thereby reducing costs to the patient, as well as providing opportunities for more individuals with depression to be treated through

drugs, rather than through the high expense of psychotherapy. The process needs provided the opportunity.

4. *Industry and Market Changes:* Often changes in laws and regulations have a significant impact on opportunities available for new companies to pursue. Changes in industry structure also create opportunity. The breakup of the nationwide monopoly held by AT&T brought significant opportunities to the telecommunications industry. Thousands of new companies took advantage of these available opportunities, installing telephones, telephone systems, and pay phones, and selling alternative local and long-distance services. The deregulation of the airline industry enabled firms like Southwest Airlines, JetBlue, and International Air to take advantage of underserved markets by requiring lower airfares, typically at underused airports and in places where demand for air transportation has been hindered by high prices.

5. *Demographic Changes:* The number and age of a population is predictable, so that understanding trends becomes a source of opportunity. The United States went through a baby boom after World War II through 1960, and then couples had fewer children from 1960 until 1980. The greater number of births during the baby boom has a predictable influence on what will occur in the economy over time. As the average age of the population increases, opportunities arise to provide services for the growing number of people over the age of 65. Also, it is important to recognize that everyone who will be in the workforce in 2020 has already been born! The "market" in the United States in 2020, therefore, is already "fixed" unless there is a significant influx of immigrants.

6. *Changes in Perception:* What people value and find important change over time. The fashion industry is an obvious example of how tastes in clothing change constantly. As the population of the United States ages, our perception of what "old age" means also changes. We now expect to live healthy and active lives into our 70s and 80s, continuing to play tennis, ski, or mountain climb. As a result, our perception of health is changing as well.

7. *New Knowledge:* Regardless of the field, the hardest and most complicated way to pursue innovation is through new knowledge. The innovations that come from discoveries in science, technology, education, and sociology take more time to develop and carry greater risk than most other factors. This concept has been documented over time, as the following quote from Nicolo Machiavelli's *The Prince,* written in 1505, proves:

> And it ought to be remembered that there is nothing more difficult to take in hand, more perilous to conduct, or more uncertain in its success, than to take the lead in the introduction of a new order of things. Because the innovator has for enemies all those who have done well under the old conditions, and lukewarm (indifferent, uninterested) defenders in those who may do well under the new.

More recently, Hillary Johnson, writing in *Inc.*, expresses a similar view in an article about her father, a visionary entrepreneur who never quite made it, despite a series of innovative ideas:

> The world does not welcome innovators or artists, though not out of malice. The problem is a structural glitch. The world is set up to function as smoothly as it can, and it doesn't recognize the difference between innovation and disaster: Either one throws a wrench into the system. Trying to make the world really better is as much a crime against society as trying to make it worse. Only small incremental improvements are rewarded and applauded. … Some people believe that good ideas always rise to the top. They're wrong. Good ideas occasionally rise, but just as many sink into oblivion. Success in the technology industry in particular, has always depended on having the right product at the right time, not necessarily on having the best product … Living with a frustrated inventor for 40 years has taught me something I didn't learn even from the cold war, and that is simply this: The scariest thing about the future is that the future isn't necessary.[5]

Trendsetters

Paying attention to how trends affect our lives, both personally and professionally, is an important way to identify potential opportunities for new businesses. Successful enterprisers tend to be more aware of trends in the environment than others. They track them on an ongoing basis and know when important changes occur.

Sources for trends are plentiful. Many magazines, from business periodicals like *Fortune* and *Business Week* to general news magazines like *Time* and *Newsweek*, feature articles on trends. *Red Herring* (http://www.redherring.com), a technology magazine, is a good source for trends relating to the intersection of technology, business, government, globalization, and investing.

In recent years, *Red Herring's* trends have covered a wide range of industries, including telecommunications, semiconductors, nanotechnology, biotechnology, venture capital, and broadband.

Several recent books document the broad changes occurring in the world. Peter Schwartz, cofounder and chairman of the Global Business Network (GBN), is a noted futurist and business strategist. GBN's website, http://www.gbn.org/, provides valuable insights about how to think about the future and which environmental factors are likely to be important. In his 2003 book *Inevitable Surprises*, he describes major trends that he believes are inevitable—but also predicts surprise twists that can create opportunities:

1. *An aging world.* In 1950, the average age at death was around 60; in 2003, it was around 77. People are likely to live and to be productive a lot longer. If people retire in their 60s and live to their 90s, they would spend nearly one-third of their lives not working. No society can afford to support this. The surprise twist: what if people don't stay healthier as they age? How do we afford significantly rising health care costs?

2. *The great flood of people.* While the average age in the United States is getting higher, this is not the case in many other parts of the world. An influx of immigrants will tend to make the country younger, more Latino, and less educated in the short term. China will face the "one child problem," and because families have tended to have boys rather than girls, there will be a significant shortage of marriageable women over the next 20 years. Europe will have to face its own immigration issues, as many more nonnationals cross borders to work and live because of the open border policies of European Union nations. The surprise twist is that Europe will face the same challenges as the United States in creating a cohesive society because many of these countries (i.e., Germany, France, Sweden) are based on a particular cultural heritage (i.e., German, French, Swedish).

3. *Return of the long boom.* Schwartz believes that technology contributes to rising rates of productivity, which improve everyone's standard of living. He believes there will be a sustainable "long boom" in prosperity. The surprise twist: Every country needs to invest in infrastructure (airports, power grids, highways, hospitals, public safety, etc.) in order for society, as a whole, to benefit.

4. *The new world order.* Can the United States, as the only superpower, work with other nations to make the world a safer place? Schwartz believes that it cannot make the world safe by going it alone. The surprise twist, then, is that U.S. strength will come through increasing commitments to cooperation among other nations.

5. *The forces of destabilization.* Will terrorism continue to rise? Will the forces that lead to terrorism, such as radical religious views, not only in the Middle East but also in South East Asia and Africa, lead to continual wars and conflict? The surprise twist: If prosperity and freedom continue to grow across the world, many of the forces that spawn terrorism and discouragement (i.e., poverty, lack of opportunity) will diminish.

6. *Benefits of science.* Schwartz sees the continuing importance of biotechnology, computers, and all other applications of science leading to significant benefits to all people in the world. The surprise twist: Every new technology brings possibilities for benefits as well as harm. For instance, the ability to manipulate atoms has led to nuclear power plants for electricity (supplying France with 70 percent of its electricity) as well as the material to make nuclear bombs.

7. *The challenge of dealing with the environment.* Will choices be made to improve the air, water, and land around the world, or not? These are political choices more than just economic choices. The surprise twist is that as the economic well-being of citizens rises in any country, their interest in improving the environmental standards of their air, water, and land also increases.

In 2006, James Canton, CEO and chairman of the Institute for Global Futures, published *The Extreme Future*, a book describing the major trends that present strategic challenges for the world's leaders over the next 5–20 years. He believes that every individual, organization, and country should be aware of and prepare for these top-ten trends, many of which echo Schwartz's earlier predictions:

1. *Energy:* The need to solve the current energy crisis and to understand energy's pivotal role in business and society.

2. *Innovation industries:* The global economy will be driven by innovation in such fields as nano-, bio-, neuro-, and information technologies.

3. *The changing workforce:* Diversity and multiculturalism will characterize the workforce of the future. A shortage of talented workers will create competition to hire and retain the best employees.

4. *Medical advances:* Biotech and genomic research are helping us stay healthy longer.

5. *Weird science:* Ongoing advances in technology will change our lives, culture, and economy. Nations and businesses that invest in future science will profit in economic growth.

6. *Reducing security risks:* Protecting ourselves from threats to our physical well-being and also to our identities has moved to the fore.

7. *Globalization:* Both opportunities and risks will increase from open global trade. China and India will gain in economic importance. Cultures and ideas will clash.

8. *The changing climate:* Global warming and pollution are changing the ecosystems. These, along with threats to biodiversity, present challenges as well as new business opportunities.

9. *Protecting individual rights:* Individuals and society must find a way to balance personal freedom, privacy, and security.

10. *America's relationship with China:* These two countries could have the greatest impact on the world's future.[6]

Economic trends are critical components of many of the trends we've discussed so far. Successful enterprisers also follow what's happening in the economy. Exhibit 6.3 lists a number of valuable websites that provide helpful information on a diverse group of economic indicators, including some more unusual ones.

As our discussion of trends demonstrates, change is guaranteed. Anyone who is looking at the future can see that some kinds of changes (demographic changes, for example) will happen. Along with change come opportunities.

exhibit 6.3 | **Tracking Economic and Demographic Trends**

These websites will link you to a wealth of economic surveys, statistics, and other information that will help you identify trends.

Indicator/Source	Link	Description
Business Roundtable's CEO Economic Outlook	http://www. businessroundtable.org	Conducts quarterly CEO Economic Outlook surveys that ask about expectations for the short-term economic outlook.
Bureau of Labor Statistics	http://www.bls.gov	A good place to find statistics on inflation and consumer spending, job growth and unemployment, earnings, productivity, business costs, and demographics.
U. S. Census Bureau	http://www.census.gov	Statistics and analysis on people, households, and businesses.
BizStats.com	http://bizstats.com	Links to a variety of business and industry statistics.
MBA Mortgage Applications Survey	http://www. mortgagebankers.org	Weekly mortgage applications survey predicts trends in home sales; economic outlook and forecasts on market environment.
Consumer Outlook	http://www. pollingreport.com/ consumer.htm	Reports the results of several consumer confidence surveys, including ABCNews/Money Consumer Comfort Index, Conference Board, AP/Ipsos Consumer Attitudes and Spending by Household (CASH) Index, Gallup surveys, and others.

6.3 Finding Opportunities (You and the Environment)

The secret for identifying an opportunity involves leveraging your own experience (background and skills) by (1) paying attention and (2) enhancing one's luck. As we will see, experience provides both pluses and minuses to an individual's ability to notice and exploit an opportunity.

Experience

The way to look at experience is to see it in light of the 4 Cs: customers, connection, consideration, and commitment. Experience involves building up your capital, or resources, with regard to the 4 Cs. For example, if you have experience as a restaurant waiter, you are likely to have some knowledge of what menu selections and drinks interest customers who come to that restaurant. You have some sense of how much the restaurant's patrons are willing to pay for a meal and those special occasions when customers are likely to splurge on a meal. So as a waiter, you would have some sense of both customers and consideration (what kinds of benefits customers enjoy: food, service, atmosphere), and you would have some sense of whether you actually enjoyed the restaurant business (your sense of your own commitment). What you might not have knowledge of as a waiter would be the connections—for example, the details of how the food is prepared, how the restaurant is actually operated, and who the best suppliers for food are.

What we find is that enterprisers work to gather up information across the 4 Cs to identify an opportunity worth pursuing. What entrepreneurs do differently is to maximize their unique capabilities and skills to generate benefits to a specific set of customers. Entrepreneurs use their experience as a starting point for identifying an opportunity and then for gathering the resources necessary to pursue that opportunity. It is rare that an enterpriser has all of the background experiences that are likely to enable him or her to completely see all aspects of the 4 Cs in an opportunity.

It is important to realize that all enterprisers "begin where they are." We emphasized this point in Chapter 3 when we talked about effectuation. With regard to experience and its influence on recognizing opportunities, people don't see opportunities outside of the boundaries of their own experiences, that is, their "prior knowledge."

A good example of this involves a research study that looked at individuals who applied for rights to license a specific technology invented at the Massachusetts Institute of Technology (MIT).[7] This technology is three-dimensional printing (3DP), which was invented by four MIT faculty members and doctoral students and patented in the United States on December 8, 1989. According to the patent documents, 3DP involves:

> a process for making a component by depositing a first layer of a fluent porous material, such as a powder, in a confined region and then depositing a binder material to selected regions of the layer of powder material to produce a layer of bonded powder material at the selected regions. Such steps are repeated in a selected number of times to produce successive layers of selected regions of bonded powder material so as to form a desired component. The un-bonded powder material is then removed … (US Patent # 5,204,055).

Having read the description of this patent idea, what kinds of customers do you think might be interested in this idea? In what ways could this idea be made into a product or service that customers would consider buying? What value would this product or service have for these customers? And, finally, can you think of a combination of customers, connections, and considerations involving this idea that you would be committed to pursuing?

The MIT Technology Licensing Office widely circulated the 3DP idea in scientific magazines and the popular press to encourage entrepreneurs to notice this idea and come up with ways to exploit it. MIT was willing to give individuals or companies exclusive rights to use the 3DP technology if they could show how they might exploit it in a particular application. Of the thousands, if not millions, of individuals who might have noticed this idea, only eight groups devoted significant effort to getting a license to use the 3DP idea to exploit an opportunity. Four of these efforts resulted in successful companies, while the other four failed. Exhibit 6.4 provides information about the companies, the opportunities, and the current status of these efforts.

Exploring the experiences and backgrounds of the entrepreneurs involved in these eight efforts reveals several key insights:

exhibit 6.4   **Entrepreneurial Opportunities for 3DP**

Company	Opportunity	Forecast Market Size, Year 5	Forecast Sales, Year 5	Forecast Operating Earnings	Current Status
Z Corp	Machine to make rapid 3-D prototypes for industrial and architectural design	$100 million	$10 million	$2 million	Privately owned and funded by founders
Therics	Pharmaceutical delivery systems	$9 billion	$2 million	–$7.5 million	Privately owned and funded by venture capital
Specific Surface Corporation	Ceramic filters for power generation	$800 million	$31.5 million	$13 million	Privately owned and funded by venture capital
Soligen	Direct shell production casting to make ceramic mold from CAD model	$20 billion	$50 million	$8.5 million	Public company
3D Partners	Provide 3-D models to clients	$10 million	Never done	Never done	Abandoned; found market too small
3D Orthopedics	Custom orthopedic devices for medical and dental markets	Never done	Never done	Never done	Abandoned; not funded by venture capital
3D Imaging	3-D models for surgeons to reduce error	Never done	Never done	Never done	Abandoned; lost $50,000 business plan competition
Conferences	Retail chain to make 3-D sculptures of people	Never done	Never done	Never done	Abandoned; technology inappropriate for intended use

Source: Reprinted by permission, Shane, Scott, "Prior Knowledge and the Discovery of Entrepreneurial Opportunities," *Organizational Science* 11 no. 4, July/August. Copyright 2002, the Institute for Operations Research and the Management Sciences (INFORMS), 7240 Parkway Drive, Suite 310, Hanover, MD 21076 USA.

- *The range of opportunities that could be generated from the 3DP process is not obvious to everyone.* When you read the patent description, did you come up with the list of eight opportunities listed in Exhibit 6.4? In fact, each enterpriser who came up with a specific opportunity to exploit the 3DP process was surprised to find out that other enterprisers had come up with other ways to use the 3DP technology. "I certainly never thought that someone would make pills with the 3DP process," said Walter Bornhorst of Z Corp. What, then, led each enterpriser to see a specific opportunity in 3DP technology that no other enterprisers saw?

- *The opportunity that each enterpriser noticed was driven by his or her prior industry experience.* Industry experience is "code" for knowledge of the 4 Cs. For example, Z Corp., which focused on applying 3DP to make three dimensional prototypes, was developed by individuals with industrial design experience who were working in a company concerned with quickly creating three dimensional prototypes. They had knowledge of customers, they had an understanding of the kinds of prototypes that customers wanted, and they were able to see how the 3DP process could serve as the connection between what these customers wanted and their specific considerations. The enterpriser for Therics had 25 years of prior experience in pharmaceutical manufacturing, product development, and regulatory approval. When he learned about 3DP technology, he could apply it to the manufacture of drugs.

- *In all eight cases, the enterprisers saw the 3DP process in relationship to solving a particular customer problem.* These enterprisers had a particular set of considerations in mind that helped them notice how an idea such as 3DP could solve these customer problems. They *recognized* the opportunity but were not searching for it. So a good way to look for an opportunity is to begin with customer problems.

- *Individuals don't explore ideas in unfamiliar areas.* For example, if we don't have experience and knowledge of biotechnology, we aren't likely to think about how an idea might become an opportunity in that area. Even the entrepreneurs who looked at the use of 3DP in orthopedics didn't broaden their approach to other medical applications. The environmental factors discussed earlier in this chapter, for example, are ideas that will broadly influence our lives. But turning these factors into opportunities requires an understanding of the specifics of the 4 Cs: Who are your customers? What do they want (consideration)? How will these needs be met (connections)? Do you want to do this (commitment)?

As the 3DP story clearly illustrates, experience is a constraint that has a major impact on opportunity recognition. It is critical to the types of connections we make among the 4 Cs. In addition, we are less likely to recognize opportunities that are outside the realm of our prior experiences. Broadening our horizons by creating varied experiences will maximize the chances of discovering business opportunities.

At the same time, developing experience-based business concepts brings other challenges. One of the most critical is ownership of opportunities that an

enterprising ethics

Whose Opportunity Is It?

As a talented research scientist at a mid-size bio-technology company specializing in drugs to treat cancer, you are known for your creative approaches to research. Working in your lab after-hours, you believe that you have discovered a new diagnostic test for multiple sclerosis, a neurological disease. Because this type of product is outside the scope of the company's mission, you plan to start your own company to market the tests. Do you own your idea, and are you within your legal rights to develop it on your own?

Or perhaps you are a financial advisor at a major brokerage firm and believe that your firm is not serving women clients well, especially those who find themselves responsible for their own investments after a divorce or death of a partner. You want to start a specialized advisory firm for these women and begin compiling a list of your current employer's female clients. Have you violated the company's code of ethics?

These are just a few examples of the complexities surrounding intellectual property (IP) and potential conflicts of interest. Conflicts of interest arise when the private interests of an employee or director interfere with those of the company in any material way. They affect both employees with ideas for a new product or service and employers who want to protect their company's IP.

While you may think IP is limited to technological discoveries, computer source code, patents, and copyrighted designs, it also includes trade secrets, business plans, marketing strategies, sales leads, price lists, lists of customers, lists of suppliers, and similar items. Trade secrets refer to proprietary knowledge—formulas, patterns, designs, software, special equipment, or processes—used in one's business that provide a competitive advantage and thus have independent economic value.

Most companies today have codes of ethics with very specific clauses concerning actual or perceived conflicts of interest and related matters. They require that employees and directors and their immediate families avoid any conflicts of interest and disclose potential conflicts of interest. Typically, the language is very broad and prohibits employees and directors from engaging in any activities that conflict with the company's business, may negatively impact the company's reputation, or prevent accomplishing assigned job responsibilities. Examples of prohibited activities include

- Receiving compensation in any form from another company or accepting personal loans, gifts, fees, favors, or other material benefits from such a company.

- Using opportunities discovered while using the company's property (including intellectual property) or the company's property for personal gain.

- Using information gained through a person's position at the company, about the company, a competitor, supplier, or customer, for personal gain.

- Insider trading (using nonpublic information for personal financial benefit or sharing that information with others who may use it as the basis for making stock trades).

- Owning equity in a company with whom the employing company has a business relationship (customer or supplier) or that competes with the employing company.

- Participating in joint ventures or similar business arrangements.

- Simultaneous employment with another company or any activities that advance another company's interests, such as marketing competitive products.

In many cases, a company will allow certain activities that have been presented to and approved by the company's audit committee or other governance group.

Discussion Questions

1. How would you react if you were the CEO at the biotechnology firm and learn that your employee is starting a side business with an idea developed in your laboratories? Do you have the right to approve whether your employee pursues the opportunity to develop the diagnostic test—and should you have this right?

2. What criteria would you use to evaluate whether an employee's opportunity is in conflict with the organization? Are employees who are mindful of the opportunities around them penalized by conflict of interest policies?

3. What kinds of experience does an employee receive from an organization, and should the organization benefit from any opportunities derived from that experience?

4. Should all employees be subject to conflict of interest policies, or only employees who are more likely to discover opportunities closely tied to the company's current products, services, and customers?

Sources: "Business Conduct and Ethics," Chevron website, http://www.chevron.com/investor/corporate_governance/biz_conduct.asp (November 30, 2006); "Code of Ethics," NTL Incorporated website, http://investors.ntl.com (November 29, 2006); Peter Fiske, "Opportunities: Intellectual Property, Part 1," *Science Careers*, November 10, 2006, http://sciencecareers.sciencemag.org; "Genentech Good Operating Principles," Genentech website, http://www.gene.com/gene/ir/governance/ggop.jsp (November 29, 2006).

enterpriser discovers while employed by someone else. Most companies have conflict of interest clauses in their corporate codes of conduct that cover this situation, as the Enterprising Ethics box explains.

Paying Attention

Ellen J. Langer's work on mindfulness provides a good description of mindfulness. She writes:

> A mindful approach to any activity has three characteristics: the continuous creation of new categories, openness to new information, and an implicit awareness of more than one perspective.[8]

mindfulness
As defined by Ellen J. Langer, an awareness of the present moment that includes openness to new information and multiple perspectives.

The concept of **mindfulness** revolves around certain psychological states that are really different versions of the same thing: (1) openness to novelty; (2) alertness to distinction; (3) sensitivity to different contexts; (4) implicit, if not explicit, awareness of multiple perspectives; and (5) orientation in the present.[9]

What are the strategies for increasing mindfulness, and why would mindfulness lead to discovering opportunities? As we've defined an aspect of opportunity recognition, we have to be able to spot things that are "different." Instead, we often become habitual in our thinking, and, we lose our ability to notice anything that is different in our situation. We can learn to be more mindful:

- *Vary the way you do things.* When you do something different, pay attention—in the moment—to how these differences change the situation. For example, many people get their best ideas when they travel because traveling puts them in entirely new situations. We need to vary how we do things, and then pay attention to what is new and different in the current situation.

- *Increase the novelty in the situation.* Look for a situation's unique features. What is different about this situation? Focus on and pay attention to differences rather than assuming that every situation is the same as every other situation.

- *View situations from different perspectives.* Become more mindful by looking at situations from other stakeholders' perspectives, for example your customers or employees. Ask yourself these questions: How would customers or suppliers look at the product? What are their needs and interests? Their perspective may be totally different from yours.

- *Turn work into play.* If it is fun and enjoyable, one pays more attention to engaging in the activity. Most entrepreneurs consider their "job" to be about fun, rather than about "work."

- *Draw distinctions.* When we look for differences, we find that we must pay attention to the specifics of the context. By being open to thinking about distinctions, we find ourselves seeing new things that wouldn't be apparent to us otherwise.

Veteran entrepreneur Norm Brodsky is a good example of mindfulness at work. He has repeatedly gone into competitive markets that others considered saturated and built successful companies. About 25 years ago, in the early days of computer usage, he started a messenger business but was having difficulty getting customers, even though he courted law firms, advertising agencies, and others that made many deliveries and passed their costs to their clients. Taking a different perspective—the customer's—he discovered that cost was not the primary concern and identified a problem he could solve. In discussions with an office manager who was a potential customer, the office manager indicated a need for receiving invoices by each client served. This change in the billing process would make the office manager's life much easier and save administrative time. Other messenger firms provided only aggregate billing information, and it took many hours to assign costs to the client. Brodsky hired a programmer and figured out how to provide invoices that grouped pickups and deliveries by client. This feature gave him the jump on his competitors and was a key factor in the company's success.[10]

Two additional ways to increase mindfulness are to think about levels of analysis that occur and to talk about scope. A problem that you may think is an issue about the individual might really be about the group or society. Asking yourself, "Is it above or below what is happening in the situation?" will help to identify the correct level.

Mindfulness is less about getting right answers than about opening yourself up to new and different ideas and situations. As Langer says,

> How can we know if we do not ask? Why should we ask if we are certain we know? All answers come out of the question. If we pay attention to our questions, we increase the power of mindful learning.[11]

Paying attention isn't necessarily about achieving a particular outcome; rather, it is about exploring the world and understanding your experience. Particularly in the process of concept development, many different alternatives could satisfy a customer's needs. The more ways you can discover through mindfulness and paying attention, the more opportunities you will find.

Making Your Own Luck

Making your own luck is very similar to the process of becoming mindful. In an experiment to uncover how lucky people act in different ways from unlucky people, researchers asked people to count photographs as they paged through a newspaper. The researchers had placed a half-page announcement on the third page of the newspaper that said: "Stop counting. There are 43 photographs in this newspaper." The lucky would notice the ad and stop counting, while the unlucky would just continue looking for photographs. In this experiment, the researchers were testing participants' ability to notice things outside of the assigned task.

They discovered several important differences between lucky and unlucky people.

- Lucky people are open to new experiences. Unlucky people are stuck in routines, and they don't pay attention.

- Lucky people are less focused. They are willing to experience different situations and do not have a specific goal in mind. They are open to different outcomes and expect success.

- Lucky people reframe experiences so that they see them as valuable outcomes. If something goes "wrong," they consider it a learning experience rather than a failure.

(For more information about the Luck Project, visit its website: http://www.luckfactor.co.uk.)

Among the ways to create better luck for yourself are the following:

1. *Maximize chance opportunities.* This is a way of saying, "get out in the world, meet people you don't normally meet, and see what happens."

2. *Listen to your lucky hunches.* Pay attention to your intuitions and don't readily discount them.

3. *Expect good fortune.* Expectations become self-fulfilling prophecies. People who keep luck journals, writing down lucky things that happen to them, notice that over time, more lucky things happen in their lives.

4. *Turn bad luck into good.* Lucky people reimagine situations where bad things happened and realize that things could have been worse. Then they move on and take control of the situation.

Making your own luck is similar to some of the strategies we discussed in Chapter 4 that focused on optimism and small wins. If you expect good things to happen to you, they do. If you continue to take actions to make your life better, it gets better. Opportunities occur to those who expect to find opportunities.

6.4 Enterprisers and Opportunities (Evaluation of Personal Fit)

Not every opportunity is worth doing. Enterprisers need to take time to evaluate whether the opportunities they consider meet their own needs. This process is often very difficult. An enterpriser's initial commitment to an opportunity can change as the enterpriser gains more experience.

Take, for example, a business student who was also a wonderful baker. By all accounts she made a fantastic peach pie, one of the best anyone had ever tasted. Everyone who had a bite of her peach pies said the same thing: "You should sell these peach pies!" So she did. She began baking pies at home and took samples to various restaurants and gourmet shops around town. Everyone who tasted her peach pies said, "How many of these pies can I get?" Soon she was baking 50 peach pies a day and had orders for many more.

She quickly moved from making peach pies at home to renting a licensed kitchen with an industrial oven. Within about three months, as the business grew, she realized she had less and less interest in wanting to bake pies as a business. While she enjoyed making one or two peach pies for herself and for her friends on the weekends, it was less fun to get up at 4 AM to begin mixing ingredients for hundreds of pies, bake them, and get them delivered. Then she had to insure that all of her clients paid their bills. As the fresh peach season came to an end, it became more and more difficult to find enough fresh peaches (or even high quality frozen peaches).

While her friends might be forgiving if one of her pies might have a blemish on top, or look slightly crooked, the restaurants and gourmet shops wanted only perfect-looking pies. After about six months, she decided to quit making pies and to work for a company that sold baking supplies to bakers. She found that she enjoyed being around other bakers, but she didn't want to have a business as a baker. What lessons can we learn from her experience?

First, find entrepreneurs who you would like to emulate. Spend time talking with them about their businesses, what they like—and don't like—about their day-to-day lives. Interviewing entrepreneurs gives you a good sense of the start-up process. You might find that some industries have really "awful" entrepreneurs and people working in them—entrepreneurs who don't return phone calls or respond to emails and are mad and unhappy when they are interviewed. This is often a good sign that getting into that kind of business will not be fun! If the people in the industry are unhappy, the odds are high that if you get into that kind of business, you will be unhappy too.

Besides finding lots of mentors and examples of entrepreneurs in the kinds of businesses that interest you, you should consider doing an internship (paid or unpaid) to get experience with the day-to-day realities of the business that interests you. Another student loved kayaking and thought it would be great to have a kayaking store. He was able to get an internship at a major outdoor adventure store that specialized in selling kayaks. He found that his time was occupied with the details of running a retail store, and he wasn't spending any time kayaking. In selling to customers, he found he was impatient to be outside kayaking and didn't particularly like talking about kayaking.

When the personal fit is there, success can follow. In the Enterprising World box, we'll meet Lionel Poilâne, whose passion for bread and vision of a bakery with global reach helped him capitalize on opportunities and earn the title of the most famous baker in Paris.

Breadwinners

An Enterprising World

How about a nice fresh loaf of bread, from the most famous bakery in Paris—without stepping on a plane? Thanks to the innovative thinking of the late Lionel Poilâne, you can order Poilâne Bakery's signature loaves or other select bakery products from its website (http://www.Poilâne.com) and have them delivered to your door via FedEx.

Lionel Poilâne began his baking career—albeit reluctantly—at age 14 as an apprentice at his father Pierre's bakery established in 1932. However, his vision went beyond "a bakery in which my horizon was an oven." Even as a young man, he wanted to "bring the world into my business." He turned the most humble of foods—bread—into a branded item that was the foundation for a £15 million business. At the same time he was building the bakery's reputation and expanding its business, he maintained Pierre's traditional baking techniques and ingredients. Poilâne's breads contain only natural ingredients—stone-ground flour, water, salt, and natural starter (for leavening)—and are still baked by hand in wood-fired ovens. The result is not the typical French baguette but a large, hearty round loaf with dense texture that weighs about four pounds.

(continued)

Lionel embraced a special creative philosophy that he termed "retro-innovation." "I'm neither a traditionalist nor a progressive: I try to create a culture using the best of tradition and the best of new technology," he said. He immersed himself in the history of bread, interviewing old French bakers to learn their techniques and refining his father's methods to produce old-fashioned, Norman-style dark bread based on an ancient regional recipe. Although the coarse bread had fallen into disfavor after World War II because of its association with deprivation, it became popular again in the 1970s.

As demand increased, Poilâne maintained quality by building a large, modern factory with 24 wood-fired ovens in the Paris suburbs rather than opening stores in multiple locations. He and his wife Irena, an interior architect, designed the building and its special clay and brick wood-fired ovens that replicate a 16th-century French design. True to his philosophy of retro-innovation, he was able to combine the local with the global, traditional methods and modern techniques. The bread is made by hand, but this modern eco-bakery uses solar power and burns waste wood in its ovens.

As the Poilâne Bakery's reputation spread, requests for his bread came from beyond Paris. He opened a bakery in London because it was close enough to visit on a day trip. To fulfill orders, he turned to FedEx for next-day delivery to stores, restaurants, and individuals in other countries. He also added other bakery products selectively—some other types of bread, brioches, tartelettes, pains au chocolat, and a special cookie—but preferred to focus on his basic loaf. "If you start to make too many things, that's extension," he said. "My motto is, Do things with intention, not with extension."

Tragically, Lionel and Irena died in a helicopter crash on November 1, 2002. Their daughter Apollonia, then just 18, immediately took over the family business and continues to manage it from her dorm room at Harvard University. "In my heart I always knew that I would take over the company and carry on the tradition," she says.

Today Poilâne produces about 7,000 loaves per day and ships about 20 percent of them to 40 countries. "The quantities may sound industrial, but the process is artisanal," says Apollonia, who has inherited her father's reverence for bread. "Bread is not just wheat, leaven, salt, and water; it is about language and culture, peace and revolution; its symbolism is central to literature and especially religion," she says. "For me, bread's relation to everyday life is what makes it thrilling."

Discussion Questions

1. What are the opportunities that Lionel Poilâne was able to discover and exploit? How can Apollonia build on this foundation?

2. What external factors led to the discovery and development of the opportunities pursued by Lionel Poilâne?

3. Why was Lionel Poilâne able to identify and pursue this opportunity while others were not?

4. What other types of businesses might be able to replicate the kinds of opportunities that Lionel Poilâne has been able to exploit?

Sources: Amanda Friedman, "Legendary Baker Poilâne Leaves Legacy of Passion for Bread," *Nation's Restaurant News*, January 13, 2003, p. 68; Tina Isaac, "Born Bread," *Evening Standard* (London, UK), June 16, 2006, p. 21; Gregory Katz, "Her Daily Bread," *American Way* magazine, July 15, 2005, p. 34; Paul Levy, "Obituary: Lionel Poilâne," *Independent* (London, UK), November 2, 2002, p. 22; John Lichfield, "Flour Power," *Independent* (London, UK), November 5, 2002, p. 4.5; Ron Lieber, "Give Us This Day Our Global Bread," *Fast Company*, February 2001, pp. 158+; and Poilâne Bakery website http://www.Poilâne.com (November 22, 2006).

exhibit 6.5   How to Achieve a Balanced Life

As you evaluate the 4Cs of a potential business opportunity, ask yourself the following questions. Use them for an annual check-up as well, to make sure that the business continues to meet your personal goals.

1. Does the business reflect my core values and what is truly important to me? Does it reflect my dreams?

2. Does the business allow me to spend enough time with my spouse and children? How will it affect my relationship with my partner?

3. When do I want to retire, and what is my exit plan at that point? Do I want to sell the business or scale back? What type of succession planning do I need to accomplish these goals?

4. What are my financial goals for the business? How much capital do I need to start and grow the company?

5. What are my personal financial goals, both now and in retirement, and can the business support them?

6. Do I have enough time for my friends? Time for my interests and hobbies?

7. Is my work fun?

8. Where do I want to live, and how does this opportunity fit with that plan?

9. Does the business allow me to maintain my health?

10. Does the business allow me to make a contribution to society and my community? Is this important to me?

Source: Inc.: The Magazine for Growing Companies by Staff. Copyright 2004 by Mansueto Ventures LLC. Reproduced with permission of Mansueto Ventures LLC in the format Textbook via Copyright Clearance Center.

It is important to ask yourself a number of questions about whether a particular opportunity, will be worth pursuing. These include broad-based questions that address major lifestyle issues you might ask when devising a life plan. Exhibit 6.5 lists some ideas to get you started.

Enterprisers 6.5

S.C.R.U.B.S.

Sue Callaway, a nurse in the neonatal intensive care unit at Children's Hospital and Health Center in San Diego, was tired of wearing the same thing to work every day. Since she was a child, Callaway had loved sewing. So she made herself scrubs from a pastel print. "Everyone wondered where I got them and wanted them, too,"

she recalls. She started Callaway Casuals in her bedroom, recruiting neighbors and friends to help make the scrubs.

At first, S.C.R.U.B.S—Simply Comfortable Really Unique Basic Scrubs—was a sideline for Callaway, who continued her nursing career. Within two years, however, she had 600
(continued)

customers. As order volume grew, Sue's husband, Rocky Cook, convinced her to turn her hobby into a business. He introduced her to Steve Epstein, a businessman with apparel manufacturing experience. "She pulled all these little cute tops out of her bag, and I was fascinated by them," says Epstein. "I saw it and a little bell went off in my head and said, 'This is a good idea.'"

In 1992, Callaway, Epstein, and their spouses pooled savings and loans from family and friends to form S.C.R.U.B.S. in the Southern California town of Santee, near San Diego. S.C.R.U.B.S. grew from a home-based business to 150 employees who handle sales, customer service, and some manufacturing functions. Callaway outsourced the sewing to another small company just a few miles away.

Callaway's scrubs became popular very quickly because they are made of 100 percent cotton and come in unusual colors and prints. At one time, institutional scrubs came only in white, green, or pale blue, and contained polyester. With some imagination, Callaway changed the look and feel of clothing for millions of health care workers.

Epstein helped Callaway make the transition from essentially a one-person operation to a thriving corporation. With his industry experience, he had the vision to see the potential for a sizable business based on the large number of health care workers. Callaway first targeted RNs and then expanded to include other health care workers, from dentists to veterinarians and physicians. "Sue's scrubs are unique and fill a need for something fun in a somber business like health care," he says.

Callaway and Cook decided to partner with Epstein and his wife Ida. "We bring four different pieces to the puzzle," Cook explains. "Sue is, in her creative way and also her personable way, the driving force behind it all. Steve is the real business mind. He brought with him computer systems, fabric knowledge, and garment industry knowledge. Ida is a personnel specialist."

To finance the start-up, the two couples tapped personal resources. They borrowed from friends and family, maxed out all their credit cards, and even sold vehicles that were paid off and leased vehicles to get the cash.

Two events converged to make the timing perfect for Callaway's success. New research showed that germs are not transported on clothing but on the hands. Therefore, uniforms don't have to be laundered at extremely high temperatures, which would fade bright colors quickly. Second, with an eye to cost cutting, hospitals began to allow health care personnel to choose their own uniforms. For years, hospitals had provided scrubs, which purchasing agents bought in solid colors in a cheaper cotton-polyester blend, which had a longer life.

Nurses also wanted more stylish uniforms that fit their personalities and lightened the atmosphere in a hospital. "It's a very difficult job, very stressful," says Cook. "If you can lighten the mood, it helps, not only for the infants that they work with and their parents, but older adult patients as well. It really starts a conversation, changes their day."

S.C.R.U.B.S. began as a mail-order catalog business, which suited a product with a highly targeted audience. As it grew, Callaway hired Kathy Murphy, who had direct mail marketing expertise. "I know before I mail what my break-even is on the catalog, and the break-even takes into account the cost of producing the catalog and mailing it, the cost of fulfilling the order, the cost of the building that we're in, and everybody's salary," says Murphy. She has a pretty good idea of the expected order rate before she mails catalogs and uses that to determine the number of catalogs in a particular mailing. "If I think it's a really strong list, I might mail 10,000. If I'm trying something new, like creative teachers—you know, teachers who teach kindergarten kids how to paint. I think they would love our scrubs, but it's really not our core market—I might only mail 5,000."

A good mail-order company needs three elements to succeed: a unique product, a good price, and good customer service. S.C.R.U.B.S. has all three. "It has very sound fundamentals," says Epstein. "We are extremely quality conscious. We don't take any shortcuts when it comes to quality. We are very customer service conscious, to the excess probably. We provide guarantees to the customer that make the purchase totally non-risk to them." One of the frustrations for customers buying from a catalog is not knowing if they will like the product. To solve that problem, S.C.R.U.B.S. developed a mailing envelope that also serves as a postage paid return envelope. The customer writes "exchange" or "refund only," reseals it, and drops it in the mailbox.

"A really small business owner might say, 'I cannot afford to give my customers $3 worth of postage if they don't like this.' You have to look past that," Callaway explains. "That customer will order 10 times more in the year maybe, or in the lifetime. Then you've got a true customer and you will make money on the customer."

S.C.R.U.B.S. was a good idea at the perfect time from a person who knew she needed help to grow. And grow S.C.R.U.B.S. did—from 11,000 catalogs mailed to 18 million in five years. What's on the horizon? "Quite a bit larger company," says Epstein. While continuing to grow the catalog business, the company opened several retail stores to capture another market segment—those who prefer to walk in and try on the clothing before buying.

For Callaway, S.C.R.U.B.S. is not just about the money. One of her greatest joys is to walk into a hospital and have a nurse say to her, "I love my scrubs." Making people happy and bringing color into their lives bring her great satisfaction. "You have to choose something that you really love, that you really enjoy doing. You'll wake up thinking it, go to bed thinking it. You'll need to spend a lot of hours, long hours every day. But that won't matter, because you'll love doing it."

Adds Cook, "It's just not a business for us that started because, 'Wow, there's a niche, maybe we can make a buck.' It's more of a, 'Wow, there's a business where we might be able to do something that we enjoy, that's good for someone and that creates a living.' "

Note: Sometimes bigger is not better. Since this case was taped for the PBS series *Small Business School*, Sue and her partner opened too many retail stores too fast and found themselves in big trouble. S.C.R.U.B.S. was bought by SmartPractice in July of 2000 and has restructured; Sue is still involved.

Discussion Questions

1. What other kinds of business concepts might Sue Callaway have recognized as a nurse in a hospital?

2. Why did Sue Callaway recognize S.C.R.U.B.S. as an opportunity versus other possible opportunities? What roles did environment, experience, and mindfulness play?

3. What is the business concept for S.C.R.U.B.S.? Demonstrate how it meets the 4 Cs test.

4. What other business concepts might S.C.R.U.B.S. pursue?

5. Why would Callaway and Cook decide to take on a business partner? How might they have been able to pursue their vision for getting into business without a partner?

Sources: Adapted with permission from Small Business School, the series on PBS, and at http://SmallBusinessSchool.com; also based on Sherry Chiger, "S.C.R.U.B.S—Crossing the Catalog Retail Line," *Catalog Age,* January 1998; and at Carla Goodman, "Medical Garb With A Smile—S.C.R.U.B.S. Grows to $16 Million-a-Year Business," *Nation's Business*, May 1999, both downloaded from http://www.findarticles.com.

6.6 Summary

1. A business idea becomes an opportunity when an enterpriser recognizes that a particular situation includes the 4 Cs: customers, consideration, connection, and commitment. Each element is essential to business success.

2. Enterprisers pay more attention to their environment and devote substantially more effort to gathering information, both from reading business and general periodicals and meeting other people.

3. Opportunities come from a variety of sources. Previous work experiences and changes in the business environments are among the most popular sources. Because each enterpriser brings different skills and experiences to the situation, the business that results will provide a unique set of benefits to customers.

4. An enterpriser can start exploring a business opportunity with any one of the 4 Cs and then move on to the others. Developing the idea into a viable business concept is a creative process that involves answering these key questions: Does this story hold up? Does it make sense? Do the 4 Cs of the story fit together? The business concept grid helps enterprisers visualize the relationship among the 4 Cs. Even if the customer, consideration, and connection elements are present, the opportunity is not likely to succeed without commitment. An enterpriser must therefore choose an opportunity that matches his or her goals and interests.

5. Peter Drucker's "systematic innovation" is a useful approach to environmental analysis. He believes that innovation is not just luck but requires discipline and hard work: knowing, not just doing. Drucker identifies seven sources of opportunity: unexpected occurrences, incongruities, process needs, changes in industry and market, demographic changes, changes in perception, and new knowledge.

6. Following trends is another good way to identify business opportunities. Many magazines report on trends, including *Red Herring,* which focuses on technologically based trends. Futurist Peter Schwartz also reports on trends. Analyzing current trends such as an aging population, obesity as a health issue, the impact of biotechnology, and economic trends and finding ways to respond to the changes helps enterprisers discover problems that need solving.

7. Enterprisers are not necessarily more creative than other people. However, they are better at leveraging their experience (background and skills). Sometimes experience can be a disadvantage, because it makes it harder to recognize opportunities that fall outside the enterpriser's field of experience.

8. Enterprisers can increase mindfulness (a form of paying attention) by being open to novelty, varying the way they do things, looking for differences, and viewing situations from multiple perspectives.

9. Enterprisers can make their own luck when they are open to new experiences and different outcomes. They reframe experiences, and even failures, to learn from them.

10. Successful enterprisers evaluate the fit between an opportunity and their personal goals before proceeding. Talking to other entrepreneurs in a particular field provides needed information, as well as potential mentors, to determine how well a business concept works for you.

Review Questions

1. Differentiate between a business idea and an opportunity. When does a business idea become an opportunity?

2. What are the 4 Cs? Define each briefly and explain how it contributes to business success.

3. A friend tells you that successful enterprisers are just luckier than other people. Based on information in the chapter, tell your friend why you disagree.

4. What is a business concept? Suggest several ways to develop business concepts. How can you evaluate a potential business concept?

5. How does the business concept grid help an enterpriser use the 4 Cs and show the relationship between them?

6. What does Peter Drucker mean by "systematic innovation?" What are his seven sources of opportunities, and how do they apply to environmental analysis?

7. Why is trend analysis a good way to find business opportunities? Where can you learn about current trends?

8. Discuss the pros and cons of leveraging your experience to identify business opportunities. How does using your experience relate to the 4 Cs?

9. Explain how mindfulness helps to discover opportunities. What strategies can you use to improve mindfulness? Include some specific examples in your answers.

10. What characteristics make some people appear luckier than others? Describe several ways to increase your luck.

11. Identify several strategies to evaluate the fit between a business opportunity and the enterpriser's personal goals. Develop a list of questions that would help you analyze a new business you might wish to pursue.

Applying What You've Learned

1. Read three of the following articles from *Inc.*:

   - "Educating Octavia": http://www.inc.com/magazine/19890601/5677.html
   - "Cookie Monsters": http://www.inc.com/magazine/19890201/5528.html
   - "The Next Big Thing": http://www.inc.com/magazine/19900701/5242.html
   - "Made in the U.S.A.": http://www.inc.com/magazine/19890101/5492.html
   - "Seeing Red": http://www.inc.com/magazine/19890501/5636.html

   Develop a spreadsheet that compares and contrasts the three start-up companies in the articles you selected across the following categories:

   (a) *Search Process*—What kind of search process did each entrepreneur use to find the idea for this business?
   (b) *Industry Experience*—Did the entrepreneurs in each case have industry experience similar to the opportunity they pursued?
   (c) *Time*—How much time did it take each entrepreneur to develop the idea into a business?
   (d) *Change*—Was there a significant change in the business opportunity over time?

2. Choose one of the companies you selected in Question 1 and answer the follow-

ing questions based on the article and additional information you can find online:

(a) How important are previous industry and work experience to discovering opportunities?

(b) When are industry and work experience likely to be important? Why?

(c) What are the characteristics of industries where previous experience is less likely to be a factor in discovering opportunities?

(d) What seem to be the characteristics of industries that have good opportunities to pursue?

(e) What are the characteristics of a good opportunity?

(f) Are the characteristics of an opportunity idiosyncratic, that is, are the characteristics of an opportunity based on the unique characteristics of the entrepreneurs who might discover them? Are you likely to spot the same opportunities as your classmates? Why, why not?

3. Develop a business concept grid for either a business you would like to start or one of the three companies you chose in Question 1.

4. The following two articles provide different viewpoints about the opportunity recognition process.

- "Where Really Bad Ideas Come From": http://www.inc.com/magazine/19981015/1114.html
- "Where Great Ideas Come From": http:// www. inc.com/magazine/19980401/908. html

   After reading these articles, answer the following questions.

(a) How are the sources of "bad" ideas different from sources of "good" ideas?

(b) What makes a bad idea? How does this compare to a good idea?

(c) What are the characteristics of good opportunities?

5. Evaluate the personal fit of the business concept you chose for Question 3. Use the questions in Exhibit 6.5 and any others you need to determine how feasible it would be for you to pursue this opportunity. Share your findings with the class.

6. Networking is a primary activity for identifying and developing your own opportunities. You can accomplish a "small win" by contacting "strangers" (individuals with whom you have not have any previous personal contact) about aspects of entrepreneurship that will benefit you. Contact three strangers about any aspect of entrepreneurship that is of benefit to you. These strangers can be entrepreneurs; experts, customers, suppliers in an industry that interests you; and venture enablers such as accountants, lawyers, and investors.

(a) Keep a log of these strangers. Provide a name and contact information (address, phone number, email) for each stranger.

(b) How did you get the name of this stranger? Why did you contact this stranger?

(c) What benefits were you hoping to offer this stranger? What benefits were you hoping this stranger would offer you?

(d) What other contacts was this stranger able to offer you to help you achieve your goals?

Enterprisers on the Web

1. A primary resource for business ideas is the U.S. Patent Office. Perform a search for patents by word, choosing an area of interest to you such as *toys*. Using the first two URLs in the list below, compile a list of many different ideas, as well as the names and addresses of individuals who have patented these ideas. Then look at a few of the other suggested sites for more ideas. After scanning these sites, consider what factors, besides the idea, will affect whether an opportunity can be developed into a successful business.

- USPTO Web Patent Database: http://www.uspto.gov/patft/index.html
  U.S. Patent Office database on patented inventions since 1976

- IBM Patent Search Database—The IBM Intellectual Property Network: http://www.patents.ibm.com/
  A user-friendly process for exploring patents and ideas

- National Inventors Hall of Fame: http://www.invent.org/
  Examples of successful inventors and assistance for finding and protecting ideas

- Inventor's Net: http://www.geocities.com/CapeCanaveral/3861/
  No-profit organization listing inventions as opportunities

- Institute of Inventors: http://members.aol.com/mikinvent/

  A United Kingdom site devoted to inventions that could be developed into businesses

2. Using several of the resources suggested in Entrepreneur.com's article, "Finding the Perfect Business Idea," http://www.entrepreneur.com/article/0,4621,304276,00.html, pick three ideas that interest you. How well does each meet the 4 Cs test? Evaluate them for personal fit using the questions in Exhibit 6.5.

3. Using three of the sites listed in Exhibit 6.2, prepare a brief overview of current economic trends.

4. Visit the Red Herring website, http://www.redherring.com. What are the top trends for the current year, and how do they compare to the ones in the chapter? (Registration, if required, is free.)

End Notes

1. Paul Farris, with assistance from Richard R. Johnson, Lauren Killgallon, and Kimberly Lockhart, "Case Study: Online Grocery: How the Internet Is Changing the Grocery Industry" (Charlottesville, VA: University of Virginia Darden School Foundation, 2002).

2. "Peapod, Inc. Opens 6th Market," Peapod, Inc., press release, March 17, 2004, http://www.peapod.com, and material from the "About Peapod" section of the corporate website, http://www.peapod.com (July 16, 2004).

3. Peter F. Drucker, *Innovation and Entrepreneurship* (New York: HarperCollins Publishers, 1985).

4. Ibid.

5. Hillary Johnson, "If at First You Don't Succeed," *Inc.*, July 2003, p. 102.

6. Adapted from James Canton, *The Extreme Future* (New York: Dutton, 2006), p. 2; and "The Top Ten Trends of the Extreme Future," Global Futurist website, http://globalfuturist.com (January 3, 2006).

7. Discussion based on Scott Shane, "Prior Knowledge and the Discovery of Entrepreneurial Opportunities," *Organization Science*, July/August 2000, pp. 448–469.

8. Ellen J. Langer, *The Power of Mindful Learning* (Cambridge, MA: Perseus Publishing, 1997), p. 4.

9. Ibid.

10. Norm Brodsky, "The Path to the Top," *Inc.*, February 2003, pp. 44–45.

11. Langer, *The Power of Mindful Learning*, p. 139.

chapter 7

Feasibility

Key Concepts

1. Feasibility analysis involves determining whether a business concept will actually work—that is, make money or satisfy the goals and interests of the enterpriser. It starts with an analysis of four key areas of a business model: revenue sources, cost drivers and cost structure, investment size, and critical success factors. Analyses of your market and sales and distribution strategy will provide knowledge about your customers, competitors, suppliers, substitutes for your product/service, and barriers to entry. A value analysis identifies the specific benefits that your customers perceive as important to them and demonstrates how well your products meet these customer needs.

2. Probably the most important factor in determining whether a new enterprise can start and grow is the commitment of the individuals involved. As you develop a detailed description of your customers, competition, and industry, and the way in which your enterprise will operate, you must seriously consider whether this kind of business meets your personal needs and goals.

3. Finally, a feasibility analysis will help you broadly identify the capital (human, financial, social) that you will need to start, operate, and grow your venture. Imagine all of the resources your business will need. This is taking a "grand tour" of your business. Often the easiest way to conduct a grand tour is to observe your competitors and make a detailed analysis of all financial, human, and social resources they seem to require to operate.

198

Suppose you major in Greek and Latin as an undergraduate, complete a law degree, and, after a few years in a law firm, discover you have some entrepreneurial interests. With some like-minded friends, you start a new mail-order catalog featuring high quality children's products. You don't have any knowledge or skills about this business, but you are willing to learn, you have plenty of determination to succeed, and you are willing to put as much work into the business as it requires. Your idea takes off, and you are so successful that one day, Robert Redford knocks on your door.

In this chapter's case study, we'll meet Harry Rosenthal, who developed Redford's business concept into the Sundance Catalog, a feasible business model that now results in annual catalog sales of $42 million a year.

7.0 Feasibility: Is This Project Doable?

Let's say that you were considering the following business concept: a delivery-only Mexican food business. Basically, you hope to become the Domino's Pizza of Mexican food. You know that there are many people who order pizza and Chinese food for delivery in your neighborhood, and a number of pizza and Chinese restaurants seem to be doing a brisk business in delivering food.

Is this concept worth pursuing? To answer this question, you will need to ask many more, among them:

- What do you have to know about your customers, their needs, and the business of preparing and delivering Mexican food?

- Might this concept be viable in other neighborhoods besides yours?

- What is the potential for this business?

- How much money do you think such a business might make?

Feasibility involves revising the business concept to test whether the business you are considering is "doable" and worth pursuing. The feasibility process is about answering the question, "Under what conditions will I go forward?" This process requires both discovery and adaptation: Will this business concept actually work? Will it make money, or satisfy the goals and interests of the enterpriser, and what aspects of the 4 Cs (customers, consideration, connection,

feasibility
Process of revising the business concept to test whether a business is worth pursuing and under which conditions.

commitment) must you change to improve the business concept and enhance success? We now add a fifth C to our analysis: capital. What are the capital resources—financial, human, and social—needed to make this business feasible? We'll discuss capital in greater detail later in this chapter.

It is important to realize that only under very rare circumstances does an enterpriser's initial business concept become the blueprint for the actual business. The entire process we describe in Chapters 6, 7, and 8 is extremely iterative. Enterprisers constantly change their original ideas as they gain more information through the concept development, feasibility, and business planning stages.

Appendix B provides a detailed framework to help you prepare a thorough feasibility study for your proposed business concept.

7.1 The Business Model: How Will This Concept Make Money?

business model

A plan that shows how all of the different major aspects of a business work together to generate a profit.

Every business operates on a **business model** that describes how the major aspects of that business—customer, consideration, connection, commitment—work together to generate a profit. Business models focus on the decisions a company makes to determine whether a particular way of doing business is profitable. A particular business is worth pursuing if it makes money—that is, the cost of providing a service or product to a customer is less than the income the customer provides. Even then, there are situations where a business concept could be profitable, but the enterpriser decides the returns and rewards of engaging in that kind of business are insufficient to proceed.

Some businesses use the same business model, while others don't. This is really a key idea in the feasibility process. Enterprisers now begin to move from just considering their own business model, to thinking about how their business model could be successful vis-à-vis other businesses and about those other business models.

No single formula works for all businesses in an industry. For example, thousands of businesses sell personal computers. How can so many businesses successfully compete and survive? There are a number of different business models in the personal computer industry. Some manufacture and sell directly to the end-user, like Dell. Others sell through third-party retailers. Yet others focus on specific types of customers.

A computer business focusing on doctors' offices would have a different configuration of customers, considerations, connections, and commitments than a computer business that focused on home computer users, insurance agents, or small retail stores. A doctor's office has specialized needs, such as a billing system for various types of insurance companies, a patient tracking system, and a system for keeping track of medical supplies. The factors that contribute to the profitability of a business that sells computers to medical offices will be different from one that sells computers to home computer users. Understanding these differences shows how various businesses in the same industry can succeed and presents an important lesson for enterprisers: individuals can be successful in many different ways, even within the same industry.

Understanding the Business Model

How do we determine the kind of business model for a proposed business? We do that through business model analysis. In developing a business concept, we begin to answer, very specifically, these three questions:

1. Who is the customer?

2. What does the customer want? (consideration)

3. How is this consideration going to be provided? (connection)

In developing a business model, we add a fourth question:

4. Can you make money doing this?

In developing a business model, the enterpriser works through a framework to consider how money is made for a particular concept considered. In the rest of the chapter, we demonstrate how one such framework can help an enterpriser analyze and refine a business model.[1]

Basically, we examine four key areas to determine how a business makes money:

*   *Revenue sources:* All the revenue streams a particular business model will produce, and the source, size, significance, and growth potential of each.

*   *Cost drivers:* The cost structure of a business model (fixed, variable, recurring, etc.), relative importance, and how it may change over time.

*   *Investment size:* Amount and timing of investment to produce positive cash flow, including cash required for startup and working capital.

*   *Critical success factors (CSFs):* Elements that have the greatest impact on the company's becoming profitable.

Let's look at each of these factors and the trade-offs they involve. Exhibit 7.1 is a summary of the questions an enterpriser should ask about each area to fully understand how it affects the business.

Revenue Sources

First, an enterpriser must consider where the many different sources of revenue from customers are coming from. These fall into four broad categories:

*   Single stream: one main revenue source

*   Multiple streams: significant revenues from several products or services

*   Interdependent: Sale of related products to generate revenues from other products

*   Loss leader: several revenue sources, but not all are equally profitable, and some may actually incur a loss while promoting sales of other, more profitable, items or services

Remember the concept grid in Chapter 6 involving selling candy at a movie theater (see page 174)? Let's use the movie theater as an example of how a business may have different sources of revenue (see Exhibit 7.2).

exhibit 7.1

Key Questions for Business Model Analysis

Sources of Revenue

1. What kind of revenue stream does this model produce?
2. If a loss leader revenue stream, how will losses be covered by other revenue streams?

Revenue Model

1. Do I have a single or hybrid revenue model?
2. How quickly will revenues increase?
3. How long does it take to collect cash following a sale?

Cost Drivers

1. What are the cost drivers of the business model?
2. How much volume can be supported with the fixed cost base?
3. Are the primary cost drivers expected to change over time?

Cost Structure

1. What are the largest cost centers for the business model?
2. What is the relative size and importance of each cost center?
3. Do any of the cost centers deliver a strategic cost advantage?

Investment Size

1. What is the maximum financing the business needs, and when is the cash needed?
2. When does positive cash flow occur?
3. When will the company reach cash breakeven?

Critical Success Factors (CSFs)

1. What are the CFSs of this business model?
2. How do these affect revenues and costs and cash?
3. What happens if any of these CSFs change?

Source: The business model analysis presented in this chapter is based on a Harvard Business School teaching note: Richard G. Hammermesh, Paul W. Marshall, and Taz Pirmohamed, "Note on Business Model Analysis for the Entrepreneur" (Boston: Harvard Business School Pubhlishing, 2002).

Therefore, when you are thinking about the revenues your business concept will generate, you need to ask yourself these two questions:

1. What kinds of revenue streams will my business have?

2. If one is a loss leader revenue stream, how will other revenue streams cover the losses?

The second consideration centers on which of these revenue streams the business actually captures. Identifying all the various revenue streams in the business is developing a **revenue model** for the business. Businesses can generate revenue in five ways: subscription membership, volume- or unit-based pricing, advertising sales, licensing fees, and transaction fees.

Let's say that you were planning to open a DVD rental business in your local neighborhood. You will need to think about how quickly you will generate revenues and from what sources, including

revenue model
All the revenue streams a business will generate from sources such as subscriptions/ memberships, volume- or unit- based pricing, advertising sales, licensing fees, and transaction fees.

exhibit 7.2	**Revenue Sources for a Movie Theater**

Category	Revenue Source
Single stream	Sale of movie tickets only.
Multiple streams	Sales of movie tickets, snacks; revenue from video game machines.
Interdependent	The multiple revenue streams are interdependent; if more people buy tickets, snack sales will be higher.
Loss leader	Paying 100 percent of ticket revenues to a movie studio during a movie's first two weeks because the revenues generated from selling snacks will make up for the expense of showing the movie; the movie is the loss leader.

- *Selling memberships:* This membership fee could be a one-time fee that gives customers the right to rent DVDs on an individual basis or a monthly membership fee that allows customers to rent an unlimited number of DVDs each month, which would then be your major revenue source.

- *Charging a rental fee per DVD (volume- or unit-based revenue stream):* The more DVDs that a customer rents, the more revenue you earn.

- *Selling ads:* You could offer free DVDs if customers were willing to watch DVDs that had ten minutes of advertising at the beginning. Advertisers could then pay your business a fee to place ads on your DVDs.

- *Licensing* your successful business model to other enterprisers.

- *Earning transaction fees:* You might set up an area where customers could sell used DVDs on a consignment basis and take a fee for each one sold.

When you are thinking about your business concept, ask yourself these three questions:

1. Do I have a single or hybrid revenue model?

2. How quickly will revenues increase?

3. How long does it take to collect cash following a sale?

Using the DVD store as an example, you would have a single revenue model if you generated revenues only from renting DVDs. You would have a hybrid model if you charged a membership fee to join and a rental fee for each DVD.

Internet-Based Revenue Models

The Internet and electronic commerce (e-commerce) have opened up new avenues for enterprisers to launch businesses and to expand existing businesses by providing additional revenue sources. At the same time, the Internet requires companies and even entire industries to rethink their business models. Just a decade ago, for example, most retailers operated with a very simple business model and limited revenue streams. They sold products to their customers at a physical location or through catalogs, with orders placed by mail or phone. As the Internet's popularity and sophistication grew, retailers created informational websites. Soon they recognized the power of bringing the store to the consumer electronically and developed merchant business models such as online store-fronts, either to supplement traditional stores or as their primary sales channel. These models include the following:

- Virtual merchants, who sell a variety of goods and services from many different manufacturers only through the Internet (Amazon.com, Overstock.com).

- Catalog merchants, who reach customers through traditional media, such as a mail-order catalogue or telemarketing, and also have websites for online browsing and ordering (Avon, Lillian Vernon).

- Clicks-and-mortar companies, with both physical locations and a Web presence (Powells Books (powellsbooks.com), Macy's (macys.com), Target (target.com), etc.).

- Bit vendors who sell and distribute digitally based products, including soft-ware and music, through the Web (iTunes.com, eBooks.com, Symantec).

- Direct merchants who sell the majority of the products they manufacture through the Internet (Dell Computer).

The ability to network with other retailers led to more revenue options and business models, such as paid advertising with clickable links to other sites and subscription models. General portal websites such as Yahoo.com, Google.com, and MySpace.com entice users to use their sites as their first stop on the Web. Advertisers who seek large numbers of Internet participants may pay the portal to post text- or graphical-based advertisements, either on the home page or on specialized pages such as Yahoo's Finance, Entertainment, Autos, or Travel pages. Classified ad sites such as Monster.com for job listings and Craigslist.com for a broad array of goods and services are just two of the many sites in this category. Subscription models provide information that users pay for on a monthly or annual basis. *The Wall Street Journal's* online edition, www.WSJ.com, is one of the most successful content subscription sites. Networking sites such as Classmates.com offer access to other individuals who share the same interests or experiences. It offers some free services, but others are available only to subscribers. This two-tiered approach is often used by financial sites as well. Affiliate models generate revenues through referral fees and commissions when a user clicks through to the affiliated merchant. For example, an online parenting community that has a book review section may establish an affiliate relationship with Barnes and Noble (www.bn.com) and will receive a percentage of all purchases made when members link to bn.com from the site.

More complex models emerged once these early models demonstrated their success. Companies can also choose from several different types of market-making (brokerage) and community models, as summarized in Exhibit 7.3. Community models generate revenue through advertising on their sites, user fees, or payments for specialized content.[2]

exhibit 7.3   **Second-Generation Web Revenue Sources**

Business Model	Forms of Model Implementation	Description	Examples
Market-Making (Brokerage)			
	Auction	Website where sellers list products on which buyers place bids. Auction site host receives a fee from the seller once an auction has been completed.	eBay
	Marketplace exchange	Electronic exchanges for business to consumer (B2C) or business to business (B2B) markets that facilitate buying and selling. Exchange host receives a fee for facilitating these transactions.	Travelocity (B2C) offers flights, hotels, and rental cars from numerous vendors; ChemConnect (B2B) is industry-based exchange.
	Buy/sell fulfillment	Website that takes orders to buy or sell products at a specific price and receives a fee or commission from the seller for completing the transaction.	CarsDirect.com
	Demand fulfillment	Online matching site where buyers make a firm bid for a product or service. If a seller meets the buyer's price, the buyer is obligated to complete the transaction.	Priceline.com
	Virtual mall	Online hosting service for other merchants; host's revenue may come from site set-up, listing fees for products or services, and transaction fees for products and services sold.	
	Transaction broker	A third-party intermediary.	
Community			
	Social networks	Websites where users can meet others who might share some common interest.	Facebook.com, Myspace.com, Friendster.com
	Open source	Develops products or services (typically software) that other users may modify, enhance, and support.	Red Hat
	Open content	Based on community generated content, where users can modify current content that is posted.	Wikipedia
	Blogs	Web logs or online journals where individuals or companies post information; blogs that create substantial traffic sell advertisements or generate revenue through specific links to other sites.	TechCrunch.com (posts about new Internet products and companies); BeautyAddict.com (cosmetics); Gizmodo.com (cutting-edge consumer electronics and gadgets)

Companies also combine models. A merchant or subscription business may also incorporate the advertising model. The Power to the People box describes how Threadless.com and its sister companies at skinnyCorp combine community and virtual merchant models.

Threadless.com

Imagine a T-shirt company that in just six years generated estimated revenues of $25 million and profits of $7 million—without a design, sales, or marketing staff. You'd be describing Threadless.com, brainchild of Jake Nickell and Jacob DeHart. The "two Jakes," as they are often called, were studying design—Nickell at the Illinois Institute of Art in Chicago and DeHart at Purdue University—when they met at an Art Institute of Chicago design course in 1999. Both had submitted designs for a T-shirt competition, which Nickell won. Nickell then decided to try the idea out on a larger scale.

With each contributing $500, the pair launched Threadless.com. The premise was simple: people submit T-shirt designs for posting on the Threadless.com website (http://www.threadless.com). The community votes for a week, and Threadless produces the highest-scoring shirts and sells them at the site. "In the beginning, we wanted to create an outlet for designers," explains Nickell. "It turned into this great business, and now we've extended the model to ties, music, cocktails. ... In 10 years, who knows where we might be?"

The idea caught on quickly, although for the first two years the founders took no salary and supported themselves with full-time jobs in Web development. Today Threadless has more than 400,000 registered users and is growing at about 20,000 new members each month. More than 150 designs pour in from around the world every day, with 90 chosen for the weekly contest. Community members vote on a one-to-five scale. The top five to seven designs become part of Threadless' inventory, with most shirts selling for about $15 to $17 each. Threadless orders print runs of 500 to 1,500 of each design from its screen-printing company. By year-end 2006, the company was selling about 80,000 shirts a month.

The winning designers receive a $1,500 cash award, plus $500 in Threadless merchandise credit. Customers who refer new buyers or send in pictures of themselves modeling Threadless shirts earn points toward store credit.

Threadless follows four basic rules. "We let the community create the content," explains DeHart. "We let the community build itself—no advertising. We let the community help with the business; we add features based on user feedback. And we reward members of the community for participating."

The high level of customer involvement is unique and keeps costs low, as does outsourcing the T-shirt production. Nickell and DeHart developed the company's order fulfillment software in-house. Profit margins run about 30 percent. "Most of the energy comes from how fast the product line is changing," says Nickell. "There's something for users to do every day—see which new designs are out, score the latest submissions, post a blog entry. It's just a very active community."

skinnyCorp currently employs about 20 people, mostly to fill orders. It operates on the basis that work should be fun, and the two Jakes are committed to the idea that having fun is more important than growth or maximizing profits. For example, they turned down offers from several major retailers to carry Threadless shirts. "We want to keep things simple and about the community," says Nickell.

Experts praise Nickell and DeHart. "It's a brilliant application of participatory culture," says Ted Byfield, associate chair of the communication, design, and technology department at Parsons. The New School for Design. Adds Harvard Business School professor Karim Lakhani, "They've recognized that knowledge and innovation reside outside the firm. People spend gazillions of dollars trying to figure out what demand is going to be. These guys have said, 'We're not even gonna try—let the community decide.' "

Threadless.com's success led the two Jakes to form a parent company, skinny-Corp, and experiment with other community-based concepts:

- 15 Megs of Fame: A music site where emerging underground musicians can post sound tracks. Visitors can listen to the music, download free audio clips, and post comments.

- Naked & Angry: Creates high quality clothing from fabric patterns submitted and chosen by the brand's audience.

- ExtraTasty: An interactive drink site with inventive bar recipes.

Another site, OMG Clothing, allowed people to submit just slogans rather than designs. It was recently merged into Threadless. In response to member demand, Threadless now offers a women's style shirt, children's sizes, sweatshirts, and hoodies for some designs.

In late 2006, skinnyCorp entered into a deal with Insight Partners, a venture capital firm, to provide funding for future expansion into other types of merchandise. However, the community remains fundamental to skinnyCorp's activities. "We don't make any moves without consulting the community."

Discussion Questions

1. Describe Threadless.com's unique business model. Why do you think it has been so successful and also profitable? Suggest other types of products that could use this model and some which could not use it effectively and explain why.

2. Who are the customers for Threadless.com? What are the benefits that different kinds of customers receive from Threadless.com? How does Threadless.com go about making money by providing these various benefits?

3. What are the cost drivers for Threadless.com and skinnyCorp? How do these cost drivers compare to a retail store selling T-shirts?

4. How has the commitment of the founders changed over the life of Threadless. com? Could the founders have predicted at the beginning of this venture how it would have evolved?

Sources: Based on Brandon Copple, "40 under 40 2006: Jake Nickell and Jacob DeHart," *Chicago Business*, October 18, 2006, http://www.chicagobusiness.com; Darren Dahl, "Nice Threads," *Southwest Airlines Spirit*, December 2006, p. 8694; Jeff Howe, "Amateurs Rank," *Print*, November/December 2006, pp. 298–300; skinnyCorp website, http://www.skinnycorp.com (December 22, 2006); Brad Spirrison, "skinnyCorp to Purchase New Threads with Venture Deal," *Chicago Sun-Times*, December 11, 2006, p. 60; and William C. Taylor, "To Charge Up Customers, Put Customers in Charge," *New York Times*, June 18, 2006. p. BU5 (L).

As you will see in the next section, you will have a number of costs associated with starting your business that will need to be covered. Generating sales and collecting cash will therefore become very important in order to pay these expenses.

Cost Drivers and Cost Structure

Now that you understand the sources of revenue for your business, you must identify the costs of providing goods and services to the enterprise's customers. It is very important to recognize that the kinds of cost drivers and cost structures of the enterprise might not be directly linked to the revenue model of the business. For example, the development of a computer game is a fixed cost, and the cost structures for the computer game are primarily payroll centered (paying programmers and designers to create the computer game) and facilities costs (the space/rent and computers to house these people and help them develop the game). There will also be minimal costs to print disks or deliver the game over the Internet. So in this business model, the majority of costs are fixed while the revenue model is likely to be volume based and therefore variable. Whether the company sells one game or ten million games, the costs are nearly the same. A game company, then, hopes to score big with a game that will sell millions of units. Once the company covers its fixed costs (reaches a breakeven point) nearly all additional revenues flow to the bottom line as profits.

A business can incur four types of costs:

- Fixed

- Semi-variable

- Variable

- Nonrecurring

fixed costs
Costs that do not vary with sales volume, such as rent.

variable costs
Costs that vary directly and proportionally with sales such as raw materials and shipping costs.

semi-variable costs
Costs that change, but not in direct relationship to sales volume.

nonrecurring costs
Fixed costs that occur only once during the life of a business.

Fixed costs are constant and not tied to the volume of goods or services produced. For example, if you were thinking of opening a restaurant, the fixed portion of your expenses would be the equipment and building. You would have these costs whether you served one customer or thousands. **Variable costs** change in relationship to your sales volume. In a restaurant, your variable costs would be the costs of the food and drink served. Every meal ordered would be composed of specific ingredients that you could specifically "cost out"—that is, you could determine the exact cost of the meat, vegetables, and other food products that go into that meal. **Semi-variable costs** change depending on certain levels of revenue generated. For example, the cost of a waiter in a restaurant is a semi-variable cost. Each waiter can serve only so many tables during a specific time period, so at times when the restaurant is crowded, such as noon to 2 PM, you would need more waiters. If you know that one waiter can handle 10 tables and your typical lunch crowd fills 12 tables, you would need two waiters, even though you have the capacity to serve 20 tables. **Nonrecurring costs** are often fixed costs that occur only once during the life of a business. For example, the purchase of your kitchen equipment—the stove, range, freezer, and cooler—is likely to be both a fixed cost and a nonrecurring cost.

The *cost drivers*—anything that affects total costs—in your business model focus on the timing of those costs and the relationship of costs to changes in revenues. As with revenue streams, you must ask several key questions about the cost drivers of your business model:

1.   What are the cost drivers of the business model?

2.   How much volume can be supported with the fixed cost base?

3.   Are the primary cost drivers expected to change over time?

The *cost structure* of your business model explores the kinds of costs your business might have. There are five broad categories of costs:

- *Direct:* Cost for individuals who are actually providing a service or producing a good for the customer.

- *Indirect (support):* Cost of individuals not directly involved in providing a good or service, but help the organization provide the service or goods.

- *Inventory:* Cost of material necessary to provide a good or service.

- *Space/Rent:* Costs to buy or rent facilities to house the business.

- *Marketing/Advertising:* Costs to attract, acquire, and retain customers.

A computer consultant working with a client or a worker on an automobile engine assembly line would be a direct cost. Members of the accounting, purchasing, and human resources departments in an organization are support costs. Steel would be an inventory cost in the manufacturing of an automobile body; pepperoni would be an inventory cost for a pizza restaurant. All businesses need a location and must make rent or mortgage payments. Some businesses, such as a restaurant, may need more space than a computer consulting business; the computer consultant might be able to operate the business out of her or his home or car. Finally, most businesses will incur marketing and advertising costs. For example, a mail-order catalog business is likely to have a significant cost for mailing catalogs and for advertising to bring the company's catalog to potential customers' attention.

Each business, then, will have a different cost structure. The three primary questions to ask about the business model for your concept are

1.   What are the largest cost centers for the business model?

2.   What is the relative size and importance of each cost center?

3.   Do any of the cost centers deliver a strategic cost advantage?

Investment Size

Some enterprises need more resources than others. For example, the costs to build a 100-seat, sit-down, gourmet restaurant might be $5 million, while the cost to build a mobile hot dog stand might be less than $5,000. And that $5,000 hot dog stand might generate more profits (revenues minus costs) than the $5 million restaurant. Now you must make an estimate for the investment necessary to support your business concept and its configuration of customers, connections, and considerations. This requires asking the following three questions:

1. What is the maximum financing the business needs, and when is the cash needed?

2. When does positive cash flow occur?

3. When will the company reach cash breakeven?

For example, let's assume that the total investment to open the hot dog stand and operate it for six months is $8,000. You would first need to buy the stand for $5,000 and obtain needed permits and licenses to operate a food stand in the desired location. Then you will have to purchase supplies such as a cash-box, paper goods, fuel for cooking, and inventory—hot dogs, buns, condiments, and beverages. You may want to print flyers to advertise your stand. And if you don't want to be tied to the stand during all the hours it is open, you will have to pay someone to staff the stand in your absence. Exhibit 7.4 summarizes the investment needs for this business venture and the timeline for the cash infusions.

At this point, you may not have the financial skills necessary to make accurate estimates of these costs. Don't worry. We will explore these issues in great detail in later chapters. For now, you should be aware of all the costs involved with providing your products or services to your customers. It is very important for you

exhibit 7.4   **Timeline for Financial Resources to Open a Hot Dog Stand**

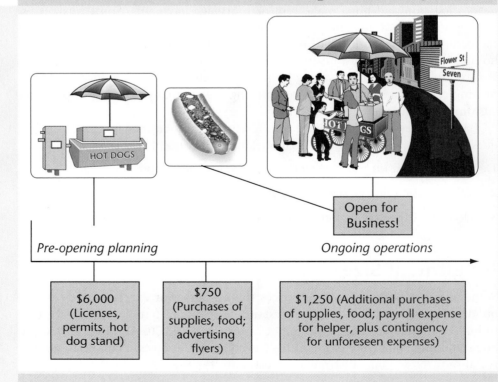

Pre-opening planning

Ongoing operations

Open for Business!

| $6,000 (Licenses, permits, hot dog stand) | $750 (Purchases of supplies, food; advertising flyers) | $1,250 (Additional purchases of supplies, food; payroll expense for helper, plus contingency for unforeseen expenses) |

to explore how other enterprises develop estimates of their revenues, costs, and investment requirements.

Critical Success Factors

Critical success factors (CSFs) are operational functions or competencies that a company must have in order for it to be profitable. Each business will have a set of critical success factors that are necessary for the business to be successful. For instance, a CFS in a high-end restaurant is a chef who can create wonderful innovative and delicious dishes, night after night, and in peak demand situations like the dinner hours of 7 PM to 9 PM. A chef who can make wonderful meals may be unable to manage a kitchen staff of eight assistants who need to serve 50 such wonderful meals an hour. Without this ability to deliver all the meals patrons order, a high-end restaurant could not charge high prices and bring in enough customers to make the business work.

critical success factors (CSFs) *Operational functions or competencies that a company requires to be profitable.*

A critical success factor might also be a piece of equipment (a restaurant needs a fully-equipped kitchen), a location (successful gas stations are typically located on streets with a lot of traffic and easy in and out access), or special knowledge (a patent or knowledge about how to make a particular product). The three major questions to ask about your critical success factors (CFS) are:

1. What are the CFSs of this business model?

2. How do these affect revenues, costs, and cash?

3. What happens if any of these changes?

You shouldn't be discouraged if you can't provide answers to all of the questions posed in the business model analysis. The rest of this chapter and the next provide a framework for getting answers to these issues and for helping you begin to take the actions necessary to take your ideas and make them real—and profitable to you!

7.2 Customers: Market Analysis

Most enterprisers will be developing businesses in markets where an identifiable base of customers *and* competitors serving those customers already exists. Most new businesses offer new products and services to an established group of customers who have unmet or insufficiently met needs. Determining sales forecasts for markets and customers that don't yet exist is a quick way to create an unviable business. To survive, all businesses need *identifiable* customers who will buy their products. If your business depends on developing a base of customers over a long period of time, consider whether you will have sufficient resources to undertake this process.

In addition, all businesses have identifiable competitors. Therefore, another important component of a market analysis is understanding your competition. Once you know who your customers and competitors are, you can describe the characteristics of the market you wish to enter. Then you should perform research using industry studies and interview industry experts who can validate forecasts for future changes in the growth of the market.

Who Will Buy?

Finding customers involves identifying specific individuals who require specific considerations through specific connections. The concept grid helps you answer a critical question: Under what conditions will customers buy?

You can learn about your customers in two ways: primary and secondary research. *Primary research* is what you learn first-hand from specific individuals such as potential and existing customers, experts who study your market, and suppliers and distributors to competitors in your market. The goal of primary research is understanding what will be necessary to sell to specific customers. Many individuals (potential customers) will often tell you that you have a good idea. What you want to discover from your primary research is whether they will *actually buy* from you. You want to get beyond compliments to contracts.

Secondary research is what you learn from others—for example, learning about your market and how your competitors already serve the customers you hope to attract. You can often find this type of information in articles and research materials at the library and on the Internet.

In testing for customers, you want to get individuals to engage in "phantom sales," to sign prospective purchase orders that indicate their willingness to buy if such a product or service was available to them. Many businesses are started because a potential customer was willing to give an enterpriser money up-front to develop a product or provide a service that the customer wanted. How sure are you that customers will actually give you money for the product or service you want to provide? Ideally, they will give you money up-front, because they are committed to you and your business concept. An acceptable test is being able to answer the question, "How sure are you that customers will buy?"

Who Is Your Competition?

Individuals who plan to sell a new product or service often believe that they have no competition and that their new company will be wildly successful because no other competitor offers a similar product or service. WRONG! *All products and services have competition. All products and services have substitutes.* What entrepreneurs create are businesses that offer products and services that offer *advantages* over other competitors. It is rare that a business can create a product or service that customers will immediately purchase without comparing it to other products or services already on the market. If you cannot identify your competition or substitutes, you need to devote substantial efforts to this task.

The intellectual framework that many enterprisers have used for exploring the competitive dynamics of their industry is Michael E. Porter's *Competitive Strategy*, published in 1980 by the Free Press. This book uses information from industrial economics to specify a set of rules that govern whether a particular company can/will be successful in a particular industry. One of the primary tenets of this book is that the profitability of a business is often determined by the characteristics of its industry. For example, nearly all companies in the pharmaceutical industry are very profitable, while companies that are in industries such as farming and coal mining are less likely to be very profitable. What are some of the factors that determine whether an industry will be profitable? How might a business take advantage of the structure of its industry to develop a "sustainable competitive advantage"?

What Drives Industry Competition?

Porter describes five forces that drive industry competition: direct competitors, barriers to entry, substitute products/services, the power of suppliers, and the power of customers. These are shown in Exhibit 7.5.

Your direct competitors are your *rivals*. The degree of rivalry in your industry varies. Industries that are more competitive (have lower overall profitability—i.e., lower margins) are likely to be composed of firms that have the following characteristics:

* Numerous or equally balanced competitors

* Slow industry growth

* High fixed costs

* Lack of differentiation or switching costs

exhibit 7.5   **Five Forces of Industry Competition**

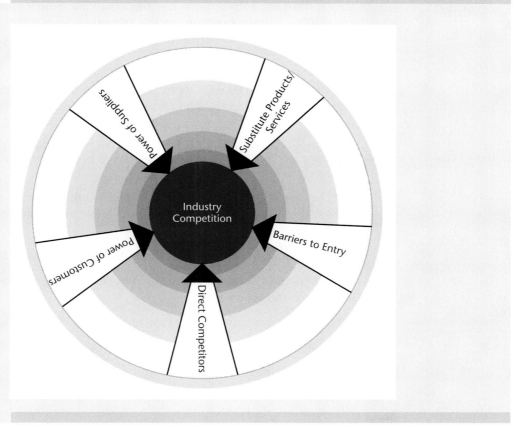

- Capacity augmented in large increments

- Diverse competitors, where each company seems to be playing by different rules of the game

- High strategic stakes

- High exit barriers such as high fixed costs to exit, specialized assets, emotional barriers, government and social restrictions, and strategic interrelationships

Barriers to entry refers to ways to keep possible new competitors out of your industry. High barriers to entry should lead to high profits. As shown in Exhibit 7.5, barriers to entry might include economies of scale, product/service differentiation, capital requirements, switching costs, access to distribution channels, government policy, cost disadvantages independent of scale (such as proprietary technologies or products), location, and "the learning curve."

Substitute products or services perform the same function as the products/ services in your industry. For example, a new boat, a ski vacation in Colorado, or a home computer might all be considered as substitutes for a home audio/video entertainment system; all provide a form of recreation. Substitute products/ services can become a major factor in determining the profitability of an industry if the price/performance ratio changes between your product/services and the substitutes. For example, could airfares decline to the point where the costs of a ski vacation are substantially less than they are now? Could the cost of boats decline? How will the functions, price, and capabilities of home computers affect sales of home audio/video entertainment systems? If the value of your product/ services is perceived to decline relative to other substitutes, your industry will become less profitable.

Customer power is the ability to drive prices lower, insist on higher quality and service, and create bidding wars among various competitors. Customers are powerful if

- Purchases are perceived as "standard" or undifferentiated.

- There are few switching costs.

- If customers can integrate backward (do what you do, such as buy direct from the manufacturer or rep, and service and install the products themselves).

- If the industry's products/services are unimportant to the buyer.

Supplier power occurs if vendors can unilaterally raise prices or reduce quality. A supplier group is powerful if:

- The supplier group is more concentrated than the industry it sells to.

- It does not have to contend with other substitutes to sell to your industry.

- Your industry is not an important customer to them.

- The supplier's product is a critical input for the success of your industry.

- The supplier's products have switching costs.

- The supplier group can forward integrate (do what you do, set up their own retail stores).

At this point, the details of the dynamics of an industry can seem overwhelming. There are so many different industry considerations that can affect how a firm can be successful. Exhibit 7.6 shows all of the competitive forces that affect your purchase of this textbook. You may have purchased this book from the college bookstore. The bookstore was one of a number of competitors that had an opportunity to sell you this book. Maybe another bookstore around your campus sells textbooks. These bookstores are direct competitors of each other. They have a physical location for you to go and purchase books for your classes. They likely purchase books from a book wholesaler, or from the book manufacturer at the same discount. Their competitive advantage is likely to be their closeness to your college, so it is convenient for you to drop by their stores, and, their ability to get information from professors about what books will need to be ordered for upcoming classes. So the local college bookstores are likely to have the books you want at a convenient location for you to purchase.

Yet you have alternatives to purchasing your books from the local bookstore. You could use the Internet and see whether you could purchase the book, perhaps at a lower price, from a company like Amazon.com, or you could search eBay and see whether there were individuals who had your book for sale, or you could talk to your friends and find out whether there might be someone who took the class already and wanted to sell you the used book. Indeed, you can substitute any one of these options for the campus bookstore to obtain the book you need.

Now let's broaden our discussion to include all the textbook publishers who publish business books for the college market. You are likely to have many

exhibit 7.6   **Customer-Stage Model for Mexican Food Delivery Business**

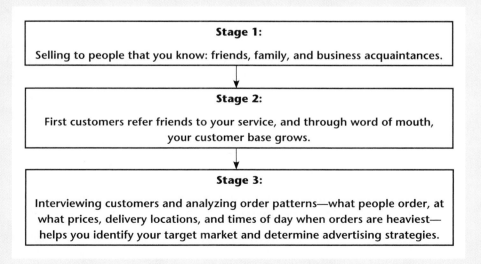

options for purchasing books on the topic of enterprise. One aspect of purchasing a college textbook is its selection by the professor. In doing so, the professor creates a monopoly for that particular book for his or her students.

As a supplier of textbooks, a textbook publisher would like to generate incentives to insure that college instructors are more likely to select and require its book for a class. The publisher might provide the teacher with additional materials (teaching manual, slides, Internet support, a help line, and other added value for students and teachers) that help to use the book more effectively. The costs to develop these additional materials can often be expensive, and the price of a new textbook can be very high to cover these costs.

Once students use a book for a class, they have the option of selling their used books to others. A textbook publisher would get no revenue from this sale to help cover the costs of developing ancillary materials that helped convince a professor to select the book for the course. This creates yet another dilemma for the publisher—over time, the number of used textbooks increases, and sales of these used textbooks compete with sales of the manufacturer's new textbooks.

You can begin to see, then, how the competitive dynamics of book publishers, book distributors, bookstores, and book buyers can get complicated. These differences and dynamics are what create opportunities for enterprisers to pursue. For example, a number of new enterprises sell used textbooks on the Internet, thereby enabling buyers to avoid the price mark-up that a retail bookstore might require. Some enterprisers act as a clearing house for students who want to sell books, while others buy review copies of new textbooks from college professors and then sell these books to bookstores or online.

Enterprisers might also consider better ways to distribute and sell the information that textbooks provide. For example, an enterprise might sell "electronic textbooks" that students purchase and read online. These could be customized to follow a professor's syllabus by reordering chapters or only including those chapters that the instructor wishes to cover. Indeed, a textbook company might sell textbooks both as "hard copies," or as electronic versions.

While new entrants are always trying to spot opportunities to exploit an industry, it is likely that companies who are already players in that industry (your rivals, suppliers, customers, and substitutes for your specific products/services) are also thinking of new ways to meet their customer's needs. How, then, are you likely to compete?

Competitive Strategies

To have a competitive strategy, an enterpriser must find or create a position that he or she can defend and maintain. The primary measure of a successful competitive strategy is your company's ability to generate profits. Porter defines two basic generic competitive strategies:

1. *Low cost:* Sell the most for less (economies of scale) to become the industry's low cost producer. Strategies to achieve this objective require finding all possible cost advantages such as economies of scale, proprietary technology, and preferential access to raw materials.

2. *Differentiation:* Have a unique product/service customer niche that other companies will have difficulty duplicating or acquiring. Such uniqueness commands a higher price.

When you consider the college textbook industry, you can see how different businesses pursue these two different strategies of low cost (eBay, Amazon.com) or differentiation (your local bookstore). As you consider your business concept and model, you need to think about whether there will be enough customers for your enterprise to generate income to both pay expenses and provide you with some income, as well. Is the potential size of the market large enough for you to make the kind of profit that you would like?

For example, if you decided at the end of the semester to sell only your own used textbooks on eBay, the revenue you received would unlikely be enough to consider living on these proceeds. To expand the idea and begin an enterprise selling used college textbooks, you would need to consider where to get a supply of used books as well as where you might find potential buyers for these books, whether you could purchase enough books at a price lower than you could sell the books to others, *and* if you could cover all of the costs of coordinating this effort, mailing the books, keeping track of the process, and so forth.

The underlying issues that an entrepreneur must explore when considering market size and competition include such questions as:

*   Is the market large enough (are there enough customers) for your business to earn the kind of profits to warrant investment?

*   How are you different (better) than your competitors?

*   What do you do better than other competitors?

*   What will it take for a competitor to gain that same competitive advantage as your business?

An ability to thoroughly describe the characteristics of the industry that your company will be competing in, as well as the details about the competitors in this industry, will help convince others about the thoughtfulness and thoroughness of your preparation to start your company. Naïve entrepreneurs often underestimate the power of competitors and companies offering substitutes to change and adapt their products and services to meet the competitive threats of new entrants. They also underestimate the loyalty of customers to established companies, goods, and services.

One way to consider the value of conducting a thorough industry analysis is to view the descriptions of competitors and substitutes as background for celebrating the benefits of your company's products and services. The more detail you can provide about other products and services on the market, the more information you have available to make valid and insightful comparisons with your company's offerings.

Often entrepreneurs fail to admit that their competition is formidable and offers products and services that provide many benefits to customers. They should be honest when they describe their competitors and substitutes. Smart entrepreneurs recognize their competitors' strengths as well as weaknesses. An established company that has been in business for a while is doing something right. Understanding why your competitors are successful can help you generate a more effective competitive strategy for your company. For example, your firm may decide to target a different customer base or offer benefits that other companies cannot provide.

Once you have completed your market analysis, you should be able to analyze the business models of each competitor. How does each competitor specify customers, connections, and consideration? Where are the similarities between competitors and your business model? Where are the differences in each of the business concepts that competitors in the industry have, or don't?

7.3 Connections: Sales and Distribution Analysis

Now let's turn our focus in the feasibility process to "how:"

- How will specific customers be identified?

- How will specific customers be targeted?

- How will these customers be attracted to purchase products/services?

You must identify the specific activities the business will undertake to generate sales. To know whether your business concept is feasible, you should be able to "walk through" the entire process—from identifying customers to collecting the cash from the purchase to providing ongoing service (if the purchase requires it). Details, details, details! The success of the business will depend on how these details are executed.

Selling to Your Customers

A *stage model* is likely to be the most viable way for describing the activities involved in identifying, targeting, and attracting customers. The model for customer acquisition has three stages:

- Stage 1: How will you identify and sell to the first customer group?

- Stage 2: How do you identify and sell to the second and third customer groups?

- Stage 3: How will you use the information from Stages 1 and 2 to identify additional customers?

As customers accumulate, they will likely reflect a pattern of similar characteristics and emerge as a "target market." These specific target markets form the business's total market.

Exhibit 7.6 shows possible stages for the Mexican food delivery business discussed at the beginning of the chapter.

Some specific details of the feasibility process involve making determinations about advertising and promotion. If sufficient effort has been undertaken in the section on identifying customers, you will have completed numerous personal interviews of potential customers. These interviews will provide you with the information you need to describe how they are alerted to new products and services and how they are likely to be reached through advertising and promotion. Some products and services will need to be sold through personal selling (e.g., medical supplies and pharmaceuticals), while other products might require an advertising campaign (e.g., groceries and soft drinks). Your customers will tell you how they buy.

Reaching Your Customers

It is also likely that the purchase process involves a channel of distribution from your business to a final customer. You will need to describe how the business's products and services will reach your final customer and how you will sell to each link in this distribution process:

- Can you sell directly to the end-user, or does your product/service require an intermediary, such as a wholesaler, or a value added reseller to reach your final customer?

- If your business sells directly, will you use an internal sales force or manufacturer's representatives?

- How will you hire, train, and reward your sales force?

- How will you select manufacturers' representatives or other kinds of intermediaries and provide them with sales support and training?

- What kinds of incentives will these intermediaries need to sell and service your products or services?

- How will you support these intermediaries to insure they can accomplish the sales goals your have specified?

As described in industry analysis, you will have already compiled detailed information on the pricing policies of your competitors (price, terms, credit policy, service, and warranty policies). This data will help you differentiate your business from others. In addition, you will be able to offer reasons why the industry prices products at certain levels and why the margins for certain products and services are as they are.

For businesses that are selling products to customers through a retail channel, you will describe the details of your merchandising strategy:

- How will products be sold in retail environments?

- Will the product require packaging?

- How will the product be displayed by retailers?

- What kinds of incentives might be required for retailers to actively sell your products?

Finally, you need to step back and look at the big picture. Be sure that the tactics involved in identifying and selling to customers make sense as a whole. For example, if you identify a certain customer type, are the methods for attracting these customers consistent with the places these customers purchase products and services? Do these customers require service and warranties that are covered in the price of the product offered?

The sales and distribution analysis of your feasibility study provides some of the strongest evidence about an entrepreneur's understanding of how the business will be successful. This section offers concrete information about the entire process of generating sales. Knowing that the possible market for a product/service may have a potential for sales in the millions of dollars is important, but showing how sales will specifically be achieved is critical.

Being able to demonstrate that you have detailed knowledge of the entire sales process is a significant undertaking. Yet describing all of the details of identifying, targeting, attracting, and selling to customers insures that sales to customers will likely occur. An in-depth and comprehensive description of all of the details of the selling process is a significant indicator that the business will be viable and successful.

While we will cover marketing and selling in a later chapter of this book, an enterpriser who is developing a feasibility study must consider *how*, specifically, to sell the product or service to a particular customer. It is one thing to know that there is a market, but it is often difficult to get specific customers to purchase your products or services. Therefore, you should consider the specific process of selling to the customers you have identified in your feasibility study. Here are five parts to the selling process that you should consider.

1. *Contact:* Basically, there needs to be contact made between the buyer and the seller. A buyer receives a phone call, is greeted at the door to a restaurant, is asked: "Can I help you?" from a clerk at a store, etc. How will this contact between you and the customer occur?

2. *Identifying the need:* Why is the customer interested in buying? Ask open-ended questions to get to the buyers' sense of what they want—"What are the problems your restaurant is facing in terms of your produce needs?"

3. *Solution:* Given your needs, these are our products or services that can solve them.

4. *Benefits:* These are the benefits of the products and services we have that can meet your needs.

5. *Closing:* The buyer purchases your product or service by offering you an approval and a commitment to buy. "Can I wrap those jeans for you now?"

Your enterprise will be successful only if you can get customers to complete a purchase: You provide them with goods or services, and they provide you with money. Remember, a market, no matter how large, doesn't give you money. *Customers* pay for goods and services.

7.4 Consideration: Value Analysis

Why will individuals want to purchase your products or services? Why are they interested in buying from you? The answers to these questions involve *value analysis.* Many enterprisers start businesses based on their love of a product or service that they, themselves, would be interested in having or using. Indeed, many product ideas originate with the creator's personal need for that product. When Monica Ramirez, a former model and beauty pageant winner from Peru, couldn't find cosmetics from existing companies in tones that were appropriate for Hispanic women's skin tones, she started her own company. Zalia Cosmetics features products with more yellow and golden tones, rather than the pink-based formulations of mainstream cosmetics companies.[3] The first product of Brian Le Gette and Ron Wilson's company, 180°s, was an ear warmer that wrapped around the back of the head instead of the top. The idea came to Wilson as he was walking across his snowy college campus: what could keep his ears warm yet not have him looking like a dork? From there he and Le Gette developed other innovative products that they wanted to use, such as running gloves with a retractable windproof "hood" for cold weather use and sunglasses whose sidepieces pivot to prevent lens scratching and breakage.[4]

If everyone else is like you, and you came up with an idea for a new product or service, then it would be likely that everyone else would buy it. But we know that we are all different, that we all have different wants and needs. Enterprisers must identify those individuals who want what they have to offer. If those potential customers do not exist, then, the enterprisers must modify their products and services so that they can sell enough to make a profit.

In assessing the value of a business concept, ask three major questions:

1. What are the benefits that you will provide your customers?

2. What are the benefits that your competitors provide your customers?

3. What is the "value chain" between you and your customers?

Benefits

In general, there are three broad reasons that individuals buy something that they don't already have: it's better, faster, and/or cheaper. *Better* means that the product or service has benefits that other competitors don't offer. For example, mobile phone companies are always touting new features to attract customers, such as more minutes for your monthly fee, better service area coverage, better games and Internet access. Many customers want *faster*, that is, they want something *now*. For example, Barnes and Noble has a service that will deliver books to individuals the same day that they are ordered if they are in stock at a local store. That is fast. Software companies may offer product downloads, again providing immediate delivery.

Finally, if buyers are going to compare products or services and their benefits are nearly equal, most people will choose the cheaper offering. Enterprisers who can compete with other companies by selling the same products or services for less can be very successful. In fact, this is often the way that many enterprisers in services compete. An enterpriser often doesn't have the same level of expenses that a big corporation might have. Take consulting as an example. A big corporation would have to pay for an expensive suite of offices and lots of staff, whereas an enterpriser may operate from a home office and not have rent or staff costs. But the enterpriser's skills as a consultant could be better than what bigger companies offer, allowing the sole practitioner to compete on price and still earn a significant profit.

Another technique to evaluate the specific needs of a customer is to consider the customers biggest "pain." No one wants to be in pain; we want to avoid it. Customers who have a "pain" in their needs have a problem they want solved *now* and are likely to pay more to have this pain go away. Ask your potential customers, "What is your biggest pain? What keeps you awake at night? What do you need solved now?" Finding how to relieve their pains will provide a significant benefit to them—and help you develop more ideas to modify your products and services to generate sales.

While is it important to identify the specific needs of a customer, it is worth thinking about what these customers are likely to value. What lies behind the needs? What goals serve as the basis for those needs? Exhibit 7.7 lists a number of possible values that drive needs.

For example, some products don't sell because buyers have to change their ways of doing things. And, some products—Microsoft Word is one—continue to sell because people don't want to change the way they do things (inertia). They prefer to stick with products and services that might not really meet their needs. The cost of making the switch may be too high, as we discussed in the competition section earlier in the chapter.

Your Competitors' Benefits

How does your competition provide benefits to your customers? If you have identified the business concepts and business models of your competitors using the process suggested in the previous section of this chapter, you already have a good idea of the answers to this question. You know about the specific customers, connections, and considerations that each of your competitors is focused on. Now you can take this information and create a grid that identifies your potential competitors and describes how each competitor meets specific customer considerations. This grid provides insights on what kinds of benefits and features each customer considers important. You would do such a grid for each customer group that you think you might be pursuing.

For example, let's go back to the concept of delivering Mexican food. You would begin with a grid that would identify all of your possible competitors who deliver food, not just any direct competitors (those that deliver only Mexican food). You would list all of the pizza, Chinese, and Thai food delivery businesses, or any other restaurants that have delivery service in the first

exhibit 7.7 | **What Customers Value**

1. Prosperity—People want to increase their wealth, so products or services that either save them money or help them make more money address this value.

2. Accomplishment—Can your product or service help people meet their goals and achieve what they want? For example, a service that helps a person learn a language is a service that enables people to accomplish something.

3. Security—Improves their sense that they won't come into any harm. Some people buy products because they fear if they don't, then they might not succeed. A salesperson could say "well your competitor has three of these machines" and a buyer might buy because to NOT have one of these machines could be a mistake.

4. Freedom—Increase one's options by purchasing something (e.g., often a value associated with buying a car—the freedom of the road, cars allow you to get away).

5. Happiness—Ask the question, how could I make your life happier? It can lead to product or service ideas from your customers.

6. Pleasure—A product or service will enable people to have more fun.

7. Self-respect—Things that make people feel good about themselves.

8. Friendship—Often, purchasing over time occurs because relationships are developed between buyers and enterprisers. This may be a very important aspect of why some buyers buy from certain providers. We buy from people we like and who we think share mutual interests.

9. Understanding—We buy if we think the sellers are listening to our needs. Listening is the beginning of understanding. The most important aspect of selling a product or service, actually, is listening. What do my customers want from me?

10. Convenience—Some people will buy if the product or service makes their lives easier.

11. Consistency—People stay in a certain direction, and feel right about that direction.

12. Inclusion—People want to be liked by other people, and be part of the fashion "in crowd." Follow the latest trends in fashion—but don't forget to put away your Ugg Boots when stilettos heels replace them!

13. Excitement—Not being bored or doing something new is important for some buyers.

14. Getting what one thinks one deserves—Often luxury products are sold because they appeal to the sense that buyers are purchasing something that they've earned, and because of their achievements, they now deserve a new watch, or jewelry, or a new car. Hotels are now marking this value. You deserve to get away and be pampered at our hotel!

15. Feeling important—We all want to be treated special. Restaurants where the host knows our name when we enter the door, or a bar that lets us past the velvet rope are all signs that we are important. In some ways, the VISA Signature card, which is being marketed now, is about feeling special and unique.

16. Knowledge—Things that help a buyer learn more.

column. Exhibit 7.8 shows a partially completed competitive grid. Across the top of the row, identify what particular customers look for in making their purchases from these restaurants, such as timeliness (how fast it takes to get an order), price, food quality, menu variety, and customer service. As you

exhibit 7.8   Competitive Benefit Grid

Restaurant	Timeliness	Price	Food Quality	Menu Variety	Customer Service
Domino's	Delivery in 30 minutes	$10–$25	Good	Pizza, soft drinks, chicken wings, bread sticks	Fast, takes credit cards
Pizza Hut			Good		Fast, takes credit cards
Papa John's			Good; Fresh ingredients		Fast, takes credit cards
Best Neighborhood Pizza	Delivery in 30–45 minutes				Cash only
New York Pizza			NY style pizza, good quality		
Tasty Thai	Delivery in 30–45 minutes				
Cheerful Chinese	Delivery in 25–45 minutes				
Sushi to Go	Delivery in 45–60 minutes	Minimum order for free delivery $15			
Taste of India	Delivery in 30–45 minutes				
Alberto's Italian					

interview customers who purchase delivered food in your prospective delivery area, you'd ask from whom do they order, and why, filling in the grid as you learn about each restaurant.

The competitive matrix can show you that buyers often buy from a variety of competitors, depending on their values at that particular moment. Sometimes a customer might want to buy on price and timeliness; at other times, quality of the food and variety may be more important. You are trying to see where your concept will fit among all of the other competing business concepts. How similar are you on price, timeliness, quality, and variety? The competitive grid also shows whether you are too much of a significant outlier in the marketplace. For example, if you decided that your Mexican food delivery service was going to offer delivery for $50 gourmet meals, your competitive matrix is likely to show that few, if any competitors are providing delivered food at that price point. Whether or not there is a market for meals in that category is a different question entirely!

The Value Chain

Every product or service begins with inputs that are processed and then delivered to a customer. How the product or service goes from inputs to the customer is its **value chain**. In a value chain analysis, one is looking for where the "value" is actually added to the product.

value chain
The process by which a product or service moves from inputs to the final customer.

For example, let's say that you want to start a data systems company that develops and sells point-of-purchase sales terminals and the related computer inventory systems to small jewelry stores. The business concept for your enterprise centers on the jewelry stores' desire to manage their inventory better. They want to immediately see what jewelry items are selling, whether they should order more of the best sellers, and to identify and mark down poorly selling items. The value chain for such your jewelry data system business would include such things as the cost of the computer components, software costs, installation, and debugging. The value chain for this project might look like the table in Exhibit 7.9.

With this information, we can identify the costs of the system and determine where the value is. As you can see, the value chain for selling a computer inventory system has most of the value added in the installation and debugging of the system. Many businesses look similar to the above example, particularly in services. Often a company might price hardware and software, initially, at close to their costs, knowing that they will make their money by providing installation and services later on.

Another example might be in automobile sales and services. An automobile dealer might sell a car at "cost" and not generate much revenue in the value chain by selling the car. Instead, the dealer may make money servicing the car, especially if the car can only be under warranty if it is serviced where it is sold. This strategy might not work if a customer could still keep the car under warranty and go to a dealer that has lower service and repair costs.

Mapping out the value chain provides you with insights into your costs and where the biggest spreads are between costs and revenues. It is at these points that enterprisers can often find opportunities to pursue. You should also develop a map for your competitors.

Certainly, one of the best examples of how this has occurred in many industries has been using the Internet to sell directly to customers without the use of middlemen such as wholesalers and retailers. For example, if Amazon sells books directly to customers in the value chain, then, the retailer markup, which

exhibit 7.9

Value Chain for Jewelry Data Systems

Item	Cost	You Charge	Value Added
Hardware	$5,000	$6,000	$1,000
Software Costs	$10,000	$12,000	$2,000
Installation and Debugging	$5,000	$17,000	$12,000
TOTAL	$20,000	$35,000	$15,000

is typically 40 percent of the wholesale cost of the book, goes to Amazon rather than through the value chain of the retailer. Amazon can keep this value added (if it sells books at the retail listed price), or provide books at a lower price and split the value between itself and its customers.

In computers and computer software, it seems that most of the value added has been in the computer chip (Intel) or in the computer software (Microsoft), and less in other components of the system (disk drives, the case, or other parts of the hardware).

7.5 Commitment: Personal Analysis

Now that we have analyzed the customers, consideration, and connections, we turn to the fourth C, commitment. Are you sure YOU want to pursue this business concept? An enterpriser might have a great business concept, but developing that concept into a viable business may not be an enjoyable prospect for that particular person. Or perhaps the concept calls for specific talents and skills.

For example, an enterpriser might come up with a business concept that requires efforts at direct sales and significant amounts of cold calling on customers to generate sales. Cold-calling and talking to people might not be significant strengths of the enterpriser. In this case the enterpriser has two options: choose not to pursue the concept or find people with these strengths to participate in the business.

Talking It Up

The best way to learn about the personal commitment required to start and run a particular type of business is to talk to entrepreneurs who are already in your chosen industry. Asking them lots of questions about the business you are considering will reveal key information about their lifestyle. Only then can you see how well your proposed business venture fits with your personal goals.

For example, if you want to spend time with family and friends and find that the enterprisers in the business you enjoy spend 18 hours a day, 7 days a week at work, it is unlikely you'll have sufficient time for friends and family. You will have to decide if you want to make this trade-off.

Please note that the startup of a business, and the effort that the startup of a business takes, may require substantially more time at the beginning, than as the business matures. Make sure to ask other enterprisers how much time it took them to start their businesses versus how much time it currently takes to operate and manage their businesses. Then ask yourself if you are willing to devote the necessary time for each phase. You could have a very good idea but not be willing to dedicate enough time to implement it. Some businesses are easy to start and hard to operate (many restaurants are this way), and many businesses, such as technology companies, are hard to start but easier to operate.

Signature Strengths

In the book *Authentic Happiness* and at his website (http://www.authentichappiness.com), Martin Seligman suggests that you will be happier if your work revolves around your signature strengths. A **signature strength** is one that you are more likely to use frequently. It makes you feel good when you use it, and so you want to discover ways to use this strength even more often. Some examples of signature strengths are curiosity/interest in the world, love of learning, integrity/genuineness/honesty, and perseverance/industry/diligence.

signature strength
A strength that you are more likely to use frequently, feel good about using, and want to use more often.

To know whether a strength is a signature strength, ask yourself, "When I use this strength, does it invigorate me or not?" If this activity provides you with more joy and enthusiasm, then it is likely to be one of your signature strengths. Take the time to identify your personal signature strengths and consider them when you evaluate a particular business concept. If the business does not help you focus on your signature strengths, you are less likely to be happy pursuing that activity. You can go to the Authentic Happiness website (http://www.authentichappiness.sas.upenn.edu) to learn more about signature strengths.

Answering Tough Questions

As you evaluate a business concept from the perspective of personal commitment, ask yourself the following questions:

- Do you have the talents for the business or know where to find people who do?

- What are your aspirations and how well does this business fit them?

- Where do you see this business in five years, and can you picture yourself running it?

- Do the activities and time commitment required for your proposed enterprise match the kind of lifestyle that you want?

These questions seem simple to answer, but when you begin to write down your responses, you may find that your personal goals and aspirations will not likely be an exact fit with the needs and requirements of starting and running the enterprise you've mapped out in the feasibility study. As you have more information about your intended enterprise, ask yourself, "Is this really what I want to do?" If you find that with each hour and day you devote to your enterprise that you find less and less enjoyment from it, you should seriously consider doing something else, or working to modify your business concept and business model to design an enterprise that will meet your needs.

We are sure you have heard the expression, "If there is a will, there is a way." The development of an enterprise will invariably have days of successes and disappointments, and days when you will need to adapt and change because what you thought would work doesn't. Enterprisers who really love what they are doing will have the enthusiasm and energy to push through the many difficulties that will occur in the startup process.

7.6 Enterprisers

Bringing Home the Sundance Concept

When you hear the name "Sundance," you probably think first of Robert Redford's independent film festival. But Sundance is also a 6,000 acre site in the Provo Canyon area of Utah that Redford bought to protect it and also to provide a place for artists to develop their craft. Redford funded his enterprise with earnings from one of his first big hits, *Butch Cassidy and the Sundance Kid*. Because Redford couldn't get a loan from a bank, he found investors who shared his vision. What started 30 years ago is today a premier place to visit, a venue for filmmakers, and a mail-order catalog company.

Redford brought Harry Rosenthal, CEO of the catalog, into the organization because of Rosenthal's success in his own catalog business. As Rosenthal tells it, he was an unlikely entrepreneur. "[At college] I majored in Greek and Latin literature, perfect background for mail order," he says jokingly. "It's so perfect that I went to law school. There's not a lot else you can do with a Greek and Latin major." After a few years as a lawyer, he and some friends who shared his entrepreneurial spirit started a mail-order catalog called Right Start, featuring high quality products and educational toys for babies and young children. "We all quit our jobs, knocked on doors, raised money," he says. "We thought that we had the range of skills necessary to start up and succeed at a business that we knew nothing about."

In fact, they succeeded in the mail order business in spite of their lack of knowledge. They found that their skills were not as applicable as they'd anticipated. Rather, their success was based on the ability to work very hard, react very quickly, and fly by the seat of their pants. "The first thing you learn, I think, when you start a new business in an area where you're inexperienced is that you really don't know anything," says Rosenthal. "The sooner you learn that, the faster you begin succeeding. It's when you think

you know things that you don't know that you run into trouble."

Once Right Start was on the road to success, Rosenthal left the company to pursue other opportunities. A mutual acquaintance who was Robert Redford's lawyer knew that Sundance was considering adding a mail-order catalog and brought Rosenthal and Sundance together. He was skeptical at first about the Sundance team's concept and discouraged them. However, Sundance was persistent and asked Rosenthal to consult and write a business plan. He agreed after clarifying that Sundance understood what the business entailed. He also recommended that they have someone on the startup team who was passionate about the business: "Someone who is going to get up in the morning and go to bed at night living and breathing that business. It helps if that person has experience, but it's more important, in a lot of cases, to have the drive and the dedication." Rosenthal offered to use his industry contacts to help Sundance find such a person but had no interest in filling that role himself.

Pleased with Rosenthal's business plan, in 1989 Sundance formed the catalog company, obtained financing, and then asked Rosenthal to head the company. After carefully considering the attractive business opportunity and the lifestyle changes it would entail to move him and his family from Southern California to Utah, he decided to join Sundance.

While both Right Start and Sundance were new catalog companies, there was a major difference: Sundance already had name recognition and the Robert Redford connection. "Redford stands for many things—support of the environment, support of the arts—that are meaningful to people in America," explains Rosenthal. This name recognition made it easier for the made it easier for the Sundance Catalog to become profitable. "Most catalog companies take four to five years to begin turning a profit," says Rosenthal. "We did it much faster than that." One reason was the merchandising expertise of Brent Beck, who was running Sundance's very successful General Store. The store's offerings reflected the Sundance area and appealed to the vacationers who stayed at the lodge. When they wore their apparel purchases at home, friends wanted to buy similar items and began calling the store to request mail orders. The Sundance Catalog filled that need very well—and also provided a means for Redford to fund the artistic and environmental disciplines that he supports.

What makes the catalog's products so marketable? All the items convey the special sense of Sundance, blending environmental responsibility, creativity, craftsmanship, support of the arts, and responsible business. "That's what Bob [Redford] lives for, what he's passionate about, and so that's the vision of this catalog." says Beck. Many items are unique and created by local artisans such as scented glass objects and sculptures based on scrap iron. Textures are important. The products reflect their Western heritage and the Sundance lifestyle.

Sundance had a big advantage in Redford's fame, but that only goes so far. In the catalog business, repeat purchases by customers are the key to profitability and success. "A spokesperson, a famous name, or a famous brand gets people to try your product or service once," says Rosenthal. "If you deliver a good quality product or service at a good price and people are satisfied with the experience they have, then they will come back. If they don't have a good experience, you won't have a successful business." In addition, Sundance tries to exceed, not just meet, customer expectations and involves customers with the community's goals—protection of the environment, the promotion of the arts—so that they feel that they are making a contribution with each purchase. This sets Sundance apart from other catalog companies. "If you're thinking of starting up anything from a corner drugstore to a software company, somebody else has tried it at least in some way;

maybe not exactly the idea that you have, but in some way," says Rosenthal.

He offers prospective enterprisers the following advice: First, learn about the business—the target market, competition, business operations. "Think about what people are doing that is similar to what you're doing, and find out all you can about them," he says. "Find out how they make their money, what works and what doesn't work." "Step number two," he says, "is to prepare a rigorous business plan that spells out capital needs." "Most businesses start out undercapitalized," he says.

"Optimism rules among entrepreneurs," Rosenthal warns. "Whatever it is, it's going to take longer and it's going to cost more. So be really rigorous in your business plan. Figure out how much capital you're really going to need, then add to it. And usually the early years of a company involve losses."

Next, be prepared for what Rosenthal says might be "five years of the most abject misery" before you succeed. If your capital runs out, you could have a few really rough years before you finally turn the corner. "Don't get discouraged," he says. "When you're new at something, you make mistakes. You'll think, 'How did I ever get into this? When am I going to come out? When is it finally going to turn the corner?' Most new businesses go through that. It's better to understand that you have problems to overcome than to live in a fool's paradise and wake up one day with a train wreck."

In the long run, the Sundance catalog's success was built on the quality products it carried. Today the company racks up more than $70 million in sales a year, mails more than 1 million catalogs each month, takes orders in its modern call center, and is now installing state-of-the-art technology to prepare for even more growth.

Note: In 2004, Robert Redford and Bruce Willard, who was CEO of the Sundance Catalog at that time, sold the profitable company to two private equity firms. Redford retained a minority share.

(continued)

Discussion Questions

1. What is the business concept for the Sundance catalog?

2. Discuss the business model for the Sundance catalog, including customers, revenue sources, cost drivers and cost structure, investment size, and critical success factors using the questions in Exhibit 7.1.

3. Outline a plan to guide Rosenthal's analysis of the market for the Sundance catalog, using Exhibit 7.5 as a guide.

4. Prepare a competitive benefit grid for Rosenthal to use in his value analysis. How does Sundance plan to differentiate itself from its competitors?

5. How does Rosenthal's advice to Sundance and then to enterprisers in general relate to the 5 Cs?

6. Go to the Sundance catalog site, http://www.sundancecatalog.com. How well has Sundance realized its business concept? What contributes to its feasibility?

Sources: Adapted with permission from the transcript of the show "More than a Catalog," Small Business School, the series on PBS, and at http://SmallBusinessSchool.com; and Paul Miller, "Sundance Catalog Sold," *Multichannel Merchant,* July 9, 2004, http://multichannelmerchant.com; and "The Sundance Catalog Story" and "Sundance Community," Sundance Catalog website, http://www.sundancecatalog.com (February 28, 2006).

7.7 Capital: The Fifth C

The final part of the feasibility process involves identifying all the resources that you will need in order to make your enterprise a reality. We call this the fifth C—Capital. Every enterprise consists of three different kinds of capital:

- *Human capital:* Your expertise, your knowledge, and the expertise and knowledge of your partners and employees.

- *Financial capital:* The specific resources, such as land, building, equipment, machines, desks, supplies, and inventory necessary to start and operate the business.

- *Social capital:* The network of relationships that you and your enterprise need for the business to succeed.

In accounting, there is a concept called *good will* that puts a value on the intangible elements of the business. These intangible parts of the business often consist of such social capital as the reputation the business has developed with customers and suppliers, the value of a strong brand, the network of advisors the business has created, the use of helpful suppliers that may be willing to extend the business longer credit terms, and buyers that provide helpful suggestions for improving your products and services. Often the inclusion of these intangibles will give a business a significantly higher value than the financial resources of the business would suggest.

The key questions to ask as you begin to examine your capital requirements are:

- What financial, human, and social capital do I need to provide customers with the considerations I've identified?

- When will these capital requirements be needed?

The Grand Tour

To answer these questions, you need to take a "grand tour" through your business concept and literally or figuratively walk around your business. As you identify everything that has to happen for the business to become real and when it has to happen, you will also discover all of the financial, human, and social requirements of your business.

Let's take, as an example, the printed T-shirt business. Your business concept involves silk-screening T-shirts and selling them at special events. In the imaginary tour, you will think about everything that your T-shirt business requires to operate. Exhibit 7.10 presents some key questions you'd want to answer.

Enterprisers can be creative in looking for ways to cut down on the specific costs for getting into business. (We will return to this later in the financing chapter of this book.) For example, in the T-shirt business, you might find that a silkscreen machine might cost $1,000, but that you could buy one used for $500, or you could rent someone else's machine for $1 per shirt.

exhibit 7.10   **"Grand Tour" Questions for a T-Shirt Business**

Human Capital:

What knowledge and skills do you bring, and what do you need to find in partners/employees?

Who will design your shirts?

How many employees will you need?

What skills should these employees have?

Who will handle the marketing, sales, financial management, and operation (management of the making of the T-shirts), as well as distribution of the t-shirts?

Social Capital:

Who are your customers?

How will you contact them (mail, personal contacts, door to door, on the phone, etc.)?

Once contacted, how long will it take to make a sale?

Who are the best suppliers?

What relationships do you already have with potential investors, customers and vendors?

How can you leverage these relationships?

Financial Capital:

Where will your facility be located?

What kind of equipment do you need to silk screen t-shirts (a printer, drying racks, boxes for the shirts)?

Where will you purchase your t-shirts, inks, and stencils?

How much will supplies, equipment, rent, utilities, labor for help, etc., cost you?

When will you need all of these items?

What sources of financing do you already have?

How much additional funding do you need?

You can learn nearly everything you need to know about how to start and successfully operate your enterprise from someone else. You need to find mentors, experts, customers, suppliers, and even competitors who can help teach you. Your competitors are actually the best place to start acquiring information about the capital needs of your business. A good way to find enterprisers who might be willing to help you is to go to another city or state where your contacts (enterprisers) won't be in direct competition to you. What kinds of resources do your competitors use to operate their businesses? How big are their facilities, what kinds of equipment do they have, how many people do they employ and at what levels or expertise, and how much are employees paid?

For example, if your concept is to start a restaurant, go in and be a customer, and watch everything that is happening. How many people are working? How were you greeted? How many tables does the restaurant have for the number of workers? What is the quality of the dishes and silverware? What is the look and quality of the menus? How big is the restaurant, how big is the kitchen? How many chefs and cooks are in the kitchen? Pay attention to everything you see. Everything you note becomes part of the information you need to complete your "grand tour" of your potential enterprise.

A trade show is another excellent resource to include as you identify your capital requirements. Attending a show in your industry provides the opportunity to see what large numbers of potential competitors are doing, the products your suppliers are likely to provide, and to meet many buyers of the products and services you might be offering.

Your goal at this stage in the feasibility process is to develop a preliminary estimate of all the possible costs of doing business. This includes more than the obvious financial costs, such as equipment and rent, but also the social and human costs of operating the business.

Your restaurant will need a talented chef. Your T-shirt business calls for a creative designer. Perhaps your enterprise requires computer experts with PhDs. You have to be able to evaluate how good your experts are at their jobs regardless of the type of specialized skills they have. If your customers are CEOs of Fortune 500 companies, you'll need to know how to gain access to these individuals to make sales.

How do you develop social capital? Make it a habit to contact at least one person every day who can help you learn more about being a successful enterpriser. We call this the "one-a-day" rule. You will build a contact list of people who might help you learn. As you call individuals on that list who will offer you some important insights about your enterprise, you can ask for names of others who might help you. For every person you contact, think about how you might be able to help the person in return or think about how you might help some other enterpriser. As you ask others for advice and assistance, you must also return the favors to other enterprisers.

Taking Stock

With this final process of identifying resources, we've gathered enough information to really begin to answer the primary feasibility question we posed at the beginning of the chapter: Under what conditions would you go forward with this enterprise?

Review what you have discovered thus far about your customers, competitors, the industry, how your enterprise will operate, the requirements the enterprise will make on you (your commitment), and the resources you will need to start and operate your enterprise over time. You should have a good sense of whether making the commitment to take the next steps and actually start your business is the right decision—or not.

You might, at this point, realize that your business concept and model isn't as feasible as you originally thought. First, congratulations! Feel good that you aren't going to invest more time, effort, and resources in something that won't work. Second, you might take the information you've gained at this point and consider how to reconfigure this business concept and model so that it might be feasible.

An important characteristic of success in the feasibility process is an ability to change and adapt your business concept and model to incorporate the new information you learn. Your customers and competitors can give you many clues about what kinds of changes might be needed to make your enterprise feasible. There is no shame in abandoning a business concept that you find unfeasible. Plenty of other opportunities await you. The time and effort you have put into the feasibility process has improved your skills at learning from customers, exploring the strengths and weaknesses of your competitors, and finding experts and mentors to help you succeed. As we talked about in Chapter 4, stopping effort on an idea that won't work gives you the time to pursue ideas that will.

7.8 Summary

1. The feasibility process involves testing the business concept to determine whether the business is worth pursuing, both in terms of making a profit and satisfying the enterpriser's personal goals. After completing an analysis, an enterpriser should know the conditions required to move ahead with the business. Discovery and adaptation are essential components of feasibility, because the enterpriser must adapt aspects of the 5 Cs—customers, consideration, connection, commitment, and capital—to improve the business concept. Enterprisers constantly change their original ideas as they gain more information through the concept development, feasibility, and business planning stages.

2. The business model focuses on the decisions a company makes to determine whether a particular way of doing business is profitable. No single formula works for all businesses, even those within the same industry. Business model analysis examines four areas to determine the profit potential of a business concept: revenue sources, cost drivers, investment size, and critical success factors.

3. Enterprisers must identify the many different revenue sources for a particular business model, such as single streams, multiple streams from several products or services, interdependent (related) streams, and loss leaders. Revenues can be generated by subscription memberships, volume- or unit-based pricing, advertising sales, licensing fees, or transaction fees. The Internet has created additional types of revenue

models, including several Web-based online merchant, advertising, and subscription models. Market-making (brokerage) and community models have become popular as the Web has developed.

4. Once enterprisers understand the revenue sources for a business concept, they can determine the costs associated with it—for example, fixed, variable, and recurring costs—their relative importance, and how the cost mix may change over time. Cost drivers affect total costs and can change over time. Five cost categories make up the cost structure of a business: direct payroll, payroll support, inventory, facility costs, and marketing and advertising. Knowing the size and importance of each cost center is a key part of this component of business model analysis.

5. An analysis of investment size will show the enterpriser the amount and timing of the required funding to start and operate a particular business concept.

6. Critical success factors (CSFs) are the elements that contribute the most to a company's profitability. These operational functions or competencies vary according to the type of business and may include specialized equipment and employee talents. Enterprisers should know how each CSF affects revenues, costs, and cash flow.

7. Market analysis uses primary and secondary research to help enterprisers identify customers for the business's goods or services. Because all goods and services have competition and substitutes, enterprisers must carefully explore the competitive environment that the proposed business will face. Understanding the competitive dynamics and characteristics of an industry and offering distinct benefits compared to the competition enhances a business's chances for success. Forces that drive industry competition are degree of rivalry, barriers to entry, threat of substitute products/services, the power of suppliers, and the power of customers. Low cost and differentiation are the two basic competitive strategies an enterpriser can choose.

8. Sales and distribution analysis focuses on how to make connections and provides critical information about the entire process of generating sales. This includes identifying and attracting customers so that they buy the company's products or services, making advertising and promotional decisions, and determining the appropriate distribution channels to get your goods or services to the end-user. The five parts of the selling process are contact, need identification, solution to those needs, product benefits, and closing the sale.

9. By performing value analysis, enterprisers gain insights into the benefits the potential business offers customers, how those benefits compare to competitors' products, and the value chain that links the business and its customers. Products that are better, faster, or less expensive provide a competitive advantage. Knowing what customers value and need will help the enterpriser refine the business concept

further. Preparing a competitive benefit grid can aid in this part of the feasibility analysis. Charting the value chain shows where the business adds value and where the biggest spreads between costs and revenues occur.

10. The best idea in the world won't become a successful business without the personal commitment on the part of the enterpriser. This requires looking carefully at whether the enterpriser's own aspirations and life-style considerations match the type of business.

11. Capital resources are the final component of feasibility analysis. In addition to financial capital, a business needs human capital (exper-tise, knowledge, skills) and social capital (networks of relationships). The enterpriser must identify not only the sources for each type of capital, but also the timing. Investigating the competition is a good way to learn about the capital requirements for a business prior to pre-paring cost estimates.

Review Questions

1. Explain the purpose and general frame-work of the feasibility process.

2. What is a business model? Discuss the four main areas of business model analysis.

3. Describe the different types of revenue streams a business can generate and how they relate to the revenue model.

4. How do the Web-based revenue models described in the chapter generate rev-enues? What types of cost structures, investment requirements, and critical success factors comprise these business models?

5. Define the four types of costs a business can incur and the five cost categories that make up a firm's cost structure. What should an enterpriser know about these cost centers when developing a business model?

6. How does investment size and timing affect a business model?

7. What are critical success factors (CSFs)? List several CSFs for a business model for a new line of exercise clothing.

8. Differentiate between primary and second-ary customer research and give examples of techniques used to gather data for each.

9. Describe the five drivers of industry com-petition and apply them to the analysis of a new chain of stores that sells teen-oriented furniture and accessories. What competitive strategy would you use for this business and why?

10. What would be involved in the sales and distribution analysis for the teen furnish-ings stores?

11. Why is value analysis such an important part of determining feasibility? Choose five types of values from the list in Exhibit 7.6 that would apply to the teen furnish-ings stores and explain the reasoning for your choices. Chart the value chain for the concept.

12. Which Web-based businesses have dis-rupted past models of the value chain for particular types of goods and services? Can you also name Web businesses that have tried in specific industries and have failed? What are the characteristics of

successful disruption of the value chain through a Web-based business?

13. You want to start a company that makes dolls with ethnic features for Hispanic, Asian, and multiracial markets. Discuss how you would analyze your competitors' benefits and develop a plan to gather the information.

14. How does personal commitment relate to feasibility analysis? How can you discover if you have enough commitment to pursue a business concept that seems interesting?

15. What is a signature strength? Pick three strengths from Exhibit 7.9 that apply to you and explain how they would be used in a business.

16. Define the three types of capital and give examples of the capital requirements for the ethnic doll company.

Applying What You've Learned

1. Select a business concept that interests you. Begin applying the "one-a-day" rule to develop the knowledge and resources you need for your business concept. Prepare a strategy to identify and contact such people. What types of people do you need to include? What resources can you use to find specific names to contact? What questions do you want to ask, and what can you provide in return?

2. It takes at least five interviews with enterprisers who have founded businesses very similar to the kind of business you want to start to gain a true sense of how a particular business is started and operated. Talk to two such enterprisers. Discuss how their businesses are similar and different. Can you come up with a similar "formula" for success for these enterprisers and their businesses?

3. Spend the equivalent of an entire day observing a major competitor. Then prepare a summary of your observations that answers such questions as, How does the company do business? What kinds of customers does your competitor have? How do employees dress? How does the staff interact with customers? If your enterprise is a store, shop at the store and see how you are treated as a customer. If your enterprise is a service business, see how your competitor responds to customers who ask them for help. Identify at least five things that your competitor is doing right and five that the business is doing wrong. For each mistake, explain what you would do differently.

4. Ask yourself, how will my competitors change their behaviors once they see how successful my business is? Identify five ways that they might change the way they operate their business once you become one of their competitors. What steps can you take to counter their actions?

5. Identify the major trade associations and trade group meetings for your industry. Which appear to be the best for your particular business concept? If you can, become a member of your industry's trade association, and attend any trade shows that your industry trade association puts on. Prepare the questions you'd ask your competitors and your prospective suppliers.

6. Identify at least five people who are known as experts in your industry. These people might be reporters who write for trade journals, suppliers, or consultants. Ask them for their insights and advice about industry trends, the strengths and weaknesses of your competitors, and any "rules of thumb" for starting and operating your business.

Enterprisers on the Web

1. Visit Martin Seligman's Authentic Happiness website: (http://www.authentichappiness.com). Take the VIA signature strengths survey (you'll have to register first). Did the results surprise you, or were the results in line with what you already knew? Do your strengths match the kinds of skills and attitudes needed to make your business concept successful? Compare your findings with your classmates.

2. Browse through the success story archives of the Service Corps of Retired Executives (SCORE) at http://www.score.org. Pick one service company and one product story. For each, describe the following:

   • revenue streams
   • investment size
   • critical success factors
   • value chain
   • enterpriser's personal commitment
   • enterpriser's signature strengths

3. Go to a business website like http://www.ceoexpress.com and search for information on the industry you are considering. Information to look for could be in annual reports of publicly held companies, so you could use the Security and Exchange Commissions website, EDGAR, http://www.sec.gov/edgar/searchedgar/webusers.htm, which provides information that all publicly held companies must file quarterly with the government about their operations.

4. Go to the U.S. Census Bureau site at http://www.census.gov/statab/www/, to find information on the demographics of customers in your area. The Census Bureau has detailed information on your state, over 5,000 data items on each country, and data of cities with a population of more than 25,000 people.

5. If you are going to be making products or your business needs specific parts or products, you can identify suppliers and other manufacturers who might be your competitors at http://www.thomasregister.com/. Look for products that are similar to the kind of product you might be offering, and get information on these products from companies that will likely have websites with information about them.

6. An easy way to find information about business organizations in your type of enterprise is to use http://dir.yahoo.com/economy/organizations/professional/. Identify all of the professional and trade associations that might be able to provide you with information on your industry and on your competitors.

7. Go to http://www.inc.com and search for articles about innovative and growing businesses in your industry. Can you find any businesses in your industry that are part of the Inc. 500 fastest privately held growing businesses? Can you find any businesses in your industry that are part of the Inc. 100 publicly held fastest growing businesses? If a company is a publicly held business, you can use EDGAR to get more information about its operations such as names of all of the top management team and a listing of their salaries. Once you have identified fast growing businesses, use any of the web search engines to locate these businesses. Write up profiles on each. Why are they successful? What kinds of customers do they focus on? What kinds of benefits do they provide? What channels do they use? Finally, how might you successfully compete against each of these fast growing businesses?

End Notes

1. The business model analysis presented in this chapter is based on a Harvard Business School teaching note: Richard G. Hammermesh, Paul W. Marshall, and Taz Pirmohamed, "Note on Business Model Analysis for the Entrepreneur" (Boston: Harvard Business School Publishing, 2002).

2. Michael Rappa, "Business Models on the Web," *Managing The Digital Enterprise*, http://digitalenterprise.org/index.html.

3. Zalia Cosmetics website, http://www.zalia.com (December 3, 2004).

4. 180's website, http://www.180s.com (December 3, 2004).

chapter **8**

Business Plans and Planning

Key Concepts

1. While many enterprisers start successful businesses without writing business plans, the chances of successfully starting a business increase by 250 percent for those who do write a plan. Just as a sports team benefits from practicing and preparing a game plan that provides a strategy for competition, a business plan provides practice before actually starting a business. It enables you to build your business on paper and record the actions—past, present, and future—you are taking to make your business a reality.

2. A business plan should demonstrate that you and your partners have the requisite skills to make the business a success, demonstrate that you understand the competitive environment in which your business will operate, explain the need for and benefits of the goods or services you plan to offer, and encourage others to get involved in your business. It should include an action plan that identifies risks and suggests strategies to minimize them. Specific forecasts based on experience—your own and what you learn from others—are another key preparatory step.

3. Most business plans have three main parts: a one- to two-page executive summary with highlights, a body describing the enterprise and its major issues, and an appendix with supporting documents. Business plans are dynamic documents. As you gain knowledge about your industry and experience in running your business, you should revise your plan to reflect this additional information.

240

You have a flair for designing products that are not only attractive but also practical. As your reputation for using good design to solve problems in unique ways spreads, many new clients want your services. You have a vision of building a company that integrates art and the social sciences with industrial design. Your employees will come from many disciplines and have few constraints placed on their creative efforts. The early years are tough, but soon your creations are winning awards at the Industrial Design Excellence Awards competition.

In this chapter, you'll meet Sohrab Voussoughi, founder of Ziba Designs, and learn how he turned his dream into reality. More than 20 years after starting his company, he is still passionate about his work. With a thoughtfully conceived business plan, you can also live your dream.

8.0 Business Plans: Why Bother?

If you have talked with other enterprisers about business plans, you probably discovered that most enterprisers did not write a business plan before starting their businesses. Yet, recent research on new venture business planning suggests that those enterprisers who write business plans are 250 percent more likely to successfully start a business.[1] While a business plan does not guarantee a new successful business (because most new businesses fail), business planning does increase your chances of success.

We want you to think about business plans and business planning in a very different way—in the same way that a team practices and a coach creates a game plan. In sports, teams not only practice before playing the game, they also have a *game plan* before competing against a specific opponent. This game plan identifies the opponent's specific strengths and weaknesses and maps out specific ways to defeat the other team. In professional football, many coaches study videos of their opponents over and over to spot weaknesses in their opponents' games. Coaches then develop a set of plays for both offense and defense to counteract each opponent's strengths and weaknesses. Some coaches, for example, have a list of plays that will be run at the beginning of the game that will be undertaken no matter what, as a way of getting their team into the game. Coaches then adjust their team's efforts once they see how their opponents respond. That is what business plans and planning are really about: practicing before playing the real game and developing a set of specific activities that can help you defeat your competition.

If you have played competitive sports, you probably spent many hours in practices before actually competing against opponents. These practices gave your team more experience to help it win. If your opponent didn't practice, your team had an advantage—and a greater chance of winning.

If both teams practiced before their games, practice alone might not lead to success. That is why, in some circumstances, enterprisers who write business plans find those plans don't help them to win. Perhaps their competitors have much more experience and knowledge (another type of practice) about competing in their industry. They have already played the game and have developed a set of actions that have helped them be successful against other competitors. In these situations writing a business plan is a necessary, but not sufficient condition for becoming successful. You need to practice, but practicing doesn't necessarily mean that you will defeat your opponent. So, why write a business plan?

A business plan and the planning process can be like practicing before playing the real game. You can try out different ways to compete against a team as you practice. You can simulate whether certain actions might work and improve the odds of winning. Just as in sports, writing a business plan serves the same purpose as practice sessions and provides an advantage in situations where your competitors are less prepared. As the competition in your industry becomes more sophisticated, you will find that your competitors are practicing and developing plans to defeat your business.

We recognize that writing a business plan is not the same thing as actually taking the actions required to start a business and operate it. At some point, every enterpriser has to show up and play the game—that is, actually start and operate the business. In many industries, that will be enough for enterprisers to succeed, and writing a business plan wouldn't necessarily help them be more successful. Why not just show up and not bother with writing a business plan?

If you think you can win at the game of enterprise without practicing or having a game plan, then don't write a business plan! Play the game of enterprise and see what happens. Or, take time now to practice how to be successful in your business, and identify those activities (have a game plan) that might lead your enterprise toward success.

We believe it is better to be prepared to be successful, rather than hope that circumstances will turn in your favor. As we said in Chapter 5, you can make you own luck, and becoming lucky involves preparation. You need to be ready for the changes in circumstances that occur while playing the game of enterprise. The best way to be ready is to engage in planning and in writing a business plan.

This chapter will show you how to "practice" being successful in the start-up and operation of your business, and to have a game plan of tactics for successfully competing in your industry.

8.1 The Feasibility Study versus the Business Plan

How is writing a business plan different from undertaking a feasibility study? In many ways they are similar. However, a business plan goes beyond the feasibility study and identifies the specific tactics and actions for enterprise success. The feasibility study collects sufficient information about a specific opportunity to determine whether you should go forward and convert your opportunity into an ongoing business. The **business plan** is a way to record your successes and failures while you practice for success at making your business a reality. And, for those enterprisers who just take action to start a business and then realize that they need a business plan, the business plan identifies what they have already accomplished. Indeed, for whatever stage of the start-up process you are in, the business plan is documentation of your actions: past, present, and future. The business plan is not the business. The underlying purpose of a business plan is to help you take the right kinds of actions for success. Your feasibility study has already helped you identify the strategy and goals for success. The business plan will specify the tactics you'll use to take concrete actions that will make your business a reality.

Two other major reasons for writing a business plan might convince you to engage in this effort. Writing a business plan helps you to

- *Get a better understanding of why your business is going to be successful.* That is, you write a business plan for yourself to become more efficient and effective. When you write down what you know about your business, you can see what you know and don't know. Writing a business plan can help you spot the flaws in your strategy and tactics for becoming successful. When you put your "game plan" on paper, you see your business. As you may recall, part of the enterprising process is creating a vision, that is, seeing what the future of your business will be like. Writing a business plan gives your vision much more clarity.

- *Engage others in your efforts.* Many enterprisers write business plans to raise money to start and grow their business. However, raising money should not be the sole purpose of writing a business plan. Money is just one of several types of capital that you will need to start your enterprise. As a document that talks about your actions (past, present, and future), the business plan can help others see where you are going and where you have been. You are more likely to get money, hire people, lock in suppliers, and get customer orders when you have something (a business plan) that you can show, rather than just talk about. The problem with writing a business plan solely for the purposes of raising money is that many enterprisers make promises to prospective investors that are not based on reality. If you write a business plan based on what you think investors want to hear, you put yourself in the position of having to deliver on issues that they think are important rather than on issues that the business must focus on.

Business plans serve as both a reality check for the enterpriser and an invitation for others to join the enterprisers' efforts. When you develop your business plan, you show others how you will implement your game plan, which helps them see what role they might play in helping you win the game. As such, the business plan is written to answer four fundamental questions:

1. *Why you?* Your response should demonstrate that *you* have the knowledge, skills, and abilities to make your opportunity become a reality. What accomplishments have you and your partners achieved that provide the basis for the future success of your enterprise? Can you successfully achieve the game plan you have mapped out?

business plan
A written plan for a business that documents an enterpriser's past, present, and future actions and helps identify the right actions for success. Shows where you are going and where you have been.

2. *Whom do you hurt?* No enterpriser starts a business that doesn't involve *competitors* in some form. In all likelihood, your success will come at the expense of someone else. Who will lose when you win? Who are these competitors? How will your entry into the market affect them? What will these competitors do in response to your entry? How will their responses affect you? Your game plan is not only about your team. It must also recognize the other teams against whom you will compete.

3. *Why now?* Is there a proven *need* for the products/services that your enterprise offers? How does your enterprise go about meeting the needs of specific customers? Why are your products/services better than those offered by your competition? What are the facts that indicate your enterprise will be successful? If you follow professional sports teams, you have probably seen situations where a team has "peaked" before the play-offs—that is, as they come up against more competitive teams, they find that they have spent their time and energy too soon and don't have the necessary attitude and effort to triumph. Your enterprise could find itself in the same position. You might be offering products or services that customers are not ready to purchase now, but might be interested in later. Can your enterprise survive the wait?

4. *Why me?* This question focuses on issues that *others* considering involvement in your effort will ask. Why should they get involved? What skills, knowledge, abilities, or resources do they provide that are necessary for your venture's success? If they do get involved, what is in it for them? Investors who provide money will want to know when they will get their money back—plus some sense of likely future earnings. Prospective employees will want to know how viable the enterprise is so that they will likely get a salary, stock options, or other forms of payment. Suppliers will want to know whether they should extend credit to your business and if your business will be an important source of their future sales growth. Your game plan provides each player (investors, employees, suppliers, customers) with an understanding of how they fit into your winning formula for enterprise success.

Answering these four questions provides you with the material to convince yourself and others to take action to successfully start and operate your business. We will explore how to answer these questions in more detail later when we survey the format for writing a business plan. Before we explore a format for a business plan, however, we want you to create action plans that methodically identify what you and your partners will need to accomplish.

8.2 Developing Action Plans

Action plans are a way to identify the primary risks facing your enterprise and the specific actions you will take to address these risks. An action plan helps you identify the right actions—the effective and efficient efforts—that will actually make a difference in the success of your enterprise. Effective actions solve important problems facing your enterprise, and efficient actions mean that you expend the least amount of effort to get the best results. You don't want to waste your time and energy on issues that may seem important, but are actually trivial for the success of your enterprise.[2]

Creating an action plan is a three-step process, where you (1) identify risks, (2) develop a response strategy, and (3) control and monitor the risks and responses. Exhibit 8.1 summarizes the action plan–preparation process.

In the first step of the action plan, you should list all of the risks you identified in your feasibility study: business concept risks, business model risks, and business feasibility risks. What were the risks inherent in your business concept? What kinds of customer, consideration, connection, and commitment risks do you face? What are the risks in your business model? What risks might prevent your enterprise from making money or generating the capital necessary to accomplish your enterprise's objectives?

What do we mean by risk? A **risk** has a condition and a consequence. A condition is a statement that describes a situation that is causing concern and/or uncertainty. A consequence is a statement that describes the possible negative outcomes that may be caused by this condition. Here is an example of a customer risk for a software company that has a product designed for manufacturing companies. The *condition* is that customers require any new production software they purchase provide demonstrated cost savings of 25 percent in the first year of use. The following are three *consequences* of this condition:

risk
A situation that causes concern and/or uncertainty and could therefore result in negative outcomes.

1. Unless we can show cost savings, customer won't buy.

2. This is a new software product and we don't have any customer history with it.

exhibit 8.1   **Three Steps to an Action Plan**

Step 3: Control and monitor the risks and responses by assigning responsibility for specific risks and actions. Use this feedback to adapt planning as required.

Step 2: Develop a response strategy identifying specific actions to address these risks. You can either accept the risk (do nothing) or monitor and prepare to take action to address the risk.

Step 1: List the risks identified during the feasibility study stage: risks inherent in your business concept; customer, consideration, connection, and commitment risks; business model risks; risks that might prevent your enterprise from raising capital or making money.

3.   Another product we produced has shown cost savings of 50 percent after two years of use.

We would then begin to identify likely outcomes of this risk. In our example, we would ask how likely it is that the customer won't buy without a "lead user," the customer won't buy without a "money-back guarantee," or the customer won't buy without some other condition.

By listing risks in such a detailed way, you can move to Step 2 and develop a response strategy that identifies specific actions you might take to deal with those particular risks. You can either accept the risk (do nothing) or take actions to reduce or eliminate the risk. In our software example, actions to address your customer risks are offering a money-back guarantee that the software will work or partnering with someone who meets the customer's criteria. Taking action should increase your odds of success.

Finally, an enterpriser needs to control and monitor these risks and responses. This third step involves assigning responsibility for specific risks and actions and indicating when reports on risks and actions need to occur. This process of identifying risks, developing responses, and controlling and monitoring them is time consuming and difficult. In the next section, we offer a way of breaking down these broad goals into specific tasks.

The Structure of Work

Your abilities and efforts should focus on specific tasks to achieve specific goals. Broadly, the goal of your business planning effort is to start and operate a successful enterprise. In looking at the structure of this work effort, ask yourself, "What tasks are necessary to complete the project?" By analyzing the specific tasks, your action plan can be broken down into smaller tasks or projects. For example, these projects include marketing, selling, finding resources to make your product or provide your service, finding employees, and so forth. Creating a feasibility study has already helped you identify the major groups of tasks you need to accomplish. As you move to the business planning process, you divide these larger groups of tasks, such as marketing, into specific projects that you can actually make sense of and accomplish. You begin to see what you need to do to be successful. "Marketing," for example, becomes a series of specific efforts and actions.

Continuing with the software company example, we have a specific project— selling software to manufacturing companies. We have identified the risks inherent in this effort and ways that we might respond to these risks. We now ask, "What are the specific tasks required?"

In answering this question we also identify the sequence of specific tasks, specify how groups of tasks are related to each other, outline a schedule for completing these tasks, indicate the resources required to complete these tasks, and then determine a budget. By putting effort into identifying tasks for each project required to reach the broad goals of starting and operating your enterprise, you can monitor the progress of your efforts and create a more accurate sense of the costs and time it will take to achieve your goals. In addition, task identification will help others see what needs to be accomplished. Marketing, selling, financing, hiring, and other required functions are no longer broad generalities. They become activities that others can see, grasp, and undertake. Rather than say, "Go out and sell" to an employee, you will establish the specific set of actions necessary to undertake the process of selling.

In thinking about the tasks required for selling, for example, you should consider what these tasks will achieve: What are the major deliverables? The sum of your deliverables equals a particular project, and the sum of a set of tasks would equal a particular deliverable. Exhibit 8.2 illustrates the relationship between these project steps.

For example, a major deliverable in selling would be to identify customers. Some of the tasks to achieve this deliverable would be identifying target industries for the manufacturing software, listing manufacturers in these industries, and getting phone numbers and names of individuals at each company who can authorize purchases of software. Another deliverable would be the sales presentation your salesforce uses, which incorporates the results of the "identify customers" deliverable. In fact, there might be many more tasks that need to be accomplished to complete the deliverable of "identifying customers." It is not easy to break down even such a simple activity as "identifying customers" without undertaking a significant amount of work to determine how much work you must actually do. Exhibit 8.3 offers several suggestions for constructing a set of tasks.

Determining the tasks for a deliverable such as identifying customers is often easier for enterprisers who have engaged in this kind of effort before. For example, a salesperson who has sold software to manufacturing companies is much more likely to know how to identify customers. If you do not have experience in accomplishing specific tasks for a particular project, you need to find

exhibit 8.2   **From Project to Task**

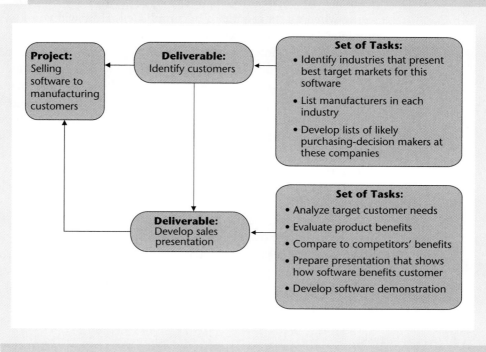

exhibit 8.3

Five Tips for Successful Task Construction

1. 8/80 rule: Tasks should be no smaller than 8 hours or no larger than 80 hours.
2. Tasks should be no longer than the time between reporting periods, for example, reported each week, or every other week. (And, at that meeting, one would report whether the task is "Complete" or "Not Complete.")
3. Smaller tasks are easier to estimate.
4. Smaller tasks are easier to assign.
5. Smaller tasks are easier to track.

individuals with the requisite expertise to help you, such as mentors, other enterprisers in your industry, and industry experts.

Determining specific actions that you and others need to take to accomplish your goals is critical. Your game plan should show how members of your team would accomplish their roles to help your enterprise win. For example, a game plan for a professional football team would show what each person would do for each particular play: which team members would block specific opponents, who would catch the ball on a pass play, and how a receiver would get "open" (away from a defender) to catch the ball. You could compare a professional team's game plan specifying each person's role and actions with an informal game among friends where the only game plan might be "run as fast as you can down the field, and I'll throw the ball to you." Wouldn't everyone involved in your enterprise feel more confident if they knew exactly what they would be doing?

Finally, an important part of specifying tasks for each project involves determining when a task is actually accomplished. How will you know when a task is complete? How will you know when a person on your team has done his or her job? Think about how you will define *success* in completing a specific set of tasks and deliverables. For example, in achieving the deliverable "identifying customers," you should consider how long it will take to identify manufacturing companies and the people in these companies who would be your buyers, and you should have some idea of how many specific companies and buyers you think are necessary to identify. Is identifying ten buyers a satisfactory completion of this task—or do you need to identify 25 buyers, or just one? It would be valuable to ask others for their feedback on what indicators work best for various tasks and to construct checklists that use these indicators to show completion of specific actions.

Specifying tasks and actions might seem to take a lot of effort, and you may wonder how exploring the minutiae of the enterprise will contribute to your successful goal achievement. Devoting adequate time to these small activities pays off. For example, preparing customer lists and telephone numbers of important contacts is a tedious task; but you cannot make a software sale unless you have specific customers to sell to! The success of your enterprise will actually be determined by how well you accomplish each of these small tasks.

The Critical Path

As you identify deliverables and tasks for each project, you will begin to understand how particular tasks and projects relate to each other. For example, if one of your projects for selling software involves demonstrating the software, this project is dependent on having software to demonstrate. As you discover which projects are related to each other and which projects must be completed before you can undertake other projects, you determine the critical path for your enterprise.

The **critical path** in the start-up of your enterprise involves thinking through the key milestones that need to be achieved. A milestone is a major project that has been accomplished. Each project will involve specifying tasks to be achieved, the people who will complete these tasks, the resources necessary for these individuals to accomplish their tasks, and the length of time you estimate for completing these tasks. Identifying resources will require you to make estimates of the equipment, materials, or other kinds of capital necessary to finish a project. We will look at how you go about making these estimates in the next section.

In generating a critical path, you begin by creating an initial schedule of all major projects necessary for the development of your enterprise. You then estimate the time it will take to accomplish each major project. As you list tasks that need to be completed on a month-to-month basis, you will see which tasks are more critical than others. For example, before you can demonstrate your software, you must develop the software, and to develop the software, you need to hire programmers to write the software. Once the programmers are hired, they need a certain amount of time to create the software.

Knowing which tasks and projects are critical, you can focus your efforts and resources on them. Otherwise, you could spend time on projects that are not crucial for your business. For example, if developing software is the most important project on your critical path, it is less important to hire sales people and develop a marketing program, particularly if software development might take a year to complete. Hiring salespeople who have nothing to sell could drain your enterprise of limited resources and negatively affect employee morale.

critical path
The activities required to complete a project and the order in which they must be completed to keep a project on track.

Forecasting Future Effort

Generating estimates of time, effort, and resources necessary to accomplish a project in the future is no easy task. "Guesstimates" are usually wrong, and usually not in your favor. When you try to pad your estimates (that is, add an arbitrary factor such as an additional 25 percent), you don't do much better. A better method for forecasting an action plan is using your personal experience or someone else's. For nearly all start-up efforts, you can find previous similar start-up efforts. If you have experience in sales, you are likely to make better judgments about the time and effort to achieve your sales goal. You can benefit from the expertise of others by asking the right questions when you interview entrepreneurs in your industry, and then applying their experiences as you generate your action plan estimates.

Whatever you plan to undertake, someone else has probably done something similar. Learn from their successes and failures! Find similar efforts to the one you are undertaking and modify your game plan based on what they have done. You don't have to create a business that is totally unique. Such a unique business actually doesn't exist.

For example, if no company has previously sold the kind of software to manufacturing companies that you plan to sell, you can still learn from companies that have sold products or services to your particular customers. You can learn how long it took to sell their products and services. You can learn what kind of sales pitch helped sell their products. You can also learn from companies that have developed a different type of software. You can learn the length of time they needed to develop and debug similar software. Even though other businesses might not be "exactly" like your business, their experiences can serve as benchmarks to determine whether the tasks you have specified can reasonably be accomplished with the people and resources you have identified.

Many novice enterprisers ignore this important step of learning from others. Big mistake! Even if your product is unique, you can benefit from looking at other companies that have sold unique products. When enterprisers say, "I am unique" they are often indicating, "I am ignorant."

With the information you learn from your competitors, you are better prepared to develop good forecasts. You can estimate the number of people you should hire, the amount of time these employees will need for specific tasks, and the equipment, facilities, and materials they will require to produce the item or service.

Forecasting, therefore, is about using the past to help predict the future. The more you know about how others have been successful in the past, the more likely you will be to accurately identify what to do in the future. Again, ignorance of the past experiences of others is your worst enemy when you are trying to forecast.

In practice, though, things don't go the way you plan. Even with all the time and effort you devote to learning from others what will be necessary to achieve your goals, your forecasts are likely to be inaccurate. As you actually play the game of business, you will find that your competitors may not respond in the ways that you predicted in your game plan. The opposing team is likely to respond to your actions and revise their efforts and activities. This does not mean that you should not make forecasts. It means that a forecast is your best understanding of what you think is likely to occur. You will need to revise your forecasts as you go forward. You don't throw out the game plan because a particular play doesn't achieve the objectives you planned. Great coaches revise their game plan as the game develops.

Revising your forecasts is a dynamic process that involves actively reestimating tasks and resources as you learn from your own experiences. As you go forward with creating your enterprise, you will likely change task assignments (for example, put more resources into software development rather than sales), add or subtract from levels of people and equipment you originally estimated, and change your criteria for determining a successful outcome. For example, you might find that the manufacturing software you planned to sell to appliance manufacturers is not appropriate for their needs and might be better suited to automobile part manufacturers. The goal of identifying buyers in the appliance industry will need to be revised to reflect your new objective of identifying buyers in the automobile part industry.

The challenge in forecasting is to be as specific as possible when making estimates of what needs to be done and when. Broad general estimates likely mean that you will not have the necessary people and resources to achieve your goals, and that you may not know what is required for success.

It is better to recognize and attempt to manage the risks your enterprise will likely face. This is not easy. We tend to minimize risks that we have not faced before. We often see this in a highly ranked team that does not take an unranked competitor seriously. The highly ranked team doesn't devote the time and effort to prepare for what they expect to be an easy game, and then find, during the actual game, the unranked opponent is tough to defeat.

The process of planning is, then, the struggle to identify what you don't know, and to realize that what you don't know is likely to significantly impact your business. The process of identifying the risks in your business and specifying actions to take is a very humbling experience. All enterprisers find that there are often significant gaps in what they know, and they discover that there will always be room for learning more about their enterprises.

8.3 Writing the Business Plan

There are knowns,
Known unknowns,
And unknown unknowns.
                    —Anonymous

As we indicated at the beginning of the chapter, you write a business plan for yourself and for others. When writing a business plan for yourself, think of the process as an effort to collect all information you know about your business in one place. We suggest that you get a three-ring binder (or binders) to house the information you collect about your business. Three-ring binders are ideal because you can update sections of your business plan as you gain more knowledge about your situation. You will then use this information to answer the questions outlined in the "Business Plan Format" section.

As you compile this information, you will see the gaps in your knowledge. For example, if your expertise is sales, you might find that your marketing and sales section is very detailed, while the finance section is missing a lot of information. These gaps provide clues to potential blind spots in developing the enterprise, and you will know to focus more attention on these particular sections.

As the quote at the beginning of this section suggests, your task in business planning is to identify the "knowns" (what you know) the "known unknowns" (what you know you don't know), and attempt to minimize the "unknown unknowns" (issues that you don't know might have an impact on your enterprise). The business plan format that we outline in section 8.5 may force you to address those aspects of your enterprise about which you really have little knowledge. Significant problems that confront many businesses are more likely to come from the "unknown unknowns." Ignorance is rarely good protection for problems that are likely to confront your business.

Filling in the Gaps: A Business Plan for Your Own Use

The development of a business plan for your own use requires that you be completely honest with yourself in terms of what you actually know or don't know. The difficultly that many enterprisers face often comes from assuming that unanswered questions are likely to be unimportant to the enterprise's subsequent success. Clearly, you will never know everything that might be important to being successful in the particular business you choose to pursue. There will always be gaps in your knowledge. Recognizing that such gaps exist—and assuming that your lack of knowledge in a particular area might create significant risks to the business—will help you develop strategies to reduce those risks and undertake the right actions in developing and operating your enterprise.

Here are a few issues that often cause enterprisers trouble when writing their business plans:

- *Making unrealistic projections:* As we mentioned earlier, it is difficult to generate accurate forecasts, particularly sales forecasts. Many enterprisers are tempted to make sales projections that fulfill other requirements for business success—for example, sales forecasts that create financial statements that show the business will make money sooner, rather than later—rather than specifying realistic sales goals that are achievable.

- *Underestimating time:* Most enterprisers assume that activities take less time than they actually do. For example, we have met enterprisers who thought that customers would purchase their product after the first sales call, and then found out that most customers took 18 months to evaluate their products and decide to purchase. If you didn't budget for an 18-month lag between the first sales call and the actual sale, your enterprise would probably run out of money paying salaries and expenses before you collect the cash from the first sale.

- *Failing to understand the competitive landscape:* Many enterprisers think that their competition will be only those businesses that sell exactly the same products or services. They forget that most buyers are likely to consider a wider range of alternatives. For example, if your enterprise is selling bottled juices, your competition is not only businesses that sell bottled juices, but also all those businesses that sell other beverages such as milk, bottled water, and soft drinks. Competitors selling other types of drinks will have a significant influence on the prices you charge for juice. Many of these competitors, such as soft drink companies, are likely to determine how much visibility your product has in a grocery store or whether your product can even be sold in certain stores or outlets.

due diligence
The process of thoroughly investigating all parties who will be involved in your business, including investors, partners, potential employees, customers, and suppliers.

- *Insufficient due diligence:* A thorough investigation of investors, partners, potential employees, customers, and suppliers, called **due diligence**, is an essential part of the start-up process. Many enterprisers do not check references or confirm the details of a person's resume. They hire people assuming they are trustworthy, only to discover later that these employees are dishonest. After an employee has stolen from the company, the enterpriser learns that this person has a history of theft. Due diligence is also required to explore how prospective investors have worked with other companies. Did other enterprisers who worked with an investor have enjoyable and satisfying experiences, or was dealing with the investor difficult?

As your enterprise goes through the process of start-up, it is tempting to hire the first person that walks through the door (because you need help "right now"), or take money from the first person that offers to invest (because you are short of cash). Please perform your due diligence and investigate the previous experience of any person you plan to be involved with. You should also investigate the reliability of your suppliers, and you need to get confirmations that materials can be delivered at a particular price and time. You don't want to be caught in a situation where you have promised your customers that you can deliver your product at a particular time, and then find out that the parts you need to manufacture your product are out of stock, or cost much more than you assumed.

Know Your Audience: Gearing a Plan to Other Readers

You will also write business plans for other people to read. Please consider who they are and why they are reading your plan. Then tailor the plan to those specific readers: employees, customers, investors, or suppliers, for example. Although you will base this business plan on the information in your personal business plan, you should not share your personal business plan with them. For example, if you were sharing your business plan with your customers, you would probably not share information on your markups for materials and labor, nor would you likely share all of the information you have obtained on your competitors (such as your competitors' strengths) that might entice your customers to buy from them. You may not need to share with prospective investors the specifics of your operations to provide your goods or services to customers. It is important, therefore, to clearly understand your readers before you send them a business plan and write your business plan accordingly. No single business plan can meet the needs of the various types of people who will be involved in your enterprise.

Here are a few issues that enterprisers should consider when writing a business plan for others:

* *A business plan is like an invitation to a dance, but it is not the dance itself.* The purpose of sharing your business plan with others is to help you engage them, in some form, in your enterprise. For example, a business plan written for a prospective investor is an opportunity to begin a dialogue about the investor's relationship with you. When you involve an investor, you are not only asking for money, you are also asking the investor for his or her personal involvement in your business: advice,

questions, phone calls, concerns. A business plan is just one of many ways to present your vision of your enterprise. A business plan is not the last word you will offer, but the first of many chances to convey your knowledge.

- *The business plan is a reflection of the enterpriser.* A business plan may be the first impression an outsider has of you. It is important to present a document that does not have spelling and grammatical errors. The plan should be easy to read, legible, and well designed. If the business plan looks like a mess, outsiders are likely to think that the enterpriser is also a mess.

- *Write in words that your reader can understand.* For example, engineers and scientists tend to use technical terms that only other engineers and scientists would understand. If the business plan is being written for investors who are not scientists, enterprisers need to help these readers understand the scientific aspects of the enterprise, but without the scientific jargon.

- *When presenting financial information, it is not quantity, but quality.* A business plan is not about the numbers; rather, it is about the *logic* of the numbers. It is easy to get caught up in the creation of financial spreadsheets that offer thousands and thousands of numbers and ten-year projections, quickly padding a business plan with pages and pages of financial data. Offering many spreadsheets is not as convincing to an outsider as identifying how you arrived at your estimates for such broad categories as sales, cost of goods sold, expenses, and the timing of the acquisition of necessary assets. The financial information you provide is, therefore, a numerical summary of the logic of your business model. The primary purpose of your financial statements is to describe how the business will make money.

- *Finally, never make promises that you can't keep.* A business plan creates expectations. If your plan promises too much and you don't meet these goals, you will find yourself with many unhappy and disappointed investors, employees, and so on. It is better to underpromise in your business plan and overdeliver in how the business actually does, than vice versa.

A Special Plan Worth Having

A traditional business plan provides the game plan for your business venture and forces you to analyze all the aspects of your proposed venture: product, customers, competition, operations, and financing. There is another important aspect to running a business, however, that requires consideration. In the aftermath of ethical and financial lapses at Enron, Tyco, Adelphia, and other corporations, there has been an increased emphasis on ethical conduct and developing formal ethical codes that define acceptable behavior for executives, board members, and employees. These documents set forth the ethical foundations on which your company is based. They provide standards to guide stakeholder actions and a framework for appropriate behavior. For example, in Chapter 6, we learned that most company codes of ethics include specific clauses about conflicts of interest.

The process of developing a code of ethics is in itself a learning experience. Just as writing a business plan requires you to confront all the issues of forming and running your enterprise, your code of ethics asks you to reconsider your mission, corporate values, and your relationship to your business environment and the larger society. The Enterprising Ethics box offers advice for preparing this important document.

enterprising ethics

Developing an Ethics Plan

As they develop business plans to guide the formation of their new companies, enterprisers also should give careful thought to the underlying corporate values and codes of conduct that they want as a foundation for ethical behavior. A formal code of ethics prepared early in the company's life defines the values and ethical responsibilities an enterpriser wants to own and communicates those expectations to anyone who becomes involved with the company. This includes shareholders, employees, customers, suppliers, and local/national community. The code of ethics serves as a management tool as well, providing guidelines for managing workplace ethics. Companies with well-crafted and effectively implemented codes of ethics are more likely to avoid ethical conflicts and dilemmas.

While every organization's code of ethics should be unique, the basic steps to develop the plan are similar. Senior management must set the tone and commit publicly to the business ethics policy. Because values and ethics are related to corporate governance, the board should also support this initiative. Involving employees and external stakeholders in the writing of the code is critical, so that it reflects their needs as well as management's and increases buy-in. A code should not be formulated and decreed by the company's board or human resources or legal departments. The best codes include topics that matter to employees. Reading examples of other codes can be very helpful in providing a framework and ideas to jump-start the development of your code, although it's essential to take the time to customize the content to your company.

Before beginning to write a code of ethics, it's important to consider some general questions:

- What is the code's purpose—to inspire or to regulate behavior? Do you want the code to guide people or to set out requirements?
- Will your ethics document include some sort of enforcement? If so, what kind?
- Who will develop your code?
- How will you identify the needs of your organization?
- What steps will you take to publicize and implement the code?
- How will you incorporate the values set forth in the code into organizational policies and practices?
- What procedures will you use to enforce the code?
- How often will you revisit the code and revise it?

The first phase in code preparation is identifying and articulating the company's key values and behaviors. Some guidelines for this difficult and critical process follow:

1. *Review all values related to laws and regulations.* Your organization should already be in compliance with them. Values that support these laws should be part of your code.

2. *Identify values important to your product, service, and industry or profession.* These may include

(continued)

product safety, confidentiality, fair pricing, community involvement, and others.

3. *Interview employees to identify values related to current workplace issues.* These might include avoiding discrimination in the workplace (age, race, gender, sexual orientation), inappropriate dress, prohibiting drug and alcoholic beverage usage on the premises, accepting personal gifts from stakeholders, and avoiding conflicts of interest. Also include values that promote desired behaviors such as teamwork, honesty, and respect, and any other issues that might have ethical repercussions for your company.

4. *Take into account ethical values relevant to stakeholders.* For example, the communities where you locate plants may consider concern for the environment an important value.

5. *Review the values developed in the preceding steps and select those with the highest priority for your company.* These might include the six ethical values named by Josephson Institute of Ethics: trustworthiness, respect, responsibility, caring, justice and fairness, and civic responsibility.

After completing the value identification process, it's time to actually write the code of ethics. Many ethics codes have two parts. The first is typically an inspirational section summarizing the organization's ideals. The second section lists the guidelines for ethical behavior, often by priority for the company. These might be classified by stakeholder group or by topic, such as compliance with law, work environment, acceptance of gifts, conflicts of interest, insider trading, and use of company assets.

The best codes include examples of behavior associated with key corporate values. A code cannot cover every type of ethical dilemma. It can, however, offer guidelines on how to resolve most ethical dilemmas. The wording should also make it clear

that the code applies to all employees. In addition to defining values and ethical behavior, the code should include a procedure for employees to discuss or report ethics-related questions.

Before finalizing and implementing the code, key executives and your legal advisors should review the document carefully. It is helpful to test the code with a few representative groups. The code can then be revised to incorporate feedback from these reviewers.

The implementation of the code must go beyond merely announcing it and distributing printed copies to all employees. The code should be a dynamic document that becomes an integral part of the way the company does business. Many companies hold special sessions to explain the code when it is first introduced and include it in new employee orientation sessions. In addition, a company's code of ethics should be reviewed annually and updated as new situations arise.

Discussion Questions

1. Why should an enterprise have a code of ethics? What are the key issues to consider when developing an ethics plan for an enterprise?

2. Outline a process for developing a code of ethics for your enterprise.

3. What kinds of ethical dilemmas might an ethics plan identify and solve as an enterprise develops and grows?

4. Using the information provided, the resources suggested below, and other online resources, write a code of ethics for your enterprise.

Suggested resources: Carter McNamara, *Complete Guide to Ethics Management: An Ethics Toolkit for Managers,* http://www.managementhelp.org/ethics/ethxgde.htm; Chris MacDonald, "Creating a Code of Ethics for Your Organization," *EthicsWeb.ca,* http://www.ethicsweb.ca/codes.

Sources: Adapted from Chris MacDonald, "Creating a Code of Ethics for Your Organization," *EthicsWeb.ca,* http://www.ethicsweb.ca/codes (January 3, 2007); Chris MacDonald, "Considerations For Writing A Code Of Ethics," in Gene Marks Ed., *Streetwise Small Business Book of Lists* (Cincinnati, OH: Adams Media, 2006); "Codes of Ethics," *Institute of Business Ethics,* http://www.ibe.org.uk/codesofconduct.html (January 6, 2007); and Carter McNamara, *Complete Guide to Ethics Management: An Ethics Toolkit for Managers,* http://www.managementhelp.org/ethics/ethxgde.htm (January 4, 2007).

Enterprisers 8.4

Integrating Design and Function at Ziba Designs

Did you ever wonder where all the gadgets and gizmos we use every day originate? Many come from Ziba Designs, an internationally known industrial design firm with a reputation for creative excellence. Headquartered in Portland, Oregon, with offices in Tokyo, Taipei, Boston, and San Jose, the company is a wonderful mix of personalities and nationalities. Sohrab Vossoughi, who is originally from Iran, started Ziba in 1984 as a brand consultancy with expertise in product development. His goal was to solve business problems with great design. "Ziba means beautiful in Farsi, the language of Persians," Vossoughi explains. "I wanted a name that was easy to say, easy to spell and at the same time has a meaning."

From humble beginnings—Ziba's first big product was the Cleret Bathroom Squeegee—the company has grown to 80 employees and over $12 million in revenues. Its client list includes Intel, Hewlett Packard, McDonald's, FedEx, Procter & Gamble, Rubbermaid, Nike, Microsoft, Ford, and Whirlpool. "Design is a continuum," Vossoughi explains. "It never ends; once you do something, you know it can be done better." He also believes that design should reflect the integration of many disciplines and hires not just industrial designers but also employees with experience in art and the social sciences. Clearly, his strategic design vision is working. In 2001, Ziba became the first firm in the world to win four Gold Awards in the annual Industrial Design Excellence Awards competition. Ziba also holds the record for the most awards per employee.

According to Bob Marchant, a friend, mentor, and customer to Ziba's founder Sohrab Voussoughi, Ziba is one of the world's top five design firms. "They have created products for leading global brands all over the world, and their products have been consistently successful," Marchant says. He believes that Ziba's focus on economics is a primary factor in its success. "Their designers understand that it does no good for a product to win an award but not make a profit for the client who is actually bringing it to the marketplace. It is not enough for the form to be interesting or exciting—or for the form to generate market acceptance. It's important for the form to be profitable, for somebody to be able to make it and for it to work reliably."

From the beginning, Vossoughi refused to place limits on what can or cannot be done. By asking many "What if?" questions, he encouraged his employees to challenge the norm. "We are our own worst competitors," he says. "We are like athletes; we try to beat our own time. We do our best for our clients, and we deliver way beyond what we promised."

The early years were difficult. "For the first six months, I didn't take a single dime out of the business," Vossoughi recalls. "We had our savings; we got rid of the house, we lived with one car, we did everything. There is a saying back home in Persia that says, 'For one year you eat bread and water—then you can eat bread and butter for the next ten years.'" His sacrifice paid off as his vision became a reality and won him the *Business Week* "Entrepreneur of the Year" award in 1992.

As a service business offering creative design capabilities, Ziba's "product" is not easily explained. Each project is unique. For example, Ziba developed the Cleret Squeegee in response to a request for a nice-looking and efficient squeegee to clean glass shower doors. The resulting design was so popular that the design client had revenues of $16 million in its second year—just from this one product! Its design was so impressive that the squeegee appears in the Smithsonian Museum's permanent collection and was sold at the Museum of Modern Art's store.

(continued)

Ziba also helped Coleman, best known for camping gear, use the strength of its brand name to break into the home market. The design team developed the Safe Keep smoke detector product line with a unique feature: an easy way to turn off the monitor in the case of a false alarm. Ziba's award-winning design was simple: a broom button allows the homeowner turn off the alarm with the push of a stick. Coleman quickly went from no presence in this market to 40 percent market share.

"This is what design should be about—defining a problem and moving a business forward," says Vossoughi. "It's all about creating the right product for the market. We design not for the manufacturer, not for the designer, but for the user. We get into people's minds. We want to understand the user's latent needs."

This dedication to integrated user-focused design and the innate understanding of human nature are major contributors to the company's ongoing success. Among Ziba's other innovative products are the Clorox ReadyMop, the Polycom conference phone, outpatient care furniture for Herman Miller's health care furniture systems, and the Stair Assist Bar and Guide Rail System to help people climb stairs without bulky in-home elevators. Ziba also worked with a Portland bank to redesign a more friendly branch atmosphere and with FedEx to create its new look, from logo to courier uniforms.

Vossoughi remains passionate about the work Ziba does. "I didn't start the business because of money; I started because I loved what I was doing," he says. "I can use my creativity and my talent for different things. I can't wait to get up in the morning and come to work. It's still fun. I love challenge. Everything that happens, every obstacle that comes up at Ziba, I look at as a challenge and a problem to solve. And that is our business—we are problem solvers."

Discussion Questions

1. How would a business plan for a service business like Zibaqfer from a business that manufactured and sold products? What are the particular challenges in preparing Ziba's business plan?

2. How might Vossoughi's personal goals for the business be different from or similar to the goals of the business? What entrepreneurial characteristics does he possess or lack?

3. Assume that you are Sohrab Voussoughi and you get in an elevator with the CEO of a company that manufactures household products. What would be your elevator pitch to this CEO if you were asked, "What do you do?" (See page 261 for a description of the elevator speech.)

4. If you owned Ziba Designs, what would be the critical issues and questions that you would focus on in writing a business plan for yourself? Could this business be sold to someone else? If so, what aspects of this business would make it valuable to others?

Sources: Adapted with permission from the video "Possibility School," Small Business School, the series on PBS, and at http://SmallBusinessSchool.com; Mary Bellotti, "Design from A to Ziba," *Portland Tribune*, August 16, 2002, http://www.ziba.com; and Joan O'C. Hamilton, "Coleman's No-Nuisance Lifesavers," *Business Week*, June 2, 1997, http://www.ziba.com.

8.5 The Business Plan Format

A business plan should follow a format that makes the most sense for the type of business you are planning to pursue and its stage of development. For example, a business plan for a company that is making a new product will likely have a greater emphasis on the stage of the product's development—for example, is the product at the idea or prototype stage? Is there a version that can be manufactured, or is the product already being manufactured? A business plan for a janitorial services business, on the other hand, will have very little about product development and more of a focus on finding customers and the process for consistently delivering janitorial services.

We are not saying that each business plan is unique and that you will not be able to find good examples of business plans from similar businesses. Rather, you must pay attention to the specifics of *your* business—and not be seduced into filling in the blanks of a business plan workbook, business plan computer program, or just substituting your information into a preexisting business plan.

A number of websites provide assistance for developing business plans; some offer business plan outlines. Exhibit 8.4 lists several sites where you can learn more about the format and structure of a business plan.

Your business plan is the story of your enterprise. When you write a business plan in your own words, describing your understanding of the most important issues facing the business, your readers will perceive you as "authentic." Most people who read business plans can quickly tell whether your plan was written from your own personal knowledge and experience or whether it seems to follow someone else's format. Remember, other people—investors, customers, employees, partners—will get involved in your enterprise because of *you*. If your plan does not have your "voice," if it does not reflect your thoughts and concerns and hopes, then other people

exhibit 8.4   Business Plan Websites

Name	URL	Description
The Business Plan: Road Map to Success	http://www.sba.gov/starting/ indexbusplans.html	Small Business Administration business plan tutorial and outline
Business Plan Components	http://www.quicken.com/small_ business/cch/tools/?topic=4& subtopic=0&article=buspln_m#article	Business Plans on Quicken.com
Creating an Effective Business Plan	http://home3.americanexpress.com/ smallbusiness/resources/starting/ biz_plan/	Business Plans on Americanexpress.com
Business Planning Tools	http://wsj.miniplan.com/	The Wall Street Journal StartupJournal.com's MiniPlan that guides you through the basics of creating a business plan
Business Plan Software and Sample Business Plans	http://www.bplans.com	Guidelines to write a plan and several sample plans

will quickly see the plan as a "fake" and not representative of your vision for the business. Would you be willing to get involved in a business where the business plan seemed to be nothing like the enterpriser who supposedly wrote the plan?

Appendix C provides a generic format for a business plan. This format is merely a guide to prompt you to think through the critical issues in developing and growing your enterprise. No business plan will follow this format exactly or address all of the questions in this outline comprehensively and thoroughly. The format identifies the important questions and issues you should address—even though you are unable to provide answers to some questions in your plan. If you ignore any of these questions, you might find that these "unknown unknowns" have a significant impact on the success of your business.

Finally, you should visualize the format of your business plan as a pyramid with three parts, as shown in Exhibit 8.5: (1) Executive Summary, (2) Body of the business plan, and (3) Supporting Materials. The top of your business plan pyramid is the Executive Summary, a one-to two-page summary of your entire business plan. The Body of the business plan should be about 20 pages long. This section provides the reader with a narrative of the major issues of your enterprise. In this section you, the writer, tell the story of your enterprise. The Supporting Materials section offers evidence for the statements made in the Body of your business plan. For example, when you discuss the size of your market and the types of customers your enterprise focuses on in the plan's Body, the Supporting Materials section will provide information that shows how you determined size of market, how you went about identifying customers, and so forth.

The pyramid structure for a business plan recognizes that few people will want to know all of the details of your proposed business at one sitting. Each section of the business plan demands a greater commitment from the reader to delve into

exhibit 8.5   **The Business Plan Pyramid**

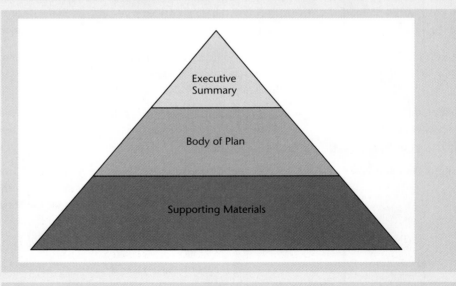

your business. Most readers will stop after the Executive Summary. Few will want to make the plunge into the Body and Supporting Materials, and it will be those few individuals who really want to be involved.

Executive Summary: The Elevator Speech

The Executive Summary is your "elevator speech" about your business. It represents the essence of your plan, what you would tell an important investor whom you happen to meet as you get into an elevator and says, "Tell me about your business." You have just two to three minutes of that investor's undivided attention to make your best pitch. You want the investor to say at the end of your pitch, "WOW! Tell me more."

The Executive Summary is your invitation to the readers of your plan to get interested enough in the highlights to read more. Attention spans are shorter and shorter. With most TV and radio commercials taking 30 seconds or less, we are conditioned to ignore most messages quickly unless they really engage us. The Executive Summary is like a commercial for your business plan. If the Executive Summary does not engage your readers immediately, you will lose their interest.

You can also think of the Executive Summary as the first impression you will likely make for many prospective investors, employees, partners, etc. Most people make decisions based on those all-important first impressions, even if they only last a few seconds. Many enterprisers put almost as much time into writing the Executive Summary as they do into the rest of the plan.

The Executive Summary is, therefore, written *after* the rest of your business plan. It distills the essentials of your business down to a sound bite of one to two pages, just like a TV advertisement tries to get you to stop and watch rather than change the channel.

Body of the Business Plan: The Full Tour

The main section, or body, of the business plan will provide the reader with a 20-page tour of the critical issues involved in your business. This tour should describe your business, analyze your market (customers and competitors), explain your value proposition and distribution strategy, discuss management's qualifications, explain how the business will be organized and why, provide an overview of operations, and present a financial plan. Your feasibility study will provide much of the necessary information for the plan's body. Appendix C provides a more complete description of the plan body.

Marketing Analysis: Who Are Our Customers?

As we discussed in Chapter 7, the identification of customers for the business is probably the most important business planning activity. The customer section of the business plan provides evidence as well as the logic you used to make sales estimates and supports the sales forecasts in the financial statements. The reliability and validity of the sales forecast depends on a thorough understanding of your customers and the reasons they will purchase your products or services. In an ideal situation, you would want commitments from customers to purchase products (purchase orders) as evidence of demand.

Interviewing actual customers is very important for describing the reasons that customers buy, as well as the selling cycle (the time from first customer contact to receipt of payment). The activities involved in moving from first customer, to second customer, to tens, and then hundreds of customers are another important consideration when estimating sales for the business.

As with all of the sections of the business plan, the evidence and logic you offer to convince your reader about the reliability and validity of your findings is very important. What facts will convince the reader that your estimates of the number of customers who will purchase your products or services are accurate? What facts are missing? Why are those facts missing?

Your business will have a number of different customer groups besides the people who buy your products and services. We categorize customer groups into two types:

- Primary customers—those people who buy your products and services.

- Secondary customers—those people who have some interest in the operation of your business.

In evaluating your primary and secondary customers, you should seek the answers to questions like those summarized in Exhibit 8.6.

To demonstrate that you thoroughly understand your customer base, you should summarize the results of your extensive interviews with potential customers and provide more complete documentation in the plan appendix. Such in-depth interviews will offer reasons why customers want to purchase your products or services, as well information about their sensitivity to price, quality, and other benefits. Offering more evidence increases the likelihood that your sales estimates are realistic and that your plan is the basis of a successful enterprise. Also, if your business depends on growing a base of customers over a long period of time, consider whether you will have sufficient resources to engage in this process.

exhibit 8.6   **Understanding Your Customers**

Primary Customers (Buyers of your goods or services)	Secondary Customers (Others interested in your business)
Who are your primary customers?	Who are your secondary customers (What other groups of people affect your business)?
What do your primary customer groups value? What value do you provide to each of these primary customer groups?	What do your secondary customer groups value? Do the strengths of the business match what each secondary customer group values? Why or why not?
Do the strengths of the business match what each primary customer group values? Why or why not?	What other groups of customers should this business be serving? Why? What are the strengths of the business that would benefit these customers?

Marketing Analysis: Who Are Our Competitors?

Do you think your product is totally new and appeals to a new market? This is probably not the case. Most entrepreneurs will develop businesses in established markets, with competitors who serve an identifiable base of customers. Often, new products and services are offered to an established group of customers who have unmet or insufficiently met needs, not customers who don't yet exist.

All products and services have both identifiable competition and substitutes. What entrepreneurs create are businesses that offer products and services that provide some advantages over what their competitors offer. Most customers will not immediately purchase your products or services but will first compare them to others already on the market. Identifying your competition or substitutes will show you how to position your goods or services relative to your competitors. This analysis will help you focus on the benefits of your company's products and services as well as help you identify weaknesses and problems your products/services may face in the marketplace.

You have many options when it comes to situating your business among various competitors and substitutes. Methodically describing the characteristics of your industry as well as the details about your competitors will help you convince others of the feasibility of your business concept. Trade associations provide a good way to gain a better understanding of the industry in which you will operate. Most markets of sufficient size have organizations that cater to the needs of businesses that serve certain types of customers. These groups often publish magazines and newsletters that offer insights into changes in the industry, lists of companies in the industry, and advertisements from suppliers offering products and services to the industry. Trade associations also provide information on changes in government regulation, plus ideas about possible trends occurring in the industry. Assume that the kind of business you are starting will be part of an industry with a trade association—and then locate it. If you cannot find a trade association, then you probably have not devoted enough effort to exploring the characteristics of your industry.

Armed with a thorough knowledge of your competition, you can now apply Michael Porter's competitive dynamics framework (explained in Chapter 7, page 216) to describe your competitive environment and set forth your competitive strategy. Your business plan will provide details about the five forces that drive industry competition: direct competitors, the threat of new entrants, substitute products/services, the power of suppliers, and the power of customers.

The competitive strategy you develop defines (or creates) a position that you can defend and maintain. The primary measure of a successful competitive strategy is your company's ability to generate profits. The underlying issues that an entrepreneur considers with regard to market size and competition are reviewed in Exhibit 8.7.

The competitive environment is dynamic, and your competitors will adapt their products and services to meet threats from new entrants. Naïve entrepreneurs often underestimate the loyalty of customers to established companies, goods, and services. Many potential customers may complain about your competitors' products or services, but these complaints may not be sufficient for them to switch to your company. Assume that your potential customers will use your

exhibit 8.7

Questions for Developing a Competitive Strategy

1. Is the market large enough (are there enough customers) for your business to earn the kinds of profits to warrant investment?
2. How are you different (better) than your competitors?
3. What do you do better than other competitors (your strengths)?
4. What are your weaknesses relative to your competition?
5. What will it take for a competitor to gain that same competitive advantage as your business?

company's products and services to force your competitors to offer them better deals. Don't be a naïve entrepreneur!

Smart enterprisers recognize their competitors' strengths. An established company has typically been in business because it is doing something right for its customers. Accurately describing why your competitors are successful can help you generate arguments for how your company can successfully compete. For example, your company may sell to different customers or offer significant product benefits that other companies cannot provide.

Marketing Strategy: How Will We Deliver Value to Our Customers?

Now the business plan shifts from "what" to "how:"

- How will you identify specific customers?

- How will you target these customers?

- How will you attract these customers to purchase your products/services?

- How will you get your products to the end-user?

This section, therefore, focuses on the activities the business will undertake to generate sales. It will lead the reader of the business plan through the entire sales cycle, from identifying customers to collecting the cash from the purchase to providing ongoing service if required. Details, details, details—but the success of the business will depend on how you execute the sales details.

The stage model you developed as part of your feasibility analysis (see Chapter 7, p. 215) forms the basis for your description of sales activities. Recall that you began by describing how you would identify and sell to the first customer and then move on to subsequent customers. As customers accumulate, they will likely reflect a pattern of similar characteristics so that patterns of similar customers define your target markets. These specific target markets combine into larger customer groups that form the business's total market. A strong business plan depicts each customer in detail and describes all of the activities involved in the sales process. The action plan you developed for selling your product or service will serve as the basis of this section of the plan.

You will also address your advertising and promotion strategies. The numerous personal interviews with potential customers provide you with information about how these people discover new products and services, which advertising and promotion strategies work best, and how they buy. Does your product require personal selling, like medical supplies and pharmaceuticals, or is it better suited to an advertising campaign, like groceries and soft drinks?

The purchase process also involves a channel of distribution from your business to a final customer. Your plan must describe how the business's products or services will reach your final customer and how you will sell to each link in this value chain. For example, if your product/service requires an intermediary, such as a wholesaler or a value-added reseller, to reach your final customer, you should explain how you would satisfy these intermediaries. What kinds of incentives will these intermediaries need to sell and service your products and services? How will these intermediaries be supported to insure they can accomplish the sales goals you have specified?

Mapping out the value chain for a single transaction for your product or service is a good way to visualize the many steps. Indicate the cost at each stage of the process, from raw materials to finished product purchased by your customer. This clearly identifies the "added value" at each stage and the revenue for each unit, as well as estimates of the fixed costs associated with producing your product or providing your service. How might the fixed or variable costs change if certain key issues in your business change? For example, if you are manufacturing a product that requires an expensive piece of machinery, the portion of your fixed costs to be allocated to each product produced will be significantly different if you are making 100 items versus 1 million items. You should begin to estimate at what level of sales (by number of items or by sales volume) you will break even. We will cover how to estimate breakeven in a later chapter.

If your business will depend on an internal sales force, the business plan will describe your plans to hire, train, and reward these individuals. If you prefer to use manufacturers' representatives or other intermediaries, your plan will describe how you will select these companies and provide sales support and training to insure that they will actively sell and service your products.

The plan's prior discussion of the business's industry, including information on your competitor's pricing policies (price, terms, credit policy, service, and warranty), will help you set your own policies and differentiate your business from others. In addition, you will be able to offer reasons for why the industry prices products at certain levels and why the margins for certain products and services are as they are.

Will your business sell its products to customers through retail channels? If so, you will now describe the details of your merchandising strategy, such as:

- How will products be sold in retail environments?

- Will the product require packaging?

- How will the product be displayed by retailers?

- What kinds of incentives might be required for retailers to actively sell your products?

Finally, be sure that your strategies to identify and sell to customers make sense as a whole. For example, if you identify a certain customer type for your product, the methods for attracting that customer must be consistent with the places this customer purchases products and services. Do these customers require service and warranties that are covered in the price of the product offered? Some products may need to be demonstrated to certain customers before they will purchase. For example, some individuals will want to hold, see, and use a laptop computer before purchasing it. You would need retail outlets where these customers could do this. In comparison, you might find that some buyers of laptops are willing to purchase their computers on the Internet, with no more than a photograph and a written description of the product listed. You will need to identify which customer group you are pursuing and specify how your sales efforts will meet their specific needs.

The "Sales Goals" section of the business plan provides some of the strongest evidence about the entrepreneur's understanding of how the business will be successful. It offers concrete information about the entire process of generating sales. Knowing that the possible market for a product/service may have a potential in the millions is important, but showing how sales will specifically be achieved is critical. Demonstrating to a reader that you have detailed knowledge of the entire sales process—identifying, targeting, attracting, and selling to customers—becomes a significant indicator that the business will be viable and successful. The action plan that you developed for generating sales will help you highlight the critical selling tasks to be accomplished.

Implementation: Management and Organization

The next two sections focus on implementation: who will manage the firm and the activities they will perform. These detailed sections on management and organization, operations, and execution can be very difficult to write, requiring an imagination and significant due diligence to describe the operations of the business in a concrete way.

An entrepreneur who assumes that he or she can learn how to operate the business as it emerges will have some costly lessons. A start-up can face critical problems that can easily overwhelm a fledgling firm. What if your suppliers are late with a critical parts delivery? What if your equipment breaks down? Perhaps your employees turn out to be less skilled or incompetent at selling to your customers or providing good service. What will happen if your customers don't pay on time? This section of the plan will indicate to the reader that you are prepared for success and know what to do when things go wrong.

The "Management and Organization" section of the business plan identifies the key managerial and organizational skills necessary to run the business and links these skill sets to positions within the organization. In addition, the plan should identify which individuals who are a part of the start-up team have these necessary skills. If the existing management team lacks some of the necessary skills, the plan explains how additional critical personnel will be hired to fill in any gaps. Organization charts of duties and responsibilities should not only cover the present situation but also show how the business may change as it grows over the next few years.

There are many ways to organize a business to successfully compete. Some businesses organize by function, with a department in charge of marketing, human resources, finance, production, and so on. Others structure along product line, type of customer, or geographic region. Companies vary in their degree of centralization and how rigidly they define their overall structure. In addition, companies can have a clearly defined chain of command with many levels of managers, or adopt a flatter structure with fewer layers. The particular configuration of resources and capabilities you select will depend on the type of business and its needs.

Few start-ups will have a team of individuals who have all of the necessary skills to successfully operate the business. Be honest about weaknesses in the skills and abilities of the current management team. Show how you will counteract these weaknesses by hiring employees, consultants, or advisors. Provide descriptions of critical outside board members, advisors, consultants, lawyers, and accountants. Describe how these individuals are involved in the management of the business and provide information on how you will compensate these individuals. Enterprisers who use experts and advisors wisely show others that they have a sound understanding of what it takes to manage the business successfully.

Implementation: Operations and Execution

The "Operations" section of the business plan provides a detailed description of the activities necessary to run the day-to-day operations of the business. The issues to consider vary depending on whether the firm makes and sells products or is a service business.

For manufacturing firms, the plan's "Operations" section describes the entire manufacturing process from the purchase of raw materials to the sales and service of the product in the field. The reader should feel as if he or she is walking through the factory. The enterpriser should identify critical problems that might occur in the manufacturing process and offer solutions for these issues. An often-ignored issue in managing a business is determining cash flow needs. The "Operations" section will identify suppliers and their capabilities, the payment terms specified by suppliers for parts and raw materials, and the likely time the business will need to collect cash from customers. This section should also list important machinery and equipment necessary to manufacture the products and the facilities required to house these machines and store raw materials, work in process, and finished good inventories. Repair and maintenance procedures and alternative methods of production in the case of critical machinery downtime are also important to include.

A service business will provide a detailed description of how it will provide services. This includes identifying the individuals responsible for providing services to customers and describing all the tasks necessary to insure customer satisfaction. How will service personnel be managed from initial customer contact through payment? How will quality control be handled? What kinds of support systems and equipment will service personnel need to complete their assignments?

For all businesses, the plan should outline the accounting and control systems necessary to operate the business. After reviewing this section, the reader should know

- Who will be responsible for managing the company's assets and cash?

- How will cash accounts be monitored to prevent fraud and malfeasance?

- How will inventory and supplies be managed?

- What business licenses and permits are required to operate the business?

- Will the location of the business need to be inspected?

- What kinds of measurement systems will the business implement to insure that the business is successful?

- What key metrics will monitor the business' critical success factors?

- What are the key indicators that the business is on the path to success? What are the key indicators that the business is failing?

- What remedial activities will the enterpriser implement if the business appears to be failing?

The "Execution" section of the business plan will indicate all of the critical milestones in the life the organization. These are the issues you addressed when you created the action plan described earlier in this chapter and developed the critical path for the business:

- When will essential employees be hired?

- When will a building and offices be rented or purchased?

- When will machinery be purchased and installed?

- When will training for key manufacturing and service tasks occur?

A timeline will help you identify the critical events that are necessary for business success and the correct sequence of these events. For example, the manufacture of a product will require that you install and test your machinery, order raw materials, and accept delivery before you begin production.

It is well worth your effort to prepare contingency plans for likely problem situations you may encounter. Possible "what if" scenarios include the following:

- What will happen if a key part necessary for the manufacture of your product is not delivered on time? Will you manage this problem by having a substantial inventory of this product, or will you have alternative sources of supply?

- What if a critical machine breaks down?

- What happens if renovations to your plant and offices take longer than anticipated?

- What if critical permits and licenses are delayed?

- What will occur if a key employee quits?

- Will your business have the resources, skills, and capabilities to weather unforeseen problems?

Start-ups tend to follow Murphy's Law: Anything that can go wrong, will. Are you prepared? Showing your readers that you have considered problems in advance indicates an ability to cover all your bases.

Many enterprisers are big-picture visionaries: good at seeing and selling the possibility of success and opportunity. The ability to grasp the specific details necessary to achieve these opportunities often requires a different mindset and skills. The successful development and growth of a business will require attention to these details. If the "Management and Organization," "Operations," and "Execution" sections of the business plan are well thought out, the ideas and vision of the business will come to life. The readers of the plan should be able to see how all of the aspects of the enterprise connect and how the enterprise will operate successfully. Invariably, as the business develops and grows, unforeseen problems and issues will arise, including those that were not considered in the business plan. The entrepreneur who demonstrates an ability to solve problems identified in the business plan will be better prepared to solve unforeseen issues and circumstances as they occur.

Financial Plan: How Will We Measure the Results?

The "Financial Plan" section of the business plan looks to be the most daunting aspect of the planning process. There is a strong temptation to create financial documents and reports by using formulas with estimations of growth rates. For example, it is easy to create a series of scenarios with good, better, and best estimations for sales and expenses, where "good" might be a 5 percent growth rate, "better" is a 15 percent growth rate, and "best" is a 50 percent growth rate. "Good, better, best" says that you don't have an accurate estimate of sales that you believe you can achieve. "Good, better, best" says to many readers that you are guessing. It is far better to struggle through the logic involved in generating each number rather than taking the easy route.

A good strategy for completing the financial statements is to start at the end. Begin by identifying all of the specific financing needs of the business and their timing. For example, list the cash outlays for salaries, rent, purchases of raw materials, machines, and all other expenses and capital investments and indicate when these cash outlays will occur. In addition, show when you will receive cash inflows from investments, loans, and the collection of cash sales and accounts receivable. These figures form the basis of your cash flow statement. The cash flow statement serves as the fundamental operating document for the day-to-day management of the business. Without cash, the business will be unable to meet its financial obligations.

For each figure listed in the financial statements, provide a footnote for how you arrived at this figure. For example, if equipment was purchased for cash, reference the "Operations" section of the business plan that describes this equipment. The business plan appendix will include documents describing this equipment—price, where the equipment will be purchased, maintenance agreements, and any other important technical data. For sales and expense estimates on the income statement, reference the marketing sections of the business plan that describe how you generated sales forecasts and support your forecasts with materials in the appendix, such as purchase orders from prospective customers and marketing research reports. For your own benefit, you want to know which figures in the financial statements are solid and which are guesses. The goal is to derive financial estimations that you can substantiate with evidence and logic.

Information on key industry ratios and standards will serve as a benchmark for the performance of your business. You will want to know whether the financial values you are specifying in your business plan are reasonable compared to other firms. For example, is the gross margin for your business similar to other competitors? Are the expenses in your business similar to other competitors'? Is your business more or less efficient than other businesses? If the financial standards of your business are significantly different from those of other businesses, you will need to offer reasons for these differences.

The Risk Management Association is one of the major sources of performance standards and publishes financial ratios by industry type and firm size. Most libraries and banks have copies of RMA materials. Most trade associations have information on the financial performance of firms in their industries. This information is often accessible to association members on websites. Other resources for generating industry standards are the *U.S. Industry and Trade Outlook*, published by NTIS, and the Small Business Advancement National Center, (http://www.sbaer.uca.edu), where you'll find 33 small business industry profiles.

If the business plan relates to an existing business, you should provide actual historical financial statements for the last two to five years. This information will show readers how the business has operated successfully (or not) in the past and why. You should include extensive footnotes to these financial statements that explain the rationale for these numbers.

You will be generating prospective financial statements for two to five years—a sufficient period to be able to determine at what point the firm will generate positive cash flow as well as satisfy its cash flow needs. The date when positive cash flow occurs is a very important milestone, and your financial estimates should continue for at least two years beyond that date. Important financial statements to include are income statements, balance sheets, cash flow statements, sources and uses of funds, and a list of all capital equipment and the dates and prices of purchase. Prepare statements showing monthly figures for the first year and quarterly figures for subsequent years.

Numbers that cannot be supported through evidence or logic should be referenced as "guesses." Don't pretend to know information. If you have problems generating specific numbers for parts of the financial plan, you probably have not done sufficient research on previous business plan sections.

Appendix (Supporting Documents)

The Appendix will provide information that supports the claims in the body of your business plan for such key issues in your enterprise as estimating sales, costing out your product or service, and demonstrating the competence and capabilities of yourself and your management team. The Appendix will include resumes of your management team and key advisors. You should also consider including such documentation as

(a) market analysis data and market research studies

(b) action plans for sales and distribution

(c) product specifications and photos

(d) action plans for production, operations, and service

(e) letters of reference

(f) census and demographic data

(g) contracts

(h) letters of commitment from customers, suppliers, and lenders

(i) buy/sell agreements among partners

A reader who delves into the Appendix will be looking for detailed evidence of how you arrived at critical numbers (e.g., sales, costs, product development process). You have to show that you have facts to back up your claims.

8.6 The Final Product

Congratulations! If you have persevered in completing the business plan in sufficient detail, you have built a business on paper. This business plan provides you with a good indication of how the business will operate and the critical issues that will determine its success or failure. It creates a road map that depicts where you will meet with success, as well as encounter difficulties.

Reading an actual business plan is perhaps the best way to understand the value of preparing your own plan. We have provided the business plan for Beau-Ties, Inc., on our website, www.thomsonedu.com/management/enterpriseonline. As you read it, you will see how a team of enterprisers presented its plan for a company that manufactures and sells bow ties. Let's take a quick tour of the plan so that you will be familiar with it and can answer the questions posed later in the chapter.

- **Executive Summary:** These enterprisers have done a good job of presenting the highlights of their business in just one page. They pique the reader's interest by mentioning the undeveloped competitive structure of the industry, low initial investment, integrated merchandising program, and high growth rate and potential profitability of the men's fashion accessory sector of the men's apparel industry.

- **Body of the Plan:** In the "Business Description" section the principals clearly and concisely present an overview of the business concept and why they believe it can succeed. By stating their specific goals, the principals demonstrate their understanding of their business venture's market and how they intend to achieve these objectives. The product description includes not only the features of the bow ties themselves, but also the merchandising program and support services that make their concept unique. The product matrix and product design matrix exhibits highlight these characteristics. A discussion of the men's fashion accessory industry, including statistics and results of interviews with retailers, follows. A table comparing other companies in this market to Beau-Ties supports the analysis of the competitive environment. The "Marketing Analysis/Strategy" section describes the two target customer groups and how Beau-Ties will market its product to each category. It also identifies the unique benefits the company's marketing and promotional strategy offers.

The next part of the business plan's body is devoted to the management team and operations. In addition to biographies of the principals, other equity participants, and consultants, this section outlines the overall company operating structure (three functional areas). The "Financials" section opens with the anticipated financial needs, proposed sources of funding, and expected rate of return for investors. It then summarizes the profitability (picture presented) in the detailed financial statements and refers readers to the exhibits for the statements themselves and the assumptions used to develop them.

- **Exhibits:** The 14 exhibits provide evidence that substantiates the claims made in the plan narrative. They cover product design, market data, marketing research, marketing strategy, qualifications of the management team, financial reports, and assumptions in the financial statements.

This business plan reflects the principals' understanding of their business at one particular moment in time: now. As they move forward, the business will change, and the knowledge and experience they gain in developing and operating Beau-Ties will require them to modify this business plan. The business plan enables them to see how the business *should* operate and helps them determine whether their assumptions are accurate.

Your business plan will help you be conscious and thoughtful, so that you do not manage your business moment to moment. It should be a useful, dynamic document. To keep it that way, you should revise it regularly—on a quarterly, semi-annual, or annual basis. Look upon these modifications as opportunities to reconsider why and how your business is successful. A reevaluation of your business plan will help you see whether your assumptions about your business are accurate, and whether new metrics and measures are needed. Typically, as your business grows, your priorities change—and so do those of your customers, suppliers, and employees.

Remember, if you don't have a road map and plan for your business, any route will get you there. Having a business plan will help you achieve the goals you set for yourself. Keeping your business plan updated will help you reexamine your goals and priorities.

8.7 Summary

1. A business plan serves as a game plan for your business. It provides an opportunity to practice operating your business and gives you experiences that provide an advantage over your competition.

2. Your business plan records the actions—past, present, and future—you are taking to make your business a reality. It goes beyond the feasibility study and identifies the specific tactics and actions for enterprise success. As you write a business plan, you will be able to visualize your business and gain a better understanding of what it will take to make it successful. It will show you what you know and what you need to know, as well as point out the flaws in your strategy. In addition to serving as a reality check, the business plan also becomes a valuable tool to engage others in your efforts.

3. A business plan should answer four key questions: Why you? Whom do you hurt? Why now? Why me? Your responses should demonstrate that you and your partners have the requisite skills to make the business a success and that you understand the competitive environment in which your business will operate, explain the need for and benefits of the goods or services you plan to offer, and encourage others to get involved in your business.

4. An action plan serves as preparation for writing a business plan. The three steps of an action plan are (1) identify risks, (2) develop a response strategy, and (3) control and monitor the risks and responses. Developing an action plan includes breaking each project down into deliverables and specific tasks necessary to accomplish your goals. The sequence of actions is another key component. Knowing how tasks relate to each other allows you to develop a critical path that shows the schedule of important milestones, the order to follow, and tasks to reach them.

5. Forecasting the future starts with understanding the past. The more specific you can be, the more useful your forecasts. Learning from others is an excellent way to improve your knowledge of the industry and business. Experience, either yours or someone else's, will help you develop meaningful forecasts of the time, people, equipment, facilities, and funding you need to start your business. Your forecasts should be dynamic. You will revise them in response to changes in your business environment. It's also important to identify gaps in your knowledge base so that you can fill them.

6. You should write the first business plan for yourself. As you prepare it, you will become aware of your knowledge gaps and can develop strategies to address them. Pitfalls to avoid include making unrealistic projections, underestimating the time it takes to accomplish various tasks, failing to understand the competitive landscape, and performing inadequate due diligence.

7. Your personal business plan forms the basis for the business plans you write to attract others to participate in your enterprise. You should customize these plans to the readers' interests and to your purpose in sharing it, choosing the appropriate language for your audience. The plans you write for others serve as introductions to your business and should encourage them to find out more. They should be a true

reflection of you as an enterpriser and focus on the quality of the information, not the quantity.

8. The business plan format should take into account the type of business and where it is in its life cycle. While each business plan will be different, most plans share certain characteristics and contain three main parts: the one- to two-page executive summary, the 20-page body of the business plan with a narrative that describes the enterprise and its major issues, and a section with supporting materials that provide evidence for the business facts you've described.

9. The Executive Summary provides the highlights of your business plan and invites the reader to delve into the body of the plan. Even though it is the shortest section, it is extremely important to your success and serves as the first impression readers get of you and your proposed business venture. While it comes first, you write it after you have prepared the rest of the report.

10. The body of the plan serves as a tour of your proposed business venture. It should describe your business, analyze your market (customers and competitors), explain your value proposition and distribution strategy, discuss management's qualifications, explain how the business will be organized and why, provide an overview of operations, and present a financial plan. Your narrative should address not only the management's perspective but also stakeholder issues.

11. Marketing analysis starts with the identification of customers, probably the most important business planning activity. In addition to primary customers—those people who buy your products and services—enterprisers should also identify the business's secondary customers, those people who have an interest in the operation of your business. Marketing analysis also includes understanding your competition and substitutes for your products or services.

12. Once you have analyzed your market, you can focus on how you will attract customers and distribute your goods and services to the ultimate user. This includes understanding your sales cycles, developing appropriate advertising and promotion strategies, setting pricing and credit policies, and selecting distribution channels. A value chain map can help identify the steps required to accomplish these objectives and demonstrate how they work together.

13. The next sections of the plan's body present the implementation program for the business. The "Management" section of the business plan describes the executive team and the capabilities they bring to the business, as well as the outside consultants and professional advisors (attorneys, accountants). This section should also include an organization chart that shows the overall business structure and who will be responsible for key functional departments. After reviewing the "Operations" section, a reader should have a clear picture of the firm's daily activities and how the firm will produce its goods or services. This section should also address potential problems and offer solutions. The

"Execution Plan" summarizes all the important activities you identified in other parts of the plan and plots them on a timeline of critical milestones. The timeline demonstrates that your activities are internally consistent and coordinated with the financial projections.

14. The "Financial Plan" includes both actual historical financial statements for an existing business and projected financial information for the next two to five years. It is important to explain the assumptions you use to develop the projected statements and indicate how the financial statements compare to industry benchmarks. This section also identifies the financing needs and their timing, as well as possible sources.

15. The Appendix contains documents that support the assumptions on which you based the plan's marketing analysis, action plans, product specifications, and financial statements. Presenting the facts that back up your claims lends credibility to your plan.

Review Questions

1. What is a business plan and why do many enterprisers start businesses without writing one? List several reasons for writing such a plan and describe the benefits of doing so.

2. Describe the four questions a business plan should answer and explain the objective for each.

3. Discuss the three steps required to prepare an action plan and the importance of each step.

4. What is a critical path and why should you identify it for the business you want to start?

5. Describe several steps enterprisers can take to increase the accuracy of their projections.

6. Differentiate between the business plan an enterpriser writes for his or her own use and the plans that are written for others. What are the key issues to consider for each type of business plan?

7. Name the three major parts of a business plan and what each should include. Why

should you write the executive summary last?

8. Summarize the key points in the business description.

9. What two broad topics are the focus of the marketing analysis section? Describe the types of information this section should include.

10. How does marketing strategy differ from marketing analysis? What are the major issues that this section addresses?

11. Describe the information you'd include in the "Management" section of a plan for a new business.

12. Why is it important to provide a detailed operations summary and execution plan in the business plan and what should these sections cover?

13. What are the drawbacks to developing a "good, better, best" financial plan? How should an enterpriser prepare financial information?

14. What is the objective of the Appendix and why should the supporting documents go here rather than in the plan's body?

Applying What You've Learned

1. Differentiate between a feasibility study and a business plan. When are business plans necessary, and when are they not?

2. Consider how the content of a business plan might differ based on the interests of the reader. What would an investor be looking for in a business plan that a potential employee might not? What would a potential supplier be looking for in a business plan that a customer might not?

Read the Beau-Ties business plan provided on our website, www.thomsonedu.com/management/ enterpriseonline, before answering the following questions.

3. You are one of the founders of Beau-Ties. You want to prepare a business plan before proceeding any further, but your partners don't think it is necessary. How would you convince them to write a plan, and why?

4. For whom do you think the Beau-Ties business plan was written, the founders or other readers, and why? How well does the plan address the issues presented in section 8.3, "Writing the Business Plan"? Explain your answer.

5. Develop a critical path chart for Beau-Ties. Include the rationale for the milestones you've chosen.

6. Write the "elevator speech" for Beau-Ties. Divide the class into teams of two to four members, with half playing the role of company founder and half taking the part of a potential investor. Make the presentation to the investor(s). Get feedback and revise the speech as needed. Pick several groups to present their final speeches to the class for more feedback.

7. Analyze the sections of the Beau-Ties business plan as follows:

   (a) *Executive Summary and Business Description.* How well do they answer the questions posed in the chapter's discussions of these sections?
   (b) *Marketing analysis and strategies.* How well do the enterprisers identify potential customers, competition, demand, and potential market size for the company?
   (c) *Management.* Is the Beau-Ties management team qualified to turn this business plan into a viable business, and why?
   (d) *Operations and execution plan.* Does it enable the company to meet its stated objectives?
   (e) *Financial plan and the assumptions.* Do they seem reasonable for the business as described in the plan?
   (f) *Exhibits.* Are the documents included as exhibits sufficient to support the business plan? What additional material would you like to see in this section?

   In your opinion, does the Beau-Ties business plan a good case, and why?

Enterprisers on the Web

1. An enterpriser can buy software designed specifically for writing business plans. Using an Internet search engine such as Google, Yahoo, Excite, or Lycos, select three such programs.

   (a) Compare their features.

   (b) See if you can find user reviews to determine how well the programs live up to their claims.
   (c) Based on your analysis, which seems to be the best, and why?
   (d) Now, read the *Inc.* article "Garbage In, Garbage Out," which discusses

advantages and disadvantages of using one of these programs to write a business plan (http://www.inc.com/magazine/19960801/1764.html). Summarize the article's arguments and compare them to your research. Do you agree and why? (While the article is old and some of the software mentioned may no longer be available, the basic information is still valid.)

2. Using resources such as the sites listed below, locate three companies in an industry (or industries) in which you might like to start a business. (You can also find annual reports at companies' websites.) How does each company describe itself? What are the goals and objectives of the companies? How do they describe their customers and competitors? How do they describe their competitive advantage?

CEOEXPRESS at http://ceoexpress.com/

Public Register's Annual Report Service at http://www.annualreportservice.com/

Hoovers Online at http://www.hoovers.com/

3. Using a general search engine such as Google, Yahoo, Excite, Askjeeves, Altavista, or hotbot), search for trade associations that cater to the industry in which you'd like to start your business.

(a) What services and publications does this trade association offer?

(b) How often does the trade association meet for trade shows?

(c) What are the dues for belonging to the trade association?

4. Now search for industry reports on your chosen industry. Who is publishing these reports? Why do they make this information available to others (e.g., they are consultants to this industry, they do mergers and acquisitions for companies in this industry, they sell stock in businesses in this industry)? Which appear to be the most valuable and why?

5. Using the industry resources you've identified thus far, answer the following questions:

(a) What companies are identified in this industry? Why are these companies identified rather than others? What constitutes the characteristics of these companies that would put them in this industry?

(b) What trends in this industry are likely to occur in the next five years?

(c) What do industry experts predict is the likely growth rate of this industry in the next five years?

End Notes

1. Frédéric Delmar and Scott Shane, "Does Business Planning Facilitate the Development of New Ventures?" *Strategic Management Journal*, December 2003, pp. 1165–1185; and Jon Liao and William B. Gartner, "The Effects of Pre-Venture Plan Timing and Perceived Environmental Uncertainty on the Persistence of Emerging Firms," *Small Business Economics*, August 2006, pp. 23–40.

2. This section is based on material in Eric Verzuh, *The Fast Forward MBA in Project Management* (New York: John Wiley and Sons, Inc., 1999).

Enterprising Strategies

chapter 9

Pathways to Enterprise Creation

1. Enterprisers can start businesses in many different ways. Pursuing opportunities involves a wide range of new venture strategies, situations, and behaviors. We all have different interests, skills, knowledge, and abilities. It is important to discover our strengths and to use them to choose the most appropriate route to entrepreneurship.

2. The use of a typology to describe new venture pathways focuses attention on the differences among enterprisers rather than on the supposed differences between enterprisers and "others."

    We can group similar businesses into eight archetypes, each of which suggests different start-up strategies and behaviors that enterprisers can apply to their start-up situations. The eight pathways to enterprise creation are:

    - Type 1—Escaping to Something New
    - Type 2—Putting the Deal Together
    - Type 3—Using Prior Skills & Contacts (Professionals)
    - Type 4—Purchasing a Firm
    - Type 5—Leveraging Expertise
    - Type 6—Aggressive Service
    - Type 7—Pursuing the Unique Idea
    - Type 8—Methodical Organizing

3. In addition to describing the archetype profiles, it is helpful to analyze them using 19 factors that cover environment, business, person, and start-up process. These archetypes can serve as broad guides for getting into business. However, your own start-up pathway is likely to be a blend of several of the eight archetypes.

Suppose as you travel to other cultures, you see how women use plant-based products for skin care. Working in a plastic surgeon's office and then as an aesthetician, you continue to increase your knowledge about natural skin care. Because you live in Colorado, you are especially interested in the healing properties of local plants and start mixing ingredients on your stove. Once you develop a formula that works, you start a home-based company to make your first product, Cowgirl Cream.

The case study in this chapter tells the story of Cowgirl Enterprises' founder Donna Baase, and follows the growth of her natural beauty products company. You'll learn about her particular path to success, and the chapter describes seven other pathways to entrepreneurial creation. Which one will you choose?

9.0 What Kind of Enterprise Are You Starting?

Just as there are no average or typical kinds of enterprises, there is no one "right" way to start a business. As we discussed in Chapter 1, enterprisers can start and successfully operate many different types of enterprises. For example, you'd start a pizza restaurant in a different way than you would a biotechnology company. A business consulting company will be started in a different way than a company that intends to make and sell ice cream. In this chapter we'll explore the different ways that enterprisers can start their businesses. You'll learn to pinpoint and focus on the specific issues for the kind of business you want to form.

To accomplish this, we group similar types of businesses into broad categories called archetypes. An **archetype** is a model or prototype from which similar things can be made. In this case, we refer to a model for an ideal business in a particular group. The archetype does not describe each individual enterprise in the group but rather the best representation of a typical business in that group. As we delve more deeply into the archetypes presented in this chapter, you will get a better sense of how the ideal type for each group is both similar to and different from the examples we use to describe actual businesses in these groups. You might also consider each archetype as a particular pathway and set of directions to use when setting off on the journey of enterprise creation.

This chapter describes eight broad archetypes for starting enterprises, as listed in Exhibit 9.1.[1] The profile for each archetype includes the three major levels of analysis we identified in Chapter 1 (individual, enterprise, environment) plus the

archetype
A model or prototype from which similar things can be made.

exhibit 9.1

Eight Archetypes for New Business Ventures

Type	Name
1	Escaping to Something New
2	Putting the Deal Together
3	Using Prior Skills & Contacts (Professionals)
4	Purchasing a Firm
5	Leveraging Expertise
6	Aggressive Service
7	Pursuing the Unique Idea
8	Methodical Organizing

Source: William B. Gartner, Terence R. Mitchell, and Karl H. Vesper, "A Taxonomy of New Business Ventures," *Journal of Business Venturing,* May 1989, pp. 169–186.

start-up process for that type of enterprise. Each archetype, therefore, answers four questions:

1. What kinds of individuals are likely to start this kind of enterprise?

2. What does this kind of enterprise look like and how does it compete?

3. In what kind of industry and environment does this enterprise compete?

4. What does the enterpriser do to start this kind of enterprise?

For these four questions, we identify 19 specific issues to help categorize the wide array of different enterprises as shown in Exhibit 9.2. An archetype will not differ from the other seven types on all 19 characteristics. The *pattern* of responses to the 19 questions is what may differ. Exhibit 9.3 illustrates the significant similarities and differences among the archetypes across the 19 questions.

exhibit 9.2

19 Questions for Business Archetypes

Individual Level

1. Did the enterpriser's previous work experiences provide opportunities for advancement? (great to none)

2. Are the enterpriser's previous work experiences similar to the work required in the new enterprise? (similar to unrelated)

3. What was the enterpriser's interest in starting a business? (always interested to never interested)

4. Did the enterpriser see much chance that the new venture would fail? (0% to 95% chance of failure)

Enterprise Level

5. Did the enterprise have any partners when it was started? (yes or no)

6. When did the enterprise begin to offer its products/services compared to its competitors? (First to after all of the others)

7. What is the quality of the enterprise's goods/services compared to its competitors? (lower to higher)

8. How similar are the enterprise's goods/services compared to its competitors? (different to same)

9. How flexible is the enterprise to adapting its goods/services compared to its competitors? (much lower to much higher)

Environmental Level

10. How complex are the technology and skills required to manufacture products or deliver services in this industry? (simple to complex)

11. How important are contacts with suppliers in this industry? (important to not important)

12. Do customers need a lot of expertise to purchase goods/services in the enterprise's industry? (high to none)

Startup Process

How much time did the enterpriser spend (a lot to none) on the following:

13. Convincing customers to buy the enterprise's products/services?

14. Seeking advice from lawyers, consultants, bankers and friends?

15. Seeking resources (loans, equity, suppliers, etc.) to start the enterprise?

16. Advertising, issuing press releases, sending out brochures?

17. Manufacturing the product or providing the service?

18. Was the enterprise purchased or is it a franchise? (yes or no)

19. At the beginning of the startup process, how much time did the enterpriser devote to starting the new enterprise? (full time to part time)

Source: William B. Gartner, Terence R. Mitchell, and Karl H. Vesper, "A Taxonomy of New Business Ventures," *Journal of Business Venturing*, May 1989, pp. 173–174.

exhibit 9.3   Profiles of New Business Ventures

				Type				
	1	**2**	**3**	**4**	**5**	**6**	**7**	**8**
	Escaping to Something New	Putting the Deal Together	Rollover Skills/ Contacts	Purchasing a Firm	Leveraging Expertise	Aggressive Service	Pursuing the Unique Idea	Methodical Organizing
Individual Characteristics								
Opportunities for advancement in previous work	Low	NS	NS	NS	NS	NS	High	High

(continued)

Similarity of previous work to work in new venture	Low	High	High	NS	High	High	Low	Low
Previous interest in starting a company	NS	NS	NS	NS	Low	High	High	NS
Perception of risk of new venture failure	NS	Low	NS	Low	Low	NS	NS	High
Organizational Characteristics								
Active partners involved in operations	Likely	No	No	No	Yes	No	Likely	Likely
Product/ service pioneer	NS	NS	NS	NS	NS	NS	Yes	NS
Relative quality of products/services	NS	NS	NS	NS	High	High	High	High
Relative similarity of products/services	NS	Unique	Similar	Similar	Unique	NS	Unique	NS
Relative flexibility to adapt to customer's needs	NS	NS	NS	High	High	High	NS	NS
Environmental Characteristics								
Technology	Simple	NS	Complex	NS	Complex	Complex	Simple	NS
Importance of contacts	NS	High	NS	NS	NS	High	NS	NS
Customer expertise in product purchasing	Low	Low	Low	Low	High	High	High	High
Process Characteristics (How much did you spend?)								
Selling	NS	NS	Low	NS	High	High	Low	High
Seeking advice	NS	Low	Low	NS	NS	High	High	High
Seeking resources	NS	NS	Low	High	NS	NS	High	High
Advertising	NS	NS	NS	NS	NS	NS	NS	NS
Manufacturing/ delivery service	NS	NS	NS	High	High	NS	High	High
Purchase firm	NS	NS	NS	Yes	NS	NS	NS	NS
Time commitment at start-up	NS	Part-time	Full-time	NS	NS	Full-time	Part-time	NS

NS, not a significant differentiating variable for this gestalt.

Source: William B. Gartner, Terence R. Mitchell, and Karl H. Vesper, "A Taxonomy of New Business Ventures," _Journal of Business Venturing,_ May 1989, pp. 176–177.

9.1 Eight Pathways to Enterprise Creation

Each archetype represents an ideal pathway that enterprisers use for getting into business. Think of these archetypes as templates for the kinds of people, firms, environments, and start-up activities that are most likely to be associated with each other. Our research shows that certain types of individuals are more likely to start particular kinds of firms in specific industries, using distinct kinds of activities to start these businesses. For example, the start-up of some businesses, such as accounting, law, and veterinary practices, requires those enterprisers to have specific skills and abilities. In addition, they also are more likely to have established a network of potential customers to whom they can provide their services. It is this cross-level combination of characteristics at the individual, organizational, and environmental levels that provides us with some important insights into the firm start-up process.

Now let's look at the characteristics of each archetype and at an example of an enterpriser who started this form of business.

Type 1: Escaping to Something New

Individuals who start enterprises often seek to escape from their previous jobs—jobs that, from their perspective, offer few rewards in terms of salary, challenging work, and promotion opportunities. The new venture is in a different industry and represents a different type of work from the enterpriser's previous job. The enterpriser begins the enterprise part time and eventually works up to a full-time commitment, meeting capital requirements through savings and loans from family and friends. The majority of the enterpriser's time is devoted to finding a location for the business and in making sales.

This is an enterpriser oriented toward the general, or average, consumer. This type of firm enters an established market and offers goods or services similar to its competitors. The goods are not technically complicated (e.g., pets, furniture, clothes), yet the industry is very competitive because of the many other firms offering similar products or services.

Janice Myers (all names disguised) and her sister, a speech therapist, took this pathway to start their pet store. Both women had become dissatisfied with their jobs. After spending several months discussing business ownership, they convinced themselves that they had the skills and resources to proceed. After taking classes on how to start a business at the local university and the Small Business Administration, the sisters spent about three months preparing to open their business. They did a market location study, found a building in a good area of town, signed a lease, and began renovating the interior. They used personal funds to finance the business.

During this time they went to other pet stores in their area and asked for advice. One owner allowed them to look at her books and introduced them to the right suppliers. The two sisters also ran this person's store for a couple of days to better understand how to operate this kind of business.

Why were these enterprisers successful in getting into business? The sisters attribute their success to their enjoyment of running a pet store, which is apparent to their customers. The sisters have established a good reputation around town for their knowledge of pets and for the service they provide. Although most of the products the sisters sell are available at lower prices at other places, their customers prefer to shop at this store because of the advice and good service the sisters provide.

Type 2: Putting the Deal Together

Enterprisers in this group assemble the different aspects of the business (suppliers, wholesale and retail channels, customers) into a "deal" designed to ensure success for each participant. Two types of enterprises make up this group. The first is the real estate developer. This enterpriser's experience putting deals together for other firms forms the basis for the business start-up. The other type of enterprise is the novelty firm start-up, where an enterpriser comes up with an idea for a product, finds a manufacturer to make the product, makes sales calls to wholesalers and retailers, and generates primary demand for the product. The novelty firm coordinates the different functions of the business among the various parties (manufacturer, wholesaler, retailer, etc.). For both types of firms, a good contact network—knowing the right kinds of people—is a critical factor. The real estate developer needs to know the land-owners, the builders, and the investors for projects. The novelty enterpriser has to know purchasing agents in key stores.

John Bosworth is a good example of a Type 2 deal maker. Using his experience developing houses for the elderly with the state housing authority, he started a real estate development company to assist other businesses in obtaining state contracts to build housing for the elderly. His firm puts deals together: arranging financing from the state to build housing, getting an architect to draw up plans for the buildings, finding a builder willing to construct the units for a given price, and locating the land. Mr. Bosworth's actions, beyond his deal-making activities, involved incorporating and investing some money in renting an office. The work he was able to get came from contacts he had from his previous work.

Type 3: Using Prior Skills and Contacts (Professionals)

Professional start-ups are formed by enterprisers who held positions in which they used technical skills and expertise similar to those required in the new business. These enterprisers did not have a long-term desire to start a business and only began to pursue the pathway of enterprise creation after discovering that job advancement and career and salary growth were blocked. They view starting a business as a risky effort. Rather than searching for capital, these enterprisers use their own money. Because the enterprisers bring industry expertise and contacts to the table, they spend very little time studying the industry or learning the technical requirements of the job. They sell to their previous customer contact base rather than devote energy to marketing or advertising. These enterprisers quit their jobs to work full time in their new business. Examples include enterprises that depend on the enterpriser's professional expertise, such as CPA firms, consultants, personnel agencies, and advertising firms. In many respects, these enterprises offer a generic service that other firms also offer. The new enterprise competes by offering better service than others.

An example of this archetype is April Burke, who started a management compensation consulting business—the same kind of work she had performed for another company for the previous six years. She believed she could provide higher quality service on her own. She first contacted a lawyer to help her incorporate her business. Then she contacted some of her previous clients to offer her services. Developing a reputation for good work was very important because most of her clients (human resource departments in large corporations) knew one another. Ms. Burke also wrote articles in trade journals to build a strong reputation in her industry.

Type 4: Purchasing a Business or Acquiring a Franchise

Both purchasing a business and acquiring a franchise are significant pathways for becoming an enterpriser. Because so many enterprisers use these two pathways to start their businesses, we will devote a chapter to each method. For now, we will outline the characteristics of enterprisers who are more likely to pursue these two routes.

Three types of firms fall into this category of new business venture: the purchase firm, a firm that is family owned or started with family assistance, and the franchise. All three types offer products and services of the same kind and quality as their competitors. These firms compete by adapting to the changing needs of their customers. The types of goods and services offered are not complex, and the entrepreneur's work background is typically similar to the venture acquired. Although enterprisers who follow this path had opportunities for advancement and growth in their previous jobs, they had long-term goals of owning a business. These enterprisers perceive the new enterprise as low risk.

With both purchasing and franchising, enterprisers must find capital to fund the business acquisition or purchase the franchise. Much of the owners' time is devoted to financial planning. Enterprisers who follow this path make a full-time commitment upon purchase or start-up of the franchise. In purchasing an ongoing concern, they view it as a turnaround situation and hope to run it more profitably than the previous owners. With an acquisition of either an independent company or a franchise, enterprisers spend a great deal of time evaluating the business' goods or services and becoming very familiar with the different aspects of the business.

A good example of a Type 4 start-up enterpriser is Lance Vermont, who purchased a bike shop. Lance describes himself as a bike person, and from childhood he dreamt of owning a bike shop. After retiring from the military, he decided to go to college. While at college he found a bike shop and bought out the owner. Why did he buy an existing business rather than start his own? He recognized that the college town could support only one bike shop. Since buying the firm, Lance has quadrupled its sales. His success is based on four factors:

(a) His enthusiasm for biking

(b) Providing better service than other bike shops in the general area

(c) Taking courses to learn how to operate a business, including marketing, for which he did a study of bike purchasing patterns for his area

(d) Absence of competition; although some department and discount stores sell bikes, he has the only store that services bikes and handles 99 percent of the repair market

Type 5: Leveraging Expertise

These enterprisers are experts, among the best in their technical field. Past work experiences provided a great deal of opportunity for growth, and the enterprisers had little previous interest in starting a business. But when an opportunity presents itself (usually an idea for a new product or for the modification of an old product that their present employer declines to pursue), they feel that pursuing such an opportunity presents little risk. Even though the business is in an established market, it offers very different products/services, of higher quality, than its competition. These enterprisers typically seek the help of partners to start the business.

The industry environment is usually characterized by high technical change and complexity. The firm is highly flexible in adapting to customer needs, because the enterprisers' expertise keeps them keenly aware of changes in the industry. Customers are purchasing agents or committees who analyze the business' products/services before purchase, making sales strategy a major focus of the business. Other firms pose a low competitive threat since the experts' products/services have special features that attract customers.

A good example of a Type 5 enterpriser is Virginia Albertson. She and several partners quit their jobs to start a business that installs a special type of inventory tracking software on PCs. Her previous work involved writing software for the same type of application, but for larger computers. As PCs became more powerful, she and her four partners saw an opportunity to start a business using the Intel/Windows platform. The enterprise is nationally known as the best supplier and installer of this type of inventory tracking software. Most of their clients are Fortune 500 corporations.

Baidu Searches for China's Market

With 132 million Internet users, the second largest online market, China attracts many companies eager for a share of its riches. Unlike other countries, however, where Google and Yahoo! fight for the lead, China has its own search giant: Baidu. Often called the Chinese Google, Baidu is the brainchild of Robin Li, who studied computer science in the United States after graduating from Beijing University. Tiring of academia once he completed his master's degree, Li joined *The Wall Street Journal's* online edition in its formative years. Intrigued by the problems involved in sorting information, he moved to InfoSeek, a search engine. By 1998, however, many firms, Infoseek and Yahoo among them, were shifting their focus from search as a business to content-driven business models.

Li believed passionately that search had a strong future. He left Infoseek, raised $1.2 million in funding from U.S. venture capital firms, and returned to China. In 2000, he and partner Eric Xu, a former Xerox employee, started Baidu as a uniquely Chinese search company. Later that year the pair raised an additional $10 million in venture capital.

The name Baidu, inspired by an ancient Chinese poem, means hundreds of times and represents the "persistent search for the ideal." Li and Xu chose the name to reinforce the company's Chinese heritage, positioning it as a local company that understands China, the Chinese, the Chinese language, and the regulatory environment. "We think search is not just about technology," explains Li, who owns 22 percent of Baidu. "It's also about language. It's also about culture." Designing a search engine that can deal with the complexities and nuances of the Chinese language was a major challenge, and one at which Baidu excelled.

Although Baidu mimicked Google's simple look, it let advertisers pay to rank higher in search results—a major cultural difference between China and the United States. The Chinese see paid results as demonstrating an advertiser's confidence in its products, whereas Americans believe that paid search compromises objectivity. "If an advertiser wants to pay a lot of money, that probably says something," Li says. "The best measure for this is our growth pattern. If users keep coming back to our service, we're doing the right thing."

Baidu often reminds users of its Chinese ownership, playing up a historical distrust of outsiders. It runs ads showing locals saying to foreigners, "You don't understand us, you don't understand us." According to Dick Wei, a JPMorgan Chase China Internet analyst, "Google is still perceived as a foreign search engine, so Chinese prefer to use Baidu when searching for anything about China. They only use Google for foreign information. Also, the relevancy of search results from Baidu is better than Google's results in China, which has helped Baidu win market share."

Understanding the Chinese business and regulatory environments gives Baidu a significant advantage over its foreign competitors. Government censorship is a particularly difficult area for companies such as Google. They are subject to strict rules and censorship, which conflict with their usual ways of conducting business. Baidu chose to let government censors oversee its site, thereby winning government support.

These reasons propelled Baidu to the top of the Chinese search market, despite its Western rivals' more sophisticated technology and management expertise. By 2006, Baidu had a 70 percent share of China's search market and a market value in

(continued)

An Enterprising World

excess of $3 billion. It has been profitable since 2004. Its market dominance continues to grow at the expense of Google, whose share has dropped from 25 percent in 2005 to about 15 percent in early 2007.

Today Baidu offers more than search, with news links, MP3 music and image searches, message boards, a wiki encyclopedia (with content provided by users), a social networking service, maps, and more. Its Post Bar feature combines online message boards and social networking. Recently it added phonetic search so that a user can enter Chinese keywords using the English alphabet. Major U.S. companies, such as Viacom and Microsoft, acknowledge Baidu's leadership in China and are forming strategic alliances to gain entry to the Chinese market. Viacom teamed with Baidu to distribute television shows and music videos through a new MTV channel at Baidu's site.

Last month, Baidu announced plans to enter Japan's search market. "Our proven strength in non-English-language search, the high Internet penetration in Japan, [and] similarities between the Chinese and Japanese languages make this market an ideal next step," Mr. Li said.

Discussion Questions

1. Using the 19 factors as a way to evaluate the Baidu story, what new venture pathway seems to best fit?

2. Which aspects of Robin Li's prior experience were helpful in starting Baidu?

3. How has emphasizing its Chinese heritage given Baidu an advantage over its competition?

4. What steps might non-Chinese Internet companies take to gain market share in China?

Sources: Based on "The Baidu Story," Baidu.com website, http://www.baidu.com (January 11, 2007); "Baidu.com, Inc." *Hoover's Company Records*, January 1, 2007, downloaded from ProQuest database (January 10, 2007); "Baidu to Enter Japanese Search Market in 2007," *Xinhua-PRNewswire*, December 4, 2007, http://www.newscom.com; David Barboza, "The Rise of Baidu (That's Chinese for Google)," *New York Times*, September 17, 2006, pp. 3.1, 3.7; Andrew Batson, "Viacom Forges Online-Video Deal With China's Baidu to Boost MTV," *The Wall Street Journal*, October 18, 2006, p. A19; David Greising, "Baidu vs. Google," *Chicago Tribune*, December 3, 2006, p. 1; Normandy Madden, "Google Is Clearly King of Search-Except in China," *Advertising Age*, January 22, 2007, p. 18; and "Microsoft Teams Up with Baidu to Deliver Paid Search Listings in China," Baidu press release, December 14, 2006, http://www.baidu.com (January 11, 2007).

Type 6: The Aggressive Service Enterprise

Compared to the Type 3 enterprise (professionals), the Type 6 enterprise is a very intense service-oriented firm. Type 6 businesses are usually consulting firms dedicated to a very specialized area such as technology transfer or certain types of executive recruiting. The enterpriser's involvement level is very high; a great deal of time is spent identifying and selling to customers, advertising, and scanning for new opportunities. Little time is spent searching for resources, because start-up costs are low or the enterpriser knows people who will contribute the necessary resources. Individuals who form Type 6 firms have always wanted to start a business to build on previous work or educational training. The environment requires that these enterprisers have specific professional or technical expertise.

The products/services are offered to a very narrow range of customers with very specific needs. Knowing the right people in this industry is very important for making sales or for gaining access to those who influence which firms have the opportunity to make sales. The firm enters a marketplace which is relatively new. The firm's products/services are somewhat better and different from those of other ventures.

Jefferson Smith's investment banking company is a good example of a Type 6 start-up. Before going into business for himself, he had been an investment banker at three different Wall Street firms. A very aggressive and outgoing person, he was always meeting new people and contacts who provided opportunities for investment banking deals.

To start his company, he filed papers of incorporation, found an office, talked with many people in the investment banking business about his new firm, and expanded his contact base using his present contacts to make others. He also developed an innovative way to provide investment banking services, which he marketed to his clients. He sought out new markets in areas of the United States that lacked the services he provided, and he sold his products/services in those areas.

Type 7: Pursuing the Unique Idea

This type of enterprise is created to pursue an idea for a new product or service. These products/services are of high quality but not technically sophisticated or difficult to manufacture. The business is flexible in changing its products to meet customer needs. Since this is the first business in the marketplace to offer this item or service, there is some uncertainty as to whether customers can be found. The work in this new business is different from the enterpriser's work in a previous job, which offered opportunities for growth and advancement. However, the enterpriser has always wanted to start and own a business and is constantly alert for new opportunities. The enterpriser doesn't know if it's possible to acquire the resources required to begin the business and to deliver the products/services with the desired high quality. Therefore, the new venture seems risky.

Franklin Boots worked in advertising and in his spare time developed his own innovative product ideas. One business that he started involved replacement collar stays, since he often needed them for his own shirts. His idea incorporated a unique package for these collar stays. Using the yellow pages, he called manufacturers of collar stays and purchased some. He then devoted a great deal of time to developing his package and label. He went on the road to generate orders, selling his product through manufacturers' representatives. Because this was a very small and unique market, he had no competitors.

Many enterprisers, however, aren't sure what steps to take to bring a product idea to reality. They may look to consultants who specialize in commercializing ideas. The Enterprising Ethics box explains how Big Idea Group acts as an idea broker for inventors and the ethical implications of doing so.

enterprising ethics

Making Money from Other People's Ideas

For many enterprisers, coming up with an exciting idea is not the difficult part. Figuring out what to do next presents a major challenge, however. Is the idea as good as it seems? Is there a large-enough market for it to build a profitable business? How should the product be priced, packaged, and sold? Is financing available to develop the business concept?

Michael Collins, a former inventor, knows just how frustrating this process can be. He started Kid Galaxy, a toy company that produced Bendos, action figures that could be posed. From his own experience he saw a need for a company to work with independent inventors who needed help commercializing promising ideas. Often innovators do not have the skills or interest to become entrepreneurs and build a company, Collins believes. These inventors are better off licensing their ideas to another company.

In 2000 he formed Big Idea Group (BIG), a Manchester, New Hampshire, company that matches inventors with companies that can manufacture and market these consumer products (http://www.bigideagroup.net). In addition to representing inventors, BIG offers corporations access to its network of more than 8,000 inventors with marketable concepts. To date BIG has helped inventors develop and market more than 50 products, including toys, cosmetics, luggage, pet products, office supplies, crafts, kitchenware, housewares, tools, and storage and organization products. The company's major corporate clients include Avon, Gillette, Fortune Brands, Staples, Sunbeam, Target, and Toys "R" Us.

Ideas come to BIG in several ways. Inventors submit them directly to BIG by mail or phone, or in person at BIG Roadshows throughout the United States. At Roadshows, inventors present their ideas privately to a panel of industry experts. BIG also conducts Idea Hunts on behalf of corporate sponsors

looking for marketable ideas in a specific industry. BIG evaluates ideas at no charge and offers advice to inventors. Its Entry Agreement includes confidentiality protection for inventors. BIG then conducts additional research and responds to inventors in about a month. "Innovators can lose objectivity when it comes to their ideas," Collins says. "My job is to guide them through the process. I ask them a series of questions, and based on the viability of their idea, help them decide what to do with it."

BIG evaluates ideas for appeal, originality, market potential, competitive environment, and compliance with safety standards. When BIG finds an idea it likes, it offers to become the inventor's agent, again at no charge. The inventor signs an agreement that gives BIG either the right to represent the idea for 180 days, or the right to commercialize or sublicense the idea. Its revenues come from royalties and advances from companies that license the idea, and they split this revenue 50-50 with the inventor. Because BIG provides most of its services for free, it is very selective in the ideas it chooses to represent: Only 1 to 3 percent of submissions become agented deals.

Discussion Questions

1. What kind of enterprise start-up pathway is Big Idea Group (BIG)? What benefits does it provide to inventors?

2. How does BIG deal with the ethical issues related to ownership of an idea with business potential?

3. How does BIG develop trust between the inventors and the clients that BIG represents?

4. As a successful entrepreneur, you've been asked to participate on BIG's Roadshow panel when it comes to your area. You receive no payment for serving on the panel and helping BIG spot marketable ideas. Would you participate, and why?

Sources: BIG Idea Group website, http://www.bigideagroup.net (January 30, 2007); D.C. Denison, "BIG Founders Aim To Be the Fathers of Invention," *Boston Globe,* April 28, 2002, p. C.2; and "Making It: Michael Collins," *Business NH,* August 2006, p. 46.

Type 8: Methodical Organizing

This type of firm takes form slowly during the start-up period. The enterpriser devotes a great deal of time to all of the aspects of the enterprise—planning, marketing, production, and finance—and has to learn the entire business from the ground up. The enterpriser's previous work experience provides excellent opportunities for job growth and salary increase, yet this person has a high desire to own a business. The new business is seen as risky since it is in an area where the enterpriser has little previous experience or expertise. The enterpriser's use of planning, both in acquiring skills and performing the tasks required for the new venture, reflect the methodical aspects of this path to business creation.

The firm's products/services are similar to those of other firms, but the firm has some new twist, either by having a slightly different way to manufacture the product or provide the service, or by selling to a slightly different type of customer. This is a very competitive environment. Customers require highly technical and competent products/services, and there are many firms trying to meet these demands. The enterpriser frequently deals with middlemen—retailers or purchasing agents—to reach customers and spends considerable time and money on advertising. Initially the enterpriser makes a part-time commitment to get the venture on its feet and earns money elsewhere to keep it afloat.

Lindsey Price started a company that manufactured collapsible baby strollers. She had a BA in English Literature, an MBA in finance and marketing, and work experience in marketing with a large food conglomerate. She quickly became dissatisfied with the corporate lifestyle. She decided to start a business in an industry meeting the following criteria:

(a) small industry

(b) not capital intensive

(c) history of a low rate of innovation

(d) little credit extension required of manufacturers to retailers

(e) weak competitors

She identified several industries that met these criteria before choosing the children's furniture industry. She conducted focus groups to learn which children's furniture products were the most unsatisfactory to consumers. Because the baby stroller was most often mentioned, Lindsey designed a collapsible baby stroller that folded into a very small size. It was the first of its type on the market. She sought out major retailers to carry this stroller. The business devoted a great deal of time to meeting the needs of the large retailers by doing things such as creating specialized packaging. Lindsey's goal was to saturate the market with her unique stroller design before other competitors entered. She contracted with another company for the initial production of the stroller. The business plan estimated sales per year and she had calculated breakeven at a certain number of units per month. Within a year, sales per month were three times breakeven, and she took over manufacture of the stroller.

9.2 What Kind of Enterpriser Are You?

As we indicated at the beginning of the chapter, exploring these eight types of business creation pathways helps enterprisers recognize the various ways to craft strategies for success. Now let's look at the differences and similarities among these pathways in greater detail. We'll compare the pathways using each of the 19 variables shown in Exhibit 9.2 (p. 282), dividing them into the four categories of individual, organization, environment, and process, as in the exhibit. In the following section, we will compare some of the archetypes as a whole to other pathways. For each category we describe, we will also provide some examples of enterprisers that seem to fit the characteristics of that category. Note that each example is in some respects unique—and that no example will fit each of the types exactly.

We believe that by making comparisons among the 19 variables and the 8 types, you will begin to realize that many kinds of businesses require a specific type of person. If you were thinking of starting an enterprise that sold real estate, it would quickly become obvious to you that you would need to devote time to obtaining a real estate license. But as we've shown in the descriptions of the eight archetypes, certain kinds of businesses—especially Type 3 (professional) businesses like real estate brokerages—require more than specific skills and knowledge. Enterprisers who start real estate brokerage businesses need an established base of contacts in the community, both buyers and sellers of houses, and a reputation for being successful at helping customers buy or sell their homes. Knowing how important it is to have skills, knowledge, contacts, and many years of work experience in the real estate industry will enable you to evaluate your skills and abilities and match them to start-up pathways that will result in a successful venture.

For example, a number of our students were interested in starting a financial planning and investing business catering to wealthy individuals. When they interviewed enterprisers who started businesses in this field, they learned that nearly everyone had first worked a minimum of five and as many as ten years in a firm that provided just these financial planning and investing services. Most of these enterprisers acquired the specific knowledge and skills necessary for this business by meeting the standards for a Certified Financial Planner's designation, developing a track record of successful investing, and establishing a network of clients who would be willing to use their services. It would be naïve for students to believe they could start a firm engaged in financial planning and investing without first putting the necessary pieces of the puzzle (skills and knowledge, certification, reputation, contacts) in place. Starting this kind of firm, therefore, would entail a five- to ten-year effort before an enterpriser could actually engage in the activities of start-up.

Exploring these archetypes in more detail will help you answer the question: What kind of enterpriser are you? It will also help you identify the kinds of skills and abilities, connections, and experiences in other firms that you might need to start the kind of business that interests you. Recognizing the variety of different ways that people start firms will help you see that everyone can become an enterpriser. There is an enterprise that is more likely to be the right kind of business for you. By better knowing yourself as well as seeing the many different ways that enterprisers start businesses, you will be better prepared to position yourself to take advantage of the opportunities that come your way.

These archetypes can serve as broad guides for getting into business and provide clues about the factors (individual, firm, environment, process) necessary to start a business. However, your own start-up pathway is likely to be a blend of some of these.

Individual Level

The variables that come into play at the individual level include opportunities for advancement at prior jobs, similarity of previous work experience to the new venture, interest in starting a business, and risk of the new venture. The variables of job advancement and similarity of work are often directly correlated. When enterprisers saw that opportunities for job advancement were low, the likelihood that they would seek opportunities in areas where they had previous work experience was also low. For example, enterprisers in Type 1 (Escape to Something New) indicated that their current jobs offered little opportunity for advancement, challenging work, or salary increases. These enterprisers saw their current careers in these jobs as a dead end and sought higher levels of job satisfaction through entrepreneurship. Conversely, when job advancement was high, the odds of enterprisers starting businesses in the same industry were also high.

A good example of an enterpriser who typifies these variables of limited job advancement coupled with business ventures in new areas is Jerry Dawson, who started a waterbed store. Jerry was 20 years old, going to college, and working at a grocery store. He decided to take some entrepreneurship courses, and through this education grew confident he could start a business. He had grown dissatisfied working for other people because he felt they were less competent than he was. He began the start-up process by searching for a retail business to start. He first thought of stereos but discovered the market was saturated with stores. He decided on waterbeds when a friend asked him about the waterbed he was currently using. Jerry decided to interview waterbed storeowners. From these interviews he learned about an excellent waterbed manufactured locally. The manufacturer, a very important contact, put him in touch with accessory suppliers. Jerry then sought out a good location, negotiated a lease, named his business, and read a lot of books about starting a business. He used his own capital, which he raised by selling most of his personal possessions, and also borrowed money from his family.

The first few months of business were slow. Jerry had never been a salesman and it took time to learn how to communicate with prospective buyers. Slowly the business began to grow. He worked long hours and spent the initial earnings of the business paying for advertisements in a local "penny savings" newspaper. He persuaded a local finance company to make consumer loans to his customers.

In contrast, the second and by far larger group of enterprisers was satisfied with their present jobs and careers. The professionals in Type 2 (Deal Makers), Type 3 (Using Prior Skills & Contacts), Type 5 (Experts), and Type 6 (Aggressive Service) were all involved in jobs that they found very satisfying. However, they found some aspect of their previous jobs limiting. For example, they would have liked more responsibility, a wider range of work experiences, and freedom to pursue their own ideas. For these professionals, starting a business was a part of the same career pathway. The work they performed in their new businesses was very similar to the work in their previous jobs.

Ann Champion, an enterpriser in the Aggressive Service category, started a company that published specialty books. This company identifies a specific audience and then develops a book to sell to that market. It handles all phases of the process—writing, publishing, and distributing the books. Ann worked part time on several books that she and a partner had published while she was working full time as a financial controller. Her part-time experience provided her with the skills to become a book publisher full time. With sales from two previously published books, she quit her job and devoted her efforts to the publishing venture. Since the company does most of the publishing functions, its overhead is low and the books are of consistent quality. The publishing industry is very competitive, but Ann's publishing company is successful because it carefully targets books to markets where sales are likely.

It should be noted that the correlation between job advancement and similarity of work is not always so direct. Enterprisers in Type 7 (Pursuing the Unique Idea) and Type 8 (Methodical Organizing) were the most highly satisfied with their jobs, yet they usually started firms in unrelated work areas. Why? These two categories of enterpriser found better opportunities for advancement and success than their current jobs could offer.

Most enterprisers indicated they had frequently thought about starting a business. The only type that had less previous business start-up interest was the experts in Type 5. Experts usually had interesting jobs in firms where their expertise was highly valued. They had little interest in starting a company until their career paths were blocked.

For example, Virginia Albertson's new venture in writing software for PCs (described earlier in Type 5) was created when her former company did not want to pursue the PC marketplace and stayed with software for mainframe computers. Robert Jones is another example of an expert who enjoyed his current job yet found he could have more freedom by starting his own company. Robert is involved in international technology transfer. His company puts together joint ventures and represents U.S. corporations in China. Mr. Jones had many years' research experience in high technology areas, as well as seven years' technology transfer experience in China, working for an R&D company. The R&D company constrained his freedom to try new projects. While pursuing his MBA at night school, he began to consider starting his own company. He quit his job to develop new projects through his own company. He found a good lawyer to work with him, since technology transfer involves contracts and securities. He also found a partner with seasoned business experience for managing the company. He then went to previous clients and sold them on his new projects.

The perception of risk was not a differentiating factor. Most enterprisers perceived a moderate level of risk in pursuing their businesses, except that Type 2 (Deal Makers), Type 4 (Purchase/Franchise), and Type 5 (Expert) perceived lower levels of risk, while Type 8 (Methodical Organizing) perceived higher levels of risk. Some enterprisers saw lower levels of risk because their new ventures would use their previous experience, skills, and contacts (Deal Makers and Experts), or the business itself was successful before its purchase or its franchise acquisition (Type 4). One of the reasons why enterprisers in Type 8 (Methodical

Organizing) perceived a higher level of risk than other types of enterprisers was that the Methodical Organizers were entering industries where they lacked experience and knowledge. The focus on business planning for Type 8 is a way for these enterprisers to identify and respond to these unknown risks.

Enterprise Level

At the enterprise level, the variables to consider include the existence of partners; comparison with competitors with regard to the timing of product introductions and quality and unique characteristics of goods and services; and flexibility of the new enterprise in adapting its offerings in response to competitors' products.

The enterprises most likely to have partners were Type 1 (Escaping to Something New), Type 5 (Experts), Type 7 (Unique Idea), and Type 8 (Methodical Start-up). The Type 1 and Type 8 enterprisers, who left their previous jobs for new and unfamiliar ventures, often took partners to provide the necessary expertise and moral support. Enterprisers in Type 5 (Leveraging Expertise) were in highly complex industries where each partner contributed a share of the needed knowledge and skills necessary for the business's success.

An example of Type 1 partnership start-up is Jennifer Rose. She started a fresh fish wholesaling business with her father, who lost his job after 26 years with a wholesale frozen fish company. As part of his termination package, he agreed to not work for any other frozen fish company. Jennifer, who was working in the marketing department of a large corporation, decided to start the wholesale fresh fish company with her dad. The initial product was fresh perch that they sold in the Midwest, where that fish is the most popular. Jennifer's father purchased fresh perch from his previous employer. He then called on his old frozen fish customers in the Midwest and convinced them to sell fresh perch. Once orders were placed, the fish was sent via air freight to the buyers. The partners located more suppliers of fresh fish, paying them as quickly as possible to insure supply in the future. Jennifer felt that her venture was successful because they placed a high priority on excellent customer service, always had access to fresh fish, and provided a full line of fresh fish to customers.

The types of start-ups where partnerships were least likely to occur were Type 2 (Deal Markers) and Type 6 (Aggressive Service Firms). In these firms, contacts with suppliers and customers were extremely important, which suggests that the network of personal relationships developed by these enterprisers is a critical success factor. While another person with as many contacts might be a good partner, he or she would have been more likely to start his/her own venture.

The product/market newness variable measures the entry position of the new venture. Businesses in Type 7 (Unique Idea) were first to offer their products in the market. Next in terms of perceived newness were firms that were purchased (Type 4). Enterprisers in this category often talked about purchasing a business with the idea of turning the business around by orienting the purchased firm's current products/services to a new market. Alisa Showers, for example, purchased a small newspaper publishing company that was printing two bi-weekly papers in a large metropolitan area. She had operated these two papers for an owner who lived 2,000 miles away. After months of negotiation, Alisa purchased the fixed assets of the company. Alisa chose to purchase the two newspapers rather than start new publications because she felt that it would take her four years to reach the same base of readers that the two purchased newspapers had. With the existing reader base, she could pursue new advertisers who would be interested in selling their products/services to her readers.

At the other end of the product/market newness scale are businesses in Type 1 (Escape to Something New), Type 5 (Experts), and Type 8 (Methodical Start-ups). Type 1 consists of retail firms and restaurants that offered the same products as their competitors. Type 5 firms (Experts) generally modified an existing product for an already established market familiar to the expert. For example, a Type 5 enterpriser started a company in which he substituted an all-electronic temperature control system technology for an electromechanical technology and offered these advanced products to his old customers. Enterprisers in Type 8 firms (Methodical Organizing) followed systematic start-up procedures to enter established markets where they could imitate or learn from existing firms. For example, one enterpriser visited other microfilming services before setting up his own firm in this field.

Almost by definition, enterprisers in Type 7 (Unique Idea) perceived their firms as offering different products/services from their competitors. Founders of Type 2 firms (Deal Makers) also believed they offered different products/services compared to competitors, because they considered each deal to be unique. Deal Makers were also the only type of firm to rank the quality of their products/services similar to their competition. Either these enterprisers found the quality of deal making difficult to ascertain, or they did not compete on the basis of quality. All other types of firms regarded their products/services as higher in quality than their competitors.

Finally, the enterprisers in all eight types rated their firms as being more flexible than their competitors. The Experts (Type 5) rated their firms as the most flexible. Since firms in the Expert category provided products/services that were often designed to the specifications of a narrow range of customers, flexibility would be an important characteristic of these firms.

Environmental Level

At the environmental level, we can compare pathways to new business ventures on the basis of complexity of technology and skills required to manufacture products or deliver services in this industry, importance of contacts with suppliers in the industry, and customer expertise as the key environmental variables.

The variable technological complexity and change differentiated the high technology businesses (Type 3—Using Prior Skills & Contacts, Type 5—Experts, and Type 6—Aggressive Service) from low technology firms (Type 1—Escape to Something New, Type 2—Deal Makers, Type 4—Purchase/Franchise, and Type 7— Unique Idea). This comes as no surprise; as we stated earlier, high technology firms were likely to be started by enterprisers with previous experience in high technology industries.

Intensity of competition proved to be highly correlated to customer contacts. In other words, firms that placed a high value on contacts with suppliers and customers were perceived to be in the most competitive environments. Enterprisers identified the customer contact variable as the one best way to separate the Type 3 firms (Using Prior Skills & Contacts) from the Type 6 firms (Aggressive Service).

Both types of firms are service firms. The Type 6 firm places a higher priority on making and maintaining contacts, while the firms in Type 3 relied more heavily on their reputations to draw new customers.

There is a high correlation between customer expertise and degree of technology in each type, except for Type 7 (Unique Idea). Type 7 enterprisers sold low technology products, but some uniqueness of the design caused the products to appeal to a narrow range of customers (expert customers). For example, Bill Sanders started a part-time business manufacturing and selling baby towels that incorporated a unique design his mother had created and made as gifts for friends. Recognizing that this product was a marketable item that no one else was selling, he bought some material and had his mother and a friend construct prototypes of the baby towel. He designed a package and took the product to stores, where buyers reacted positively to his design. Then he contracted with a clothing manufacturer to produce the baby towels.

Start-Up Process

The variables in Exhibit 9.2 that relate to the start-up process describe the time allocated to selling and promoting the product or service, seeking advice and resources, producing the item, and purchasing a business or franchise versus starting a totally new business. Another key factor is whether the enterpriser made a full- or part-time commitment to the new venture.

Two of the eight types of start-up pathways were defined, primarily, in terms of the behaviors of the enterprisers. The enterprisers in Type 8 (Methodical Organizing) performed more of the seven behaviors listed in this section than enterprisers in any of the other seven types. Enterprisers in Type 8 felt that they were entering complex industries with little or no previous experience, and therefore, believed they had the double burden of learning the business as they started it. The primary characteristic of Type 4 (Purchase/Franchise) was also largely identified by a specific behavior—purchase or franchise.

Enterprisers in Type 7 (Unique Product/Market) spent the least amount of time marketing/selling. They believed that their idea so perfectly fit a product/market niche. They either did not feel a need to convince customers to buy the product or felt that it would be impossible to convince unwilling customers to buy their products. A good example of this conundrum involved a Type 7 firm that manufactured a unique silk-screened fabric that was sold to a limited number of high fashion clothing designers.

On the other hand, enterprisers in Type 6 (Aggressive Service) spent significantly more time marketing/selling than did the professionals in Type 3. This characteristic, along with the importance of contacts factor previously discussed, further differentiated these two groups of enterprisers who possessed expertise. Taking both of these variables into account, we can conclude that marketing/selling behaviors were a key route to establishing contacts with customers.

The amount of time devoted to resource acquisition varied among the eight pathways. Enterprisers who purchased firms (Type 4) spend a great deal of time seeking resources. Acquiring resources was also important to enterprisers in Type 2 (Deal Makers) and Type 7 (Unique Idea). Frequently, a crucial part of the Deal

Maker's transaction involved lining up resources (from insurance companies, banks, builders, landowners). The unique idea/market (Type 7) was frequently all that the enterpriser had, so that the process of acquiring resources to realize the idea was a high priority. For example, two women who decided to open the first cookie store in their city (their unique idea) indicated that the acquisition of sufficient resources (a store, oven, supplies) was critical for their idea to succeed.

As we would expect, service-oriented firms (Type 3—Professionals and Type 6—Aggressive Service Firms) are less capital intensive and spend little or no time seeking resources. The Experts (Type 5) also spent little time seeking resources, because these firms were the most likely to have partners who invested in the new venture. Experts are recognized as the best in their field, and, as discussed earlier, these experts were developing products that were perceived to have a high probability of success, making it easier to find investors for such ventures.

The time commitment to the new venture varied across types. Enterprisers in both service-oriented categories (Professionals and Aggressive Service) quit their jobs and devoted all their time to their new ventures. Since these enterprisers frequently tapped customers from their previous jobs, a definite break with the old employer would be an important factor. On the other hand, Deal Makers (Type 2) typically began their businesses part time. The part-time group was, for example, largely composed of real estate brokers. The nature of the real estate industry makes it possible for them to arrange deals on the side. The other group of Type 2 ventures, novelty firms, are similar to firms in Type 7 (Unique Idea). Both types of enterpriser based the start-up on a novel idea and worked at the new firm on a part-time basis. The new concept took some time to develop and catch on, and enterprisers worked full time at something else until they were ready to give all their attention to the new business.

The enterprisers who purchased or franchised firms spent the most time involved in the manufacturing/operational aspects of starting their businesses. We surmise that these enterprisers devoted more time to manufacturing and operations so that they could understand how the firms they purchased/franchised actually operated. The enterprisers who devoted the least amount of time to manufacturing and operations were Type 1 (Escaping to Something New) firms. These firms were more likely to be focused in the retail industry.

9.3 Enterprisers

Cowgirl Enterprises Rides to Success

What do you think of when you hear the term *cowgirl*? Like Donna Baase, at first you might picture somebody in boots on a horse. But Donna realized that the term conveys much more and chose to name her natural beauty products company Cowgirl Enterprises. "To me, it has to do with independence, resourcefulness, staying in the saddle, taking the reins, making use of the natural resources around us," she explains. "I meet cowgirls of all walks of life. It's about really driving your own life."

Started in Boulder, Colorado, in 1994, Cowgirl Enterprises offers customers a full line of unique natural skincare products based on healing desert botanicals. Its products, which soothe and nourish dry, weather-stressed skin, have been praised by a wide customer base, including climbers to Mt. Everest, scientists in Antarctica, women's track teams, New York City firemen, and everyday cowgirls and cowboys.

Donna's interest in plants and their healing properties started when she was a child and her family had a garden. "I grew up with a lot of beauty around me. My mother was very inspiring and we had a lot of flowers," she recalls. In the early '70s, she traveled extensively. In India and South America, she noticed how women incorporated plants into their beauty routines and for medicine. "I watched women comb coconut oil into their hair, and pretty soon we were doing that, too," she says. "This period of travel profoundly influenced my outlook on beauty, health and how plants are the source of medicine, cosmetics and well-being and became the seed for the Cowgirl products."

She returned to the United States and for eight years worked for a plastic surgeon in Miami, who became her mentor. "I probably was the first paramedical makeup artist in Miami in the early '70s, using makeup to alleviate bad medical conditions, such as bad burns or terrible scarring from accidents," she says. "I learned how the body healed." When she and her family moved to Boulder, she continued working in skincare as a licensed aesthetician. She also took advantage of Boulder's extensive network of people in alternative therapies and studied skincare, herbalism, and aromatherapy. "Then I started teaching classes in how to make your own cosmetics—for example, how to take some yogurt and egg yolk, mix in a couple of drops of lavender, and you have a mask," she says. "It is really using food for the skin."

Donna recognized the historical roots of what she was doing and wanted to continue this tradition in the modern world. "The whole skin-care industry and beauty business started in the kitchen," she explains. "After women made their candles, their soaps, their cough syrups and put up their preserves for the winter, they might have some time left over to take chamomile and infuse it in some olive oil. Here in Colorado, they would have found horsetail

(or bottle brush) and infused that to make a salve for wound healing. You could take aloe vera and sunflower oil and you might add a little bit of the lavender from your garden, and then you have a beautiful, natural oil for the skin."

The idea for the natural beauty products company came when Donna's family was driving home after a vacation in Oregon. "I started asking myself, 'What the heck did people put on their skin?' I wondered what native people, the indigenous women, the pioneer women, cowgirls riding those horses, did to protect their skin in the bleak winters and also those rough summers," she remembers. "I also thought about the plants that grow in the West, and how they really heal the skin. And a light bulb went off in my head—Cowgirl Cream!"

Donna mixed the first batch of Cowgirl Cream in her kitchen and operated as a home-based business for about six months. As it grew, Donna realized that she couldn't run the business out of her house, with employees working at her kitchen table. "Between the packing boxes and peanut bags, my house was just being taken over." The move to her present location was a big step. "It felt frightening because it was a commitment to pay the rent," Donna says. "But as soon as we got here, business increased."

The idea for Donna's next product after the cream was the Ranch Hand Cream, which she developed after a friend brought her an olive oil and beeswax bar from Italy. "This is brilliant," Donna thought. "Every product for hand and body care, hand creams particularly, comes in pump bottles, as liquid or lotion. I came up with a formula for a solid cake to heal chapped hands. Beeswax is difficult and messy to work with; if you spill it, it immediately dries. So you need a place where you can really be sloppy with beeswax—not your kitchen!" Donna also realized that she needed outside resources to make the product and others she wanted to create, such as a cleanser to go with Cowgirl Cream.

Donna consulted with Ben Fuchs, a pharmacist and owner of the Rocky Mountain Natural Laboratories, which produces her liquid products. "I develop a very strong personal bond with all my customers," Fuchs says. "I learned what Donna

(continued)

needed, not just as a businesswoman, but also from a personal standpoint, so I could provide the best service. I love my customers, working with creative people." Donna arranged for Ben's company to help her craft her products and then manufacture and bottle them, paying him on a fee basis.

Next Donna developed a three-channel distribution strategy: independent sales reps, contacts from trade shows, and cold-calling. She began by selling her products at local Boulder natural product stores and their branches around the Denver area. Then she expanded to Santa Fe, another good market for natural products. "I had really terrific sales reps that took our product line on the road. We sent press releases, and I made presentations when I went on the road locally. Then we started getting into the gift market. We found a showroom down at the Denver Merchandise Mart selling Western apparel and accessories and they agreed to carry the products. Sales came in right away, and suddenly we were in the gift market—a whole new world. They didn't even know how great the ingredients were until later. They just thought they were adorable little boxes. And they liked the name." Gift stores at spas also began carrying Cowgirl products.

The company's third product was an herbal rub for sore muscles. "We called it the Trail Boss Bar because on a trail ride the boss would have the medicine kit. The same concept applies to Ranch Hand Cream. It has a beeswax base and sunflower oil, but we added to that some wonderful herbal ingredients that are known to promote circulation and wound healing. It's not greasy, it doesn't have a heavy aroma, and it brings warmth and circulation."

Customers love Donna's products. "They want pure products and they want the natural ingredients," says Jennifer Biller, a sales rep. "Donna doesn't use any fillers or synthetic chemicals. It's all natural and very concentrated." As one storeowner commented, "We're fortunate to carry Cowgirl products because we have a customer demand for it. Especially living here in Boulder, where it is very dry and women need it. At first, they're attracted to the packaging, it's beautiful. They give it as gifts or take it home. But once they try it, they're back for more."

Cowgirl Enterprises also uses direct mail to keep its name in front of customers. "We use direct mail to let our customers know about new promotions," says Kendra Harris, Trail Boss (operations manager). "Every six to eight weeks, we put together a program and design postcards to send to our retail accounts and our mail-order customers. We've learned that our customers really like seeing product photographs rather than line drawings, and they buy more. It costs more but it's definitely worth it. We use inventory codes and our software tracks order sources, and we can see which marketing programs are producing results."

Running a small business brings a special set of challenges, such as finding sources of labor. "I would also say that some of the difficulties come from sales," Kendra says. "We don't have a solid distribution network set up yet. We're in the process of doing that and that takes a lot of work for a small company." Donna has been creative in tapping unusual labor pools, such as using inmates in the Boulder County Jail to package products.

Currently Cowgirl Enterprises makes seven items: Cowgirl Cream, Extreme Cream, Trail Boss Bar, Ranch Hand Cream, Cowgirl Lip Balm, Desert Recovery Serum, and Round Up Gel. The company first sold through retailers but began selling online in 1999. Growth has been slow but steady.

However, Donna does not want to run a manufacturing plant. Instead, she built a virtual corporation that operates with a minimal number of full- and part-time employees and four business alliances. She outsources the manufacturing, with one lab making the liquid products and two other companies producing the bars and lip balm. And, of course, jail prisoners do packaging. This concept represents a new way to run a business: do what you do best, then find others to do the rest. Forming alliances is efficient and saves you from burdening yourself with infrastructure and overhead. For now, Donna is glad to have teams of people who don't work for her, but with her, as well as consultants to advise her.

For example, Cathy Price, also a customer, is Donna's insurance adviser. "One of the main concerns in cosmetics is the pollution exposure. … That's a real concern when you're the insurer.

The other real high-risk end of cosmetics is how it can possibly hurt a customer. ... The beauty of Donna's product is it's all natural ingredients."

Despite the small size of Cowgirl Enterprises, Donna wants everyone involved to enjoy working there and to have fun. "I often will walk in and say, 'Hey, what do you think of this?' I want everyone's opinion. It's important that we all buy the Cowgirl way, to see this through my filter in a sense." Her employees agree. "Donna has great ideas and she believes in herself," says Paula Gardner, who handles customer service. "We all believe in her. We believe in the product. And we've seen the success because she's motivated, she has tenacity, she just keeps on going." At the same time, Donna allows room for self-expression. "But ultimately, I have to be the one leading it," she says. "That's kind of where I am. Just be me. And just hold the reins."

Discussion Questions

1. In which of the eight archetypes does Cowgirl Enterprises fall? Could it fall into more than one? Briefly explain your answer. Are there other ways that Donna could have started Cowgirl Enterprises? How would her background, skills, activities, and competitive strategy be different if she were to choose another pathway?

2. As best possible, use the information in the case to answer the 19 questions in the Exhibit 9.2 as they apply to Cowgirl Enterprises. Create a table that summarizes your answers. Compare your table to your classmates' and discuss any differences.

3. Based on the table you created in question 2, select the archetype that most closely resembles Cowgirl Enterprises. Does it match the one you chose in question 1? Why or why not?

4. Discuss the advantages and disadvantages of operating Cowgirl Enterprises as a virtual corporation. Do you agree with Donna's decision to use this form? When should she consider bringing more operations in-house? What questions could she ask to help her choose if and how to accomplish this?

Sources: Adapted with permission from the video "Staying in the Saddle: Cowgirl Enterprises," Small Business School, the series on PBS, and at http://SmallBusinessSchool.com; "About Cowgirl Enterprises," Cowgirl Enterprises website, http://www.cowgirlenterprises.com (January 10, 2007); and Nettie Hartsock, "Interview with Donna Baase," *iBizInterviews.com,* January 2001, http://www.ibizinterviews.com/donnab1.htm.

9.4 Finding the Best Pathway for You

As this chapter explains, nearly all enterprises that people start will follow one of the eight pathways we've described. Now that we have a fuller understanding of the eight pathways and their defining characteristics, we can use it to make better enterprising decisions.

Let's go back and look over the 19 questions that differentiate the eight archetypes, listed in Exhibit 9.2 on page 282. These questions will help you figure out how to approach the development of your potential enterprise.

We believe that the primary issue for most enterprisers is the choice to start a particular kind of enterprise that will satisfy their own interests. The individual-level questions are the first questions to ask yourself: Will you use your previous work experience, and will you be satisfied starting an enterprise based on this work experience? If you like the kind of work you are doing and the industry you are currently in, the next critical issue you need to address involves whether you want to continue working for your current employer. If you don't see opportunities for advancement in your current position, and you don't seem to get much satisfaction from working for your current employer, you might be in the position to take your current skills and apply them in your own enterprise, serving your current customers or customers similar to your current customers.

A decision tree can help you visualize your own route to enterprise formation. Exhibit 9.4 illustrates a sample decision tree based on the answer to one of the questions on individual characteristics: Do you want to use your prior work experience in your new venture? If you answer "yes," then you might consider whether you are satisfied with your work and have opportunities for advancement in your current position. A "yes" answer may mean that you don't have a strong desire to start a new business. If you are not happy at your present job yet want to use the same skills and contacts, you would begin exploring Types 2, 3, 5, and 6 (based on the profiles in Exhibit 9.3, page 283). You'd proceed by asking yourself some of the other questions posed in Exhibit 9.2 and could create another decision tree to guide you.

exhibit 9.4   Choosing a Path

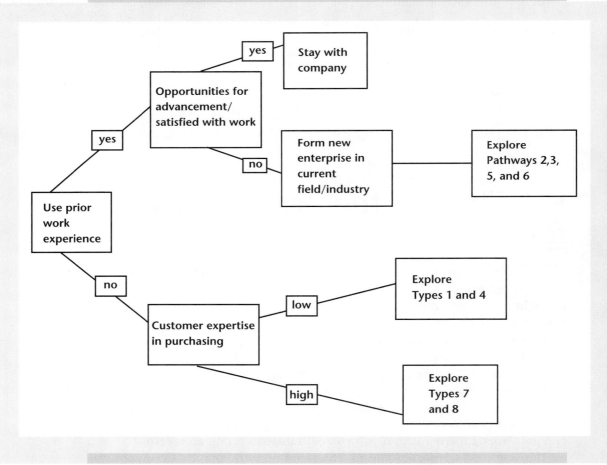

Suppose you want to try something different. Then you might follow the lower path on the decision tree. As Exhibit 9.4 shows, your options include Types 1, 4, 7, and 8. You might consider customer expertise as the next factor to consider in narrowing your search. If you want to sell goods or services that do not require customer expertise in purchasing, you'd investigate Types 1 and 4. If your interests lie with products that call for educated customers, you'd move toward Types 7 and 8.

If you are reading this book because you are serious about enterprising, you should explore another very important question: Is your current situation—job or school—leading you toward what you want to do in the future? Are the skills and knowledge you are acquiring creating more satisfaction in your life?

For example, let's say that you are studying accounting and expect to become a CPA. However, you may discover that you really have difficulty handling the many details and number-crunching that accounting requires. As you worked as an intern in an accounting firm, you got a taste of the profession. Now you can ask yourself more specific questions, such as whether you like auditing and if you can work the long hours that are often necessary around tax time. Do you like working with individuals at firms that need accounting help? If you don't like accounting now, it is unlikely that your experience in an accounting firm would help you start an accounting business and enjoy running it.

As you have seen in the description of the eight pathways, some require that you have previous work experience involving the acquisition of knowledge and skills as well as connections to clients who are likely to become your customers. One of the challenges, then, that you face is choosing jobs in areas that provide you with satisfaction with doing that kind of job (e.g., accounting, real estate sales or investing, information technology consulting) so that you gain the necessary skills, knowledge and contacts. Pathways 3 (Professionals), 5 (Leveraging Expertise), and 6 (Aggressive Service) are all based on individuals who have first gained experience in an area they truly enjoy, so that they pursue opportunities to develop enterprises that use those skills.

Pathway 4 (Purchase) typically involves enterprisers who seek to purchase a business in an industry that they are already familiar with and enjoy—even though the profile of Type 4 shows that this characteristic is not significant. Enterprisers who don't have industry experience may miss the problems and flaws in an established business that could lead to failure. As we will see in the next chapter on purchasing a business, enterprisers often seek to purchase a business in an industry where they have experience. They know how to exploit new opportunities at an established business, increasing the odds of success.

9.5 Summary

1. Enterprisers can start their businesses in many different ways. Pursuing opportunities involves a wide range of new venture strategies, situations, and behaviors. We group similar types of businesses into eight broad archetypes for starting enterprises. The eight pathways to enterprise creation are the following: Type 1—Escaping to Something New; Type 2—Putting the Deal Together; Type 3—Using Prior Skills & Contacts (Professionals); Type 4—Purchasing a Firm; Type 5—Leveraging Expertise; Type 6—Aggressive Service; Type 7—Pursuing the

Unique Idea; and Type 8—Methodical Organizing. These eight pathways present a repertoire of different start-up strategies and behaviors.

2. The profile for each archetype includes four levels of analysis: individual, enterprise, environment, and start-up process. These categories are further divided into 19 factors, as shown in Exhibit 9.2. The profiles (summarized in Exhibit 9.3) describe the types of individuals who are likely to start this kind of enterprise, what the business looks like, how it competes, the industry environment, and the start-up process. By understanding the differences and similarities between archetypes, an enterpriser can choose the best route to business ownership.

3. Enterprisers who choose Type 1 (Escape to Something New) have limited opportunities for advancement in their current jobs and are dissatisfied with their jobs. They generally gravitate to industries different from their prior work experience and may begin with a part-time commitment to the business. Competition is high because these businesses operate in established markets, offering low-technology products that target the general consumer. Funding for these firms comes form the enterprisers themselves, along with loans from family and friends.

4. Type 2 (Putting the Deal Together) enterprisers assemble the different aspects of the business (suppliers, wholesale and retail channels, customers). Typically they have experience in their chosen field. Real estate developers and novelty firms that outsource the manufacturing and distribution of the enterpriser's product idea are the two businesses that fall into Type 2. Both types of firms depend on good contact networks. Unlike Type 1 businesses, the services or products of Type 2 firms are unique.

5. Professionals who decide to go into business for themselves create Type 3 (Using Prior Skills & Contacts) companies. Because they stay in a familiar industry, they draw on the technical skills, expertise, and contacts acquired in previous positions. Like Type 1 enterprisers, they use their own money to finance the firm. Examples include CPA firms, attorneys, consultants, personnel agencies, and advertising firms. Type 3 firms differentiate themselves from the competition by offering better service.

6. Type 4 (Purchasing a Business or Acquiring a Franchise) is a popular route to entrepreneurship, especially for those who like the industry where they work but want to own a business. Firms in this archetype offer low-tech products and services similar to their competitors and differentiate themselves by adapting to the changing needs of their customers. Financial issues take up a lot of the owners' time. Enterprisers who buy existing businesses hope to improve it and increase profits.

7. Experts with technical knowledge form Type 5 businesses when they identify a new product opportunity in their industry. They often team up with partners to start the business. The industry environment is typically characterized by high technical change and complexity, and successful Type 5 firms are flexible in adapting products to customer needs.

8. Type 6, or Aggressive Service, enterprises are service-oriented firms such as specialized consulting firms. The enterpriser builds on prior work

experience or training and is intensely involved in all phases of operations, such as business development, advertising, and product offerings. Start-up costs for these knowledge-based companies are low. The enterpriser's networks are an important resource.

9. Certain enterprisers start Type 7 companies to pursue new ideas for low tech but high quality goods or services in different industries. Since this is the first business in the marketplace to offer this item or service, there is some uncertainty as to whether customers can be found, making these ventures seem risky.

10. The Type 8 firm, Methodical Organizing, starts up slowly as the enterpriser spends considerable time learning about all aspects of the enterprise—planning, marketing, production and finance. Enterprisers who chose this category typically have a long-standing desire to own a business and look to a new industry rather than continuing in the same one. The firm's products/services are similar to those of other firms but with some new twist to make it stand out in a very competitive environment.

11. Comparing pathways to new businesses in terms of the 19 variables helps enterprisers determine the best fit for their individual needs. For example, many kinds of businesses require a specific type of person, experience, or skill set. Certain patterns emerge, such as the high correlation between limited opportunities for advancement in a current job and starting a business in a different industry. Enterprisers in the Deal Maker, Professional, Expert, and, Aggressive Service categories generally continue to build on experience and stay in the same industry. Types 1, 5, 7, and 8 are more likely to have partners than the other four archetypes; unique products characterize Types 2, 5, and 7. Exhibit 9.3 summarizes the similarities and differences across all 19 factors.

12. Looking across the whole archetype gives enterprisers a more complete picture of which types are best for them. Some archetypes seem quite similar, such as Type 3 (Professionals) and Type 6 (Aggressive Service).

Review Questions

1. How does grouping enterprises into broad categories help enterprisers choose a pathway to new business formation?

2. Why should enterprisers analyze businesses on four different levels—individual, enterprise, environment, and start-up process?

3. Describe the key characteristics of Type 1—Escaping to Something New.

4. Which two types of companies comprise Type 2—Putting the Deal Together? Why are they grouped together?

5. Compare and contrast the major characteristics of Type 3, Using Prior Skills & Contacts (Professionals), and Type 5, Leveraging Expertise. How does Type 6, Aggressive Service, compare?

6. Explain, using the 19 factors in Exhibit 9.2, why Type 4, Purchasing a Firm or Franchise, is such a popular pathway.

7. What types of products would you find at a Type 7 firm? Differentiate between the enterprise characteristics of Type 7 and Type 1.

8. Which archetype is most similar to Type 8—Methodical Organizing? Which form differs most from this pathway? Explain your answers.

9. Explain how you can apply your understanding of the eight archetypes to choose a pathway to entrepreneurship.

Applying What You've Learned

1. Review the eight pathways to new business formation and choose the one that appeals to you most. Explain your reasons and why you think this is most suitable. What is your second choice? Describe one or more businesses that you might start for each of these archetypes.

2. Which of the 19 variables in Exhibit 9.2 were the most important in making your choices in question 1, and why?

3. After leaving Laser Diagnostic Technologies, a company he founded, Andre Dreher was looking for a new business opportunity. Recognizing the potential of applying wavefront-guided technology to improve visual acuity, he obtained commercial rights from the company that developed it and formed Opthonix, a vision care company, in 2000. Dreher arranged for financing from several leading venture capital firms. Ophthonix's patented high definition vision technology is the first fully customized form of vision correction and uses the Z-View™ Aberrometer to measure the patient's eyes for both low and high order aberrations. The Z-View then generates a fully customized prescription that is used to produce customized eyeglasses and contact lenses that optimize vision. In 2004 Ophthonix entered into a strategic alliance with Optical Connection, a San Jose company. Optical Connection will use wavefront-guided technology to produce contact lenses for distribution by Ophthonix.[2]

   (a) Which archetype best describes Ophthonix? Explain why you selected this pathway, including the most significant of the 19 variables.
   (b) Compare your answer with your classmates' and discuss the different selections. Does a different archetype seem more appropriate?

4. Robert Warfield (not his real name) started an executive-search consulting firm. Rather than following the traditional "headhunting" process (finding an individual to fill a job and receiving a fee based on the placed person's salary), he chose to work with a company's upper management to develop a strategy for executive recruitment and compensation. Mr. Warfield has many years' experience as a recruiter in government and private industry and worked hard to develop a strong base of individuals on whom he could call in the future. Once he started his company, he let his network know he was available for executive search consulting. This led to several contracts and an expanding client base. Mr. Warfield is well regarded as a qualified specialist who can solve management's personnel problems, and his firm has a solid track record of success.[3]

   (a) Evaluate this company on the 19 variables and assign it to an archetype.
   (b) Compare your answer with your classmates' and discuss the different selections. Does a different archetype seem more appropriate?
   (c) You instructor will now give you the classifications assigned by a computer model and the entrepreneur himself. How do these compare with your selection?

   (Note: Both were Type 8, Methodical Organizing.)

5. Marilyn Brooks and four partners started a company that developed a process to print on mylar. One of her partners had developed the special technology. Although they worked as a team, each partner was responsible for a functional area in which he or she had expertise: marketing

development, art, production, innovation, and general marketing. The first market they identified was labels for lawn mowers, because the metal labels then in use were not attractive, and paper labels fell off. Mylar labels looked better, were more durable, and cost the same as metal labels. The partner in charge of general marketing negotiated a deal with a lawn mower manufacturer. After this first success, the company expanded into other areas.[4]

(a) Evaluate this company on the 19 variables and assign it to an archetype.
(b) Compare your answer with your classmates' and discuss the different selections. Does a different archetype seem more appropriate?
(c) You instructor will now give you the classifications assigned by a computer model and the entrepreneur himself. How do these compare with your selection? (Note: Both were Type 5, The Expert.)

Enterprisers on the Web

1. Visit the archive of success stories at the Service Corps of Retired Executives (SCORE) website, http://www.score.org/success_story_archive.html. Select two companies in different industry groups.

    (a) Summarize the enterprisers' start-up stories.
    (b) Evaluate these companies on the 19 variables and assign each to an archetype.
    (c) Discuss your answer with classmates. How well do these firms fit into the pathways?

2. The *Wall Street Journal's* http://www.StartupJournal.com lists many businesses and franchises for sale. Go to the Startup Journal's home page, http://www.startupjournal.com, and navigate to the businesses for sale page. Fill in the form with your preferences as to industry and location. Review the list of businesses and choose one that interests you. What qualifications do you have to operate this type of company? What would you need to do to make this venture feasible?

3. Select the pathway that seems best for you. Then choose an industry of interest and search the Web for businesses that fall into this industry and archetype. Pick two and summarize the characteristics that place them in the archetype.

4. Go to the *Inc.* website and look for the current listing of the Inc. 500 (the 500 privately held companies with the highest growth in sales): http://www.inc.com/resources/inc500/2006. Select 5 of the top 25 fastest growing companies.

    (a) Which of the eight pathways to success do these companies follow?
    (b) Are there some pathways that are not likely to result in high growth firms?

5. *Entrepreneur's* website features stories of successful start-ups at http://www.entrepreneur.com/startingabusiness/successstories/index.html. Select 5 success stories that interest you and identify the pathway that each followed. Are the pathways to success for companies profiled by *Entrepreneur* different from the Inc. 500 companies? How are they similar or different? Why?

End Notes

1. This chapter is based on William B. Gartner, Terence R. Mitchell, and Karl H. Vesper, "A Taxonomy of New Business Ventures," *Journal of Business Venturing*, May 1989, pp. 169–186.

2. Based on information from Ophthonix' website, http://www.ophthonix.com (March 29, 2005).

3. William Baum Gartner, *An Empirical Model of the Business Startup and Eight Entrepreneurial Archetypes*, Ph.D. dissertation, Graduate School of Business Administration, University of Washington, 1982, p. 209.

4. Ibid., p. 203.

chapter 10

Purchasing a Business

Key Concepts

1. Purchasing a business is one of the most popular ways to become an enterpriser, and buying an existing firm can be a faster and more cost-effective route to business ownership than a start-up. Before making a business purchase, however, enterprisers must perform a thorough analysis of the business, from business model to market environment, operations, and financial feasibility. This due diligence process is similar to evaluating a new venture, except that it applies to a going concern. The objective is the same: to determine if the enterpriser can successfully operate the business and earn an appropriate return on the investment of time and money.

2. A business's value is ultimately what a buyer is willing to pay for it and depends upon many factors. The value of an ongoing business should be based on the business's ability to generate earnings. Enterprisers can choose from different valuation techniques, such as asset-based (book value, replacement value, liquidation value), market-based, earnings formulas, and cash flow methods. Each has advantages and disadvantages.

3. The terms negotiated between the buyer and seller can be as important as the price for the business. These include whether the buyer acquires only the assets or the entire business and the payment terms, each of which carries different tax implications for the parties. Often sellers provide financing for the purchase; they may also take a portion of the payment in future payments of either a percentage of profits, a noncompete fee, or an employment contract. Enterprisers should consult both an accountant and an attorney during the extensive due diligence process.

Suppose you are laid off from your position in sales and marketing of food products. Although you have many years' experience in this field, you have a desire to innovate that hasn't been satisfied working for large corporations. You and your wife, who also has a marketing background, want more time for your family. Rather than look for another job, you decide to buy a company.

In this chapter you'll meet Paul and Vickie Scharfman, who bought the Heim Cheese Company in 1991 after in-depth research into the cheese industry and due diligence into the company's operations. They focused on niche markets such as underserved ethnic groups, developing natural cheeses for Hispanic, Middle Eastern, and Indian consumers. By following the Scharfmans' example, you can learn how to assess an ongoing business, apply valuation techniques, and negotiate satisfactory terms to buy a business.

10.0 Make or Buy?

As we indicated in Chapter 9, purchasing a business or a franchise (Type 4) is one of the eight pathways to business ownership—and a major way for enterprisers to go into business. Why is this pathway such a popular route? Stop and think for a minute about all the different types of businesses in your area. Any of them might be for sale at some point. That opens up a lot of options! Many enterprisers have found that buying a going concern is a simpler and faster way to get into business than creating one. In some cases it may even be less expensive than starting from scratch. While buying a business with a track record does not guarantee future success, the enterpriser begins with fewer unknowns and less risk. Although there are many similarities between buying an independent business and a franchise outlet, we'll look at each option separately. We'll focus on purchasing a business in this chapter and the franchising process in Chapter 11.

Deciding whether to purchase a business rather than start a new one is similar to buying a home. Prospective homeowners have two choices: build a new house or buy an existing home. They will find more existing houses on the market than new or to-be-built houses. If they were interested in living in a particular area, they might only find existing homes available. In the same way, enterprisers may discover that it is easier to purchase a business in a particular industry sector than to create one.

We can also look at the purchase versus start-up decision as a make or buy decision. Just as some companies decide to make all the component parts of a product, enterprisers who choose an independent start-up are essentially making their own businesses. They do everything themselves: identify an opportunity, develop a product or service from this opportunity, find customers, determine channels of distribution, develop a marketing plan, acquire resources to execute their plan, and operate the business. Or, like other companies who outsource all or part of the manufacturing process, they could find a business that has all the desired attributes and purchase it.

In evaluating a potential business purchase, enterprisers must explore what makes a successful business. Before deciding to buy a business, they have to ask a critical question: "Can this business be successful?" Answering it requires delving into the fundamentals we discussed in earlier chapters: the business model, feasibility, and the business plan. Only by getting a complete picture of the business and how it operates—the customers, competitors, operations, employees, products/services—will they be able to determine its future profitability. The due diligence process is quite extensive and includes many of the same issues involved in a start-up, along with some new ones. For example, is the business priced fairly, and what is the basis for the valuation? What is the reputation of the current owners? The more thorough the research, the fewer surprises later.

Industry studies show that most enterprisers who begin exploring the purchase option search about 18 months for a business to buy and fewer than 10 percent actually complete the purchase. In the rest of the chapter we'll help you determine whether the purchase route is right for you, and if so, how to increase the odds of success.

10.1 Why Buy a Business?

Enterprisers buy businesses for many reasons, including the speed with which they can get into business for themselves and economic factors. Here are several motives they often cite for choosing the purchase option:

1. *Buying a proven business concept.* A business that is already profitable has proven that it works, and there is less uncertainty about whether it will be successful. The business may have significant market share, and if not, the enterpriser can develop a plan to increase it. The odds are in the enterpriser's favor, although of course it depends on a number of factors such as customer loyalty, employee retention, and the response of competing firms. Overall, buying an established business should mean less risk to a purchaser compared to a start-up situation.

2. *Getting into business for yourself more quickly.* The business is already established and operating, which makes it easier to finance. Your business has name recognition, trained employees, a vendor network, and an established base of customers already buying your products or services, all of which take a great deal of time to develop. Operating procedures are in place as well.

3. *Purchasing is often less expensive than a start-up.* Marketing and sales costs for an existing business should be lower than for a new venture. When an enterpriser buys a business, the client list is usually one of the intangible assets. For example, many professionals such as dentists, doctors,

and accountants often buy established practices. While clients may prefer the old dentist/doctor/accountant, the new owner of the business gets the opportunity to develop a new relationship with these clients, who are already in the habit of visiting that office. Buying the firm's fixed assets also saves money. Operating costs should be lower than in a start-up situation.

4. *Generating positive cash.* By purchasing a going concern, the enterpriser acquires inventory and receivables, as well as assets. These produce immediate cash flow when the business sells the products in inventory and collects the receivables owed.

5. *Improving an undervalued business.* Enterprisers often find businesses that need changes and improvements for sale at a good price. With some effort and skill, enterprisers can implement these changes and make the business more valuable. This is similar to buying a rundown house, fixing it up, and then selling it for a profit. For example, you might come across a house for $150,000 that you can renovate for $50,000 in materials and your time, and then sell it for $275,000. Likewise, some enterprisers are actually in the business of buying businesses, turning them around, and then selling them for a higher price.

6. *Counseling from the seller.* Because sellers often finance part of the business purchase price, they have a keen interest in the new owner's success. They will share their knowledge to help the new owner get off to a good start.

In addition, it may make more sense to purchase rather than start certain types of businesses. Service businesses, for instance, fall into this category because they bring established clients. Buying businesses situated in a prime location or with a dominant position in a particular market makes sense—if the purchasing rights to the location or market are included as well. Later in this chapter we will look at the various parts of a business that one might consider purchasing rather than creating.

Buyer Beware

Of course, buying a business has its risks, too:

1. *Obtaining large initial financial outlay.* The selling price of a going concern reflects the investment the current owner has made to build the business. The cost may be higher than starting from scratch when financing needs occur over a longer time period. Closing costs, transfer fees, and other costs can drive the financial outlay even higher.

2. *Setting the right price.* Determining whether the seller's asking price is fair can be difficult. The valuation process has many variables, and there are different methods of valuing a business. However, the future earning power of the business should be your primary focus, as we will discuss later in this chapter.

3. *Discovering problems after the fact.* Owners who want to present their businesses favorably may hide or fail to disclose problems that could reduce

the value of a business. For example, the balance sheet may include accounts receivable that cannot be collected. The business may have credit problems with its banks and vendors. The business may have had negative publicity. A new competitor may be entering the market. The city might be considering new taxes or zoning regulations. The main product may be at the end of its life cycle. These are just a few possible pitfalls that could await the new owner. Being extremely thorough when performing your due diligence and researching every aspect of the business is the best way to protect yourself. We suggest you review the feasibility study questions in Chapter 7 as a format for evaluating any business you might plan to purchase.

4. *Underestimating the commitment required to operate the business.* In their eagerness to buy a firm, enterprisers may not consider carefully the realities of running a particular type of business—and the commitment it will take in both time and money. As a result, they may find themselves spending long hours dealing with unexpected problems or facing a financial crisis because they didn't provide adequate working capital.

5. *Verifying the seller's claims.* Some business owners may overstate their company's advantages and downplay the negatives. It is up to you to get all the information you can, from objective sources when possible, before buying. If the owner brags about extra income that was not reported to the IRS and wants to include it when valuing the business, watch out! Not only is there no way to determine the accuracy of such cash income, but this practice is illegal. An owner who tells you about cheating the government may be stretching the truth in other areas as well.

Should You Buy?

In addition to understanding the pros and cons of a business purchase, an enterpriser must also consider personal motivation and goals. Because buying a business requires a major financial commitment, you should take your time to make sure it makes sense for you. Exhibit 10.1 provides a list of questions to get you thinking about the many issues that are involved. For example, you may want to own a company to supplement your current job rather than replace it. Knowing that ahead of time will help you focus your search on businesses that you can run part time. Also note that the primary issues involved with buying a business are similar to issues one would face in starting a business. The viability of the business concept (Chapter 6), the feasibility of the business model (Chapter 7), and the implementation and ongoing operations of the business (Chapter 8) will need the same level of diligence before you buy. You'll need to understand the industry you are considering, which means going to trade shows, industry association meetings, site visits to similar businesses, and interviewing business owners. When you evaluate management, you'll want to consider whether a poorly managed company offers an opportunity to turn around the business.

exhibit 10.1	**First Questions to Ask Before Buying a Business**

1. What are your primary reasons for taking the purchase route to business ownership? Keep them in mind as you look at various businesses.

2. Are you buying a business as a full-time or a part-time endeavor? What are your income expectations?

3. Would you prefer to buy a business in your current industry or go into a new field?

4. What appeals to you about a particular industry? How well have you researched this field?

5. Why does this particular business opportunity excite you? Would you feel proud to own this type of business?

6. Why is the owner selling this business?

7. What skills and experience do you bring to the business? Do you need to hire people to provide expertise in specific areas?

8. Can you identify ways to improve the business to make it more successful?

9. Will you need partners to help you finance or operate the business successfully? If so, do you want to work with partners or would you prefer solo ownership?

10. Does the business make sense financially? What factors indicate the potential of revenue and earnings growth?

11. On what are the valuation and price based? Do they seem reasonable?

12. How easily will it be for you to obtain the financing you'll need to buy the business?

13. How well has the business been managed? Do you want to keep many of the current managers or employees?

14. Does it make sense to buy rather than start this type of business?

Use these questions to make some basic decisions about (1) whether to purchase a business and (2) the type of business to seek. Try not to limit yourself in these early stages. You may think you want to own a party-planning business until you learn that you will be working most weekends and have to sacrifice important family time. Rather than give up, think about what interested you in this type of business and see if there are other ways to follow your passion. For example, you might want to start with corporate events that take place mostly during the week.

Then you can go more deeply into the overall feasibility, examining the business model, market environment, value proposition, and capital considerations. In the final analysis, only you can decide if a business purchase meets your personal goals and is a good fit for your particular situation.

10.2 Business for Sale

Before you buy a business, you should find out as much as possible about the owner's motives for selling. Knowing the circumstances behind the sale is critical information for your evaluation of the enterprise's future profit potential. If, for example, the owner has neglected the business for a while, you may be able to implement immediate changes that quickly increase revenues. An owner who wants to cash out and move to another venture may hand over a thriving business that is still growing rapidly—or that has reached its mature stage.

People decide to sell businesses for many reasons. The owner may want to move on to a new venture, be ready to retire, or be in poor health and decide that he or she no longer wants to operate the business. If no family members or employees are interested in taking over the company, the owner may have no choice but to sell.

Life Cycle Issues

As we described in Chapter 1, every enterprise has its own life cycle that is often tied to the life cycle of the enterpriser. As enterprisers get older, their interests and abilities to successfully operate a business may diminish. Let's face it—most people, enterprisers included, after a certain age, aren't that interested in having a full-time job and working long hours each day. Operating a successful business takes considerable time and energy. At some point, it becomes too much for many business owners, and they decide to sell their businesses. Also, if an owner dies, the business may owe significant estate taxes upon transfer to family members. The heirs may need to sell the business to pay taxes.

In many situations, an enterpriser's family might be interested in taking over the business. The enterpriser may groom a relative to own and manage the business. This doesn't always occur, however. Family members may have other career opportunities they wish to pursue. For example, an enterpriser might own a café at which his or her children worked as they grew up. As both the café and the owner mature, the kids might decide that they have had enough of the restaurant business and its particular problems and challenges. The same circumstances can apply to the café's employees, who may not have either the inclination or the financial resources to buy the business.

Working in a business where the owner is likely to sell the business can be an excellent way to acquire a business. Many enterprisers have joined businesses with an understanding, often through a written contract, that the enterpriser will take over the business from the owner at a specified price and time. This is certainly a very viable strategy when no family members or other employees are interested in running the business.

Even if family members might want to take over the business, the current owner might decide that it would be better for a non-family member to own the business, and pay the current owner and family. A family member might not have the necessary resources to purchase the business, or the business might be split into so many ownership shares among a family that it would make more sense (for the benefit of the business) if an outsider purchased all of the family's interests for a fair price.

Also, family members often end up disagreeing about how the business should be run, which can lead to disastrous results. A good example of this is the Haft family in Washington, D.C., which at one point owned a very large drug store chain, as well as Crown Books, one of the first discount book chains. Father and son disagreed about how to run these businesses; the mother sided with the son, and the father sued both the mother and the son for control of these businesses. Legal disputes took so much of the family's time that no one was minding the store—literally—and these businesses subsequently went into bankruptcy. These enterprises might have survived if the family had sold them to an outsider to manage.

New Interests

Starting a business doesn't mean that the enterpriser will always want to run that type of business. Enterprisers thrive on challenges, so it is not unusual for them to lose interest after running a business for a while. They may become bored with doing the same thing day after day, whether it is making pizzas, selling hardware, or developing a new compound to fight disease. Or they may discover a different opportunity that seems more appealing.

Many enterprisers want to move on to something else, and they actually plan on selling their businesses as a part of their enterprising strategy. A good example of a serial entrepreneur is Terry Allen, author of *No Cash, No Fear,* who has probably started over 50 businesses. He quickly recognized that he had a talent for starting profitable businesses but was not very good at running them. So he always looked for exit strategies, such as selling the business to employees or to an outsider, freeing him to move on to the next start-up opportunity.

Management Problems

Some owners don't have the managerial, financial, and operational capabilities to run businesses. For example, most businesses need enterprisers who can understand financial statements and manage the cash in the business. Some individuals just can't figure out how cash flows through the firm and how their actions affect profitability. Sometimes they hit on a formula for success. But as the competition changes and they try to adapt to changing customer needs and competitive pressures, the formula no longer works. The enterpriser is clueless about what changes to make in the business model to ensure success.

Poor Businesses

And, finally, there are some businesses that are dogs—poor choices, literally and figuratively! They will not be successful no matter what a new owner does. The reason may be changing customer needs. Take, for example, a small appliance repair business. It is probably cheaper to purchase a new coffee maker for $20 at the local discount store than to fix a broken one. In fact, it could be *more* expensive to repair it! The same holds true for audio equipment, computers, and electronics. Because people prefer to buy new rather than repair, owning a repair business might just not be feasible, no matter what the enterpriser does to make the business a success.

Ethical considerations also have a bearing on the decision to buy a business. The basic issue is one of information asymmetries between the buyer and the seller. The owner usually knows more about the nature of the business for sale than the prospective buyer and also has other types of information about the business that the buyer doesn't. Typically, we say "buyers beware" and place most of the risk on the buyer to do as much due diligence as possible. But is it ethical for a seller to withhold information that might significantly affect the purchase price of a business, its operations, or its potential growth in the future? The Enterprising Ethics box presents some ethical dilemmas a seller might face.

enterprising ethics

Buyer Beware—The Ethics of Selling a Business

For the past 30 years, you have enjoyed owning and operating a upscale clothing store in an affluent suburb. You started with women's clothes and expanded into juniors at the request of your customers. When the adjacent store became available, you leased that space as well. You enlarged the original store to include more lines of women's clothing and used the new space to begin selling high-quality children's apparel as well.

Over the past year, managing the store and its ten employees has become increasingly stressful for you. You are open seven days a week from 10 AM until 6 PM, and until 8 PM on Thursday. The long days are taking a toll on your health. It might be time to sell the business, retire, and finally have time to travel. As you begin to prepare sales materials for potential buyers, you discover several matters that could be troublesome for a new owner.

The business is conveniently located on a busy street with a high volume of pedestrian and vehicle traffic and plenty of parking. Last month, however, you received a notice that the city is planning to widen the road in front of your business. Construction will take at least a year, and access to your business and the parking lot is likely to be affected by this.

Even though you have employees to help you at the store, you have been its primary manager. Of your ten staff members, two are long-term employees whom you can trust to open and close the store and oversee other employees in your absence. Two others are also trustworthy, dependable, and good with customers. You are not so sure about the other six and suspect that one or two might be stealing from the business—an easy thing to do because

about one-third of your sales are for cash. However, you don't have concrete proof of this.

One of the reasons for your store's success is its exclusive right to sell a prestigious designer's clothes. No other store in a 20-mile radius is allowed to sell this clothing line. Nor does the designer sell on the Web, believing that a strong retail network with trained sales representatives helps customers coordinate clothing and accessories. Last week, the designer's representative told you that the designer was considering constructing his or her own boutiques to showcase the fashions. Your store derives 25 percent of its revenue from this designer's products, and because the line has a high markup, it accounts for about 40 percent of your profits. You also sell many accessories, such as scarves, jewelry, and belts that compliment the designer items and will likely lose sales for these products as well. You might be looking at a 50 percent reduction in sales, and an even greater reduction in the profits.

Discussion Questions

1. In your opinion, how much information should a seller disclose to a prospective buyer about the business for sale? What general guidelines would you suggest?

2. Do you have an obligation to tell a prospective buyer about the following, or should you assume that the buyer will find out through due diligence?

   a. The city's plans to widen the road.

   b. The rumor concerning the opening of designer boutiques that would compete with your store.

   What are the implications of your decision? What could you include in the seller's agreement to protect yourself from lawsuits if there are significant changes arising from either of these situations?

3. A buyer indicates that he plans to keep the current employees after purchasing the store. What, if anything, should you say about your employees to him, and why? Should you express your concerns about the two employees you

suspect may be stealing, even though you aren't sure about this? Could you be sued by these employees if they were let go by the new owner?

4. Another option is to sell the business "as is," so that as the seller you are not responsible or liable for any changes in the performance of the business after the sale. Do you think this would be ethical? Why or why not?

10.3 Finding Businesses for Sale

Once you decide to buy a business, you have to find the right one. You can consult a professional whose expertise is buying and selling companies or go it alone by reading classified ads in newspapers and magazines or attending business opportunity trade shows.

Professionals who specialize in business purchases fall into several categories. Those involved in buying and selling large businesses (like Fortune 1,000 businesses) are called investment bankers. They have the capital and connections to broker billion-dollar transactions. For the smaller deals that account for most of the business purchase activity in the United States, an enterpriser would look for a *business broker*. Merger and acquisition specialists concentrate on the middle range between these extremes.

Business Brokers

Business brokers are similar to real estate agents. They act as agents for sellers of businesses, listing businesses for sale. In that role, they may also be a consultant to the seller of the business, providing advice and expertise about valuing the business and presenting the business to prospective buyers. Business brokers often qualify potential buyers for sellers, screening buyers to ensure they have the financial resources and requisite expertise to complete a purchase.

There are many different kinds of business brokers. Brokers often focus on a particular business segment, such as:

- Certain types of businesses (doctor's offices, restaurants, service businesses, retail stores).

- Specific size categories (for example, businesses priced under $100,000, or over $1 million).

- A geographic region (city, county, state, or region).

Finding a business broker is easy; just search for "business broker" using any major Internet search engine, and it'll generate a long list of sites offering businesses for sale. State business broker associations and the yellow pages of your local phone book are additional resources. Membership in the International Business Brokers Association (IBBA), a nonprofit organization that promotes professionalism in the buying and selling of businesses, is an important credential for a broker to have. The IBBA offers educational courses and a certification program. In addition to a member database searchable by geography, it lists over 3,000 businesses for sale that can be searched by geographic location, firm and industry type, and purchase price. Another site is the World M&A Network, which lists businesses by industry and type.

Browsing several broker-sponsored "business for sale" sites is a good way for prospective enterprisers to learn what kinds of businesses are sold, reasons that owners of businesses sell them, and the terms business owners offer a prospective purchaser. While the formats of these listings vary from site to site, most include similar information. They provide a quick overview of many different types of businesses, along with asking price and financial highlights such as gross revenue and **cash flow**, the cash generated by the business after subtracting taxes and adding back noncash expenses such as depreciation. The representative listings in Exhibit 10.2 are typical of what you will find.

Typically, a business broker will enter into an agreement with the seller to list the business for sale. The agreement usually includes

cash flow
Cash generated by the business after subtracting taxes and adding back noncash expenses such as depreciation.

---

exhibit 10.2   **Business for Sale Listings**

While hypothetical, the following listings are based on actual business for sale ads from a variety of sources.

Children's Gymnastics & Activity Center

Offers full range of gymnastics, tumbling & trampoline classes, as well as Day Camps, Parties, Special Events, and Indoor Rock Climbing option. Great business with low down payment, and seller financing possible to qualified buyer. Established 1980.

Industry:	Educational
Industry Segment:	Other Educational
Geography:	United States/Midwest
Asking Price:	$650,000
Gross Revenue/Trend:	$955,188/Increasing
Cash Flow:	$180,648
Cash Flow Type:	Seller's Discretionary Earnings
Value of Equipment:	$184,000 (Included in asking price)
Seller Financing:	Negotiable
Mgmt. Training/Support:	Owner will train
Reason for Selling:	Retiring and pursuing other interests
Facilities:	23,450 sf with option for another 5,800 sf for Indoor Rock Climbing. Owner offers favorable long-term lease.
Market Outlook/Competition:	Excellent; business has set high barrier to entry for similar businesses, and has room to expand.

Bagel Shop

Beautiful, well-equipped bagel shop serving breakfast (60%) and lunch (40%) in a comfortable 60-seat dining area. Bagels represent about 70% of the business. Located in an extremely busy, upscale shopping center in Orange County, CA, with many high traffic tenants, including Long's Drugs. Business is being run semi-absentee; a full-time, hands-on owner could certainly build upon the current operation.

Asking Price:	$130,000
Industry:	Food & Beverage: Coffee, Cafe, Dessert
Reason for Selling:	Other business interests
Year Established:	1991
# of Employees:	7
Yearly Revenues:	$300,000
Yearly Cash Flow:	$54,000

Additional Details:

- The property is leased.

- The owner is willing to train/assist the new owner.

- The owner is not willing to work for the new owner.

- This is not a franchise opportunity.

- This is not a distressed business or bankruptcy situation.

Energy Conservation Project Management

East Coast Energy Conservation Project Management business with excellent growth potential. Home-based business; can be relocated anywhere in the country; the best sites are Atlanta, Baltimore, Florida, and North Carolina. National client base of big box companies and department stores; projects require travel to all parts of the country and typically take 2 days to 3 weeks.. Current project contracts, mostly in eastern United States, extend through next year, with solid project pipeline. Sales will exceed $1 million. The usual project will last 3 days to 3 weeks.

Industry:	Professional Services
Industry Segment:	Consulting
Asking Price:	$210,000
Gross Revenue:	$672,400
Cash Flow:	$121,000
Value of Equipment:	$5,000 (Included in Asking Price)
Seller Financing:	Seller will provide financing, with $60K down
Year Established:	1993
Number of Employees:	6 full time
Home Based:	Yes
Mgmt. Training/Support:	Seller will provide training
Reason For Selling:	Other Interests
Facilities:	Home Based

- What is offered for sale (assets such as equipment, inventory, facilities, patents; stock).

- Initial offering price and terms (for example, 100 percent cash payment; seller financing offered).

- Broker's commission rate: These vary but typically a business broker would receive 10 to 15 percent of the sales price up to a certain amount (often $1 million), and a sliding scale commission on the sales price above $1 million, such as 5 percent. The seller pays the broker's commission.

- Financing fee if a broker arranges financing for the buyer. This can range from 2.5 to 5 percent of the financing amount.

- Length of time the broker has exclusive rights to sell the business.

Other Resources

In addition to searching the Internet and contacting business brokers, several other avenues can help enterprisers locate businesses for sale:

- *Realtors.* Some real estate brokerage companies selling commercial properties also sell businesses that are "attached" to the property. Many kinds of retail firms fit this category. A realtor tries to find a buyer to buy the business and the location that goes with it, or buy the location and get the business as well.

- *People knowledgeable about an industry.* These would include anyone in the deal flow, such as supply chain contacts (suppliers and customers), competitors, and industry associations. Tapping into these and similar networks often turns up good leads.

- *Business owners.* Enterprisers can ask owners of businesses they like whether they would consider selling. This direct route often works, as we will see.

- *Business valuation seminars.* Attending a seminar designed to help business owners value their companies is a good way to meet enterprisers who want to sell their businesses.

- *"Business wanted" ads.* Placing an ad that summarizes the type of business you want to buy brings sellers to you. You may also hear from owners who have not yet decided to sell but are interested in exploring their options.

10.4 Valuation: What Is a Business Worth?

Finding a business to buy is just the first step. Next, an enterpriser must analyze the business and value it based on what it will earn. A business's value is ultimately what a buyer is willing to pay for it and depends upon a lot of factors: how long it's been in operation, how many employees, quality of physical assets (i.e., equipment, facilities, supplies, and inventory), market considerations, customer base and loyalty, and earning potential. You want to buy a business that you believe has all the necessary parts to operate successfully, both hard assets and goodwill. Goodwill represents intangibles, such as the value of the business's reputation and similar factors that come with a going concern, and can be difficult to ascertain.

Buying a business is similar to purchasing any asset that will generate some rate of return. If you purchased a $10,000 bond, you would expect the bond to pay you interest every year and return your principle when you sold the bond. It's the same for a business. When you buy a business for $10,000, you expect a return for your investment and the time and effort you spend working in the business. Otherwise, you'd be better off, financially, working for a salary elsewhere and looking for a separate investment that would generate money. (Of course, there are other reasons to be in business, but we believe that enterprisers should also make money doing what they love.)

The critical factor in determining a particular value for a business is earnings, or potential earnings—not the business's physical assets. As we explain the various valuation methods that enterprisers might apply to a particular business, please keep in mind that the *ultimate value of buying an ongoing business must be based on the business's ability to generate earnings.*

As we have covered in Chapters 6, 7, and 8, valuing a business begins with considering

- the value of the opportunity.

- the enterprise's business model.

- the future feasibility of the enterprise.

- the specific ways the business operates—the business plan.

In purchasing a business, enterprisers should undertake the same types of analysis they would go through to start a business. Therefore, you should use the frameworks we provided in those chapters as guides for evaluating businesses you seek to purchase. We will refer to many of the same topics regarding the business model, feasibility, and business plan (customers, intensity of competitors, channels, benefits, etc.) at the end of this chapter, when we look at the nonfinancial issues that constitute the real value of purchasing a business.

The financial aspects of a business are, in many respects, a summary of the success (or failure) of the business over time. The financial figures represent the business—but they are not the business itself. Because the financial characteristics of the business reflect the critical success factors in the way the business operates, we have waited to introduce many of the financial aspects of the enterprising process until you were familiar with nonfinancial factors.

Some enterprisers hire a professional appraiser to do a formal business valuation, especially if they are interested in a large or complex business. However, enterprisers should always perform their own valuation analysis and not rely on the broker or the seller to give you the numbers. It's the best way to understand a business, get a frame of reference before proceeding, and avoid overpaying. Exhibit 10.3 lists some of the financial and legal documentation an enterpriser should request prior to beginning the valuation process.

There are many different valuation formulas, and some are more applicable to certain types of businesses. It's a good idea to calculate value using several

exhibit 10.3

Financial and Legal Documents to Request when Purchasing a Business

- All financial statements for the past five years
- Income tax statements for the past five years
- List of equipment and the depreciation schedule
- List of Accounts Receivables and their age (when they were due)
- List of Accounts Payables and their age (when they were due)
- Inventory list
- Any leases (rental agreements, equipment leases, automobile leases)
- Any contracts (customer, supplier, employment, loan agreements, labor contracts, royalty agreements, franchise agreements)
- List of partners and stockholders (indicating percentage of business owned and/or amount of stock held)
- Compensation for owners of the business (salaries and perks)
- Insurance documents
- Legal documents (articles of incorporation, partnership agreement)
- Copies of licenses and other documents pertaining to government regulations
- Tax payments for federal, state, and local governments

methods to get a feel for a price range. Because valuation is a very complex topic, with whole books devoted to it, we will provide an overview of four popular bases of valuation: assets, market, earnings, and cash flow. Even if you choose to hire a professional to appraise a business for you, this basic knowledge will help you understand the benefits and limitations of each technique and be able to ask the right questions.

Asset-Based Valuations

asset-based valuation
Determination of a business's value based on the company's assets.

Asset-based valuation approaches begin with placing a value on the business's assets. This category has several variations, with some using replacement or market value rather than book (depreciated) value. In addition to buildings, land, and equipment, these assets include improvements to leased space and all inventory (raw materials, parts, work-in-progress, finished goods). For example, in valuing a printing company, you'd look at the buildings, presses and copiers, as well as ink, paper, and other supplies in inventory. Intangible assets include goodwill, logos, trademarks, and patents. Exhibit 10.4 briefly describes the four categories of asset-based valuations.

    While these methods are relatively easy to calculate, they take a narrow look at a business, focusing on assets alone. They assign no value to the business's ability to use those assets to generate revenues. While modifying the asset values to either current market or replacement value provides a better estimate than book value, they are not as helpful as other valuation methods we discuss in the next section.

exhibit 10.4 | **Asset-Based Valuation Methods**

1. **Book value:** The value according to the business' current financial statements, as shown on the balance sheet (financial statement listing assets and liabilities).
2. **Modified book value:** The asset values adjusted to their actual, or current, values.
3. **Replacement value:** The amount required to replace, at current market rates, the assets the business owns.
4. **Liquidation value:** The value of the assets if the business needed to be sold immediately. The liquidation value is likely to be much lower than the replacement value of these assets. This is not an especially useful figure, as why sell a business for the same amount you would receive for liquidating it?

Market-Based Valuations

Essentially, **market-based valuations** are determined by what other people will pay for this business or similar businesses. Industry valuation and multiplier formula valuations are two categories of market-based valuation.

In a perfect world, a business would be sold for its **fair market value,** or the price that a business would command from a knowledgeable buyer and seller with the relevant information about the business and willingness to undertake the transaction. In some respects, one doesn't know the fair market value of a business until it is actually sold. So we have a catch-22: we can't determine fair market value until the business is sold, and the actual selling price of the business is the fair market value!

Market value includes a number of factors, and each may be viewed differently by various sellers and buyers. The value of a business, then, often lies in the eyes of the beholder:

1. *Different estimates of future earnings.* As we mentioned earlier, a good valuation technique must account for the future earnings of the business. The challenge for a buyer purchasing a business is estimating accurately the actual earnings for the business at some future date. Different buyers will no doubt have different earnings estimates for the same business. How could that be? One buyer might have 25 years of sales experience in the same industry and project rapid revenue growth based on the addition of revenues from many new clients. Another buyer might lack the industry experience and include only current clients in the earnings estimates.

2. *Risk perception.* Given that each buyer brings different skills, experience, and industry knowledge, the perceived risk of the enterprise to achieve estimated earnings levels will vary. A buyer with less experience in a particular business might view the purchase as more of a risk and therefore would likely pay less for something that might not achieve the earnings objectives. The buyer with considerable experience operating the same kind of business expects to meet the revenue and earnings goals and may be willing to pay more.

market-based valuation
Valuation method that looks at process paid for comparable firms. Industry valuation and multiplier formula valuations are two categories of market-based valuation.

fair market value
The price that a business would command from a knowledgeable buyer and a seller with the relevant information about the business and willingness to undertake the transaction.

3. *Tax considerations.* Any sale of a business is likely to involve paying taxes to federal, state, and local governments. How a sale is structured can result in widely varying tax rates for both the seller and buyer of a business. We will discuss tax implications later when we look at how deals are structured. Clearly, the payment or avoidance of taxes can be a significant factor in whether a business is sold or not.

4. *Buyer synergies.* A buyer who has businesses in a similar industry may want to add another complimentary business. For example, a business that manufactures furniture might purchase a chain of furniture retail stores to provide a direct channel of distribution to the final customer. The retail furniture business might be more valuable to a furniture manufacturer than to someone who doesn't own any related businesses.

A number of sources provide valuation guidelines to help an enterpriser determine what a particular type of business might be worth. For example, *Inc.* magazine publishes a valuation matrix that enterprisers can download from its website (http://www.inc.com/valuation). It lists different types of businesses and median revenue, sales price, and a price range. Multiple factors determine the price for each type of business—total assets, liabilities, and earnings. In early 2007, for example, a lawn and garden services business had median annual revenues of $250,000 and a median sale price of $165,000, while a gasoline service station will have median revenues of $1,800,000 and a median sale price of $341,000.[1]

Earnings Valuations

Even though asset-based, market-based, and industry valuation techniques have some merit, the primary way to value a business is by exploring the past, current and future earnings of the business. Assets are meaningless if they don't generate earnings! As we have indicated in the chapters on the business model and feasibility, it is important to understand not only how much the business earns but also how the business creates these earnings. In addition, earnings will reflect the contribution of intangibles such as goodwill.

Cash Flow Valuation

discounted cash flow (DCF)
Valuation technique that finds the present value of a future cash flow stream at a specified discount rate.

discount rate
A rate that represents the buyer's expected cost of capital (the interest rate for a loan to buy the company), as well as the desired return on investment and an adjustment for inflation.

Cash flow valuations are perhaps the most realistic approach to determining a business's value. After all, the future cash flows the business will generate are the basis of its financial success. As we will see in later chapters, it is better to operate a business that has more cash flow than one that has low cash flow—even if its income statement shows higher profits.

This method, also called **discounted cash flow (DCF)**, is more difficult to calculate. It requires an estimate of future cash flow and then applies a **discount rate** that represents the buyer's expected cost of capital (the interest rate for a loan to buy the company) as well as the desired return on investment. The resulting calculation provides the current value of the future cash flow stream.

10.5 Structuring the Deal

Structuring the purchase is often more art than science and requires considerable negotiating between the parties, whose preferences may be quite different. In fact, the purchase terms can be just as important as the price of the business.

It's important to note that the *face value*, or listed purchase price for a business, is often quite different from the *cash value* of the deal. Let's say that a buyer offered $1 million to purchase a firm that manufactured plastic garden equipment. The $1 million represents the face value of the purchase. Rarely are businesses sold for an all cash price at the time of transaction. Many sellers offer the buyer a loan to purchase the business or let the buyer pay for the business over time.

Let's now look at some of the decisions that affect the structure of a business purchase transaction.

What Are You Buying?

One of the first decisions an enterpriser makes when structuring a purchase transaction is whether to buy the entire business or only its assets. Usually buying the whole business is structured as a *stock sale* and includes the assets, liabilities, and owner's equity. The new owner is liable for any debts of the business. An *asset sale* is just what it implies: the buyer acquires only the business's assets. In this case, the seller must settle any outstanding debts. With an asset sale, the new owner avoids being saddled with unknown liabilities. The purchaser could choose to assume specific debts, such as a lease or mortgage on the facilities, if the terms were advantageous.

Tax considerations play a major role in the decision of what to buy, and the interests of buyer and seller may conflict. A seller usually prefers a stock sale, which would be taxed at lower capital gain rates. With an asset sale, any amount the seller receives for the assets that exceeds the book value on the balance sheet would be taxed at higher than ordinary income tax rates. A buyer, however, would prefer an asset sale because the purchase price of the assets becomes the value that the buyer can then list on the business's balance sheet. A higher asset valuation would mean that the buyer could likely deduct higher amounts of depreciation expenses, which would minimize the business's future tax liabilities.

Arranging Financing

While sellers would most likely prefer to sell their businesses for all cash, most buyers will not have the necessary funds to pay the full price up-front. To finance the purchase, the enterpriser must obtain financing from a bank or other lender, an investor group, or the seller. Regardless of the funding source, incurring debt to buy the business increases its risk by adding a high priority fixed obligation—the loan payment.

The availability of bank financing will depend on the type of business, the enterpriser's creditworthiness and experience, collateral offered, and similar factors. Banks prefer to make loans for specific asset purchases. For example, a loan for a delivery truck to the new owner of a furniture delivery service would be easier to obtain than one to cover rent and salaries for a tutoring company. The bank would take the truck as collateral (security) for the loan. If the delivery company fails to make its payments, the bank can repossess the truck. If the tutoring business fails to attract students and can't generate the revenues it projected, the bank has no other source of loan repayment.

Many sellers offer the buyer a note to help finance a portion of the business purchase. The buyer repays the note over a specified length of time at a specified interest rate. The seller often becomes the lender, rather than an outside lender such as a bank, for various reasons:

- Many small businesses have such poor financial records that other lenders (such as a bank) are unsure of what theses businesses can actually earn.

- Privately held corporations often report income and expenses in a way that the financial statements show little profit. For example, the owner of the business can pay high salaries to themselves and their family, which is a business expense that would lower net income.

- If accurate financial statements are generated for the business, the owner could be subject to an IRS audit if the figures are significantly different than those submitted earlier.

- Many buyers purchase businesses that they have less experience in operating, putting the business at a higher risk—a risk that many outsider lenders are unwilling to take.

Like a bank note, a note from the seller will include an interest rate that provides an acceptable return—typically, a rate based on current market conditions. Taking a note for part of the purchase price of a business puts the seller in a risky position. What if the buyer cannot make payments to the seller at some point in the future? Most sellers are advised to include covenants in the purchase contract that require the buyer to limit salaries and other expenses so that the payment of the note is a priority. If the buyer cannot make payments, most sellers often specify that the business's assets or all of the business's stock must be put up as collateral for the loan. Should the loan go into default, the seller regains ownership of the business—not really what someone who is selling a business wants!

Many sellers may be willing to accept stock in the buyer's new company as partial payment for the value of the business. The new stock is a tax-free exchange of stock. In the U.S. tax system, the exchange of old shares of the selling company for new shares in the buying company are not taxed until they are sold. This can be an important tax advantage to a seller. Again, the seller has to believe that the buyer will grow the business in such a way that the shares in the buyer's business have more value than the shares in the old business.

earn-out
Payment strategy that gives the seller of a business a certain amount of the future earnings of the business over a specified time period.

Earn-outs

With an **earn-out,** the seller takes part of the payment as a certain amount of the future earnings of the business over a period of time. For example, a seller might want an earn-out of 50 percent of the profits of the business over a period of five years. The seller and buyer would determine what might be reasonable expenses to be charged, so that the business would generate profits. In an earn-out, the seller shares in the future risk of the business and the buyer's ability to generate earnings. Such a deal might occur because the buyer is uncertain about the business's ability to generate a specific level of cash payment over time (to make fixed payments of principal and interest on a note). In nearly all earn-out agreements, the seller manages part of the risk of this arrangement by keeping ownership of the business until the buyer has met the terms of the earn-out agreement.

Noncompete Agreements and Employment Contracts

Buyers often want sellers to agree to a **noncompete agreement** that prohibits the seller from engaging in a similar kind of business for a set time period within the geographic area in which the purchased business competes. There may be an annual payment to the seller for this agreement. Besides noncompete agreements, many buyers ask sellers to take employment contracts as part of the price of the business. An employment contract is another tax-deductible expense to the business.

noncompete agreement
Agreement prohibiting the seller from entering into a similar kind of business for a set time period within the geographic area in which the purchased business competes.

Once again, tax considerations come into play. Sellers prefer receiving cash for the business, which is taxed at the lower capital gains rate. Payments for a noncompete agreement or employment contract are taxed as current income to the seller. The buyer, on the other hand, likes these options because such payouts are expenses to the business that lower taxable income.

As these examples show, a business purchase transaction can be very complex and can take many different forms. The buyer and seller may have conflicts arising from competing interests. Deals are often limited only by the imagination of the buyer and sellers involved in the agreement. With so many complexities and tax implications in the purchase of a business, we advise you to involve a lawyer, an accountant, and a business appraiser in the process.

10.6 Other Considerations

As this chapter demonstrates, buying a business is a multifaceted process that includes both financial and non-financial considerations. Your analysis includes the same issues you'd consider if you were planning to start a business—the topics we discussed in Chapters 6 through 9. Here, though, we are performing the analysis on an ongoing business. For example, instead of looking at the financing required to start a company, the enterpriser would evaluate financial feasibility based on the purchase price and the terms of the deal. The bottom line is the same: Given everything the enterpriser now knows about the business, can he or she operate it successfully in the future and earn an adequate return on the investment of time and money?

The primary concern for a prospective purchaser involves determining whether the business model is sound and will generate future earnings. Begin by asking yourself the four broad questions we posed in Chapter 7:

1. Who is the customer?

2. What does the customer want? (consideration)

3. How is this consideration going to be provided? (connection)

4. Can you make money doing this?

When investigating the purchase of a business, a savvy enterpriser should interview customers of the business to explore whether these customers are satisfied with the business's goods and services. If these customers are unhappy, the business may have a lower value because dissatisfied customers might go to competitors. Understanding the market environment is also important. Is the industry undergoing significant changes that could have an impact on current connections? For example, the desirability of buying a retail children's clothing store would change if a new Babies-R-Us store was under construction nearby, or if more people chose to buy children's clothes online. Attending industry meetings and talking to other business owners will provide valuable insights. The prospective purchaser needs to have a clear sense of how the business makes money, and what key factors determine whether the business will generate profits.

As mentioned earlier, professionals should help you with your due diligence. An accountant can audit the financial characteristics of the business, while an attorney should review a number of other issues, as Exhibit 10.5 demonstrates.

Like those who choose to start businesses from scratch, business buyers must perform extensive due diligence before buying any business. It is very easy to overlook critical success factors that might be necessary for the business to be successful such as key employees, knowledge of how the business works, and knowledge of how to sell to prospective customers. Another important question to ask is whether the business is a good fit for your experience, skills, and

exhibit 10.5

Accounting and Legal Issues to Examine

An audit would explore such issues as

- Collectability and age of accounts receivable
- Age, condition, and value of inventory
- Age, condition, and value of equipment and physical plant
- Unknown liabilities
- Credit problems
- Tax payments

On the legal front, an attorney can review

- Compliance with local zoning and environmental regulations
- Validity of all required licenses and similar documents
- Current leases and contracts
- Insurance policies
- Existing and pending lawsuits against the business

personal goals. Paying proper attention to all the key factors will increase the likelihood that an enterpriser will be successful in both acquiring a business at a fair price and achieving desired operational and financial objectives in the future.

Whereas buying a business in the United States is a complex process, purchasing one in a foreign country is even more complicated. The Enterprising World box introduces you to the many issues you'd encounter if you wanted to own a business in France.

Working and Living Outside the United States

Like many Americans, you love to travel and have spent many happy vacations hiking and bicycling in Europe. You often daydream about moving overseas to live and work. Now you may be able to make your dream a reality, because an uncle has left you a generous bequest—enough for the down payment on a business venture in France, your favorite country. After browsing the business for sale listings, you discover what could be the perfect solution: A recently established cycle tour company and large farmhouse in Normandy. While the business is new, it is operational and has already developed a brand identity. Unexpected family health issues make it difficult for the founding owner, who lives in London, to spend enough time in France operating the company.

The business can be run from a home office, and the five-bedroom farmhouse has been renovated with modern kitchen and bathrooms. In addition to the main house, the property also has an adjacent building suitable for six more bedrooms and a gym equipped for cycle training. You and your spouse could live there and also develop a small inn to house your cycle tour participants.

Intrigued by the possibility of combining your passion for cycling with a business venture, you research the issues involved in buying a business in another country. Right away, you realize that the French business and legal environment is quite different from what you've experienced in the United States. First, the legal system in France is based on the Napoleonic Code, or civil law, rather than the common law system used in the United States and the United Kingdom. The public sector is large and bureaucratic, with many levels to negotiate. Public law covers municipal and tax law, and there are also private laws that govern commercial and corporate aspects of the transaction from construction and sale and purchase agreements to mortgages. You will be subject to French income tax regulations, which will also vary from U.S. tax laws.

The usual forms of business organization are unfamiliar to you and include:

- Enterprise individuelle (E.I.)—a one-person business

- Entreprise Unipersonnelle à Responsabilité Limitée (E.U.R.L.)—a private limited company under sole ownership

- Société à Responsabilité Limitée (S.A.R.L.)—a limited liability company

In addition, the law divides small businesses into three categories based on the main activity: Artisan (craftsmen) with no more than ten employees; Libéral, generally professionals such as physicians, attorneys, or consultants; and Commerçant (tradesmen).

Property sales procedures are different as well. For example, in France you are expected to sign a binding preliminary contract of sale prior to performing the

(continued)

An Enterprising World

various legal and other searches. In the United States typically you conduct your searches before signing any sales contract.

These are just a few issues you encounter in a quick search for information on buying a business in France. You wonder what else you need to know before proceeding further.

Discussion Questions

1. Prepare a list of questions you would want to ask before purchasing this business, including those relating to the business and its operations as well as the problems you might encounter in trying to purchase a French business. How would owning your own business in France be different from working for an employer based in France?

Now, use a Web search engine to find information to answer the following questions:

2. What regulations apply to non–European Union persons purchasing a business in a European Union country like France? What are the visa, residency, and work permit requirements for a non–European Union citizen to work in France?

3. Because your bicycle business is seasonal, you plan to live part of the year in France, and part of the year in the United States, how would your tax liability for each country be determined?

4. Let's assume that the bicycle tour/inn business you purchased tripled in value over a five-year period, and, now you have decided to sell the property. What kinds of problems might you encounter selling a business in France? What tax liabilities would you face in France and the United States?

Sources: Businesses for Sale, http://www.businessesforsale.com (February 6, 2007); "Buying a Business in France," *Christie+Co.*, http://www.christie.com/christie/index.asp (February 3, 2007); and "Running *a Gite* Business in France," *FrenchEntrée.com*, http://www.frenchentree.com (February 6, 2007).

10.7 Enterprisers

The Small Cheese

In a state known for cheese, Specialty Cheese Company is somewhat unique. Based in Lowell, Wisconsin, the company makes over 35 varieties of cheese that cater to diverse ethnic populations. From its four cheese plants, among the oldest and smallest in the United States, 110 employees, including ten Wisconsin-licensed cheese makers, produce both traditional and innovative award-winning products.

Owners Vicki and Paul Scharfman were newcomers to small business. Both have MBAs in marketing and many years' experience in big corporations and nonprofit organizations. Until he was laid off in January 1991, Paul had been the sales and marketing manager for the Louis Kampf Seafood subsidiary of Oscar Mayer, and before that he'd been a marketing manager for Oscar Mayer, Kraft, and General Foods. "An outplacement counselor gave me a battery of tests," he says. "None of them were terribly useful, but in total they helped me identify something that I could really believe in. I learned that I like to start things, to initiate, to innovate, to get going." He and Vickie also liked living in the Madison, Wisconsin, area and wanted to find a better balance between work and family life. Putting those factors together with Paul's skills in food marketing, the Scharfmans began looking for a company to purchase.

The Heim Cheese Company, Wisconsin's oldest continuously running cheese factory, appeared to meet the Scharfmans' needs. Before buying it, however, the enterprising couple used their marketing backgrounds to extensively research the cheese industry. "I identified a company that fit my desires; they wanted to sell out, needed equity, needed marketing help," Paul recalls. "And I went to that firm and said, 'So what do you do well? What can I build on?' Well, I could say what they didn't do well—sales were dropping. The big question was, what do they do well?"

Heim already made very good cheese, including a Cuban cheese. That became the starting point for the Scharfmans' research. They analyzed census data and conducted extensive consumer research to identify underserved but high-growth niche markets, the largest of which was the Hispanic market.

Then they went directly to the potential customer and interviewed former residents of Mexico and South America. By asking what they liked and didn't like about the cheeses available in American grocery stores, the Scharfmans learned that Hispanic cheeses look, cook, and taste different from American or European cheeses. Hispanics found cooking with American cheese very frustrating because it melts when heated, whereas Hispanic cheese becomes soft and creamy but holds its shape.

Several months and many thousands of dollars later, they confirmed that there was an as-yet untapped market for ethnic cheeses for Hispanic customers from several areas, including the Caribbean and Latin America. Paul recognized that the current producers weren't offering the variety that the market was asking for, and customer service was inadequate.

With these facts in hand, the Scharfmans bought Fred Heim's cheese company in 1991 and renamed it Specialty Cheese. Instead of going head to head with the large food companies like Kraft, they focused on natural cheeses for selected ethnic markets. "We make good cheese in small batches," says Paul. "But our most important ingredient is information."

They started the La Vaca Rica (The Rich Cow) line with what became their biggest seller: Queso Blanco. "I bought a bunch of cheeses from Houston, Los Angeles, New York, and Miami, and brought them back to my cheese makers," explains Paul. "They were good enough to figure out how to make them." This fresh white cheese was an instant hit in major cities with large Hispanic populations.

Paul understood that he had inherited a valuable resource: talented employees. What the Scharfmans brought to the table was marketing flair, an understanding of how markets change, and how to tailor the products. "You guys make the cheese," Paul told the cheese makers. "My job is to represent the consumer, be it a housewife, an individual, a chef, a restaurant owner, and find out what the consumer needs."

As Paul explains, "The gist of it is simple: ask. People love talking. Ask them about something that they care about, and they will tell you more than you want to know. If you want to become a manufacturer of golf balls, start by asking people who play golf a lot about the product. It's free. You can do it." The Scharfmans conducted focus groups where people could see and taste the test products. From that they learned how to change their cheeses to improve marketability.

"The products that we inherited from the previous owner were on target, but they were maybe the wrong shape or the wrong color or the wrong name," says Vicki. They took slightly different versions of the products to the focus groups, until they began to get "Ahas."

From that base, the Scharfmans looked for other unique markets to which their master cheese makers could apply their skills. "We asked, 'Which cultures eat cheese,'" says Vicki. To find the answer, they hired someone to go through census data to learn the major languages people speak at home in this country. The result of that research was two additional product lines: The Rich Cow brand Middle Eastern cheeses and Bharatma brand Indian cheeses.

(continued)

In a departure from its fresh cheese products, the company developed a new line called Just the Cheese™ Crunchy Baked Cheese™. The innovative, all-natural 100 percent cheese-baked cheese snacks have a potato chip-like crunch—"sort of a cheese and cracker combination all in one," Paul says. The first attempts to market Just the Cheese met with lackluster response. "It failed miserably," Scharfman says. "The world wasn't waiting for another gourmet snack."

However, the product's introduction in 1997 coincided with the growing popularity of low carbohydrate diets. A Wisconsin doctor told the Scharfmans that there was indeed a market for no-carbohydrate, high calcium Crunchy Baked Cheese—as a diet food. A tie-in with the Atkins Diet helped the product, which comes in white cheddar, garlic and herb, sour cream and onion, jalapeno, and nacho flavors. "On the Atkins Diet you can't have anything crunchy or salty—no chips, crackers, or pretzels. We have invented the salty snack category for people on this diet," Paul says. Customers from all over the world flocked to the Specialty Cheese website to order cases of the crunchy cheese chips, which now account for about 15 percent of the company's sales.

"We do niches," Paul says. "One set of niches is the ethnic market. By luck, we ended up in the diet niche with patented products." Although many of the company's market niches are small, the market research the Scharfmans performed helped them choose ones with potential that are strong and steady. Today's consumers are increasingly willing to express their desires about food products and have a strong interest in ethnic foods. They believe in "tribal marketing," a term Paul developed to describe marketing efforts geared towards different ethnic groups who have unmet product needs.

As Vicki explains, "There are many people who go out and say, 'I have God's gift to the product world. I have this fabulous invention. Everyone's going to love it. I'm going to make a mint. I'm gonna sell a gazillion of them.' They go out and they make this wonderful product, and it sits there and nothing happens. They can't understand why people aren't buying it. That is the backwards approach to marketing." Instead, she advises enterprisers to start with qualitative research to find out what your consumer wants and needs and what they are not getting from the current offerings in the marketplace. "Go out and tailor your dream to what they want," she says. "That's the fit that sells product."

Discussion Questions

1. What were the advantages to the Scharfmans of buying Heim Cheese rather than starting a new cheese company from scratch? The disadvantages? How well did the Heim Cheese Company fit with the Scharfman's personal goals? Suggest several reasons that Fred Heim might be selling his company.

2. What are the critical success factors for successfully running a cheese business? What skills and abilities and resources do the new owners bring to this business? What critical success factors don't they possess, and how will they insure that the business continues to have them?

3. What valuation technique would you recommend that the Scharfmans use to set a value for the Heim Cheese Company, and why?

4. You are helping the Scharfmans prepare a proposal for financing to buy Heim Cheese Company. Prepare an executive summary that describes the company's business model, marketing strategy, and other key points. What are some ways that they can structure a financial package to purchase the company? Suggest a number of ways they might be able to secure financing beyond their own resources.

Sources: Adapted with permission from "Meet the MBAs of Marketing Who Turned Around the Oldest Cheese Factory in Wisconsin," Small Business School, the series on PBS, and at http://SmallBusinessSchool.com; Carole Ashkinaze, "Spies Like Us," *Businessweek Online*, June 16, 2000, http://www.businessweek.com/smallbiz/0006/ma3685105.htm; Kate Sander, "Specialty Cheese Co. Stands Ready to Expand Market for Its 'Diet' Cheese," *Cheese Market News*, February 11, 2000, http://www.cheesemarketnews.com; Specialty Cheese Company website, http://www.specialcheese.com (June 22, 2005); *The Specialty Cheese Market* (Lincoln, Nebraska: Food Processing Center, Institute of Agriculture and Natural Resources, University of Nebraska, Lincoln, October 2001), http://www.farmprofitability.org/cheese.htm; and Linda Spice, "Cheese, Hispanic Style," *Milwaukee Journal Sentinel*, June 27, 2004, http://www.jsonline.com.

10.8 Summary

1. Purchasing a business or a franchise (Type 4) is one of the eight pathways to business ownership—and a major way for enterprisers to go into business. Before making such a purchase, enterprisers must thoroughly analyze the business model, feasibility, and business plan.

2. Enterprisers choose to buy a going concern rather than start a business for several reasons. Buying a proven business concept lowers risk because the enterpriser has more knowledge of the firm's operations, market, and customer base. The speed with which they can get into business appeals to many enterprisers. An established business has a track record and may be easier to finance. It may cost less to purchase and operate a business than to start one from scratch, and the enterprise may already be producing a positive cash flow. The potential to improve an undervalued business is a factor for some enterprisers, who have a clear vision of changes they can make to increase profitability.

3. Drawbacks to buying a business include raising the financing, which can often be quite a large amount, and setting the right price. Sometimes sellers are overly optimistic when they describe their company and may also fail to disclose problems prior to the purchase. An enterpriser may discover that operating the new business requires more time or money than originally expected. Thorough analysis prior to entering into a purchase contract can avoid unpleasant surprises after the fact.

4. Other factors to consider before buying a business include the enterpriser's personal motivation and goals, the time the business will require to be managed, the owner's reasons for selling, and whether the enterpriser will need to bring in partners.

5. Before buying a business, the enterpriser should know why the current owner is selling. The owner may be ready to retire or be in poor health. Some enterprisers prefer to start businesses and then move on to new ventures once they are up and running. Lack of managerial expertise is another factor that leads to business sales.

6. Enterprisers can find businesses for sale through classified ads in newspapers, magazines, and online or by using a business broker. Brokers will pre-qualify buyers and use this information to match potential buyers and sellers.

7. A business's value is ultimately what a buyer is willing to pay for it and should be based on the firm's ability to generate earnings. Valuing a business begins with considering the value of the opportunity, the enterprise's business model, the future feasibility of the enterprise, and the business plan. Many factors influence the valuation process, including the age and size of the business, quality of physical assets, market considerations, customer base and loyalty, and earning potential.

Intangibles, such as the value of the business's reputation and similar factors that come with a going concern, also affect the business value.

8. Asset-based approaches to valuation begin with placing a value on the business's assets. This category has several variations, with some using replacement or market value rather than book (depreciated) value. These methods are relatively easy to calculate. However, they focus on assets alone and assign no value to the business's ability to use these assets to generate revenues.

9. Market-based valuations are determined by what other people will pay for this business or similar businesses. Industry valuation and multiplier formula valuations are two categories of market-based valuation. Industry valuations begin with sales of comparable businesses. Multiplier formulas use sales, income, or other financial statistics, taking into account business characteristics and the prices paid for similar businesses. Because no two businesses are exactly alike, market-based methods must be applied with care.

10. The primary way to value a business is by exploring the past, current, and future earnings of the business and applying a multiplier of earnings. Multipliers are often based on sales prices of comparable businesses and vary across industry sectors. The riskiness of a business also affects the multiplier.

11. Although they are the most difficult to calculate, valuations based on cash flow can be the most accurate. The value takes into account the present value of future cash flows by applying a discount rate that includes the purchaser's cost of capital, desired return, and future inflation.

12. The purchase terms for a business are as important as the price and require considerable negotiation between buyer and seller. For example, the decision to buy the entire business (assets and liabilities, usually done as a stock sale) rather than buying just the assets has a different tax implication for each party. The buyer may not be able to pay for the business in cash up-front and may want an installment sale. Sellers often provide financing in the form of a note to be repaid over a defined time period. Earn-outs offer another way to pay for the business over time; the seller receives a stated percentage of future profits for a set time period.

13. The purchase agreement may also include a noncompete agreement that prevents the seller from operating a similar business in the same market area for a certain time period. A seller may also agree to take a portion of the sales price in the form of an employment contract, which becomes a tax-deductible expense to the new owner.

14. Before signing a purchase agreement, enterprisers should perform extensive due diligence. This process should include both an accountant and an attorney, who can audit financial records and review legal issues.

Review Questions

1. What are the advantages of buying an existing business compared to starting a new one?

2. What disadvantages might an enterpriser encounter when buying a business?

3. Summarize the key questions an enterpriser should ask when evaluating his or her personal motivation and goals for purchasing a business. What other factors come into play?

4. Why is the owner's reason for selling an important consideration? Describe some of the common reasons for selling a business.

5. How would you search for potential businesses to buy? Would you use business brokers, and why?

6. What factors go into the valuation of a business? Which is the most important, and why?

7. What are the calculations involved in asset-based valuation techniques, and what are their pros and cons?

8. Describe how market-based methods set business valuations and briefly describe the two main types of market-based valuation models.

9. Why are earnings valuations considered the best indicator of a business's worth? How do cash flow techniques incorporate earnings into their models?

10. How does the structure of a business purchase transaction affect the price and the terms? List several possible deal structures and their implications.

11. What sources of financing are available for business purchases? How does an earnout affect the selling price of a business, and why?

12. Why might a purchase agreement include a noncompete agreement or an employment contract?

13. What other steps should a buyer take before finalizing a business purchase? What legal and accounting issues may arise?

Applying What You've Learned

1. The following *Inc.* article provides a number of insights into the criteria an entrepreneur should consider when purchasing an established business, as well as into the process involved in purchasing and operating it:

    Jay Finegan, "The Insider's Guide: 15 Steps to Owning the Company that's Right for You," *Inc.*, October 1991, http://www.inc.com/magazine/19911001/4874.html

    Now read the following articles, which describe Hendrix Niemann's efforts to buy a business.

2. Hendrix F. C. Niemann, "Buying a Business," *Inc.*, February 1990, http://www.inc.com/magazine/19900201/5028.html

3. Hendrix F. C. Niemann, "The Rest of the Story," *Inc.*, October 1991, http://www.inc.com/magazine/19911001/4875.html
    After reading Niemann's story, answer the following questions:

    (a) How many of the criteria in the "Insider's Guide" did Mr. Niemann follow in purchasing the business? What did Mr. Niemann do right? What did Mr. Niemann do wrong?

    (b) How well did Mr. Niemann operate the business? What did he do wrong?

    (c) What were the major mistakes that Mr. Niemann made during the search, purchase, and operation of this business?

How many of these mistakes could he have avoided?

4. Now consider the Niemann business purchase transaction from the seller's point of view.

   (a) Did Mr. Klosky receive full value for the sale of his business?
   (b) Suggest actions that Mr. Klosky could have performed to achieve a higher price for the business.
   (c) What other alternatives did Mr. Klosky have for "harvesting" his business?

5. Look in the "Businesses for Sale" part of the Classified Ads section of your local newspaper. Note that there are likely to be more advertisements in the Sunday edition of the newspaper than on weekdays. What kinds of businesses are for sale? Who is offering those businesses (e.g., owners, business brokers, accountants, lawyers)? Make some inquires about these advertisements to find out more about these businesses. Why are they being sold? What kinds of prices are they asking, and how are they planning on structuring the deals for these businesses? Prepare a brief summary to share with your classmates.

6. Select a particular kind of business that you would be interested in either starting or buying. Interview business owners to find out whether they started these businesses or purchased them. How might these two types of business owners (start-ups versus purchasers) be different in terms of their backgrounds, skills, and abilities? Why did some of these enterprisers start businesses while others purchased? What advice do both of these groups offer you about being successful as enterprisers?

7. Market-based valuations of different types of businesses vary widely. For example, an accounting practice may sell for 100 to 125 percent of its annual revenues, but a travel agency may typically sell for 40 to 60 percent of annual sales. In the retail sector, a bookstore might sell for 15 percent of annual sales plus inventory, whereas a coffee shop price is based on 40 to 45 percent of annual sales plus inventory.[2] In your opinion, why are these multipliers different, and why would someone be willing to pay more for one kind of business versus another?

Enterprisers on the Web

1. Many sites offer searchable databases of businesses for sale. Explore the following sites and browse the listings.

   (a) International Business Brokers Association, http://www.ibba.org
   (b) Business Broker.net, http://www.businessbroker.net/
   (c) StartupJournal, http://bizbuysell.startupjournal.com

   Now prepare a table that compares the sites in the following areas: Number of listings, how listings are categorized, content of individual listings, ease of navigation, search capabilities, and any other areas you choose.

   Rank the sites based on your findings and explain the rationale for your choices. Why do you prefer your number one site?

2. Pick an industry or business category that appeals to you. Using search engines like Google, Yahoo!, AltaVista, or Lycos, find sites for its trade associations. Visit them to learn more about the industries and summarize your findings. Based on your research, explain why you would or would not continue to look for a business to buy in that industry.

3. Go to the site you liked best from question 1. Search for businesses in at least two different industries located in either

your current area or one where you'd like to live. Choose three and compare them in terms of purchase price, reasons for sale, financial information, and other available information. What other information would you need before starting a serious investigation of these businesses?

4. Using any source of business for sale listings, pick one company that interests you. Read the article "What's Your Company Worth Now?" *Inc.*, August 2004, http://www.inc.com/magazine/20040801/valuations_index.html. Then refer to "The Ultimate Valuation Guide" (http://www.inc.com/valuation) and look at prices of comparable businesses. Determine whether the asking price is reasonable. What valuation method seems most appropriate for this company, and why?

5. Use either the International Business Brokers Association (http://www.ibba.org) or Business Broker.net (http://www.businessbroker.net) site to identify business brokers in your area. Select three and interview them to find out more about the kinds of owners who are willing to sell their businesses, as well as the kinds of buyers business brokers are looking for. Based on these interviews, what will you need to do in order for a business broker to want to sell a business to you?

End Notes

1. "The Most, and the Least, Valuable Businesses in America," *Inc.*, January 2007, pp. 102–103.

2. Based on information in *The 2001 Business Reference Guide*, Business Brokerage Press, cited on "Valuing Your Business," http://www.bizhelp24.com/small_business/selling_a_business_5.shtml.

chapter 11

Franchising

Key Concepts

1. Buying a franchise enables enterprisers to sell brand-name goods and services by entering into a contractual business relationship with a franchisor, the parent business. Franchisees can own one unit or obtain the rights to develop multiple units in a territory. The Federal Trade Commission regulates the offer and sale of franchises, and many states have their own franchise laws.

2. Choosing a franchise requires the same careful due diligence process as other prospective business ventures. Franchising's benefits include training, help and support, system synergies, financing assistance, and economies of scale. However, the franchisee must comply with the franchisor's operating restrictions and contractual obligations and pay the franchisor an initial fee as well as ongoing fees and royalties.

3. Entrepreneurs with an easily replicated business model, a strong brand or trademark, and a unique concept can use franchising to grow their businesses quickly. Other enterprisers become franchisees and provide talent and capital. While becoming a franchisor can be quite profitable, the franchisor loses some profits to the franchisees and also gives up a degree of operating control. Successful franchisors know what it takes to be a good franchisee, have systems in place to recruit and train franchisees, and work closely with system members.

Suppose you and your wife both work and have a new baby to care for. You can no longer go out to dinner whenever you choose. Wouldn't it be great if the restaurants came to you instead?

This was the idea behind Takeout Taxi, a food delivery service started in 1987 by Kevin Abt. He conducted market research to test his idea and learned that other than pizza, there weren't many choices for home delivery. As he refined his business concept, he found that restaurant owners as well as customers liked the idea. The business grew, so Abt decided to franchise his concept in other areas.

As you'll learn in this chapter's case, Takeout Taxi expanded to 15 states. However, it was unable to manage its growth and ran into major problems. The chapter provides information on both how to buy a franchise and how to use franchising to grow your business, to help you avoid the difficulties Abt encountered.

11.0 The Franchise Route to Business Ownership

As you go about your day, you might have breakfast at McDonald's, mail a package from the UPS Store, get your car's brakes repaired at Midas, order a pizza from Domino's, and get a haircut at Supercuts. Meanwhile, you arranged for California Closets to install cabinets in your garage and for Merry Maids to clean your house. At work you contacted Management Recruiters for help finding a sales manager. And a Century 21 realtor found you the house you bought last year. Did you know that in each case you were dealing with a franchised business?

Purchasing a franchise is another way for individuals to become enterprisers. Franchising is a type of business ownership where a parent business (the franchisor) provides an investor (the franchisee) with the rights to sell its products or services and use its trademark and operating procedures. In return, the franchisee pays up-front fees and/or ongoing royalty payments. The term **franchise** refers to the agreement or license between the franchisor and franchisee. A strong and growing franchise has to provide benefits for both franchisors and franchisees. We will see how a franchise system needs to be a win-win for both parties.

The franchising concept has a long history, tracing its origins to the guilds of the Middle Ages. Kings and lords gave certain individuals exclusive rights to engage in such activities as ironwork, stone cutting and masonry work, and

franchise
The rights to offer specific products or services under explicit guidelines at a certain location for a declared period of time.

341

barrel making. In the 1840s, German breweries began to offer franchises to tavern owners, giving them exclusive rights to sell their beer. In what would be considered the precursor of many of the activities involved with modern forms of franchising, in 1851 the Singer Sewing Machine Company developed written contracts and sold franchisees exclusive distribution rights to sell its sewing machines from local stores. These early franchise contracts became the model for today's Prospectus or United Offering Circular, which retains much of the same language and format. By the early 1900s, automobile manufacturers followed Singer's lead, and soon oil companies saw franchising as a good way to grow. The first franchised restaurant chain opened in 1924 and was, in fact, a drive-in: A&W Root Beer® drive-in restaurants.[1]

Much of the growth of franchising has occurred since the 1950s, when some of today's major franchisors opened for business. For example, Kentucky Fried Chicken began operations in 1952, followed by Burger King and McDonald's in 1955, Midas Muffler in 1956, and H&R Block in 1958.

Most early franchises centered on the fast food and hotel industries. During the 1960s and 1970s, the franchise concept experienced dynamic growth and expanded into a broader range of business categories. Today, 765,000 franchised businesses from more than 1,200 franchisors span 75 industries, from restaurants to technology consulting. Exhibit 11.1 shows the distribution of franchises across

exhibit 11.1   **Franchises by Industry Category**

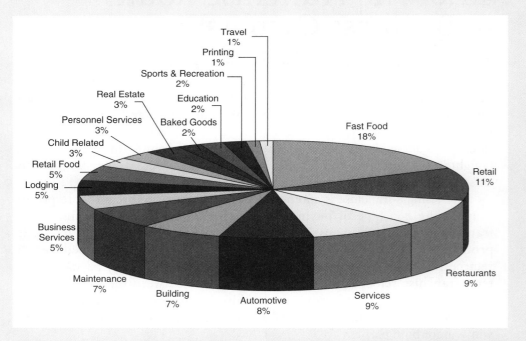

Note: The Fast Food category includes fast food and frozen desserts. Retail includes beauty, clothing, computer, party, pet, photo, and video. Services includes health and fitness, publications, security. Building includes building, construction, home décor.

Source: The Profile of Franchising (Washington, DC: Frandata Corp. and IFA Educational Foundation, February 2000), pp. 26–27.

18 major industry sectors. Food-related industries—fast food, baked goods, retail food, and restaurants—account for 34 percent of all franchise systems and the highest number of new concepts.

In some industries, franchises are a significant portion of the total number of businesses that compete. For example, nearly one-third of all retail sales are made through franchised firms. In terms of the number of business establishments, franchise units represent over 56 percent of all fast food restaurants, 18 percent of all hotels and motels, 14 percent of retail food stores, and 13 percent of full service restaurants.[2]

Franchising has become a major contributor to the world economy. Exhibit 11.2 illustrates the direct impact of franchising on just the U.S. economy. With almost 10 million jobs, the franchising sector represents the second largest category of direct employment, just behind durable goods manufacturing. In addition, franchising indirectly affects these areas of the economy. For example, restaurant franchises require food and other supplies. According to a study commissioned by the International Franchise Association, the indirect and direct impact of franchising accounts for almost 14 percent of the nation's employment and $1.53 trillion in economic output.

Although the big national brands are the first names that come to mind when we think of franchising, most franchisors are in fact small- to medium-sized businesses with 200 units or less. Only about 8 percent of all franchise systems have more than 500 units, while 25 percent have 11–50 units, and 17 percent have ten or fewer units.[3]

Franchising continues to grow as franchisors find new brands to offer and consumers want more specialized services—for example, adult day care, beauty and skin treatments, entertainment, health and home care, and spas. This form of business ownership is gaining popularity among aging baby boomers, who often choose to start new careers rather than retire. Franchisors report that franchisee applicants today present better qualifications than in the past, with more management experience and education.[4]

In this chapter we will explore this route to business ownership, starting with the basics of franchising and the legal aspects of franchising. We will look at both sides of the franchising equation: becoming either a franchisee or franchisor. We

exhibit 11.2

Direct Contribution of Franchising to the U.S. Economy

Category	In Franchised Businesses	Percent of the Private Sector Economy
Jobs	9,797,117	7.4%
Payroll	$229.1 billion	5.0%
Output	$624.6 billion	3.9%

Source: Economic Impact of Franchised Businesses, a study conducted by PricewaterhouseCoopers for the IFA Educational Foundation, 2004.

will first discuss how individuals should select a franchise for purchase. Then we will explain how some enterprisers might take their established business and create a franchise system.

11.1 How Franchising Works

Franchising represents a business relationship between the franchisor and franchisee. All franchises share three basic elements: a brand, a business system, and fees. Within that relationship structure, however, franchises have several alternatives from which to choose: the type of franchise (business format or product and trademark) and the number of units the franchisee wishes to own.

Franchise Formats

Franchises fall into two major categories: *business format franchises* and *product and trademark* (also called *product distribution*) *franchises.* About 80 percent of all franchises and jobs fall into the business format category.

business format franchise
A type of franchise where the franchisee purchases a product and a complete system to operate the business.

In the **business format franchise,** the franchisee purchases a plan, or format, for running the business. In addition to the brand name, the franchisor provides the franchisee with training in how to manage and grow the business, guidelines for operating the business, local and national advertising, and other forms of assistance such as help in locating a site, guidance on building and outfitting the store, and financing. Business format franchisors make their money through fees and royalties. We'll cover the cost elements in greater detail later in the chapter, when we discuss how to evaluate a franchise.

Franchisors offer varying degrees of assistance. Not all franchisors offer financing, for instance. Some have very specific guidelines on how to conduct every aspect of the business. For example, a Subway restaurant will have specific guidelines on how to greet customers, bake the bread for the sandwiches, and place meats, cheeses, and other toppings on each sandwich. Many franchisors require their franchisees to link their cash registers to the franchisor's main computer, so that the franchisor can monitor sales and also help the franchisee order supplies. Other franchisors provide little guidance beyond the operations manual on specific aspects of managing the business.

While fast food restaurants rank first among business format franchises in number of people employed, the business services sector has the most units and generates the highest output of any franchise type.

affiliation or conversion franchising
A business format franchise in which an operating business becomes part of a franchise system to take advantage of the brand but has more flexibility with regard to operating format. The unit name may reflect both the franchisor and the local entity.

Affiliation or conversion franchising is a special type of business format franchise. The owner of an operating business joins forces with a franchisor to benefit from the power of the brand and some elements of the operating format. In affiliation franchising, the franchisee may combine the local company's name with the franchisor's brand. This is particularly common in real estate brokerage franchises, which might use a name such as Coldwell Banker/Lynn Lawrence Realty, and in hotel chains—Best Western Any Town Inn.

Product and trademark (or product distribution) franchises provide franchisees with the right to buy, sell, and advertise the products under the manufacturer's trademarked name. These franchisees create a dealer network for the manufacturer. Unlike business format franchises, which have stringent operating requirements, product and trademark franchisees have considerable latitude in how they run their businesses. The franchisors earn their profits by selling products to the distributors. Because these franchises typically deal with big-ticket purchases, they generate about 30 percent of all franchise payroll and 26 percent of total franchise output.[5]

Automobile and truck dealerships are by far the largest industry group within product and trademark franchises, accounting for 70 percent of the category's output and more than 18 percent of total franchise output.[6] For example, the Ford Motor Company designs and builds automobiles and sells them to franchised dealerships. These dealerships both sell and service automobiles under the Ford brand. The Ford Motor Company earns its revenues from the sales of automobiles and parts to its dealerships. Ford also advertises its automobiles so that people will buy its cars. The dealerships make money by selling automobiles and parts for a higher price than they paid to Ford and by providing repairs and services.

Other types of product distribution franchises include the sales and distribution of oil and gasoline (Chevron, Shell, ExxonMobil), tire centers (Firestone, Goodyear), soft drink bottlers (Coca-Cola, Pepsi), and heavy equipment manufacturers (John Deere, Caterpillar).

Franchise Purchase Options

Franchisors offer different purchase options to potential franchisees, ranging from the basic single-unit franchise to the multiple-unit area development and master franchise arrangements. The **unit franchise** is the simplest form: the franchisor grants the franchisee the right to open an individual franchise, often in a particular location. Many franchisors prefer to work with *multiple-unit franchisees* that own two or more units of the same franchise. Because those franchisees have more experience operating that particular franchise, the franchisor doesn't have to devote as much time and energy training new franchisees.

Multiple-unit ownership can take one of two forms:

- *Area development franchise:* The franchisor grants the franchisee, or area developer, the rights to open and operate a specific number of franchises within a particular geographic region. The two parties agree on a time schedule for the franchise development. Franchisees sign an area development agreement that defines the region and the timing for the new units and a unit franchise agreement when each individual franchise is developed. Failure to maintain the development timetable may result in termination of the area development agreement. The franchisee usually retains any established units.

- *Master franchise (subfranchising):* A master franchise goes one step further than area development franchising. In addition to granting rights over a particular territory, the franchisor also gives the master franchisee

---

product and trademark (product distribution) franchise
Franchise arrangement under which manufacturers grant franchisees, or dealers, the right to buy, sell, and advertise the products under the manufacturer's trademarked name.

unit franchise
Agreement to open one unit in a particular location.

area development franchise
Rights to open and operate a specific number of franchises within a particular geographic region.

master franchise (subfranchising)
A three-party arrangement that grants a master franchisee rights to open franchises in a particular territory, along with right to sell franchises to other unit franchisees.

subfranchisor
A franchisee who contracts with a master franchisee to open a franchise within the same territory.

the right to either open franchise units or sell franchises to other unit franchisees, called **subfranchisors**, in that particular territory. This three-party form of franchising is often used by American franchisors who wish to expand internationally. For example, Jim Bryant holds the master franchise for Subway in China. His agreement with the company allows him to open his own stores, sell to local subfranchisees, and serve as liaison between his subfranchisees and the parent company. In return, he is entitled to 50 percent of the initial fee and one-third of the royalty fees.[7]

Multiple franchise ownership may vary from these traditional forms. Rather than specify a geographic territory, a franchisor may grant the right to sell to a particular customer category—for example, doctors, elementary schools, or an industry sector.

11.2 Legal Aspects of Franchising

Despite the popularity of franchising, the industry is not as heavily regulated as you might expect. Congress passed the first laws in the 1950s to regulate auto and petroleum franchise sales, but other types of franchises remained essentially unregulated. As complaints against fraudulent sales practices rose, California became the first state with a Franchise Investment Law covering disclosure by franchisors to potential investors.

The Federal Trade Commission (FTC) regulates the offer and sale of franchises at the federal level. Laws covering franchise operations vary, however, from state to state. Because franchises commonly fall within the legal definition of a "business opportunity," they are subject to business opportunity laws in about 25 states. Some states have general franchise investment or relationship statutes and others may have industry-specific regulations. Franchise relationships also are regulated by antitrust laws and by general business regulations such as contract law.

Is current franchise regulation adequate? Well-known franchise attorney Lewis Rudnick believes it is. "The disclosure laws have gotten rid of fly-by-night, poorly conceived business models," he says. Franchisee advocates such as the American Franchising Association (AFA) disagree, however. According to AFA president Susan Kezios, current laws do not address key issues such as encroachment (opening another franchised- or company-owned store in close proximity of an existing franchise); product sourcing (requiring franchisees to buy products only from approved suppliers regardless of price); and restrictions on selling a franchise to another franchisee. Since 1995, Congress has attempted without success to amend franchise regulations (Rule 436).

Rule 436
Federal Trade Commission regulation that governs disclosure requirements for the offer and sale of franchises in all 50 states.

Federal Regulation of Franchise Sales

Since 1979, the FTC has been responsible for regulating the purchase and sale of franchises under FTC **Rule 436**, which mandates minimum disclosure requirements. The basic provisions of the rule include the following:

(a) *Basic Requirement:* Franchisors must provide potential franchisees with written disclosures of important information about the franchisor, the franchised business, and the franchise relationship, and give them at least ten business days to review it before investing.

(b) *Disclosure Option:* Franchisors have two options for the mandatory disclosures: the rule's disclosure format or the Uniform Franchise Offering Circular Guidelines prepared by state franchise law officials.

(c) *Coverage:* Rule 436 primarily covers both business format and product and trademark franchises, as well as vending machine or display rack business opportunity ventures.

(d) *No Filing:* Rule 436 does not require the franchisor to register, file, or have reviewed or approved by the FTC any disclosure documents, advertising, or agreements. (State disclosure laws may differ in this regard.)

(e) *Remedies:* Rule 436 has the full force and effect of federal law and may be enforced only by the FTC, which may seek injunctions, civil penalties, and consumer redress for violations.

(f) *Purpose:* Rule 436 ensures that potential franchisees receive adequate information to evaluate the risks and benefits of a particular franchise prior to investing.[8]

In addition, Rule 436 imposes six requirements related to any "advertising, offering, licensing, contracting, sale, or other promotion" of a franchise that affects commerce:

1. *Basic Disclosures:* Franchisors must give potential investors a basic disclosure document at the earliest of either the first face-to-face meeting or ten business days before any money is paid or an agreement is signed in connection with the investment.

2. *Earnings Claims:* Any historical or forecasted earnings claims a franchisor makes must be based on reasonable assumptions, which must be disclosed along with other required documents.

3. *Advertised Claims:* Ads including an earnings claim must disclose the number and percentage of existing franchisees that have achieved the claimed results, along with cautionary language. These ads are subject to the earnings claims disclosure rules.

4. *Franchise Agreements:* The franchisor must give franchisees a review copy of all standard franchise agreements along with the basic disclosures and execution copies no less than five business days before signing.

5. *Refunds:* Franchisors must make refunds of deposits and initial payments to potential investors in accordance with refund terms stated in the disclosure document.

6. *Contradictory Claims:* No written or oral claims the franchisor makes may contradict information provided in the required disclosure document.[9]

All franchisors must provide prospective franchisees with a written **Uniform Franchise Offering Circular (UFOC)** that covers 23 items a franchisor must

Uniform Franchise Offering Circular (UFOC)
A document prepared by franchisor for prospective franchisees that includes 23 issues that disclose background information and financial condition of the franchisor.

disclose to a franchisee. Exhibit 11.3 provides a brief description of what the UFOC covers. The standardization of the UFOC format allows investors to compare offerings from different franchise companies.

The FTC requires that franchisors comply with the UFOC regulations and grants franchisees certain legal rights if the franchisor fails to comply. The FTC does not review the contents or accuracy of UFOCs. Therefore, potential franchisees must

exhibit 11.3   **Summary of the Uniform Franchise Offering Circular (UFOC)**

Section	Description
Cover Page	Must clearly state FRANCHISE OFFERING CIRCULAR and include: franchisor's name, type of business organization, principal business address and telephone number, a sample of the primary business trademark, logotype, trade name, or commercial label or symbol under which the franchisee will conduct its business in upper left-hand corner of the cover page, brief description of the franchised business, total amounts of Franchisee's Initial Franchisee Fee or Other Payment and Franchisee's Initial Investment, specified disclaimer statements, and effective date.
1. The Franchisor, Its Predecessors and Affiliates	Information about the franchisor and its affiliates and their business experience.
2. Business Experience	A description of the business experience of the franchisor's officers, directors and management personnel responsible for the franchise system.
3. Litigation	Information on prior or current lawsuits involving the franchisor, its officers, directors and management personnel. (Note: Nearly all franchises of a certain age or above a certain size will have had lawsuits with its franchisees.)
4. Bankruptcy	History of any bankruptcies involving the franchisor, its officers, directors and management personnel.
5. Initial Franchise Fee	Information on the fees due the franchisor that are required to obtain the franchise.
6. Other Fees	There may be other fees involved with the purchase of the franchise besides the initial franchise fee. These fees will be listed in this section (and these fees can be very substantial!).
7. Initial Investment	A indication of the total funds necessary to invest in this franchise.
8. Restrictions on Sources of Products and Services	Information on the franchisor's requirements for purchases of goods or services. Many franchisors will require that franchisees purchase all goods and services from the franchisor.
9. Franchisee's Obligations	Information on what the franchisee will be required to do.
10. Financing	A description of any financing the franchisor might offer the franchisee.
11. Franchisor's Obligations	Information on assistance the franchisor may offer the franchisee, such as help in starting up, training, marketing, and advertising.
12. Territory	Information on the geographic area (if any) a franchisee might have exclusive rights to.
13. Trademarks	A description of the franchisor's trademarks and under what conditions the franchisee may use these trademarks.

14. Patents, Copyrights, and Proprietary Information	A description of the franchisor's patents, copyrights, and proprietary information and the conditions the franchisee may use them.
15. Obligation to Participate in the Actual Operation of the Franchise Business	Most franchisors will require that franchisees be actively involved in the operations of their franchise units. Most franchisors will want investor/operators, rather than investors as the owners of their franchise units.
16. Restrictions on What the Franchisee May Sell	The agreement specifies what goods and services the franchisee may offer for sale.
17. Renewal, Termination, Transfer, and Dispute Resolution	Critical information on how a franchisee license can be renewed (most franchise agreements have a limited life, such as 20 years); the criteria for terminating a franchise agreement; the conditions for transferring a franchise agreement to either the franchisor or another party; the process for resolving disagreements between the franchisor and franchisee.
18. Public Figures	Information on whether any public figures are involved in the franchise, either through advertising or other activities.
19. Earnings Claims	Information about the financial performance of franchise units. This information may include data indicating the percentage of franchises that have achieved these projected earnings.
20. List of Outlets	A comprehensive list of all franchise units: (1) company owned units, (2) franchised units—with names of franchise owners and addresses, (3) estimates of number of units to be sold in the next year, and (4) names and addresses of franchisees who have dropped out of the franchise system in the past three years.
21. Financial Statements	A minimum of two years of the franchisor's audited financial statements.
22. Contracts	Copies of the contracts the franchisee will sign to purchase the franchise.
23. Receipt	A form the franchisee will sign and return to the franchisor indicating the UFOC has been received.
Exhibits	A. Franchise Agreement
	B. Equipment Lease
	C. Lease for Premises
	D. Loan Agreement

Source: "The Uniform Franchise Offering Circular Guidelines," Federal Trade Commission, July 12, 2005, http:www.ftc.gov.

perform their own careful due diligence of the UFOC information. We will discuss how to approach this process later in the chapter.

The FTC's website pages on franchises and business opportunities (http://www.ftc.gov/bcp/menu-fran.htm) contain valuable information for both franchisees and franchisors.

exhibit 11.4   **State Regulation of Franchises**

Regulation	States
Must file disclosure statement with a state agency	California, Hawaii, Illinois, Indiana, Maryland, Minnesota, New York, North Dakota, Rhode Island, South Dakota, Virginia, Washington, Wisconsin
No filing	Oregon
Notice only	Michigan
Business Opportunity Law applies	Connecticut, Florida, Nebraska, Texas, Utah

Source: "State Offices Administering Franchise Disclosure Laws," Federal Trade Commission, http://www.ftc.gov/bcp/franchise/netdiscl.htm (February 15, 2007).

State Regulation

Many states have their own franchise rules and regulations requiring a higher level of franchisor disclosure. The degree of state regulation of franchises varies. Certain states require that franchisors file and register pre-sale offering circulars, while others require appropriate disclosure documents but no filing with a state agency. The most restrictive states apply the same rules to franchises as to security sales. Exhibit 11.4 lists the states in each category.

As you can see, the amount of control and regulation provided in certain states varies. Michigan, for example, requires only that franchisors tell the state that they are selling franchises in the state, while a state such as California requires franchisors to file a disclosure similar to the FTC UFOC with the state before selling franchises.

States with franchise regulations protect franchisees through state courts, which may be a less expensive and faster resolution process. Many states have courts that can hear and judge such cases faster than the federal court system.

11.3 Why Buy a Franchise?

Franchising provides a middle ground between starting your own business and purchasing an existing one. Will franchising be right for you? "A true entrepreneur has an idea and takes a risk," says Steve Hockett, president of FranChoice, Inc., a consulting firm that works with potential franchisees. "But not all of us wake up in the morning with a great idea and know how to make it into a business. Franchisers know they need people who have motivation and a dream. [Franchisees] have time, talent, skills, energy, and desire. But they don't want to spend years building an idea."[10]

In many respects, the decision criteria for choosing the franchising path to entrepreneurship are similar to those you would consider when either buying or starting an independent business. You would first reflect on your personal and financial goals, how much money you have to invest, your abilities, and your interests. Then you would investigate the operating characteristics, size, growth, profitability, and complexity of the businesses you are considering. In addition, you must add to these a thorough investigation of the franchisor. Let's review some of the key questions you should ask yourself as you begin to research the franchise option.

- *What are your personal goals?* How important is leisure time, involvement with family, personal growth, financial success, involvement with friends, and social contribution? What do you envision in each of these areas over the next 2, 5, 10, and 25 years?

- *What are your family goals?* What do you envision in each of these goals over the next 2, 5, 10, and 25 years?

- *What are your business goals?* What field do you want to pursue? Which would you rather sell: goods or services? What kind of work do you enjoy most? Would you rather work with people or things? How much annual income do you need? Will you rely solely on the franchise for your income or have other sources? Can you see yourself running this business for 10, 15, or 20 years? Do you want to become an area developer or stick with a single unit?

- *What abilities do you bring to this business venture?* Do you have the education or business experience the franchise requires? How well does the industry fit your prior skills and knowledge? What other skills do you need to successfully run the business, and do you have them (computer literacy, accounting, human relations, management)? Strong interpersonal skills will contribute to your success as a franchisee, helping you to work effectively with your employees and create loyal customers. Can you develop the skills you lack?

- *How much money can you invest in a business?* What percentage of your assets are you willing to put at risk? Will you need or want partners?

- *How much involvement do you want in operating the business?* Do you want to operate the business yourself or hire a manager? This is a particularly important issue when considering a franchise. Some franchisors require that franchisee owners themselves work full time in the franchises they purchase. Other companies are looking for enterprisers who can own and manage a number of franchise locations.

- *Can you take direction from the franchisor?* A franchise involves a very specific way of doing business. Many franchises have operating manuals that provide detailed directions about how the franchise will operate (e.g., how food will be prepared, what items will be on the menu, how customers will be greeted, how the store location will look, the kinds of fixtures that each location will have). Do you like having a proven method of operating your business, and are you willing to learn best practices from others? Then you have the potential to be a successful franchisee. On the other hand, if you prefer to "do your own thing" and can't imagine owning a business that looks and operates exactly like many other franchise locations, then purchasing a franchise is probably not the best form of enterprise for you.

- *Can you be a member rather than the leader?* A franchisee belongs to a system along with many other franchisees. As such, you will likely be required to contribute to marketing efforts that support the franchise system overall, not just your specific unit. Consider the advertising campaign for Subway. TV advertisements are paid for by fees collected from all franchisees, and decisions about when ads will run and the look of these advertisements, as well as the kinds of "deals" that are offered (i.e., sandwich, chips, and a drink combos for a certain price) are determined by the franchisor. You will have to go along with decisions made by all of the franchisees and the franchisor.

Benefits of Franchising

As with any form of business enterprise, franchising offers several distinct advantages for the enterpriser.

- *Proven business model.* A franchise offers a product/service (benefits), and a way of providing those benefits (channel) to a specific market (customers). An enterpriser can evaluate the performance of existing franchisees to learn how well the system's business concept works.

- *Brand name and recognition.* An important value in belonging to a franchise system is the awareness that comes with an organization that engages in joint advertising and marketing. Wherever their franchise is located, such brands as McDonald's, Subway, Kentucky Fried Chicken, and H&R Block have instant recognition for the value of their products and services.

- *Training and support.* A franchisor provides training and operational, marketing, financial, and managerial expertise to help franchisees successfully start and operate their franchise units. A franchisee does not have to invent the entire start-up process alone. Some franchisors, for example, provide help in selecting a location for the franchise, as well as require that prospective franchisees work at other franchise locations to learn how to effectively manage the business, deal with employees, and sell to customers.

- *Financing.* Some franchisors provide help in purchasing one of their franchises. Often financial institutions and investors become familiar with certain franchise systems and are willing to loan money or make equity investments to assist franchisees.

- *System synergies.* Membership in a franchise system creates a supportive network where franchisees can learn from each other. You are in business for yourself, but not by yourself. Most franchise systems have ways for franchisees to meet and share their experiences as well as offer ways for each franchise to compete more efficiently and effectively. Many product and service innovations are first initiated by an individual franchisee, who then shares this with other franchisees in the franchise system. A good example of this is the Egg McMuffin, created by a franchisee who wanted to serve breakfast items.

- *Economies of scale.* As one of many other franchisees in a franchise system, franchisees benefit from the system's ability to make volume purchases of supplies, standardize specific kinds of equipment and building materials, purchase medical and dental insurance, and offer other system discounts. Operating costs will therefore be lower than if an enterpriser were to operate the same business as an independent startup.

The Downside to Franchising

Although these benefits contribute to franchising success, franchising has its negative aspects.

- *Operating restrictions.* A franchise is a particular way of doing business. When you purchase a franchise, you are agreeing to operate the business according to the franchisor's guidelines. While this can be an advantage, it can also be a disadvantage if competitive and market conditions change and the franchise system's way of doing business does not meet the current needs of your customers.

- *Costs.* Purchasing a franchise can be quite expensive. In addition to the initial purchase price, the investment in facilities and equipment may add up to a significant financial outlay. The franchisee also pays ongoing fees and royalties to the franchisor and may have to contribute to national advertising. These mandatory expenses reduce the enterpriser's profits—and must be paid whether or not the individual franchise unit is profitable. With an independent business, the owner has greater control over the expense outlay and retains all the profits.

- *Interdependence.* Being a member of the franchise system is not without risks. The actions of the other franchisees will have a significant impact on each member's success. If a number of franchisees provide poor service and products, it will reflect on other members of the franchise system. Suppose a franchisee in California prepares food items incorrectly and many customers become sick. This mistake will affect the sales of all franchisees across the country. In addition, some franchisors have failed, leaving the franchisees in the difficult position of being in a franchise without the support and help they promised.

- *Contractual obligations.* Most franchise agreements are likely to restrict a franchisee's ability to terminate the franchise agreement or sell the franchise to others without the approval of the franchisor. Many franchisors require that franchisees agree to a "noncompete" clause that prevents a franchisee from starting or purchasing a similar business (or franchise). Also, many franchise agreements have a limited life. The franchise rights might be only 20 years long, after which the franchisor may have rights to repurchase the franchise for a specified amount.

- *Business risks.* As with any business, franchises carry risks. A proven business concept does not guarantee success. Recent research shows that franchising may not lead to higher success and growth rates than individual businesses. According to Scott Shane, who conducted a study of franchise systems that started offering franchises for sales in 1983, new franchise systems fail at roughly the same rate as all new businesses. After 10 years, less than 25 percent of the initial group of franchisors he studied was still franchising. "If you buy a new franchise from a new franchisor, there is a 75 percent chance the person who sold it to you won't be around to support you in 10 years," Shane explains. "So, it's very important that people thinking of buying a franchise outlet differentiate from long-standing franchisors and those that just started this year or last year."[11] Particularly with new franchises, the franchisor may misrepresent the franchise's potential or be overly optimistic in the financial projections.

- *Missed expectations.* Many promises are made between the franchisor and the franchisee (both verbally and in writing) that the franchisor may not meet, such as expected levels of support and help, advertising, and system growth. For example, the franchisor may tell a franchisee that the system will grow by 1,000 units in the next three years, and these expectations might not be fulfilled. If the franchisee was hoping that the growth in extra units would generate synergies in purchasing, advertising, and branding, the franchisee may be very disappointed (and, may also seek damages through a law suit).

Situations like these can lead to franchisee discontent and lawsuits against the franchisor. This was the case with Quiznos, a fast food franchisor whose problems are described in the Enterprising Ethics box.

enterprising ethics

Quiznos' Franchisees Lose their Appetites

Starting with recipes developed in the kitchen of an Italian restaurant, Denver-based Quiznos Subs opened its first sandwich shop in 1981. Two years later it began franchising new locations to expand the chain. By 1994, Quiznos Toasted Subs was named a "Hot Concept" by *Nation's Restaurant News*. The chain grew quickly, working its way up in *Entrepreneur*'s Franchise 500 rankings, reaching the top ten in 2001 and the number two spot in 2006. Quiznos was also one of the top ten fastest growing franchises for many years and the number two global franchise in 2006. Today the chain has almost 5,000 restaurants, including 500 international locations in 21 countries.

However, the rosy scene these numbers paint does not portray the whole picture. The franchisor is the defendant in numerous lawsuits from franchisees who claim that Quiznos made many promises that it didn't meet.

A New Jersey case claims that the growth statistics are a sham. Although Quiznos sold about 350 licenses from 2003 to 2005 and collected $7 million in fees, none of the franchisees ever opened a restaurant. "They duped these people into thinking they were getting site assistance, but after they plunked down their $25,000, Quiznos would disappear," said Justin M. Klein, lawyer for the New Jersey plaintiffs.

High operating costs are at the center of other lawsuits. The licensing agreement requires franchisees to buy supplies and services only from Quiznos-designated suppliers, at inflated prices. These vendors, some of whom are owned by the parent, then pay "rebates" to the corporation. Franchisees were squeezed because they were unable to set retail prices high enough to make up for the inflated supply prices. "My food cost has gone up 10 percent in a year," says Melody Cox, who operated a Quiznos in Evansville, Indiana. She and her husband owned two units which closed in January 2007.

Encroachment, or opening units in close proximity, is another major complaint. Quiznos' franchise agreement does not offer franchisees exclusive rights to a specific territory or restrict the company from opening franchises within the proximity of existing locations. Former CEO Rick Schaden defended Quiznos' actions. "We're a convenience item and we're putting restaurants where consumers can grab a quick lunch," he explained. "In the country, that may be four miles apart, but in the city, it may be every five blocks."

Franchisee Glenn Keane, who owns a Quiznos shop in Derby, Connecticut, is one of the dissatisfied franchisees. "When Quiznos allowed a second franchisee to open here last summer, my sales dropped from $15,000 a week to $8,000," he says. "Instead of taking money out of the franchise, I'm now putting my own money in, just to keep going."

In California, Bhupinder and Ratt Baber formed a franchisee organization to advocate for franchisee rights and filed a breach of contract suit against Quiznos in 2004 because the franchisor opened new units within two miles of their restaurants. Quiznos attempted to close the Babers' locations while the case was pending, but a California judge found for the Babers. "There is an implied covenant of good faith and fair dealing that says you don't dump competition on top of your existing franchisees," said Fred Pardes, attorney for the Babers. The problems between the Babers and Quiznos did not end there, however. Sales at the Babers' locations declined 30 percent as new Quiznos stores cannibalized revenues. The Babers refinanced their house to make ends meet. In January 2007, Baber was so distraught over his precarious financial situation that he committed suicide.

Discussion Questions

1. The Quiznos franchise agreement does not include any prohibitions against encroachment, so the franchisor believes it has the right to open new locations where it chooses. Don Boroian, a franchise consultant with Francorp, disagrees, saying that franchisors have an obligation to prevent locations from encroaching on each other's territory. With whom do you agree, and why?

2. Why do most franchise systems require that franchisees buy supplies and services only from approved sources? Where did Quiznos cross the line with its vendor situation? Suggest ways a franchisor can keep franchisees happy with regard to supplier sources.

3. Review the International Franchise Association's Code of Ethics at the IFA site, http://www.franchise.org. Based on information in the box and from your own research, discuss Quiznos' compliance with the code.

4. Quiznos is not the only franchisor facing lawsuits from its franchisees. Using search tools find examples of other cases. What can franchisees do to protect themselves from ethical breaches?

Sources: Based on Julie Bennett, "Pitfalls People May Face When Buying a Franchise," *StartupJournal.com*, March 6, 2006; Amanda Bronstad, "Quiznos Finds Fast Growth Has Its Costs as It Battles Franchisees in Court," *Los Angeles Business Journal*, September 19, 2005, p. 5; Julie Creswell, "Some Quiznos Franchisees Take Chain to Court," *New York Times*, February 24, 2007, p. C1; Bill Medley, "Loss of Quiznos Store Irks Owner," *Evansville Courier & Press* (Indiana), January 27, 2007, p. B6; Carol Tice, "Find Your Franchise Match," *Entrepreneur*, January 2007, http://www.entrepreneur.com; and Toasted Subs Franchise Association, http://www.toastedsubs.info/ (February 23, 2007).

As a franchisee, you are an independent business owner but must pay franchise fees and operate within the franchisor's system. "You have to have the entrepreneurial spirit to quit your job, and you get a check only after you make money," notes Sam Chamberlain, vice president of sales with franchise consultant Fransmart LLC. "However, franchising is about being in a system, and once you are in a system, you cannot change it."[12] Enterprisers who like to do things their own way may find the franchise path restricts their creativity and choose to pursue an independent business venture instead.

This was the case for Betsy Ludlow, a former Fortune 500 marketing executive, who loved working out at Curves, one of the fastest growing fitness franchises. When corporate life became too stressful, she decided to investigate owning a Curves franchise. As she evaluated the system's UFOC, contract, and other materials, she thought carefully about how she would like to run her own Curves facility. "I didn't like feeling boxed in with someone else's concept," she said. Instead she chose to open an independent exercise studio. Working with exercise experts to develop her own format, she opened the first Slim and Tone in 2002, advertising it as "A Better 30 Minute Workout." Her concept caught on, and she soon had a chain of four exercise clubs.[13]

11.4 Selecting the Right Franchise

With more than 1,200 franchise concepts covering 75 industries, enterprisers who have decided to go the franchising route have a wealth of options from which to choose. You may want to consider a franchise that you visit frequently and already know and like. Exploring the listings for franchise opportunities in newspapers, magazines such as *Entrepreneur* and *Inc.*, and on the Web is a good way for an enterpriser to narrow the field. Most websites have search features to help you find franchises in a particular industry or price range. Business brokers are another source of franchise offerings.

Take time to research a variety of franchises. You will discover different conceptual approaches and operating methods, even within the same industry. Educating yourself before you buy will help you choose a franchise that meets your personal and business goals. Most Web-based franchise directories provide company background, costs and fees, financing options, training and support, and contact information, along with educational articles and other resources. Be aware that featured franchisors often pay for sponsored listings. Some of the more popular sites include:

- *Entrepreneur's* FranchiseZone (http://www.entrepreneur.com/franchise/): Publishes the Franchise 500 and special lists for top home-based, low cost, new, fastest growing, and global franchises. You can browse by category, and it has links to *FranchiseZone* magazine and how-to articles.

- *StartupJournal.com* (http://www.startupjournal.com/franchising/): Part of *The Wall Street Journal* center for entrepreneurs, it has articles profiling franchisors, franchise-for-sale listings, and general articles about franchising.

- International Franchise Association (IFA) (http://www.franchise.org): Search for more than 1,000 different franchises by industry and subcategories, with information on company background and costs; extensive franchising resources.

- *FranchiseHandbook.com* (http://www.franchisehandbook.com): Publishes the *Franchise Handbook* and offers a searchable Web directory.

- *Franchise.com* (http://www.franchise.com): Includes *Franchise Matchmaker* search feature and several directories.

- *FranchiseWorks.com* (http://www.franchiseworks.com): Lists franchises by category; offers help from franchise consultants.

Attending a franchise trade show or exposition is another excellent way to learn about many different franchising opportunities. For example, each year the IFA cosponsors the International Franchise Expo, a three-day event held in Washington, D.C. The IFA also sponsors regional franchise shows. To make the most of these events, have a general idea of how much you can invest and the industry categories that interest you. You can then focus your efforts on specific franchisors and compare what they offer.

Franchise Costs

As with any business start-up or purchase, an enterpriser who buys a franchise wants to develop a profitable business. The total cost to buy a franchise unit depends on many factors such as the industry, products sold, type of physical facilities, and location, and can be less than $20,000 to more than $1 million for lodging franchises. The enterpriser must weigh the extra costs against the benefits gained by becoming a franchisee. Exhibit 11.5 shows the costs involved in starting a franchise in a representative sample of franchise systems. In addition to the initial capital investment, franchisees must also consider the ongoing cost obligations, such as fees and royalties, when calculating the overall return from this investment. Even within the same industry, the total investment and special conditions may vary considerably, as comparisons between Subway and Quiznos and Curves and Jazzercise demonstrate.

Let's take a closer look at seven different cost categories for business format franchises:

1. *Initial franchise fee:* May be nonrefundable and range from a few thousand to several hundred thousand dollars. Most franchise fees—70 percent of systems—are less than $40,000.

2. *Capital costs:* May include costs for real estate, construction or rental of facilities, equipment, and inventory.

3. *Other start-up costs:* Business permits and operating licenses; insurance; some franchisors charge a special promotional fee for a "grand opening."

exhibit 11.5 — Costs to Buy a Franchise

Franchisor	Industry	Total investment	Initial franchise fee	Royalty payments	Term in years	Comments
Subway	Submarine sandwiches & salads	$74,900–$222,800	$15,000	8%	20	Net worth requirement $30,000–$90,000; 65% of franchisees own multiple units; no absentee ownership
Curves	Women's fitness and weight loss	$31.4K–53.5K	$24.9K–39.9K	5%/6%	5	$75,000 net worth requirement; half of all franchisees own multiple units; no financial assistance offered
Quiznos Sub	Submarine sandwiche, soups, salads	$71.7K–251.1K	$10K–25K	7%	15	Few franchisees own multiple units; absentee ownership allowed
Jani-King	Commercial cleaning services	$11.3K–34.1K	$8.6K–16.3K+	10%	20	
Jazzercise	Exercise	$2.99K–33.1K	$500/$1K	To 20%	5	
Liberty Tax Service	Tax preparation	$33.4K–59.9K	$15K–30K	Varies	Perpetual	50% of all franchisees own more than one unit
Kumon Math & Reading Centers	Educational services	$30K–110K	$1K	$30+/student/month	2 years	

Source: Entrepreneur magazine's Franchise Zone, http:www.entrepreneur.com/franchise.

4. *Royalty payments:* Most franchisors collect royalties for the ongoing use of the brand name and trademark for the period covered by the franchise contract. These are based on a percentage of the unit's weekly or monthly gross income. Royalty payments are due regardless of the level of net income (income after expenses). In other words, the franchisee could be operating at a loss and still owe royalties. Royalties typically range from 5 to 8 percent of gross sales.

5. *Advertising fees:* Many franchise systems require franchisees to pay 3 percent of gross sales for local advertising, as well as a minimum of

1 percent for publications, promotional materials, and national and regional advertising.

6. *Other fees:* May include continuing education and training.

7. *Purchase of supplies:* Franchisees may be required to purchase supplies from the franchisor.

Evaluating a Potential Franchise Opportunity

You've assessed your personal characteristics and skills, researched the universe of franchise opportunities, and decided that a franchise in the lawn care industry/category appeals to you most. After reading the basics on all five franchisors (Lawn Doctor, Scotts Lawn Service, U.S. Lawns, Spring-Green Lawn, and Truly Nolen), you've selected the two that sound best. How do you choose the one that best suits your needs?

Dick Rennick, chairman of the board of the IFA and chief executive officer of the American Leak Detection franchise system, advises franchisees to be thorough in researching a potential franchisor. He compares the franchisor–franchisee relationship to being part of a sports team. "The franchiser is like the team owner or coach, and you have to stay within the rules of the game, or go find another game to play," he says.[14]

As noted earlier, the due diligence involved in purchasing a franchise is similar to the process for other types of business enterprises. Appendix D, Before You Purchase a Franchise, offers many questions that apply to franchising, especially the sections covering economic and industry trends. The following guidelines, which cover the market environment and move on to franchise-specific issues, will help you get started.[15]

- *Demand:* How great is the demand for the franchisor's goods or services in your area? Are the franchise's products technologically current and competitive? Is the current level of demand likely to continue, or is it a passing fad? Is the business year-round or seasonal?

- *Competition:* How much competition is there locally and nationally for the franchisor's products, and how do these products compare to the competition's in terms of quality and price? How well known are the competing companies? Does the franchisor already have many units in your community and where are they located?

- *Brand equity:* How strong is the franchisor's name recognition? How long has it been operating? What is the general reputation associated with this brand—for quality or service, for example? Does the brand attract customers?

- *Franchisor's background:* How long has the franchisor been running this franchise system? What is its track record in its industry and in managing franchisees? How solid is the system's financial condition? Are you confident that the franchisor's management team can provide a high level of assistance and support to its franchisees? How fast is it growing, and does it have adequate financial strength to support this growth?

- *Training and support:* How much training and ongoing support services does the franchisor provide, and at what levels? Is it sufficient to prepare you to compete effectively in your industry? How does your background compare to that of existing franchise owners? If you lack any of the technical or other skills required or suggested to operate a successful franchise, can you acquire them?

- *Operating restrictions:* How extensive are the franchisor's operating restrictions as defined by the license agreement? Are you comfortable complying with these limitations?

- *Other questions:* Does the franchise require professional licenses or other special business experience? What is the process for terminating the franchise relationship?

Don't overlook the economics of operating a specific franchise unit. Look for objective measures to provide clues to the overall operating health of a franchise system. "The numbers don't lie," says Dan Rowe, president and CEO of Fransmart. "Get out the ruler, and make a chart. [See] what the per-unit sales volume has been for the last five years. Then extend that line out a couple more inches, and get a sense of where it's going. Is the food cost going up or going down? Is the check average going up or going down?" Other statistics to check include the number of units opened and closed in the past three to five years. The number of multiunit franchisees is another good indicator of a franchise's success. "To get rich in the franchise business, you never do it on one store; you always do it on multiples. You're building a franchise company," explains Rowe.[16]

Site Visits

Once you have finished your background research, you are ready to see for yourself how well the franchisor lives up to its UFOC claims. When you visit the franchisor's headquarters to meet with the franchisor's management team, ask detailed questions about the company and its background, financial condition, management, and what it offers its franchisees for training and support.

Perhaps the most important part of the due diligence process is visiting actual franchise units and talking to franchisees. This reality check is essential to understanding how the franchise system operates. For example, you may be counting on the franchisor's training programs to fill in your knowledge gaps. "Many franchisees think they will get a lot of training, but find out it's a one-week crash course," says Marko Grunhagen, a franchising specialist at Southern Illinois University–Edwardsville. "One day it's marketing, and one day it's accounting."[17]

When you visit franchise units, look at them from both the owner/manager's and the customer's perspective. Imagine yourself running the unit. Would you enjoy this type of business? Does the physical store appeal to you? Are the employees happy and providing good customer service? Would you want to buy what the company offers? Asking questions about the actual operation of the franchise provides insights into the nuts and bolts of managing the franchise. For example, you can learn whether your financial projections are realistic, the extent and adequacy of the training programs, and how well the franchisor lives up to its promises and supports the system's franchisees.

11.5 Acquiring a Franchise

You have finished your due diligence and chosen the franchise system you wish to join. The next step in the process involves meeting with a franchise attorney to insure that you understand all of the legal details involved with the franchise license agreement and the UFOC.

The Franchise License Agreement

The franchise license agreement is the document that gives the franchisee the right to use the franchisor's registered brands and trademarks together with a specific business operating system. The license is granted for a specified time period—typically eight to ten years—and requires payments that are explicitly set forth in the agreement along with the operating restrictions that apply to the franchisee's use of the brand and the running of the franchise unit.

It's important for a potential franchisee to understand that executing a franchise agreement is not the same as buying a business entity. In fact, the agreement will clearly state that the franchise company retains all ownership rights to the brand, trademarks, and proprietary business operating systems. The franchisee who invests in personal or real property required to operate the franchised business will have an ownership interest based on the proportional share of the investment. However, many franchise agreements require the franchisee to sell such property, often at its depreciated value, back to the franchise company when the franchise agreement terminates.

The Purchase Process

If you understand what you are buying when you sign the franchise agreement, and your franchise attorney is comfortable with the legal issues involved with the franchise agreement and the UFOC, then you are ready to sign the franchise agreement. Once you have signed the franchise agreement and paid the franchisor all of the applicable fees, you will attend training sessions as well as begin the process of opening your franchise.

Other Considerations

As you narrow your choices to a particular industry and then down to a few franchisors within that industry, there are other issues to consider. For example, should you choose the older, more established national franchise or the up-and-coming regionally focused franchise? The answer may not be obvious. According to Kevin Hogan, president of Liberty Development Consulting LLC, who works with the Whattaburger franchise, "It's a matter of individual location, brand awareness, marketing power, and media efficiency."

Smaller franchise systems with local appeal can be a good choice. Sam Fangary opted to buy a California-based hamburger franchise called Farmer Boys instead of a McDonald's or Burger King. Although the franchisor was young and only had seven franchise units, his research showed that local customers loved the chain's hamburgers. "I'd rather invest in a company that's growing—not a company that's already huge—so I have a chance to grow with them," he says. "When Farmer Boys gets as big as some of the big franchisors out there, I can have 20 stores—that's my goal."[18]

You may also find that the opportunity you seek involves working not with the franchisor but with a master franchisee. Some franchisors see the master franchise route as a faster way to grow than contracting directly with numerous individual franchisees. In that case, the master franchisee becomes the major contact point for the franchisee and provides the training and support. When this is the case, a prospective franchisee should investigate not only the franchise system but also the master franchisee's organization. In addition to the ability to recruit additional franchisees, the master franchisee must also be able to provide the requisite training and operating support for its franchisees.

Franchise experts advise visiting franchise units in the general system and also those in the region of the master franchisee you are considering. By doing both, a prospective franchisee will be able to assess the overall quality of the franchise system as a whole and also how well the master franchisee manages its territory. If the franchisor is sound but the problems lie with a specific master franchisee, you would be better off choosing a different master franchisee with whom to work.[19]

11.6 Starting a Franchise System

It is worth considering how and why enterprisers might pursue the development of a franchise system as a way to expand their businesses. Developing a franchise system can be a way to quickly expand a successful business model by attracting both capital investment from potential franchisees and their managerial and operational talents in running their own units. Developing a franchise system requires a significant investment of time and resources by a prospective franchisor. In nearly all instances where enterprisers seek to develop a particular business into a franchise, they will need to involve both a franchise lawyer and a franchise development consultant to help them work through the creation of the UFOC and develop other aspects of the franchise system.

Why would an enterpriser consider becoming a franchisor? Franchising offers a way to

- Expand the business through the use of other people's capital and talents.

- Shorten the time to bring the business concept to a larger market.

- Generate income through fees and royalties from franchisees.

- Harness the effort and creativity of motivated owner/managers.

- Share costs of advertising and other expenses.

- Increase buying power.

By building a network of motivated franchisees who have a personal stake in the success of the franchise system, an enterpriser can often use franchising to create a high-growth business enterprise more easily than opening multiple company-owned locations.

Franchising can be a profitable venture. As we explained earlier, franchisees must pay the franchisor initial fees averaging $20,000 to $30,000 and royalties ranging from 5 to 8 percent. Studies by the International Franchise Association show that the typical new franchisor will sell six to eight units the first year of operation, increasing to as many as 20 a year going forward. If each unit has gross sales of $500,000 and the franchisor sells seven units, the minimum revenue for the first year, assuming a $20,000 fee and 5 percent royalties, will be $315,000 ($140,000 in fees and $175,000 in royalties). By the time a franchisor has 17 units, it will have earned $340,000 from fees and received ongoing royalties of $425,000. In addition, franchisors often earn profits from a mark-up of 10 to 20 percent on sales of proprietary goods to franchisees.[20]

As tempting as these numbers sound, franchising has its downside for the franchisor who will

- Lose a portion of profits to franchisees.

- Lose some control over operations to franchisees.

- Face the difficulty of keeping franchisees happy as the franchise grows and changes over time.

- Expend significant time and energy to grow the franchise system.

- Incur significant legal costs to develop the franchise system.

When to Franchise

Some business situations are better suited to franchising than others. An enterpriser should consider growing a business through the development of a franchise system where the enterpriser has

- A business model that can be replicated in other areas.

- A business that will have a strong brand or trademark.

- A unique concept.

- A business that can be taught easily to others who may not have experience in the industry.

- A business that others can manage.

A franchise offers others an opportunity to both own and manage a business that will be similar to the business a prospective franchisor already operates. An enterpriser who already successfully operates a minimum of three to four other stores (units) might consider creating a franchise. Many enterprisers can often effectively manage two stores through direct supervision—dividing time between each of the two stores. Once the chain reaches three or four locations, most enterprisers can no longer directly manage all of these units. They must therefore hire managers as well as develop operations guides and procedures to insure that each location operates similarly.

Before embarking on the franchise route, enterprisers have to thoughtfully explore the reasons for their business success as well as identify specifically how these businesses operate. The challenge in building a franchise system is developing the operating manuals and procedures that make the business system obvious to others. Creating a franchise requires the enterpriser to specify all of those successful "tricks of the trade" and activities that contributed to the enterpriser's success. If the enterpriser cannot identify the unique formula for success, then, it will be difficult to create a franchise system where others can replicate the enterpriser's success.

Remember Betsy Ludlow, the marketing executive who opened her own exercise studio rather than buying a Curves franchise? The success of her small chain led her to follow the franchise route to growth and develop a website to market franchises online. "I sold 68 clubs working out of my bedroom," she reports. The Slim and Tone franchise now has over 140 units and operates as a division of Nutri-Systems Inc., which acquired the system in 2004. The initial investment of about $32,000, including the franchise fee, includes the exercise machines required to set up the exercise club.[21]

Steps to Franchising a Business

Enterprisers who determine that they have an established business that can be expanded into a franchise system should follow these eight steps:

1. *Develop a business plan for the franchise system.* A franchise system business plan envisions how the franchise system will expand and grow over time. It explains why growth through franchising is more appropriate than other ways of expansion.

2. *Hire a franchise attorney and a franchise development consultant.* Creating the UFOC and all the materials necessary to insure that potential franchisees can successfully develop and operate your prospective franchises is a very complicated process. It is fraught with many legal consequences if you do things incorrectly. As we indicated earlier in this chapter, the FTC and state agencies regulate franchising, but they do not approve or review franchising documents. In other words, the FTC will become involved after the fact—when something goes wrong and the franchisor violates the franchising regulations. It is better to involve franchising experts at the outset to make sure that your franchising system meets all

legal requirements than to be sued by disappointed franchisees or have to pay penalties to the FTC or state agencies.

3. *Identify the intellectual property that serves as the basis for the franchise system.* Such intellectual property would include the business's name, trade names, trademarks, trade secrets, operating manuals, training manuals, operating processes and procedures, or any other information that is critical to the success of your business.

4. *Develop the UFOC and the franchise agreement.* It is necessary to have your franchise attorney and franchise development consultant review these documents for omissions and mistakes so that you avoid very costly legal problems later on.

5. *Develop all operating manuals and procedures necessary for a potential franchisee to successfully run a franchise unit.* You should develop a process for training franchisees to execute the franchise operating plans and procedures as specified. In addition, the material on the development of the franchise system will include information on how the franchise will grow through marketing, advertising, and unit expansion.

6. *Identify your franchise development team.* This executive group will identify potential franchisees, train them, and work with them to start and grow their franchise units. If a franchisor is serious about expanding a franchise system, the franchise development team should consist of individuals who are solely devoted to the franchise development effort. A franchisor cannot expect the manager of a store to both manage a store and also help potential franchisees start and grow their franchise units. Most franchisees will require help and guidance to learn the franchise system and effectively run their franchises. Not providing ongoing training, help, and guidance to franchisees often leads to disaster, as franchisees will then not follow franchise system guidelines, or complain (and file lawsuits) if they feel they are not getting the help they expected.

7. *Create a process for attracting prospective franchisees.* Consider how individuals might learn that your business provides a franchise opportunity. Develop an advertising campaign, attend franchise trade fairs, place newspaper advertisements, and make full use of your website and other Internet resources.

8. *Work closely with franchisees.* Help them find locations for franchise units and build units that meet the franchise system specifications. Train them to start and expand their businesses.

This list of activities requires a significant commitment by a franchisor to help the system's franchisees become successful. As we indicated at the beginning of the chapter, a good franchise opportunity is a win-win situation for both the franchisor and the franchisee. A franchisor will be successful if franchisees grow and are profitable. The franchisor benefits because the franchisees are paying royalties on sales from these successful units.

One of the most critical decisions that a franchisor will make is selecting potential franchisees. Ideally, franchisees will be willing to implement the vision and processes of the franchisor as well as provide the necessary capital to grow the number of franchise units. Franchisees are partners in the franchise system and, in some respects, "co-owners" in the success and growth of the franchise overall. A franchisor should look for franchisees who are willing to be partners in the business, as well as individuals who are willing to take direction.

Clearly, franchising isn't a simple process. Nor does operating a successful business—a restaurant, for example—guarantee success in franchising. In addition to issues related to the suitability of the business concept to franchising, an enterpriser must consider the significant regulatory burden of preparing and living up to the UFOC. Relationships with franchisees can be even more complex than other types of business partnerships.

11.7 Enterprisers

Takeout Taxi Breaks Down

Too busy to cook dinner, but don't want to go out? You are not alone, and one entrepreneur trusted his instincts to build a thriving business that is now an industry leader.

The birth of Kevin Abt's daughter in 1987 was a precipitating factor behind the Takeout Taxi concept. He and his wife both worked and often went out to dinner after work. But with a baby, that was no longer practical. Abt, a former marketing executive at Sprint Corp. says, "When I left my corporate career, I was on the fast track, and my peer network looked at me and said, 'Kevin, you know, have you fallen on the ice? What are you doing? You're gonna leave to go schlep pizzas in Herndon, Virginia?' And I said, 'No, no, no, no, no, no.'"

He recognized that many people have to run their lives around their meal schedule, rather than being able to fit their meal into their life schedule. Takeout Taxi, whose slogan was "we bring the restaurants to you," was a business idea that could be national in scope. His timing was right, because off-premise dining is one of the biggest segments of the $160 billion-a-year food-service industry.

Kevin didn't simply assume that everyone else felt the same way that he did. While he thought that was a good starting place, he tested his idea by going back into his corporate network and talked to his friends and affiliates about the idea. "This time famine—is this me or is this us? Is everybody else having home-cooked meals at 5:30, seven days a week or not?" he wondered. "And lo and behold, I heard a resounding mimic of my own life from my entire network. Everybody was saying, 'Look, the only thing we can get delivered to our house is a pizza.' I listened to that and I said they're telling me there's massive demand for real food delivered to the home."

Want something other than pizza? Takeout Taxi can satisfy those cravings. Customers order from 20 to 50 restaurant menus, from local eateries to national chains such as Bennigan's, Fuddruckers, TGI Friday's, Chili's, and Steak and Ale. The orders go into Takeout Taxi's computers and are faxed to the restaurant. The sophisticated computer system not only tracks orders but also helps dispatchers arrange deliveries efficiently. Customers pay the regular menu price plus a delivery charge, and Takeout Taxi receives a commission, typically 30 percent, from the restaurant.

Takeout Taxi developed a targeted marketing strategy that focused on territories covering a

10- to 15-minute driving time and about 30,000–40,000 people. It used direct mail to tell customers about the service, sending restaurant menus, discount coupons for new customers, and contact information for Takeout Taxi. When a customer placed an order, the company fed the information into a database that became the basis of future marketing efforts. Restaurants could work with Takeout Taxi on special promotions.

Takeout Taxi marketed to both restaurants and patrons. "It's been a huge side benefit for us, because it has helped us develop a sense of who our customers are," said Chuck Curcio, owner of a Tortilla Factory restaurant in Herndon, Virginia. "We've been able to use the information for all sorts of direct marketing: birthday clubs, Christmas cards, and direct-mailing pieces about summer specials." Curcio also realized that sales from Takeout Taxi were incremental to onsite revenues and added significantly to his bottom line.

Abt chose to expand his company by selling franchises for an initial fee of $25,000 for rights to serve a guaranteed territory, plus ongoing royalties. In addition to training and one week's help from a corporate specialist to learn how to negotiate with restaurants, franchisees received the hardware and software for the company's computerized ordering system.

The idea proved popular and the company grew rapidly. In 1992, Takeout Taxi had 41 units in 15 states. In 1994, Abt raised $3 million in equity from a venture capital firm to finance an aggressive expansion program. By 1995, company revenues topped $70 million as 101 franchisees delivered meals in 200 locations across 30 states and Canada, for 4,000 restaurants. *Fortune* featured Takeout Taxi in an article about problems in the franchise industry as a company that did franchising the right way.

Why was Takeout Taxi's multirestaurant delivery service a success? Not only did Kevin Abt have a concept for a service with broad market appeal, but he knew how to turn that plan into reality. "Concepts are cheap," he says. "It's really the execution of the details. In new concepts and new ventures, there is a minefield of details between the concept and the bottom line of profits. We spent four long, hard years debugging the concept before we started franchising."

Kevin Abt's basic idea was sound. People liked the idea of calling a meal delivery service to get lunch or dinner brought directly to their homes or offices. Today over 120 restaurant delivery businesses operate in the United States. However, rapid expansion took its toll on the company. Franchisees became dissatisfied about the services they received from corporate headquarters. In 1996 Abt was replaced as CEO by William Howe, who promised to improve the company's systems and overall service to its three types of customers: franchisees, restaurants, and consumers.

Flash forward to 2003. Takeout Taxi filed for Chapter 7 bankruptcy (liquidation of assets). The following year, 15 of the system's franchisees formed a limited liability company called Brand Solutions, LLC, and purchased the trademarks and other key assets from the former franchisor. Brand Solutions then licensed its members to operate their individually owned territories in 18 major markets under the Takeout Taxi trademark.[22]

Discussion Questions

1. Using the five criteria in "When to Franchise" in section 11.6 (p. 363), evaluate the suitability of the Takeout Taxi concept for growth through franchising. Was Takeout Taxi a good candidate for this method of growth, and why or why not?

2. Kevin Abt has hired you as his director of franchisee recruitment. Develop a list of criteria you would look for in prospective franchisees. Include personal characteristics as well as business background.

3. What should the training program for Takeout Taxi franchisees cover? Prepare an outline for the one-week curriculum for new franchisees and one for a one-day refresher course for experienced franchisees.

(continued)

4. As a prospective franchisee, what would you want to know about Takeout Taxi before buying a franchise? Describe your due diligence plan in detail.

5. Meal delivery services have become a popular service business. However, Takeout Taxi was unable to survive as a large-scale franchisor. What factors might have contributed to its demise? Suggest some steps Abt and his management team could have taken to avoid filing for bankruptcy.

6. If you were considering starting an independent business based on the Takeout Taxi concept, estimate the costs and the time to develop a system similar to the Takeout Taxi franchise system. How much do you estimate it would cost you in resources and time to develop your own system versus purchasing the franchise system from Takeout Taxi?

Source: Adapted with permission from Small Business School, the series on PBS, and at http://SmallBusinessSchool.com.

11.8 International Franchising

If you have done any foreign travel, you realize that franchising is now an international form of business. Fast food franchises like McDonald's and Pizza Hut are quickly becoming as common in Moscow and Madrid as in Minneapolis. Not only have U.S. franchise systems expanded into other countries, but overseas franchisors have also brought their concepts to the U.S. Cartridge World, which refills printer ink cartridges, originated in Australia, while Shred-It, a mobile document shredding franchise, is Toronto-based. Japan's Kumon Math and Reading Centers is the largest foreign-based franchise in the United States. In either situation, crossing national borders increases the complexity, because franchisors must now consider the franchising laws of both countries. Franchising may not be a familiar concept in other countries such as China, where franchisees may not understand the need to adhere to the franchisor's operating system. China recently passed its first franchise laws, which should help overseas franchisors in their quest to tap this huge market.

Many U.S. franchisors who venture abroad discover the benefits of partnering with local business people who can smooth the path through the local business customs. In certain countries, a local partner is a requirement for foreign-based businesses.

Some franchise concepts must be adapted to suit local customs. Bark Busters, a dog-training method from Australia, had to take into account the differences in the way pet owners in each country treat their dogs. In Australia, most dogs are outdoor animals, whereas in the United States, people bring dogs inside and treat them more like children. Others, like Computer Troubleshooters U.S.A., the U.S. arm of an Australian franchisor with units in over 200 countries, find that few adjustments are necessary. The Enterprising World box discusses the franchising strategy of Wagamama, a chain of Japanese noodle restaurants that started in London.

Food franchises, of course, must take into account native tastes. McDonald's added a spicy chicken burger to its Chinese menus, and KFC replaced coleslaw with local vegetable side dishes. When Jim Bryant, master franchisee for Subway in China, opened the first unit in Beijing, he had to print instructions cards to explain to Chinese customers how to order sandwiches, a foreign concept. Overall the sandwich concept has been slow to catch on, and local franchisees criticized the franchisor for not finding ways to adapt the menu. "Subway should have at least one item tailored to Chinese tastes to show that they are respecting the local culture," says franchisee Luo Bing Ling. Time is helping, as a uniquely American item, tuna salad, is now the most popular item.[23]

Wagamama Uses Its Noodle

To the surprise of the editors of *Zagat's 2006 London Restaurant Guides*, the most popular restaurant in the city was not the upscale Gordon Ramsay or Ivy, but a chain of Japanese noodle restaurants called Wagamama. Modeled on the ramen shops popular in Japan for over 200 years, Wagamama's menu features Oriental-style thin noodles with toppings, served either in soups or fried on a grill. Rounding out the menu are rice dishes, fresh juices, and side dishes such as dumplings, chicken skewers, fried shrimp, and salads.

Wagamama prides itself on using the freshest ingredients and preparing all food onsite. The restaurant décor is sleek yet simple, and service is friendly and fast. Patrons sit at communal tables and at most locations can also order food to take out. Good food, affordable prices, and the consistently high level of service bring customers back. In addition to the accolades from *Zagat's* readers, Wagamama was named *Time Out* guide's best family restaurant.

Restaurateur Alan Yau opened the first Wagamama restaurant in London in 1992. Customers liked its concept, and soon the noodle bars appeared in most major UK cities. Yau sold the business to Ian Neil, Wagamama's current chief executive, in 1997 and moved on to other restaurant ventures.

As Wagamama's popularity grew, its owners raised venture capital funding from Graphite Capital for the chain's initial expansion efforts. The investment was a good one for Graphite, which earned a 500 percent return when it sold a portion of its interest to Hutton Collins, an investment bank. In 2005, Graphite sold its majority interest to Lion Capital, another private equity firm. "Lion Capital has a big international brand perspective," says Neil. "They also own Jimmy Choo shoes and Weetabix Cereals. I think this experience will help us develop our overseas business." With Lion's backing, Wagamama began its next expansion phase.

By February 2007, the chain had about 45 locations in the UK and 16 international locations in Europe, Australia, New Zealand, and the Middle East. The company owns all its UK restaurants but decided to franchise its international operations. The company seeks owner-operators with prior multiunit restaurant experience as franchisees. For example, Luke Fryer, an experienced fast food franchise operator, is responsible for bringing Wagamama to Australia. "In 1998 I opened the first Burger King franchise at the Sydney Airport. It was on a trip to London when I first heard about Wagamama and saw the huge potential for here."

In 2007 Wagamama opened the first of its U.S. locations in Boston. "We chose Boston because we know the area and because of the interesting mix of communities in the region, including universities, finance, and business," explained Neil. "It's

An Enterprising World

(continued)

also easy to access from the UK." Unlike its other overseas units, the U.S. operations will be company-owned. "The U.S. market, should it be successful, is enormous. We believe we'll get better value for our shareholders by controlling the business directly," said Neil.

Discussion Questions

1. Why has Wagamama chosen to franchise its international restaurant operations? What are some of the reasons that Wagamama wants to own and operate its U.S. restaurant sites?

2. How could Wagamama insure that a franchisee in Auckland, New Zealand, is operating a restaurant to the company's standards?

3. Why would a private equity firm be interested in an investment in Wagamama? How might Lion Capital get a return on its investment in the future?

4. What are the advantages and disadvantages of getting private equity money from investors versus using a franchise system to grow Wagamama?

Sources: Based on "Clocking on ... Luke Fryer of Wagamama," *Hospitality,* March 1, 2006, p. 16; Amanda Mosle Friedman, "Having Words with Ian Neill, Chief Executive, Wagamama," *Nation's Restaurant News,* October 10, 2005, p. 114; "Graphite Makes Partial Exit from Wagamama," *European Venture Capital Journal,* October 2004, p. 13; "Noodle Migration," *Restaurants & Institutions,* February 15, 2006, p. 13; "Wagamama Changes Hands and Sets Out to Conquer the USA," *Caterer & Hotelkeeper,* June 23, 2005, p. 8; "Wagamama Gets £13m to Fund Its Expansion Drive," *Caterer & Hotelkeeper,* September 9, 2004, p. 9; and "Wagamama Set to Take On U.S. Market," *Caterer & Hotelkeeper,* January 19, 2006, p. 8.

11.9 Summary

1. Franchising is a popular form of business ownership that makes a significant contribution to the national economy. It spans 75 industry groups, from fast food to health care services to pet stores. In a franchise relationship, a parent business (the *franchisor*) provides an investor (the *franchisee*) with the rights to sell its products or services and use its trademark and operating procedures. In return, the franchisee pays up-front fees and/or ongoing royalty payments. About one-third of all franchise outlets are in food-related industries.

2. Business format franchises account for 80 percent of all franchises. The franchisor provides the franchisee a defined format under which to operate the franchise unit, as well as training and other types of support, such as help in locating a site, guidance on building and outfitting the store, and financing. The franchisee also acquires the rights to use the brand name and related trademarks. Franchisees pay fees and royalties to the franchisor. They must adhere to the franchisor's operating guidelines in managing their units.

3. With a product and trademark (or product distribution) franchise, franchisees have the right to buy, sell, and advertise trademarked products and serve as a dealer network for the manufacturer. Product and trademark franchisees have greater operating freedom than business

format franchisees. Vehicle dealerships are the most common type of franchise, followed by oil and gas distributorships.

4. The Federal Trade Commission (FTC) under Rule 436 regulates disclosures related to the offer and sale of franchises at the federal level. The law sets forth the minimum disclosure requirements but does not require franchisors to register their filings. Franchisors must provide prospective franchisees with a Uniform Franchise Offering Circular (UFOC) that covers 23 items in a standard format. Because the FTC does not review the contents or accuracy of UFOCs, prospective franchisees are responsible for their own review. State laws vary in the degree of regulation, with some states requiring that franchisors register their UFOCs.

5. Deciding whether to buy a franchise or another type of business requires the same type of review process as any new business venture, including personal goals, interests, skills, investment requirements, type of business opportunity, industry characteristics, and market environment. A prospective franchisee must also investigate the franchisor to make sure that it can deliver on its promises. The benefits of franchising include a proven business model, brand name and trademarks, training and support from the franchisor, financing assistance, system synergies, and economies of scale. Disadvantages include the need to follow the franchisor's operating systems, costs such as franchise fees and ongoing royalties, inability to act independently of the system, limitations on the sale or termination of the franchise contract, business risks, and unfulfilled expectations on the part of the franchisor.

6. Choosing a franchise opportunity requires substantial research into different franchise concepts. Costs vary considerably, even within the same industry, and depend on the type of unit and required equipment, franchise fee, ongoing royalty payments, and other fees such as contributions to a systemwide advertising fund. Other areas of comparison include demand for the products, competition, brand equity, amount of training and support, and degree of operating restrictions. Site visits, to both the franchisor's headquarters and to individual franchise units, are an essential part of the due diligence process.

7. The *franchise license agreement* gives the franchisee the right to use the franchisor's registered brands and trademarks and business operating system. It specifies the contract term, franchisee payments, and operating restrictions.

8. Franchising also offers a way for an enterpriser to grow a business more quickly by using the talent and capital of other enterprisers, who become franchisees. While becoming a franchisor can be quite profitable, the franchisor loses some profits to the franchisees and also gives up a degree of operating control. Businesses that are well suited to grow by franchising should have an easily replicated business model, a strong brand or trademark, and a unique concept. In addition, the business should be easy for others to learn and manage. The franchisor

must be able to identify the qualities that make the business successful and prepare detailed operating manuals to guide the system's franchisees in duplicating them.

9. Developing a franchise system calls for a significant commitment on the part of the franchisor and starts with a business plan. Working with a franchise attorney and development consultant, the franchisor must prepare the UFOC and supporting materials in accordance with federal and state regulations, identify the system's intellectual property (brand, trademarks, procedures), write operating manuals and procedures, hire a franchise development team to recruit and train franchisees, create a marketing strategy, and work closely with franchisees on a continuing basis.

10. The franchise concept has become global in scope, with U.S. franchisors opening units overseas and foreign-based franchises coming to the United States to build their systems. Some types of franchises translate easily to new countries, while others—food-related franchises in particular—require adaptation to local tastes and customs.

Review Questions

1. What makes a franchise different from other paths to entrepreneurship?

2. What is the relationship between the franchisor and the franchisee? Name the three basic elements in a franchise.

3. Differentiate between business format and product and trademark franchises.

4. Describe the two types of multiple-unit ownership options.

5. To what extent are franchises regulated at the federal and state level? How do federal and state regulations differ?

6. What is the Uniform Franchise Offering Circular and what must it contain to conform to FTC disclosure requirements?

7. What advantages does franchising offer to the franchisee? What are the negatives in choosing the franchise route?

8. Describe the process for selecting a franchise opportunity. What areas should an enterpriser take into account with regard to personal characteristics

and the business itself before buying a franchise?

9. What costs are involved in the purchase and operation of a franchise unit?

10. Why are site visits to the franchisor's headquarters and to existing franchisees integral to the due diligence process? List the questions a prospective franchisee would ask at each type of meeting.

11. What is a franchise license agreement? How does it treat the franchisee's investments in property?

12. Why would an entrepreneur decide to use franchising as a way to grow a business? What characteristics should a business have to be suitable for franchising?

13. Briefly describe the process involved in becoming a franchisor.

14. Discuss the issues facing U.S. franchisors who wish to expand abroad. What additional concerns might a U.S. enterpriser have in buying a franchise from a foreign-based franchisor?

Applying What You've Learned

1. Your friend has just been laid off from her job as a software support specialist. She has heard about a franchise opportunity that provides computer training to individuals and small businesses. However, she is unsure whether to buy a franchise or to set up her own company and asks for your advice. Describe the pros and cons of each alternative for her. Explain what she can expect in the way of assistance from the franchisor and suggest a game plan for her to follow to evaluate the franchise. What questions should she ask the franchisor? Current franchisees?

2. The IFA (International Franchise Association) is the trade association that works to promote and regulate franchising in ways that benefit all franchisors and franchisees. Visit its website, http://www.franchise.org, and click on the Government Relations section. What are the top regulatory issues currently facing the franchise industry? Summarize the types of legislation that are under consideration at both the state and federal levels.

3. Select five franchises in at least three different industries that have outlets in your community. (Refer to *Entrepreneur*'s Franchise 500 lists, http://www.entrepreneur.com/franchise/, if you are not sure whether a business is franchised or independent.) After visiting the stores, choose two you like best and explain why you prefer these franchises. Arrange interviews with the owners and speak to employees. What impressed you about these franchises? Could you see yourself owning a similar franchise? Summarize your findings.

4. Not all kinds of businesses and industries are well suited to establishing a franchise. What kind of business could not be expanded by developing a franchise system and selling it to others? Look through the many listings of different franchises and consider what businesses and industries do not appear to be represented. How do these industries and businesses seem to be different from industries and businesses with a high percentage of franchise systems?

5. Six years ago you opened Scoop Shop, an ice cream parlor patterned after a 1950s soda fountain. The concept was so popular that you opened five more stores in nearby towns. Soon people were approaching you about expanding Scoop Shop to their area, so you decided to become a franchisor. Today you have 33 stores in a three-state region. The Center for Entrepreneurship at your state university has asked you to speak to its students about your success. Prepare a presentation that includes the key factors you considered before deciding to franchise Scoop Shops and how you developed your franchise system. What were the most difficult aspects you faced, and what advice can you give students from the franchisor's perspective about buying a franchise?

6. Some enterprises have focused on purchasing franchises as a way to grow. A good example of this is AutoNation (http://www.autonation.com), which was founded by Wayne Huizenga, who had previously started Waste Management and Blockbuster Video. AutoNation is the largest car dealer in the United States, with over 350 new vehicle franchises in more than 15 states and offers no-haggle sales policies and online sales through http://www.autonation.com and individual dealer websites. How could a company that owns many different automobile franchise systems (e.g., Ford, General Motors, Toyota, Nissan, Honda) become successful in the marketplace? Are there other industries with a high percentage of franchises where the AutoNation strategy might also work?

Enterprisers on the Web

1. Is franchising the right business venture for you? Take the first section (Questions 1–33) of the quiz you'll find in the article "Are You Suited to Be a Franchisee?" *Entrepreneur*'s FranchiseZone, April 19, 2004, http://www.entrepreneur.com/franzone/article/0,5847,315261,00.html. What did you discover about yourself? Were you surprised at the results?

2. Another site that can help you evaluate the franchising option for yourself is the International Franchise Association (http://www.franchise.org) resource site. There are seven readings that provide a good overview of franchising issues. Please be sure to cover the last two readings: "Most Frequently Asked Questions About Franchising" and "Self-Evaluation: Is Franchising for You?"

3. The Federal Trade Commission is the government agency responsible for monitoring and regulating franchises. The FTC site (http://www.ftc.gov) provides links to many resources on franchising, including details on the legal responsibilities of franchisors and franchisees. What kinds of problems should a prospective franchisee look out for when considering a franchise? What kinds of scams are typical in the franchise industry?

4. *Entrepreneur* conducts a number of surveys of the franchise industry and reports on new franchising trends and issues. At the *Entrepreneur* magazine's FranchiseZone site (http://www.entrepreneur.com/franzone/), browse the Franchise 500, as well as the special lists of Top New Franchises, Fast-Growing Franchises, Low-Cost Franchises, and so on. Find three franchise opportunities that are of interest to you. Read their profiles and visit the franchisor websites. Compare these three franchise opportunities in either chart or narrative format. Include the following information for each franchise opportunity:

   Resources necessary to participate

   Up-front costs

   Ongoing costs

   Capabilities of the entrepreneurs these franchises seek

   Advantages that each franchise promotes

   Type of help and support offered

   Of the franchises you analyzed, which franchise seems to be better than the others? Does it meet your needs and suit your background and personality? Explain your rationale in detail.

5. Revisit the three franchisor websites from the previous question, plus any others that interest you. Which websites seemed to be the most appealing to you? What features and information in these websites were more likely to convince you to become a franchisee? Which websites seemed to do a poor job of convincing you to become a franchisee? What are the critical features and information that a franchisor needs to provide to prospective franchisees on their websites?

6. *Inc.* magazine (http://www.inc.com/guides/buy_biz/20674.html) offers insights into how franchisors and franchisees can better manage their businesses. Using the site's resources, discuss ways the owner of a franchise can help motivate employees. What specific expenses and revenue items should you monitor daily in a franchise restaurant business to insure that you are profitable?

End Notes

1. Julie Bennett, "Franchise Regulation: Past, Present and Future," *StartupJournal.com*, January 9, 2002, http:www.startupjournal.com; "Important Facts about Franchising," Franchise Opportunities.com, http://www.franchiseopportunities.com (July 3, 2005).

2. "Answers to the 20 Most Frequently Asked Questions about Franchising," International Franchising Association, 2005, http://www.franchise.org.

3. *The Profile of Franchising* (Washington, DC: Frandata Corp and IFA Educational Foundation, February 2000), p. 5.

4. Jerry Wilkerson, "2005 Franchise Business Development Forecast and Industry Trends Analysis: 14th Annual Franchise Study," Franchise Recruiters Ltd., March 6, 2005, http://franchiserecruiters.com.

5. *Economic Impact of Franchised Businesses—Policymakers Digest*, IFA Educational Foundation, 2005, p. 3.

6. Ibid.

7. Carlye Adler, "How China Eats a Sandwich," *Fortune*, March 21, 2005, p. F210[B].

8. "Rule Overview," *Guide to the FTC Franchise Rule*, Federal Trade Commission, http://www.ftc.gov/bcp/franchise/netrule.htm (July 12, 2005).

9. "Rule requirements," *Guide to the FTC Franchise Rule*," Federal Trade Commission, http://www.ftc.gov/bcp/franchise/netrule.htm (July 12, 2005).

10. Gene J. Koprowski, "Successful Franchisees Embrace 'The System'," *StartupJournal Online*, March 8, 2004, http://www.startupjournal.com/franchising/.

11. Lea McLees, "Flourishing New Franchises," *Research Horizons* 13, no. 3 (Winter 1996), pp. 14–16.

12. Koprowski, "Successful Franchisees Embrace 'The System'," *StartupJournal Online*, March 8, 2004, http://www.startupjournal.com/franchising/.

13. Paulette Thomas, "Franchise Sparks Idea to Create a New Firm," *Wall Street Journal*, May 31, 2005, p. B12.

14. Koprowski, "Successful Franchisees Embrace 'The System'," *StartupJournal Online*, March 8, 2004, http://www.startupjournal.com/franchising/.

15. Adapted from *A Consumer Guide to Buying a Franchise*, Federal Trade Commission, http://www.ftc.gov/bcp/conline/pubs/invest/buyfran.htm (July 15, 2005).

16. April Y. Pennington, "Would You Like a Franchise with That?" *Entrepreneur*, January 2005, http://www.entrepreneur.com.

17. Richard Gibson, "Franchise Fever Jumps to Overseas Markets," *Wall Street Journal Online*, February 24, 2004, http://www.startupjournal.com/franchising/.

18. Pennington, "Would You Like a Franchise with That?" *Entrepreneur*, January 2005, http://www.entrepreneur.com.

19. Jeff Elgin, "What is a Master Franchisee?" *Entrepreneur*, September 7, 2004, http://www.entrepreneur.com.

20. "Becoming a Franchisor," Franchise Consulting, http://www.franchiseconsulting.net/intro.html (July 3, 2005).

21. Thomas, "Franchise Sparks Idea to Create a New Firm," *Wall Street Journal*, May 31, 2005, p. B12.

22. Sources: Adapted from the Small Business School video "Take Out Taxi" and related materials http:smallbusinessschool.org; "Services That Deliver—Home Meal Replacement," *Nation's Restaurant News*, March 16, 1998, http://www.findarticles.com; "Takeout Taxi: Howe Jumps into Driver's Seat," *Restaurants & Institutions*, March 15, 1996, p. 26; and "Takeout Taxi Speeds up Delivery Sales for Operators," *Nation's Restaurant News*, November 23, 1992, http://www.findarticles.com.

23. Carlye Adler, "How China Eats a Sandwich," *Fortune*, March 21, 2005, p. F210[B].

The Enterprising Mind

The Enterprising Mind

chapter **12**

Key Concepts

1. After exploring business opportunities, it is time to make the transition from dreams to realities, which requires a shift in focus—from how and why to goals and values. Enterprisers must determine what's important and make sure their actions and commitments correlate with their goals.

2. The way we tell our life stories—where we came from and where we are going—defines our self-perceptions. Telling a more positive story can transform how we think about ourselves and how others think about us, leading to a more successful outcome. A good story uses past experiences to demonstrate how an enterpriser will meet new challenges. It's normal to have many fears as you embark on your enterprising journey, which has many unknowns.

3. Focusing more on the limitations of a particular situation than on the possibilities it presents is a restrictive mind-set that can hinder future success. Ways to improve our mind-set include assuming that everyone wants to do "A" work, believing that we can contribute, not taking ourselves so seriously, and being passionate about what we do.

4. One of the challenges of being an enterpriser is trying to satisfy four different goals: achievement, significance, legacy, and happiness. It's impossible to maximize all four, and we should set priorities and seek success in many arenas: work, family, self, and community.

Suppose you are an action-oriented person who has overcome many difficulties in your life. After a string of 30 jobs in a variety of fields, you are working for a computer sales company. Because you do not agree with management's values and ethics, you decide to leave yet another job—this time to start your own company. Raising financing for your used computer sales business was tough, but you didn't give up. You believed in yourself and your business model.

In this chapter's case, we'll meet Tom Pace, who built PaceButler Corporation into a leading reseller of used computer equipment. He later refocused the company's resales expertise to become a broker for used cellular phones. A factor in his success is the company's "atmosphere statement," developed in 1990 to establish a values orientation that emphasizes an employee-centric, positive, working environment. In 2003, Pace took full responsibility for a major computer problem that almost put the company out of business. His story shows how setting goals, knowing your values, focusing on possibilities, and taking action lead to success.

12.0 Taking Stock

In the preceding 11 chapters, you have learned a lot about business opportunities and the steps required to turn them into actual businesses. You have the tools to execute your dreams—but what, exactly, are your dreams? As you have looked at various opportunities, you have probably reconsidered your goals based on this new information about what might be possible for your life as an enterpriser. The many possibilities that are now available to you can be overwhelming. This chapter is designed to help you take stock of your situation so you can move forward to realize your dreams.

Most enterprisers experience a transition point when they move from the activities involved in starting a business to the actual process of operating and managing an ongoing business. Even from conversations with enterprisers, it is difficult to know when, specifically, they move from starting the business to actually being in business. In many retail establishments and restaurants, you'll notice a dollar bill pasted on the wall next to the cash register. When you ask the business owner about it, you are likely to hear a story related to how he or she earned that dollar, which represents the company's first sale. Often, that marks the enterprise's first day of business.

A good description of this transition period from start-up to ongoing business appears in one of the first studies of the enterprising process undertaken by Orvis Collins and David Moore in the 1960s. They studied individuals who started small manufacturing businesses—basically, machine shops that made parts for the automobile and furniture industries in the Michigan area. In what is a pretty dry study of these enterprisers, they point to this period of transition with these words:

> *In this period of fear and doubt, however, these men found creativity. At a time when it became necessary for them to reorganize their lives and to re-establish their futures, they had the capacity not only to dream but to transmute their dreams into action. They created the business of which they were dreaming. Between the idea and the act falls the shadow. This shadow, which these men had to explore, and out of which they had to hammer a reality, lay immediately ahead. They had now to organize the universe around them in such a way that they could progress in establishing their new business. The first act in this direction is what we will call the act of creation.*[1]

That is a somewhat moody soliloquy, yet it speaks to what nearly all enterprisers go through during the process of turning their dreams into reality. There is a gap—what Collins and Moore call "the shadow"—that lies between our present situation and a vision of our future. In our mind's eye, we might be able to actually see where we want to be in the future. But the specific process of getting there is likely to be less clear. We can see ourselves owning a 100-room hotel, we can imagine what each of the rooms look like, we can see the lobby and the front desk, and we can walk around the hotel in our imagination. The actual process of moving from dreaming about owning a hotel to actually owning a hotel is the "shadow" that we must walk through to make our vision come into existence. Taking your dreams and turning them into reality takes more than action. While you now have tools for spotting opportunities, evaluating them, and developing the plans to make those opportunities into enterprises, you must also consider your values: What do you really want? The challenge is to transform *your thinking* so you can take in all of the possibilities available to you.

Some aspects of this chapter are similar to the issues we raised in Chapter 3, Enterprising Fundamentals. However, in the earlier chapter we focused more on the *how*. Now we ask you to concentrate on your values and goals—the *why*—and begin to act in ways that support them. For example, in Chapter 3 the focus on time management was *how* to manage your time. In this chapter we approach time management from a different perspective, on *why* we really want to pursue a particular opportunity. Our actions and commitments should reflect our values and goals. Shifting our focus to values takes some effort. We tend to take action, which sets us on a particular course. We find ourselves on autopilot and may not make the necessary course corrections as we proceed on our journey. Often we realize that our destination is changing: our course is set for London, but we really want to go to Paris. This chapter is about being conscious of our goals and values as we move toward our dreams. As we have identified the opportunities we want to pursue in our lives (through our efforts in Chapters 6 through 8), we will need to make these mid-course corrections in our lives. We need insure that the direction of our opportunities matches the direction of our goals and values.

12.1 What Are Your Commitments?

Commitments are choices that bind you to some future course of action.[2] Often, we think about a commitment as a big or important choice that has future implications. For example, if you take out a loan to purchase a car, you've made a commitment to make monthly payments to the bank for the next five years to pay off that loan. Buying the car and taking out the loan are choices that constrain your actions, because you'll need to earn income to make the loan payments. The action also opens up opportunities for you: you now have a car that gives you mobility. You can drive where you want, when you want, and you might even use your car to make money—delivering pizzas, driving to a job—to pay for the car.

Larger commitments tend to require other obligations of time, money, and energy as well. For example, if you purchase the car, you are also making a commitment to keep it maintained, which means tune-ups and new tires and parts; the car will require gasoline when you drive it; it will have to be washed and cleaned; and it will need a parking place and insurance. We often underestimate these other minor commitments.

Remember your goals? In Chapter 3 we provided exercises to help you discover your goals and priorities. Now let's see whether your actions and activities are well correlated to these goals. To do this, ask yourself the following questions: What is important to you? What do you really care about (what are your goals and values)?

List these on a piece of paper using the format in Exhibit 12.1. As we suggested in the goal setting section of Chapter 3, try to be as specific as possible about what matters to you. For example, if you write down "family," then begin to identify what goals you have with your family, such as "having fun" with your family, versus "making sure kids in the family get an education." For each goal, then ask yourself what your commitment in money, time, and energy is to accomplish that. Include what you are doing about that goal now. For example, if one of your

exhibit 12.1 **What Is Important to Me?**

Goal	Money	Time	Energy
Good health	$100 a month for gym	Go twice a week after work	Research most convenient gyms
	Buy more fresh fruits and vegetables	Trips to grocery store	Find best sources, scout out farmer's markets
Learn new skills required to start own business	Tuition for additional courses	3–5 hours a week in class per semester plus studying	Determine which courses will help most
		Enrich current job, take advantage of training opportunities	Find a mentor, seminars, etc.

goals is to be physically fit, you would note how much time, money, and energy you currently devote to keeping fit. Maybe you pay for a gym membership fee as your financial commitment, but you only go to the gym once a month.

In going through this exercise to identify what you find important and where you've been spending money, time, and energy, you can begin to see whether your commitments correspond to your goals and values. Using Exhibit 12.1 as an example, if you really value your health and you are not taking time to exercise and eat well, your commitments clearly don't match your values.

As you develop the opportunities in your life, it is easy to get caught up in activities that, over time, do not bring you closer to the values and goals that matter most to you. Just like in Chapter 3, we encourage you to work smarter rather than work harder. Working harder may not bring you any closer to achieving your goals. For example, we all have a desire to be better off financially, and so we set financial goals. Yet how much time and energy do we really devote to meeting our financial goals? If we are spending only ten minutes a month balancing our checkbook, then our actions do not reflect much time or energy spent to improve our financial situation.

Once we've identified mismatches between our values and goals and our commitments in money, time, and energy, how do we begin to change them? Just being aware of the mismatches is an important first step. Next, consider your current commitments and how they influence your investment of that time, money, and energy. Suppose you find that you are spending most of your time at work but need to spend more time with your family. Before you cut back your hours, you'll have to talk with your boss and coworkers about your plans. If you suddenly decide to cut back on your work effort without telling anyone, you are likely to be perceived as slacking off—when in fact you've made a conscious choice to emphasize other priorities in your life. Realize that others might not always share your excitement about devoting less time and energy to things you've been involved with in the past. Another benefit of sharing your plans: you create a path for yourself (as we will see in the next section).

Second, clear your clutter. Basically, as you review your activities, the money you spend, and the places you put your energy, you should begin to cull things from your list. As we indicated in Chapter 3's section on time management, you can't take on new things unless you get rid of old activities. If one of the things you value in your life is spending time painting and want an hour a day to paint, you have to take that hour from something else on your schedule. A good rule of thumb in evaluating your commitments and making new commitments is to take on a new commitment only when you've ended another.

By looking at your commitments, then, you'll see how your actions match your values and goals. If your goal is to start and own a business, are you putting time, money, and energy into accomplishing this? To be a business owner, you need to act like a business owner. This means you will have to make a commitment to

- devote x number of hours a week to the development and (eventual) operation of your business.

- invest a certain amount of your resources into creating the business.

- put some of your best efforts into making the business a reality.

For example, if your day is devoted entirely to completing school work and being with friends and family, and your only free time to develop your business is late at night (between midnight and 2 AM), you might not be able to devote your best energy to your business. Nor will most customers, suppliers, or others be available at those hours. To do your best on a commitment, then, you will have to rearrange your schedule so you can spend your best time, the time when you have the most energy, to starting a business, so that the circumstances are also best for insuring your success.

In this section we've helped you identify the gaps between what you want and what you need to do. Yet while we know that we need to take action to move closer to our goals, we get stuck doing the same things we have always done. For example, to create an enterprise we need to build a network of supportive people to help us firm up our business plans. We need to do the cold-calling necessary to identify "strangers" who can eventually become supportive advisors. But we spend the day with our friends and family—people we already know. Inertia keeps us stuck in our old patterns. Part of the reason for being stuck is that we are held back by how we see ourselves and our ideas, as well as the way that others view us. It's easier to keep thinking and acting the same way we have done until now.

12.2 What Is Your Story?

As Zig Ziglar, a well-known business and sales training consultant and author, reminds us, "You cannot consistently perform in a manner which is inconsistent with the way you see yourself." Not only do we need to begin acting like enterprisers and engaging in activities to start and grow businesses, we also need to change how we think and talk about being enterprisers. The way we tell our life stories—where we came from and where we are going—serves as a lever for creating the changes necessary to achieve our goals and dreams.

The stories we relate to others create an overview of where we've been in the past and how those events and experiences of the past will propel us forward into the future.[3] Our personal stories define our self-perceptions. If I tell the story about my life as a series of struggles, about how I overcame many obstacles and difficulties to finally triumph, I'm telling others—and myself—that I'm persistent, hardworking, and will get things done. If instead I tell a story about my life that says that I don't complete tasks, that I don't like to work, and that I'm lazy, that story tells other people how I behaved in the past and am likely to behave in the future. So changing the way you tell that story can help you transform your view of yourself and how others think about you.

A Model for Your Story

The task at hand, then, is to develop the story about how your current opportunities will become real through your efforts and the help of others. Creating your story will not only help you think through issues for yourself but also convey to others where you are in the process of transforming your dreams into realities.

Where do you begin your story about your life? Good stories have drama, an element of suspense. They describe how the main character of the story is confronted with challenges and then solves them. Many enterprisers often suggest using the David and Goliath story as the template for their business start-up struggles. We, too, will use this model to outline the basic aspects of what a story should contain.

As you'll recall, this story begins with David, the youngest of eight sons of Jesse and a shepherd. David spends most of his days and nights outside the city where his family lives, guarding the sheep from lions and wolves. With these responsibilities, David learns many skills to protect his sheep from harm. One day his father asks David to take food to his brothers, who are soldiers in the army of King Saul that is fighting the Philistines. The Philistines are led by Goliath, a giant who challenges King Saul to send one man to fight him. The outcome of this fight will determine who will win the war. When he arrives at the army camp and hears Goliath making this challenge, David volunteers to fight. Everyone in Saul's army is surprised by the young boy's offer, but no one else volunteers to fight, so David is chosen. Rather than using the heavy armor that most of the soldiers use for fighting, David approaches the giant only with a sling-shot and five stones. The giant is surprised that he will fight a young boy with no armor or weapons and mocks his opponents "Am I a dog that you would come at me with sticks?" In response to Goliath's taunt, David puts a stone in his sling-shot and swings it at Goliath, hits him in the head, and kills him. Goliath's death routs the Philistine army.

The story begins with a protagonist, or main character, and is told in such a way that we can relate to the issues the main character faces. Here we see how a boy can overcome great odds by doing things differently. If David had put on armor and used the kinds of weapons that Goliath was using, David would have surely been killed. By using a sling-shot, something that Goliath did not expect, David won the contest.

Our stories often have similar elements. The main character will face a problem that needs to be solved. In great stories, the main character will solve this problem in an innovative way. Your challenge, then, is to tell your story about developing your business opportunity and the new kinds of problems that you face as you embark on your journey to become an enterpriser.

Developing Your Story

Telling a story about your new path to entrepreneurship is particularly challenging, because you aren't currently at the end of the story. In some respects, you are at the beginning or the middle of the story. You are David, who has just arrived at the camp of Saul's army and realizes that the challenge will be to fight Goliath. Your story will not have an outcome yet, and your challenges may not be specific enough to identify. Yet you still must talk about your new journey—and how the challenges you've met successfully in the past have prepared you for this undertaking.

For example, Albert Jennings had been a poor student during high school and college, and he had then worked at numerous jobs in various industries. What kind of story could Albert tell that would engage others in his journey to become an enterpriser? First, Albert could talk about his struggles to learn new skills and to explore different jobs and businesses that he thought he might enjoy. He can then talk about what he learned and how these previous struggles have helped him better understand what he wants as an enterpriser. His story can tell of his journey of discovery to realize what he wants to do—rather than focusing on his inability to do well in school and hold a job for any length of time.

Here are five suggestions to develop a story that will help you to become the enterpriser you imagine yourself to be:

1. *Be coherent.* Explain the events and the experiences in your past so that they support your view of what you will become. For example, David could describe how his life as a shepherd taught him how to defend his sheep from lions and wolves. These past incidents would support his view that he could also fight a giant. David has learned fighting skills that he can use now, to meet the current challenges he faces.

2. *Explain your motivations for change and be sure they are consistent with your values and beliefs.* Most stories of enterprisers center on their discovery of what they love and enjoy doing and how they pursued this discovery. Offer consistent reasons to illustrate why these new changes are occurring in your life. For example, you could say, "I discovered in my previous jobs and in my school work that I'm really good at. …"

3. *Use your past to help explain what you now want to do.* The more we can point to incidents in our past, the more plausible our story becomes to others. As David can explain, "I may have been a shepherd, but I have had practice fighting lions and wolves, which prepared me to meet the challenge of fighting a giant." We probably will never have the skills and experiences to be fully prepared for many of the challenges confronting us, but we can look to find incidents in our past that have provided some of the requisite capabilities.

4. *Reframe your past experiences to demonstrate how you can meet the new challenges.* While David could tell a story about how skilled he is at tending sheep and guiding them to new areas to graze, he should tell stories that focus on his fighting abilities to convince others of his fighting skills. Look into your past and think about which incidents in your life support your story of becoming an enterpriser.

5. *Begin telling the story of your journey as an enterpriser and get feedback.* The more you tell your story, the more you will learn from others whether your story makes sense to them, and how they, too, might become a part of your journey. We all like to hear stories of success and how people have overcome difficult odds to triumph. Most people would like to help others become successful. As you tell your story, you will learn what additional information others need to know about your past events and experiences and how they support achieving your goals. You'll also discover the skills and abilities you still need to acquire to convince others that you will succeed.

Telling your story is a way to help you to believe in yourself, and for helping others believe in you as well. It goes back to the quote from the beginning of

Charles Dickens' *David Copperfield*: "Whether I shall turn out to be the hero of my own life, or whether that station will be held by anybody else, these pages must show." A key challenge, then, in becoming an enterpriser is to tell a story about your life where you are the main character, and that your life is unfolding in a way that you can meet the challenges and problems that are now facing you.

12.3 Facing Your Fears

Frankly, any transition is difficult. When we embark on a new journey, a new effort, we can't be prepared for all of the challenges that might confront us. This is particularly true in the enterprising process. Opportunity recognition, developing a business model, generating a feasibility study and a business plan—there are so many unknowns that will cause anxiety. We have a vision of where we want to go, we've made plans about how we think we might get there—but we aren't there yet, are we?

Being in "fear and doubt," as Collins and Moore suggest, is really very normal. There are a number of reasons why, at this stage of implementing our dreams, we may have fears and doubts. But we must face those fears and overcome them.

Suppose you fear that you don't have the talents, skills, and abilities to actually achieve your goals and dreams. For example, you might see yourself as the owner of a tour company that offers adventure tours throughout the world, but right now, you may have only been a tour guide, or maybe haven't even gone on a tour! At this early stage, it's hard to know whether you can gain the necessary experience to develop your business. It's one thing to be an expert in the field you've chosen for your enterprise, but in fact most beginning enterprisers are not experts or the best in their fields when they develop their business opportunities. So, you are not alone when you wonder, "Do I have the talent to start this enterprise? Am I good enough?"

A common story about how individuals choose the types of opportunities for their new venture investments goes something like this. If given the choice between investing in an "A" opportunity with a "B" team, or an "A" team with a "B" opportunity, most investors are likely to pick the "A" team with the "B" opportunity. The theory is that investors believe that "A" level enterprisers are more likely to make "B" level opportunities successful. "B" level enterprisers, even with "A" level opportunities, won't have the talents and skills to make their new enterprises work. This story is likely to cause fledgling enterprisers to wonder whether they are "A" level enterprisers. It would be great if before starting out they had ten years of experience in their selected industries, along with all of the connections to investors, suppliers, customers, employees, and advisors. It would be great if they had already started an enterprise in those fields—and even better if those business start-ups succeeded and were exactly like the ones they plan to start.

That is the irony. If you are doing something new, you won't have the experience and knowledge you need to begin your effort. So, it is important to realize that *you begin your journey where you are.* You start with what you have.

Whatever talents and skills and knowledge you have, right now, is sufficient for you to begin.

This goes back to Chapter 2, when we talked about "effectual" thinking. The critical task for an enterpriser is *to begin,* to take actions and steps toward enterprising. No situation that you are in is likely to be optimal for developing your opportunity, and you simply will never have all the skills and knowledge you need to pursue your goals and dreams. You may be involved in situations where you are "way over your head" in terms of what you need to be successful. Yet in the reality of enterprising, it's better to take action, to engage in enterprising—even when you might know that you are in over your head—than to not engage in the process at all.

Using a sports analogy: You can't learn to hit the ball in baseball unless you are willing to go to the plate and try. You can practice hitting and simulate the process, but at some point, to play the game you have to go to the plate, face a pitcher, and see whether you can hit the ball. There is no substitute for actually playing the game, and that is how you improve your ability to play. We know that in baseball, not every trip to home plate results in getting a hit. Many times we strike out. But we can't let our fears of whether we are good enough to get a hit prevent us from stepping up to the plate and trying.

We get better at the things we need to do by trying, by practicing. You might not be "good enough" to achieve what you would like, but, if you use your fear that you aren't "good enough" to keep you from trying, then you will never get better.

Many people assume that entrepreneurs have the "right stuff"—and that is what differentiates entrepreneurs from others. Often this belief gets in the way and seems to be an excuse for people to avoid taking action. But is there ever enough "right stuff" for enterprising? We don't think so. There isn't any magic to becoming an enterpriser. We don't need to be more than we are to engage in the activities that enable us to succeed. We all have the "right stuff" necessary for success.

The Great Imposter

Let's say that you are looking to start a business that modifies cars into high performance automobiles. When you spend time with many successful enterprisers in this field, you might fear that you are just pretending that you could be a successful enterpriser in this area. You see what others are doing in your field, and you begin to doubt that you are one of them. Or you want to start a restaurant and you meet a successful restaurateur who has a highly visible restaurant with many favorable reviews in national gourmet and travel magazines. It is humbling to consider that your initial effort at starting a restaurant could put you in the same class. As a result, you might feel like an imposter in the role of an enterpriser.

This feeling arises because you are developing the skills and knowledge necessary to create your enterprise. At the same time, there is much uncertainty about how the process of enterprise creation is going to turn out. Am I really an enterpriser if, at this stage, I'm really a fledgling enterpriser? If I haven't really started a restaurant, am I really a restaurateur?

If you are working at developing an enterprise, you *are* an enterpriser. If you are working to start a restaurant, then you *are* a restaurateur. By doing the work, you become what you are. Going back to our baseball analogy: If you are playing baseball, you are hitting, pitching, and catching. When you are performing those tasks, you aren't pretending—you are playing baseball. So to begin feeling like you are an enterpriser, do the work of an enterpriser. You can't pretend when you are talking with customers, meeting with suppliers, and asking investors for money. Those actions mean that you are an enterpriser.

Expecting Perfection

As an enterpriser, you should have vision of where you want to go and goals for what you want to achieve. Expecting perfection from your efforts can quickly derail your hard work and make you experience the "fear and doubt" we mentioned at the start of this section. Your efforts are probably never going to be perfect in the way you imagine.

Let's say that your enterprise is an event management firm and you will be planning a wedding with 100 guests. While you can imagine the perfect wedding event—perfect cake, perfect flower arrangements, perfectly served food, great tables and chairs, and everything being just right—the odds of that happening are slim to none. Something in the wedding event is likely to go wrong, or turn our differently than expected or planned. For some individuals, the fact that things don't turn out exactly as planned or imagined can be devastating. It can be so disheartening when what you so clearly see in your mind isn't what actually occurs. Some people just give up when they don't achieve what they imagined. They somehow want to have that perfect restaurant, or the perfect bed and breakfast, or the perfect retail store, and they continually disappoint themselves when what they do have doesn't match their vision.

The challenge is to continue to do your work and expect that as you work at being an enterpriser, you will improve over time. If you are doing events, the more events you plan, the better each event is likely to become—even though there may be events along the way that are complete disasters. In many fields, what you might consider a flaw isn't even noticed by the customer. Your expectations might be so much higher than your customer's. While it would be great if our goal was to achieve a "wow" experience for all of our customers, and each time we did something for a customer, they said, "Wow!", but we can still meet our customers' needs without the "wow."

If we seek perfection in everything we do, then, frankly, we probably won't do anything. Most of what we do often won't meet the standards we imagine. Operate using the premise "Anything worth doing is worth doing"—not "Anything worth doing is worth doing well." We strive to do the best we can, but it may not always be "the best."

To combat your fear that your efforts aren't good enough and the outcome of the process isn't perfect, the best thing to do is try. We don't get better at anything unless we undertake the activity. Fearing that your enterprise is not worth doing unless it is perfect is just a recipe for not doing it at all.

How can you identify and defuse your fears, negative beliefs, and self-doubts as you move forward as an enterpriser? Imagine the worst fears and the biggest doubts you have about enterprising. Write them down in the left column of a two-column chart. Then in the right column, answer each with a possible solution or another way of looking at the situation. Exhibit 12.2 shows a sample chart for a hypothetical enterpriser. This exercise is a valuable method to gain insights about what specifically is holding you back and to develop ways to counter these negatives.

Need for Approval

Wouldn't it be great if, before you start, someone who was really knowledgeable about your business gave you a "seal of approval"? Wouldn't it be terrific to have experts in your area tell you that your proposed venture will be a success? On the other hand, how would you feel if that really knowledgeable person told you that your idea was stupid and that you should not do your venture, at all?

While it is nice to get advice from others about the future success or failure of your venture, such input is not always correct or insightful. This is not to say that you should ignore the advice of others, or that you can't gain valuable insights into your business's potential. What you learn from others can be helpful, but it should not be the determining factor of whether or not you pursue your opportunity.

A story about how an actual entrepreneur got into business will help drive this point home. Many years ago, John Morse, an MBA student, approached one of his professors about an idea to start an ice-cream company similar to Ben and Jerry's in the Pacific Northwest. John asked the professor for his advice

exhibit 12.2   Analyzing Your Fears

Fear/Doubt/Negative Belief	Response
I will be alone a lot as an enterpriser.	I will be involved with many people, including customers, suppliers, friends, and other supportive people.
	I can join a business networking association to make new contacts.
I don't have enough industry knowledge to succeed.	I'm a fast learner.
	I can do research online to acquire more information.
	I can subscribe to a trade journal for my industry.
I have no accounting skills.	I can buy books that will teach me the basics or take a class at the community college.
My business idea is not that good.	I can do a feasibility study that analyzes the market for my idea. With that information I can make an informed decision about how to improve my idea.

about whether to pursue this idea or not. The professor recommended looking for another opportunity for the following reason: If a company like Hagen-Das, which makes ice cream in New Jersey, can sell it successfully in the Pacific Northwest, why would there be any competitive advantage to starting an ice-cream company locally?

Based on this advice, Richard began researching many different business opportunities. After a year, he realized that he had spent 12 months *not* pursuing his dream of starting an ice-cream company. Upon graduating from the MBA program, he took a job as a bartender (so his days would be free), teamed up with his brother, and began looking for dairies in the Pacific Northwest to produce their ice cream. At the same time, they developed recipes for ice creams, contacted local grocery stores to carry their ice creams, and held many in-store samplings to get prospective customers to buy. After 12 dairies turned them down, the 13th said "yes." Their ice-cream company, Fratelli's, became a big success in the Pacific Northwest, and it eventually led to John becoming a frozen desert distributor and a major specialty food distributor. Although his professor had some insights into whether an ice-cream company might or might not work, he couldn't predict whether John could be successful as an ice-cream enterpriser.

The moral of this story is that even highly respected professors of entrepreneurship won't always be right. You will never know whether a particular opportunity will be successful unless you take the effort to find out whether customers will buy your product or service. All opinions, even from experts, are just opinions, not necessarily facts. Perhaps we are less likely to believe in ourselves as we start out, or because our own ideas are not yet as clear or developed as they will be in the end. Rather than give up too easily, we need to be persistent and focus our efforts into discovering, through trial and error, whether our vision for the enterprise is accurate or not.

Don't let advice from others about whether you should go forward with your idea discourage you. No one is likely to be as excited about your idea as you are. You'll always encounter people along the way who will "rain on your parade" and tell you that what you are thinking of doing isn't worth pursuing. Sometimes it is worth taking the next steps to test the advice. Even if the advice is true, the knowledge you've gained can help you modify or change your ideas so that you might be more successful with the revised opportunity.

Be persistent and pursue your ideas. Work at getting beyond other people's opinions. Probe for the specific reasons they believe your idea won't work. Like John Morse, seek evidence to test these opinions. If an advisor says that your opportunity won't work, ask "Why?" Suppose your consultant doesn't think customers would pay the price you have set for your service. Go out and talk to people to learn whether they will become customers and if they are willing to pay for the service at your price point. Treat opinions that people give you about your opportunities as hypotheses: think of other people's judgments about your opportunity as issues that you can test to determine if they are true or not. Opinions are not necessarily facts. Your goal is always to generate evidence. (This is the purpose of doing the feasibility study.)

Exhibit 12.3 provides suggestions for overcoming your fears.

exhibit 12.3 | **Overcoming Your Fears**

- Look for experiences in your life where you have had encouragement. Who offered you compliments along the way? When, and what did people say that you were affirmed for?

- If you think you might be a "great imposter," study how others "play" their roles as enterprisers. As you watch and interview other entrepreneurs, how do they "play" out their role? What kinds of "performances" have you seen other enterprisers play?

- Do you have to be "perfect" in all that you do? Identify what you consider perfection to be for the kind of enterprise that you want. What will it take for you to accomplish this? Can perfection, at this point, be achieved? Probably not. Then, take each part of your perfect enterprise, and ask yourself what you might settle for, today, in terms of what you could achieve. Much as in the strategy of "small wins" in Chapter 3, identify what small achievements you can accomplish now that would move you further down the road to achieving your goals.

- Identify all of the people from whom you seek approval: parents, other family members, friends, teachers, etc. Explore how these individuals support your progress toward achieving your goals. Do they offer positive and supportive insights that help you move forward with your goals, or do some give you negative and critical feedback that makes you feel that you can't move forward at all? While every plan may have problems, the solution to most plans is not inaction or negativity. If you have friends and others around you who are not providing you with support and help, consider whether the time and energy you devote to maintaining these relationships will help you achieve your goals. Instead, find people who want to help you be successful and are supportive when you pursue your dreams.

12.4 The Mind-set for Change

Now let's turn our attention to changing our thinking and our actions. The insights we'll provide in this section will help you take full advantage of the new possibilities that you'll encounter on your journey as enterprisers.[4]

First, it is important to realize that our current situations are "invented." We take for granted the facts of the situation we are in and often don't think very consciously about what those facts are—and whether they are actually true. To underscore this concept, ask yourself this question, which comes from *The Art of Possibility* by Zander and Zander:[5]

> *What assumption am I making,*
> *That I'm not aware I'm making,*
> *That gives me what I see?*

When you have an answer to that question, think about this one:

> *What might I now invent,*
> *That I haven't yet invented,*
> *That would give me other choices?*

What this exercise does is shift the framework of assumptions about your situation and challenge you to speculate about other choices for yourself. For example, what assumptions have you made about the people you've contacted regarding the creation of your enterprise? When you meet people with businesses that might be similar to the one you would like to own, do you think of them as competitors—or as people who might also be colleagues and friends who want you to succeed in developing your dreams?

In the restaurant industry, research shows that many of the founders and owners of restaurants know each other, often have worked for other restaurants, and help each other out. Restaurant owners define their dining business in terms of getting customers to eat more meals out. As the number of restaurants increases, patrons have more choices to eat out rather than at home. Rather than considering that new restaurants mean *less* business for existing restaurants, restaurateurs see them as *expanding* the overall market. What assumptions, then, are you making about your competition? Do you view them as helpful? If you think about your competition in this way, how will you act toward them? Will your behaviors be different than if you thought of your competition in only negative terms?

Not everyone agrees with this approach. In his book *Only the Paranoid Survive,* Andy Grove, former chairman of Intel Corp., suggests that to be competitive we must assume that there is always a competitor out there who is seeking to destroy your business. If you can't identify this competitor, it just means that the competitor is so crafty that you'll be even more surprised and unprepared when this competitor surfaces. Consider the differences between these two views of competition and the way each affects how you would deal with your competitors. Our perceptions color our worldview. What we look for, we find. For example, if we think that the world is full of cheaters, then we tend to see a lot of cheaters—and we are more likely to feel cheated. Awareness of the kind of world we invent, then, can prevent negativism from derailing our efforts.

Next, we can begin to "invent the possible." We tend to think about the limitations of a particular situation as the "givens" of that situation. If we assume that we have a limit on the number of customers, ideas, and resources, then we won't be as open to seeing the many additional options available to us.

During the feasibility and business planning process, we often get stuck analyzing what we see as "already there"—how our customers currently buy products and services, and how our competitors currently meet these customer needs. When we think about the givens and apply the metrics that others use for their success, we often restrict ourselves and fail to consider other ways of being successful.

For example, let's look at the retail industry. For many years, enterprisers focused on selling goods and services to customers in a store. Then they thought of different ways to connect with customers: mail-order catalogues, direct mail, websites, telephone orders, television shopping networks. New businesses arose from these new methods of reaching customers, many of which are now quite large. The bottom line is basic: Things may be one way now—but they don't have to stay that way!

Making Changes

Numerous strategies can help change your mind-set. We'll get you started by describing several approaches, from doing "A" work to living your passion. You can choose the methods that suit you best. Doing these activities can "jumpstart" your thinking about how to pursue your dreams in a new way and give you new ways to think about a situation. When we pursue new opportunities, it's very easy to get stuck in our old ways of thinking, because they are our only frame of reference. These creative approaches will encourage you to think outside the box and prevent falling back on old patterns.

Doing "A" Work

Assume that everyone around you wants to do "A" work. By giving an "A" to people at the outset of your interactions with them, you send a very positive message about your expectations. Doing so enables them to aspire higher and accomplish more. As Zander and Zander explain, "This A is not an expectation to live up to, but a possibility to live into."[6] They suggest performing a simple exercise to reinforce the "A"-work mind-set: Tell yourself and others that you/ they will get "A"s for *future* work—but you/they must write a letter *now*, and date it *after* completing the work. The letter begins, "I received an A because..."

Karl Weick describes this kind of writing as the "future perfect" tense.[7] We are writing about a future moment, something that has already been accomplished. If we can project ourselves into the future and then look back on the events of the "past," the actual future, in some respects, is less uncertain or frightening. Because we've already lived it in our imagination, we have less anxiety about acting to create the future. We have some idea of what can happen. Giving one's self and others "A"s helps relax us about whether we have the ability to achieve an "A." We won't have as much anxiety because we can project ourselves into the future and see that we've been able to accomplish what we believed we could. Basically, if you can't see yourself as a winner, it's unlikely that you will become a winner.

You Are the Solution

As we indicated in earlier chapters, opportunities exist because there are individuals (customers) who have problems that need to be solved. Opportunities specify the benefits of solving these problems. When we think of ourselves as part of the solution, we put ourselves in a position to create benefits for others: If I believe that I can make a contribution, I'll think and act in ways to make that contribution. With this strategy, we create a mind-set to take action. If we don't think we will make a difference, we won't take any actions to make a difference, and this negative mind-set becomes a self-fulfilling prophecy.

Lighten Up

An important way to change your mind-set is Zander and Zander's rule number 6: "Don't take yourself so ... seriously."[8] This viewpoint is somewhat similar to the "give yourself an A" lesson. Taking ourselves too seriously increases our anxiety about whether we can control the situation and gets in the way of accomplishing our goals. Once again, a sports example makes this very clear. When you think too much about whether you will make a particular basketball shot, if you get overly anxious about it, you are more likely to miss the basket. When you relax and don't worry as much about the situation, you will probably make the shot.

Being Present

Another way to improve your mind-set is to be in the present. This does not mean resigning yourself to the "things are as they are" mind-set, ignoring negative feelings, or pretending to like something you can't stand. Rather, it means "being present without resistance; being present to what is happening and present to your reactions, no matter how intense." We start from what is, not from what should be.⁹ We get stuck by thinking too much about "what should be," because the "should" is filled with expectations and judgments about our situation. Here are several ways to be in the present:

- Clearing "shoulds"

- Closing the exits: escape, denial, and blame

- Clearing judgments

- Distinguishing physical from conceptual reality

Often our expectations of what we think *should* happen get in the way of actually seeing what *has* happened and what *is* happening. To be open to new possibilities, we need to be aware of the present. One of the things that most people fear is failure. We don't like to admit that things are not working out the way we planned. We don't like it when we make a wrong turn, get lost, are late, make mistakes, or lose money.

Think about a situation where you found it difficult to admit that you were lost even though you didn't have a clue where you were. Because you didn't want to admit that you were lost, you continued in the same direction, and got even more lost! You would only ask for directions if you were lost. People who aren't lost don't ask for directions because they know where they are.

But the first step to finding your way is admitting that you are lost. Once you do that, you stop blaming yourself (well, I got lost because I wasn't paying attention, I didn't get a map beforehand, and so on), and can move ahead to make changes. Basically, we can't change directions in our lives if we don't admit that we might not be on the right path to begin with.

By actually paying attention to what is occurring in the situation, we increase our awareness of the possibilities that might come our way. Suppose you are unhappy that no one you have contacted has been willing to invest in the business. That might be a clue that the business model is incorrect or that others can't see clearly how this business will make money. Perhaps you need to rethink what you are going to do, and why. Or maybe the lesson is that you can develop the enterprise in another way, without investors, and that the business itself might be better operated without outside funding. So rather than blaming the investors who turned you down for not seeing the potential of your opportunity, consider *why* they didn't invest. Pay attention! We can learn to be more mindful and in doing so, open ourselves up to new and different ideas.

Passion Lights Sparks

Do you believe in what you are doing? When you do, you bring a sense of passion to your tasks. If you don't believe in your future, in your opportunities, you are unlikely to convince others to believe in you, and it becomes very difficult to accomplish what you need to do.

To become passionate, you must first notice where you are holding back—and let go. Then you can participate more fully in the activity you want to do. Suppose the business that you want to start involves consulting with retailers about how to provide their sales staff with a more customer-focused orientation. As we discussed earlier in the chapter, your fears might be stopping you from pitching this idea passionately to retail store owners: "Maybe store owners won't think I have the experience necessary to pay me to improve their customer service. Maybe I'm an imposter and not really a consultant." But in fact, nothing stops you from being passionate about providing this consulting service and having clients pay you for these services. When we authentically communicate to others what we love, other people can see that passion, and they respond to it. When you believe in yourself, others will believe in you, too. If you don't believe in yourself, others can see that hesitancy as well, and they won't get involved, say "yes," or become your customers.

Passion is infectious. When you are passionate about your enterprising activities, you generate sparks so that others see the possibilities and become eager to join you. Passion and excitement breed more of the same, so light a spark within yourself and among your friends and colleagues.

Frameworks for Possibility

New thinking creates frameworks for possibility. As we have mentioned many times throughout this book, the first step in making your dreams real is expressing a vision, which in turn provides real power to achieving that dream. To have a vision is to see something special that is not bounded by time, place, audience, or product. It is not about the right or wrong way to do things but is rather a "long line of possibility."[10] The process of enterprising, then, is more like a journey rather than the actual destination. As you work to see the future of your dreams and to make them real, you become an adventurer taking steps along the way, day to day.

What do you see in your vision of your future enterprise? Can you describe it so that others can see your vision as well? Framing your vision involves several steps, such as seeing your vision in the realm of possibility, distinguishing what is on track from what is off track, and staying focused on what moves you toward your goals.[11] What you can see of your vision now can help you and others move forward. Your vision provides direction, but it is not necessarily the end goal of the process. As you move forward, you see new things on the horizon, and new possibilities will likely be open to you—if you are open to them.

One final note: The fundamental process of enterprising, of identifying and pursuing opportunities, involves other people. The most basic ideas require enterprisers to pay attention to customers (others) to recognize and meet their needs. Enterprising, then, is not just about oneself; it requires that you accomplish something that is of value to someone else. In a broad sense, successful enterprising is more about *we* than about *me*. The story of Muhammad Yunus and Grameen Bank, "Making a World of Difference," offers an excellent example of an enterprise that focuses on the *we* and making a change.

enterprising ethics

Making a World of Difference

When he began making very small loans for income-generating activities to individuals or groups in his native Bangladesh, Muhammad Yunus did not expect to revolutionize traditional financial norms. His efforts to break the cycle of poverty in rural Bangladesh, however, have had a major impact on the world. In 2006, he and Grameen Bank, which he founded to provide these loans, shared the 2006 Nobel Peace Prize.

After studying in the United States, Yunus returned to Bangladesh to chair the economics department at the University of Chittagong. As he explained in his Nobel Peace Prize acceptance speech, he "found it difficult to teach elegant theories of economics in the university classroom, in the backdrop of a terrible famine in Bangladesh. Suddenly, I felt the emptiness of those theories in the face of crushing hunger and poverty." Observing that unscrupulous lenders took advantage of the poor and charged such exorbitant interest that borrowers couldn't pay off their debts, he saw a way to help.

In 1976 he personally loaned $27 to 42 villagers to pay off their debts. Their joy at his gesture convinced him that these small loans could be good business—and also provide a way to make the villagers self-reliant. He continued making small loans to other villagers for activities such as making crafts or buying farm animals. He required no collateral and charged no interest but instead based the loans on personal trust. All the villagers repaid their loans on time, so Yunus began lending in other villages and then took his program to more districts. Unable to find regular banks that agreed with his belief in the creditworthiness of the poor, he established Grameen Bank in 1983 to expand the program throughout Bangladesh.

Since then Grameen Bank has developed into a profitable and self-financing institution. The largest bank serving the poor, it lends about $800 million each year, in amounts averaging $100 per loan, to 7 million borrowers. By 2006 it had lent close to $6 billion in total, and an astounding 99 percent

had been repaid. The depositors own 94 percent of the bank, and the Government of Bangladesh owns the remaining 6 percent. In addition to micro-loans for enterprise, Grameen Bank also provides no-collateral loans for housing and education, along with savings, pension funds, and insurance products. It charges interest of up to 20 percent to cover the high costs of administration for so many small loans.

The principles on which Yunus founded Grameen Bank run counter to traditional banking concepts. It lends funds to poor Bangladeshis based only on "mutual trust, accountability, participation, and creativity." As Yunus explains, "Lend the poor money in amounts which suit them, teach them a few sound financial principles, and they manage on their own."

At the heart of his groundbreaking idea is the idea that micro-credit can break the cycle of poverty and raise living standards by promoting entrepreneurship and recognizing potential. "Poverty is a denial of human rights, and this is not natural," says Yunus. "The current institutional and societal set ups fail to enable people to discover creativity, which remains buried in them. Poverty needs to be addressed by providing bank credit. The poor are denied access to credit and this is a global phenomenon. Two-thirds of the world population is being rejected access to credit by conventional bankers. They are often cited as not creditworthy. It's now time for bankers to turn the wheel and position themselves as people-worthy." With micro-credit, people gain control of their lives and future well-being. Grameen's high repayment rates prove that Yunus' trust was not misplaced.

Yunus also broke with tradition by focusing his attention on women, who account for about 97 percent of Grameen's borrowers. Most banks in developing countries lend only to men. "We found giving loans to women always brought more benefits to the family," he says. Women spend on food and clothes for their families, while men are more likely to spend on themselves. Grameen's loans to women have had a dramatic impact on Bangladesh society. Once they can feed their families, the women send the children to school, creating a better-educated next generation. Grameen encouraged this by establishing a scholarship program.

Other bank programs creatively expand the micro-credit concept. For example, Grameen's telephone lady project gave women funds to buy cell phones to sell in their villages. The women gained both a business opportunity and a desirable occupation, and the villagers received access to phone service that was previously not available. Today 300,000 women sell Grameen's phone services to 10 million subscribers. Grameen's Struggling Beggars program provides loans to the poorest Bangladeshis and arranges credit to buy items for resale. The goal is to move them from begging to business activities.

As word of Yunus' success with micro-credit spread, other countries began to follow his lead. Today about 100 nations have micro-credit programs modeled on Grameen. Individuals have also been inspired by Yunus' example to support programs such as Yunus' Grameen Foundation, which provides guarantees to banks for micro-loans. The Michael and Susan Dell Foundation, Google. org, and the Bill and Melinda Gates Foundation are among the charitable organizations to set up microfinance programs.

Others have chosen a different route for their efforts to help the poor. They believe they can fund social impact businesses and also make a profit. Acción International, a network of Latin-American institutions, was one of the first for-profit ventures. Formed in the 1990s, its goal was to commercialize microfinance and gain access to capital markets to raise funds. Today Acción's partners cover the globe and include Bolivia's BancoSol, Mexico's Financiera Compartamos, and Ghana's Ecobank.

Pierre Omidyar, founder of eBay, also believes in microfinance. "It's a self-sustaining, profitable model, which opens the door to reaching large numbers of people who need to be reached by this tool of access to capital," he says. He established the Omidyar Network to foster "individual self-empowerment on a global scale" by commercializing microfinance—a term he prefers over *micro-credit*. (This contrasts with Yunus' primary mission of eliminating poverty.) The network makes for-profit investments and charitable donations. In 2005, he gave $100 million to Tufts University to create the Omidyar-Tufts Microfinance Fund (for international microfinance initiatives). Omidyar's intent is to show other institutional investors that microfinance is a viable investment. As loans are repaid with interest, the funds can be lent to new borrowers. In ten years, he estimates that the $100 million could grow to reach $1 billion. Citigroup also set up a microfinance business division in 2005.

Yunus takes issue with the for-profit model. While he recognizes that these programs also help the poor, he maintains that profit maximization is an inappropriate goal for organizations that make micro-credit loans.

Discussion Questions

1. How did Muhammad Yunus get the idea to start a bank that would lend money to the extremely poor? Do you believe in Yunus' view that poverty can be eliminated through social business initiatives? Why, or why not?

2. What entrepreneurial characteristics does it take to start and grow an enterprise that can affect so many millions of people?

3. What are the kinds of business models that are used to create a sustainable enterprise that loans money to the extremely poor?

4. How does Muhammad Yunus "face his fears" in the creation of Grameen Bank? What could have gone wrong and how might Yunus have dealt with these fears? How does Muhammad Yunus demonstrate a "mind-set for change?"

5. What are the advantages of a "for-profit" business that would make money from lending to the extremely poor? What are the

(continued)

disadvantages? Is making money from lending to the extremely poor as a for-profit business morally right?

6. Robert Annibale, head of Citigroup's microfinance unit, believes that this sector is large enough to support multiple approaches such as for-profit initiatives, sustainable programs, and subsidies. Do you agree and why? Why was Citigroup interested in entering the microfinance sphere?

7. Visit the websites of Grameen Bank, http://www.grameen-info.org, and Citigroup's Microfinance unit, http://www.citigroup.com/citigroup/citizen/microfinance/index.htm. Using the sites' resources, including articles by Muhammad Yunis on Grameen's site, summarize the similarities and differences between the banks. Which approach do you support and why?

Sources: Based on Connie Bruck, "Millions for Millions," *New Yorker*, October 30, 2006, pp. 62–73; Riva Froymovich, "Maximizing Microfinance's Cachet," *Investment News*, January 15, 2007, p. 6; Grameen Bank website, http://www.grameen-info.org (February 24, 2007); Professor Ole Danbolt Mjøs, Presentation Speech, Nobel Peace Prize, December 10, 2006, http://www.nobelprize.org; "The Nobel Peace Prize for 2006," press release, October 13, 2006, http://www.nobelprize.org; Michelle Yvonne Szpara, Iftikhar Ahmad, and Patricia Velde Pederson, "Nobel Peace Laureate Muhammad Yunus: A Banker Who Believes Credit Is a Human Right," *Social Education*, January–February 2007, p. 9+; and Muhammad Yunus, Nobel Lecture, Nobel Peace Prize, December 10, 2006, http://www.nobelprize.org.

12.5 The Balanced Life

Thinking about actually pursuing your possibilities can be energizing. On the other hand, the scope and depth of all these possibilities can be overwhelming. How can you be successful at filling many roles: enterpriser, spouse, parent, citizen? Can you really have it all when your dreams seem to be bigger than life?

What you are trying to do is to satisfy four different goals: achievement, significance, legacy, and happiness. But you cannot maximize all four. You could probably get what you want—but do you really want what you get? Yes, you could achieve great things in your enterprise, but at what cost? Perhaps your business success would come only at the expense of your personal happiness. For example, many enterprisers run into marital difficulties as they devote more and more hours to growing their businesses. To lead a personally successful life, you must first determine your own priorities.[12] Start by asking some basic questions about your efforts:

- *Achievement: Is this challenging?* Will the goals you intend to accomplish engage all your capabilities? Are you challenged to learn new things, for example? Success often includes stretching our knowledge, skills, and abilities in new ways. We need to set challenging goals (as we discussed in Chapter 3), and we need to achieve them.

- *Significance: Will this make a difference in the world?* We view our actions as successful when they make a difference to other people. It is important to consider what others care about and to engage in activities that meet others' needs and wants.

- *Legacy: Will this be enduring?* We all want to engage in activities that will have a lasting effect in the world. We want to know that our efforts will have an impact beyond the present moment.

- *Happiness: Is this enjoyable to you?* Many tasks may be valuable to others, challenging to you, and endure into the future. But will engaging in those activities actually make you happy or satisfied? What you are doing may not be enjoyable to you. If not, then you need to ask yourself: Why am I doing this activity if it really doesn't give me much personal satisfaction?

Given that we can't maximize all four goals simultaneously, how can we address all four issues to some degree of satisfaction? Begin by looking at how activities involved with work, family, self, and community might satisfy aspects of those four broad measures of success. For achievement, what challenges have you mastered at work, with your family, for yourself, and for your community? Using a chart like the one in Exhibit 12.4, list activities that made a difference in each of these areas. When you engage in this exercise, you typically discover that you have placed more emphasis on certain areas. This helps you identify what you would like to achieve in each of the four areas of success and in each of the four areas of work, family, self, and community. What would you like to see in each of these areas next week, next month, next year, and in your life? Exhibit 12.4 shows what the charts might look like for a 29-year-old married sales representative at a sporting equipment manufacturer who wants to start a retail sporting goods business. What did your charts reveal?

As you focus on your achievements, you will begin to see overlaps in activities that meet several of these goals. For example, coaching the soccer team fills most of our sales representative's family-related goals. We often get stuck because we look only at one category with one measure of success. We may look for achievement only from our work, rather than seek it in other areas as well, for example in our family time and leisure pursuits. A legacy does not only come from big accomplishments.

A balanced life includes variety and involves many different measures of success across a range of categories. There is no one measure of success, and no one particular area where success can or must be achieved. This broad sense of success offers us a wider sense of who we are and what we can become.

The following lines by German author Johann Wolfgang von Goethe provide an excellent summary of this chapter's concepts. It describes the need to adopt an orientation toward action and realizing our dreams. Such action helps us to shape our environment into a reality that actually supports the development of those dreams. Will you accept its challenge and begin now?

> *Until one is committed, there is hesitancy,*
> *the chance to draw back, always ineffectiveness.*
> *Concerning all acts of initiative (and creation),*
> *there is one elementary truth the ignorance of which*
> *kills countless ideas and splendid plans:*
> *That the moment one definitely commits oneself,*

then providence moves too.
All sorts of things occur to help one that would
never otherwise have occurred.
A whole stream of events issues from the decision,
raising in one's favor all manner of unforeseen
incidents and meetings and material assistance,
which no man could have dreamed would have come his way.
Whatever you do or dream you can,
Begin,
Boldness has genius, power, and magic in it.
Begin it now.

exhibit 12.4   Achieving Your Goals

Current Activities

Goal	Work	Family	Self	Community
Achievement	Brought in three new customers	Coaching daughter's soccer team		One of the founders of youth soccer program
Significance	Contributed to department's quarterly sales goals	Spend additional time in fun activity		
Legacy		Teaching kids teamwork will help them develop skills		
Happiness	Like meeting new people	Enjoy working with kids		

Commitments to Reach Goals/Timeframe

Goal	Work	Family	Self	Community
Achievement	Attend any classes and workshops offered that add to knowledge of sporting goods industry		Take business classes at university extension program/ start next semester	Join Rotary, Chamber of Commerce, or other organizations to help build contact base/now
Significance			Gain knowledge to use in opening own business	
Legacy				
Happiness	Travel less	Spend more time at home		Make new friends

Enterprisers 12.6

Leading through Values

In 1987, Tom Pace started PaceButler Corporation to buy, refurbish, and resell computers—even though he knew nothing about computers. He had just left a short stint at a similar company because he disagreed with management's ethical practices, or lack thereof. "I don't always have to reinvent the wheel," he explains. "Someone else has already invented the wheel. I just took it under my own wing and took action from there. ... I saw a business model that I thought would really work. I got a legal pad and I wrote out a business plan. That was it."

With $62.53 in his bank account, courage, and integrity, he set out to build his company. Banks would not loan him money, so he scraped together $11,000 in seed capital from private sources to fund his start-up.

The first few years were tough. "In 1990, the atmosphere at our company was terrible," Pace says. "We were on the edge of bankruptcy. That's what happens when you create a company with no knowledge and no capital and the business is changing fast. Nobody wanted to work there. Everybody was dissatisfied. I was dissatisfied. I wanted to give up."

Pace brought in Louis Gandra, a business consultant, to help refocus his efforts. They worked together to make sure that people and their skills matched their positions. Many were in the wrong jobs. "We reorganized from top to bottom," says Pace. "Secretaries became sales people. Some people left."

Gandra encouraged Pace to ask his employees to write an "atmosphere statement" that describes what people experience when they come into the company. The statement his employees prepared in 1990 is still in place today and emphasizes providing "a positive, successful, and healthy atmosphere" that motivates "by enthusiasm, knowledge, and skill" in "an atmosphere that nurtures confidence, love, and power—a climate that produces creative ideas and plans that allow us to easily reach our objectives, goals, and values." Through this value system, employees can accomplish and achieve "excellence in all areas of our lives. ... We have an abundance of finances, health, relationships, and family life. We speak the language of faith."

With that values orientation in place, Pace wrote a mission statement, company values, and company goals. The mission statement focuses on quality and customer service: "PaceButler Corporation contributes to the local and worldwide community by providing top quality products and service. We are dedicated to customer satisfaction through constant improvement of systems and procedures. When our customers profit, we profit, resulting in a win/win situation."

With these employee-centric foundations in place, Pace was ready to move forward. By 1992, PaceButler had grown to 30 employees and had sales of $3.5 million. In 1999, the company received the Oklahoma Quality Award and Tom Pace won the model CEO award from the Council of Growing Companies. The company's growth continued, and by 2002 Pace/Butler had 65 employees, a national client base, and sales of $22 million.

Not bad for a kid who got lousy grades and who didn't graduate from college. What Pace had, however, was a belief in himself that came after many difficult years. "I've had over 30 jobs. A friend of mine said, 'No wonder you had to start your own business.' I said, 'Why?' He said, 'No one would hire you with that kind of background.'"

Pace has a commitment to his employees and nurturing their success. "We're all capable of success if we choose to be successful and if we have the right knowledge," Pace says. "The more we use our resources, the stronger the resources get."

Today Pace asks any job applicant who considers coming to work at PaceButler to review the

(continued)

atmosphere statement, mission statement, values, and goals. The idea is to see how close the alignment is between the person and the company principles. If the alignment isn't there, PaceButler is probably not going to be a good fit for that person.

Encouraging positive attitudes, being receptive to new ideas, and remaining passionate about his business has helped PaceButler survive. Pace also recognizes the relationship between success and taking action. In 2002, Pace added a new line of business, purchasing and refurbishing old cell phones, to his major one of selling used business technology systems worldwide. Because Pace expects the best from his employees, he often gets it. "In a corporate society, we need to raise the level of mutual trust and respect. Success breeds success. ... It's very, very important to be around other people who share the same values and the same goals and that we can reinforce one another. ... It's very easy to say, 'It's not going to work out,' and to give up."

Early in 2003, however, he came close to giving up. Pace had to lay off 55 workers—85 percent of his staff—because of a major computer problem. Pace took full responsibility for the technical

glitches, citing "bad business decisions that Tom Pace made in regards to accounting software, which led to the problem of inventory control and cash management," he explained. Instead of welcoming employees to work, he helped them find new jobs. He sold the company's office building and cut back operations to focus on cell phones. Today the company is still in business, with its values intact.

Discussion Questions

1. How did values drive the building and structuring of Tom Pace's business?

2. What values were important to Tom Pace in turning the company around in 1990? Were they congruent with his actions then and in later years? Explain your answer.

3. Tom Pace has asked for your help in telling his story. Make suggestions of how he should frame his life and business experiences.

4. What characteristics of entrepreneurial success does Pace exhibit? Cite examples from the case that relate to the chapter material.

Sources: Adapted with permission from the video "Leading through Values," Small Business School, the series on PBS, and at http://SmallBusinessSchool.com; Elizabeth Camacho, "Edmond, Okla., Computer Resale Firm Forced to Lay Off 55 Due to Software Error," *Daily Oklahoman*, January 29, 2003, http://www.dailyoklahoman.com; Sonya Colberg, "Bottomed-Out Businessman Nearer Top—Owner's Successful Present Imitates No Past Lessons," *Daily Oklahoman*, October 14, 2001, http://www.pacebutler.com. (November 25, 2005); Jon Denton, "Used Computer Dealer Thrives," *Daily Oklahoman*, October 3, 1996, http://www.pacebutler.com. (November 25, 2005); and Paula Burkes Erickson, "Oklahoma City-Area Companies Escape Perils of Hard Times," *Daily Oklahoman*, November 28, 2003, http://www.dailyoklahoman.com.

12.7 Summary

1. After identifying many different business opportunities, enterprisers must reevaluate their goals. Making the transition from dreams to reality can be difficult. It requires a shift in focus. Not only must enterprisers take action, they must also take into account their values: not just the *how,* but also the *why.* Their actions and commitments—choices that bind them to a future course of action—should be congruent with these goals and values. It's important not to underestimate the many commitments enterprisers make when developing a new venture.

2. To pinpoint your goals and values, take the time to make written lists and charts of what is important to you. Once you have a picture of what is

important to you, look at the commitments that relate to each item. You'll quickly see whether your commitments are congruent with your goals and values. If not, analyze the gaps and make changes that bring the two closer together and eliminate mismatches. Before taking on new commitments, cut back on others that are not in line with your goals and values.

3. A critical step in becoming a successful enterpriser is picturing yourself in such a role. Your personal story and how you tell it play an important role in how you perceive yourself. Recasting your story to focus on how you will develop your business opportunity and the steps you'll take to overcome any obstacles will highlight the characteristics that contribute to your future success.

4. Telling the story of your entrepreneurial success is difficult because you are still in the middle of the plot. Imagine yourself having succeeded and tell a story that supports your accomplishments. The story should be a coherent description of how and why you will create your business that emphasizes how your past experiences contribute to your ability to reach your business goals.

5. Tell your entrepreneurial story to others and ask for feedback. This will help you revise and fine-tune it—and at the same time build your network of contacts. The story development process will also help you believe in yourself more strongly and enhance your confidence.

6. It's normal to wonder whether you have the ability to develop your business opportunity and to fear that you lack the requisite skills to make it happen. No one ever has all the skills and knowledge at hand when they start a business. Don't let your fears stop you from acting like an enterpriser. Unless you take the first steps and try, you will never be able to improve.

7. By working at developing an enterprise, you become an enterpriser. Accept that you will have to overcome your fears and doubts, and avoid placing unrealistic expectations on yourself. Rather than seeking perfection, focus on meeting customers' needs and look for signs of improvement as you work at being an enterpriser.

8. Advice from others, especially if they have experience in your field, can be helpful. But even the experts can be wrong, so take the time to ask questions, evaluate the advice, and do your own research and feasibility analysis. Your persistence in generating evidence will pay off.

9. Shift your focus from the limitations of a particular situation to the possibilities it presents. Don't let a restrictive mind-set and assumptions that may no longer hold true hinder your future success. Instead of getting bogged down in old ways of thinking, look for ways to "invent the possible." Change can be good! When you expect the best from those around you, they are likely to accomplish more. Believing in your ability to solve problems and not worrying about a situation will help you take actions with positive results. Don't get stuck in the "what should be" mentality, which just gets in the way of being receptive to

new possibilities. Finally, believe in what you are doing and let your passion show. Use your vision of a successful enterprise as a framework for moving forward.

10. One of the challenges of being an enterpriser is trying to satisfy four different goals: achievement, significance, legacy, and happiness. It's impossible to maximize all four at the same time. You should set priorities and seek success in many arenas: work, family, self, and community.

Review Questions

1. What are some of the barriers that make it difficult for enterprisers to turn dreams into reality?

2. Why should enterprisers focus on goals and values as they prepare to start their new ventures?

3. Discuss the importance of achieving congruence between actions and goals. Choose one of your goals and give examples of actions that reflect the goal and some that are out of step with the goal.

4. What are commitments, and why should commitments also match your goals and priorities in life? How can you take steps to eliminate mismatches?

5. What elements in the David and Goliath story make it a good model to use in developing your own story? How can a well-scripted story help you reframe how you see yourself?

6. Describe five ways to develop a strong story that will contribute to your entrepreneurial success.

7. How do fears hold us back from taking action? What can you do to change your thinking so that you overcome fears and doubts?

8. What are the advantages and disadvantages of seeking the opinions of experts in your chosen field? How should you use the information you gather?

9. Compare Zander and Zander's approach to assumptions with Grove's. With which do you agree and why?

10. Describe several ways to develop a positive mind-set. Give a specific example of how you would apply one of these methods.

11. Define the four principal goals that contribute to living a personally successful life. Which are most important to you now, and how are you satisfying them? What changes can you make in your life to achieve more satisfaction in one area?

Applying What You've Learned

1. How much personal time and energy does it take to start and manage your own enterprise? Develop a chart that lists your current activities including school, work, family, and personal interests, and how much time you allocate to them. Review your chart and determine how much time will you have each week to devote to enterprising.

2. Now create a similar chart that identifies the specific tasks you'll need to undertake to take the first steps toward developing your enterprise. Include time estimates for these tasks that show how much time you'll

need to spend each week and also the overall time frame. For example, you may wish to dedicate three to five hours a week to interviewing enterprisers and spend two months on this phase of the project.

3. Using the charts you created in Exercises 1 and 2, compare the free time you identified in Exercise 1 with the time you'll need for your enterprising activities. Do you have enough time to begin? If not, what changes can you make to free up time for business development?

4. Identify enterprisers that have the kind of life that you would like to emulate. Ask if you can spend a day "shadowing" two of these people to identify what activities they engage in throughout the day. How much of their time is devoted to aspects of their enterprise? What activities fill the day—for example, meetings with employees, suppliers, customers; administrative and operational matters; solving enterprise problems; talking on the phone; answering e-mails? How much time do these individuals have for their families, friends, and other activities? What are the major commitments that you see these enterprisers have made?

5. Interview the same two enterprisers you chose in Exercise 4 or different ones to learn experiences leading up to and during the development of their enterprises. Prepare summaries of their stories that include the five elements listed on page 385 to help refine their stories. Are there common elements among these stories? What lessons do you see from these stories that can help you write your own?

6. Write a hypothetical story about a successful enterpriser who started the type of business you are most interested in developing. How closely can you match your story to your ideal?

7. Which of the different types of fears mentioned in the chapter—being a great

imposter, expecting perfection, needing approval—apply to you? Create a chart like the sample in Exhibit 12.2, being as specific as possible about your self-doubts as they relate to your chosen business venture. Consider why and where these fears came from. Review it often to remind yourself of your talents to take action.

8. An important part of working on your fears is having the imagination to see yourself in a different way. Affirmations that describe who you will be can help you change your mind-set. For example, if your goal is to be a successful restaurateur, write out ten times: "I am a successful restaurateur!" and say this to yourself several times a day. Write out five affirmations that support your business goals that you will say to yourself each day for the next month.

9. Identify all of the areas in your life where you feel stuck, where you think you can't make any changes. What do you believe about these situations that makes you feel you are stuck? Imagine what it would be like if you were "unstuck." What about each of these situations has changed in your "unstuck" world? What would you now have to do to live in the "unstuck" world?

10. Imagine yourself five years from today. Now, look back and write out the story of the achievement of your goals and accomplishments during that time. What happened to you along the way? Write out your story as specifically as possible. Now consider using this story as your game plan for the next five years. You might also consider writing out your life story. Think of yourself 20 years from today. Now, look back and write out that story!

11. Write down all of the ways that you might be the solution to someone else's problems and issues. Consider whether your being the solution to any of these situations

might be the genesis for the development of your enterprise.

12. Identify all of the "shoulds" that you believe must happen in your life. Where do these "shoulds" come from? Are these "shoulds" that you believe are important, or are these "shoulds" other people have told you are important? Now, identify what "is" happening in your life. What aspects of your life are you happy with? What aspects of your life are you not? Compare the "shoulds" to the "is." How different are they?

Enterprisers on the Web

1. Need help setting goals? Go to TopAchievement.com, http://www.topachievement.com, and click on "7 Steps to Powerful Goals." Read the article and use it to create personal goals in the six areas listed in point 3. While still at TopAchievement.com, click on "Goal Setting Articles" and select three to read. How did they expand your knowledge of goal setting?

2. The Life Work Transitions website, http://lifeworktransitions.com, is another site with good exercises that will help you identify and refine your goals. Start at the Exercises page, http://lifeworktransitions.com/exercises/exercs.html, and do the three exercises for Chapter 4, Goal Setting. Did you come up with different goals than you did in Exercise 1?

3. The Life Work Transitions website, http://lifeworktransitions.com, also has activities that will help you tell your story. From the Exercises page, http://lifeworktransitions.com/exercises/exercs.html, do the Accomplishments Inventory to help you summarize your achievements and Guidelines for Your Spiritual Autobiography, which deals with values. What did these exercises reveal?

4. How committed are you to achieving your goals? Find out by taking the Perseverance Quotient quiz at TopAchievement.com, http://www.topachievement.com/persevere.html. What did you learn about yourself?

5. What are your values? Using a search engine like Google, Dogpile, Yahoo!, or Lycos, find two sites with questionnaires you can fill out. Then list your three top values. Break up into small groups to discuss your findings with classmates.

6. How satisfied are you with your life, and what would it take to make yourself happier? Explore the resources and questionnaires at the Authentic Happiness site, http://www.authentichappiness.com, to learn how to take a more positive approach to life. (You'll have to register to use the questionnaires; it's free.) What suggestions would be most useful to you?

End Notes

1. O. F. Collins and D. G. Moore. *The Enterprising Man* (East Lansing, MI: MSU Business Studies, Michigan State University, 1964), p. 160.

2. This section is based on material in Donal N. Sull and Dominic Houlder, "Do Your Commitments Match Your Convictions?" *Harvard Business Review*, January 2005, pp. 82–91.

3. This section is adapted from Herminia Ibarra and Kent Lineback, "What's Your Story?" *Harvard Business Review*, January 2005, pp. 65–71.

4. This section is based on R. S. Zander and
    B. Zander, *The Art of Possibility* (Boston, MA:
    Harvard Business School Press, 2000).

5. Ibid., p. 15.

6. Ibid., p. 26.

7. Karl E. Weick. *The Social Psychology of
    Organizing*, 2nd ed. (New York: Random House,
    1979).

8. Zander and Zander, *The Art of Possibility*, p. 79.

9. Ibid., pp. 100, 103.

10. Ibid., p. 170.

11. Ibid., p. 163.

12. Adapted from material in Laura Nash and
    Howard Stevenson, "Success that Lasts,"
    Harvard Business Review, February 2004,
    pp. 102–109.

Time Management

How Do You Manage Your Time?

How well do you manage your time? The quiz in Exhibit A.1 will give you more clues to how well you manage time.

Where Did the Day Go?

Before you determine how to use time better, you have to understand how you currently spend your time. This process starts with recording everything you do on a time log.[1] An easy way to track your time is on a chart that divides your day into 30-minute segments. Keep the log for at least two weeks, and longer if your work follows a monthly cycle. You may want to track your whole day, including personal time, or just focus on work-related activities. Armed with your detailed log, analyze how you spent your time.

- **Set up task categories**. Divide your tasks into relevant categories, such as commuting, staff meetings, client meetings, business phone calls/email, personal phone calls/email, writing proposals, personal errands, family time, and new business development. Add up the time spent for each category and calculate the percentage of time you spend on each task category. You will quickly see where your time went!

- **Classify categories into three or four broader groups**. These can relate to Covey's four quadrants (Exhibit 3.2, p. 69), or you may prefer to divide them into A-B-C groups; for example, A tasks: important and urgent/planning and development; B tasks: either important or urgent/ongoing projects; C tasks: routine tasks. Determine how much time you spend in each group. Studies indicate that most of us devote about 60 percent of our time to routine tasks (Quadrants 3 and 4), 25 percent to ongoing projects (Quadrant 1), and a mere 15 percent to planning and development (Quadrant 2). The "ideal" distribution is, in fact, the opposite, with 60 percent spent on activities that further your career or business or contribute to your personal growth, and only 15 percent on routine matters.

exhibit A.1   How Time-Worthy Are You?

Assessing Your Ability

The key of successful management is the possession of good time-management skills. Think about how well you manage your time by responding to the following statements, then mark the options that are closest to your experience. Be as honest as you can: If your answer is "never," mark Option 1; if your answer is "always," mark Option 4; and so on. Add your scores together, then refer to the Analysis to see how you scored. Use your answers to identify the areas that need the most improvement.

OPTIONS
1 Never
2 Occasionally
3 Frequently
4 Always

1 I arrive on time and prepared for meetings. [1] [2] [3] [4]

2 I ensure that a clock is visible in the room where meetings are held. [1] [2] [3] [4]

3 The meetings I organize achieve their purpose. [1] [2] [3] [4]

4 The meetings I organize finish on time. [1] [2] [3] [4]

5 I open my mail as soon as it arrives on my desk. [1] [2] [3] [4]

6 I skim any relevant newspaper and magazine articles. [1] [2] [3] [4]

7 I cross my name off the circulation list for magazines and journals I do not read. [1] [2] [3] [4]

8 I read my faxes on the day on which I receive them. [1] [2] [3] [4]

9 I am able to complete tasks without interruptions from colleagues. [1] [2] [3] [4]

10 I decide how many times I can be interrupted in a day. [1] [2] [3] [4]

11 I reserve certain hours for visits from colleagues. [1] [2] [3] [4]

12 I close my office door when I want to think strategically. [1] [2] [3] [4]

13 I tell telephone callers that I will return their calls, and I do so. [1] [2] [3] [4]

14 I limit the duration of my telephone calls. [1] [2] [3] [4]

15 I allow a colleague or secretary to screen my telephone calls. [1] [2] [3] [4]

16 I decide how many telephone calls I can deal with personally in a day. [1] [2] [3] [4]

(continued)

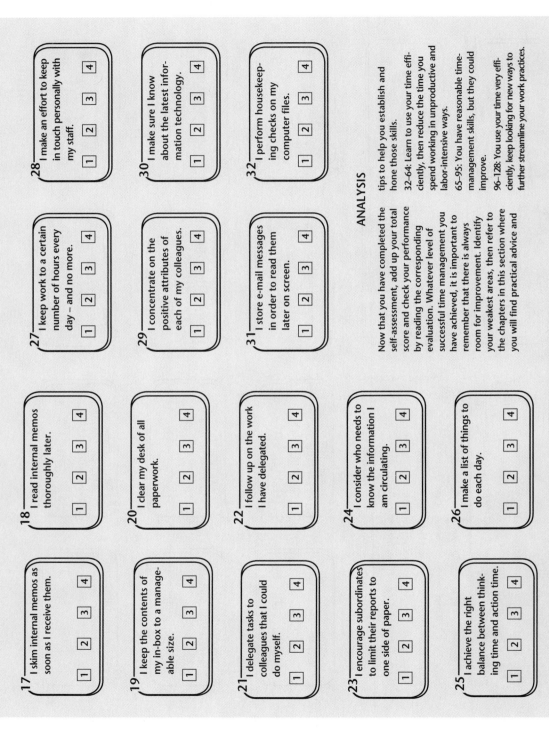

17 I skim internal memos as soon as I receive them.

1 ☐ 2 ☐ 3 ☐ 4 ☐

18 I read internal memos thoroughly later.

1 ☐ 2 ☐ 3 ☐ 4 ☐

28 I make an effort to keep in touch personally with my staff.

1 ☐ 2 ☐ 3 ☐ 4 ☐

19 I keep the contents of my in-box to a manageable size.

1 ☐ 2 ☐ 3 ☐ 4 ☐

20 I clear my desk of all paperwork.

1 ☐ 2 ☐ 3 ☐ 4 ☐

27 I keep work to a certain number of hours every day – and no more.

1 ☐ 2 ☐ 3 ☐ 4 ☐

30 I make sure I know about the latest information technology.

1 ☐ 2 ☐ 3 ☐ 4 ☐

21 I delegate tasks to colleagues that I could do myself.

1 ☐ 2 ☐ 3 ☐ 4 ☐

22 I follow up on the work I have delegated.

1 ☐ 2 ☐ 3 ☐ 4 ☐

29 I concentrate on the positive attributes of each of my colleagues.

1 ☐ 2 ☐ 3 ☐ 4 ☐

32 I perform housekeeping checks on my computer files.

1 ☐ 2 ☐ 3 ☐ 4 ☐

23 I encourage subordinates to limit their reports to one side of paper.

1 ☐ 2 ☐ 3 ☐ 4 ☐

24 I consider who needs to know the information I am circulating.

1 ☐ 2 ☐ 3 ☐ 4 ☐

31 I store e-mail messages in order to read them later on screen.

1 ☐ 2 ☐ 3 ☐ 4 ☐

25 I achieve the right balance between thinking time and action time.

1 ☐ 2 ☐ 3 ☐ 4 ☐

26 I make a list of things to do each day.

1 ☐ 2 ☐ 3 ☐ 4 ☐

ANALYSIS

Now that you have completed the self-assessment, add up your total score and check your performance by reading the corresponding evaluation. Whatever level of successful time management you have achieved, it is important to remember that there is always room for improvement. Identify your weakest areas, then refer to the chapters in this section where you will find practical advice and tips to help you establish and hone those skills.

32–64: Learn to use your time efficiently, then reduce the time you spend working in unproductive and labor-intensive ways.

65–95: You have reasonable time-management skills, but they could improve.

96–128: You use your time very efficiently, keep looking for new ways to further streamline your work practices.

Source: Robert Heller and Tim Hindle, *Essential Manager's Manual*, pp. 92–95, November 1998, DK Adult. Reproduced by permission of Dorting Kindersley Ltd.

- **Look for patterns**. Review your time logs in detail to analyze your current time usage compared to your ideal. Also note whether you finish tasks in the allocated time frame and when you do things during the day. If you have slow periods at the same time most days, schedule activities that require concentration and creativity in those periods. Organize your day so that your workflow is relatively consistent.

Time Management Strategies

Now that you've set goals, established priorities, and assessed how you use your time, you're ready to take control of your time. While we can't provide a complete time management course in this book, we can start you on the right path.

A Sharper Focus

Imagine that a genie has granted your wish for more hours in the day. Poof! Your day now has 27 hours and your time management problems are over. Unfortunately, having more hours isn't the answer. Your 27-hour-day time logs will probably show that you have continued to allocate your time to the same tasks, wasting even larger blocks of time.

It's not more time you need, but more effective use of what you already have. Don't confuse being busy with making progress. The key to effective time management is *focus*. To stay focused on what's important:

- *Consult your personal mission statement and goals often.* These should be the foundation of your weekly schedule and will keep you focused on activities that move you closer to your goals.

- *Make and use a weekly plan and a daily "to-do" list.* Label each task with its priority code (more on this in the next section).

- *Make appointments with yourself.* Schedule important tasks and *ignore interruptions* when you work on a project.

- *Just say no.* Otherwise you will take on more than you can accomplish. Ask yourself if the new task or responsibility is a better use of your time than what you're already doing.

- *Delegate.* You can't—and shouldn't—do it all yourself. Determine what you do best, and delegate everything else.

- *Set realistic time estimates.* Build in a cushion, because tasks usually take much more time than you expect. Keep track of how long you actually need for specific tasks, so the next time you can allocate an appropriate amount of time and won't get off schedule.

- *Build in time for yourself.* Your health and your productivity will suffer if you try to work 24/7. Breaks during your work day, whether a quick walk around the block or a trip to the gym, will keep you stay fresh. You also need time for family and personal interests, as well as planned vacations.

Your Weekly Plan

A weekly decision-making framework forms the basis of your time management plan.[2] Go back to your mission statement and goals and ask yourself, "What is the most important thing I could do in each role this week to have the greatest positive impact?" Then prepare a weekly schedule with daily to-do lists and time blocks—large, interchangeable chunks of time—for specific and important activities. Leave open time and be flexible. Crises will crop up, and you need time to deal with them. When you focus on your mission statement, roles, and key goals, you put the most important (Quadrant 2) goals first. Remember to *enter the most important tasks first*. Build your calendar around these activities, and *then* fit in the Quadrant 1 and 3 goals. Otherwise you will fritter away time on less important tasks.

Why take a weekly view, instead of going from your mission and goals to a daily view? When you focus on each day as a separate time unit, you tend to do what's most pressing and urgent—the crises become the priorities. This approach doesn't help you reach your goals. The weekly perspective allows you to connect the big picture to your daily activities and achieve a better balance in your life. It retains some immediacy but also places the activities in a larger context so that you do not lose sight of future goals.[3]

Many companies offer time management systems and diaries. Investigate several options to find the one that best serves your needs and style: a simple or a complete system; a page-a-day format or week-at-a-time; a personal digital assistant (PDA); or personal information manager (PIM) software. A $300 PDA is worthless if you haven't updated it for three weeks. Technophobes may find a more traditional paper-based planner easier to maintain. If you enjoy using the latest technology, the PDA is a good way to go. Exhibit A.2 lists several good time management resources.

---

exhibit A.2 | **Time Management Resources**

You'll find many good time management resources at your local bookstore. Here are a few websites and books to get you started.

- Day-Timer: **http://www.daytimer.com**. The Library page of this time management product company has a good selection of time management articles, productivity tips, and other time-related information.

- Franklin Covey: **http://www.franklincovey.com**. Another leading time management services company, it offers articles, learning tools, courses, and other time management resources.

- "Managing Time" in Robert Heller and Tim Hindle, *Essential Manager's Manual* (New York: DK Publishing, Inc., 1998), pp. 82–149: A comprehensive time management reference, including analyzing time and work patterns, using time planners, and practical tips to be more efficient in all aspects of your life.

- Stephen R. Covey, A. Roger Merrill, and Rebecca R. Merrill, *First Things First* (New York: Simon & Schuster, 1995).

Revisit your weekly schedule each day and update it as you complete tasks and begin new ones. You may want to review a day's activities at the end of the day, or first thing in the morning. Either way, identifying the Quadrant 1 and 2 activities will reinforce your priorities. Then assess your progress at the end of the week and update your progress toward reaching your goals. You may not achieve all your goals by the end of the week, but you will learn from the process where you went off course and can make changes.

The A List

As you prepare your weekly plan, you create your daily to-do lists, the five to ten items you want to accomplish during a particular day. Be realistic about what you can do in a day. Then assign each task a priority using the system you chose when grouping your tasks in your time log, and write this priority on the weekly plan. You may want to create a daily schedule that lists the highest priority tasks first. When assigning priorities, evaluate the task's payoff in terms of meeting your goals. Don't try to do all the high priority tasks first and then move down the list. You will get more done by spreading the tasks out and giving yourself a break from the most demanding tasks.

You should also chart your daily energy levels. Schedule the highest priority and most difficult tasks when you are at your physical and mental best, whether it's first thing in the morning or late afternoon. Work on strategic projects during your first peak period. Not only does that put you in a positive frame of mind, but you will also have accomplished something significant and feel good about moving your life forward. Build in the flexibility to modify your priorities and schedule when the situation changes. For example, the presentation to a new client moves down the list when the meeting is rescheduled for next week instead of tomorrow. Exhibit A.3 offers more tips for better time management.

Your reaction to reading all these suggestions for organizing your time may be, "I'm too busy to do all this planning!" However, the feeling that you are too busy to be productive is a clear indication that it's time to set priorities.

exhibit A.3   **Tips to Organize Your Time**

- **Schedule thinking and quiet time each day, and make sure you aren't interrupted.**
- **Follow through on task completion.**
- **Use different colors for each priority category.**
- **Estimate how long a task will take and then compare it to the actual time required to develop better estimates in the future.**
- **Delegate more effectively by defining the task's objectives and setting realistic deadlines.**
- **Break large projects into smaller tasks.**
- **Schedule specific times to answer phone calls and emails—and stick to them!**
- **Do a little each day on big projects—it will add up over time.**
- **Have a list of tasks to do when time unexpectedly frees up.**
- **At the end of the day, prioritize and schedule tasks for tomorrow.**

(continued)

- Don't get bogged down in "administrivia," those routine-task time hogs.
- Reduce clutter. An organized work space, a good filing system, and regular attention to maintaining order go a long way in improving time management.
- Before calling a meeting, consider other ways to accomplish the business matters.
- Plan meetings carefully in terms of who needs to attend. Develop an agenda with a time allocated to each topic.
- Reduce shopping time: Keep a list, combine errands, order online, have things picked up or delivered whenever possible, even if is more expensive. Time is money!
- Reduce drive time. Have appointments at your office rather than away if possible. Schedule off-site meetings at the beginning or end of the day.
- Give yourself time for family and leisure activities.

End Notes

1. Adapted from Robert Heller and Tim Hindle, "Analyzing Use of Time," *Essential Manager's Manual* (New York: DK Publishing, Inc., 1998), pp. 88–91.

2. Lori Ioannou, "Stephen Covey on Time Management," *FSB* (*Fortune Small Business*), June 1, 2002, p. 73.

3. Stephen R. Covey, A. Roger Merrill, and Rebecca R. Merrill, *First Things First* (New York: Simon & Schuster, 1995), pp. 154–156.

Feasibility Studies

Feasibility Study Format Guidelines

The following outline provides a framework to prepare a feasibility study for your proposed business concept.

Cover Page

Identify the "title" (name of the business) of your feasibility study.

Identify the names of the team members involved in the feasibility study.

Contact information (mailing address, phone number, and e-mail address).

Executive Summary

This is a summary of the entire feasibility study (in 250 words or less).

The Executive Summary should be no more than two pages long.

A well-written Executive Summary is less than a page.

Table of Contents

1. Feasibility Decision
2. The Business Model
3. Industry/Market Analyses
4. Product/Service Development Plan

5. Management Team and Organization

6. Financial Plan

7. Timeline to Launch/Implementation Risk

8. Sources of Information and Appendixes

Feasibility Decision

Briefly describe the business you are considering.

Describe the conditions under which you are willing to go forward.

Briefly describe the major risks (customers, benefits, channel, and implementation) that are involved and how these risks might be overcome (or not).

Indicate a YES or a NO about your decision to pursue your feasibility project in the future and what major contingencies influence this decision.

The Business Model

What is the business?

Describe the value proposition of the business: the specific benefits/features that you will offer through specific channels to specific customers.

Describe your customers in detail.

Why were these customers chosen versus others?

What are the revenue sources from these customers?

Describe the benefits provided to your customers in detail.

Why were these benefits chosen versus others?

What are the cost drivers for providing these benefits?

Describe the distribution channel in detail.

Why was this channel (or channels) chosen versus others?

What are the cost drivers for using these channels?

How will this business make money?

Briefly provide an overview of investment size (maximum financing needs, and when there will be positive cash flow and cash breakeven)

What are the critical success factors for this business?

Describe, in detail, the major risks in this business and how you plan to address them. Point to other sections of the feasibility study where these risks are identified and dealt with.

Industry/Market Analyses

Describe the industry/competition.

What are the business models that exist in the industry you will be competing in? (Identify business models of specific rivals.)

What are the business models of the substitutes of your business?

If there are no businesses similar to your business, then provide business models of businesses that would be analogous to your business model.

Identify how and why each of these businesses makes money.

Provide a competitive grid highlighting key success attributes and weaknesses among all players (rivals and substitutes).

Describe the market and customers.

What are the various types of customers in this industry?

Provide a customer profile.

Why were these customers chosen versus others?

Provide a customer grid highlighting the key attributes of each of the customer segments.

Describe the distribution channels.

Describe the value chains of competitors, substitutes, and analogues.

Identify specific costs and revenues at each point in the value chain.

Show your value chain and compare and contrast this value chain to the others.

Initial sales plan.

How will the first customers buy your product/service?

Provide a timeline for the selling cycle.

When will cash from your first customers be received?

Product/Service Development Plan

Describe the features of your product/service that meet the benefits provided to your customers.

What is the current status of product/service development?

Identify the specific tasks that will need to be accomplished (and when) in order for your product/service to be ready for sale.

Provide a specific timeline of critical events in product/service development (identify specific resources, people involved, activities).

Management Team and Organization

Who will be involved in this business and why?

What are the qualifications of the founding team members and how do their skills and abilities match the needs of the business?

What are the critical skills and abilities needed to start and run the proposed business?

Who has these critical skills and abilities on the founding team?

If the founding team does not have these critical skills and abilities, how will other people be involved (employees, professional advisors, board of directors, independent contracts)?

Financial Plan

What are the key assumptions (based on information provided in other sections of the plan) for how and why this business will make money?

What kinds of resources will be needed for this business (and when will they be needed)?

Provide a pro-forma income statement (one to three years).

Identify critical financial categories of the business only.

Provide footnotes for each financial category and identify the assumptions used to develop the figures in the financial estimates.

Provide a break-even analysis.

When will the business reach positive cash flow?

How much income will this business likely provide (and when) and is this level of income sufficient for the time and resources involved?

Timeline to Launch/Implementation Risk

What needs to be accomplished (and when) in order to get the business up and running?

What tasks incur the most risk of not getting accomplished and how will these risks be managed?

Sources of Information and Appendixes

Provide endnotes and a bibliography of the sources of the information used to support your idea.

Provide support for the earlier sections of the feasibility study (resumes, market surveys, questionnaires, customer lists, quotes, and bids for critical services or equipment needed).

Business Plans

Business Plan Outline

Cover Page

1. Your name
2. Company name
3. Address
4. Phone number
5. Month and year plan issued
6. Copy number
7. Statement of plan's confidentiality

Executive Summary

A one- to two-page summary of the Business Plan. It should provide an overview of the entire business plan and describe the plan's highlights and significant details. Most readers will only read the Executive Summary. A good Executive Summary should be able to serve as a stand-alone document. It should be short, but comprehensive and thorough.

Table of Contents

1. Business Description
2. Market Analysis/Marketing Strategy
3. Management and Organization

4. Operations

5. Execution Plan

6. Financial Plan

7. Appendix (supporting documents)

Business Description

1. Describe the kind of business you are in.

2. Explain the goals and objectives of this business.

3. Describe your products/services in detail (customer need fulfilled, unique features, industry perception).

4. Discuss competitive products/services on the market (compare quality and features, why customers buy, pricing strategies).

5. Provide a chart that compares your product lines, product categories, and services to other product lines, product categories, and services offered by competitors by price and benefits. Describe the benefits in detail. For example:

Product	Price	Benefit A	Benefit B	Benefit C
Your Product	$$$	Details	Details	Details
Product X	$$	Details	Details	Details
Product Y	$$$$	Details	Details	Details
Service	Price	Benefit A	Benefit B	Benefit C
Your Service	$$$	Details	Details	Details
Service X	$$	Details	Details	Details
Service Y	$$$$	Details	Details	Details

6. Indicate the business' mix of products/services by percent of sales.

7. Summarize the expected costs and profits for product line, product category, and service.

8. Assess the life cycle of each product line, product category, and service.

Market Analysis/Marketing Strategy

1. Describe current and potential types of customers: (a) Who are they (location and demographics)? (b) Why will they purchase? (c) What is their sensitivity to price, quality, service, features?

2. Describe your market: (a) size, (b) state of growth, (c) history, (d) forecast for future, (e) trends.

3. Describe your competition (list major participants by critical success factors—CSFs).

   a. Provide a chart that compares your company to your competitors. For example:

Company	CSF1	CSF2	CSF3
Your company	Details	Details	Details
Competitor A	Details	Details	Details
Competitor B	Details	Details	Details

   b. Discuss the chart and point out strengths and weaknesses of your company and that of your competitors.

   c. Describe the barriers to entry and growth in this industry.

   d. How will changes in the economy affect the industry?

   e. What is the role of innovation and change?

   f. What roles does government regulation play?

4. Describe sales goals and their rationale.

   a. How will you identify, target, and attract customers?

   b. For advertising and promotion, where (media selection) will you spend your dollars? How much will you spend? How often will you spend? What is your message? How will you measure the results?

   c. What are your pricing options (price, terms, credit policy, service and warranty policies)?

   d. Who will sell the product and what kind of training is needed to enable them to be effective?

   e. What is your merchandising strategy?

   f. Is there "congruence" among your advertising and promotion strategy, pricing options, selling strategy, and merchandising strategy?

Management and Organization

1. What are the key skills required for this business to succeed?

2. Who are the key managers (and employees) who have these key skills and what are their backgrounds? (Provide resumes in the Appendix.)

3. If you don't have all the key personnel, how will you attract them?

4. What other experts and advisors are important to the company?

Operations

1. How will the business sell its product and deliver its service? (Describe how the sales and service functions are undertaken, the personnel needed to accomplish these tasks and the training necessary for each role.)

2. What kinds of training for sales and service personnel are necessary to attract and retain customers?

3. Describe critical elements, likely bottlenecks, quality, supply, sales, service, delivery, inventory, and cash flow issues.

4. Identify necessary resources and equipment likely to be required.

5. Identify the systems (e.g., sales management, inventory control) necessary to operate the business.

Execution Plan

1. Provide a timeline of important activities that were identified in other parts of the plan. The timeline will show that your activities are internally consistent and coordinated with the financial projections.

Financial Plan

1. Present any past financial statements for the past two to five years.

2. Present prospective financial information for the next two to five years: Income statements, balance sheets, cash flow statements. Prepare statements showing monthly figures for the first year and quarterly for years two to five.

3. For all financial statements, provide key assumptions, such as your goals for profits and sales. The best way to do this is to footnote all items.

4. Link your financial statements to key industry ratios and standards.

5. Identify your financing needs.

Appendix (Supporting Documents)

1. Include resumes of the management team.

2. Provide documentation for assumptions you make in the body of the plan.

    a. market analysis data and market research studies

    b. action plans for sales and distribution

    c. product specifications and photos

    d. action plans for production, operations, and service

    e. letters of reference

    f. census and demographic data

    g. contracts

    h. letters of commitment from customers, suppliers, and lenders

    i. buy/sell agreements among partners

Before You Purchase a Franchise

A Pre-Purchase Checklist

The following questions provide a useful outline when performing due diligence on a potential business purchase.

The Economy

- What are current national, regional, and local economic trends? If interest rates are rising, for example, this may decrease sales for businesses dependent on customers getting loans such as automobiles and houses.

- What are local and regional economic trends? If your business is dependent on local sales, is the area that your business is in an area that is growing? Are industries in your area poised to grow, or are they declining?

Industry Characteristics

- Channels of Distribution: Are the ways that customers buy products/services in your industry changing? Is the business you plan to buy likely to be competitive in those channels?

- Technology: Are the products/services in your industry changing? Are the ways that these products or services are created rapidly changing? How is the business's technology (both products/services and ability to create) up to date?

- Competition: How is competition changing in your industry? Can new businesses enter into the same industry as your business?

- Regulations: Many businesses need specific licenses to operate. Is your business in compliance? For example, if you are planning on purchasing a bakery, the bakery is likely to need a health permit as well as zoning approvals for the bakery's location. Are these current? Many localities limit the number of liquor permits in their area, so, if you were planning on buying a restaurant in that locality, will the liquor permit be transferable to you? Also, there may be upcoming regulatory changes that may affect the business. For example, you may be considering purchasing a business that restores automobiles. As part of the process, you'll need to spray-paint them. Many localities regulate the use of spray paints. You may find that you will need to install special hoods and filters to capture the paint fumes. The current business might be "grandfathered" into past regulations about spray painting, but, in a transfer of business ownership, you may need to meet new current regulations.

- Products/Services: Are the products or services offered by the business current and competitive? Are competitors likely to offer products/services that are better, faster, and cheaper?

- Intellectual Property: Does the business depend on patents, copyrights, and trademarks for its success? Are these intellectual property rights up to date and defensible?

- Service and Warranty Obligations: What kinds of liabilities might the business incur from sales of products/services that may still be under a service or warranty obligation? If you purchase a business that sold a defective part in the past, you may be obligated to replace all of these defective parts in the future.

Suppliers

- Contracts: Does the business have contracts with suppliers for the purchase of goods or services? These contracts may be a benefit or a liability. You might be required to purchase goods or services from a supplier at prices higher than what you could purchase these products for on the open market.

- Exclusivity: The business you are looking at may have exclusive relationships with certain suppliers. For example, you may be looking at an outdoor kayaking store that sells lines of kayaks that no other stores can sell in your state. Will this exclusive relationship continue if you purchase the store?

Customers

- Continuity: Will the business's current customers continue to purchase products/services from you?

- Growth: Can the number of customers be expanded for your products/services?

- Purchase Criteria: Will customers purchase your enterprise's current products/services given their quality, price, and performance characteristics?

Management and Employees

- Key Employees: Are there certain employees that have critical knowledge about customers, service, product development, and manufacturing? Will these employees continue with the business if it is purchased? If not, do these employees have noncompete agreements? How will this knowledge be transferred to other people in your organization?

- Compensation: Is compensation too high or too low for current employees?

- Number: Is the business overstaffed or understaffed?

- Climate: Are employees happy? Are there conflicts and fighting among them? Do employees work together well? Have many employees recently left the organization?

Plant and Equipment

- Condition: Do buildings and equipment need repair or updating?

- Utilities: Are utilities adequate to operate the business?

- Size: Are plant and equipment large enough to handle any growth the business may have?

- Leases: How long is the business obligated to stay at a particular place? What happens to the lease if the business is purchased? Will the lease expire, or will the rental price rise?

Ownership

Many businesses are owned by more than one individual. Will you be purchasing the ownership of all of the partners of the business? Will some of the owners be unwilling to sell their shares or percentage of the partnership to you? Will you be purchasing a majority interest in the business or minority interest? If you have a majority interest, you will have more control over making decisions about the business. But even with a majority interest, you will need to take into consideration the interests of your minority partners and shareholders.

glossary

a

administrative agencies Organizations created by all levels of government to develop, implement, and enforce regulations pertinent to a specialized area.

affiliation or conversion franchising A business format franchise in which an operating business becomes part of a franchise system to take advantage of the brand but has more flexibility with regard to operating format. The unit name may reflect both the franchisor and the local entity.

agency Situation where one party, the *agent,* agrees to represent and act on behalf of another party, the *principal.*

alternative dispute resolution (ADR) Nonjudicial method of resolving disputes.

arbitration Out-of-court method of dispute resolution whereby an impartial third party (the *arbitrator* or *arbitration panel*) hears the evidence and makes a ruling.

archetype A model or prototype from which similar things can be made.

area development franchise Rights to open and operate a specific number of franchises within a particular geographic region.

asset-based valuation Determination of a business's value based on the company's assets.

b

bankruptcy Situation where an individual or business cannot meet financial obligations and seeks legal protection to repay or restructure debts.

BATNA (best alternative to a negotiated agreement) What each party will do if the negotiation process fails to reach an acceptable agreement.

board of directors A group of people elected by the stockholders to handle the overall management of a corporation, such as setting corporate goals and policies, hiring corporate officers, and overseeing the firm's operations and finances.

breach of contract When one party does not perform as required under the contract terms.

business An organization that is started and operated for the purposes of its owners.

business ethics Application of moral standards and values to business situations.

business format franchise A type of franchise where the franchisee purchases a product and a complete system to operate the business.

business law Regulations that provide a standardized environment to conduct commercial dealings.

business model A plan that shows how all of the different major aspects of a business work together to generate a profit.

business plan A written plan for a business that documents an enterpriser's past, present, and future actions and helps identify the right actions for success. Shows where you are going and where you have been.

buyer cooperatives Consumer-owned or business cooperatives that combine members' purchasing power to buy goods or services in volume, at lower prices.

c

C corporation A conventional or basic corporate form of organization.

cash flow Cash generated by the business after subtracting taxes and adding back noncash expenses such as depreciation.

cognition Thought process that reveals what and how you think, significantly influencing what you are likely to do.

cognitive characteristics Intellectual rather than physical traits—the ability to think, learn, and remember. Examples include comprehension, reasoning, perception, decision making, planning, and learning.

commitment The enterpriser's dedication to the idea and willingness to implement it.

community A collection of related industries.

compensatory damages Monetary award to repay the victim for actual loss and suffering.

connection How enterprisers will identify and reach specific customers.

consideration The exchange of something of value; must be present to have a valid contract.

consumerism A social movement that emphasizes strengthening buyer rights and powers with regard to sellers.

contract A legally enforceable agreement between two or more parties with regard to the performance of a specific action.

cooperatives Legal entities typically formed by people with similar interests, such as customers or suppliers, to reduce costs and gain economic power. A cooperative has limited liability, an unlimited life span, an elected board of directors, and an administrative staff; all profits are distributed to the member-owners in proportion to their contributions.

copyright Gives the creator of an original work the exclusive rights to publish, perform, copy, or sell the work.

corporation A legal entity with an existence and life separate from its owners who are not personally liable for the entity's debts. A corporation is chartered by the state in which it is formed and can own property, enter into contracts, sue and be sued, and engage in business operations under the terms of its charter.

critical path The activities required to complete a project and the order in which they must be completed to keep a project on track.

critical success factors (CSFs) Operational functions or competencies that a company requires to be profitable.

customers Those who buy an enterpriser's goods or services.

d

deed Written document that transfers ownership of real property from one party to another.

discounted cash flow (DCF) Valuation technique that finds the present value of a future cash flow stream at a specified discount rate.

discount rate A rate that represents the buyer's expected cost of capital (the interest rate for a loan to buy the company), as well as the desired return on investment and an adjustment for inflation.

disposition A set of personality characteristics that generally remains stable in nearly all situations, such as a person's temperament, character, or personality.

dispositional characteristics A person's natural or acquired habits or characteristic tendencies.

due diligence The process of thoroughly investigating all parties who will be involved in your business, including investors, partners, potential employees, customers, and suppliers.

e

earn-out Payment strategy that gives the seller of a business a certain amount of the future earnings of the business over a specified time period.

emergence The first stage of a business's life cycle: New venture formation.

enterpriser An individual who engages in activities to initiate and then direct an organization to serve his or her purposes.

entrepreneur An individual involved in the start-up of a business.

environment The entire context of activities that surrounds the operation of a business.

ethics A set of moral standards and values that helps individuals choose between right and wrong.

express warranties Indications by the seller that the buyer can interpret as fact, such as descriptions of an item, promises of quality and performance, or samples of products; written warranties must indicate whether they are full or limited.

f

fair market value The price that a business would command from a knowledgeable buyer and a seller with the relevant information about the business and willingness to undertake the transaction.

feasibility Process of revising the business concept to test whether a business is worth pursuing and under which conditions.

fixed costs Costs that do not vary with sales volume, such as rent.

franchise The rights to offer specific products or services under explicit guidelines at a certain location for a declared period of time.

franchisee The individual or company that owns one or more franchises and sells goods or services in accordance with the terms set by the *franchisor*.

franchise license agreement The principal legal document that defines the terms of the relationship between the franchisor and franchisee, including the license to use the franchisor's brand for a specified time period, payment terms, and operating restrictions.

franchising A form of business ownership involving a contractual arrangement where a parent business (the *franchisor*) provides an investor (the *franchisee*) with the rights to sell products or services in exchange for fees and/or royalty payments.

franchisor Parent company that owns and controls the rights to offer the franchise's product concept to the *franchisee*.

g

general partnership All individuals share in the profits and the management responsibilities of the business, as well as any liabilities that the business might generate.

i

implied warranties Unwritten warranties specified by law that grant certain protections to the buyer, including warranties of title, merchantability (merchandise will perform as advertised), and fitness for a particular purpose (the item will serve its intended purpose).

industry A group of businesses producing similar products and services.

intellectual property Property arising from a person's creative activities.

intentional tort Deliberate action that could injure another party.

j

joint venture An alliance between two or more companies to pursue a specific project for a specified time period.

judiciary Branch of government that interprets and applies the law to resolve disputes for individuals, enterprises, and government. It uses a multilevel court system to accomplish these objectives.

l

law A statute enacted and enforced to establish rules of conduct for a society.

lease Written agreement that temporarily transfers interest in real estate or other tangible assets to the user for a specified time period.

life cycle of enterprise The three stages of an enterprise's life: emergence, newness, and transition.

limited liability company (LLC) A hybrid organization that offers the same liability protection as a corporation but may be taxed as either a partnership or a corporation.

limited partnership There are two types of partners: general partners, who share in profits, management responsibilities, and all liabilities; and limited partners, who do not share in the management of the business.

m

market-based valuation Valuation method that looks at process paid for comparable firms. Industry valuation and multiplier formula valuations are two categories of market-based valuation.

master franchise (subfranchising) A three-party arrangement that grants a master franchisee rights to open franchises in a particular territory, along with right to sell franchises to other unit franchisees.

mediation Less formal dispute resolution process that uses a neutral third party (the *mediator*) to help the parties negotiate a mutually agreeable solution.

mindfulness As defined by Ellen J. Langer, an awareness of the present moment that includes openness to new information and multiple perspectives.

n

nascent entrepreneurs Individuals who undertake the efforts necessary to initiate and start new businesses.

negligence Failure to use a reasonable amount of care to protect others from injury.

negotiation Back-and-forth communication process by which two parties try to reach a mutually acceptable solution to a problem or to accomplish something that neither party could do on its own.

network The total of a person's relationships and connections with other people.

networking The process of asking people you know (or could get to know through others) for information, advice, ideas, or help, as you plan and pursue your goals.

newness The stage in a business's life cycle that involves developing and managing a fledgling business so that it survives and flourishes.

noncompete agreement Agreement prohibiting the seller from entering into a similar kind of business for a set time period within the geographic area in which the purchased business competes.

nonrecurring costs Fixed costs that occur only once during the life of a business.

not-for-profit organization An organization that is exempt from most state and federal income taxes and has a purpose that that will benefit others.

o

officers In a corporation, these individuals are hired by the board and responsible for achieving corporate goals and policies. They include top management such as the president and chief executive officer (CEO), vice-presidents, treasurer, and secretary.

opportunity or business concept Favorable events involving customers, consideration, connection, and commitment (the 4 Cs) that have the potential to become a successful business.

optimist A person who believes that good things will happen.

organization An entity that involves people doing work for a purpose.

organizational behavior The study of people and how they act in organizations.

organizational imperative Concept that a business has its own needs and objectives separate from the needs and objectives of any of the business's other stakeholders.

p

partnership An association of two or more persons who agree to operate a business together for profit.

patent Exclusive right to make, use, or sell the product or process for 20 years from the date the patent application was filed.

personal property All property other than real property.

persuasion Deliberately seeking attitude change through communication—using your personal influence to get someone to do or believe something.

product and trademark (product distribution) franchise Franchise arrangement under which manufacturers grant franchisees, or dealers, the right to buy, sell, and advertise the products under the manufacturer's trademarked name.

product liability Concept which holds manufacturers and sellers responsible for injuries caused by defects in their products.

profit The money left over after all expenses are paid.

punitive damages Monetary payments that greatly exceed actual losses; intended to punish the wrongdoer.

r

real property Land and anything permanently attached to it.

revenue model All the revenue streams a business will generate from sources such as subscriptions/memberships, volume- or unit-based pricing, advertising sales, licensing fees, and transaction fees.

risk A situation that causes concern and/or uncertainty and could therefore result in negative outcomes.

Rule 436 Federal Trade Commission regulation that governs disclosure requirements for the offer and sale of franchises in all 50 states.

s

S corporation A hybrid entity that is organized like a corporation, with stockholders, directors, and officers, but taxed like a partnership, with income and losses flowing through to the stockholders and taxed as their personal income.

seller (producer-owned) cooperatives Individual producers who join together to compete more effectively with large producers. Members jointly support market development, national advertising, and other business activities.

semi-variable costs Costs that change, but not in direct relationship to sales volume.

seven intelligences The seven different types of intelligences that people may possess, as categorized by Howard Gardner: musical, bodily-kinesthetic, logical-mathematical, linguistic, spatial, interpersonal, and intrapersonal.

signature strength A strength that you are more likely to use frequently, feel good about using, and want to use more often.

small wins Achievable, tangible accomplishments that are within a person's capabilities and produce visible results.

sole-proprietorship A business that is established, owned, operated, and often financed by one person.

stakeholder An entity that has a legitimate interest in the processes and activities of a business.

statutory law Law written by legislative bodies (the U.S. Congress, state legislatures, local governments); incorporation and bankruptcy laws are examples of statutory laws.

stockholders The owners of a corporation who hold shares of stock that provide certain rights; also known as *shareholders*.

strict liability Type of liability that holds a manufacturer or seller liable for *any* defects in a product, even if these parties have exercised reasonable care in designing, making, and selling the product.

structural holes Gaps in the connections among people, where opportunities for success occur.

subfranchisor A franchisee who contracts with a master franchisee to open a franchise within the same territory.

systematic innovation As defined by Peter Drucker, a purposeful and organized search for and analysis of changes and the opportunities these changes create.

t

tort Civil (noncriminal) act that injures a person or property and does not arise from a breach of contract.

trademark Words, names, slogans, packaging, colors, or symbols that identify a company and its goods and services.

transformation The transitions a business goes through during its life cycle to adapt to changing circumstances.

u

Uniform Commercial Code (UCC) Set of business laws that provide a standard way for businesses to operate.

Uniform Franchise Offering Circular (UFOC) A document prepared by franchisor for prospective franchisees that includes 23 issues that disclose background information and financial condition of the franchisor.

unit franchise Agreement to open one unit in a particular location.

v

value chain The process by which a product or service moves from inputs to the final customer.

variable costs Costs that vary directly and proportionally with sales such as raw materials and shipping costs.

w

worker-owned cooperatives Employee–owned and controlled businesses.

index